Stoic Six Pack – *Meditations* by Marcus Aurelius and More

Marcus Aurelius

Seneca

Epictetus

Stoic Six Pack – Meditations by Marcus Aurelius and More. By Marcus Aurelius, Seneca and Epictetus. *Meditations* by Marcus Aurelius, translated by George Long. First published 1862. *The Golden Sayings* and *Fragments* of Epictetus, translated by Hastings Crossley. First published in 1909. *Discourses* of Epictetus translated by George Long. First published as *The Discourses of Epictetus, with the Encheridion and Fragments* in 1877. *Letters from a Stoic: Epistulae Morales AD Lucilium. All Three Volumes.* By Lucius Annaeus Seneca. Translated by Richard Mott Gummere. Volume 1 first published in 1917; Volume 2 published in 1920; Volume 3 published 1925. *The Enchiridion* of Epictetus. Translated by P. E. Matheson. First published in 1916. Marcus Aurelius biography by John Lord. From *Beacon Lights of History, Volume IV: Imperial Antiquity*. First published in 1883.

Stoic Six Pack – Meditations by Marcus Aurelius and More.

ISBN-10: 1503259439
ISBN-13: 978-1503259430

CONTENTS

MEDITATIONS

BY MARCUS AURELIUS

BOOK ONE

FROM my grandfather Verus I learned good morals and the government of my temper. From the reputation and remembrance of my father, modesty and a manly character. From my mother, piety and beneficence, and abstinence, not only from evil deeds, but even from evil thoughts; and further, simplicity in my way of living, far removed from the habits of the rich.

From my great-grandfather, not to have frequented public schools, and to have had good teachers at home, and to know that on such things a man should spend liberally.

From my governor, to be neither of the green nor of the blue party at the games in the Circus, nor a partisan either of the Parmularius or the Scutarius at the gladiators' fights; from him too I learned endurance of labour, and to want little, and to work with my own hands, and not to meddle with other people's affairs, and not to be ready to listen to slander.

From Diognetus, not to busy myself about trifling things, and not to give credit to what was said by miracle-workers and jugglers about incantations and the driving away of demons and such things; and not to breed quails for fighting, nor to give myself up passionately to such things; and to endure freedom of speech; and to have become intimate with philosophy; and to have been a hearer, first of Bacchius, then of Tandasis and Marcianus; and to have written dialogues in my youth; and to have desired a plank bed and skin, and whatever else of the kind belongs to the Grecian discipline.

From Rusticus I received the impression that my character required improvement and discipline; and from him I learned not to be led astray to sophistic emulation, nor to writing on speculative matters, nor to delivering little hortatory orations, nor to showing myself off as a man who practises much discipline, or does benevolent acts in order to make a display; and to abstain from rhetoric, and poetry, and fine writing; and not to walk about in the house in my outdoor dress, nor to do other things of the kind; and to write my letters with simplicity, like the letter which Rusticus wrote from Sinuessa to my mother; and with respect to those who have offended me by words, or done me wrong, to be easily disposed to be pacified and reconciled, as soon as they have shown a readiness to be reconciled; and to read carefully, and not to be satisfied with a superficial understanding of a book; nor hastily to give my assent to those who talk overmuch; and I am indebted to him for being acquainted with the discourses of Epictetus, which he communicated to me out of his own collection.

From Apollonius I learned freedom of will and undeviating steadiness of purpose; and to look to nothing else, not even for a moment, except to reason; and to be always the same, in sharp pains, on the occasion of the loss of a child, and in long illness; and to see clearly in a living example that the same man can be both most resolute and yielding, and not peevish in giving his instruction; and to have had before my eyes a man who clearly considered his experience and his skill in expounding philosophical principles as the smallest of his merits; and from him I learned how to receive from friends what are esteemed favours, without being either humbled by them or letting them pass unnoticed.

From Sextus, a benevolent disposition, and the example of a family governed in a fatherly manner, and the idea of living conformably to nature; and gravity without affectation, and to look carefully after the interests of friends, and to tolerate ignorant persons, and those who form opinions without consideration: he had the power of readily accommodating himself to all, so that intercourse with him was more agreeable than any flattery; and at the same time he was most highly venerated by those who associated with him: and he had the faculty both of discovering and ordering, in an intelligent and methodical way, the principles necessary for life; and he never showed anger or any other passion, but was entirely free from passion, and also most affectionate; and he could express approbation without noisy display, and he possessed much knowledge without ostentation.

From Alexander the grammarian, to refrain from fault-finding, and not in a reproachful way to chide those who uttered any barbarous or solecistic or strange-sounding expression; but dexterously to introduce the very expression which ought to have been used, and in the way of answer or giving confirmation, or joining in an inquiry about the thing itself, not about the word, or by some other fit suggestion.

From Fronto I learned to observe what envy, and duplicity, and hypocrisy are in a tyrant, and that generally those among us who are called Patricians are rather deficient in paternal affection.

From Alexander the Platonic, not frequently nor without necessity to say to any one, or to write in a letter, that I have no leisure; nor continually to excuse the neglect of duties required by our relation to those with whom we live, by alleging urgent occupations.

From Catulus, not to be indifferent when a friend finds fault, even if he should find fault without reason, but to try to restore him to his usual disposition; and to be ready to speak well of teachers, as it is reported of Domitius and Athenodotus; and to love my children truly.

From my brother Severus, to love my kin, and to love truth, and to love justice; and through him I learned to know Thrasea, Helvidius, Cato, Dion, Brutus; and from him I received the idea of a polity in which there is the same law for all, a polity administered with regard to equal rights and equal freedom of speech, and the idea of a kingly government which respects most of all the freedom of the governed; I learned from him also consistency and undeviating steadiness in my regard for philosophy; and a disposition to do good, and to give to others readily, and to cherish good hopes, and to believe that I am loved by my friends; and in him I observed no concealment of his opinions with respect to those whom he condemned, and that his friends had no need to conjecture what he wished or did not wish, but it was quite plain.

From Maximus I learned self-government, and not to be led aside by anything; and cheerfulness in all circumstances, as well as in illness; and a just admixture in the moral character of sweetness and dignity, and to do what was set before me without complaining. I observed that everybody believed that he thought as he spoke, and that in all that he did he never had any bad intention;

and he never showed amazement and surprise, and was never in a hurry, and never put off doing a thing, nor was perplexed nor dejected, nor did he ever laugh to disguise his vexation, nor, on the other hand, was he ever passionate or suspicious. He was accustomed to do acts of beneficence, and was ready to forgive, and was free from all falsehood; and he presented the appearance of a man who could not be diverted from right rather than of a man who had been improved. I observed, too, that no man could ever think that he was despised by Maximus, or ever venture to think himself a better man. He had also the art of being humorous in an agreeable way.

In my father I observed mildness of temper, and unchangeable resolution in the things which he had determined after due deliberation; and no vainglory in those things which men call honours; and a love of labour and perseverance; and a readiness to listen to those who had anything to propose for the common weal; and undeviating firmness in giving to every man according to his deserts; and a knowledge derived from experience of the occasions for vigorous action and for remission. And I observed that he had overcome all passion for boys; and he considered himself no more than any other citizen; and he released his friends from all obligation to sup with him or to attend him of necessity when he went abroad, and those who had failed to accompany him, by reason of any urgent circumstances, always found him the same. I observed too his habit of careful inquiry in all matters of deliberation, and his persistency, and that he never stopped his investigation through being satisfied with appearances which first present themselves; and that his disposition was to keep his friends, and not to be soon tired of them, nor yet to be extravagant in his affection; and to be satisfied on all occasions, and cheerful; and to foresee things a long way off, and to provide for the smallest without display; and to check immediately popular applause and all flattery; and to be ever watchful over the things which were necessary for the administration of the empire, and to be a good manager of the expenditure, and patiently to endure the blame which he got for such conduct; and he was neither superstitious with respect to the gods, nor did he court men by gifts or by trying to please them, or by flattering the populace; but he showed sobriety in all things and firmness, and never any mean thoughts or action, nor love of novelty. And the things which conduce in any way to the commodity of life, and of which fortune gives an abundant supply, he used without arrogance and without excusing himself; so that when he had them, he enjoyed them without affectation, and when he had them not, he did not want them. No one could ever say of him that he was either a sophist or a home-bred flippant slave or a pedant; but every one acknowledged him to be a man ripe, perfect, above flattery, able to manage his own and other men's affairs.

Besides this, he honoured those who were true philosophers, and he did not reproach those who pretended to be philosophers, nor yet was he easily led by them. He was also easy in conversation, and he made himself agreeable without any offensive affectation. He took a reasonable care of his body's health, not as one who was greatly attached to life, nor out of regard to personal appearance, nor yet in a careless way, but so that, through his own attention, he very seldom stood in need of the physician's art or of medicine or external applications. He was most ready to give way without envy to those who possessed any particular faculty, such as that of eloquence or knowledge of the law or of morals, or of anything else; and he gave them his help, that each might enjoy reputation according to his deserts; and he always acted conformably to the institutions of his country, without showing any affectation of doing so.

Further, he was not fond of change nor unsteady, but he loved to stay in the same places, and to employ himself about the same things; and after his paroxysms of headache he came immediately fresh and vigorous to his usual occupations. His secrets were not but very few and very rare, and these only about public matters; and he showed prudence and economy in the exhibition of the public spectacles and the construction of public buildings, his donations to the people, and in such things, for he was a man who looked to what ought to be done, not to the reputation which is got by a man's acts. He did not take the bath at unseasonable hours; he was not fond of building houses, nor curious about what he ate, nor about the texture and colour of his clothes, nor about the beauty of his slaves. His dress came from Lorium, his villa on the coast, and from Lanuvium generally. We know how he behaved to the toll-collector at Tusculum who asked his pardon; and such was all his behaviour. There was in him nothing harsh, nor implacable, nor violent, nor, as one may say, anything carried to the sweating point; but he examined all things severally, as if he had abundance of time, and without confusion, in an orderly way, vigorously and consistently.

And that might be applied to him which is recorded of Socrates, that he was able both to abstain from, and to enjoy, those things which many are too weak to abstain from, and cannot enjoy without excess. But to be strong enough both to bear the one and to be sober in the other is the mark of a man who has a perfect and invincible soul, such as he showed in the illness of Maximus.

To the gods I am indebted for having good grandfathers, good parents, a good sister, good teachers, good associates, good kinsmen and friends, nearly everything good. Further, I owe it to the gods that I was not hurried into any offence against any of them, though I had a disposition which, if opportunity had offered, might have led me to do something of this kind; but, through their favour, there never was such a concurrence of circumstances as put me to the trial.

Further, I am thankful to the gods that I was not longer brought up with my grandfather's concubine, and that I preserved the flower of my youth, and that I did not make proof of my virility before the proper season, but even deferred the time; that I was subjected to a ruler and a father who was able to take away all pride from me, and to bring me to the knowledge that it is possible for a man to live in a palace without wanting either guards or embroidered dresses, or torches and statues, and such-like show; but that it is in such a man's power to bring himself very near to the fashion of a private person, without being for this reason either meaner in thought, or more remiss in action, with respect to the things which must be done for the public interest in a manner that befits a ruler. I thank the gods for giving me such a brother, who was able by his moral character to rouse me to vigilance over myself, and who, at the same time, pleased me by his respect and affection; that my children have not been stupid nor deformed in body; that I did not make more proficiency in rhetoric, poetry, and the other studies, in which I should perhaps have been completely engaged, if I had seen that I was making progress in them; that I made haste to place those who brought me up in the station of honour, which they seemed to desire, without putting them off with hope of my doing it some time after, because they were then still young; that I knew Apollonius, Rusticus, Maximus; that I received clear and frequent impressions about living according to nature, and what kind of a life that is, so that, so far as depended on the gods, and their gifts, and help, and inspirations, nothing hindered me from forthwith living according to nature, though I still fall short of it through my own fault, and through not observing the admonitions of the gods, and, I may almost say, their direct instructions; that my body has held out so long in such a kind of life; that I never touched either Benedicta or Theodotus, and that, after having fallen into amatory passions, I was cured; and, though I was often out of humour with Rusticus, I never did anything of which I had occasion to repent; that, though it was my mother's fate to die young, she spent the last years of her life with me; that, whenever I wished to help any man in his need, or on any other occasion, I was never told that I had not the means of doing it; and that to myself the same necessity never happened, to receive anything from another; that I have such a wife, so obedient, and so affectionate, and so simple; that I had abundance of good masters for my children; and that remedies have been shown to me by dreams, both others, and against bloodspitting and giddiness...; and that, when I had an inclination to philosophy, I did not fall into the hands of any sophist, and that I did not waste my time on writers of histories, or in the resolution of syllogisms, or occupy myself about the investigation of appearances in the heavens; for all these things require the help of the gods and fortune. Among the Quadi at the Granua.

BOOK TWO

BEGIN the morning by saying to thyself, I shall meet with the busybody, the ungrateful, arrogant, deceitful, envious, unsocial. All these things happen to them by reason of their ignorance of what is good and evil. But I who have seen the nature of the good that it is beautiful, and of the bad that it is ugly, and the nature of him who does wrong, that it is akin to me, not only of the same blood or seed, but that it participates in the same intelligence and the same portion of the divinity, I can neither be injured by any of them, for no one can fix on me what is ugly, nor can I be angry with my kinsman, nor hate him, For we are made for co-operation, like feet, like hands, like eyelids, like the rows of the upper and lower teeth. To act against one another then is contrary to nature; and it is acting against one another to be vexed and to turn away.

Whatever this is that I am, it is a little flesh and breath, and the ruling part. Throw away thy books; no longer distract thyself: it is not allowed; but as if thou wast now dying, despise the flesh; it is blood and bones and a network, a contexture of nerves, veins, and arteries. See the breath also, what kind of a thing it is, air, and not always the same, but every moment sent out and again sucked in. The third then is the ruling part: consider thus: Thou art an old man; no longer let this be a slave, no longer be pulled by the strings like a puppet to unsocial movements, no longer either be dissatisfied with thy present lot, or shrink from the future. All that is from the gods is full of Providence. That which is from fortune is not separated from nature or without an interweaving and involution with the things which are ordered by Providence. From thence all things flow; and there is besides necessity, and that which is for the advantage of the whole universe, of which thou art a part. But that is good for every part of nature which the nature of the whole brings, and what serves to maintain this nature. Now the universe is preserved, as by the changes of the elements so by the changes of things compounded of the elements. Let these principles be enough for thee, let them always be fixed opinions. But cast away the thirst after books, that thou mayest not die murmuring, but cheerfully, truly, and from thy heart thankful to the gods.

Remember how long thou hast been putting off these things, and how often thou hast received an opportunity from the gods, and yet dost not use it. Thou must now at last perceive of what universe thou art a part, and of what administrator of the universe thy existence is an efflux, and that a limit of time is fixed for thee, which if thou dost not use for clearing away the clouds from thy mind, it will go and thou wilt go, and it will never return.

Every moment think steadily as a Roman and a man to do what thou hast in hand with perfect and simple dignity, and feeling of affection, and freedom, and justice; and to give thyself relief from all other thoughts. And thou wilt give thyself relief, if thou doest every act of thy life as if it were the last, laying aside all carelessness and passionate aversion from the commands of reason, and all hypocrisy, and self-love, and discontent with the portion which has been given to thee. Thou seest how few the things are, the which if a man lays hold of, he is able to live a life which flows in quiet, and is like the existence of the gods; for the gods on their part will require nothing more from him who observes these things. Do wrong to thyself, do wrong to thyself, my soul; but thou wilt no longer have the opportunity of honouring thyself. Every man's life is sufficient. But thine is nearly finished, though thy soul reverences not itself but places thy felicity in the souls of others.

Do the things external which fall upon thee distract thee? Give thyself time to learn something new and good, and cease to be whirled around. But then thou must also avoid being carried about the other way. For those too are triflers who have wearied themselves in life by their activity, and yet have no object to which to direct every movement, and, in a word, all their thoughts.

Through not observing what is in the mind of another a man has seldom been seen to be unhappy; but those who do not observe the movements of their own minds must of necessity be unhappy.

This thou must always bear in mind, what is the nature of the whole, and what is my nature, and how this is related to that, and what kind of a part it is of what kind of a whole; and that there is no one who hinders thee from always doing and saying the things which are according to the nature of which thou art a part.

Theophrastus, in his comparison of bad acts - such a comparison as one would make in accordance with the common notions of mankind - says, like a true philosopher, that the offences which are committed through desire are more blameable than those which are committed through anger. For he who is excited by anger seems to turn away from reason with a certain pain and unconscious contraction; but he who offends through desire, being overpowered by pleasure, seems to be in a manner more intemperate and more womanish in his offences. Rightly then, and in a way worthy of philosophy, he said that the offence which is committed with pleasure is more blameable than that which is committed with pain; and on the whole the one is more like a person who has been first wronged and through pain is compelled to be angry; but the other is moved by his own impulse to do wrong, being carried towards doing something by desire.

Since it is possible that thou mayest depart from life this very moment, regulate every act and thought accordingly. But to go away from among men, if there are gods, is not a thing to be afraid of, for the gods will not involve thee in evil; but if indeed they do not exist, or if they have no concern about human affairs, what is it to me to live in a universe devoid of gods or devoid of Providence? But in truth they do exist, and they do care for human things, and they have put all the means in man's power to enable him not to fall into real evils. And as to the rest, if there was anything evil, they would have provided for this also, that it should be altogether in a man's power not to fall into it. Now that which does not make a man worse, how can it make a man's life worse? But neither through ignorance, nor having the knowledge, but not the power to guard against or correct these things, is it possible that the nature of the universe has overlooked them; nor is it possible that it has made so great a mistake, either through want of power or want of skill, that good and evil should happen indiscriminately to the good and the bad. But death certainly, and life, honour and dishonour, pain and pleasure, all these things equally happen to good men and bad, being things which make us neither better nor worse. Therefore they are neither good nor evil.

How quickly all things disappear, in the universe the bodies themselves, but in time the remembrance of them; what is the nature of all sensible things, and particularly those which attract with the bait of pleasure or terrify by pain, or are noised abroad by vapoury fame; how worthless, and contemptible, and sordid, and perishable, and dead they are - all this it is the part of the intellectual faculty to observe. To observe too who these are whose opinions and voices give reputation; what death is, and the fact that, if a man looks at it in itself, and by the abstractive power of reflection resolves into their parts all the things which present themselves to the imagination in it, he will then consider it to be nothing else than an operation of nature; and if any one is afraid of an operation of nature, he is a child. This, however, is not only an operation of nature, but it is also a thing which conduces to the purposes of nature. To observe too how man comes near to the deity, and by what part of him, and when this part of man is so disposed.

Nothing is more wretched than a man who traverses everything in a round, and pries into the things beneath the earth, as the poet says, and seeks by conjecture what is in the minds of his neighbours, without perceiving that it is sufficient to attend to the daemon within him, and to reverence it sincerely. And reverence of the daemon consists in keeping it pure from passion and thoughtlessness, and dissatisfaction with what comes from gods and men. For the things from the gods merit veneration for their excellence; and the things from men should be dear to us by reason of kinship; and sometimes even, in a manner, they move our pity by reason of men's ignorance of good and bad; this defect being not less than that which deprives us of the power of distinguishing things that are white and black. Though thou shouldst be going to live three thousand years, and as many times ten thousand years, still remember that no man loses any other life than this which he now lives, nor lives any other than this which he now loses. The longest and shortest are thus brought to the same. For the present is the same to all, though that which perishes is not the same; and so that which is lost appears to be a mere moment. For a man cannot lose either the past or the future: for what a man has not, how can any one take this from him? These two things then thou must bear in mind; the one, that all things from eternity are of like forms and come round in a circle, and that it makes no difference whether a man shall see the same things during a hundred years or two hundred, or an infinite time; and the second, that the longest liver and he who will die soonest lose just the same. For the present is the only thing of which a man can be deprived, if it is true that this is the only thing which he has, and that a man cannot lose a thing if he has it not.

Remember that all is opinion. For what was said by the Cynic Monimus is manifest: and manifest too is the use of what was said, if a man receives what may be got out of it as far as it is true.

The soul of man does violence to itself, first of all, when it becomes an abscess and, as it were, a tumour on the universe, so far as it can. For to be vexed at anything which happens is a separation of ourselves from nature, in some part of which the natures of all other things are contained. In the next place, the soul does violence to itself when it turns away from any man, or even moves towards him with the intention of injuring, such as are the souls of those who are angry. In the third place, the soul does violence to itself when it is overpowered by pleasure or by pain. Fourthly, when it plays a part, and does or says anything insincerely and untruly.

Fifthly, when it allows any act of its own and any movement to be without an aim, and does anything thoughtlessly and without considering what it is, it being right that even the smallest things be done with reference to an end; and the end of rational animals is to follow the reason and the law of the most ancient city and polity. Of human life the time is a point, and the substance is in a flux, and the perception dull, and the composition of the whole body subject to putrefaction, and the soul a whirl, and fortune hard to divine, and fame a thing devoid of judgement. And, to say all in a word, everything which belongs to the body is a stream, and what belongs to the soul is a dream and vapour, and life is a warfare and a stranger's sojourn, and after-fame is oblivion. What then is that which is able to conduct a man? One thing and only one, philosophy. But this consists in keeping the daemon within a man free from violence and unharmed, superior to pains and pleasures, doing nothing without purpose, nor yet falsely and with hypocrisy, not feeling the need of another man's doing or not doing anything; and besides, accepting all that happens, and all that is allotted, as coming from thence, wherever it is, from whence he himself came; and, finally, waiting for death with a cheerful mind, as being nothing else than a dissolution of the elements of which every living being is compounded. But if there is no harm to the elements themselves in each continually changing into another, why should a man have any apprehension about the change and dissolution of all the elements? For it is according to nature, and nothing is evil which is according to nature. This in Carnuntum.

BOOK THREE

WE OUGHT to consider not only that our life is daily wasting away and a smaller part of it is left, but another thing also must be taken into the account, that if a man should live longer, it is quite uncertain whether the understanding will still continue sufficient for the comprehension of things, and retain the power of contemplation which strives to acquire the knowledge of the divine and the human.

For if he shall begin to fall into dotage, perspiration and nutrition and imagination and appetite, and whatever else there is of the kind, will not fail; but the power of making use of ourselves, and filling up the measure of our duty, and clearly separating all appearances, and considering whether a man should now depart from life, and whatever else of the kind absolutely requires a disciplined reason, all this is already extinguished. We must make haste then, not only because we are daily nearer to death, but also because the conception of things and the understanding of them cease first.

We ought to observe also that even the things which follow after the things which are produced according to nature contain something pleasing and attractive. For instance, when bread is baked some parts are split at the surface, and these parts which thus open, and have a certain fashion contrary to the purpose of the baker's art, are beautiful in a manner, and in a peculiar way excite a desire for eating. And again, figs, when they are quite ripe, gape open; and in the ripe olives the very circumstance of their being near to rottenness adds a peculiar beauty to the fruit. And the ears of corn bending down, and the lion's eyebrows, and the foam which flows from the mouth of wild boars, and many other things- though they are far from being beautiful, if a man should examine them severally- still, because they are consequent upon the things which are formed by nature, help to adorn them, and they please the mind; so that if a man should have a feeling and deeper insight with respect to the things which are produced in the universe, there is hardly one of those which follow by way of consequence which will not seem to him to be in a manner disposed so as to give pleasure. And so he will see even the real gaping jaws of wild beasts with no less pleasure than those which painters and sculptors show by imitation; and in an old woman and an old man he will be able to see a certain maturity and comeliness; and the attractive loveliness of young persons he will be able to look on with chaste eyes; and many such things will present themselves, not pleasing to every man, but to him only who has become truly familiar with nature and her works.

Hippocrates after curing many diseases himself fell sick and died.

The Chaldaei foretold the deaths of many, and then fate caught them too. Alexander, and Pompeius, and Caius Caesar, after so often completely destroying whole cities, and in battle cutting to pieces many ten thousands of cavalry and infantry, themselves too at last departed from life. Heraclitus, after so many speculations on the conflagration of the universe, was filled with water internally and died smeared all over with mud. And lice destroyed

Democritus; and other lice killed Socrates. What means all this? Thou hast embarked, thou hast made the voyage, thou art come to shore; get out. If indeed to another life, there is no want of gods, not even there.

But if to a state without sensation, thou wilt cease to be held by pains and pleasures, and to be a slave to the vessel, which is as much inferior as that which serves it is superior: for the one is intelligence and deity; the other is earth and corruption.

Do not waste the remainder of thy life in thoughts about others, when thou dost not refer thy thoughts to some object of common utility. For thou losest the opportunity of doing something else when thou hast such thoughts as these, What is such a person doing, and why, and what is he saying, and what is he thinking of, and what is he contriving, and whatever else of the kind makes us wander away from the observation of our own ruling power. We ought then to check in the series of our thoughts everything that is without a purpose and useless, but most of all the over-curious feeling and the malignant; and a man should use himself to think of those things only about which if one should suddenly ask, What hast thou now in thy thoughts? With perfect openness thou mightest, immediately answer, This or That; so that from thy words it should be plain that everything in thee is simple and benevolent, and such as befits a social animal, and one that cares not for thoughts about pleasure or sensual enjoyments at all, nor has any rivalry or envy and suspicion, or anything else for which thou wouldst blush if thou shouldst say that thou hadst it in thy mind. For the man who is such and no longer delays being among the number of the best, is like a priest and minister of the gods, using too the deity which is planted within him, which makes the man uncontaminated by pleasure, unharmed by any pain, untouched by any insult, feeling no wrong, a fighter in the noblest fight, one who cannot be overpowered by any passion, dyed deep with justice, accepting with all his soul everything which happens and is assigned to him as his portion; and not often, nor yet without great necessity and for the general interest, imagining what another says, or does, or thinks. For it is only what belongs to himself that he makes the matter for his activity; and he constantly thinks of that which is allotted to himself out of the sum total of things, and he makes his own acts fair, and he is persuaded that his own portion is good. For the lot which is assigned to each man is carried along with him and carries him along with it. And he remembers also that every rational animal is his kinsman, and that to care for all men is according to man's nature; and a man should hold on to the opinion not of all, but of those only who confessedly live according to nature. But as to those who live not so, he always bears in mind what kind of men they are both at home and from home, both by night and by day, and what they are, and with what men they live an impure life. Accordingly, he does not value at all the praise which comes from such men, since they are not even satisfied with themselves. Labour not unwillingly, nor without regard to the common interest, nor without due consideration, nor with distraction; nor let studied ornament set off thy thoughts, and be not either a man of many words, or busy about too many things. And further, let the deity which is in thee be the guardian of a living being, manly and of ripe age, and engaged in matter political, and a Roman, and a ruler, who has taken his post like a man waiting for the signal which summons him from life, and ready to go, having need neither of oath nor of any man's testimony. Be cheerful also, and seek not external help nor the tranquility which others give. A man then must stand erect, not be kept erect by others.

If thou findest in human life anything better than justice, truth, temperance, fortitude, and, in a word, anything better than thy own mind's self-satisfaction in the things which it enables thee to do according to right reason, and in the condition that is assigned to thee without thy own choice; if, I say, thou seest anything better than this, turn to it with all thy soul, and enjoy that which thou hast found to be the best. But if nothing appears to be better than the deity which is planted in thee, which has subjected to itself all thy appetites, and carefully examines all the impressions, and, as Socrates said, has detached itself from the persuasions of sense, and has submitted itself to the gods, and cares for mankind; if thou findest everything else smaller and of less value than this, give place to nothing else, for if thou dost once diverge and incline to it, thou wilt no longer without distraction be able to give the preference to that good thing which is thy proper possession and thy own; for it is not right that anything of any other kind, such as praise from the many, or power, or enjoyment of pleasure, should come into competition with that which is rationally and politically or practically good. All these things, even though they may seem to adapt themselves to the better things in a small degree, obtain the superiority all at once, and carry us away. But do thou, I say, simply and freely choose the better, and hold to it.- But that which is useful is the better.- Well then, if it is useful to thee as a rational being, keep to it; but if it is only useful to thee as an animal, say so, and maintain thy judgement without arrogance: only take care that thou makest the inquiry by a sure method.

Never value anything as profitable to thyself which shall compel thee to break thy promise, to lose thy self-respect, to hate any man, to suspect, to curse, to act the hypocrite, to desire anything which needs walls and curtains: for he who has preferred to everything intelligence and daemon and the worship of its excellence, acts no tragic part, does not groan, will not need either solitude or much company; and, what is chief of all, he will live without either pursuing or flying from death; but whether for a longer or a shorter time he shall have the soul inclosed in the body, he cares not at all: for even if he must depart immediately, he will go as readily as if he were going to do anything else which can be done with decency and order; taking care of this only all through life, that his thoughts turn not away from anything which belongs to an intelligent animal and a member of a civil community.

In the mind of one who is chastened and purified thou wilt find no corrupt matter, nor impurity, nor any sore skinned over. Nor is his life incomplete when fate overtakes him, as one may say of an actor who leaves the stage before ending and finishing the play. Besides, there is in him nothing servile, nor affected, nor too closely bound to other things, nor yet detached from other things, nothing worthy of blame, nothing which seeks a hiding-place.

Reverence the faculty which produces opinion. On this faculty it entirely depends whether there shall exist in thy ruling part any opinion inconsistent with nature and the constitution of the rational animal. And this faculty promises freedom from hasty judgement, and friendship towards men, and obedience to the gods.

Throwing away then all things, hold to these only which are few; and besides bear in mind that every man lives only this present time, which is an indivisible point, and that all the rest of his life is either past or it is uncertain. Short then is the time which every man lives, and small the nook of the earth where he lives; and short too the longest posthumous fame, and even this only continued by a succession of poor human beings, who will very soon die, and who know not even themselves, much less him who died long ago.

To the aids which have been mentioned let this one still be added:-

Make for thyself a definition or description of the thing which is presented to thee, so as to see distinctly what kind of a thing it is in its substance, in its nudity, in its complete entirety, and tell thyself its proper name, and the names of the things of which it has been compounded, and into which it will be resolved. For nothing is so productive of elevation of mind as to be able to examine methodically and truly every object which is presented to thee in life, and always to look at things so as to see at the same time what kind of universe this is, and what kind of use everything performs in it, and what value everything has with reference to the whole, and what with reference to man, who is a citizen of the highest city, of which all other cities are like families; what each thing is, and of what it is composed, and how long it is the nature of this thing to endure which now makes an impression on me, and what virtue I have need of with respect to it, such as gentleness, manliness, truth, fidelity, simplicity, contentment, and the rest. Wherefore, on every occasion a man should say: this comes from God; and this is according to the apportionment and spinning of the thread of destiny, and such-like coincidence and chance; and this is from one of the same stock, and a kinsman and partner, one who knows not however what is according to his nature. But I know; for this reason I behave towards him according to the natural law of fellowship with benevolence and justice. At the same time however in things indifferent I attempt to ascertain the value of each.

If thou workest at that which is before thee, following right reason seriously, vigorously, calmly, without allowing anything else to distract thee, but keeping thy divine part pure, as if thou shouldst be bound to give it back immediately; if thou holdest to this, expecting nothing, fearing nothing, but satisfied with thy present activity according to nature, and with heroic truth in every word and sound which thou utterest, thou wilt live happy. And there is no man who is able to prevent this.

As physicians have always their instruments and knives ready for cases which suddenly require their skill, so do thou have principles ready for the understanding of things divine and human, and for doing everything, even the smallest, with a recollection of the bond which unites the divine and human to one another. For neither wilt thou do anything well which pertains to man without at the same time having a reference to things divine; nor the contrary.

No longer wander at hazard; for neither wilt thou read thy own memoirs, nor the acts of the ancient Romans and Hellenes, and the selections from books which thou wast reserving for thy old age.

Hasten then to the end which thou hast before thee, and throwing away idle hopes, come to thy own aid, if thou carest at all for thyself, while it is in thy power.

They know not how many things are signified by the words stealing, sowing, buying, keeping quiet, seeing what ought to be done; for this is not effected by the eyes, but by another kind of vision.

Body, soul, intelligence: to the body belong sensations, to the soul appetites, to the intelligence principles. To receive the impressions of forms by means of appearances belongs even to animals; to be pulled by the strings of desire belongs both to wild beasts and to men who have made themselves into women, and to a Phalaris and a Nero: and to have the intelligence that guides to the things which appear suitable belongs also to those who do not believe in the gods, and who betray their country, and do their impure deeds when they have shut the doors. If then everything else is common to all that I have mentioned, there remains that which is peculiar to the good man, to be pleased and content with what happens, and with the thread which is spun for him; and not to defile the divinity which is planted in his breast, nor disturb it by a crowd of images, but to preserve it tranquil, following it obediently as a god, neither saying anything contrary to the truth, nor doing anything contrary to justice. And if all men refuse to believe that he lives a simple, modest, and contented life, he is neither angry with any of them, nor does he deviate from the way which leads to the end of life, to which a man ought to come pure, tranquil, ready to depart, and without any compulsion perfectly reconciled to his lot.

BOOK FOUR

THAT which rules within, when it is according to nature, is so affected with respect to the events which happen, that it always easily adapts itself to that which is and is presented to it. For it requires no definite material, but it moves towards its purpose, under certain conditions however; and it makes a material for itself out of that which opposes it, as fire lays hold of what falls into it, by which a small light would have been extinguished: but when the fire is strong, it soon appropriates to itself the matter which is heaped on it, and consumes it, and rises higher by means of this very material.

Let no act be done without a purpose, nor otherwise than according to the perfect principles of art.

Men seek retreats for themselves, houses in the country, sea-shores, and mountains; and thou too art wont to desire such things very much. But this is altogether a mark of the most common sort of men, for it is in thy power whenever thou shalt choose to retire into thyself. For nowhere either with more quiet or more freedom from trouble does a man retire than into his own soul, particularly when he has within him such thoughts that by looking into them he is immediately in perfect tranquility; and I affirm that tranquility is nothing else than the good ordering of the mind. Constantly then give to thyself this retreat, and renew thyself; and let thy principles be brief and fundamental, which, as soon as thou shalt recur to them, will be sufficient to cleanse the soul completely, and to send thee back free from all discontent with the things to which thou returnest. For with what art thou discontented? With the badness of men? Recall to thy mind this conclusion, that rational animals exist for one another, and that to endure is a part of justice, and that men do wrong involuntarily; and consider how many already, after mutual enmity, suspicion, hatred, and fighting, have been stretched dead, reduced to ashes; and be quiet at last.- But perhaps thou art dissatisfied with that which is assigned to thee out of the universe.- Recall to thy recollection this alternative; either there is providence or atoms, fortuitous concurrence of things; or remember the arguments by which it has been proved that the world is a kind of political community, and be quiet at last.- But perhaps corporeal things will still fasten upon thee.- Consider then further that the mind mingles not with the breath, whether moving gently or violently, when it has once drawn itself apart and discovered its own power, and think also of all that thou hast heard and assented to about pain and pleasure, and be quiet at last.- But perhaps the desire of the thing called fame will torment thee.- See how soon everything is forgotten, and look at the chaos of infinite time on each side of the present, and the emptiness of applause, and the changeableness and want of judgement in those who pretend to give praise, and the narrowness of the space within which it is circumscribed, and be quiet at last. For the whole earth is a point, and how small a nook in it is this thy dwelling, and how few are there in it, and what kind of people are they who will praise thee. This then remains: Remember to retire into this little territory of thy own, and above all do not distract or strain thyself, but be free, and look at things as a man, as a human being, as a citizen, as a mortal. But among the things readiest to thy hand to which thou shalt turn, let there be these, which are two. One is that things do not touch the soul, for they are external and remain immovable; but our perturbations come only from the opinion which is within. The other is that all these things, which thou seest, change immediately and will no longer be; and constantly bear in mind how many of these changes thou hast already witnessed. The universe is transformation: life is opinion.

If our intellectual part is common, the reason also, in respect of which we are rational beings, is common: if this is so, common also is the reason which commands us what to do, and what not to do; if this is so, there is a common law also; if this is so, we are fellow-citizens; if this is so, we are members of some political community; if this is so, the world is in a manner a state. For of what other common political community will any one say that the whole human race are members? And from thence, from this common political community comes also our very intellectual faculty and reasoning faculty and our capacity for law; or whence do they come?

For as my earthly part is a portion given to me from certain earth, and that which is watery from another element, and that which is hot and fiery from some peculiar source (for nothing comes out of that which is nothing, as nothing also returns to non-existence), so also the intellectual part comes from some source.

Death is such as generation is, a mystery of nature; a composition out of the same elements, and a decomposition into the same; and altogether not a thing of which any man should be ashamed, for it is not contrary to the nature of a reasonable animal, and not contrary to the reason of our constitution.

It is natural that these things should be done by such persons, it is a matter of necessity; and if a man will not have it so, he will not allow the fig-tree to have juice. But by all means bear this in mind, that within a very short time both thou and he will be dead; and soon not even your names will be left behind.

Take away thy opinion, and then there is taken away the complaint, "I have been harmed." Take away the complaint, "I have been harmed," and the harm is taken away. That which does not make a man worse than he was, also does not make his life worse, nor does it harm him either from without or from within.

The nature of that which is universally useful has been compelled to do this.

Consider that everything which happens, happens justly, and if thou observest carefully, thou wilt find it to be so. I do not say only with respect to the continuity of the series of things, but with respect to what is just, and as if it were done by one who assigns to each thing its value. Observe then as thou hast begun; and whatever thou doest, do it in conjunction with this, the being good, and in the sense in which a man is properly understood to be good. Keep to this in every action.

Do not have such an opinion of things as he has who does thee wrong, or such as he wishes thee to have, but look at them as they are in truth.

A man should always have these two rules in readiness; the one, to do only whatever the reason of the ruling and legislating faculty may suggest for the use of men; the other, to change thy opinion, if there is any one at hand who sets thee right and moves thee from any opinion. But this change of opinion must proceed only from a certain persuasion, as of what is just or of common advantage, and the like, not because it appears pleasant or brings reputation.

Hast thou reason? I have.- Why then dost not thou use it? For if this does its own work, what else dost thou wish?

Thou hast existed as a part. Thou shalt disappear in that which produced thee; but rather thou shalt be received back into its seminal principle by transmutation.

Many grains of frankincense on the same altar: one falls before, another falls after; but it makes no difference.

Within ten days thou wilt seem a god to those to whom thou art now a beast and an ape, if thou wilt return to thy principles and the worship of reason.

Do not act as if thou wert going to live ten thousand years. Death hangs over thee. While thou livest, while it is in thy power, be good.

How much trouble he avoids who does not look to see what his neighbour says or does or thinks, but only to what he does himself, that it may be just and pure; or as Agathon says, look not round at the depraved morals of others, but run straight along the line without deviating from it.

He who has a vehement desire for posthumous fame does not consider that every one of those who remember him will himself also die very soon; then again also they who have succeeded them, until the whole remembrance shall have been extinguished as it is transmitted through men who foolishly admire and perish. But suppose that those who will remember are even immortal, and that the remembrance will be immortal, what then is this to thee? And I say not what is it to the dead, but what is it to the living? What is praise except indeed so far as it has a certain utility? For thou now rejectest unseasonably the gift of nature, clinging to something else...

Everything which is in any way beautiful is beautiful in itself, and terminates in itself, not having praise as part of itself. Neither worse then nor better is a thing made by being praised. I affirm this also of the things which are called beautiful by the vulgar, for example, material things and works of art. That which is really beautiful has no need of anything; not more than law, not more than truth, not more than benevolence or modesty. Which of these things is beautiful because it is praised, or spoiled by being blamed? Is such a thing as an emerald made worse than it was, if it is not praised? Or gold, ivory, purple, a lyre, a little knife, a flower, a shrub?

If souls continue to exist, how does the air contain them from eternity?- But how does the earth contain the bodies of those who have been buried from time so remote? For as here the mutation of these bodies after a certain continuance, whatever it may be, and their dissolution make room for other dead bodies; so the souls which are removed into the air after subsisting for some time are transmuted and diffused, and assume a fiery nature by being received into the seminal intelligence of the universe, and in this way make room for the fresh souls which come to dwell there. And this is the answer which a man might give on the hypothesis of souls continuing to exist. But we must not only think of the number of bodies which are thus buried, but also of the number of animals which are daily eaten by us and the other animals. For what a number is consumed, and thus in a manner buried in the bodies of those who feed on them! And nevertheless this earth receives them by reason of the changes of these bodies into blood, and the transformations into the aerial or the fiery element.

What is the investigation into the truth in this matter? The division into that which is material and that which is the cause of form, the formal.

Do not be whirled about, but in every movement have respect to justice, and on the occasion of every impression maintain the faculty of comprehension or understanding.

Everything harmonizes with me, which is harmonious to thee, O Universe. Nothing for me is too early nor too late, which is in due time for thee. Everything is fruit to me which thy seasons bring, O Nature: from thee are all things, in thee are all things, to thee all things return. The poet says,

Dear city of Cecrops; and wilt not thou say, Dear city of Zeus?

Occupy thyself with few things, says the philosopher, if thou wouldst be tranquil.- But consider if it would not be better to say, Do what is necessary, and whatever the reason of the animal which is naturally social requires, and as it requires. For this brings not only the tranquility which comes from doing well, but also that which comes from doing few things. For the greatest part of what we say and do being unnecessary, if a man takes this away, he will have more leisure and less uneasiness. Accordingly on every occasion a man should ask himself, Is this one of the unnecessary things? Now a man should take away not only unnecessary acts, but also, unnecessary thoughts, for thus superfluous acts will not follow after.

Try how the life of the good man suits thee, the life of him who is satisfied with his portion out of the whole, and satisfied with his own just acts and benevolent disposition.

Hast thou seen those things? Look also at these. Do not disturb thyself. Make thyself all simplicity. Does any one do wrong? It is to himself that he does the wrong. Has anything happened to thee?

Well; out of the universe from the beginning everything which happens has been apportioned and spun out to thee. In a word, thy life is short. Thou must turn to profit the present by the aid of reason and justice. Be sober in thy relaxation.

Either it is a well-arranged universe or a chaos huddled together, but still a universe. But can a certain order subsist in thee, and disorder in the All? And this too when all things are so separated and diffused and sympathetic.

A black character, a womanish character, a stubborn character, bestial, childish, animal, stupid, counterfeit, scurrilous, fraudulent, tyrannical.

If he is a stranger to the universe who does not know what is in it, no less is he a stranger who does not know what is going on in it. He is a runaway, who flies from social reason; he is blind, who shuts the eyes of the understanding; he is poor, who has need of another, and has not from himself all things which are useful for life. He is an abscess on the universe who withdraws and separates himself from the reason of our common nature through being displeased with the things which happen, for the same nature produces this, and has produced thee too: he is a piece rent asunder from the state, who tears his own soul from that of reasonable animals, which is one.

The one is a philosopher without a tunic, and the other without a book: here is another half naked: Bread I have not, he says, and I abide by reason.- And I do not get the means of living out of my learning, and I abide by my reason.

Love the art, poor as it may be, which thou hast learned, and be content with it; and pass through the rest of life like one who has intrusted to the gods with his whole soul all that he has, making thyself neither the tyrant nor the slave of any man.

Consider, for example, the times of Vespasian. Thou wilt see all these things, people marrying, bringing up children, sick, dying, warring, feasting, trafficking, cultivating the ground, flattering, obstinately arrogant, suspecting, plotting, wishing for some to die, grumbling about the present, loving, heaping

22

up treasure, desiring counsulship, kingly power. Well then, that life of these people no longer exists at all. Again, remove to the times of Trajan. Again, all is the same. Their life too is gone. In like manner view also the other epochs of time and of whole nations, and see how many after great efforts soon fell and were resolved into the elements. But chiefly thou shouldst think of those whom thou hast thyself known distracting themselves about idle things, neglecting to do what was in accordance with their proper constitution, and to hold firmly to this and to be content with it. And herein it is necessary to remember that the attention given to everything has its proper value and proportion. For thus thou wilt not be dissatisfied, if thou appliest thyself to smaller matters no further than is fit.

The words which were formerly familiar are now antiquated: so also the names of those who were famed of old, are now in a manner antiquated, Camillus, Caeso, Volesus, Leonnatus, and a little after also Scipio and Cato, then Augustus, then also Hadrian and Antoninus. For all things soon pass away and become a mere tale, and complete oblivion soon buries them. And I say this of those who have shone in a wondrous way. For the rest, as soon as they have breathed out their breath, they are gone, and no man speaks of them. And, to conclude the matter, what is even an eternal remembrance? A mere nothing. What then is that about which we ought to employ our serious pains? This one thing, thoughts just, and acts social, and words which never lie, and a disposition which gladly accepts all that happens, as necessary, as usual, as flowing from a principle and source of the same kind.

Willingly give thyself up to Clotho, one of the Fates, allowing her to spin thy thread into whatever things she pleases.

Everything is only for a day, both that which remembers and that which is remembered.

Observe constantly that all things take place by change, and accustom thyself to consider that the nature of the Universe loves nothing so much as to change the things which are and to make new things like them. For everything that exists is in a manner the seed of that which will be. But thou art thinking only of seeds which are cast into the earth or into a womb: but this is a very vulgar notion.

Thou wilt soon die, and thou art not yet simple, not free from perturbations, nor without suspicion of being hurt by external things, nor kindly disposed towards all; nor dost thou yet place wisdom only in acting justly.

Examine men's ruling principles, even those of the wise, what kind of things they avoid, and what kind they pursue.

What is evil to thee does not subsist in the ruling principle of another; nor yet in any turning and mutation of thy corporeal covering. Where is it then? It is in that part of thee in which subsists the power of forming opinions about evils. Let this power then not form such opinions, and all is well. And if that which is nearest to it, the poor body, is burnt, filled with matter and rottenness, nevertheless let the part which forms opinions about these things be quiet, that is, let it judge that nothing is either bad or good which can happen equally to the bad man and the good. For that which happens equally to him who lives contrary to nature and to him who lives according to nature, is neither according to nature nor contrary to nature.

Constantly regard the universe as one living being, having one substance and one soul; and observe how all things have reference to one perception, the perception of this one living being; and how all things act with one movement; and how all things are the cooperating causes of all things which exist; observe too the continuous spinning of the thread and the contexture of the web.

Thou art a little soul bearing about a corpse, as Epictetus used to say.

It is no evil for things to undergo change, and no good for things to subsist in consequence of change.

Time is like a river made up of the events which happen, and a violent stream; for as soon as a thing has been seen, it is carried away, and another comes in its place, and this will be carried away too.

Everything which happens is as familiar and well known as the rose in spring and the fruit in summer; for such is disease, and death, and calumny, and treachery, and whatever else delights fools or vexes them.

In the series of things those which follow are always aptly fitted to those which have gone before; for this series is not like a mere enumeration of disjointed things, which has only a necessary sequence, but it is a rational connection: and as all existing things are arranged together harmoniously, so the things which come into existence exhibit no mere succession, but a certain wonderful relationship.

Always remember the saying of Heraclitus, that the death of earth is to become water, and the death of water is to become air, and the death of air is to become fire, and reversely. And think too of him who forgets whither the way leads, and that men quarrel with that with which they are most constantly in communion, the reason which governs the universe; and the things which daily meet with seem to them strange: and consider that we ought not to act and speak as if we were asleep, for even in sleep we seem to act and speak; and that we ought not, like children who learn from their parents, simply to act and speak as we have been taught.

If any god told thee that thou shalt die to-morrow, or certainly on the day after to-morrow, thou wouldst not care much whether it was on the third day or on the morrow, unless thou wast in the highest degree mean-spirited- for how small is the difference?- So think it no great thing to die after as many years as thou canst name rather than to-morrow.

Think continually how many physicians are dead after often contracting their eyebrows over the sick; and how many astrologers after predicting with great pretensions the deaths of others; and how many philosophers after endless discourses on death or immortality; how many heroes after killing thousands; and how many tyrants who have used their power over men's lives with terrible insolence as if they were immortal; and how many cities are entirely dead, so to speak, Helice and Pompeii and Herculaneum, and others innumerable. Add to the reckoning all whom thou hast known, one after another. One man after burying another has been laid out dead, and another buries him: and all this in a short time. To conclude, always observe how ephemeral and worthless human things are, and what was yesterday a little mucus to-morrow will be a mummy or ashes. Pass then through this little space of time conformably to nature, and end thy journey in content, just as an olive falls off when it is ripe, blessing nature who produced it, and thanking the tree on which it grew.

Be like the promontory against which the waves continually break, but it stands firm and tames the fury of the water around it.

Unhappy am I because this has happened to me.- Not so, but happy am I, though this has happened to me, because I continue free from pain, neither crushed by the present nor fearing the future. For such a thing as this might have happened to every man; but every man would not have continued free from pain on such an occasion. Why then is that rather a misfortune than this a good fortune? And dost thou in all cases call that a man's misfortune, which is not a deviation from man's nature? And does a thing seem to thee to be a deviation from man's nature, when it is not contrary to the will of man's nature? Well, thou knowest the will of nature. Will then this which has happened prevent thee from being just, magnanimous, temperate, prudent, secure against inconsiderate opinions and falsehood; will it prevent thee from having modesty, freedom, and everything else, by the presence of which man's nature obtains all that is its own? Remember too on every occasion which leads thee to vexation to apply this principle: not that this is a misfortune, but that to bear it nobly is good fortune.

It is a vulgar, but still a useful help towards contempt of death, to pass in review those who have tenaciously stuck to life. What more then have they gained than those who have died early? Certainly they lie in their tombs somewhere at last, Cadicianus, Fabius, Julianus, Lepidus, or any one else like them, who have carried out many to be buried, and then were carried out themselves. Altogether the interval is small between birth and death; and consider with how much trouble, and in company with what sort of people and in what a feeble body this interval is laboriously passed. Do not then consider life a thing of any value. For look to the immensity of time behind thee, and to the time which is before thee, another boundless space. In this infinity then what is the difference between him who lives three days and him who lives three generations?

Always run to the short way; and the short way is the natural: accordingly say and do everything in conformity with the soundest reason. For such a purpose frees a man from trouble, and warfare, and all artifice and ostentatious display.

BOOK FIVE

IN THE morning when thou risest unwillingly, let this thought be present- I am rising to the work of a human being. Why then am I dissatisfied if I am going to do the things for which I exist and for which I was brought into the world? Or have I been made for this, to lie in the bed-clothes and keep myself warm?- But this is more pleasant.- Dost thou exist then to take thy pleasure, and not at all for action or exertion? Dost thou not see the little plants, the little birds, the ants, the spiders, the bees working together to put in order their several parts of the universe? And art thou unwilling to do the work of a human being, and dost thou not make haste to do that which is according to thy nature?- But it is necessary to take rest also.- It is necessary: however nature has fixed bounds to this too: she has fixed bounds both to eating and drinking, and yet thou goest beyond these bounds, beyond what is sufficient; yet in thy acts it is not so, but thou stoppest short of what thou canst do. So thou lovest not thyself, for if thou didst, thou wouldst love thy nature and her will. But those who love their several arts exhaust themselves in working at them unwashed and without food; but thou valuest thy own own nature less than the turner values the turning art, or the dancer the dancing art, or the lover of money values his money, or the vainglorious man his little glory. And such men, when they have a violent affection to a thing, choose neither to eat nor to sleep rather than to perfect the things which they care for. But are the acts which concern society more vile in thy eyes and less worthy of thy labour?

How easy it is to repel and to wipe away every impression which is troublesome or unsuitable, and immediately to be in all tranquility.

Judge every word and deed which are according to nature to be fit for thee; and be not diverted by the blame which follows from any people nor by their words, but if a thing is good to be done or said, do not consider it unworthy of thee. For those persons have their peculiar leading principle and follow their peculiar movement; which things do not thou regard, but go straight on, following thy own nature and the common nature; and the way of both is one.

I go through the things which happen according to nature until I shall fall and rest, breathing out my breath into that element out of which I daily draw it in, and falling upon that earth out of which my father collected the seed, and my mother the blood, and my nurse the milk; out of which during so many years I have been supplied with food and drink; which bears me when I tread on it and abuse it for so many purposes.

Thou sayest, Men cannot admire the sharpness of thy wits.- Be it so: but there are many other things of which thou canst not say, I am not formed for them by nature. Show those qualities then which are altogether in thy power, sincerity, gravity, endurance of labour, aversion to pleasure, contentment with thy portion and with few things, benevolence, frankness, no love of superfluity, freedom from trifling magnanimity. Dost thou not see how many qualities thou art immediately able to exhibit, in which there is no excuse of natural incapacity and unfitness, and yet thou still remainest voluntarily below the mark? Or art thou compelled through being defectively furnished by nature to murmur, and to be stingy, and to flatter, and to find fault with thy poor body, and to try to please men, and to make great display, and to be so restless in thy mind? No, by the gods: but thou mightest have been delivered from these things long ago. Only if in truth thou canst be charged with being rather slow and dull of comprehension, thou must exert thyself about this also, not neglecting it nor yet taking pleasure in thy dulness.

One man, when he has done a service to another, is ready to set it down to his account as a favour conferred. Another is not ready to do this, but still in his own mind he thinks of the man as his debtor, and he knows what he has done. A third in a manner does not even know what he has done, but he is like a vine which has produced grapes, and seeks for nothing more after it has once produced its proper fruit. As a horse when he has run, a dog when he has tracked the game, a bee when it has made the honey, so a man when he has done a good act, does not call out for others to come and see, but he goes on to another act, as a vine goes on to produce again the grapes in season.- Must a man then be one of these, who in a manner act thus without observing it?- Yes.- But this very thing is necessary, the observation of what a man is doing: for, it may be said, it is characteristic of the social animal to perceive that he is working in a social manner, and indeed to wish that his social partner also should perceive it.- It is true what thou sayest, but thou dost not rightly understand what is now said: and for this reason thou wilt become one of those of whom I spoke before, for even they are misled by a certain show of reason. But if thou wilt choose to understand the meaning of what is said, do not fear that for this reason thou wilt omit any social act.

A prayer of the Athenians: Rain, rain, O dear Zeus, down on the ploughed fields of the Athenians and on the plains.- In truth we ought not to pray at all, or we ought to pray in this simple and noble fashion.

Just as we must understand when it is said, That Aesculapius prescribed to this man horse-exercise, or bathing in cold water or going without shoes; so we must understand it when it is said, That the nature of the universe prescribed to this man disease or mutilation or loss or anything else of the kind. For in the first case Prescribed means something like this: he prescribed this for this man as a thing adapted to procure health; and in the second case it means: That which happens to (or, suits) every man is fixed in a manner for him suitably to his destiny. For this is what we mean when we say that things are suitable to us, as the workmen say of squared stones in walls or the pyramids, that they are suitable, when they fit them to one another in some kind of connexion. For there is altogether one fitness, harmony. And as the universe is made up out of all bodies to be such a body as it is, so out of all existing causes necessity (destiny) is made up to be such a cause as it is. And even those who are completely ignorant understand what I mean, for they say, It (necessity, destiny) brought this to such a person.- This then was brought and this was precribed to him. Let us then receive these things, as well as those which Aesculapius prescribes. Many as a matter of course even among his prescriptions are disagreeable, but we accept them in the hope of health. Let the perfecting and accomplishment of the things, which the common nature judges to be good, be judged by thee to be of the same kind as thy health. And so accept everything which happens, even if it seem disagreeable, because it leads to this, to the health of the universe and to the prosperity and felicity of Zeus (the universe).

For he would not have brought on any man what he has brought, if it were not useful for the whole. Neither does the nature of anything, whatever it may be, cause anything which is not suitable to that which is directed by it. For two reasons then it is right to be content with that which happens to thee; the one, because it was done for thee and prescribed for thee, and in a manner had reference to thee, originally from the most ancient causes spun with thy destiny; and the other, because even that which comes severally to every man is to the power which administers the universe a cause of felicity and perfection, nay even of its very continuance. For the integrity of the whole is mutilated, if thou cuttest off anything whatever from the conjunction and the continuity either of the parts or of the causes.

And thou dost cut off, as far as it is in thy power, when thou art dissatisfied, and in a manner triest to put anything out of the way.

Be not disgusted, nor discouraged, nor dissatisfied, if thou dost not succeed in doing everything according to right principles; but when thou hast failed, return back again, and be content if the greater part of what thou doest is consistent with man's nature, and love this to which thou returnest; and do not return to philosophy as if she were a master, but act like those who have sore eyes and apply a bit of sponge and egg, or as another applies a plaster, or drenching with water. For thus thou wilt not fail to obey reason, and thou wilt repose in it. And remember that philosophy requires only the things which thy nature requires; but thou wouldst have something else which is not according to nature.- It may be objected, Why what is more agreeable than this which I am doing?- But is not this the very reason why pleasure deceives us? And consider if magnanimity, freedom, simplicity, equanimity, piety, are not more agreeable. For what is more agreeable than wisdom itself, when thou thinkest of the security and the happy course of all things which depend on the faculty of understanding and knowledge?

Things are in such a kind of envelopment that they have seemed to philosophers, not a few nor those common philosophers, altogether unintelligible; nay even to the Stoics themselves they seem difficult to understand. And all our assent is changeable; for where is the man who never changes? Carry thy thoughts then to the objects themselves, and consider how short-lived they are and worthless, and that they may be in the possession of a filthy wretch or a whore or a robber.

Then turn to the morals of those who live with thee, and it is hardly possible to endure even the most agreeable of them, to say nothing of a man being hardly able to endure himself. In such darkness then and dirt and in so constant a flux both of substance and of time, and of motion and of things moved, what there is worth being highly prized or even an object of serious pursuit, I cannot imagine. But on the contrary it is a man's duty to comfort himself, and to wait for the natural dissolution and not to be vexed at the delay, but to rest in these principles only: the one, that nothing will happen to me which is not conformable to the nature of the universe; and the other, that it is in my power never to act contrary to my god and daemon: for there is no man who will compel me to this.

About what am I now employing my own soul? On every occasion I must ask myself this question, and inquire, what have I now in this part of me which they call the ruling principle? And whose soul have I now? That of a child, or of a young man, or of a feeble woman, or of a tyrant, or of a domestic animal, or of a wild beast?

What kind of things those are which appear good to the many, we may learn even from this. For if any man should conceive certain things as being really good, such as prudence, temperance, justice, fortitude, he would not after having first conceived these endure to listen to anything which should not be in harmony with what is really good. But if a man has first conceived as good the things which appear to the many to be good, he will listen and readily receive as very applicable that which was said by the comic writer. Thus even the many perceive the difference. For were it not so, this saying would not offend and would not be rejected in the first case, while we receive it when it is said of wealth, and of the means which further luxury and fame, as said fitly and wittily. Go on then and ask if we should value and think those things to be good, to which after their first conception in the mind the words of the comic writer might be aptly applied- that he who has them, through pure abundance has not a place to ease himself in.

I am composed of the formal and the material; and neither of them will perish into non-existence, as neither of them came into existence out of non-existence. Every part of me then will be reduced by change into some part of the universe, and that again will change into another part of the universe, and so on for ever. And by consequence of such a change I too exist, and those who begot me, and so on for ever in the other direction. For nothing hinders us from saying so, even if the universe is administered according to definite periods of revolution.

Reason and the reasoning art (philosophy) are powers which are sufficient for themselves and for their own works. They move then from a first principle which is their own, and they make their way to the end which is proposed to them; and this is the reason why such acts are named catorthoseis or right acts, which word signifies that they proceed by the right road.

None of these things ought to be called a man's, which do not belong to a man, as man. They are not required of a man, nor does man's nature promise them, nor are they the means of man's nature attaining its end. Neither then does the end of man lie in these things, nor yet that which aids to the accomplishment of this end, and that which aids towards this end is that which is good. Besides, if any of these things did belong to man, it would not be right for a man to despise them and to set himself against them; nor would a man be worthy of praise who showed that he did not want these things, nor would he who stinted himself in any of them be good, if indeed these things were good. But now the more of these things a man deprives himself of, or of other things like them, or even when he is deprived of any of them, the more patiently he endures the loss, just in the same degree he is a better man.

Such as are thy habitual thoughts, such also will be the character of thy mind; for the soul is dyed by the thoughts. Dye it then with a continuous series of such thoughts as these: for instance, that where a man can live, there he can also live well. But he must live in a palace;- well then, he can also live well in a palace. And again, consider that for whatever purpose each thing has been constituted, for this it has been constituted, and towards this it is carried; and its end is in that towards which it is carried; and where the end is, there also is the advantage and the good of each thing. Now the good for the reasonable animal is society; for that we are made for society has been shown above. Is it not plain that the inferior exist for the sake of the superior? But the things which have life are superior to those which have not life, and of those which have life the superior are those which have reason.

To seek what is impossible is madness: and it is impossible that the bad should not do something of this kind.

Nothing happens to any man which he is not formed by nature to bear. The same things happen to another, and either because he does not see that they have happened or because he would show a great spirit he is firm and remains unharmed. It is a shame then that ignorance and conceit should be stronger than wisdom.

Things themselves touch not the soul, not in the least degree; nor have they admission to the soul, nor can they turn or move the soul: but the soul turns and moves itself alone, and whatever judgements it may think proper to make, such it makes for itself the things which present themselves to it.

In one respect man is the nearest thing to me, so far as I must do good to men and endure them. But so far as some men make themselves obstacles to my proper acts, man becomes to me one of the things which are indifferent, no less than the sun or wind or a wild beast. Now it is true that these may impede my action, but they are no impediments to my affects and disposition, which have the power of acting conditionally and changing: for the mind converts and changes every hindrance to its activity into an aid; and so that which is a hindrance is made a furtherance to an act; and that which is an obstacle on the road helps us on this road.

Reverence that which is best in the universe; and this is that which makes use of all things and directs all things. And in like manner also reverence that which is best in thyself; and this is of the same kind as that. For in thyself also, that which makes use of everything else, is this, and thy life is directed by this.

That which does no harm to the state, does no harm to the citizen. In the case of every appearance of harm apply this rule: if the state is not harmed by this, neither am I harmed. But if the state is harmed, thou must not be angry with him who does harm to the state.

Show him where his error is.

Often think of the rapidity with which things pass by and disappear, both the things which are and the things which are produced. For substance is like a river in a continual flow, and the activities of things are in constant change, and the causes work in infinite varieties; and there is hardly anything which stands still. And consider this which is near to thee, this boundless abyss of the past and of the future in which all things disappear. How then is he not a fool who is puffed up with such things or plagued about them and makes himself miserable? for they vex him only for a time, and a short time.

Think of the universal substance, of which thou hast a very small portion; and of universal time, of which a short and indivisible interval has been assigned to thee; and of that which is fixed by destiny, and how small a part of it thou art.

Does another do me wrong? Let him look to it. He has his own disposition, his own activity. I now have what the universal nature wills me to have; and I do what my nature now wills me to do.

Let the part of thy soul which leads and governs be undisturbed by the movements in the flesh, whether of pleasure or of pain; and let it not unite with them, but let it circumscribe itself and limit those affects to their parts. But when these affects rise up to the mind by virtue of that other sympathy that naturally exists in a body which is all one, then thou must not strive to resist the sensation, for it is natural: but let not the ruling part of itself add to the sensation the opinion that it is either good or bad.

Live with the gods. And he does live with the gods who constantly shows to them, his own soul is satisfied with that which is assigned to him, and that it does all that the daemon wishes, which Zeus hath given to every man for his guardian and guide, a portion of himself.

And this is every man's understanding and reason.

Art thou angry with him whose armpits stink? Art thou angry with him whose mouth smells foul? What good will this danger do thee? He has such a mouth, he has such arm-pits: it is necessary that such an emanation must come from such things- but the man has reason, it will be said, and he is able, if he takes pain, to discover wherein he offends- I wish thee well of thy discovery. Well then, and thou hast reason: by thy rational faculty stir up his rational faculty; show him his error, admonish him. For if he listens, thou wilt cure him, and there is no need of anger. Neither tragic actor nor whore...

As thou intendest to live when thou art gone out,...so it is in thy power to live here. But if men do not permit thee, then get away out of life, yet so as if thou wert suffering no harm. The house is smoky, and I quit it. Why dost thou think that this is any trouble? But so long as nothing of the kind drives me out, I remain, am free, and no man shall hinder me from doing what I choose; and I choose to do what is according to the nature of the rational and social animal.

The intelligence of the universe is social. Accordingly it has made the inferior things for the sake of the superior, and it has fitted the superior to one another. Thou seest how it has subordinated, co-ordinated and assigned to everything its proper portion, and has brought together into concord with one another the things which are the best.

How hast thou behaved hitherto to the gods, thy parents, brethren, children, teachers, to those who looked after thy infancy, to thy friends, kinsfolk, to thy slaves? Consider if thou hast hitherto behaved to all in such a way that this may be said of thee: Never has wronged a man in deed or word.

And call to recollection both how many things thou hast passed through, and how many things thou hast been able to endure: and that the history of thy life is now complete and thy service is ended: and how many beautiful things thou hast seen: and how many pleasures and pains thou hast despised; and how many things called honourable thou hast spurned; and to how many ill-minded folks thou hast shown a kind disposition.

Why do unskilled and ignorant souls disturb him who has skill and knowledge? What soul then has skill and knowledge? That which knows beginning and end, and knows the reason which pervades all substance and through all time by fixed periods (revolutions) administers the universe.

Soon, very soon, thou wilt be ashes, or a skeleton, and either a name or not even a name; but name is sound and echo. And the things which are much valued in life are empty and rotten and trifling, and like little dogs biting one another, and little children quarrelling, laughing, and then straightway weeping. But fidelity and modesty and justice and truth are fled

Up to Olympus from the wide-spread earth.

What then is there which still detains thee here? If the objects of sense are easily changed and never stand still, and the organs of perception are dull and easily receive false impressions; and the poor soul itself is an exhalation from blood. But to have good repute amidst such a world as this is an empty thing. Why then dost thou not wait in tranquility for thy end, whether it is extinction or removal to another state? And until that time comes, what is sufficient? Why, what else than to venerate the gods and bless them, and to do good to men, and to practise tolerance and self-restraint; but as to everything which is beyond the limits of the poor flesh and breath, to remember that this is neither thine nor in thy power.

Thou canst pass thy life in an equable flow of happiness, if thou canst go by the right way, and think and act in the right way. These two things are common both to the soul of God and to the soul of man, and to the soul of every rational being, not to be hindered by another; and to hold good to consist in the disposition to justice and the practice of it, and in this to let thy desire find its termination.

If this is neither my own badness, nor an effect of my own badness, and the common weal is not injured, why am I troubled about it? And what is the harm to the common weal?

Do not be carried along inconsiderately by the appearance of things, but give help to all according to thy ability and their fitness; and if they should have sustained loss in matters which are indifferent, do not imagine this to be a damage. For it is a bad habit. But as the old man, when he went away, asked back his foster-child's top, remembering that it was a top, so do thou in this case also.

When thou art calling out on the Rostra, hast thou forgotten, man, what these things are?- Yes; but they are objects of great concern to these people- wilt thou too then be made a fool for these things?- I was once a fortunate man, but I lost it, I know not how.- But fortunate means that a man has assigned to himself a good fortune: and a good fortune is good disposition of the soul, good emotions, good actions.

BOOK SIX

THE substance of the universe is obedient and compliant; and the reason which governs it has in itself no cause for doing evil, for it has no malice, nor does it do evil to anything, nor is anything harmed by it. But all things are made and perfected according to this reason.

Let it make no difference to thee whether thou art cold or warm, if thou art doing thy duty; and whether thou art drowsy or satisfied with sleep; and whether ill-spoken of or praised; and whether dying or doing something else. For it is one of the acts of life, this act by which we die: it is sufficient then in this act also to do well what we have in hand.

Look within. Let neither the peculiar quality of anything nor its value escape thee.

All existing things soon change, and they will either be reduced to vapour, if indeed all substance is one, or they will be dispersed.

The reason which governs knows what its own disposition is, and what it does, and on what material it works.

The best way of avenging thyself is not to become like the wrong doer.

Take pleasure in one thing and rest in it, in passing from one social act to another social act, thinking of God.

The ruling principle is that which rouses and turns itself, and while it makes itself such as it is and such as it wills to be, it also makes everything which happens appear to itself to be such as it wills.

In conformity to the nature of the universe every single thing is accomplished, for certainly it is not in conformity to any other nature that each thing is accomplished, either a nature which externally comprehends this, or a nature which is comprehended within this nature, or a nature external and independent of this.

The universe is either a confusion, and a mutual involution of things, and a dispersion; or it is unity and order and providence. If then it is the former, why do I desire to tarry in a fortuitous combination of things and such a disorder? And why do I care about anything else than how I shall at last become earth? And why am I disturbed, for the dispersion of my elements will happen whatever I do. But if the other supposition is true, I venerate, and I am firm, and I trust in him who governs.

When thou hast been compelled by circumstances to be disturbed in a manner, quickly return to thyself and do not continue out of tune longer than the compulsion lasts; for thou wilt have more mastery over the harmony by continually recurring to it.

If thou hadst a step-mother and a mother at the same time, thou wouldst be dutiful to thy step-mother, but still thou wouldst constantly return to thy mother. Let the court and philosophy now be to thee step-mother and mother: return to philosophy frequently and repose in her, through whom what thou meetest with in the court appears to thee tolerable, and thou appearest tolerable in the court.

When we have meat before us and such eatables we receive the impression, that this is the dead body of a fish, and this is the dead body of a bird or of a pig; and again, that this Falernian is only a little grape juice, and this purple robe some sheep's wool dyed with the blood of a shell-fish: such then are these impressions, and they reach the things themselves and penetrate them, and so we see what kind of things they are. Just in the same way ought we to act all through life, and where there are things which appear most worthy of our approbation, we ought to lay them bare and look at their worthlessness and strip them of all the words by which they are exalted. For outward show is a wonderful perverter of the reason, and when thou art most sure that thou art employed about things worth thy pains, it is then that it cheats thee most.

Consider then what Crates says of Xenocrates himself. Most of the things which the multitude admire are referred to objects of the most general kind, those which are held together by cohesion or natural organization, such as stones, wood, fig-trees, vines, olives. But those which are admired by men who are a little more reasonable are referred to the things which are held together by a living principle, as flocks, herds. Those which are admired by men who are still more instructed are the things which are held together by a rational soul, not however a universal soul, but rational so far as it is a soul skilled in some art, or expert in some other way, or simply rational so far as it possesses a number of slaves. But he who values rational soul, a soul universal and fitted for political life, regards nothing else except this; and above all things he keeps his soul in a condition and in an activity conformable to reason and social life, and he co-operates to this end with those who are of the same kind as himself.

Some things are hurrying into existence, and others are hurrying out of it; and of that which is coming into existence part is already extinguished. Motions and changes are continually renewing the world, just as the uninterrupted course of time is always renewing the infinite duration of ages. In this flowing stream then, on which there is no abiding, what is there of the things which hurry by on which a man would set a high price? It would be just as if a man should fall in love with one of the sparrows which fly by, but it has already passed out of sight. Something of this kind is the very life of every man, like the exhalation of the blood and the respiration of the air. For such as it is to have once drawn in the air and to have given it back, which we do every moment, just the same is it with the whole respiratory power, which thou didst receive at thy birth yesterday and the day before, to give it back to the element from which thou didst first draw it.

Neither is transpiration, as in plants, a thing to be valued, nor respiration, as in domesticated animals and wild beasts, nor the receiving of impressions by the appearances of things, nor being moved by desires as puppets by strings, nor assembling in herds, nor being nourished by food; for this is just like the act of separating and parting with the useless part of our food. What then is worth being valued? To be received with clapping of hands? No. Neither must we value the clapping of tongues, for the praise which comes from the many is a clapping of tongues. Suppose then that thou hast given up this worthless thing called fame, what remains that is worth valuing? This in my opinion, to move thyself and to restrain thyself in conformity to thy proper constitution, to which end both all employments and arts lead. For every art aims at this, that the thing which has been made should be adapted to the work for which it has been made; and both the vine-planter who looks after the vine, and the horse-breaker, and he who trains the dog, seek this end. But the education and the teaching of youth aim at something. In this then is the value of the education and the teaching. And if this is well, thou wilt not seek anything else. Wilt thou not cease to value many other things too? Then thou wilt be neither free, nor sufficient for thy own happiness, nor without passion. For of necessity thou must be envious, jealous, and suspicious of those who can take away those things, and plot against those who have that which is valued by thee. Of necessity a man must be altogether in a state of perturbation who wants any of these things; and besides, he must often find fault with the gods. But to reverence and honour thy own mind will make thee content with thyself, and in harmony with society, and in agreement with the gods, that is, praising all that they give and have ordered.

Above, below, all around are the movements of the elements. But the motion of virtue is in none of these: it is something more divine, and advancing by a way hardly observed it goes happily on its road.

How strangely men act. They will not praise those who are living at the same time and living with themselves; but to be themselves praised by posterity, by those whom they have never seen or ever will see, this they set much value on. But this is very much the same as if thou shouldst be grieved because those who have lived before thee did not praise thee.

If a thing is difficult to be accomplished by thyself, do not think that it is impossible for man: but if anything is possible for man and conformable to his nature, think that this can be attained by thyself too.

In the gymnastic exercises suppose that a man has torn thee with his nails, and by dashing against thy head has inflicted a wound. Well, we neither show any signs of vexation, nor are we offended, nor do we suspect him afterwards as a treacherous fellow; and yet we are on our guard against him, not however as an enemy, nor yet with suspicion, but we quietly get out of his way. Something like this let thy behaviour be in all the other parts of life; let us overlook many things in those who are like antagonists in the gymnasium. For it is in our power, as I said, to get out of the way, and to have no suspicion nor hatred.

If any man is able to convince me and show me that I do not think or act right, I will gladly change; for I seek the truth by which no man was ever injured. But he is injured who abides in his error and ignorance.

I do my duty: other things trouble me not; for they are either things without life, or things without reason, or things that have rambled and know not the way.

As to the animals which have no reason and generally all things and objects, do thou, since thou hast reason and they have none, make use of them with a generous and liberal spirit. But towards human beings, as they have reason, behave in a social spirit. And on all occasions call on the gods, and do not perplex thyself about the length of time in which thou shalt do this; for even three hours so spent are sufficient.

Alexander the Macedonian and his groom by death were brought to the same state; for either they were received among the same seminal principles of the universe, or they were alike dispersed among the atoms.

Consider how many things in the same indivisible time take place in each of us, things which concern the body and things which concern the soul: and so thou wilt not wonder if many more things, or rather all things which come into existence in that which is the one and all, which we call Cosmos, exist in it at the same time.

If any man should propose to thee the question, how the name Antoninus is written, wouldst thou with a straining of the voice utter each letter? What then if they grow angry, wilt thou be angry too?

Wilt thou not go on with composure and number every letter? just so then in this life also remember that every duty is made up of certain parts. These it is thy duty to observe and without being disturbed or showing anger towards those who are angry with thee to go on thy way and finish that which is set before thee.

How cruel it is not to allow men to strive after the things which appear to them to be suitable to their nature and profitable! And yet in a manner thou dost not allow them to do this, when thou art vexed because they do wrong. For they are certainly moved towards things because they suppose them to be suitable to their nature and profitable to them.- But it is not so.- Teach them then, and show them without being angry.

Death is a cessation of the impressions through the senses, and of the pulling of the strings which move the appetites, and of the discursive movements of the thoughts, and of the service to the flesh.

It is a shame for the soul to be first to give way in this life, when thy body does not give way.

Take care that thou art not made into a Caesar, that thou art not dyed with this dye; for such things happen. Keep thyself then simple, good, pure, serious, free from affectation, a friend of justice, a worshipper of the gods, kind, affectionate, strenuous in all proper acts. Strive to continue to be such as philosophy wished to make thee. Reverence the gods, and help men. Short is life. There is only one fruit of this terrene life, a pious disposition and social acts. Do everything as a disciple of Antoninus. Remember his constancy in every act which was conformable to reason, and his evenness in all things, and his piety, and the serenity of his countenance, and his sweetness, and his disregard of empty fame, and his efforts to understand things; and how he would never let anything pass without having first most carefully examined it and clearly understood it; and how he bore with those who blamed him unjustly without blaming them in return; how he did nothing in a hurry; and how he listened not to calumnies, and how exact an examiner of manners and actions he was; and not given to reproach people, nor timid, nor suspicious, nor a sophist; and with how little he was satisfied, such as lodging, bed, dress, food, servants; and how laborious and patient; and how he was able on account of his sparing diet to hold out to the evening, not even requiring to relieve himself by any evacuations except at the usual hour; and his firmness and uniformity in his friendships; and how he tolerated freedom of speech in those who opposed his opinions; and the pleasure that he had when any man showed him anything better; and how religious he was without superstition.

Imitate all this that thou mayest have as good a conscience, when thy last hour comes, as he had. Return to thy sober senses and call thyself back; and when thou hast roused thyself from sleep and hast perceived that they were only dreams which troubled thee, now in thy waking hours look at these (the things about thee) as thou didst look at those (the dreams).

I consist of a little body and a soul. Now to this little body all things are indifferent, for it is not able to perceive differences.

But to the understanding those things only are indifferent, which are not the works of its own activity. But whatever things are the works of its own activity, all these are in its power. And of these however only those which are done with reference to the present; for as to the future and the past activities of the mind, even these are for the present indifferent.

Neither the labour which the hand does nor that of the foot is contrary to nature, so long as the foot does the foot's work and the hand the hand's. So then neither to a man as a man is his labour contrary to nature, so long as it does the things of a man. But if the labour is not contrary to his nature, neither is it an evil to him. How many pleasures have been enjoyed by robbers, patricides, tyrants.

Dost thou not see how the handicraftsmen accommodate themselves up to a certain point to those who are not skilled in their craft- nevertheless they cling to the reason (the principles) of their art and do not endure to depart from it? Is it not strange if the architect and the physician shall have more respect to the reason (the principles) of their own arts than man to his own reason, which is common to him and the gods?

Asia, Europe are corners of the universe: all the sea a drop in the universe; Athos a little clod of the universe: all the present time is a point in eternity. All things are little, changeable, perishable. All things come from thence, from that universal ruling power either directly proceeding or by way of sequence. And accordingly the lion's gaping jaws, and that which is poisonous, and every harmful thing, as a thorn, as mud, are after-products of the grand and beautiful. Do not then imagine that they are of another kind from that which thou dost venerate, but form a just opinion of the source of all.

He who has seen present things has seen all, both everything which has taken place from all eternity and everything which will be for time without end; for all things are of one kin and of one form.

Frequently consider the connexion of all things in the universe and their relation to one another. For in a manner all things are implicated with one another, and all in this way are friendly to one another; for one thing comes in order after another, and this is by virtue of the active movement and mutual conspiration and the unity of the substance.

Adapt thyself to the things with which thy lot has been cast: and the men among whom thou hast received thy portion, love them, but do it truly, sincerely.

Every instrument, tool, vessel, if it does that for which it has been made, is well, and yet he who made it is not there. But in the things which are held together by nature there is within and there abides in them the power which made them; wherefore the more is it fit to reverence this power, and to think, that, if thou dost live and act according to its will, everything in thee is in conformity to intelligence. And thus also in the universe the things which belong to it are in conformity to intelligence.

Whatever of the things which are not within thy power thou shalt suppose to be good for thee or evil, it must of necessity be that, if such a bad thing befall thee or the loss of such a good thing, thou wilt blame the gods, and hate men too, those who are the cause of the misfortune or the loss, or those who are suspected of being likely to be the cause; and indeed we do much injustice, because we make a difference between these things. But if we judge only those things which are in our power to be good or bad, there remains no reason either for finding fault with God or standing in a hostile attitude to man.

We are all working together to one end, some with knowledge and design, and others without knowing what they do; as men also when they are asleep, of whom it is Heraclitus, I think, who says that they are labourers and co-operators in the things which take place in the universe. But men co-operate after different fashions: and even those co-operate abundantly, who find fault with what happens and those who try to oppose it and to hinder it; for the universe had need even of such men as these. It remains then for thee to understand among what kind of workmen thou placest thyself; for he who rules all things will certainly make a right use of thee, and he will receive thee among some part of the co-operators and of those whose labours conduce to one end. But be not thou such a part as the mean and ridiculous verse in the play, which Chrysippus speaks of.

Does the sun undertake to do the work of the rain, or Aesculapius the work of the Fruit-bearer (the earth)? And how is it with respect to each of the stars, are they not different and yet they work together to the same end?

If the gods have determined about me and about the things which must happen to me, they have determined well, for it is not easy even to imagine a deity without forethought; and as to doing me harm, why should they have any desire towards that? For what advantage would result to them from this or to the whole, which is the special object of their providence? But if they have not determined about me individually, they have certainly determined about the whole at least, and the things which happen by way of sequence in this general arrangement I ought to accept with pleasure and to be content with them. But if they determine about nothing- which it is wicked to believe, or if we do believe it, let us neither sacrifice nor pray nor swear by them nor do anything else which we do as if the gods were present and lived with us- but if however the gods determine about none of the things which concern us, I am able to determine about myself, and I can inquire about that which is useful; and that is useful to every man which is conformable to his own constitution and nature. But my nature is rational and social; and my city and country, so far as I am Antoninus, is Rome, but so far as I am a man, it is the world. The things then which are useful to these cities are alone useful to me. Whatever happens to every man, this is for the interest of the universal: this might be sufficient. But further thou wilt observe this also as a general truth, if thou dost observe, that whatever is profitable to any man is profitable also to other men. But let the word profitable be taken here in the common sense as said of things of the middle kind, neither good nor bad.

As it happens to thee in the amphitheatre and such places, that the continual sight of the same things and the uniformity make the spectacle wearisome, so it is in the whole of life; for all things above, below, are the same and from the same. How long then?

Think continually that all kinds of men and of all kinds of pursuits and of all nations are dead, so that thy thoughts come down even to Philistion and Phoebus and Origanion. Now turn thy thoughts to the other kinds of men. To that place then we must remove, where there are so many great orators, and so many noble philosophers, Heraclitus, Pythagoras, Socrates; so many heroes of former days, and so many generals after them, and tyrants; besides these, Eudoxus,

Hipparchus, Archimedes, and other men of acute natural talents, great minds, lovers of labour, versatile, confident, mockers even of the perishable and ephemeral life of man, as Menippus and such as are like him. As to all these consider that they have long been in the dust. What harm then is this to them; and what to those whose names are altogether unknown? One thing here is worth a great deal, to pass thy life in truth and justice, with a benevolent disposition even to liars and unjust men.

When thou wishest to delight thyself, think of the virtues of those who live with thee; for instance, the activity of one, and the modesty of another, and the liberality of a third, and some other good quality of a fourth. For nothing delights so much as the examples of the virtues, when they are exhibited in the morals of those who live with us and present themselves in abundance, as far as is possible.

Wherefore we must keep them before us.

Thou art not dissatisfied, I suppose, because thou weighest only so many litrae and not three hundred. Be not dissatisfied then that thou must live only so many years and not more; for as thou art satisfied with the amount of substance which has been assigned to thee, so be content with the time.

Let us try to persuade them (men). But act even against their will, when the principles of justice lead that way. If however any man by using force stands in thy way, betake thyself to contentment and tranquility, and at the same time employ the hindrance towards the exercise of some other virtue; and remember that thy attempt was with a reservation, that thou didst not desire to do impossibilities. What then didst thou desire?- Some such effort as this.- But thou attainest thy object, if the things to which thou wast moved are accomplished.

He who loves fame considers another man's activity to be his own good; and he who loves pleasure, his own sensations; but he who has understanding, considers his own acts to be his own good.

It is in our power to have no opinion about a thing, and not to be disturbed in our soul; for things themselves have no natural power to form our judgements.

Accustom thyself to attend carefully to what is said by another, and as much as it is possible, be in the speaker's mind.

That which is not good for the swarm, neither is it good for the bee.

If sailors abused the helmsman or the sick the doctor, would they listen to anybody else; or how could the helmsman secure the safety of those in the ship or the doctor the health of those whom he attends?

How many together with whom I came into the world are already gone out of it.

To the jaundiced honey tastes bitter, and to those bitten by mad dogs water causes fear; and to little children the ball is a fine thing. Why then am I angry? Dost thou think that a false opinion has less power than the bile in the jaundiced or the poison in him who is bitten by a mad dog?

No man will hinder thee from living according to the reason of thy own nature: nothing will happen to thee contrary to the reason of the universal nature.

What kind of people are those whom men wish to please, and for what objects, and by what kind of acts? How soon will time cover all things, and how many it has covered already.

BOOK SEVEN

WHAT is badness? It is that which thou hast often seen. And on the occasion of everything which happens keep this in mind, that it is that which thou hast often seen. Everywhere up and down thou wilt find the same things, with which the old histories are filled, those of the middle ages and those of our own day; with which cities and houses are filled now. There is nothing new: all things are both familiar and short-lived.

How can our principles become dead, unless the impressions (thoughts) which correspond to them are extinguished? But it is in thy power continuously to fan these thoughts into a flame. I can have that opinion about anything, which I ought to have. If I can, why am I disturbed? The things which are external to my mind have no relation at all to my mind.- Let this be the state of thy affects, and thou standest erect. To recover thy life is in thy power. Look at things again as thou didst use to look at them; for in this consists the recovery of thy life.

The idle business of show, plays on the stage, flocks of sheep, herds, exercises with spears, a bone cast to little dogs, a bit of bread into fish-ponds, labourings of ants and burden-carrying, runnings about of frightened little mice, puppets pulled by strings- all alike. It is thy duty then in the midst of such things to show good humour and not a proud air; to understand however that every man is worth just so much as the things are worth about which he busies himself.

In discourse thou must attend to what is said, and in every movement thou must observe what is doing. And in the one thou shouldst see immediately to what end it refers, but in the other watch carefully what is the thing signified.

Is my understanding sufficient for this or not? If it is sufficient, I use it for the work as an instrument given by the universal nature. But if it is not sufficient, then either I retire from the work and give way to him who is able to do it better, unless there be some reason why I ought not to do so; or I do it as well as I can, taking to help me the man who with the aid of my ruling principle can do what is now fit and useful for the general good. For whatsoever either by myself or with another I can do, ought to be directed to this only, to that which is useful and well suited to society.

How many after being celebrated by fame have been given up to oblivion; and how many who have celebrated the fame of others have long been dead.

Be not ashamed to be helped; for it is thy business to do thy duty like a soldier in the assault on a town. How then, if being lame thou canst not mount up on the battlements alone, but with the help of another it is possible?

Let not future things disturb thee, for thou wilt come to them, if it shall be necessary, having with thee the same reason which now thou usest for present things.

All things are implicated with one another, and the bond is holy; and there is hardly anything unconnected with any other thing. For things have been co-ordinated, and they combine to form the same universe (order). For there is one universe made up of all things, and one God who pervades all things, and one substance, and one law, one common reason in all intelligent animals, and one truth; if indeed there is also one perfection for all animals which are of the same stock and participate in the same reason.

Everything material soon disappears in the substance of the whole; and everything formal (causal) is very soon taken back into the universal reason; and the memory of everything is very soon overwhelmed in time.

To the rational animal the same act is according to nature and according to reason.

Be thou erect, or be made erect.

Just as it is with the members in those bodies which are united in one, so it is with rational beings which exist separate, for they have been constituted for one co-operation. And the perception of this will be more apparent to thee, if thou often sayest to thyself that I am a member (melos) of the system of rational beings. But if (using the letter r) thou sayest that thou art a part (meros) thou dost not yet love men from thy heart; beneficence does not yet delight thee for its own sake; thou still doest it barely as a thing of propriety, and not yet as doing good to thyself.

Let there fall externally what will on the parts which can feel the effects of this fall. For those parts which have felt will complain, if they choose. But I, unless I think that what has happened is an evil, am not injured. And it is in my power not to think so.

Whatever any one does or says, I must be good, just as if the gold, or the emerald, or the purple were always saying this, Whatever any one does or says, I must be emerald and keep my colour.

The ruling faculty does not disturb itself; I mean, does not frighten itself or cause itself pain. But if any one else can frighten or pain it, let him do so. For the faculty itself will not by its own opinion turn itself into such ways. Let the body itself take care, if it can, that is suffer nothing, and let it speak, if it suffers.

But the soul itself, that which is subject to fear, to pain, which has completely the power of forming an opinion about these things, will suffer nothing, for it will never deviate into such a judgement. The leading principle in itself wants nothing, unless it makes a want for itself; and therefore it is both free from perturbation and unimpeded, if it does not disturb and impede itself.

Eudaemonia (happiness) is a good daemon, or a good thing. What then art thou doing here, O imagination? Go away, I entreat thee by the gods, as thou didst come, for I want thee not. But thou art come according to thy old fashion. I am not angry with thee: only go away.

Is any man afraid of change? Why what can take place without change? What then is more pleasing or more suitable to the universal nature? And canst thou take a bath unless the wood undergoes a change? And canst thou be nourished, unless the food undergoes a change? And can anything else that is useful be accomplished without change? Dost thou not see then that for thyself also to change is just the same, and equally necessary for the universal nature?

Through the universal substance as through a furious torrent all bodies are carried, being by their nature united with and cooperating with the whole, as the parts of our body with one another.

How many a Chrysippus, how many a Socrates, how many an Epictetus has time already swallowed up? And let the same thought occur to thee with reference to every man and thing.

One thing only troubles me, lest I should do something which the constitution of man does not allow, or in the way which it does not allow, or what it does not allow now.

Near is thy forgetfulness of all things; and near the forgetfulness of thee by all.

It is peculiar to man to love even those who do wrong. And this happens, if when they do wrong it occurs to thee that they are kinsmen, and that they do wrong through ignorance and unintentionally, and that soon both of you will die; and above all, that the wrong-doer has done thee no harm, for he has not made thy ruling faculty worse than it was before.

The universal nature out of the universal substance, as if it were wax, now moulds a horse, and when it has broken this up, it uses the material for a tree, then for a man, then for something else; and each of these things subsists for a very short time. But it is no hardship for the vessel to be broken up, just as there was none in its being fastened together.

A scowling look is altogether unnatural; when it is often assumed, the result is that all comeliness dies away, and at last is so completely extinguished that it cannot be again lighted up at all. Try to conclude from this very fact that it is contrary to reason. For if even the perception of doing wrong shall depart, what reason is there for living any longer?

Nature which governs the whole will soon change all things which thou seest, and out of their substance will make other things, and again other things from the substance of them, in order that the world may be ever new.

When a man has done thee any wrong, immediately consider with what opinion about good or evil he has done wrong. For when thou hast seen this, thou wilt pity him, and wilt neither wonder nor be angry.

For either thou thyself thinkest the same thing to be good that he does or

42

another thing of the same kind. It is thy duty then to pardon him. But if thou dost not think such things to be good or evil, thou wilt more readily be well disposed to him who is in error.

Think not so much of what thou hast not as of what thou hast: but of the things which thou hast select the best, and then reflect how eagerly they would have been sought, if thou hadst them not. At the same time however take care that thou dost not through being so pleased with them accustom thyself to overvalue them, so as to be disturbed if ever thou shouldst not have them.

Retire into thyself. The rational principle which rules has this nature, that it is content with itself when it does what is just, and so secures tranquility.

Wipe out the imagination. Stop the pulling of the strings. Confine thyself to the present. Understand well what happens either to thee or to another. Divide and distribute every object into the causal (formal) and the material. Think of thy last hour. Let the wrong which is done by a man stay there where the wrong was done.

Direct thy attention to what is said. Let thy understanding enter into the things that are doing and the things which do them.

Adorn thyself with simplicity and modesty and with indifference towards the things which lie between virtue and vice. Love mankind.

Follow God. The poet says that Law rules all.- And it is enough to remember that Law rules all.

About death: Whether it is a dispersion, or a resolution into atoms, or annihilation, it is either extinction or change.

About pain: The pain which is intolerable carries us off; but that which lasts a long time is tolerable; and the mind maintains its own tranquility by retiring into itself, and the ruling faculty is not made worse. But the parts which are harmed by pain, let them, if they can, give their opinion about it.

About fame: Look at the minds of those who seek fame, observe what they are, and what kind of things they avoid, and what kind of things they pursue. And consider that as the heaps of sand piled on one another hide the former sands, so in life the events which go before are soon covered by those which come after.

From Plato: The man who has an elevated mind and takes a view of all time and of all substance, dost thou suppose it possible for him to think that human life is anything great? it is not possible, he said.- Such a man then will think that death also is no evil.- Certainly not. From Antisthenes: It is royal to do good and to be abused.

It is a base thing for the countenance to be obedient and to regulate and compose itself as the mind commands, and for the mind not to be regulated and composed by itself.

It is not right to vex ourselves at things, For they care nought about it.To the immortal gods and us give joy. Life must be reaped like the ripe ears of corn: One man is born; another dies. If gods care not for me and for my children, There is a reason for it. For the good is with me, and the just. No joining others in their wailing, no violent emotion.

From Plato: But I would make this man a sufficient answer, which is this:

Thou sayest not well, if thou thinkest that a man who is good for anything at all ought to compute the hazard of life or death, and should not rather look to this only in all that he does, whether he is doing what is just or unjust, and the works of a good or a bad man.

For thus it is, men of Athens, in truth: wherever a man has placed himself thinking it the best place for him, or has been placed by a commander, there in my opinion he ought to stay and to abide the hazard, taking nothing into the reckoning, either death or anything else, before the baseness of deserting his post.

But, my good friend, reflect whether that which is noble and good is not something different from saving and being saved; for as to a man living such or such a time, at least one who is really a man, consider if this is not a thing to be dismissed from the thoughts: and there must be no love of life: but as to these matters a man must intrust them to the deity and believe what the women say, that no man can escape his destiny, the next inquiry being how he may best live the time that he has to live.

Look round at the courses of the stars, as if thou wert going along with them; and constantly consider the changes of the elements into one another; for such thoughts purge away the filth of the terrene life.

This is a fine saying of Plato: That he who is discoursing about men should look also at earthly things as if he viewed them from some higher place; should look at them in their assemblies, armies, agricultural labours, marriages, treaties, births, deaths, noise of the courts of justice, desert places, various nations of barbarians, feasts, lamentations, markets, a mixture of all things and an orderly combination of contraries.

Consider the past; such great changes of political supremacies. Thou mayest foresee also the things which will be. For they will certainly be of like form, and it is not possible that they should deviate from the order of the things which take place now: accordingly to have contemplated human life for forty years is the same as to have contemplated it for ten thousand years. For what more wilt thou see? That which has grown from the earth to the earth, But that which has sprung from heavenly seed, Back to the heavenly realms returns.

This is either a dissolution of the mutual involution of the atoms, or a similar dispersion of the unsentient elements.

With food and drinks and cunning magic arts Turning the channel's course to 'scape from death.

The breeze which heaven has sent

We must endure, and toil without complaining.

Another may be more expert in casting his opponent; but he is not more social, nor more modest, nor better disciplined to meet all that happens, nor more considerate with respect to the faults of his neighbours.

Where any work can be done conformably to the reason which is common to gods and men, there we have nothing to fear: for where we are able to get profit by means of the activity which is successful and proceeds according to our constitution, there no harm is to be suspected.

Everywhere and at all times it is in thy power piously to acquiesce in thy present condition, and to behave justly to those who are about thee, and to exert thy skill upon thy present thoughts, that nothing shall steal into them without being well examined.

Do not look around thee to discover other men's ruling principles, but look straight to this, to what nature leads thee, both the universal nature through the things which happen to thee, and thy own nature through the acts which must be done by thee. But every being ought to do that which is according to its constitution; and all other things have been constituted for the sake of rational beings, just as among irrational things the inferior for the sake of the superior, but the rational for the sake of one another.

The prime principle then in man's constitution is the social. And the second is not to yield to the persuasions of the body, for it is the peculiar office of the rational and intelligent motion to circumscribe itself, and never to be overpowered either by the motion of the senses or of the appetites, for both are animal; but the intelligent motion claims superiority and does not permit itself to be overpowered by the others. And with good reason, for it is formed by nature to use all of them. The third thing in the rational constitution is freedom from error and from deception. Let then the ruling principle holding fast to these things go straight on, and it has what is its own.

Consider thyself to be dead, and to have completed thy life up to the present time; and live according to nature the remainder which is allowed thee.

Love that only which happens to thee and is spun with the thread of thy destiny. For what is more suitable?

In everything which happens keep before thy eyes those to whom the same things happened, and how they were vexed, and treated them as strange things, and found fault with them: and now where are they?

Nowhere. Why then dost thou too choose to act in the same way? And why dost thou not leave these agitations which are foreign to nature, to those who cause them and those who are moved by them? And why art thou not altogether intent upon the right way of making use of the things which happen to thee? For then thou wilt use them well, and they will be a material for thee to work on. Only attend to thyself, and resolve to be a good man in every act which thou doest: and remember...

Look within. Within is the fountain of good, and it will ever bubble up, if thou wilt ever dig.

The body ought to be compact, and to show no irregularity either in motion or attitude. For what the mind shows in the face by maintaining in it the expression of intelligence and propriety, that ought to be required also in the whole body. But all of these things should be observed without affectation.

The art of life is more like the wrestler's art than the dancer's, in respect of this, that it should stand ready and firm to meet onsets which are sudden and unexpected.

Constantly observe who those are whose approbation thou wishest to have, and what ruling principles they possess. For then thou wilt neither blame those who offend involuntarily, nor wilt thou want their approbation, if thou lookest to the sources of their opinions and appetites.

Every soul, the philosopher says, is involuntarily deprived of truth;

consequently in the same way it is deprived of justice and temperance and benevolence and everything of the kind. It is most necessary to bear this constantly in mind, for thus thou wilt be more gentle towards all.

In every pain let this thought be present, that there is no dishonour in it, nor does it make the governing intelligence worse, for it does not damage the intelligence either so far as the intelligence is rational or so far as it is social. Indeed in the case of most pains let this remark of Epicurus aid thee, that pain is neither intolerable nor everlasting, if thou bearest in mind that it has its limits, and if thou addest nothing to it in imagination: and remember this too, that we do not perceive that many things which are disagreeable to us are the same as pain, such as excessive drowsiness, and the being scorched by heat, and the having no appetite. When then thou art discontented about any of these things, say to thyself, that thou art yielding to pain.

Take care not to feel towards the inhuman, as they feel towards men.

How do we know if Telauges was not superior in character to Socrates? For it is not enough that Socrates died a more noble death, and disputed more skilfully with the sophists, and passed the night in the cold with more endurance, and that when he was bid to arrest Leon of Salamis, he considered it more noble to refuse, and that he walked in a swaggering way in the streets-though as to this fact one may have great doubts if it was true. But we ought to inquire, what kind of a soul it was that Socrates possessed, and if he was able to be content with being just towards men and pious towards the gods, neither idly vexed on account of men's villainy, nor yet making himself a slave to any man's ignorance, nor receiving as strange anything that fell to his share out of the universal, nor enduring it as intolerable, nor allowing his understanding to sympathize with the affects of the miserable flesh.

Nature has not so mingled the intelligence with the composition of the body, as not to have allowed thee the power of circumscribing thyself and of bringing under subjection to thyself all that is thy own; for it is very possible to be a divine man and to be recognised as such by no one. Always bear this in mind; and another thing too, that very little indeed is necessary for living a happy life. And because thou hast despaired of becoming a dialectician and skilled in the knowledge of nature, do not for this reason renounce the hope of being both free and modest and social and obedient to God.

It is in thy power to live free from all compulsion in the greatest tranquility of mind, even if all the world cry out against thee as much as they choose, and even if wild beasts tear in pieces the members of this kneaded matter which has grown around thee. For what hinders the mind in the midst of all this from maintaining itself in tranquility and in a just judgement of all surrounding things and in a ready use of the objects which are presented to it, so that the judgement may say to the thing which falls under its observation: This thou art in substance (reality), though in men's opinion thou mayest appear to be of a different kind; and the use shall say to that which falls under the hand: Thou art the thing that I was seeking; for to me that which presents itself is always a material for virtue both rational and political, and in a word, for the exercise of art, which belongs to man or God. For everything which happens has a relationship either to God or man, and is neither new nor difficult to handle, but usual and apt matter to work on.

The perfection of moral character consists in this, in passing every day as the last, and in being neither violently excited nor torpid nor playing the hypocrite.

The gods who are immortal are not vexed because during so long a time they must tolerate continually men such as they are and so many of them bad; and besides this, they also take care of them in all ways. But thou, who art destined to end so soon, art thou wearied of enduring the bad, and this too when thou art one of them?

It is a ridiculous thing for a man not to fly from his own badness, which is indeed possible, but to fly from other men's badness, which is impossible.

Whatever the rational and political (social) faculty finds to be neither intelligent nor social, it properly judges to be inferior to itself.

When thou hast done a good act and another has received it, why dost thou look for a third thing besides these, as fools do, either to have the reputation of having done a good act or to obtain a return?

No man is tired of receiving what is useful. But it is useful to act according to nature. Do not then be tired of receiving what is useful by doing it to others.

The nature of the An moved to make the universe. But now either everything that takes place comes by way of consequence or continuity; or even the chief things towards which the ruling power of the universe directs its own movement are governed by no rational principle. If this is remembered it will make thee more tranquil in many things.

BOOK EIGHT

THIS reflection also tends to the removal of the desire of empty fame, that it is no longer in thy power to have lived the whole of thy life, or at least thy life from thy youth upwards, like a philosopher; but both to many others and to thyself it is plain that thou art far from philosophy. Thou hast fallen into disorder then, so that it is no longer easy for thee to get the reputation of a philosopher; and thy plan of life also opposes it. If then thou hast truly seen where the matter lies, throw away the thought, How thou shalt seem to others, and be content if thou shalt live the rest of thy life in such wise as thy nature wills. Observe then what it wills, and let nothing else distract thee; for thou hast had experience of many wanderings without having found happiness anywhere, not in syllogisms, nor in wealth, nor in reputation, nor in enjoyment, nor anywhere. Where is it then? In doing what man's nature requires. How then shall a man do this? If he has principles from which come his affects and his acts. What principles? Those which relate to good and bad: the belief that there is nothing good for man, which does not make him just, temperate, manly, free; and that there is nothing bad, which does not do the contrary to what has been mentioned.

On the occasion of every act ask thyself, How is this with respect to me?

Shall I repent of it? A little time and I am dead, and all is gone. What more do I seek, if what I am now doing is work of an intelligent living being, and a social being, and one who is under the same law with God?

Alexander and Gaius and Pompeius, what are they in comparison with Diogenes and Heraclitus and Socrates? For they were acquainted with things, and their causes (forms), and their matter, and the ruling principles of these men were the same. But as to the others, how many things had they to care for, and to how many things were they slaves?

Consider that men will do the same things nevertheless, even though thou shouldst burst.

This is the chief thing: Be not perturbed, for all things are according to the nature of the universal; and in a little time thou wilt be nobody and nowhere, like Hadrian and Augustus. In the next place having fixed thy eyes steadily on thy business look at it, and at the same time remembering that it is thy duty to be a good man, and what man's nature demands, do that without turning aside; and speak as it seems to thee most just, only let it be with a good disposition and with modesty and without hypocrisy.

The nature of the universal has this work to do, to remove to that place the things which are in this, to change them, to take them away hence, and to carry them there. All things are change, yet we need not fear anything new. All things are familiar to us; but the distribution of them still remains the same.

Every nature is contented with itself when it goes on its way well; and a rational nature goes on its way well, when in its thoughts it assents to nothing false or uncertain, and when it directs its movements to social acts only, and when it confines its desires and aversions to the things which are in its power, and when it is satisfied with everything that is assigned to it by the common nature.

For of this common nature every particular nature is a part, as the nature of the leaf is a part of the nature of the plant; except that in the plant the nature of the leaf is part of a nature which has not perception or reason, and is subject to be impeded; but the nature of man is part of a nature which is not subject to impediments, and is intelligent and just, since it gives to everything in equal portions and according to its worth, times, substance, cause (form), activity, and incident. But examine, not to discover that any one thing compared with any other single thing is equal in all respects, but by taking all the parts together of one thing and comparing them with all the parts together of another.

Thou hast not leisure or ability to read. But thou hast leisure or ability to check arrogance: thou hast leisure to be superior to pleasure and pain: thou hast leisure to be superior to love of fame, and not to be vexed at stupid and ungrateful people, nay even to care for them.

Let no man any longer hear thee finding fault with the court life or with thy own.

Repentance is a kind of self-reproof for having neglected something useful; but that which is good must be something useful, and the perfect good man should look after it. But no such man would ever repent of having refused any sensual pleasure. Pleasure then is neither good nor useful.

This thing, what is it in itself, in its own constitution? What is its substance and material? And what its causal nature (or form)? And what is it doing in the world? And how long does it subsist?

When thou risest from sleep with reluctance, remember that it is according to thy constitution and according to human nature to perform social acts, but sleeping is common also to irrational animals. But that which is according to each individual's nature is also more peculiarly its own, and more suitable to its nature, and indeed also more agreeable.

Constantly and, if it be possible, on the occasion of every impression on the soul, apply to it the principles of Physic, of Ethic, and of Dialectic.

Whatever man thou meetest with, immediately say to thyself: What opinions has this man about good and bad? For if with respect to pleasure and pain and the causes of each, and with respect to fame and ignominy, death and life, he has such and such opinions, it will seem nothing wonderful or strange to me, if he does such and such things; and I shall bear in mind that he is compelled to do so.

Remember that as it is a shame to be surprised if the fig-tree produces figs, so it is to be surprised if the world produces such and such things of which it is productive; and for the physician and the helmsman it is a shame to be surprised, if a man has a fever, or if the wind is unfavourable.

Remember that to change thy opinion and to follow him who corrects thy error is as consistent with freedom as it is to persist in thy error. For it is thy own, the activity which is exerted according to thy own movement and judgement, and indeed according to thy own understanding too.

If a thing is in thy own power, why dost thou do it? But if it is in the power of another, whom dost thou blame? The atoms (chance) or the gods? Both are foolish. Thou must blame nobody. For if thou canst, correct that which is the cause; but if thou canst not do this, correct at least the thing itself; but if thou canst not do even this, of what use is it to thee to find fault? For nothing should be done without a purpose.

That which has died falls not out of the universe. If it stays here, it also changes here, and is dissolved into its proper parts, which are elements of the universe and of thyself. And these too change, and they murmur not.

Everything exists for some end, a horse, a vine. Why dost thou wonder? Even the sun will say, I am for some purpose, and the rest of the gods will say the same. For what purpose then art thou? To enjoy pleasure? See if common sense allows this.

Nature has had regard in everything no less to the end than to the beginning and the continuance, just like the man who throws up a ball. What good is it then for the ball to be thrown up, or harm for it to come down, or even to have fallen? And what good is it to the bubble while it holds together, or what harm when it is burst? The same may be said of a light also.

Turn it (the body) inside out, and see what kind of thing it is; and when it has grown old, what kind of thing it becomes, and when it is diseased.

Short-lived are both the praiser and the praised, and the rememberer and the remembered: and all this in a nook of this part of the world; and not even here do all agree, no, not any one with himself: and the whole earth too is a

49

point.

Attend to the matter which is before thee, whether it is an opinion or an act or a word.

Thou sufferest this justly: for thou choosest rather to become good to-morrow than to be good to-day.

Am I doing anything? I do it with reference to the good of mankind. Does anything happen to me? I receive it and refer it to the gods, and the source of all things, from which all that happens is derived.

Such as bathing appears to thee- oil, sweat, dirt, filthy water, all things disgusting- so is every part of life and everything. Lucilla saw Verus die, and then Lucilla died. Secunda saw Maximus die, and then Secunda died. Epitynchanus saw Diotimus die, and

Epitynchanus died. Antoninus saw Faustina die, and then Antoninus died. Such is everything. Celer saw Hadrian die, and then Celer died. And those sharp-witted men, either seers or men inflated with pride, where are they? For instance the sharp-witted men, Charax and

Demetrius the Platonist and Eudaemon, and any one else like them. All ephemeral, dead long ago. Some indeed have not been remembered even for a short time, and others have become the heroes of fables, and again others have disappeared even from fables. Remember this then, that this little compound, thyself, must either be dissolved, or thy poor breath must be extinguished, or be removed and placed elsewhere.

It is satisfaction to a man to do the proper works of a man. Now it is a proper work of a man to be benevolent to his own kind, to despise the movements of the senses, to form a just judgement of plausible appearances, and to take a survey of the nature of the universe and of the things which happen in it.

There are three relations between thee and other things: the one to the body which surrounds thee; the second to the divine cause from which all things come to all; and the third to those who live with thee.

Pain is either an evil to the body- then let the body say what it thinks of it- or to the soul; but it is in the power of the soul to maintain its own serenity and tranquility, and not to think that pain is an evil. For every judgement and movement and desire and aversion is within, and no evil ascends so high.

Wipe out thy imaginations by often saying to thyself: now it is in my power to let no badness be in this soul, nor desire nor any perturbation at all; but looking at all things I see what is their nature, and I use each according to its value.- Remember this power which thou hast from nature.

Speak both in the senate and to every man, whoever he may be, appropriately, not with any affectation: use plain discourse.

Augustus' court, wife, daughter, descendants, ancestors, sister, Agrippa, kinsmen, intimates, friends, Areius, Maecenas, physicians and sacrificing priests- the whole court is dead. Then turn to the rest, not considering the death of a single man, but of a whole race, as of the Pompeii; and that which is inscribed on the tombs- The last of his race. Then consider what trouble those before them have had that they might leave a successor; and then, that of necessity some one must be the last. Again here consider the death of a whole race.

It is thy duty to order thy life well in every single act; and if every act does its duty, as far as is possible, be content; and no one is able to hinder thee so that each act shall not do its duty.- But something external will stand in the way.- Nothing will stand in the way of thy acting justly and soberly and considerately.- But perhaps some other active power will be hindered.- Well, but by acquiescing in the hindrance and by being content to transfer thy efforts to that which is allowed, another opportunity of action is immediately put before thee in place of that which was hindered, and one which will adapt itself to this ordering of which we are speaking.

Receive wealth or prosperity without arrogance; and be ready to let it go.

If thou didst ever see a hand cut off, or a foot, or a head, lying anywhere apart from the rest of the body, such does a man make himself, as far as he can, who is not content with what happens, and separates himself from others, or does anything unsocial. Suppose that thou hast detached thyself from the natural unity- for thou wast made by nature a part, but now thou hast cut thyself off- yet here there is this beautiful provision, that it is in thy power again to unite thyself. God has allowed this to no other part, after it has been separated and cut asunder, to come together again. But consider the kindness by which he has distinguished man, for he has put it in his power not to be separated at all from the universal; and when he has been separated, he has allowed him to return and to be united and to resume his place as a part.

As the nature of the universal has given to every rational being all the other powers that it has, so we have received from it this power also. For as the universal nature converts and fixes in its predestined place everything which stands in the way and opposes it, and makes such things a part of itself, so also the rational animal is able to make every hindrance its own material, and to use it for such purposes as it may have designed.

Do not disturb thyself by thinking of the whole of thy life. Let not thy thoughts at once embrace all the various troubles which thou mayest expect to befall thee: but on every occasion ask thyself, What is there in this which is intolerable and past bearing? For thou wilt be ashamed to confess. In the next place remember that neither the future nor the past pains thee, but only the present.

But this is reduced to a very little, if thou only circumscribest it, and chidest thy mind, if it is unable to hold out against even this.

Does Panthea or Pergamus now sit by the tomb of Verus? Does Chaurias or Diotimus sit by the tomb of Hadrian? That would be ridiculous.

Well, suppose they did sit there, would the dead be conscious of it? And if the dead were conscious, would they be pleased? And if they were pleased, would that make them immortal? Was it not in the order of destiny that these persons too should first become old women and old men and then die? What then would those do after these were dead? All this is foul smell and blood in a bag.

If thou canst see sharp, look and judge wisely, says the philosopher.

In the constitution of the rational animal I see no virtue which is opposed to justice; but I see a virtue which is opposed to love of pleasure, and that is temperance.

If thou takest away thy opinion about that which appears to give thee pain, thou thyself standest in perfect security.- Who is this self?- The reason.- But I am not reason.- Be it so. Let then the reason itself not trouble itself. But if any other part of thee suffers, let it have its own opinion about itself.

Hindrance to the perceptions of sense is an evil to the animal nature. Hindrance to the movements (desires) is equally an evil to the animal nature. And something else also is equally an impediment and an evil to the constitution of plants. So then that which is a hindrance to the intelligence is an evil to the intelligent nature.

Apply all these things then to thyself. Does pain or sensuous pleasure affect thee? The senses will look to that.- Has any obstacle opposed thee in thy efforts towards an object? if indeed thou wast making this effort absolutely (unconditionally, or without any reservation), certainly this obstacle is an evil to thee considered as a rational animal. But if thou takest into consideration the usual course of things, thou hast not yet been injured nor even impeded. The things however which are proper to the understanding no other man is used to impede, for neither fire, nor iron, nor tyrant, nor abuse, touches it in any way. When it has been made a sphere, it continues a sphere.

It is not fit that I should give myself pain, for I have never intentionally given pain even to another. Different things delight different people. But it is my delight to keep the ruling faculty sound without turning away either from any man or from any of the things which happen to men, but looking at and receiving all with welcome eyes and using everything according to its value.

See that thou secure this present time to thyself: for those who rather pursue posthumous fame do consider that the men of after time will be exactly such as these whom they cannot bear now; and both are mortal. And what is it in any way to thee if these men of after time utter this or that sound, or have this or that opinion about thee?

Take me and cast me where thou wilt; for there I shall keep my divine part tranquil, that is, content, if it can feel and act conformably to its proper constitution. Is this change of place sufficient reason why my soul should be unhappy and worse than it was, depressed, expanded, shrinking, affrighted? And what wilt thou find which is sufficient reason for this?

Nothing can happen to any man which is not a human accident, nor to an ox which is not according to the nature of an ox, nor to a vine which is not according to the nature of a vine, nor to a stone which is not proper to a stone. If then there happens to each thing both what is usual and natural, why shouldst thou complain? For the common nature brings nothing which may not be borne by thee.

If thou art pained by any external thing, it is not this thing that disturbs thee, but thy own judgement about it. And it is in thy power to wipe out this judgement now. But if anything in thy own disposition gives thee pain, who hinders thee from correcting thy opinion? And even if thou art pained because thou art not doing some particular thing which seems to thee to be right, why dost thou not rather act than complain?- But some insuperable obstacle is in the way?- Do not be grieved then, for the cause of its not being done depends not on thee.- But it is not worth while to live if this cannot be done.- Take thy departure then from life contentedly, just as he dies who is in full activity, and well pleased too with the things which are obstacles.

Remember that the ruling faculty is invincible, when self-collected it is satisfied with itself, if it does nothing which it does not choose to do, even if it resist from mere obstinacy.

What then will it be when it forms a judgement about anything aided by reason and deliberately? Therefore the mind which is free from passions is a citadel, for man has nothing more secure to which he can fly for, refuge and for the future be inexpugnable. He then who has not seen this is an ignorant man; but he who has seen it and does not fly to this refuge is unhappy.

Say nothing more to thyself than what the first appearances report. Suppose that it has been reported to thee that a certain person speaks ill of thee. This has been reported; but that thou hast been injured, that has not been reported. I see that my child is sick. I do see; but that he is in danger, I do not see. Thus then always abide by the first appearances, and add nothing thyself from within, and then nothing happens to thee. Or rather add something, like a man who knows everything that happens in the world.

A cucumber is bitter.- Throw it away.- There are briars in the road.- Turn aside from them.- This is enough. Do not add, And why were such things made in the world? For thou wilt be ridiculed by a man who is acquainted with nature, as thou wouldst be ridiculed by a carpenter and shoemaker if thou didst find fault because thou seest in their workshop shavings and cuttings from the things which they make. And yet they have places into which they can throw these shavings and cuttings, and the universal nature has no external space; but the wondrous part of her art is that though she has circumscribed herself, everything within her which appears to decay and to grow old and to be useless she changes into herself, and again makes other new things from these very same, so that she requires neither substance from without nor wants a place into which she may cast that which decays.

She is content then with her own space, and her own matter and her own art.

Neither in thy actions be sluggish nor in thy conversation without method, nor wandering in thy thoughts, nor let there be in thy soul inward contention nor external effusion, nor in life be so busy as to have no leisure.

Suppose that men kill thee, cut thee in pieces, curse thee. What then can these things do to prevent thy mind from remaining pure, wise, sober, just? For instance, if a man should stand by a limpid pure spring, and curse it, the spring never ceases sending up potable water; and if he should cast clay into it or filth, it will speedily disperse them and wash them out, and will not be at all polluted. How then shalt thou possess a perpetual fountain and not a mere well? By forming thyself hourly to freedom conjoined with contentment, simplicity and modesty.

He who does not know what the world is, does not know where he is. And he who does not know for what purpose the world exists, does not know who he is, nor what the world is. But he who has failed in any one of these things could not even say for what purpose he exists himself. What then dost thou think of him who avoids or seeks the praise of those who applaud, of men who know not either where they are or who they are?

Dost thou wish to be praised by a man who curses himself thrice every hour? Wouldst thou wish to please a man who does not please himself? Does a man please himself who repents of nearly everything that he does?

No longer let thy breathing only act in concert with the air which surrounds thee, but let thy intelligence also now be in harmony with the intelligence which embraces all things. For the intelligent power is no less diffused in all parts and pervades all things for him who is willing to draw it to him than the aerial power for him who is able to respire it.

Generally, wickedness does no harm at all to the universe; and particularly, the wickedness of one man does no harm to another. It is only harmful to him who has it in his power to be released from it, as soon as he shall choose.

To my own free will the free will of my neighbour is just as indifferent as his poor breath and flesh. For though we are made especially for the sake of one another, still the ruling power of each of us has its own office, for otherwise my neighbour's wickedness would be my harm, which God has not willed in order that my unhappiness may not depend on another.

The sun appears to be poured down, and in all directions indeed it is diffused, yet it is not effused. For this diffusion is extension: Accordingly its rays are called Extensions [aktines] because they are extended [apo tou ekteinesthai]. But one may judge what kind of a thing a ray is, if he looks at the sun's light passing through a narrow opening into a darkened room, for it is extended in a right line, and as it were is divided when it meets with any solid body which stands in the way and intercepts the air beyond; but there the light remains fixed and does not glide or fall off. Such then ought to be the out-pouring and diffusion of the understanding, and it should in no way be an effusion, but an extension, and it should make no violent or impetuous collision with the obstacles which are in its way; nor yet fall down, but be fixed and enlighten that which receives it. For a body will deprive itself of the illumination, if it does not admit it.

He who fears death either fears the loss of sensation or a different kind of sensation. But if thou shalt have no sensation, neither wilt thou feel any harm; and if thou shalt acquire another kind of sensation, thou wilt be a different kind of living being and thou wilt not cease to live.

Men exist for the sake of one another. Teach them then or bear with them.

In one way an arrow moves, in another way the mind. The mind indeed, both when it exercises caution and when it is employed about inquiry, moves straight onward not the less, and to its object.

Enter into every man's ruling faculty; and also let every other man enter into thine.

BOOK NINE

54

HE WHO acts unjustly acts impiously. For since the universal nature has made rational animals for the sake of one another to help one another according to their deserts, but in no way to injure one another, he who transgresses her will, is clearly guilty of impiety towards the highest divinity. And he too who lies is guilty of impiety to the same divinity; for the universal nature is the nature of things that are; and things that are have a relation to all things that come into existence. And further, this universal nature is named truth, and is the prime cause of all things that are true. He then who lies intentionally is guilty of impiety inasmuch as he acts unjustly by deceiving; and he also who lies unintentionally, inasmuch as he is at variance with the universal nature, and inasmuch as he disturbs the order by fighting against the nature of the world; for he fights against it, who is moved of himself to that which is contrary to truth, for he had received powers from nature through the neglect of which he is not able now to distinguish falsehood from truth. And indeed he who pursues pleasure as good, and avoids pain as evil, is guilty of impiety. For of necessity such a man must often find fault with the universal nature, alleging that it assigns things to the bad and the good contrary to their deserts, because frequently the bad are in the enjoyment of pleasure and possess the things which procure pleasure, but the good have pain for their share and the things which cause pain. And further, he who is afraid of pain will sometimes also be afraid of some of the things which will happen in the world, and even this is impiety. And he who pursues pleasure will not abstain from injustice, and this is plainly impiety. Now with respect to the things towards which the universal nature is equally affected- for it would not have made both, unless it was equally affected towards both- towards these they who wish to follow nature should be of the same mind with it, and equally affected. With respect to pain, then, and pleasure, or death and life, or honour and dishonour, which the universal nature employs equally, whoever is not equally affected is manifestly acting impiously. And I say that the universal nature employs them equally, instead of saying that they happen alike to those who are produced in continuous series and to those who come after them by virtue of a certain original movement of Providence, according to which it moved from a certain beginning to this ordering of things, having conceived certain principles of the things which were to be, and having determined powers productive of beings and of changes and of such like successions.

It would be a man's happiest lot to depart from mankind without having had any taste of lying and hypocrisy and luxury and pride.

However to breathe out one's life when a man has had enough of these things is the next best voyage, as the saying is. Hast thou determined to abide with vice, and has not experience yet induced thee to fly from this pestilence? For the destruction of the understanding is a pestilence, much more indeed than any such corruption and change of this atmosphere which surrounds us. For this corruption is a pestilence of animals so far as they are animals; but the other is a pestilence of men so far as they are men.

Do not despise death, but be well content with it, since this too is one of those things which nature wills. For such as it is to be young and to grow old, and to increase and to reach maturity, and to have teeth and beard and grey hairs, and to beget, and to be pregnant and to bring forth, and all the other natural operations which the seasons of thy life bring, such also is dissolution. This, then, is consistent with the character of a reflecting man, to be neither careless nor impatient nor contemptuous with respect to death, but to wait for it as one of the operations of nature. As thou now waitest for the time when the child shall come out of thy wife's womb, so be ready for the time when thy soul shall fall out of this envelope. But if thou requirest also a vulgar kind of comfort which shall reach thy heart, thou wilt be made best reconciled to death by observing the objects from which thou art going to be removed, and the morals of those with whom thy soul will no longer be mingled. For it is no way right to be offended with men, but it is thy duty to care for them and to bear with them gently; and yet to remember that thy departure will be not from men who have the same principles as thyself. For this is the only thing, if there be any, which could draw us the contrary way and attach us to life, to be permitted to live with those who have the same principles as ourselves. But now thou seest how great is the trouble arising from the discordance of those who live together, so that thou mayest say, Come quick, O death, lest perchance I, too, should forget myself.

He who does wrong does wrong against himself. He who acts unjustly acts unjustly to himself, because he makes himself bad.

He often acts unjustly who does not do a certain thing; not only he who does a certain thing.

Thy present opinion founded on understanding, and thy present conduct directed to social good, and thy present disposition of contentment with everything which happens- that is enough.

Wipe out imagination: check desire: extinguish appetite: keep the ruling faculty in its own power.

Among the animals which have not reason one life is distributed; but among reasonable animals one intelligent soul is distributed: just as there is one earth of all things which are of an earthy nature, and we see by one light, and breathe one air, all of us that have the faculty of vision and all that have life.

All things which participate in anything which is common to them all move towards that which is of the same kind with themselves. Everything which is earthy turns towards the earth, everything which is liquid flows together, and everything which is of an aerial kind does the same, so that they require something to keep them asunder, and the application of force. Fire indeed moves upwards on account of the elemental fire, but it is so ready to be kindled together with all the fire which is here, that even every substance which is somewhat dry, is easily ignited, because there is less mingled with it of that which is a hindrance to ignition. Accordingly then everything also which participates in the common intelligent nature moves in like manner towards that which is of the same kind with itself, or moves even more. For so much as it is superior in comparison with all other things, in the same degree also is it more ready to mingle with and to be fused with that which is akin to it.

Accordingly among animals devoid of reason we find swarms of bees, and herds of cattle, and the nurture of young birds, and in a manner, loves; for even in animals there are souls, and that power which brings them together is seen to exert itself in the superior degree, and in such a way as never has been observed in plants nor in stones nor in trees. But in rational animals there are political communities and friendships, and families and meetings of people; and in wars, treaties and armistices. But in the things which are still superior, even though they are separated from one another, unity in a manner exists, as in the stars. Thus the ascent to the higher degree is able to produce a sympathy even in things which are separated. See, then, what now takes place. For only intelligent animals have now forgotten this mutual desire and inclination, and in them alone the property of flowing together is not seen. But still though men strive to avoid this union, they are caught and held by it, for their nature is too strong for them; and thou wilt see what I say, if thou only observest. Sooner, then, will one find anything earthy which comes in contact with no earthy thing than a man altogether separated from other men.

Both man and God and the universe produce fruit; at the proper seasons each produces it. But if usage has especially fixed these terms to the vine and like things, this is nothing. Reason produces fruit both for all and for itself, and there are produced from it other things of the same kind as reason itself.

If thou art able, correct by teaching those who do wrong; but if thou canst not, remember that indulgence is given to thee for this purpose. And the gods, too, are indulgent to such persons; and for some purposes they even help them to get health, wealth, reputation; so kind they are. And it is in thy power also; or say, who hinders thee?

Labour not as one who is wretched, nor yet as one who would be pitied or admired: but direct thy will to one thing only, to put thyself in motion and to check thyself, as the social reason requires.

To-day I have got out of all trouble, or rather I have cast out all trouble, for it was not outside, but within and in my opinions.

All things are the same, familiar in experience, and ephemeral in time, and worthless in the matter. Everything now is just as it was in the time of those whom we have buried.

Things stand outside of us, themselves by themselves, neither knowing aught of themselves, nor expressing any judgement. What is it, then, which does judge about them? The ruling faculty.

Not in passivity, but in activity lie the evil and the good of the rational social animal, just as his virtue and his vice lie not in passivity, but in activity.

For the stone which has been thrown up it is no evil to come down, nor indeed any good to have been carried up.

Penetrate inwards into men's leading principles, and thou wilt see what judges thou art afraid of, and what kind of judges they are of themselves.

All things are changing: and thou thyself art in continuous mutation and in a manner in continuous destruction, and the whole universe too.

It is thy duty to leave another man's wrongful act there where it is.

Termination of activity, cessation from movement and opinion, and in a sense their death, is no evil. Turn thy thoughts now to the consideration of thy life, thy life as a child, as a youth, thy manhood, thy old age, for in these also every change was a death. Is this anything to fear? Turn thy thoughts now to thy life under thy grandfather, then to thy life under thy mother, then to thy life under thy father; and as thou findest many other differences and changes and terminations, ask thyself, Is this anything to fear? In like manner, then, neither are the termination and cessation and change of thy whole life a thing to be afraid of.

Hasten to examine thy own ruling faculty and that of the universe and that of thy neighbour: thy own that thou mayest make it just: and that of the universe, that thou mayest remember of what thou art a part; and that of thy neighbour, that thou mayest know whether he has acted ignorantly or with knowledge, and that thou mayest also consider that his ruling faculty is akin to thine.

As thou thyself art a component part of a social system, so let every act of thine be a component part of social life. Whatever act of thine then has no reference either immediately or remotely to a social end, this tears asunder thy life, and does not allow it to be one, and it is of the nature of a mutiny, just as when in a popular assembly a man acting by himself stands apart from the general agreement.

Quarrels of little children and their sports, and poor spirits carrying about dead bodies, such is everything; and so what is exhibited in the representation of the mansions of the dead strikes our eyes more clearly.

Examine into the quality of the form of an object, and detach it altogether from its material part, and then contemplate it; then determine the time, the longest which a thing of this peculiar form is naturally made to endure.

Thou hast endured infinite troubles through not being contented with thy ruling faculty, when it does the things which it is constituted by nature to do. But enough of this.

When another blames thee or hates thee, or when men say about thee anything injurious, approach their poor souls, penetrate within, and see what kind of men they are. Thou wilt discover that there is no reason to take any trouble that these men may have this or that opinion about thee. However thou must be well disposed towards them, for by nature they are friends. And the gods too aid them in all ways, by dreams, by signs, towards the attainment of those things on which they set a value.

The periodic movements of the universe are the same, up and down from age to age. And either the universal intelligence puts itself in motion for every separate effect, and if this is so, be thou content with that which is the result of its activity; or it puts itself in motion once, and everything else comes by way of sequence in a manner; or indivisible elements are the origin of all things.- In a word, if there is a god, all is well; and if chance rules, do not thou also be governed by it.

Soon will the earth cover us all: then the earth, too, will change, and the things also which result from change will continue to change for ever, and these again for ever. For if a man reflects on the changes and transformations which follow one another like wave after wave and their rapidity, he will despise everything which is perishable.

The universal cause is like a winter torrent: it carries everything along with it. But how worthless are all these poor people who are engaged in matters political, and, as they suppose, are playing the philosopher! All drivellers. Well then, man: do what nature now requires. Set thyself in motion, if it is in thy power, and do not look about thee to see if any one will observe it; nor yet expect Plato's Republic: but be content if the smallest thing goes on well, and consider such an event to be no small matter. For who can change men's opinions? And without a change of opinions what else is there than the slavery of men who groan while they pretend to obey?

Come now and tell me of Alexander and Philip and Demetrius of Phalerum. They themselves shall judge whether they discovered what the common nature required, and trained themselves accordingly. But if they acted like tragedy heroes, no one has condemned me to imitate them. Simple and modest is the work of philosophy. Draw me not aside to indolence and pride.

Look down from above on the countless herds of men and their countless solemnities, and the infinitely varied voyagings in storms and calms, and the differences among those who are born, who live together, and die. And consider, too, the life lived by others in olden time, and the life of those who will live after thee, and the life now lived among barbarous nations, and how many know not even thy name, and how many will soon forget it, and how they who perhaps now are praising thee will very soon blame thee, and that neither a posthumous name is of any value, nor reputation, nor anything else.

Let there be freedom from perturbations with respect to the things which come from the external cause; and let there be justice in the things done by virtue of the internal cause, that is, let there be movement and action terminating in this, in social acts, for this is according to thy nature.

Thou canst remove out of the way many useless things among those which disturb thee, for they lie entirely in thy opinion; and thou wilt then gain for thyself ample space by comprehending the whole universe in thy mind, and by contemplating the eternity of time, and observing the rapid change of every several thing, how short is the time from birth to dissolution, and the illimitable time before birth as well as the equally boundless time after dissolution.

All that thou seest will quickly perish, and those who have been spectators of its dissolution will very soon perish too. And he who dies at the extremest old age will be brought into the same condition with him who died prematurely.

What are these men's leading principles, and about what kind of things are they busy, and for what kind of reasons do they love and honour? Imagine that thou seest their poor souls laid bare. When they think that they do harm by their blame or good by their praise, what an idea!

Loss is nothing else than change. But the universal nature delights in change, and in obedience to her all things are now done well, and from eternity have been done in like form, and will be such to time without end. What, then, dost thou say? That all things have been and all things always will be bad, and that no power has ever been found in so many gods to rectify these things, but the world has been condemned to be found in never ceasing evil?

The rottenness of the matter which is the foundation of everything! Water, dust, bones, filth: or again, marble rocks, the callosities of the earth; and gold and silver, the sediments; and garments, only bits of hair; and purple dye, blood; and everything else is of the same kind. And that which is of the nature of breath is also another thing of the same kind, changing from this to that.

Enough of this wretched life and murmuring and apish tricks. Why art thou disturbed? What is there new in this? What unsettles thee? Is it the form of the thing? Look at it. Or is it the matter? Look at it. But besides these there is nothing. Towards the gods, then, now become at last more simple and better. It is the same whether we examine these things for a hundred years or three.

If any man has done wrong, the harm is his own. But perhaps he has not done wrong.

Either all things proceed from one intelligent source and cometogether as in one body, and the part ought not to find fault with what is done for the benefit of the whole; or there are only atoms, and nothing else than mixture and dispersion. Why, then, art thou disturbed? Say to the ruling faculty, Art thou dead, art thou corrupted, art thou playing the hypocrite, art thou become a beast, dost thou herd and feed with the rest?

Either the gods have no power or they have power. If, then, they have no power, why dost thou pray to them? But if they have power, why dost thou not pray for them to give thee the faculty of not fearing any of the things which thou fearest, or of not desiring any of the things which thou desirest, or not being pained at anything, rather than pray that any of these things should not happen or happen? For certainly if they can co-operate with men, they can co-operate for these purposes. But perhaps thou wilt say, the gods have placed them in thy power. Well, then, is it not better to use what is in thy power like a free man than to desire in a slavish and abject way what is not in thy power? And who has told thee that the gods do not aid us even in the things which are in our power? Begin, then, to pray for such things, and thou wilt see. One man prays thus: How shall I be able to lie with that woman? Do thou pray thus: How shall I not desire to lie with her? Another prays thus: How shall I be released from this? Another prays: How shall I not desire to be released? Another thus: How shall I not lose my little son? Thou thus: How shall I not be afraid to lose him? In fine, turn thy prayers this way, and see what comes.

Epicurus says, In my sickness my conversation was not about my bodily sufferings, nor, says he, did I talk on such subjects to those who visited me; but I continued to discourse on the nature of things as before, keeping to this main point, how the mind, while participating in such movements as go on in the poor flesh, shall be free from perturbations and maintain its proper good. Nor did I, he says, give the physicians an opportunity of putting on solemn looks, as if they were doing something great, but my life went on well and happily. Do, then, the same that he did both in sickness, if thou art sick, and in any other circumstances; for never to desert philosophy in any events that may befall us, nor to hold trifling talk either with an ignorant man or with one unacquainted with nature, is a principle of all schools of philosophy; but to be intent only on that which thou art now doing and on the instrument by which thou doest it.

When thou art offended with any man's shameless conduct, immediately ask thyself, Is it possible, then, that shameless men should not be in the world? It is not possible. Do not, then, require what is impossible. For this man also is one of those shameless men who must of necessity be in the world. Let the same considerations be present to thy mind in the case of the knave, and the faithless man, and of every man who does wrong in any way. For at the same time that thou dost remind thyself that it is impossible that such kind of men should not exist, thou wilt become more kindly disposed towards every one individually. It is useful to perceive this, too, immediately when the occasion arises, what virtue nature has given to man to oppose to every wrongful act. For she has given to man, as an antidote against the stupid man, mildness, and against another kind of man some other power. And in all cases it is possible for thee to correct by teaching the man who is gone astray; for every man who errs misses his object and is gone astray. Besides wherein hast thou been injured? For thou wilt find that no one among those against whom thou art irritated has done anything by which thy mind could be made worse; but that which is evil to thee and harmful has its foundation only in the mind. And what harm is done or what is there strange, if the man who has not been instructed does the acts of an uninstructed man? Consider whether thou shouldst not rather blame thyself, because thou didst not expect such a man to err in such a way. For thou hadst means given thee by thy reason to suppose that it was likely that he would commit this error, and yet thou hast forgotten and art amazed that he has erred. But most of all when thou blamest a man as faithless or ungrateful, turn to thyself. For the fault is manifestly thy own, whether thou didst trust that a man who had such a disposition would keep his promise, or when conferring thy kindness thou didst not confer it absolutely, nor yet in such way as to have received from thy very act all the profit. For what more dost thou want when thou hast done a man a service? Art thou not content that thou hast done something conformable to thy nature, and dost thou seek to be paid for it? Just as if the eye demanded a recompense for seeing, or the feet for walking. For as these members are formed for a particular purpose, and by working according to their several constitutions obtain what is their own; so also as man is formed by nature to acts of benevolence, when he has done anything benevolent or in any other way conducive to the common interest, he has acted conformably to his constitution, and he gets what is his own.

BOOK TEN

WILT thou, then, my soul, never be good and simple and one and naked, more manifest than the body which surrounds thee? Wilt thou never enjoy an affectionate and contented disposition? Wilt thou never be full and without a want of any kind, longing for nothing more, nor desiring anything, either animate or inanimate, for the enjoyment of pleasures? Nor yet desiring time wherein thou shalt have longer enjoyment, or place, or pleasant climate, or society of men with whom thou mayest live in harmony? But wilt thou be satisfied with thy present condition, and pleased with all that is about thee, and wilt thou convince thyself that thou hast everything and that it comes from the gods, that everything is well for thee, and will be well whatever shall please them, and whatever they shall give for the conservation of the perfect living being, the good and just and beautiful, which generates and holds together all things, and contains and embraces all things which are dissolved for the production of other like things? Wilt thou never be such that thou shalt so dwell in community with gods and men as neither to find fault with them at all, nor to be condemned by them?

Observe what thy nature requires, so far as thou art governed by nature only: then do it and accept it, if thy nature, so far as thou art a living being, shall not be made worse by it.

And next thou must observe what thy nature requires so far as thou art a living being. And all this thou mayest allow thyself, if thy nature, so far as thou art a rational animal, shall not be made worse by it. But the rational animal is consequently also a political (social) animal. Use these rules, then, and trouble thyself about nothing else.

Everything which happens either happens in such wise as thou art formed by nature to bear it, or as thou art not formed by nature to bear it. If, then, it happens to thee in such way as thou art formed by nature to bear it, do not complain, but bear it as thou art formed by nature to bear it. But if it happens in such wise as thou art not formed by nature to bear it, do not complain, for it will perish after it has consumed thee. Remember, however, that thou art formed by nature to bear everything, with respect to which it depends on thy own opinion to make it endurable and tolerable, by thinking that it is either thy interest or thy duty to do this.

If a man is mistaken, instruct him kindly and show him his error. But if thou art not able, blame thyself, or blame not even thyself. Whatever may happen to thee, it was prepared for thee from all eternity; and the implication of causes was from eternity spinning the thread of thy being, and of that which is incident to it. Whether the universe is a concourse of atoms, or nature is a system, let this first be established, that I am a part of the whole which is governed by nature; next, I am in a manner intimately related to the parts which are of the same kind with myself. For remembering this, inasmuch as I am a part, I shall be discontented with none of the things which are assigned to me out of the whole; for nothing is injurious to the part, if it is for the advantage of the whole. For the whole contains nothing which is not for its advantage; and all natures indeed have this common principle, but the nature of the universe has this principle besides, that it cannot be compelled even by any external cause to generate anything harmful to itself.

By remembering, then, that I am a part of such a whole, I shall be content with everything that happens. And inasmuch as I am in a manner intimately related to the parts which are of the same kind with myself, I shall do nothing unsocial, but I shall rather direct myself to the things which are of the same kind with myself, and I shall turn an my efforts to the common interest, and divert them from the contrary. Now, if these things are done so, life must flow on happily, just as thou mayest observe that the life of a citizen is happy, who continues a course of action which is advantageous to his fellow-citizens, and is content with whatever the state may assign to him.

The parts of the whole, everything, I mean, which is naturally comprehended in the universe, must of necessity perish; but let this be understood in this sense, that they must undergo change. But if this is naturally both an evil and a necessity for the parts, the whole would not continue to exist in a good condition, the parts being subject to change and constituted so as to perish in various ways. For whether did nature herself design to do evil to the things which are parts of herself, and to make them subject to evil and of necessity fall into evil, or have such results happened without her knowing it? Both these suppositions, indeed, are incredible. But if a man should even drop the term Nature (as an efficient power), and should speak of these things as natural, even then it would be ridiculous to affirm at the same time that the parts of the whole are in their nature subject to change, and at the same time to be surprised or vexed as if something were happening contrary to nature, particularly as the dissolution of things is into those things of which each thing is composed. For there is either a dispersion of the elements out of which everything has been compounded, or a change from the solid to the earthy and from the airy to the aerial, so that these parts are taken back into the universal reason, whether this at certain periods is consumed by fire or renewed by eternal changes. And do not imagine that the solid and the airy part belong to thee from the time of generation. For all this received its accretion only yesterday and the day before, as one may say, from the food and the air which is inspired. This, then, which has received the accretion, changes, not that which thy mother brought forth. But suppose that this which thy mother brought forth implicates thee very much with that other part, which has the peculiar quality of change, this is nothing in fact in the way of objection to what is said.

When thou hast assumed these names, good, modest, true, rational, a man of equanimity, and magnanimous, take care that thou dost not change these names; and if thou shouldst lose them, quickly return to them. And remember that the term Rational was intended to signify a discriminating attention to every several thing and freedom from negligence; and that Equanimity is the voluntary acceptance of the things which are assigned to thee by the common nature; and that Magnanimity is the elevation of the intelligent part above the pleasurable or painful sensations of the flesh, and above that poor thing called fame, and death, and all such things. If, then, thou maintainest thyself in the possession of these names, without desiring to be called by these names by others, thou wilt be another person and wilt enter on another life. For to continue to be such as thou hast hitherto been, and to be tom in pieces and defiled in such a life, is the character of a very stupid man and one overfond of his life, and like those half-devoured fighters with wild beasts, who though covered with wounds and gore, still intreat to be kept to the following day, though they will be exposed in the same state to the same claws and bites. Therefore fix thyself in the possession of these few names: and if thou art able to abide in them, abide as if thou wast removed to certain islands of the Happy. But if thou shalt perceive that thou fallest out of them and dost not maintain thy hold, go courageously into some nook where thou shalt maintain them, or even depart at once from life, not in passion, but with simplicity and freedom and modesty, after doing this one laudable thing at least in thy life, to have gone out of it thus. In order, however, to the remembrance of these names, it will greatly help thee, if thou rememberest the gods, and that they wish not to be flattered, but wish all reasonable beings to be made like themselves; and if thou rememberest that what does the work of a fig-tree is a fig-tree, and that what does the work of a dog is a dog, and that what does the work of a bee is a bee, and that what does the work of a man is a man.

Mimi, war, astonishment, torpor, slavery, will daily wipe out those holy principles of thine. How many things without studying nature dost thou imagine, and how many dost thou neglect? But it is thy duty so to look on and so to do everything, that at the same time the power of dealing with circumstances is perfected, and the contemplative faculty is exercised, and the confidence which comes from the knowledge of each several thing is maintained without showing it, but yet not concealed. For when wilt thou enjoy simplicity, when gravity, and when the knowledge of every several thing, both what it is in substance, and what place it has in the universe, and how long it is formed to exist and of what things it is compounded, and to whom it can belong, and who are able both to give it and take it away?

A spider is proud when it has caught a fly, and another when he has caught a poor hare, and another when he has taken a little fish in a net, and another when he has taken wild boars, and another when he has taken bears, and another when he has taken Sarmatians. Are not these robbers, if thou examinest their opinions?

Acquire the contemplative way of seeing how all things change into one another, and constantly attend to it, and exercise thyself about this part of philosophy. For nothing is so much adapted to produce magnanimity. Such a man has put off the body, and as he sees that he must, no one knows how soon, go away from among men and leave everything here, he gives himself up entirely to just doing in all his actions, and in everything else that happens he resigns himself to the universal nature. But as to what any man shall say or think about him or do against him, he never even thinks of it, being himself contented with these two things, with acting justly in what he now does, and being satisfied with what is now assigned to him; and he lays aside all distracting and busy pursuits, and desires nothing else than to accomplish the straight course through the law, and by accomplishing the straight course to follow God.

What need is there of suspicious fear, since it is in thy power to inquire what ought to be done? And if thou seest clear, go by this way content, without turning back: but if thou dost not see clear, stop and take the best advisers. But if any other things oppose thee, go on according to thy powers with due consideration, keeping to that which appears to be just. For it is best to reach this object, and if thou dost fail, let thy failure be in attempting this.

He who follows reason in all things is both tranquil and active at the same time, and also cheerful and collected.

Inquire of thyself as soon as thou wakest from sleep, whether it will make any difference to thee, if another does what is just and right. It will make no difference.

Thou hast not forgotten, I suppose, that those who assume arrogant airs in bestowing their praise or blame on others, are such as they are at bed and at board, and thou hast not forgotten what they do, and what they avoid and what they pursue, and how they steal and how they rob, not with hands and feet, but with their most valuable part, by means of which there is produced, when a man chooses, fidelity, modesty, truth, law, a good daemon (happiness)?

To her who gives and takes back all, to nature, the man who is instructed and modest says, Give what thou wilt; take back what thou wilt. And he says this not proudly, but obediently and well pleased with her.

Short is the little which remains to thee of life. Live as on a mountain. For it makes no difference whether a man lives there or here, if he lives everywhere in the world as in a state (political community). Let men see, let them know a real man who lives according to nature. If they cannot endure him, let them kill him. For that is better than to live thus as men do. No longer talk at all about the kind of man that a good man ought to be, but be such.

Constantly contemplate the whole of time and the whole of substance, and consider that all individual things as to substance are a grain of a fig, and as to time, the turning of a gimlet.

Look at everything that exists, and observe that it is already in dissolution and in change, and as it were putrefaction or dispersion, or that everything is so constituted by nature as to die.

Consider what men are when they are eating, sleeping, generating, easing themselves and so forth. Then what kind of men they are when they are imperious and arrogant, or angry and scolding from their elevated place. But a short time ago to how many they were slaves and for what things; and after a little time consider in what a condition they will be.

That is for the good of each thing, which the universal nature brings to each. And it is for its good at the time when nature brings it.

"The earth loves the shower"; and "the solemn aether loves": and the universe loves to make whatever is about to be. I say then to the universe, that I love as thou lovest. And is not this too said, that "this or that loves (is wont) to be produced"?

Either thou livest here and hast already accustomed thyself to it, or thou art going away, and this was thy own will; or thou art dying and hast discharged thy duty. But besides these things there is nothing. Be of good cheer, then.

Let this always be plain to thee, that this piece of land is like any other; and that all things here are the same with things on top of a mountain, or on the sea-shore, or wherever thou choosest to be.

For thou wilt find just what Plato says, Dwelling within the walls of a city as in a shepherd's fold on a mountain.

What is my ruling faculty now to me? And of what nature am I now making it? And for what purpose am I now using it? Is it void of understanding? Is it loosed and rent asunder from social life? Is it melted into and mixed with the poor flesh so as to move together with it?

He who flies from his master is a runaway; but the law is master, and he who breaks the law is a runaway. And he also who is grieved or angry or afraid, is dissatisfied because something has been or is or shall be of the things which are appointed by him who rules all things, and he is Law, and assigns to every man what is fit. He then who fears or is grieved or is angry is a runaway.

A man deposits seed in a womb and goes away, and then another cause takes it, and labours on it and makes a child. What a thing from such a material! Again, the child passes food down through the throat, and then another cause takes it and makes perception and motion, and in fine life and strength and other things; how many and how strange I Observe then the things which are produced in such a hidden way, and see the power just as we see the power which carries things downwards and upwards, not with the eyes, but still no less plainly.

Constantly consider how all things such as they now are, in time past also were; and consider that they will be the same again. And place before thy eyes entire dramas and stages of the same form, whatever thou hast learned from thy experience or from older history; for example, the whole court of Hadrian, and the whole court of Antoninus, and the whole court of Philip, Alexander, Croesus; for all those were such dramas as we see now, only with different actors.

Imagine every man who is grieved at anything or discontented to be like a pig which is sacrificed and kicks and screams.

Like this pig also is he who on his bed in silence laments the bonds in which we are held. And consider that only to the rational animal is it given to follow voluntarily what happens; but simply to follow is a necessity imposed on all.

Severally on the occasion of everything that thou doest, pause and ask thyself, if death is a dreadful thing because it deprives thee of this.

When thou art offended at any man's fault, forthwith turn to thyself and reflect in what like manner thou dost err thyself; for example, in thinking that money is a good thing, or pleasure, or a bit of reputation, and the like. For by attending to this thou wilt quickly forget thy anger, if this consideration also is added, that the man is compelled: for what else could he do? or, if thou art able, take away from him the compulsion.

When thou hast seen Satyron the Socratic, think of either Eutyches or Hymen, and when thou hast seen Euphrates, think of Eutychion or Silvanus, and when thou hast seen Alciphron think of Tropaeophorus, and when thou hast seen Xenophon think of Crito or Severus, and when thou hast looked on thyself, think of any other Caesar, and in the case of every one do in like manner. Then let this thought be in thy mind, Where then are those men? Nowhere, or nobody knows where. For thus continuously thou wilt look at human things as smoke and nothing at all; especially if thou reflectest at the same time that what has once changed will never exist again in the infinite duration of time. But thou, in what a brief space of time is thy existence? And why art thou not content to pass through this short time in an orderly way? What matter and opportunity for thy activity art thou avoiding? For what else are all these things, except exercises for the reason, when it has viewed carefully and by examination into their nature the things which happen in life? Persevere then until thou shalt have made these things thy own, as the stomach which is strengthened makes all things its own, as the blazing fire makes flame and brightness out of everything that is thrown into it.

Let it not be in any man's power to say truly of thee that thou art not simple or that thou are not good; but let him be a liar whoever shall think anything of this kind about thee; and this is altogether in thy power. For who is he that shall hinder thee from being good and simple? Do thou only determine to live no longer, unless thou shalt be such. For neither does reason allow thee to live, if thou art not such.

What is that which as to this material (our life) can be done or said in the way most conformable to reason. For whatever this may be, it is in thy power to do it or to say it, and do not make excuses that thou art hindered. Thou wilt not cease to lament till thy mind is in such a condition that, what luxury is to those who enjoy pleasure, such shall be to thee, in the matter which is subjected and presented to thee, the doing of the things which are conformable to man's constitution; for a man ought to consider as an enjoyment everything which it is in his power to do according to his own nature.

And it is in his power everywhere. Now, it is not given to a cylinder to move everywhere by its own motion, nor yet to water nor to fire, nor to anything else which is governed by nature or an irrational soul, for the things which check them and stand in the way are many. But intelligence and reason are able to go through everything that opposes them, and in such manner as they are formed by nature and as they choose. Place before thy eyes this facility with which the reason will be carried through all things, as fire upwards, as a stone downwards, as a cylinder down an inclined surface, and seek for nothing further. For all other obstacles either affect the body only which is a dead thing; or, except through opinion and the yielding of the reason itself, they do not crush nor do any harm of any kind; for if they did, he who felt it would immediately become bad. Now, in the case of all things which have a certain constitution, whatever harm may happen to any of them, that which is so affected becomes consequently worse; but in the like case, a man becomes both better, if one may say so, and more worthy of praise by making a right use of these accidents. And finally remember that nothing harms him who is really a citizen, which does not harm the state; nor yet does anything harm the state, which does not harm law (order); and of these things which are called misfortunes not one harms law. What then does not harm law does not harm either state or citizen.

To him who is penetrated by true principles even the briefest precept is sufficient, and any common precept, to remind him that he should be free from grief and fear. For example- Leaves, some the wind scatters on the ground- So is the race of men.

Leaves, also, are thy children; and leaves, too, are they who cry out as if they were worthy of credit and bestow their praise, or on the contrary curse, or secretly blame and sneer; and leaves, in like manner, are those who shall receive and transmit a man's fame to aftertimes. For all such things as these "are produced in the season of spring," as the poet says; then the wind casts them down; then the forest produces other leaves in their places. But a brief existence is common to all things, and yet thou avoidest and pursuest all things as if they would be eternal. A little time, and thou shalt close thy eyes; and him who has attended thee to thy grave another soon will lament. The healthy eye ought to see all visible things and not to say, I wish for green things; for this is the condition of a diseased eye. And the healthy hearing and smelling ought to be ready to perceive all that can be heard and smelled. And the healthy stomach ought to be with respect to all food just as the mill with respect to all things which it is formed to grind. And accordingly the healthy understanding ought to be prepared for everything which happens; but that which says, Let my dear children live, and let all men praise whatever I may do, is an eye which seeks for green things, or teeth which seek for soft things.

There is no man so fortunate that there shall not be by him when he is dying some who are pleased with what is going to happen. Suppose that he was a good and wise man, will there not be at last some one to say to himself, Let us at last breathe freely being relieved from this schoolmaster? It is true that he was harsh to none of us, but I perceived that he tacitly condemns us.- This is what is said of a good man. But in our own case how many other things are there for which there are many who wish to get rid of us. Thou wilt consider this then when thou art dying, and thou wilt depart more contentedly by reflecting thus: I am going away from such a life, in which even my associates in behalf of whom I have striven so much, prayed, and cared, themselves wish me to depart, hoping perchance to get some little advantage by it. Why then should a man cling to a longer stay here? Do not however for this reason go away less kindly disposed to them, but preserving thy own character, and friendly and benevolent and mild, and on the other hand not as if thou wast torn away; but as when a man dies a quiet death, the poor soul is easily separated from the body, such also ought thy departure from men to be, for nature united thee to them and associated thee. But does she now dissolve the union? Well, I am separated as from kinsmen, not however dragged resisting, but without compulsion; for this too is one of the things according to nature.

Accustom thyself as much as possible on the occasion of anything being done by any person to inquire with thyself, For what object is this man doing this? But begin with thyself, and examine thyself first.

Remember that this which pulls the strings is the thing which is hidden within: this is the power of persuasion, this is life, this, if one may so say, is man. In contemplating thyself never include the vessel which surrounds thee and these instruments which are attached about it. For they are like to an axe, differing only in this that they grow to the body. For indeed there is no more use in these parts without the cause which moves and checks them than in the weaver's shuttle, and the writer's pen and the driver's whip.

BOOK ELEVEN

THESE are the properties of the rational soul: it sees itself, analyses itself, and makes itself such as it chooses; the fruit which it bears itself enjoys- for the fruits of plants and that in animals which corresponds to fruits others enjoy- it obtains its own end, wherever the limit of life may be fixed. Not as in a dance and in a play and in such like things, where the whole action is incomplete, if anything cuts it short; but in every part and wherever it may be stopped, it makes what has been set before it full and complete, so that it can say, I have what is my own. And further it traverses the whole universe, and the surrounding vacuum, and surveys its form, and it extends itself into the infinity of time, and embraces and comprehends the periodical renovation of all things, and it comprehends that those who come after us will see nothing new, nor have those before us seen anything more, but in a manner he who is forty years old, if he has any understanding at all, has seen by virtue of the uniformity that prevails all things which have been and all that will be. This too is a property of the rational soul, love of one's neighbour, and truth and modesty, and to value nothing more more than itself, which is also the property of Law. Thus then right reason differs not at all from the reason of justice. Thou wilt set little value on pleasing song and dancing and the pancratium, if thou wilt distribute the melody of the voice into its several sounds, and ask thyself as to each, if thou art mastered by this; for thou wilt be prevented by shame from confessing it: and in the matter of dancing, if at each movement and attitude thou wilt do the same; and the like also in the matter of the pancratium. In all things, then, except virtue and the acts of virtue, remember to apply thyself to their several parts, and by this division to come to value them little: and apply this rule also to thy whole life.

What a soul that is which is ready, if at any moment it must be separated from the body, and ready either to be extinguished or dispersed or continue to exist; but so that this readiness comes from a man's own judgement, not from mere obstinacy, as with the Christians, but considerately and with dignity and in a way to persuade another, without tragic show.

Have I done something for the general interest? Well then I have had my reward. Let this always be present to thy mind, and never stop doing such good.

What is thy art? To be good. And how is this accomplished well except by general principles, some about the nature of the universe, and others about the proper constitution of man?

At first tragedies were brought on the stage as means of reminding men of the things which happen to them, and that it is according to nature for things to happen so, and that, if you are delighted with what is shown on the stage, you should not be troubled with that which takes place on the larger stage. For you see that these things must be accomplished thus, and that even they bear them who cry out "O Cithaeron." And, indeed, some things are said well by the dramatic writers, of which kind is the following especially:-

Me and my children if the gods neglect,
This has its reason too.

And again-

We must not chale and fret at that which happens.

And

Life's harvest reap like the wheat's fruitful ear.

And other things of the same kind.

After tragedy the old comedy was introduced, which had a magisterial freedom of speech, and by its very plainness of speaking was useful in reminding men to beware of insolence; and for this purpose too Diogenes used to take from these writers.

But as to the middle comedy which came next, observe what it was, and again, for what object the new comedy was introduced, which gradually sunk down into a mere mimic artifice. That some good things are said even by these writers, everybody knows: but the whole plan of such poetry and dramaturgy, to what end does it look! How plain does it appear that there is not another condition of life so well suited for philosophising as this in which thou now happenest to be.

A branch cut off from the adjacent branch must of necessity be cut off from the whole tree also. So too a man when he is separated from another man has fallen off from the whole social community. Now as to a branch, another cuts it off, but a man by his own act separates himself from his neighbour when he hates him and turns away from him, and he does not know that he has at the same time cut himself off from the whole social system. Yet he has this privilege certainly from Zeus who framed society, for it is in our power to grow again to that which is near to us, and be to come a part which helps to make up the whole. However, if it often happens, this kind of separation, it makes it difficult for that which detaches itself to be brought to unity and to be restored to its former condition. Finally, the branch, which from the first grew together with the tree, and has continued to have one life with it, is not like that which after being cut off is then ingrafted, for this is something like what the gardeners mean when they say that it grows with the rest of the tree, but that it has not the same mind with it.

As those who try to stand in thy way when thou art proceeding according to right reason, will not be able to turn thee aside from thy proper action, so neither let them drive thee from thy benevolent feelings towards them, but be on thy guard equally in both matters, not only in the matter of steady judgement and action, but also in the matter of gentleness towards those who try to hinder or otherwise trouble thee. For this also is a weakness, to be vexed at them, as well as to be diverted from thy course of action and to give way through fear; for both are equally deserters from their post, the man who does it through fear, and the man who is alienated from him who is by nature a kinsman and a friend.

There is no nature which is inferior to art, for the arts imitate the nature of things. But if this is so, that nature which is the most perfect and the most comprehensive of all natures, cannot fall short of the skill of art. Now all arts do the inferior things for the sake of the superior; therefore the universal nature does so too. And, indeed, hence is the origin of justice, and in justice the other virtues have their foundation: for justice will not be observed, if we either care for middle things (things indifferent), or are easily deceived and careless and changeable.

If the things do not come to thee, the pursuits and avoidances of which disturb thee, still in a manner thou goest to them. Let then thy judgement about them be at rest, and they will remain quiet, and thou wilt not be seen either pursuing or avoiding.

The spherical form of the soul maintains its figure, when it is neither extended towards any object, nor contracted inwards, nor dispersed nor sinks down, but is illuminated by light, by which it sees the truth, the truth of all things and the truth that is in itself.

Suppose any man shall despise me. Let him look to that himself. But I will look to this, that I be not discovered doing or saying anything deserving of contempt. Shall any man hate me? Let him look to it. But I will be mild and benevolent towards every man, and ready to show even him his mistake, not reproachfully, nor yet as making a display of my endurance, but nobly and honestly, like the great

Phocion, unless indeed he only assumed it. For the interior parts ought to be such, and a man ought to be seen by the gods neither dissatisfied with anything nor complaining. For what evil is it to thee, if thou art now doing what is agreeable to thy own nature, and art satisfied with that which at this moment is suitable to the nature of the universe, since thou art a human being placed at thy post in order that what is for the common advantage may be done in some way?

Men despise one another and flatter one another; and men wish to raise themselves above one another, and crouch before one another. How unsound and insincere is he who says, I have determined to deal with thee in a fair way.- What art thou doing, man? There is no occasion to give this notice. It will soon show itself by acts. The voice ought to be plainly written on the forehead. Such as a man's character is, he immediately shows it in his eyes, just as he who is beloved forthwith reads everything in the eyes of lovers. The man who is honest and good ought to be exactly like a man who smells strong, so that the bystander as soon as he comes near him must smell whether he choose or not. But the affectation of simplicity is like a crooked stick. Nothing is more disgraceful than a wolfish friendship (false friendship). Avoid this most of all. The good and simple and benevolent show all these things in the eyes, and there is no mistaking.

As to living in the best way, this power is in the soul, if it be indifferent to things which are indifferent. And it will be indifferent, if it looks on each of these things separately and all together, and if it remembers that not one of them produces in us an opinion about itself, nor comes to us; but these things remain immovable, and it is we ourselves who produce the judgements about them, and, as we may say, write them in ourselves, it being in our power not to write them, and it being in our power, if perchance these judgements have imperceptibly got admission to our minds, to wipe them out; and if we remember also that such attention will only be for a short time, and then life will be at an end. Besides, what trouble is there at all in doing this? For if these things are according to nature, rejoice in them, and they will be easy to thee: but if contrary to nature, seek what is conformable to thy own nature, and strive towards this, even if it bring no reputation; for every man is allowed to seek his own good.

Consider whence each thing is come, and of what it consists, and into what it changes, and what kind of a thing it will be when it has changed, and that it will sustain no harm.

If any have offended against thee, consider first: What is my relation to men, and that we are made for one another; and in another respect, I was made to be set over them, as a ram over the flock or a bull over the herd. But examine the matter from first principles, from this: If all things are not mere atoms, it is nature which orders all things: if this is so, the inferior things exist for the sake of the superior, and these for the sake of one another.

Second, consider what kind of men they are at table, in bed, and so forth: and particularly, under what compulsions in respect of opinions they are; and as to their acts, consider with what pride they do what they do.

Third, that if men do rightly what they do, we ought not to be displeased; but if they do not right, it is plain that they do so involuntarily and in ignorance. For as every soul is unwillingly deprived of the truth, so also is it unwillingly deprived of the power of behaving to each man according to his deserts. Accordingly men are pained when they are called unjust, ungrateful, and greedy, and in a word wrong-doers to their neighbours.

Fourth, consider that thou also doest many things wrong, and that thou art a man like others; and even if thou dost abstain from certain faults, still thou hast the disposition to commit them, though either through cowardice, or concern about reputation, or some such mean motive, thou dost abstain from such faults.

Fifth, consider that thou dost not even understand whether men are doing wrong or not, for many things are done with a certain reference to circumstances. And in short, a man must learn a great deal to enable him to pass a correct judgement on another man's acts.

Sixth, consider when thou art much vexed or grieved, that man's life is only a moment, and after a short time we are all laid out dead.

Seventh, that it is not men's acts which disturb us, for those acts have their foundation in men's ruling principles, but it is our own opinions which disturb us. Take away these opinions then, and resolve to dismiss thy judgement about an act as if it were something grievous, and thy anger is gone. How then shall I take away these opinions? By reflecting that no wrongful act of another brings shame on thee: for unless that which is shameful is alone bad, thou also must of necessity do many things wrong, and become a robber and everything else.

Eighth, consider how much more pain is brought on us by the anger and vexation caused by such acts than by the acts themselves, at which we are angry and vexed.

Ninth, consider that a good disposition is invincible, if it be genuine, and not an affected smile and acting a part. For what will the most violent man do to thee, if thou continuest to be of a kind disposition towards him, and if, as opportunity offers, thou gently admonishest him and calmly correctest his errors at the very time when he is trying to do thee harm, saying, Not so, my child: we are constituted by nature for something else: I shall certainly not be injured, but thou art injuring thyself, my child.- And show him with gentle tact and by general principles that this is so, and that even bees do not do as he does, nor any animals which are formed by nature to be gregarious. And thou must do this neither with any double meaning nor in the way of reproach, but affectionately and without any rancour in thy soul; and not as if thou wert lecturing him, nor yet that any bystander may admire, but either when he is alone, and if others are present...

Remember these nine rules, as if thou hadst received them as a gift from the Muses, and begin at last to be a man while thou livest. But thou must equally avoid flattering men and being vexed at them, for both are unsocial and lead to harm. And let this truth be present to thee in the excitement of anger, that to be moved by passion is not manly, but that mildness and gentleness, as they are more agreeable to human nature, so also are they more manly; and he who possesses these qualities possesses strength, nerves and courage, and not the man who is subject to fits of passion and discontent. For in the same degree in which a man's mind is nearer to freedom from all passion, in the same degree also is it nearer to strength: and as the sense of pain is a characteristic of weakness, so also is anger. For he who yields to pain and he who yields to anger, both are wounded and both submit.

But if thou wilt, receive also a tenth present from the leader of the Muses (Apollo), and it is this- that to expect bad men not to do wrong is madness, for he who expects this desires an impossibility.

But to allow men to behave so to others, and to expect them not to do thee any wrong, is irrational and tyrannical.

There are four principal aberrations of the superior faculty against which thou shouldst be constantly on thy guard, and when thou hast detected them, thou shouldst wipe them out and say on each occasion thus: this thought is not necessary: this tends to destroy social union: this which thou art going to say comes not from the real thoughts; for thou shouldst consider it among the most absurd of things for a man not to speak from his real thoughts. But the fourth is when thou shalt reproach thyself for anything, for this is an evidence of the diviner part within thee being overpowered and yielding to the less honourable and to the perishable part, the body, and to its gross pleasures.

Thy aerial part and all the fiery parts which are mingled in thee, though by nature they have an upward tendency, still in obedience to the disposition of the universe they are overpowered here in the compound mass (the body).

73

And also the whole of the earthy part in thee and the watery, though their tendency is downward, still are raised up and occupy a position which is not their natural one. In this manner then the elemental parts obey the universal, for when they have been fixed in any place perforce they remain there until again the universal shall sound the signal for dissolution. Is it not then strange that thy intelligent part only should be disobedient and discontented with its own place? And yet no force is imposed on it, but only those things which are conformable to its nature: still it does not submit, but is carried in the opposite direction. For the movement towards injustice and intemperance and to anger and grief and fear is nothing else than the act of one who deviates from nature. And also when the ruling faculty is discontented with anything that happens, then too it deserts its post: for it is constituted for piety and reverence towards the gods no less than for justice. For these qualities also are comprehended under the generic term of contentment with the constitution of things, and indeed they are prior to acts of justice.

He who has not one and always the same object in life, cannot be one and the same all through his life. But what I have said is not enough, unless this also is added, what this object ought to be. For as there is not the same opinion about all the things which in some way or other are considered by the majority to be good, but only about some certain things, that is, things which concern the common interest; so also ought we to propose to ourselves an object which shall be of a common kind (social) and political. For he who directs all his own efforts to this object, will make all his acts alike, and thus will always be the same.

Think of the country mouse and of the town mouse, and of the alarm and trepidation of the town mouse.

Socrates used to call the opinions of the many by the name of Lamiae, bugbears to frighten children. The Lacedaemonians at their public spectacles used to set seats in the shade for strangers, but themselves sat down anywhere. Socrates excused himself to Perdiccas for not going to him, saying, It is because I would not perish by the worst of all ends, that is, I would not receive a favour and then be unable to return it. In the writings of the Ephesians there was this precept, constantly to think of some one of the men of former times who practised virtue.

The Pythagoreans bid us in the morning look to the heavens that we may be reminded of those bodies which continually do the same things and in the same manner perform their work, and also be reminded of their purity and nudity. For there is no veil over a star.

Consider what a man Socrates was when he dressed himself in a skin, after Xanthippe had taken his cloak and gone out, and what Socrates said to his friends who were ashamed of him and drew back from him when they saw him dressed thus.

Neither in writing nor in reading wilt thou be able to lay down rules for others before thou shalt have first learned to obey rules thyself. Much more is this so in life.

A slave thou art: free speech is not for thee.

And my heart laughed within.

And virtue they will curse, speaking harsh words.

To look for the fig in winter is a madman's act: such is he who looks for his child when it is no longer allowed.

When a man kisses his child, said Epictetus, he should whisper to himself, "To-morrow perchance thou wilt die."- But those are words of bad omen.- "No word is a word of bad omen," said Epictetus, "which expresses any work of nature; or if it is so, it is also a word of bad omen to speak of the ears of corn being reaped."

The unripe grape, the ripe bunch, the dried grape, all are changes, not into nothing, but into something which exists not yet.

No man can rob us of our free will.

Epictetus also said, A man must discover an art (or rules) with respect to giving his assent; and in respect to his movements he must be careful that they be made with regard to circumstances, that they be consistent with social interests, that they have regard to the value of the object; and as to sensual desire, he should altogether keep away from it; and as to avoidance (aversion) he should not show it with respect to any of the things which are not in our power.

The dispute then, he said, is not about any common matter, but about being mad or not.

Socrates used to say, What do you want? Souls of rational men or irrational?- Souls of rational men.- Of what rational men? Sound or unsound?- Sound.- Why then do you not seek for them?- Because we have them.- Why then do you fight and quarrel?

BOOK TWELVE

ALL those things at which thou wishest to arrive by a circuitous road, thou canst have now, if thou dost not refuse them to thyself.

And this means, if thou wilt take no notice of all the past, and trust the future to providence, and direct the present only conformably to piety and justice. Conformably to piety, that thou mayest be content with the lot which is assigned to thee, for nature designed it for thee and thee for it. Conformably to justice, that thou mayest always speak the truth freely and without disguise, and do the things which are agreeable to law and according to the worth of each. And let neither another man's wickedness hinder thee, nor opinion nor voice, nor yet the sensations of the poor flesh which has grown about thee; for the passive part will look to this. If then, whatever the time may be when thou shalt be near to thy departure, neglecting everything else thou shalt respect only thy ruling faculty and the divinity within thee, and if thou shalt be afraid not because thou must some time cease to live, but if thou shalt fear never to have begun to live according to nature- then thou wilt be a man worthy of the universe which has produced thee, and thou wilt cease to be a stranger in thy native land, and to wonder at things which happen daily as if they were something unexpected, and to be dependent on this or that.

God sees the minds (ruling principles) of all men bared of the material vesture and rind and impurities. For with his intellectual part alone he touches the intelligence only which has flowed and been derived from himself into these bodies. And if thou also usest thyself to do this, thou wilt rid thyself of thy much trouble. For he who regards not the poor flesh which envelops him, surely will not trouble himself by looking after raiment and dwelling and fame and such like externals and show.

The things are three of which thou art composed, a little body, a little breath (life), intelligence. Of these the first two are thine, so far as it is thy duty to take care of them; but the third alone is properly thine. Therefore if thou shalt separate from thyself, that is, from thy understanding, whatever others do or say, and whatever thou hast done or said thyself, and whatever future things trouble thee because they may happen, and whatever in the body which envelops thee or in the breath (life), which is by nature associated with the body, is attached to thee independent of thy will, and whatever the external circumfluent vortex whirls round, so that the intellectual power exempt from the things of fate can live pure and free by itself, doing what is just and accepting what happens and saying the truth: if thou wilt separate, I say, from this ruling faculty the things which are attached to it by the impressions of sense, and the things of time to come and of time that is past, and wilt make thyself like Empedocles' sphere, All round, and in its joyous rest reposing; and if thou shalt strive to live only what is really thy life, that is, the present- then thou wilt be able to pass that portion of life which remains for thee up to the time of thy death, free from perturbations, nobly, and obedient to thy own daemon (to the god that is within thee).

I have often wondered how it is that every man loves himself more than all the rest of men, but yet sets less value on his own opinion of himself than on the opinion of others. If then a god or a wise teacher should present himself to a man and bid him to think of nothing and to design nothing which he would not express as soon as he conceived it, he could not endure it even for a single day. So much more respect have we to what our neighbours shall think of us than to what we shall think of ourselves.

How can it be that the gods after having arranged all things well and benevolently for mankind, have overlooked this alone, that some men and very good men, and men who, as we may say, have had most communion with the divinity, and through pious acts and religious observances have been most intimate with the divinity, when they have once died should never exist again, but should be completely extinguished?

But if this is so, be assured that if it ought to have been otherwise, the gods would have done it. For if it were just, it would also be possible; and if it were according to nature, nature would have had it so. But because it is not so, if in fact it is not so, be thou convinced that it ought not to have been so:- for thou seest even of thyself that in this inquiry thou art disputing with the diety; and we should not thus dispute with the gods, unless they were most excellent and most just;- but if this is so, they would not have allowed anything in the ordering of the universe to be neglected unjustly and irrationally.

Practise thyself even in the things which thou despairest of accomplishing. For even the left hand, which is ineffectual for all other things for want of practice, holds the bridle more vigorously than the right hand; for it has been practised in this.

Consider in what condition both in body and soul a man should be when he is overtaken by death; and consider the shortness of life, the boundless abyss of time past and future, the feebleness of all matter.

Contemplate the formative principles (forms) of things bare of their coverings; the purposes of actions; consider what pain is, what pleasure is, and death, and fame; who is to himself the cause of his uneasiness; how no man is hindered by another; that everything is opinion.

In the application of thy principles thou must be like the pancratiast, not like the gladiator; for the gladiator lets fall the sword which he uses and is killed; but the other always has his hand, and needs to do nothing else than use it.

See what things are in themselves, dividing them into matter, form and purpose.

What a power man has to do nothing except what God will approve, and to accept all that God may give him.

With respect to that which happens conformably to nature, we ought to blame neither gods, for they do nothing wrong either voluntarily or involuntarily, nor men, for they do nothing wrong except involuntarily. Consequently we should blame nobody.

How ridiculous and what a stranger he is who is surprised at anything which happens in life.

Either there is a fatal necessity and invincible order, or a kind Providence, or a confusion without a purpose and without a director (Book IV). If then there is an invincible necessity, why dost thou resist? But if there is a Providence which allows itself to be propitiated, make thyself worthy of the help of the divinity. But if there is a confusion without governor, be content that in such a tempest thou hast in thyself a certain ruling intelligence. And even if the tempest carry thee away, let it carry away the poor flesh, the poor breath, everything else; for the intelligence at least it will not carry away.

Does the light of the lamp shine without losing its splendour until it is extinguished; and shall the truth which is in thee and justice and temperance be extinguished before thy death?

When a man has presented the appearance of having done wrong, say, How then do I know if this is a wrongful act? And even if he has done wrong, how do I know that he has not condemned himself? and so this is like tearing his own face. Consider that he, who would not have the bad man do wrong, is like the man who would not have the fig-tree to bear juice in the figs and infants to cry and the horse to neigh, and whatever else must of necessity be. For what must a man do who has such a character? If then thou art irritable, cure this man's disposition.

If it is not right, do not do it: if it is not true, do not say it. For let thy efforts be.

In everything always observe what the thing is which produces for thee an appearance, and resolve it by dividing it into the formal, the material, the purpose, and the time within which it must end.

Perceive at last that thou hast in thee something better and more divine than the things which cause the various affects, and as it were pull thee by the strings. What is there now in my mind? Is it fear, or suspicion, or desire, or anything of the kind?

First, do nothing inconsiderately, nor without a purpose. Second, make thy acts refer to nothing else than to a social end. Consider that before long thou wilt be nobody and nowhere, nor will any of the things exist which thou now seest, nor any of those who are now living. For all things are formed by nature to change and be turned and to perish in order that other things in continuous succession may exist.

Consider that everything is opinion, and opinion is in thy power. Take away then, when thou choosest, thy opinion, and like a mariner, who has doubled the promontory, thou wilt find calm, everything stable, and a waveless bay.

Any one activity whatever it may be, when it has ceased at its proper time, suffers no evil because it has ceased; nor he who has done this act, does he suffer any evil for this reason that the act has ceased. In like manner then the whole which consists of all the acts, which is our life, if it cease at its proper time, suffers no evil for this reason that it has ceased; nor he who has terminated this series at the proper time, has he been ill dealt with. But the proper time and the limit nature fixes, sometimes as in old age the peculiar nature of man, but always the universal nature, by the change of whose parts the whole universe continues ever young and perfect.

And everything which is useful to the universal is always good and in season. Therefore the termination of life for every man is no evil, because neither is it shameful, since it is both independent of the will and not opposed to the general interest, but it is good, since it is seasonable and profitable to and congruent with the universal. For thus too he is moved by the deity who is moved in the same manner with the deity and moved towards the same things in his mind.

These three principles thou must have in readiness. In the things which thou doest do nothing either inconsiderately or otherwise than as justice herself would act; but with respect to what may happen to thee from without, consider that it happens either by chance or according to Providence, and thou must neither blame chance nor accuse Providence. Second, consider what every being is from the seed to the time of its receiving a soul, and from the reception of a soul to the giving back of the same, and of what things every being is compounded and into what things it is resolved. Third, if thou shouldst suddenly be raised up above the earth, and shouldst look down on human things, and observe the variety of them how great it is, and at the same time also shouldst see at a glance how great is the number of beings who dwell around in the air and the aether, consider that as often as thou shouldst be raised up, thou wouldst see the same things, sameness of form and shortness of duration. Are these things to be proud of?

Cast away opinion: thou art saved. Who then hinders thee from casting it away?

When thou art troubled about anything, thou hast forgotten this, that all things happen according to the universal nature; and forgotten this, that a man's wrongful act is nothing to thee; and further thou hast forgotten this, that everything which happens, always happened so and will happen so, and now happens so everywhere; forgotten this too, how close is the kinship between a man and the whole human race, for it is a community, not of a little blood or seed, but of intelligence. And thou hast forgotten this too, that every man's intelligence is a god, and is an efflux of the deity; and forgotten this, that nothing is a man's own, but that his child and his body and his very soul came from the deity; forgotten this, that everything is opinion; and lastly thou hast forgotten that every man lives the present time only, and loses only this.

Constantly bring to thy recollection those who have complained greatly about anything, those who have been most conspicuous by the greatest fame or misfortunes or enmities or fortunes of any kind: then think where are they all now? Smoke and ash and a tale, or not even a tale. And let there be present to thy mind also everything of this sort, how Fabius Catullinus lived in the country, and Lucius Lupus in his gardens, and Stertinius at Baiae, and Tiberius at Capreae and Velius Rufus (or Rufus at Velia); and in fine think of the eager pursuit of anything conjoined with pride; and how worthless everything is after which men violently strain; and how much more philosophical it is for a man in the opportunities presented to him to show.

THE GOLDEN SAYINGS

OF EPICTETUS

I

Are these the only works of Providence within us? What words suffice to praise or set them forth? Had we but understanding, should we ever cease hymning and blessing the Divine Power, both openly and in secret, and telling of His gracious gifts? Whether digging or ploughing or eating, should we not sing the hymn to God:—

Great is God, for that He hath given us such instruments to till the ground withal: Great is God, for that He hath given us hands and the power of swallowing and digesting; of unconsciously growing and breathing while we sleep!

Thus should we ever have sung; yea and this, the grandest and divinest hymn of all:—

Great is God, for that He hath given us a mind to apprehend these things, and duly to use them!

What then! seeing that most of you are blinded, should there not be some one to fill this place, and sing the hymn to God on behalf of all men? What else can I that am old and lame do but sing to God? Were I a nightingale, I should do after the manner of a nightingale. Were I a swan, I should do after the manner of a swan. But now, since I am a reasonable being, I must sing to God: that is my work: I do it, nor will I desert this my post, as long as it is granted me to hold it; and upon you too I call to join in this self-same hymn.

II

How then do men act? As though one returning to his country who had sojourned for the night in a fair inn, should be so captivated thereby as to take up his abode there.

"Friend, thou hast forgotten thine intention! This was not thy destination, but only lay on the way thither."

"Nay, but it is a proper place."

"And how many more of the sort there may be; only to pass through upon thy way! Thy purpose was to return to thy country; to relieve thy kinsmen's fears for thee; thyself to discharge the duties of a citizen; to marry a wife, to beget offspring, and to fill the appointed round of office. Thou didst not come to choose out what places are most pleasant; but rather to return to that wherein thou wast born and where wert appointed to be a citizen."

III

Try to enjoy the great festival of life with other men.

IV

But I have one whom I must please, to whom I must be subject, whom I must obey:—God, and those who come next to Him. He hath entrusted me with myself: He hath made my will subject to myself alone and given me rules for the right use thereof.

V

Rufus used to say, If you have leisure to praise me, what I say is naught. In truth he spoke in such wise, that each of us who sat there, though that some one had accused him to Rufus:—so surely did he lay his finger on the very deeds we did: so surely display the faults of each before his very eyes.

VI

But what saith God?—"Had it been possible, Epictetus, I would have made both that body of thine and thy possessions free and unimpeded, but as it is, be not deceived:—it is not thine own; it is but finely tempered clay. Since then this I could not do, I have given thee a portion of Myself, in the power of desiring and declining and of pursuing and avoiding, and in a word the power of dealing with the things of sense. And if thou neglect not this, but place all that thou hast therein, thou shalt never be let or hindered; thou shalt never lament; thou shalt not blame or flatter any. What then? Seemeth this to thee a little thing?"—God forbid!—"Be content then therewith!"
And so I pray the Gods.

VII

What saith Antisthenes? Hast thou never heard?— It is a kingly thing, O Cyrus, to do well and to be evil spoken of.

VIII

"Aye, but to debase myself thus were unworthy of me."
"That," said Epictetus, "is for you to consider, not for me. You know yourself what you are worth in your own eyes; and at what price you will sell yourself. For men sell themselves at various prices. This was why, when Florus was deliberating whether he should appear at Nero's shows, taking part in the performance himself, Agrippinus replied, 'But why do not you appear?' he answered, 'Because I do not even consider the question.' For the man who has once stooped to consider such questions, and to reckon up the value of external things, is not far from forgetting what manner of man he is. Why, what is it that you ask me? Is death preferable, or life? I reply, Life. Pain or pleasure? I reply, Pleasure."
"Well, but if I do not act, I shall lose my head."
"Then go and act! But for my part I will not act."
"Why?"
"Because you think yourself but one among the many threads which make up the texture of the doublet. You should aim at being like men in general—just as your thread has no ambition either to be anything distinguished compared with the other threads. But I desire to be the purple—that small and shining

part which makes the rest seem fair and beautiful. Why then do you bid me become even as the multitude? Then were I no longer the purple."

IX

If a man could be thoroughly penetrated, as he ought, with this thought, that we are all in an especial manner sprung from God, and that God is the Father of men as well as of Gods, full surely he would never conceive aught ignoble or base of himself. Whereas if Caesar were to adopt you, your haughty looks would be intolerable; will you not be elated at knowing that you are the son of God? Now however it is not so with us: but seeing that in our birth these two things are commingled—the body which we share with the animals, and the Reason and Thought which we share with the Gods, many decline towards this unhappy kinship with the dead, few rise to the blessed kinship with the Divine. Since then every one must deal with each thing according to the view which he forms about it, those few who hold that they are born for fidelity, modesty, and unerring sureness in dealing with the things of sense, never conceive aught base or ignoble of themselves: but the multitude the contrary. Why, what am I?—A wretched human creature; with this miserable flesh of mine. Miserable indeed! but you have something better than that paltry flesh of yours. Why then cling to the one, and neglect the other?

X

Thou art but a poor soul laden with a lifeless body.

XI

The other day I had an iron lamp placed beside my household gods. I heard a noise at the door and on hastening down found my lamp carried off. I reflected that the culprit was in no very strange case. "Tomorrow, my friend," I said, "you will find an earthenware lamp; for a man can only lose what he has."

XII

The reason why I lost my lamp was that the thief was superior to me in vigilance. He paid however this price for the lamp, that in exchange for it he consented to become a thief: in exchange for it, to become faithless.

XIII

But God hath introduced Man to be a spectator of Himself and of His works; and not a spectator only, but also an interpreter of them. Wherefore it is a shame for man to begin and to leave off where the brutes do. Rather he should begin there, and leave off where Nature leaves off in us: and that is at contemplation, and understanding, and a manner of life that is in harmony with herself.

See then that ye die not without being spectators of these things.

XIV

You journey to Olympia to see the work of Phidias; and each of you holds it a misfortune not to have beheld these things before you die. Whereas when there is no need even to take a journey, but you are on the spot, with the works before you, have you no care to contemplate and study these?
Will you not then perceive either who you are or unto what end you were born: or for what purpose the power of contemplation has been bestowed on you?
"Well, but in life there are some things disagreeable and hard to bear."
And are there none at Olympia? Are you not scorched by the heat? Are you not cramped for room? Have you not to bathe with discomfort? Are you not drenched when it rains? Have you not to endure the clamor and shouting and such annoyances as these? Well, I suppose you set all this over against the splendour of the spectacle and bear it patiently. What then? have you not received greatness of heart, received courage, received fortitude? What care I, if I am great of heart, for aught that can come to pass? What shall cast me down or disturb me? What shall seem painful? Shall I not use the power to the end for which I received it, instead of moaning and wailing over what comes to pass?

XV

If what philosophers say of the kinship of God and Man be true, what remains for men to do but as Socrates did:—never, when asked one's country, to answer, "I am an Athenian or a Corinthian," but "I am a citizen of the world."

XVI

He that hath grasped the administration of the World, who hath learned that this Community, which consists of God and men, is the foremost and mightiest and most comprehensive of all:—that from God have descended the germs of life, not to my father only and father's father, but to all things that are born and grow upon the earth, and in an especial manner to those endowed with Reason (for those only are by their nature fitted to hold communion with God, being by means of Reason conjoined with Him)—why should not such an one call himself a citizen of the world? Why not a son of God? Why should he fear aught that comes to pass among men? Shall kinship with Caesar, or any other of the great at Rome, be enough to hedge men around with safety and consideration, without a thought of apprehension: while to have God for our Maker, and Father, and Kinsman, shall not this set us free from sorrows and fears?

XVII

I do not think that an old fellow like me need have been sitting here to try and prevent your entertaining abject notions of yourselves, and talking of yourselves in an abject and ignoble way: but to prevent there being by chance among you any such young men as, after recognising their kindred to the Gods, and their bondage in these chains of the body and its manifold necessities, should desire to cast them off as burdens too grievous to be borne, and depart their true kindred. This is the struggle in which your Master and Teacher, were he worthy of the name, should be engaged. You would come to me and say: "Epictetus, we can no longer endure being chained to this wretched body, giving food and drink and rest and purification: aye, and for its sake forced to be subservient to this man and that. Are these not things indifferent and nothing to us? Is it not true that death is no evil? Are we not in a manner kinsmen of the Gods, and have we not come from them? Let us depart thither, whence we came: let us be freed from these chains that confine and press us down. Here are thieves and robbers and tribunals: and they that are called tyrants, who deem that they have after a fashion power over us, because of the miserable body and what appertains to it. Let us show them that they have power over none."

XVIII

And to this I reply:—

"Friends, wait for God. When He gives the signal, and releases you from this service, then depart to Him. But for the present, endure to dwell in the place wherein He hath assigned you your post. Short indeed is the time of your habitation therein, and easy to those that are minded. What tyrant, what robber, what tribunals have any terrors for those who thus esteem the body and all that belong to it as of no account? Stay; depart not rashly hence!"

XIX

Something like that is what should pass between a teacher and ingenuous youths. As it is, what does pass? The teacher is a lifeless body, and you are lifeless bodies yourselves. When you have had enough to eat today, you sit down and weep about tomorrow's food. Slave! if you have it, well and good; if not, you will depart: the door is open—why lament? What further room is there for tears? What further occasion for flattery? Why should one envy another? Why should you stand in awe of them that have much or are placed in power, especially if they be also strong and passionate? Why, what should they do to us? What they can do, we will not regard: what does concern us, that they cannot do. Who then shall rule one that is thus minded?

XX

Seeing this then, and noting well the faculties which you have, you should say,—"Send now, O God, any trial that Thou wilt; lo, I have means and powers given me by Thee to acquit myself with honour through whatever comes to pass!"—No; but there you sit, trembling for fear certain things should come to pass, and moaning and groaning and lamenting over what does come to pass. And then you upbraid the Gods. Such meanness of spirit can have but one result—impiety.

Yet God has not only given us these faculties by means of which we may bear everything that comes to pass without being crushed or depressed thereby; but like a good King and Father, He has given us this without let or hindrance, placed wholly at our own disposition, without reserving to Himself any power of impediment or restraint. Though possessing all these things free and all you own, you do not use them! you do not perceive what it is you have received nor whence it comes, but sit moaning and groaning; some of you blind to the Giver, making no acknowledgment to your Benefactor; others basely giving themselves to complaints and accusations against God.

Yet what faculties and powers you possess for attaining courage and greatness of heart, I can easily show you; what you have for upbraiding and accusation, it is for you to show me!

XXI

How did Socrates bear himself in this regard? How else than as became one who was fully assured that he was the kinsman of Gods?

XXII

If God had made that part of His own nature which He severed from Himself and gave to us, liable to be hindered or constrained either by Himself or any other, He would not have been God, nor would He have been taking care of us as He ought . . . . If you choose, you are free; if you choose, you need blame no man—accuse no man. All things will be at once according to your mind and according to the Mind of God.

XXIII

Petrifaction is of two sorts. There is petrifaction of the understanding; and also of the sense of shame. This happens when a man obstinately refuses to acknowledge plain truths, and persists in maintaining what is self-contradictory. Most of us dread mortification of the body, and would spare no pains to escape anything of that kind. But of mortification of the soul we are utterly heedless. With regard, indeed, to the soul, if a man is in such a state as to be incapable of following or understanding anything, I grant you we do think him in a bad way. But mortification of the sense of shame and modesty we go so far as to dub strength of mind!

XXIV

If we were as intent upon our business as the old fellows at Rome are upon what interests them, we too might perhaps accomplish something. I know a man older than I am, now Superintendent of the Corn-market at Rome, and I remember when he passed through this place on his way back from exile, what an account he gave me of his former life, declaring that for the future, once home again, his only care should be to pass his remaining years in quiet and tranquility. "For how few years have I left!" he cried. "That," I said, "you will not do; but the moment the scent of Rome is in your nostrils, you will forget it all; and if you can but gain admission to Court, you will be glad enough to elbow your way in, and thank God for it." "Epictetus," he replied, "if ever you find me setting as much as one foot within the Court, think what you will of me."

Well, as it was, what did he do? Ere ever he entered the city, he was met by a despatch from the Emperor. He took it, and forgot the whole of his resolutions. From that moment, he has been piling one thing upon another. I should like to be beside him to remind him of what he said when passing this way, and to add, How much better a prophet I am than you!

What then? do I say man is not made for an active life? Far from it! . . . But there is a great difference between other men's occupations and ours. . . . A glance at theirs will make it clear to you. All day long they do nothing but calculate, contrive, consult how to wring their profit out of food-stuffs, farm-plots and the like. . . . Whereas, I entreat you to learn what the administration of the World is, and what place a Being endowed with reason holds therein: to consider what you are yourself, and wherein your Good and Evil consists.

XXV

A man asked me to write to Rome on his behalf who, as most people thought, had met with misfortune; for having been before wealthy and distinguished, he had afterwards lost all and was living here. So I wrote about him in a humble style. He however on reading the letter returned it to me, with the words: "I asked for your help, not for your pity. No evil has happened unto me."

XXVI

True instruction is this:—to learn to wish that each thing should come to pass as it does. And how does it come to pass? As the Disposer has disposed it. Now He has disposed that there should be summer and winter, and plenty and dearth, and vice and virtue, and all such opposites, for the harmony of the whole.

XXVII

Have this thought ever present with thee, when thou losest any outward thing, what thou gainest in its stead; and if this be the more precious, say not, I have suffered loss.

XXVIII

Concerning the Gods, there are who deny the very existence of the Godhead; others say that it exists, but neither bestirs nor concerns itself nor has forethought for anything. A third party attributes to it existence and forethought, but only for great and heavenly matters, not for anything that is on earth. A fourth party admit things on earth as well as in heaven, but only in general, and not with respect to each individual. A fifth, of whom were Ulysses and Socrates are those that cry:—
I move not without Thy knowledge!

XXIX

Considering all these things, the good and true man submits his judgment to Him that administers the Universe, even as good citizens to the law of the State. And he that is being instructed should come thus minded:—How may I in all things follow the Gods; and, How may I rest satisfied with the Divine Administration; and, How may I become free? For he is free for whom all things come to pass according to his will, and whom none can hinder. What then, is freedom madness? God forbid. For madness and freedom exist not together.
"But I wish all that I desire to come to pass and in the manner that I desire."
—You are mad, you are beside yourself. Know you not that Freedom is a glorious thing and of great worth? But that what I desired at random I should wish at random to come to pass, so far from being noble, may well be exceeding base.

XXX

You must know that it is no easy thing for a principle to become a man's own, unless each day he maintain it and hear it maintained, as well as work it out in life.

XXXI

You are impatient and hard to please. If alone, you call it solitude: if in the company of men, you dub them conspirators and thieves, and find fault with your very parents, children, brothers, and neighbours. Whereas when by yourself you should have called it Tranquillity and Freedom: and herein deemed yourself like unto the Gods. And when in the company of many, you should not have called it a wearisome crowd and tumult, but an assembly and a tribunal; and thus accepted all with contentment.

XXXII

What then is the chastisement of those who accept it not? To be as they are. Is any discontented with being alone? let him be in solitude. Is any discontented with his parents? let him be a bad son, and lament. Is any discontented with his children? let him be a bad father.—"Throw him into prison!"—What prison?—Where he is already: for he is there against his will; and wherever a man is against his will, that to him is a prison. Thus Socrates was not in prison, since he was there with his own consent.

XXXIII

Knowest thou what a speck thou art in comparison with the Universe?—That is, with respect to the body; since with respect to Reason, thou art not inferior to the Gods, nor less than they. For the greatness of Reason is not measured by length or height, but by the resolves of the mind. Place then thy happiness in that wherein thou art equal to the Gods.

XXXIV

Asked how a man might eat acceptably to the Gods, Epictetus replied:—If when he eats, he can be just, cheerful, equable, temperate, and orderly, can he not thus eat acceptably to the Gods? But when you call for warm water, and your slave does not answer, or when he answers brings it lukewarm, or is not even found to be in the house at all, then not to be vexed nor burst with anger, is not that acceptable to the Gods?
"But how can one endure such people?"
Slave, will you not endure your own brother, that has God to his forefather, even as a son sprung from the same stock, and of the same high descent as yourself? And if you are stationed in a high position, are you therefor forthwith set up for a tyrant? Remember who you are, and whom you rule, that they are by nature your kinsmen, your brothers, the offspring of God.
"But I paid a price for them, not they for me."
Do you see whither you are looking—down to the earth, to the pit, to those despicable laws of the dead? But to the laws of the Gods you do not look.

XXXV

When we are invited to a banquet, we take what is set before us; and were one to call upon his host to set fish upon the table or sweet things, he would be deemed absurd. Yet in a word, we ask the Gods for what they do not give; and that, although they have given us so many things!

XXXVI

Asked how a man might convince himself that every single act of his was under the eye of God, Epictetus answered:—
"Do you not hold that things on earth and things in heaven are continuous and in unison with each other?"
"I do," was the reply.

"Else how should the trees so regularly, as though by God's command, at His bidding flower; at His bidding send forth shoots, bear fruit and ripen it; at His bidding let it fall and shed their leaves, and folded up upon themselves lie in quietness and rest? How else, as the Moon waxes and wanes, as the Sun approaches and recedes, can it be that such vicissitude and alternation is seen in earthly things?

"If then all things that grow, nay, our own bodies, are thus bound up with the whole, is not this still truer of our souls? And if our souls are bound up and in contact with God, as being very parts and fragments plucked from Himself, shall He not feel every movement of theirs as though it were His own, and belonging to His own nature?"

XXXVII

"But," you say, "I cannot comprehend all this at once."

"Why, who told you that your powers were equal to God's?"

Yet God hath placed by the side of each a man's own Guardian Spirit, who is charged to watch over him—a Guardian who sleeps not nor is deceived. For to what better or more watchful Guardian could He have committed which of us? So when you have shut the doors and made a darkness within, remember never to say that you are alone; for you are not alone, but God is within, and your Guardian Spirit, and what light do they need to behold what you do? To this God you also should have sworn allegiance, even as soldiers unto Caesar. They, when their service is hired, swear to hold the life of Caesar dearer than all else: and will you not swear your oath, that are deemed worthy of so many and great gifts? And will you not keep your oath when you have sworn it? And what oath will you swear? Never to disobey, never to arraign or murmur at aught that comes to you from His hand: never unwillingly to do or suffer aught that necessity lays upon you.

"Is this oath like theirs?"

They swear to hold no other dearer than Caesar: you, to hold our true selves dearer than all else beside.

XXXVIII

"How shall my brother cease to be wroth with me?"

Bring him to me, and I will tell him. But to thee I have nothing to say about his anger.

XXXIX

When one took counsel of Epictetus, saying, "What I seek is this, how even though my brother be not reconciled to me, I may still remain as Nature would have me to be," he replied: "All great things are slow of growth; nay, this is true even of a grape or of a fig. If then you say to me now, I desire a fig, I shall answer, It needs time: wait till it first flower, then cast its blossom, then ripen. Whereas then the fruit of the fig-tree reaches not maturity suddenly nor yet in a single hour, do you nevertheless desire so quickly, and easily to reap the fruit of the mind of man?—Nay, expect it not, even though I bade you!"

XL

Epaphroditus had a shoemaker whom he sold as being good-for-nothing. This fellow, by some accident, was afterwards purchased by one of Caesar's men, and became a shoemaker to Caesar. You should have seen what respect Epaphroditus paid him then. "How does the good Felicion? Kindly let me know!" And if any of us inquired, "What is Epaphroditus doing?" the answer was, "He is consulting about so and so with Felicion."—Had he not sold him as good-for-nothing? Who had in a trice converted him into a wiseacre?
This is what comes of holding of importance anything but the things that depend on the Will.

XLI

What you shun enduring yourself, attempt not to impose on others. You shun slavery—beware of enslaving others! If you can endure to do that, one would think you had been once upon a time a slave yourself. For Vice has nothing in common with virtue, nor Freedom with slavery.

XLII

Has a man been raised to tribuneship? Every one that he meets congratulates him. One kisses him on the eyes, another on the neck, while the slaves kiss his hands. He goes home to find torches burning; he ascends to the Capitol to sacrifice.—Who ever sacrificed for having had right desires; for having conceived such inclinations as Nature would have him? In truth we thank the Gods for that wherein we place our happiness.

XLIII

A man was talking to me to-day about the priesthood of Augustus. I said to him, "Let the thing go, my good Sir; you will spend a good deal to no purpose."
"Well, but my name will be inserted in all documents and contracts."
"Will you be standing there to tell those that read them, That is my name written there? And even if you could now be there in every case, what will you do when you are dead?"
"At all events my name will remain."
"Inscribe it on a stone and it will remain just as well. And think, beyond Nicopolis what memory of you will there be?"
"But I shall have a golden wreath to wear."
"If you must have a wreath, get a wreath of roses and put it on; you will look more elegant!"

XLIV

Above all, remember that the door stands open. Be not more fearful than children; but as they, when they weary of the game, cry, "I will play no more," even so, when thou art in the like case, cry, "I will play no more" and depart. But if thou stayest, make no lamentation.

XLV

Is there smoke in the room? If it be slight, I remain; if grievous, I quit it. For you must remember this and hold it fast, that the door stands open.
"You shall not dwell at Nicopolis!"
Well and good.
"Nor at Athens."
Then I will not dwell at Athens either.
"Nor at Rome."
Nor at Rome either.
"You shall dwell in Gyara!"
Well: but to dwell in Gyara seems to me like a grievous smoke; I depart to a place where none can forbid me to dwell: that habitation is open unto all! As for the last garment of all, that is the poor body; beyond that, none can do aught unto me. This why Demetrius said to Nero: "You threaten me with death; it is Nature who threatens you!"

XLVI

The beginning of philosophy is to know the condition of one's own mind. If a man recognises that this is in a weakly state, he will not then want to apply it to questions of the greatest moment. As it is, men who are not fit to swallow even a morsel, buy whole treatises and try to devour them. Accordingly they either vomit them up again, or suffer from indigestion, whence come gripings, fluxions, and fevers. Whereas they should have stopped to consider their capacity.

XLVII

In theory it is easy to convince an ignorant person: in actual life, men not only object to offer themselves to be convinced, but hate the man who has convinced them. Whereas Socrates used to say that we should never lead a life not subjected to examination.

XLVIII

This is the reason why Socrates, when reminded that he should prepare for his trial, answered: "Thinkest thou not that I have been preparing for it all my life?"

"In what way?"

"I have maintained that which in me lay!"

"How so?"

"I have never, secretly or openly, done a wrong unto any."

XLIX

In what character dost thou now come forward?

As a witness summoned by God. "Come thou," saith God, "and testify for me, for thou art worthy of being brought forward as a witness by Me. Is aught that is outside thy will either good or bad? Do I hurt any man? Have I placed the good of each in the power of any other than himself? What witness dost thou bear to God?"

"I am in evil state, Master, I am undone! None careth for me, none giveth me aught: all men blame, all speak evil of me."

Is this the witness thou wilt bear, and do dishonour to the calling wherewith He hath called thee, because He hath done thee so great honour, and deemed thee worthy of being summoned to bear witness in so great a cause?

L

Wouldst thou have men speak good of thee? speak good of them. And when thou hast learned to speak good of them, try to do good unto them, and thus thou wilt reap in return their speaking good of thee.

LI

When thou goest in to any of the great, remember that Another from above sees what is passing, and that thou shouldst please Him rather than man. He therefore asks thee:—

"In the Schools, what didst thou call exile, imprisonment, bonds, death and shame?"

"I called them things indifferent."

"What then dost thou call them now? Are they at all changed?"

"No."

"Is it then thou that art changed?"

"No."

"Say then, what are things indifferent?"

"Things that are not in our power."

"Say then, what follows?"

"That things which are not in our power are nothing to me."

"Say also what things you hold to be good."

"A will such as it ought to be, and a right use of the things of sense."

"And what is the end?"

"To follow Thee!"

LII

"That Socrates should ever have been so treated by the Athenians!"
Slave! why say "Socrates"? Speak of the thing as it is: That ever then the poor body of Socrates should have been dragged away and haled by main force to prison! That ever hemlock should have been given to the body of Socrates; that that should have breathed its life away!—Do you marvel at this? Do you hold this unjust? Is it for this that you accuse God? Had Socrates no compensation for this? Where then for him was the ideal Good? Whom shall we hearken to, you or him? And what says he?
"Anytus and Melitus may put me to death: to injure me is beyond their power." And again:—
"If such be the will of God, so let it be."

LIII

Nay, young man, for heaven's sake; but once thou hast heard these words, go home and say to thyself:—"It is not Epictetus that has told me these things: how indeed should he? No, it is some gracious God through him. Else it would never have entered his head to tell me them—he that is not used to speak to any one thus. Well, then, let us not lie under the wrath of God, but be obedient unto Him."—Nay, indeed; but if a raven by its croaking bears thee any sign, it is not the raven but God that sends the sign through the raven; and if He signifies anything to thee through human voice, will He not cause the man to say these words to thee, that thou mayest know the power of the Divine—how He sends a sign to some in one way and to others in another, and on the greatest and highest matters of all signifies His will through the noblest messenger?
What else does the poet mean:—
I spake unto him erst Myself, and sent
Hermes the shining One, to check and warn him,
The husband not to slay, nor woo the wife!

LIV

In the same way my friend Heraclitus, who had a trifling suit about a petty farm at Rhodes, first showed the judges that his cause was just, and then at the finish cried, "I will not entreat you: nor do I care what sentence you pass. It is you who are on your trial, not I!"—And so he ended the case.

LV

As for us, we behave like a herd of deer. When they flee from the huntsman's feathers in affright, which way do they turn? What haven of safety do they make for? Why, they rush upon the nets! And thus they perish by confounding what they should fear with that wherein no danger lies. . . . Not death or pain is to be feared, but the fear of death or pain. Well said the poet therefore:—
Death has no terror; only a Death of shame!

LVI

How is it then that certain external things are said to be natural, and other contrary to Nature?

Why, just as it might be said if we stood alone and apart from others. A foot, for instance, I will allow it is natural should be clean. But if you take it as a foot, and as a thing which does not stand by itself, it will beseem it (if need be) to walk in the mud, to tread on thorns, and sometimes even to be cut off, for the benefit of the whole body; else it is no longer a foot. In some such way we should conceive of ourselves also. What art thou?—A man.—Looked at as standing by thyself and separate, it is natural for thee in health and wealth long to live. But looked at as a Man, and only as a part of a Whole, it is for that Whole's sake that thou shouldest at one time fall sick, at another brave the perils of the sea, again, know the meaning of want and perhaps die an early death. Why then repine? Knowest thou not that as the foot is no more a foot if detached from the body, so thou in like case art no longer a Man? For what is a Man? A part of a City:—first of the City of Gods and Men; next, of that which ranks nearest it, a miniature of the universal City. . . . In such a body, in such a world enveloping us, among lives like these, such things must happen to one or another. Thy part, then, being here, is to speak of these things as is meet, and to order them as befits the matter.

LVII

That was a good reply which Diogenes made to a man who asked him for letters of recommendation.—"That you are a man, he will know when he sees you;—whether a good or bad one, he will know if he has any skill in discerning the good or bad. But if he has none, he will never know, though I write him a thousand times."—It is as though a piece of silver money desired to be recommended to some one to be tested. If the man be a good judge of silver, he will know: the coin will tell its own tale.

LVIII

Even as the traveller asks his way of him that he meets, inclined in no wise to bear to the right rather than to the left (for he desires only the way leading whither he would go), so should we come unto God as to a guide; even as we use our eyes without admonishing them to show us some things rather than others, but content to receive the images of such things as they present to us. But as it is we stand anxiously watching the victim, and with the voice of supplication call upon the augur:—"Master, have mercy on me: vouchsafe unto me a way of escape!" Slave, would you then have aught else then what is best? is there anything better than what is God's good pleasure? Why, as far as in you lies, would you corrupt your Judge, and lead your Counsellor astray?

LIX

God is beneficent. But the Good also is beneficent. It should seem then that where the real nature of God is, there too is to be found the real nature of the Good. What then is the real nature of God?—Intelligence, Knowledge, Right Reason. Here then without more ado seek the real nature of the Good. For surely thou dost not seek it in a plant or in an animal that reasoneth not.

LX

Seek then the real nature of the Good in that without whose presence thou wilt not admit the Good to exist in aught else.—What then? Are not these other things also works of God?—They are; but not preferred to honour, nor are they portions of God. But thou art a thing preferred to honour: thou art thyself a fragment torn from God:—thou hast a portion of Him within thyself. How is it then that thou dost not know thy high descent—dost not know whence thou comest? When thou eatest, wilt thou not remember who thou art that eatest and whom thou feedest? In intercourse, in exercise, in discussion knowest thou not that it is a God whom thou feedest, a God whom thou exercisest, a God whom thou bearest about with thee, O miserable! and thou perceivest it not. Thinkest thou that I speak of a God of silver or gold, that is without thee? Nay, thou bearest Him within thee! all unconscious of polluting Him with thoughts impure and unclean deeds. Were an image of God present, thou wouldest not dare to act as thou dost, yet, when God Himself is present within thee, beholding and hearing all, thou dost not blush to think such thoughts and do such deeds, O thou that art insensible of thine own nature and liest under the wrath of God!

LXI

Why then are we afraid when we send a young man from the Schools into active life, lest he should indulge his appetites intemperately, lest he should debase himself by ragged clothing, or be puffed up by fine raiment? Knows he not the God within him; knows he not with whom he is starting on his way? Have we patience to hear him say to us, Would I had thee with me!—Hast thou not God where thou art, and having Him dost thou still seek for any other! Would He tell thee aught else than these things? Why, wert thou a statue of Phidias, an Athena or a Zeus, thou wouldst bethink thee both of thyself and thine artificer; and hadst thou any sense, thou wouldst strive to do no dishonour to thyself or him that fashioned thee, nor appear to beholders in unbefitting guise. But now, because God is thy Maker, is that why thou carest not of what sort thou shalt show thyself to be? Yet how different the artists and their workmanship! What human artist's work, for example, has in it the faculties that are displayed in fashioning it? Is it aught but marble, bronze, gold, or ivory? Nay, when the Athena of Phidias has put forth her hand and received therein a Victory, in that attitude she stands for evermore. But God's works move and breathe; they use and judge the things of sense. The workmanship of such an Artist, wilt thou dishonor Him? Ay, when he not only fashioned thee, but placed thee, like a ward, in the care and guardianship of thyself alone, wilt thou not only forget this, but also do dishonour to what is committed to thy care! If God had entrusted thee with an orphan, wouldst thou have thus neglected him? He hath delivered thee to thine own care, saying, I had none more faithful than myself: keep this man for me such as Nature hath made him—modest, faithful, high-minded, a stranger to fear, to passion, to perturbation. . . .

Such will I show myself to you all.—"What, exempt from sickness also: from age, from death?"—Nay, but accepting sickness, accepting death as becomes a God!

LXII

No labour, according to Diogenes, is good but that which aims at producing courage and strength of soul rather than of body.

LXIII

A guide, on finding a man who has lost his way, brings him back to the right path—he does not mock and jeer at him and then take himself off. You also must show the unlearned man the truth, and you will see that he will follow. But so long as you do not show it him, you should not mock, but rather feel your own incapacity.

LXIV

It was the first and most striking characteristic of Socrates never to become heated in discourse, never to utter an injurious or insulting word—on the contrary, he persistently bore insult from others and thus put an end to the fray. If you care to know the extent of his power in this direction, read Xenophon's Banquet, and you will see how many quarrels he put an end to. This is why the Poets are right in so highly commending this faculty:—

Quickly and wisely withal even bitter feuds would he settle.

Nevertheless the practice is not very safe at present, especially in Rome. One who adopts it, I need not say, ought not to carry it out in an obscure corner, but boldly accost, if occasion serve, some personage of rank or wealth.

"Can you tell me, sir, to whose care you entrust your horses?"

"I can."

"Is it to the first comer, who knows nothing about them?"

"Certainly not."

"Well, what of the man who takes care of your gold, your silver or your raiment?"

"He must be experienced also."

"And your body—have you ever considered about entrusting it to any one's care?"

"Of course I have."

"And no doubt to a person of experience as a trainer, a physician?"

"Surely."

"And these things the best you possess, or have you anything more precious?"

"What can you mean?"

"I mean that which employs these; which weights all things; which takes counsel and resolve."

"Oh, you mean the soul."

"You take me rightly; I do mean the soul. By Heaven, I hold that far more precious than all else I possess. Can you show me then what care you bestow on a soul? For it can scarcely be thought that a man of your wisdom and consideration in the city would suffer your most precious possession to go to ruin through carelessness and neglect."

"Certainly not."

"Well, do you take care of it yourself? Did any one teach you the right method, or did you discover it yourself?"

Now here comes in the danger: first, that the great man may answer, "Why, what is that to you, my good fellow? are you my master?" And then, if you persist in troubling him, may raise his hand to strike you. It is a practice of which I was myself a warm admirer until such experiences as these befell me.

LXV

When a youth was giving himself airs in the Theatre and saying, "I am wise, for I have conversed with many wise men," Epictetus replied, "I too have conversed with many rich men, yet I am not rich!"

LXVI

We see that a carpenter becomes a carpenter by learning certain things: that a pilot, by learning certain things, becomes a pilot. Possibly also in the present case the mere desire to be wise and good is not enough. It is necessary to learn certain things. This is then the object of our search. The Philosophers would have us first learn that there is a God, and that His Providence directs the Universe; further, that to hide from Him not only one's acts but even one's thoughts and intentions is impossible; secondly, what the nature of God is. Whatever that nature is discovered to be, the man who would please and obey Him must strive with all his might to be made like unto him. If the Divine is faithful, he also must be faithful; if free, he also must be free; if beneficent, he also must be beneficent; if magnanimous, he also must be magnanimous. Thus as an imitator of God must he follow Him in every deed and word.

LXVII

If I show you, that you lack just what is most important and necessary to happiness, that hitherto your attention has been bestowed on everything rather than that which claims it most; and, to crown all, that you know neither what

God nor Man is—neither what Good or Evil is: why, that you are ignorant of everything else, perhaps you may bear to be told; but to hear that you know nothing of yourself, how could you submit to that? How could you stand your ground and suffer that to be proved? Clearly not at all. You instantly turn away in wrath. Yet what harm have I done to you? Unless indeed the mirror harms the ill-favoured man by showing him to himself just as he is; unless the physician can be thought to insult his patient, when he tells him:—"Friend, do you suppose there is nothing wrong with you? why, you have a fever. Eat nothing to-day, and drink only water." Yet no one says, "What an insufferable insult!" Whereas if you say to a man, "Your desires are inflamed, your instincts of rejection are weak and low, your aims are inconsistent, your impulses are not in harmony with Nature, your opinions are rash and false," he forthwith goes away and complains that you have insulted him.

LXVIII

Our way of life resembles a fair. The flocks and herds are passing along to be sold, and the greater part of the crowd to buy and sell. But there are some few who come only to look at the fair, to inquire how and why it is being held, upon what authority and with what object. So too, in this great Fair of life, some, like the cattle, trouble themselves about nothing but the fodder. Know all of you, who are busied about land, slaves and public posts, that these are nothing but fodder! Some few there are attending the Fair, who love to contemplate what the world is, what He that administers it. Can there be no Administrator? is it possible, that while neither city nor household could endure even a moment without one to administer and see to its welfare, this Fabric, so fair, so vast, should be administered in order so harmonious, without a purpose and by blind chance? There is therefore an Administrator. What is His nature and how does He administer? And who are we that are His children and what work were we born to perform? Have we any close connection or relation with Him or not?
Such are the impressions of the few of whom I speak. And further, they apply themselves solely to considering and examining the great assembly before they depart. Well, they are derided by the multitude. So are the lookers-on by the traders: aye, and if the beasts had any sense, they would deride those who thought much of anything but fodder!

LXIX

I think I know now what I never knew before—the meaning of the common saying, A fool you can neither bend nor break. Pray heaven I may never have a wise fool for my friend! There is nothing more intractable.—"My resolve is fixed!"—Why so madman say too; but the more firmly they believe in their delusions, the more they stand in need of treatment.

LXX

—"O! when shall I see Athens and its Acropolis again?"—Miserable man! art thou not contented with the daily sights that meet thine eyes? canst thou behold aught greater or nobler than the Sun, Moon, and Stars; than the outspread Earth and Sea? If indeed thou apprehendest Him who administers the universe, if thou bearest Him about within thee, canst thou still hanker after mere fragments of stone and fine rock? When thou art about to bid farewell to the Sun and Moon itself, wilt thou sit down and cry like a child? Why, what didst thou hear, what didst thou learn? why didst thou write thyself down a philosopher, when thou mightest have written what was the fact, namely, "I have made one or two Compendiums, I have read some works of Chrysippus, and I have not even touched the hem of Philosophy's robe!"

LXXI

Friend, lay hold with a desperate grasp, ere it is too late, on Freedom, on Tranquility, on Greatness of soul! Lift up thy head, as one escaped from slavery; dare to look up to God, and say:—"Deal with me henceforth as Thou wilt; Thou and I are of one mind. I am Thine: I refuse nothing that seeeth good to Thee; lead on whither Thou wilt; clothe me in what garb Thou pleasest; wilt Thou have me a ruler or a subject—at home or in exile—poor or rich? All these things will I justify unto men for Thee. I will show the true nature of each. . . ."

Who would Hercules have been had he loitered at home? no Hercules, but Eurystheus. And in his wanderings through the world how many friends and comrades did he find? but nothing dearer to him than God. Wherefore he was believed to be God's son, as indeed he was. So then in obedience to Him, he went about delivering the earth from injustice and lawlessness.

But thou art not Hercules, thou sayest, and canst not deliver others from their iniquity—not even Theseus, to deliver the soil of Attica from its monsters? Purge away thine own, cast forth thence—from thine own mind, not robbers and monsters, but Fear, Desire, Envy, Malignity, Avarice, Effeminacy, Intemperance. And these may not be cast out, except by looking to God alone, by fixing thy affections on Him only, and by consecrating thyself to His commands. If thou choosest aught else, with sighs and groans thou wilt be forced to follow a Might greater than thine own, ever seeking Tranquillity without, and never able to attain unto her. For thou seekest her where she is not to be found; and where she is, there thou seekest her not!

LXXII

If a man would pursue Philosophy, his first task is to throw away conceit. For it is impossible for a man to begin to learn what he has a conceit that he already knows.

LXXIII

Give me but one young man, that has come to the School with this intention, who stands forth a champion of this cause, and says, "All else I renounce, content if I am but able to pass my life free from hindrance and trouble; to raise my head aloft and face all things as a free man; to look up to heaven as a friend of God, fearing nothing that may come to pass!" Point out such a one to me, that I may say, "Enter, young man, into possession of that which is thine own. For thy lot is to adorn Philosophy. Thine are these possessions; thine these books, these discourses!"

And when our champion has duly exercised himself in this part of the subject, I hope he will come back to me and say:—"What I desire is to be free from passion and from perturbation; as one who grudges no pains in the pursuit of piety and philosophy, what I desire is to know my duty to the Gods, my duty to my parents, to my brothers, to my country, to strangers."

"Enter then on the second part of the subject; it is thine also."

"But I have already mastered the second part; only I wished to stand firm and unshaken—as firm when asleep as when awake, as firm when elated with wine as in despondency and dejection."

"Friend, you are verily a God! you cherish great designs."

LXXIV

"The question at stake," said Epictetus, "is no common one; it is this:—Are we in our senses, or are we not?"

LXXV

If you have given way to anger, be sure that over and above the evil involved therein, you have strengthened the habit, and added fuel to the fire. If overcome by a temptation of the flesh, do not reckon it a single defeat, but that you have also strengthened your dissolute habits. Habits and faculties are necessarily affected by the corresponding acts. Those that were not there before, spring up: the rest gain in strength and extent. This is the account which Philosophers give of the origin of diseases of the mind:—Suppose you have once lusted after money: if reason sufficient to produce a sense of evil be applied, then the lust is checked, and the mind at once regains its original authority; whereas if you have recourse to no remedy, you can no longer look for this return—on the contrary, the next time it is excited by the corresponding object, the flame of desire leaps up more quickly than before. By frequent repetition, the mind in the long run becomes callous; and thus this mental disease produces confirmed Avarice.

One who has had fever, even when it has left him, is not in the same condition of health as before, unless indeed his cure is complete. Something of the same sort is true also of diseases of the mind. Behind, there remains a legacy of traces and blisters: and unless these are effectually erased, subsequent blows on the same spot will produce no longer mere blisters, but sores. If you do not wish to be prone to anger, do not feed the habit; give it nothing which may tend its increase. At first, keep quiet and count the days when you were not angry: "I used to be angry every day, then every other day: next every two, next every three days!" and if you succeed in passing thirty days, sacrifice to the Gods in thanksgiving.

LXXVI

How then may this be attained?—Resolve, now if never before, to approve thyself to thyself; resolve to show thyself fair in God's sight; long to be pure with thine own pure self and God!

LXXVII

That is the true athlete, that trains himself to resist such outward impressions as these.
"Stay, wretched man! suffer not thyself to be carried away!" Great is the combat, divine the task! you are fighting for Kingship, for Liberty, for Happiness, for Tranquillity. Remember God: call upon Him to aid thee, like a comrade that stands beside thee in the fight.

LXXVIII

Who then is a Stoic—in the sense that we call a statue of Phidias which is modelled after that master's art? Show me a man in this sense modelled after the doctrines that are ever upon his lips. Show me a man that is sick—and happy; an exile—and happy; in evil report—and happy! Show me him, I ask again. So help me Heaven, I long to see one Stoic! Nay, if you cannot show me one fully modelled, let me at least see one in whom the process is at work—one whose bent is in that direction. Do me that favour! Grudge it not to an old man, to behold a sight he has never yet beheld. Think you I wish to see the Zeus or Athena of Phidias, bedecked with gold and ivory?—Nay, show me, one of you, a human soul, desiring to be of one mind with God, no more to lay blame on God or man, to suffer nothing to disappoint, nothing to cross him, to yield neither to anger, envy, nor jealousy—in a word, why disguise the matter? one that from a man would fain become a God; one that while still imprisoned in this dead body makes fellowship with God his aim. Show me him!—Ah, you cannot! Then why mock yourselves and delude others? why stalk about tricked out in other men's attire, thieves and robbers that you are of names and things to which you can show no title!

LXXIX

If you have assumed a character beyond your strength, you have both played a poor figure in that, and neglected one that is within your powers.

LXXX

Fellow, you have come to blows at home with a slave: you have turned the household upside down, and thrown the neighbourhood into confusion; and do you come to me then with airs of assumed modesty—do you sit down like a sage and criticise my explanation of the readings, and whatever idle babble you say has come into my head? Have you come full of envy, and dejected because nothing is sent you from home; and while the discussion is going on, do you sit brooding on nothing but how your father or your brother are disposed towards you:—"What are they saying about me there? at this moment they imagine I am making progress and saying, He will return perfectly omniscient! I wish I could become omniscient before I return; but that would be very troublesome. No one sends me anything—the baths at Nicopolis are dirty; things are wretched at home and wretched here." And then they say, "Nobody is any the better for the School."—Who comes to the School with a sincere wish to learn: to submit his principles to correction and himself to treatment? Who, to gain a sense of his wants? Why then be surprised if you carry home from the School exactly what you bring into it?

LXXXI

"Epictetus, I have often come desiring to hear you speak, and you have never given me any answer; now if possible, I entreat you, say something to me."
"Is there, do you think," replied Epictetus, "an art of speaking as of other things, if it is to be done skilfully and with profit to the hearer?"
"Yes."
"And are all profited by what they hear, or only some among them? So that it seems there is an art of hearing as well as of speaking. . . . To make a statue needs skill: to view a statue aright needs skill also."
"Admitted."
"And I think all will allow that one who proposes to hear philosophers speak needs a considerable training in hearing. Is that not so? The tell me on what subject your are able to hear me."
"Why, on good and evil."
"The good and evil of what? a horse, an ox?"
"No; of a man."
"Do we know then what Man is? what his nature is? what is the idea we have of him? And are our ears practised in any degree on the subject? Nay, do you understand what Nature is? can you follow me in any degree when I say that I shall have to use demonstration? Do you understand what Demonstration is? what True or False is? . . . must I drive you to Philosophy? . . . Show me what good I am to do by discoursing with you. Rouse my desire to do so. The sight of a pasture it loves stirs in a sheep the desire to feed: show it a stone or a bit of bread and it remains unmoved. Thus we also have certain natural desires, aye, and one that moves us to speak when we find a listener that is worth his salt: one that himself stirs the spirit. But if he sits by like a stone or a tuft of grass, how can he rouse a man's desire?"
"Then you will say nothing to me?"
"I can only tell you this: that one who knows not who he is and to what end he was born; what kind of world this is and with whom he is associated therein; one who cannot distinguish Good and Evil, Beauty and Foulness, . . . Truth

and Falsehood, will never follow Reason in shaping his desires and impulses and repulsions, nor yet in assent, denial, or suspension of judgement; but will in one word go about deaf and blind, thinking himself to be somewhat, when he is in truth of no account. Is there anything new in all this? Is not this ignorance the cause of all the mistakes and mischances of men since the human race began? . . ."

"This is all I have to say to you, and even this against the grain. Why? Because you have not stirred my spirit. For what can I see in you to stir me, as a spirited horse will stir a judge of horses? Your body? That you maltreat. Your dress? That is luxurious. You behavior, your look?—Nothing whatever. When you want to hear a philosopher, do not say, You say nothing to me'; only show yourself worthy or fit to hear, and then you will see how you will move the speaker."

LXXXII

And now, when you see brothers apparently good friends and living in accord, do not immediately pronounce anything upon their friendship, though they should affirm it with an oath, though they should declare, "For us to live apart in a thing impossible!" For the heart of a bad man is faithless, unprincipled, inconstant: now overpowered by one impression, now by another. Ask not the usual questions, Were they born of the same parents, reared together, and under the same tutor; but ask this only, in what they place their real interest— whether in outward things or in the Will. If in outward things, call them not friends, any more than faithful, constant, brave or free: call them not even human beings, if you have any sense. . . . But should you hear that these men hold the Good to lie only in the Will, only in rightly dealing with the things of sense, take no more trouble to inquire whether they are father and son or brothers, or comrades of long standing; but, sure of this one thing, pronounce as boldly that they are friends as that they are faithful and just: for where else can Friendship be found than where Modesty is, where there is an interchange of things fair and honest, and of such only?

LXXXIII

No man can rob us of our Will—no man can lord it over that!

LXXXIV

When disease and death overtake me, I would fain be found engaged in the task of liberating mine own Will from the assaults of passion, from hindrance, from resentment, from slavery.

Thus would I fain to be found employed, so that I may say to God, "Have I in aught transgressed Thy commands? Have I in aught perverted the faculties, the senses, the natural principles that Thou didst give me? Have I ever blamed Thee or found fault with Thine administration? When it was Thy good pleasure, I fell sick—and so did other men: by my will consented. Because it was Thy pleasure, I became poor: but my heart rejoiced. No power in the State was mine, because Thou wouldst not: such power I never desired! Hast Thou ever seen me of more doleful countenance on that account? Have I not ever drawn nigh unto Thee with cheerful look, waiting upon Thy commands, attentive to Thy signals? Wilt Thou that I now depart from the great Assembly of men? I go: I give Thee all thanks, that Thou hast deemed me worthy to take part with Thee in this Assembly: to behold Thy works, to comprehend this Thine administration."

Such I would were the subject of my thoughts, my pen, my study, when death overtakes me.

LXXXV

Seemeth it nothing to you, never to accuse, never to blame either God or Man? to wear ever the same countenance in going forth as in coming in? This was the secret of Socrates: yet he never said that he knew or taught anything. . . . Who amongst you makes this his aim? Were it indeed so, you would gladly endure sickness, hunger, aye, death itself.

LXXXVI

How are we constituted by Nature? To be free, to be noble, to be modest (for what other living thing is capable of blushing, or of feeling the impression of shame?) and to subordinate pleasure to the ends for which Nature designed us, as a handmaid and a minister, in order to call forth our activity; in order to keep us constant to the path prescribed by Nature.

LXXXVII

The husbandman deals with land; physicians and trainers with the body; the wise man with his own Mind.

LXXXVIII

Which of us does not admire what Lycurgus the Spartan did? A young citizen had put out his eye, and been handed over to him by the people to be punished at his own discretion. Lycurgus abstained from all vengeance, but on the contrary instructed and made a good man of him. Producing him in public in the theatre, he said to the astonished Spartans:—"I received this young man at your hands full of violence and wanton insolence; I restore him to you in his right mind and fit to serve his country."

LXXXIX

A money-changer may not reject Caesar's coin, nor may the seller of herbs, but must when once the coin is shown, deliver what is sold for it, whether he will or no. So is it also with the Soul. Once the Good appears, it attracts towards itself; evil repels. But a clear and certain impression of the Good the Soul will never reject, any more than men do Cæsar's coin. On this hangs every impulse alike of Man and God.

XC

Asked what Common Sense was, Epictetus replied:—
As that may be called a Common Ear which distinguishes only sounds, while that which distinguishes musical notes is not common but produced by training; so there are certain things which men not entirely perverted see by the natural principles common to all. Such a constitution of the Mind is called Common Sense.

XCI

Canst thou judge men? . . . then make us imitators of thyself, as Socrates did. Do this, do not do that, else will I cast thee into prison; this is not governing men like reasonable creatures. Say rather, As God hath ordained, so do; else thou wilt suffer chastisement and loss. Askest thou what loss? None other than this: To have left undone what thou shouldst have done: to have lost the faithfulness, the reverence, the modesty that is in thee! Greater loss than this seek not to find!

XCII

"His son is dead."
What has happened?
"His son is dead."
Nothing more?
"Nothing."
"His ship is lost."
"He has been haled to prison."
What has happened?
"He has been haled to prison."
But that any of these things are misfortunes to him, is an addition which every one makes of his own. But (you say) God is unjust is this.—Why? For having given thee endurance and greatness of soul? For having made such things to be no evils? For placing happiness within thy reach, even when enduring them? For open unto thee a door, when things make not for thy good?—Depart, my friend and find fault no more!

XCIII

You are sailing to Rome (you tell me) to obtain the post of Governor of Cnossus. You are not content to stay at home with the honours you had before; you want something on a larger scale, and more conspicuous. But when did you ever undertake a voyage for the purpose of reviewing your own principles and getting rid of any of them that proved unsound? Whom did you ever visit for that object? What time did you ever set yourself for that? What age? Run over the times of your life—by yourself, if you are ashamed before me. Did you examine your principles when a boy? Did you not do everything just as you do now? Or when you were a stripling, attending the school of oratory and practising the art yourself, what did you ever imagine you lacked? And when you were a young man, entered upon public life, and were pleading causes and making a name, who any longer seemed equal to you? And at what moment would you have endured another examining your principles and proving that they were unsound? What then am I to say to you? "Help me in this matter!" you cry. Ah, for that I have no rule! And neither did you, if that was your object, come to me as a philosopher, but as you might have gone to a herb-seller or a cobbler.—"What do philosophers have rules for, then?"— Why, that whatever may betide, our ruling faculty may be as Nature would have it, and so remain. Think you this a small matter? Not so! but the greatest thing there is. Well, does it need but a short time? Can it be grasped by a passer-by?—grasp it, if you can!

Then you will say, "Yes, I met Epictetus!"

Aye, just as you might a statue or a monument. You saw me! and that is all. But a man who meets a man is one who learns the other's mind, and lets him see his in turn. Learn my mind—show me yours; and then go and say that you met me. Let us try each other; if I have any wrong principle, rid me of it; if you have, out with it. That is what meeting a philosopher means. Not so, you think; this is only a flying visit; while we are hiring the ship, we can see Epictetus too! Let us see what he has to say. Then on leaving you cry, "Out on Epictetus for a worthless fellow, provincial and barbarous of speech!" What else indeed did you come to judge of?

XCIV

Whether you will or no, you are poorer than I!

"What then do I lack?"

What you have not: Constancy of mind, such as Nature would have it be: Tranquillity. Patron or no patron, what care I? but you do care. I am richer than you: I am not racked with anxiety as to what Caesar may think of me; I flatter none on that account. This is what I have, instead of vessels of gold and silver! your vessels may be of gold, but your reason, your principles, your accepted views, your inclinations, your desires are of earthenware.

XCV

To you, all you have seems small: to me, all I have seems great. Your desire is insatiable, mine is satisfied. See children thrusting their hands into a narrow-necked jar, and striving to pull out the nuts and figs it contains: if they fill the hand, they cannot pull it out again, and then they fall to tears.—"Let go a few of them, and then you can draw out the rest!"—You, too, let your desire go!

covet not many things, and you will obtain.

XCVI

Pittacus wronged by one whom he had it in his power to punish, let him go free, saying, Forgiveness is better than revenge. The one shows native gentleness, the other savagery.

XCVII

"My brother ought not to have treated me thus."
True: but he must see to that. However he may treat me, I must deal rightly by him. This is what lies with me, what none can hinder.

XCVIII

Nevertheless a man should also be prepared to be sufficient unto himself—to dwell with himself alone, even as God dwells with Himself alone, shares His repose with none, and considers the nature of His own administration, intent upon such thoughts as are meet unto Himself. So should we also be able to converse with ourselves, to need none else beside, to sigh for no distraction, to bend our thoughts upon the Divine Administration, and how we stand related to all else; to observe how human accidents touched us of old, and how they touch us now; what things they are that still have power to hurt us, and how they may be cured or removed; to perfect what needs perfecting as Reason would direct.

XCIX

If a man has frequent intercourse with others, either in the way of conversation, entertainment, or simple familiarity, he must either become like them, or change them to his own fashion. A live coal placed next a dead one will either kindle that or be quenched by it. Such being the risk, it is well to be cautious in admitting intimacies of this sort, remembering that one cannot rub shoulders with a soot-stained man without sharing the soot oneself. What will you do, supposing the talk turns on gladiators, or horses, or prize-fighters, or (what is worse) on persons, condemning this and that, approving the other? Or suppose a man sneers and jeers or shows a malignant temper? Has any among us the skill of the lute-player, who knows at the first touch which strings are out of tune and sets the instrument right: has any of you such power as Socrates had, in all his intercourse with men, of winning them over to his own convictions? Nay, but you must needs be swayed hither and thither by the uninstructed. How comes it then that they prove so much stronger than you? Because they speak from the fulness of the heart—their low, corrupt views are their real convictions: whereas your fine sentiments are but from the lips, outwards; that is why they are so nerveless and dead. It turns one's stomach to listen to your exhortations, and hear of your miserable Virtue, that you prate of up and down. Thus it is that the Vulgar prove too strong for you. Everywhere strength, everywhere victory waits your conviction!

C

In general, any methods of discipline applied to the body which tend to modify its desires or repulsions, are good—for ascetic ends. But if done for display, they betray at once a man who keeps an eye on outward show; who has an ulterior purpose, and is looking for spectators to shout, "Oh what a great man!" This is why Apollonius so well said: "If you are bent upon a little private discipline, wait till you are choking with heat some day—then take a mouthful of cold water, and spit it out again, and tell no man!"

CI

Study how to give as one that is sick: that thou mayest hereafter give as one that is whole. Fast; drink water only; abstain altogether from desire, that thou mayest hereafter conform thy desire to Reason.

CII

Thou wouldst do good unto men? then show them by thine own example what kind of men philosophy can make, and cease from foolish trifling. Eating, do good to them that eat with thee; drinking, to them that drink with thee; yield unto all, give way, and bear with them. Thus shalt thou do them good: but vent not upon them thine own evil humour!

CIII

Even as bad actors cannot sing alone, but only in chorus: so some cannot walk alone.
Man, if thou art aught, strive to walk alone and hold converse with thyself, instead of skulking in the chorus! at length think; look around thee; bestir thyself, that thou mayest know who thou art!

CIV

You would fain be victor at the Olympic games, you say. Yes, but weigh the conditions, weigh the consequences; then and then only, lay to your hand—if it be for your profit. You must live by rule, submit to diet, abstain from dainty meats, exercise your body perforce at stated hours, in heat or in cold; drink no cold water, nor, it may be, wine. In a word, you must surrender yourself wholly to your trainer, as though to a physician.
Then in the hour of contest, you will have to delve the ground, it may chance dislocate an arm, sprain an ankle, gulp down abundance of yellow sand, be scourge with the whip—and with all this sometimes lose the victory. Count the cost—and then, if your desire still holds, try the wrestler's life. Else let me tell

you that you will be behaving like a pack of children playing now at wrestlers, now at gladiators; presently falling to trumpeting and anon to stage-playing, when the fancy takes them for what they have seen. And you are even the same: wrestler, gladiator, philosopher, orator all by turns and none of them with your whole soul. Like an ape, you mimic what you see, to one thing constant never; the thing that is familiar charms no more. This is because you never undertook aught with due consideration, nor after strictly testing and viewing it from every side; no, your choice was thoughtless; the glow of your desire had waxed cold . . . .

Friend, bethink you first what it is you would do, and then what your own nature is able to bear. Would you be a wrestler, consider your shoulders, your thighs, your loins—not all men are formed to the same end. Think you to be a philosopher while acting as you do? think you go on thus eating, thus drinking, giving way in like manner to wrath and to displeasure? Nay, you must watch, you must labour; overcome certain desires; quit your familiar friends, submit to be despised by your slave, to be held in derision by them that meet you, to take the lower place in all things, in office, in positions of authority, in courts of law.

Weigh these things fully, and then, if you will, lay to your hand; if as the price of these things you would gain Freedom, Tranquillity, and passionless Serenity.

CV

He that hath no musical instruction is a child in Music; he that hath no letters is a child in Learning; he that is untaught is a child in Life.

CVI

Can any profit be derived from these men? Aye, from all.
"What, even from a reviler?"
Why, tell me what profit a wrestler gains from him who exercises him beforehand? The very greatest: he trains me in the practice of endurance, of controlling my temper, of gentle ways. You deny it. What, the man who lays hold of my neck, and disciplines loins and shoulders, does me good, . . . while he that trains me to keep my temper does me none? This is what it means, not knowing how to gain advantage from men! Is my neighbour bad? Bad to himself, but good to me: he brings my good temper, my gentleness into play. Is my father bad? Bad to himself, but good to me. This is the rod of Hermes; touch what you will with it, they say, and it becomes gold. Nay, but bring what you will and I will transmute it into Good. Bring sickness, bring death, bring poverty and reproach, bring trial for life—all these things through the rod of Hermes shall be turned to profit.

CVII

Till then these sound opinions have taken firm root in you, and you have gained a measure of strength for your security, I counsel you to be cautious in associating with the uninstructed. Else whatever impressions you receive upon the tablets of your mind in the School will day by day melt and disappear, like wax in the sun. Withdraw then somewhere far from the sun, while you have these waxen sentiments.

CVIII

We must approach this matter in a different way; it is great and mystical: it is no common thing; nor given to every man. Wisdom alone, it may be, will not suffice for the care of youth: a man needs also a certain measure of readiness—an aptitude for the office; aye, and certain bodily qualities; and above all, to be counselled of God Himself to undertake this post; even as He counselled Socrates to fill the post of one who confutes error, assigning to Diogenes the royal office of high reproof, and to Zeno that of positive instruction. Whereas you would fain set up for a physician provided with nothing but drugs! Where and how they should be applied you neither know nor care.

CIX

If what charms you is nothing but abstract principles, sit down and turn them over quietly in your mind: but never dub yourself a Philosopher, nor suffer others to call you so. Say rather: He is in error; for my desires, my impulses are unaltered. I give in my adhesion to what I did before; nor has my mode of dealing with the things of sense undergone any change.

CX

When a friend inclined to Cynic views asked Epictetus, what sort of person a true Cynic should be, requesting a general sketch of the system, he answered:—"We will consider that at leisure. At present I content myself with saying this much: If a man put his hand to so weighty a matter without God, the wrath of God abides upon him. That which he covets will but bring upon him public shame. Not even on finding himself in a well-ordered house does a man step forward and say to himself, I must be master here! Else the lord of that house takes notice of it, and, seeing him insolently giving orders, drags him forth and chastises him. So it is also in this great City, the World. Here also is there a Lord of the House, who orders all things:—
"Thou are the Sun! in thine orbit thou hast
power to make the year and the seasons;
to bid the fruits of the earth to grow
and increase, the winds arise and fall;
thou canst in due measure cherish with
thy warmth the frames of men; go make
thy circuit, and thus minister unto all
from the greatest to the least! . . ."

"Thou canst lead a host against Troy; be Agamemnon!"

111

"Thou canst meet Hector in single combat; be Achilles!"
"But had Thersites stepped forward and claimed the chief command, he had been met with a refusal, or obtained it only to his own shame and confusion of face, before a cloud of witnesses."

CXI

Others may fence themselves with walls and houses, when they do such deeds as these, and wrap themselves in darkness—aye, they have many a device to hide themselves. Another may shut his door and station one before his chamber to say, if any comes, He has gone forth! he is not at leisure! But the true Cynic will have none of these things; instead of them, he must wrap himself in Modesty: else he will but bring himself to shame, naked and under the open sky. That is his house; that is his door; that is the slave that guards his chamber; that is his darkness!

CXII

Death? let it come when it will, whether it smite but a part of the whole: Fly, you tell me—fly! But whither shall I fly? Can any man cast me beyond the limits of the World? It may not be! And whithersoever I go, there shall I still find Sun, Moon, and Stars; there I shall find dreams, and omens, and converse with the Gods!

CXIII

Furthermore the true Cynic must know that he is sent as a Messenger from God to men, to show unto them that as touching good and evil they are in error; looking for these where they are not to be found, nor ever bethinking themselves where they are. And like Diogenes when brought before Philip after the battle of Chaeronea, the Cynic must remember that he is a Spy. For a Spy he really is—to bring back word what things are on Man's side, and what against him. And when he had diligently observed all, he must come back with a true report, not terrified into announcing them to be foes that are no foes, nor otherwise perturbed or confounded by the things of sense.

CXIV

How can it be that one who hath nothing, neither raiment, nor house, nor home, nor bodily tendance, nor servant, nor city, should yet live tranquil and contented? Behold God hath sent you a man to show you in act and deed that it may be so. Behold me! I have neither house nor possessions nor servants: the ground is my couch; I have no wife, no children, no shelter—nothing but earth and sky, and one poor cloak. And what lack I yet? am I not untouched by sorrow, by fear? am I not free? . . . when have I laid anything to the charge of God or Man? when have I accused any? hath any of you seen me with a sorrowful countenance? And in what wise treat I those of whom you stand in fear and awe? Is it not as slaves? Who when he seeth me doth not think that he beholdeth his Master and his King?

CXV

Give thyself more diligently to reflection: know thyself: take counsel with the Godhead: without God put thine hand unto nothing!

CXVI

"But to marry and to rear offspring," said the young man, "will the Cynic hold himself bound to undertake this as a chief duty?"
Grant me a republic of wise men, answered Epictetus, and perhaps none will lightly take the Cynic life upon him. For on whose account should he embrace that method of life? Suppose however that he does, there will then be nothing to hinder his marrying and rearing offspring. For his wife will be even such another as himself, and likewise her father; and in like manner will his children be brought up.
But in the present condition of things, which resembles an Army in battle array, ought not the Cynic to be free from all distraction and given wholly to the service of God, so that he can go in and out among men, neither fettered by the duties nor entangled by the relations of common life? For if he transgress them, he will forfeit the character of a good man and true; whereas if he observe them, there is an end to him as the Messenger, the Spy, the Herald of the Gods!

CXVII

Ask me if you choose if a Cynic shall engage in the administration of the State. O fool, seek you a nobler administration that that in which he is engaged? Ask you if a man shall come forward in the Athenian assembly and talk about revenue and supplies, when his business is to converse with all men, Athenians, Corinthians, and Romans alike, not about supplies, not about revenue, nor yet peace and war, but about Happiness and Misery, Prosperity and Adversity, Slavery and Freedom?
Ask you whether a man shall engage in the administration of the State who has engaged in such an Administration as this? Ask me too if he shall govern; and again I will answer, Fool, what greater government shall he hold than he holds already?

CXVIII

Such a man needs also to have a certain habit of body. If he appears consumptive, thin and pale, his testimony has no longer the same authority. He must not only prove to the unlearned by showing them what his Soul is that it is possible to be a good man apart from all that they admire; but he must also show them, by his body, that a plain and simple manner of life under the open sky does no harm to the body either. "See, I am proof of this! and my body also." As Diogenes used to do, who went about fresh of look and by the very appearance of his body drew men's eyes. But if a Cynic is an object of pity, he seems a mere beggar; all turn away, all are offended at him. Nor should he be slovenly of look, so as not to scare men from him in this way either; on the contrary, his very roughness should be clean and attractive.

CXIX

Kings and tyrants have armed guards wherewith to chastise certain persons, though they themselves be evil. But to the Cynic conscience gives this power—not arms and guards. When he knows that he has watched and laboured on behalf of mankind: that sleep hath found him pure, and left him purer still: that his thoughts have been the thought of a Friend of the Gods— of a servant, yet one that hath a part in the government of the Supreme God: that the words are ever on his lips:—
Lead me, O God, and thou, O Destiny!
as well as these:—
If this be God's will, so let it be!
Why should he not speak boldly unto his own brethren, unto his children—in a word, unto all that are akin to him!

CXX

Does a Philosopher apply to people to come and hear him? does he not rather, of his own nature, attract those that will be benefited by him—like the sun that warms, the food that sustains them? What Physician applies to men to come and be healed? (Though indeed I hear that the Physicians at Rome do nowadays apply for patients—in my time they were applied to.) I apply to you to come and hear that you are in evil case; that what deserves your attention most is the last thing to gain it; that you know not good from evil, and are in short a hapless wretch; a fine way to apply! though unless the words of the Philosopher affect you thus, speaker and speech are alike dead.

CXXI

A Philosopher's school is a Surgery: pain, not pleasure, you should have felt therein. For on entering none of you is whole. One has a shoulder out of joint, another an abscess: a third suffers from an issue, a fourth from pains in the head. And am I then to sit down and treat you to pretty sentiments and empty flourishes, so that you may applaud me and depart, with neither shoulder, nor head, nor issue, nor abscess a whit the better for your visit? Is it then for this that young men are to quit their homes, and leave parents, friends, kinsmen and substance to mouth out Bravo to your empty phrases!

CXXII

If any be unhappy, let him remember that he is unhappy by reason of himself alone. For God hath made all men to enjoy felicity and constancy of good.

CXXIII

Shall we never wean ourselves—shall we never heed the teachings of Philosophy (unless perchance they have been sounding in our ears like an enchanter's drone):—
This World is one great City, and one is the substance whereof it is fashioned: a certain period indeed there needs must be, while these give place to those; some must perish for others to succeed; some move and some abide: yet all is full of friends—first God, then Men, whom Nature hath bound by ties of kindred each to each.

CXXIV

Nor did the hero weep and lament at leaving his children orphans. For he knew that no man is an orphan, but it is the Father that careth for all continually and for evermore. Not by mere report had he heard that the Supreme God is the Father of men: seeing that he called Him Father believing Him so to be, and in all that he did had ever his eyes fixed upon Him. Wherefore in whatsoever place he was, there is was given him to live happily.

CXXV

Know you not that the thing is a warfare? one man's duty is to mount guard, another must go out to reconnoitre, a third to battle; all cannot be in one place, nor would it even be expedient. But you, instead of executing you Commander's orders, complain if aught harsher than usual is enjoined; not understanding to what condition you are bringing the army, so far as in you lies. If all were to follow your example, none would dig a trench, none would cast a rampart around the camp, none would keep watch, or expose himself to danger; but all turn out useless for the service of war. . . . Thus it is here also. Every life is a warfare, and that long and various. You must fulfil a soldier's duty, and obey each order at your commander's nod: aye, if it be possible, divine what he would have done; for between that Command and this, there is no comparison, either in might or in excellence.

CXXVI

Have you again forgotten? Know you not that a good man does nothing for appearance' sake, but for the sake of having done right? . . .
"Is there no reward then?"

Reward! do you seek any greater reward for a good man than doing what is right and just? Yet at the Great Games you look for nothing else; there the victor's crown you deem enough. Seems it to you so small a thing and worthless, to be a good man, and happy therein?

CXXVII

It befits thee not to be unhappy by reason of any, but rather to be happy by reason of all men, and especially by reason of God, who formed us to this end.

CXXVIII

What, did Diogenes love no man, he that was so gentle, so true a friend to men as cheerfully to endure such bodily hardships for the common weal of all mankind? But how loved he them? As behoved a minister of the Supreme God, alike caring for men and subject unto God.

CXXIX

I am by Nature made for my own good; not for my own evil.

CXXX

Remind thyself that he whom thou lovest is mortal—that what thou lovest is not thine own; it is given thee for the present, not irrevocably nor for ever, but even as a fig or a bunch of grapes at the appointed season of the year. . . .
"But these are words of evil omen.". . .
What, callest thou aught of evil omen save that which signifies some evil thing? Cowardice is a word of evil omen, if thou wilt, and meanness of spirit, and lamentation and mourning, and shamelessness. . . .
But do not, I pray thee, call of evil omen a word that is significant of any natural thing:—as well call of evil omen the reaping of the corn; for that means the destruction of the ears, though not of the World!—as well say that the fall of the leaf is of evil omen; that the dried fig should take the place of the green; that raisins should be made from grapes. All these are changes from a former state into another; not destruction, but an ordered economy, a fixed administration. Such is leaving home, a change of small account; such is Death, a greater change, from what now is, not to what is not, but to what is not now.
"Shall I then no longer be?"
Not so; thou wilt be; but something different, of which the World now hath need. For thou too wert born not when thou chosest, but when the World had need of thee.

CXXXI

Wherefore a good man and true, bearing in mind who he is and whence he came and from whom he sprang, cares only how he may fill his post with due discipline and obedience to God.

Wilt thou that I continue to live? Then will I live, as one that is free and noble, as Thou wouldst have me. For Thou hast made me free from hindrance in what appertaineth unto me. But hast Thou no further need of me? I thank Thee! Up to this hour have I stayed for Thy sake and none other's: and now in obedience to Thee I depart.

"How dost thou depart?"

Again I say, as Thou wouldst have me; as one that is free, as Thy servant, as one whose ear is open unto what Thou dost enjoin, what Thou dost forbid.

CXXXII

Whatsoever place or post Thou assignest me, sooner will I die a thousand deaths, as Socrates said, than desert it. And where wilt Thou have me to be? At Rome or Athens? At Thebes or on a desert island? Only remember me there! Shouldst Thou send me where man cannot live as Nature would have him, I will depart, not in disobedience to Thee, but as though Thou wert sounding the signal for my retreat: I am not deserting Thee—far be that from me! I only perceive that thou needest me no longer.

CXXXIII

If you are in Gyaros, do not let your mind dwell upon life at Rome, and all the pleasures it offered to you when living there, and all that would attend your return. Rather be intent on this—how he that lives in Gyaros may live in Gyaros like a man of spirit. And if you are at Rome, do not let your mind dwell upon the life at Athens, but study only how to live at Rome.

Finally, in the room of all other pleasures put this—the pleasure which springs from conscious obedience to God.

CXXXIV

To a good man there is no evil, either in life or death. And if God supply not food, has He not, as a wise Commander, sounded the signal for retreat and nothing more? I obey, I follow—speaking good of my Commander, and praising His acts. For at His good pleasure I came; and I depart when it pleases Him; and while I was yet alive that was my work, to sing praises unto God!

CXXXV

Reflect that the chief source of all evils to Man, and of baseness and cowardice, is not death, but the fear of death.

Against this fear then, I pray you, harden yourself; to this let all your reasonings, your exercises, your reading tend. Then shall you know that thus alone are men set free.

CXXXVI

He is free who lives as he wishes to live; to whom none can do violence, none hinder or compel; whose impulses are unimpeded, whose desires are attain their purpose, who falls not into what he would avoid. Who then would live in error?—None. Who would live deceived and prone to fall, unjust, intemperate, in abject whining at his lot?—None. Then doth no wicked man live as he would, and therefore neither is he free.

CXXXVII

Thus do the more cautious of travellers act. The road is said to be beset by robbers. The traveller will not venture alone, but awaits the companionship on the road of an ambassador, a quaestor or a proconsul. To him he attaches himself and thus passes by in safety. So doth the wise man in the world. Many are the companies of robbers and tyrants, many the storms, the straits, the losses of all a man holds dearest. Whither shall he fall for refuge—how shall he pass by unassailed? What companion on the road shall he await for protection? Such and such a wealthy man, of consular rank? And how shall I be profited, if he is stripped and falls to lamentation and weeping? And how if my fellow-traveller himself turns upon me and robs me? What am I to do? I will become a friend of Caesar's! in his train none will do me wrong! In the first place—O the indignities I must endure to win distinction! O the multitude of hands there will be to rob me! And if I succeed, Caesar too is but a mortal. While should it come to pass that I offend him, whither shall I flee from his presence? To the wilderness? And may not fever await me there? What then is to be done? Cannot a fellow-traveller be found that is honest and loyal, strong and secure against surprise? Thus doth the wise man reason, considering that if he would pass through in safety, he must attach himself unto God.

CXXXVIII

"How understandest thou attach himself to God?"
That what God wills, he should will also; that what God wills not, neither should he will.
"How then may this come to pass?"
By considering the movements of God, and His administration.

CXXXIX

And dost thou that hast received all from another's hands, repine and blame the Giver, if He takes anything from thee? Why, who art thou, and to what end comest thou here? was it not He that made the Light manifest unto thee, that gave thee fellow-workers, and senses, and the power to reason? And how brought He thee into the world? Was it not as one born to die; as one bound to live out his earthly life in some small tabernacle of flesh; to behold His administration, and for a little while share with Him in the mighty march of this great Festival Procession? Now therefore that thou hast beheld, while it was permitted thee, the Solemn Feast and Assembly, wilt thou not cheerfully depart, when He summons thee forth, with adoration and thanksgiving for what thou hast seen and heard?—"Nay, but I would fain have stayed longer at the Festival."—Ah, so would the mystics fain have the rites prolonged; so perchance would the crowd at the Great Games fain behold more wrestlers still. But the Solemn Assembly is over! Come forth, depart with thanksgiving and modesty—give place to others that must come into being even as thyself.

CXL

Why art thou thus insatiable? why thus unreasonable? why encumber the world?—"Aye, but I fain would have my wife and children with me too."—What, are they then thine, and not His that gave them—His that made thee? Give up then that which is not thine own: yield it to One who is better than thou. "Nay, but why did He bring one into the world on these conditions?"—If it suits thee not, depart! He hath no need of a spectator who finds fault with his lot! Them that will take part in the Feast he needeth—that will lift their voices with the rest that men may applaud the more, and exalt the Great Assembly in hymns and songs of praise. But the wretched and the fearful He will not be displeased to see absent from it: for when they were present, they did not behave as at a Feast, nor fulfil their proper office; but moaned as though in pain, and found fault with their fate, their fortune and their companions; insensible to what had fallen to their lot, insensible to the powers they had received for a very different purpose—the powers of Magnanimity, Nobility of Heart, of Fortitude, or Freedom!

CXLI

Art thou then free? a man may say. So help me heaven, I long and pray for freedom! But I cannot look my masters boldly in the face; I still value the poor body; I still set much store on its preservation whole and sound.
But I can point thee out a free man, that thou mayest be no more in search of an example. Diogenes was free. How so? Not because he was of free parentage (for that, indeed, was not the case), but because he was himself free. He had cast away every handle whereby slavery might lay hold of him to enslave him, nor was it possible for any to approach and take hold of him to enslave him. All things sat loose upon him—all things were to him attached by but slender ties. Hadst thou seized upon his possessions, he would rather have let them go than have followed thee for them—aye, had it been even a limb, or mayhap his whole body; and in like manner, relatives, friends, and country. For he knew whence they came—from whose hands and on what terms he had received them. His true forefathers, the Gods, his true Country, he never would have

abandoned; nor would he have yielded to any man in obedience and submission to the one nor in cheerfully dying for the other. For he was ever mindful that everything that comes to pass has its source and origin there; being indeed brought about for the weal of that his true Country, and directed by Him in whose governance it is.

CXLII

Ponder on this—on these convictions, on these words: fix thine eyes on these examples, if thou wouldst be free, if thou hast thine heart set upon the matter according to its worth. And what marvel if thou purchase so great a thing at so great and high a price? For the sake of this that men deem liberty, some hang themselves, others cast themselves down from the rock; aye, time has been when whole cities came utterly to an end: while for the sake of Freedom that is true, and sure, and unassailable, dost thou grudge to God what He gave, when He claims it? Wilt thou not study, as Plato saith, to endure, not death alone, but torture, exile, stripes—in a word, to render up all that is not thine own? Else thou wilt be a slave amid slaves, wert thou ten thousand times a consul; aye, not a whit the less, though thou climb the Palace steps. And thou shalt know how true the saying of Cleanthes, that though the words of philosophers may run counter to the opinions of the world, yet have they reason on their side.

CXLIII

Asked how a man should best grieve his enemy, Epictetus replied, "By setting himself to live the noblest life himself."

CXLIV

I am free, I am a friend of God, ready to render Him willing obedience. Of all else I may set store by nothing—neither by mine own body, nor possessions, nor office, nor good report, nor, in a word, aught else beside. For it is not His Will, that I should so set store by these things. Had it been His pleasure, He would have placed my Good therein. But now He hath not done so: therefore I cannot transgress one jot of His commands. In everything hold fast to that which is thy Good—but to all else (as far as is given thee) within the measure of Reason only, contented with this alone. Else thou wilt meet with failure, ill success, let and hindrance. These are the Laws ordained of God—these are His Edicts; these a man should expound and interpret; to these submit himself, not to the laws of Masurius and Cassius.

CXLV

Remember that not the love of power and wealth sets us under the heel of others, but even the love of tranquillity, of leisure, of change of scene—of learning in general, it matters not what the outward thing may be—to set store by it is to place thyself in subjection to another. Where is the difference then between desiring to be a Senator, and desiring not to be one: between thirsting for office and thirsting to be quit of it? Where is the difference between crying, Woe is me, I know not what to do, bound hand and foot as I am to my books so that I cannot stir! and crying, Woe is me, I have not time to read! As though a book were not as much an outward thing and independent of the will, as office and power and the receptions of the great.

Or what reason hast thou (tell me) for desiring to read? For if thou aim at nothing beyond the mere delight of it, or gaining some scrap of knowledge, thou art but a poor, spiritless knave. But if thou desirest to study to its proper end, what else is this than a life that flows on tranquil and serene? And if thy reading secures thee not serenity, what profits it?—"Nay, but it doth secure it," quoth he, "and that is why I repine at being deprived of it."—And what serenity is this that lies at the mercy of every passer-by? I say not at the mercy of the Emperor or Emperor's favorite, but such as trembles at a raven's croak and piper's din, a fever's touch or a thousand things of like sort! Whereas the life serene has no more certain mark than this, that it ever moves with constant unimpeded flow.

CXLVI

If thou hast put malice and evil speaking from thee, altogether, or in some degree: if thou hast put away from thee rashness, foulness of tongue, intemperance, sluggishness: if thou art not moved by what once moved thee, or in like manner as thou once wert moved—then thou mayest celebrate a daily festival, to-day because thou hast done well in this manner, to-morrow in that. How much greater cause is here for offering sacrifice, than if a man should become Consul or Prefect?

CXLVII

These things hast thou from thyself and from the Gods: only remember who it is that giveth them—to whom and for what purpose they were given. Feeding thy soul on thoughts like these, dost thou debate in what place happiness awaits thee? in what place thou shalt do God's pleasure? Are not the Gods nigh unto all places alike; see they not alike what everywhere comes to pass?

CXLVIII

To each man God hath granted this inward freedom. These are the principles that in a house create love, in a city concord, among nations peace, teaching a man gratitude towards God and cheerful confidence, wherever he may be, in dealing with outward things that he knows are neither his nor worth striving after.

CXLIX

If you seek Truth, you will not seek to gain a victory by every possible means; and when you have found Truth, you need not fear being defeated.

CL

What foolish talk is this? how can I any longer lay claim to right principles, if I am not content with being what I am, but am all aflutter about what I am supposed to be?

CLI

God hath made all things in the world, nay, the world itself, free from hindrance and perfect, and its parts for the use of the whole. No other creature is capable of comprehending His administration thereof; but the reasonable being Man possesses faculties for the consideration of all these things—not only that he is himself a part, but what part he is, and how it is meet that the parts should give place to the whole. Nor is this all. Being naturally constituted noble, magnanimous, and free, he sees that the things which surround him are of two kinds. Some are free from hindrance and in the power of the will. Other are subject to hindrance, and depend on the will of other men. If then he place his own good, his own best interest, only in that which is free from hindrance and in his power, he will be free, tranquil, happy, unharmed, noble-hearted, and pious; giving thanks to all things unto God, finding fault with nothing that comes to pass, laying no charge against anything. Whereas if he place his good in outward things, depending not on the will, he must perforce be subject to hindrance and restraint, the slave of those that have power over the things he desires and fears; he must perforce be impious, as deeming himself injured at the hands of God; he must be unjust, as ever prone to claim more than his due; he must perforce be of a mean and abject spirit.

CLII

Whom then shall I fear? the lords of the Bedchamber, lest they should shut me out? If they find me desirous of entering in, let them shut me out, if they will. "Then why comest thou to the door?"
Because I think it meet and right, so long as the Play lasts, to take part therein.
"In what sense art thou then shut out?"
Because, unless I am admitted, it is not my will to enter: on the contrary, my will is simply that which comes to pass. For I esteem what God wills better than what I will. To Him will I cleave as His minister and attendant; having the same movements, the same desires, in a word the same Will as He. There is no such thing as being shut out for me, but only for them that would force their way in.

CLIII

But what says Socrates?—"One man finds pleasure in improving his land, another his horses. My pleasure lies in seeing that I myself grow better day by day."

CLIV

The dress is suited to the craft; the craftsman takes his name from the craft, not from the dress. For this reason Euphrates was right in saying, "I long endeavoured to conceal my following the philosophic life; and this profited me much. In the first place, I knew that what I did aright, I did not for the sake of lookers-on, but for my own. I ate aright—unto myself; I kept the even tenor of my walk, my glance composed and serene—all unto myself and unto God. Then as I fought alone, I was alone in peril. If I did anything amiss or shameful, the cause of Philosophy was not in me endangered; nor did I wrong the multitude by transgressing as a professed philosopher. Wherefore those that knew not my purpose marvelled how it came about, that whilst all my life and conversation was passed with philosophers without exception, I was yet none myself. And what harm that the philosopher should be known by his acts, instead of mere outward signs and symbols?"

CLV

First study to conceal what thou art; seek wisdom a little while unto thyself. Thus grows the fruit; first, the seed must be buried in the earth for a little space; there it must be hid and slowly grow, that it may reach maturity. But if it produce the ear before the jointed stalk, it is imperfect—a thing from the garden of Adonis. Such a sorry growth art thou; thou hast blossomed too soon: the winter cold will wither thee away!

CLVI

First of all, condemn the life thou art now leading: but when thou hast condemned it, do not despair of thyself—be not like them of mean spirit, who once they have yielded, abandon themselves entirely and as it were allow the torrent to sweep them away. No; learn what the wrestling masters do. Has the boy fallen? "Rise," they say, "wrestle again, till thy strength come to thee." Even thus should it be with thee. For know that there is nothing more tractable than the human soul. It needs but to will, and the thing is done; the soul is set upon the right path: as on the contrary it needs but to nod over the task, and all is lost. For ruin and recovery alike are from within.

CLVII

It is the critical moment that shows the man. So when the crisis is upon you, remember that God, like a trainer of wrestlers, has matched you with a rough and stalwart antagonist.—"To what end?" you ask. That you may prove the victor at the Great Games. Yet without toil and sweat this may not be!

CLVIII

If thou wouldst make progress, be content to seem foolish and void of understanding with respect to outward things. Care not to be thought to know anything. If any should make account of thee, distrust thyself.

CLIX

Remember that in life thou shouldst order thy conduct as at a banquet. Has any dish that is being served reached thee? Stretch forth thy hand and help thyself modestly. Doth it pass thee by? Seek not to detain it. Has it not yet come? Send not forth thy desire to meet it, but wait until it reaches thee. Deal thus with children, thus with wife; thus with office, thus with wealth—and one day thou wilt be meet to share the Banquets of the Gods. But if thou dost not so much as touch that which is placed before thee, but despisest it, then shalt thou not only share the Banquets of the Gods, but their Empire also.

CLX

Remember that thou art an actor in a play, and of such sort as the Author chooses, whether long or short. If it be his good pleasure to assign thee the part of a beggar, a ruler, or a simple citizen, thine it is to play it fitly. For thy business is to act the part assigned thee, well: to choose it, is another's.

CLXI

Keep death and exile daily before thine eyes, with all else that men deem terrible, but more especially Death. Then wilt thou never think a mean though, nor covet anything beyond measure.

CLXII

As a mark is not set up in order to be missed, so neither is such a thing as natural evil produced in the World.

CLXIII

Piety toward the Gods, to be sure, consists chiefly in thinking rightly concerning them—that they are, and that they govern the Universe with goodness and justice; and that thou thyself art appointed to obey them, and to submit under all circumstances that arise; acquiescing cheerfully in whatever may happen, sure it is brought to pass and accomplished by the most Perfect Understanding. Thus thou wilt never find fault with the Gods, nor charge them with neglecting thee.

CLXIV

Lose no time in setting before you a certain stamp of character and behaviour both when by yourself and in company with others. Let silence be your general rule; or say only what is necessary and in few words. We shall, however, when occasion demands, enter into discourse sparingly. avoiding common topics as gladiators, horse-races, athletes; and the perpetual talk about food and drink. Above all avoid speaking of persons, either in way of praise or blame, or comparison.

If you can, win over the conversation of your company to what it should be by your own. But if you find yourself cut off without escape among strangers and aliens, be silent.

CLXV

Laughter should not be much, nor frequent, nor unrestrained.

CLXVI

Refuse altogether to take an oath if you can, if not, as far as may be.

CLXVII

Banquets of the unlearned and of them that are without, avoid. But if you have occasion to take part in them, let not your attention be relaxed for a moment, lest you slip after all into evil ways. For you may rest assured that be a man ever so pure himself, he cannot escape defilement if his associates are impure.

CLXVIII

Take what relates to the body as far as the bare use warrants—as meat, drink, raiment, house and servants. But all that makes for show and luxury reject.

CLXIX

If you are told that such an one speaks ill of you, make no defence against what was said, but answer, He surely knew not my other faults, else he would not have mentioned these only!

CLXX

When you visit any of those in power, bethink yourself that you will not find him in: that you may not be admitted: that the door may be shut in your face: that he may not concern himself about you. If with all this, it is your duty to go, bear what happens, and never say to yourself, It was not worth the trouble! For that would smack of the foolish and unlearned who suffer outward things to touch them.

CLXXI

In company avoid frequent and undue talk about your own actions and dangers. However pleasant it may be to you to enlarge upon the risks you have run, others may not find such pleasure in listening to your adventures. Avoid provoking laughter also: it is a habit from which one easily slides into the ways of the foolish, and apt to diminish the respect which your neighbors feel for you. To border on coarse talk is also dangerous. On such occasions, if a convenient opportunity offer, rebuke the speaker. If not, at least by relapsing into silence, colouring, and looking annoyed, show that you are displeased with the subject.

CLXXII

When you have decided that a thing ought to be done, and are doing it, never shun being seen doing it, even though the multitude should be likely to judge the matter amiss. For if you are not acting rightly, shun the act itself; if rightly, however, why fear misplaced censure?

CLXXIII

It stamps a man of mean capacity to spend much time on the things of the body, as to be long over bodily exercises, long over eating, long over drinking, long over other bodily functions. Rather should these things take the second place, while all your care is directed to the understanding.

CLXXIV

Everything has two handles, one by which it may be borne, the other by which it may not. If your brother sin against you lay not hold of it by the handle of injustice, for by that it may not be borne: but rather by this, that he is your brother, the comrade of your youth; and thus you will lay hold on it so that it may be borne.

CLXXV

Never call yourself a Philosopher nor talk much among the unlearned about Principles, but do that which follows from them. Thus at a banquet, do not discuss how people ought to eat; but eat as you ought. Remember that Socrates thus entirely avoided ostentation. Men would come to him desiring to be recommended to philosophers, and he would conduct them thither himself—so well did he bear being overlooked. Accordingly if any talk concerning principles should arise among the unlearned, be you for the most part silent. For you run great risk of spewing up what you have ill digested. And when a man tells you that you know nothing and you are not nettled at it, then you may be sure that you have begun the work.

CLXXVI

When you have brought yourself to supply the needs of the body at small cost, do not pique yourself on that, nor if you drink only water, keep saying on each occasion, I drink water! And if you ever want to practise endurance and toil, do so unto yourself and not unto others—do not embrace statues!

CLXXVII

When a man prides himself on being able to understand and interpret the writings of Chrysippus, say to yourself:—
If Chrysippus had not written obscurely, this fellow would have had nothing to be proud of. But what is it that I desire? To understand Nature, and to follow her! Accordingly I ask who is the Interpreter. On hearing that it is Chrysippus, I go to him. But it seems I do not understand what he wrote. So I seek one to interpret that. So far there is nothing to pride myself on. But when I have found my interpreter, what remains is to put in practice his instructions. This itself is the only thing to be proud of. But if I admire the interpretation and that alone, what else have I turned out but a mere commentator instead of a lover of wisdom?—except indeed that I happen to be interpreting Chrysippus instead of Homer. So when any one says to me, Prithee, read me Chrysippus, I am more inclined to blush, when I cannot show my deeds to be in harmony and accordance with his sayings.

CLXXVIII

At feasts, remember that you are entertaining two guests, body and soul. What you give to the body, you presently lose; what you give to the soul, you keep for ever.

CLXXIX

At meals, see to it that those who serve be not more in number than those who are served. It is absurd for a crowd of persons to be dancing attendance on half a dozen chairs.

CLXXX

It is best to share with your attendants what is going forward, both in the labour of preparation and in the enjoyment of the feast itself. If such a thing be difficult at the time, recollect that you who are not weary are being served by those that are; you who are eating and drinking by those who do neither; you who are talking by those who are silent; you who are at ease by those who are under constraint. Thus no sudden wrath will betray you into unreasonable conduct, nor will you behave harshly by irritating another.

CLXXXI

When Xanthippe was chiding Socrates for making scanty preparation for entertaining his friends, he answered:—"If they are friends of ours they will not care for that; if they are not, we shall care nothing for them!"

CLXXXII

Asked, Who is the rich man? Epictetus replied, "He who is content."

CLXXXIII

Favorinus tells us how Epictetus would also say that there were two faults far graver and fouler than any others—inability to bear, and inability to forbear, when we neither patiently bear the blows that must be borne, nor abstain from the things and the pleasures we ought to abstain from. "So," he went on, "if a man will only have these two words at heart, and heed them carefully by ruling and watching over himself, he will for the most part fall into no sin, and his life will be tranquil and serene." He meant the words [Greek: Anechou kai apechou]—"Bear and Forbear."

CLXXXIV

On all occasions these thoughts should be at hand:—

Lead me, O God, and Thou, O Destiny
Be what it may the goal appointed me,
Bravely I'll follow; nay, and if I would not,
I'd prove a coward, yet must follow still!

Again:

Who to Necessity doth bow aright,
Is learn'd in wisdom and the things of God.

Once more:—

Crito, if this be God's will, so let it be. As for me,
Anytus and Meletus can indeed put me to death, but injure me, never!

CLXXXV

We shall then be like Socrates, when we can indite hymns of praise to the Gods in prison.

CLXXXVI

It is hard to combine and unite these two qualities, the carefulness of one who is affected by circumstances, and the intrepidity of one who heeds them not.

But it is not impossible: else were happiness also impossible. We should act as we do in seafaring.

"What can I do?"—Choose the master, the crew, the day, the opportunity. Then comes a sudden storm. What matters it to me? my part has been fully done. The matter is in the hands of another—the Master of the ship. The ship is foundering. What then have I to do? I do the only thing that remains to me—to be drowned without fear, without a cry, without upbraiding God, but knowing that what has been born must likewise perish. For I am not Eternity, but a human being—a part of the whole, as an hour is part of the day. I must come like the hour, and like the hour must pass!

CLXXXVII

And now we are sending you to Rome to spy out the land; but none send a coward as such a spy, that, if he hear but a noise and see a shadow moving anywhere, loses his wits and comes flying to say, The enemy are upon us!

So if you go now, and come and tell us: "Everything at Rome is terrible: Death is terrible, Exile is terrible, Slander is terrible, Want is terrible; fly, comrades! the enemy are upon us!" we shall reply, Get you gone, and prophesy to yourself! we have but erred in sending such a spy as you. Diogenes, who was sent as a spy long before you, brought us back another report than this. He says that Death is no evil; for it need not even bring shame with it. He says that Fame is but the empty noise of madmen. And what report did this spy bring us of Pain, what of Pleasure, what of Want? That to be clothed in sackcloth is better than any purple robe; that sleeping on the bare ground is the softest couch; and in proof of each assertion he points to his own courage, constancy, and freedom; to his own healthy and muscular frame. "There is no enemy near," he cries, "all is perfect peace!"

CLXXXVIII

If a man has this peace—not the peace proclaimed by Caesar (how indeed should he have it to proclaim?), nay, but the peace proclaimed by God through reason, will not that suffice him when alone, when he beholds and reflects:— Now can no evil happen unto me; for me there is no robber, for me no earthquake; all things are full of peace, full of tranquillity; neither highway nor city nor gathering of men, neither neighbor nor comrade can do me hurt. Another supplies my food, whose care it is; another my raiment; another hath given me perceptions of sense and primary conceptions. And when He supplies my necessities no more, it is that He is sounding the retreat, that He hath opened the door, and is saying to thee, Come!—Wither? To nought that thou needest fear, but to the friendly kindred elements whence thou didst spring. Whatsoever of fire is in thee, unto fire shall return; whatsoever of earth, unto earth; of spirit, unto spirit; of water, unto water. There is no Hades, no fabled rivers of Sighs, of Lamentation, or of Fire: but all things are full of Beings spiritual and divine. With thoughts like these, beholding the Sun, Moon, and Stars, enjoying earth and sea, a man is neither helpless nor alone!

CLXXXIX

What wouldst thou be found doing when overtaken by Death? If I might choose, I would be found doing some deed of true humanity, of wide import, beneficent and noble. But if I may not be found engaged in aught so lofty, let me hope at least for this—what none may hinder, what is surely in my power—that I may be found raising up in myself that which had fallen; learning to deal more wisely with the things of sense; working out my own tranquillity, and thus rendering that which is its due to every relation of life. . . . If death surprise me thus employed, it is enough if I can stretch forth my hands to God and say, "The faculties which I received at Thy hands for apprehending this thine Administration, I have not neglected. As far as in me lay, I have done Thee no dishonour. Behold how I have used the senses, the primary conceptions which Thou gavest me. Have I ever laid anything to Thy charge? Have I ever murmured at aught that came to pass, or wished it otherwise? Have I in anything transgressed the relations of life? For that Thou didst beget me, I thank Thee for that Thou hast given: for the time during which I have used the things that were Thine, it suffices me. Take them back and place them wherever Thou wilt! They were all Thine, and Thou gavest them me."—If a man depart thus minded, is it not enough? What life is fairer and more noble, what end happier than his?

FRAGMENTS ATTRIBUTED

TO EPICTETUS

I

A life entangled with Fortune is like a torrent. It is turbulent and muddy; hard to pass and masterful of mood: noisy and of brief continuance.

II

The soul that companies with Virtue is like an ever-flowing source. It is a pure, clear, and wholesome draught; sweet, rich, and generous of its store; that injures not, neither destroys.

III

It is a shame that one who sweetens his drink with the gifts of the bee, should embitter God's gift Reason with vice.

IV

Crows pick out the eyes of the dead, when the dead have no longer need of them; but flatterers mar the soul of the living, and her eyes they blind.

V

Keep neither a blunt knife nor an ill-disciplined looseness of tongue.

VI

Nature hath given men one tongue but two ears, that we may hear from others twice as much as we speak.

VII

Do not give sentence in another tribunal till you have been yourself judged in the tribunal of Justice.

VIII

If is shameful for a Judge to be judged by others.

IX

Give me by all means the shorter and nobler life, instead of one that is longer but of less account!

X

Freedom is the name of virtue: Slavery, of vice. . . . None is a slave whose acts are free.

XI

Of pleasures, those which occur most rarely give the most delight.

XII

Exceed due measure, and the most delightful things become the least delightful.

XIII

The anger of an ape—the threat of a flatterer:—these deserve equal regard.

XIV

Chastise thy passions that they avenge not themselves upon thee.

XV

No man is free who is not master of himself.

XVI

A ship should not ride on a single anchor, nor life on a single hope.

XVII

Fortify thyself with contentment: that is an impregnable stronghold.

XVIII

No man who is a lover of money, of pleasure, of glory, is likewise a lover of Men; but only he that is a lover of whatsoever things are fair and good.

XIX

Think of God more often than thou breathest.

XX

Choose the life that is noblest, for custom can make it sweet to thee.

XXI

Let thy speech of God be renewed day by day, aye, rather than thy meat and drink.

XXII

Even as the Sun doth not wait for prayers and incantations to rise, but shines forth and is welcomed by all: so thou also wait not for clapping of hands and shouts and praise to do thy duty; nay, do good of thine own accord, and thou wilt be loved like the Sun.

XXIII

Let no man think that he is loved by any who loveth none.

XXIV

If thou rememberest that God standeth by to behold and visit all that thou doest; whether in the body or in the soul, thou surely wilt not err in any prayer or deed; and thou shalt have God to dwell with thee.

THE DISCOURSES OF EPICTETUS

A Selection

OF THE THINGS WHICH ARE IN OUR POWER AND NOT IN OUR POWER

Of all the faculties (except that which I shall soon mention), you will find not one which is capable of contemplating itself, and, consequently, not capable either of approving or disapproving. How far does the grammatic art possess the contemplating power? As far as forming a judgment about what is written and spoken. And how far music? As far as judging about melody. Does either of them then contemplate itself? By no means. But when you must write something to your friend, grammar will tell you what words you should write; but whether you should write or not, grammar will not tell you. And so it is with music as to musical sounds; but whether you should sing at the present time and play on the lute, or do neither, music will not tell you. What faculty then will tell you? That which contemplates both itself and all other things. And what is this faculty? The rational faculty; for this is the only faculty that we have received which examines itself, what it is, and what power it has, and what is the value of this gift, and examines all other faculties: for what else is there which tells us that golden things are beautiful, for they do not say so themselves? Evidently it is the faculty which is capable of judging of appearances. What else judges of music, grammar, and the other faculties, proves their uses, and points out the occasions for using them? Nothing else.

What then should a man have in readiness in such circumstances? What else than this? What is mine, and what is not mine; and what is permitted to me, and what is not permitted to me. I must die. Must I then die lamenting? I must be put in chains. Must I then also lament? I must go into exile. Does any man then hinder me from going with smiles and cheerfulness and contentment? Tell me the secret which you possess. I will not, for this is in my power. But I will put you in chains. Man, what are you talking about? Me, in chains? You may fetter my leg, but my will not even Zeus himself can overpower. I will throw you into prison. My poor body, you mean. I will cut your head off. When then have I told you that my head alone cannot be cut off? These are the things which philosophers should meditate on, which they should write daily, in which they should exercise themselves.

What then did Agrippinus say? He said, "I am not a hindrance to myself." When it was reported to him that his trial was going on in the Senate, he said:

"I hope it may turn out well; but it is the fifth hour of the day"—this was the time when he was used to exercise himself and then take the cold bath,—"let us go and take our exercise." After he had taken his exercise, one comes and tells him, "You have been condemned." "To banishment," he replies, "or to death?" "To banishment." "What about my property?" "It is not taken from you." "Let us go to Aricia then," he said, "and dine."

HOW A MAN ON EVERY OCCASION CAN MAINTAIN HIS PROPER CHARACTER

To the rational animal only is the irrational intolerable; but that which is rational is tolerable. Blows are not naturally intolerable. How is that? See how the Lacedaemonians endure whipping when they have learned that whipping is consistent with reason. To hang yourself is not intolerable. When then you have the opinion that it is rational, you go and hang yourself. In short, if we observe, we shall find that the animal man is pained by nothing so much as by that which is irrational; and, on the contrary, attracted to nothing so much as to that which is rational.

Only consider at what price you sell your own will: if for no other reason, at least for this, that you sell it not for a small sum. But that which is great and superior perhaps belongs to Socrates and such as are like him. Why then, if we are naturally such, are not a very great number of us like him? Is it true then that all horses become swift, that all dogs are skilled in tracking footprints? What then, since I am naturally dull, shall I, for this reason, take no pains? I hope not. Epictetus is not superior to Socrates; but if he is not inferior, this is enough for me; for I shall never be a Milo, and yet I do not neglect my body; nor shall I be a Croesus, and yet I do not neglect my property; nor, in a word, do we neglect looking after anything because we despair of reaching the highest degree.

HOW A MAN SHOULD PROCEED FROM THE PRINCIPLE OF GOD BEING THE FATHER OF ALL MEN TO THE REST

If a man should be able to assent to this doctrine as he ought, that we are all sprung from God in an especial manner, and that God is the father both of men and of gods, I suppose that he would never have any ignoble or mean thoughts about himself. But if Caesar (the emperor) should adopt you, no one could endure your arrogance; and if you know that you are the son of Zeus, will you not be elated? Yet we do not so; but since these two things are mingled in the generation of man, body in common with the animals, and reason and intelligence in common with the gods, many incline to this kinship, which is miserable and mortal; and some few to that which is divine and happy. Since then it is of necessity that every man uses everything according to the opinion which he has about it, those, the few, who think that they are formed for fidelity and modesty and a sure use of appearances have no mean or ignoble thoughts about themselves; but with the many it is quite the contrary. For they say, What am I? A poor, miserable man, with my wretched bit of flesh. Wretched, indeed; but you possess something better than your bit of flesh. Why then do you neglect that which is better, and why do you attach yourself to this?

Through this kinship with the flesh, some of us inclining to it become like wolves, faithless and treacherous and mischievous; some become like lions, savage and bestial and untamed; but the greater part of us become foxes, and other worse animals. For what else is a slanderer and malignant man than a fox, or some other more wretched and meaner animal? See then and take care that you do not become some one of these miserable things.

OF PROGRESS OR IMPROVEMENT

He who is making progress, having learned from philosophers that desire means the desire of good things, and aversion means aversion from bad things; having learned too that happiness and tranquillity are not attainable by man otherwise than by not failing to obtain what he desires, and not falling into that which he would avoid; such a man takes from himself desire altogether and confers it, but he employs his aversion only on things which are dependent on his will. For if he attempts to avoid anything independent of his will, he knows that sometimes he will fall in with something which he wishes to avoid, and he will be unhappy. Now if virtue promises good fortune and tranquillity and happiness, certainly also the progress towards virtue is progress towards each of these things. For it is always true that to whatever point the perfecting of anything leads us, progress is an approach towards this point.

How then do we admit that virtue is such as I have said, and yet seek progress in other things and make a display of it? What is the product of virtue? Tranquillity. Who then makes improvement? Is it he who has read many books of Chrysippus? But does virtue consist in having understood Chrysippus? If this is so, progress is clearly nothing else than knowing a great deal of Chrysippus. But now we admit that virtue produces one thing, and we declare that approaching near to it is another thing, namely, progress or improvement. Such a person, says one, is already able to read Chrysippus by himself. Indeed, sir, you are making great progress. What kind of progress? But why do you mock the man? Why do you draw him away from the perception of his own misfortunes? Will you not show him the effect of virtue that he may learn where to look for improvement? Seek it there, wretch, where your work lies. And where is your work? In desire and in aversion, that you may not be disappointed in your desire, and that you may not fall into that which you would avoid; in your pursuit and avoiding, that you commit no error; in assent and suspension of assent, that you be not deceived. The first things, and the most necessary are those which I have named. But if with trembling and lamentation you seek not to fall into that which you avoid, tell me how you are improving.

Do you then show me your improvement in these things? If I were talking to an athlete, I should say, Show me your shoulders; and then he might say, Here are my Halteres. You and your Halteres look to that. I should reply, I wish to see the effect of the Halteres. So, when you say: Take the treatise on the active powers ([Greek: hormea]), and see how I have studied it, I reply: Slave, I am not inquiring about this, but how you exercise pursuit and avoidance, desire and aversion, how you design and purpose and prepare yourself, whether conformably to nature or not. If conformably, give me evidence of it, and I will say that you are making progress; but if not conformably, be gone, and not only expound your books, but write such books yourself; and what will you gain by it? Do you not know that the whole book costs only five denarii? Does then the expounder seem to be worth more than five denarii? Never then look for the matter itself in one place, and progress towards it in another. Where then is progress? If any of you, withdrawing himself from externals, turns to his own will ([Greek: proairesis]) to exercise it and to improve it by labor, so as to make it conformable to nature, elevated, free, unrestrained, unimpeded, faithful, modest; and if he has learned that he who desires or avoids the things which are not in his power can neither be faithful nor free, but of necessity he must change with them and be tossed about with them as in a tempest, and of necessity must subject himself to others who have the power to procure or prevent what he desires or would avoid; finally, when he rises in the morning, if he observes and keeps these rules, bathes as a man of fidelity, eats as a modest man; in like manner, if in every matter that occurs he works out his chief principles ([Greek: ta proaegoumena]) as the runner does with reference to running, and the trainer of the voice with reference to the voice—this is the man who truly makes progress, and this is the man who has not travelled in vain. But if he has strained his efforts to the practice of reading books, and labors only at this, and has travelled for this, I tell him to return home immediately, and not to neglect his affairs there; for this for which he has travelled is nothing. But the other thing is something, to study how a man can rid his life of lamentation and groaning, and saying, Woe to me, and wretched that I am, and to rid it also of misfortune and disappointment, and to learn what death is, and exile, and prison, and poison, that he may be able to say when he is in fetters, Dear Crito, if it is the will of the gods that it be so, let it be so; and not to say, Wretched am I, an old man: have I kept my gray hairs for this? Who is it that speaks thus? Do you think that I shall name some man of no repute and of low condition? Does not Priam say this? Does not Oedipus say this? Nay, all kings say it! For what else is tragedy than the perturbations ([Greek: pathae]) of men who value externals exhibited in this kind of poetry? But if a man must learn by fiction that no external things which are independent of the will concern us, for my part I should like this fiction, by the aid of which I should live happily and undisturbed. But you must consider for yourselves what you wish.

What then does Chrysippus teach us? The reply is, to know that these things are not false, from which happiness comes and tranquillity arises. Take my books, and you will learn how true and conformable to nature are the things which make me free from perturbations. O great good fortune! O the great benefactor who points out the way! To Triptolemus all men have erected temples and altars, because he gave us food by cultivation; but to him who discovered truth and brought it to light and communicated it to all, not the truth which shows us how to live, but how to live well, who of you for this reason has built an altar, or a temple, or has dedicated a statue, or who worships God for this? Because the gods have given the vine, or wheat, we sacrifice to them; but because they have produced in the human mind that fruit by which they designed to show us the truth which relates to happiness, shall we not thank God for this?

AGAINST THE ACADEMICS

If a man, said Epictetus, opposes evident truths, it is not easy to find arguments by which we shall make him change his opinion. But this does not arise either from the man's strength or the teacher's weakness; for when the man, though he has been confuted, is hardened like a stone, how shall we then be able to deal with him by argument?

Now there are two kinds of hardening, one of the understanding, the other of the sense of shame, when a man is resolved not to assent to what is manifest nor to desist from contradictions. Most of us are afraid of mortification of the body, and would contrive all means to avoid such a thing, but we care not about the soul's mortification. And indeed with regard to the soul, if a man be in such a state as not to apprehend anything, or understand at all, we think that he is in a bad condition; but if the sense of shame and modesty are deadened, this we call even power (or strength).

OF PROVIDENCE

From everything, which is or happens in the world, it is easy to praise Providence, if a man possesses these two qualities: the faculty of seeing what belongs and happens to all persons and things, and a grateful disposition. If he does not possess these two qualities, one man will not see the use of things which are and which happen: another will not be thankful for them, even if he does know them. If God had made colors, but had not made the faculty of seeing them, what would have been their use? None at all. On the other hand, if he had made the faculty of vision, but had not made objects such as to fall under the faculty, what in that case also would have been the use of it? None at all. Well, suppose that he had made both, but had not made light? In that case, also, they would have been of no use. Who is it then who has fitted this to that and that to this?

What, then, are these things done in us only? Many, indeed, in us only, of which the rational animal had peculiar need; but you will find many common to us with irrational animals. Do they then understand what is done? By no means. For use is one thing, and understanding is another; God had need of irrational animals to make use of appearances, but of us to understand the use of appearances. It is therefore enough for them to eat and to drink, and to copulate, and to do all the other things which they severally do. But for us, to whom he has given also the intellectual faculty, these things are not sufficient;

for unless we act in a proper and orderly manner, and conformably to the nature and constitution of each thing, we shall never attain our true end. For where the constitutions of living beings are different, there also the acts and the ends are different. In those animals then whose constitution is adapted only to use, use alone is enough; but in an animal (man), which has also the power of understanding the use, unless there be the due exercise of the understanding, he will never attain his proper end. Well then God constitutes every animal, one to be eaten, another to serve for agriculture, another to supply cheese, and another for some like use; for which purposes what need is there to understand appearances and to be able to distinguish them? But God has introduced man to be a spectator of God and of his works; and not only a spectator of them, but an interpreter. For this reason it is shameful for man to begin and to end where irrational animals do; but rather he ought to begin where they begin, and to end where nature ends in us; and nature ends in contemplation and understanding, and in a way of life conformable to nature. Take care then not to die without having been spectators of these things.

But you take a journey to Olympia to see the work of Phidias, and all of you think it a misfortune to die without having seen such things. But when there is no need to take a journey, and where a man is, there he has the works (of God) before him, will you not desire to see and understand them? Will you not perceive either what you are, or what you were born for, or what this is for which you have received the faculty of sight? But you may say, There are some things disagreeable and troublesome in life. And are there none at Olympia? Are you not scorched? Are you not pressed by a crowd? Are you not without comfortable means of bathing? Are you not wet when it rains? Have you not abundance of noise, clamor, and other disagreeable things? But I suppose that setting all these things off against the magnificence of the spectacle, you bear and endure. Well then and have you not received faculties by which you will be able to bear all that happens? Have you not received greatness of soul? Have you not received manliness? Have you not received endurance? And why do I trouble myself about anything that can happen if I possess greatness of soul? What shall distract my mind, or disturb me, or appear painful? Shall I not use the power for the purposes for which I received it, and shall I grieve and lament over what happens?

Come, then, do you also having observed these things look to the faculties which you have, and when you have looked at them, say: Bring now, O Zeus, any difficulty that thou pleasest, for I have means given to me by thee and powers for honoring myself through the things which happen. You do not so; but you sit still, trembling for fear that some things will happen, and weeping, and lamenting, and groaning for what does happen; and then you blame the gods. For what is the consequence of such meanness of spirit but impiety? And yet God has not only given us these faculties, by which we shall be able to bear everything that happens without being depressed or broken by it; but, like a good king and a true father, He has given us these faculties free from hindrance, subject to no compulsion, unimpeded, and has put them entirely in our own power, without even having reserved to Himself any power of hindering or impeding. You, who have received these powers free and as your own, use them not; you do not even see what you have received, and from whom; some of you being blinded to the giver, and not even acknowledging your benefactor, and others, through meanness of spirit, betaking yourselves to fault-finding and making charges against God. Yet I will show to you that you have powers and means for greatness of soul and manliness; but what powers you have for finding fault making accusations, do you show me.

HOW FROM THE FACT THAT WE ARE AKIN TO GOD A MAN MAY PROCEED TO THE CONSEQUENCES

I indeed think that the old man ought to be sitting here, not to contrive how you may have no mean thoughts nor mean and ignoble talk about yourselves, but to take care that there be not among us any young men of such a mind, that when they have recognized their kinship to God, and that we are fettered by these bonds, the body, I mean, and its possessions, and whatever else on account of them is necessary to us for the economy and commerce of life, they should intend to throw off these things as if they were burdens painful and intolerable, and to depart to their kinsmen. But this is the labor that your teacher and instructor ought to be employed upon, if he really were what he should be. You should come to him and say: Epictetus, we can no longer endure being bound to this poor body, and feeding it, and giving it drink and rest, and cleaning it, and for the sake of the body complying with the wishes of these and of those. Are not these things indifferent and nothing to us; and is not death no evil? And are we not in a manner kinsmen of God, and did we not come from him? Allow us to depart to the place from which we came; allow us to be released at last from these bonds by which we are bound and weighed down. Here there are robbers and thieves and courts of justice, and those who are named tyrants, and think that they have some power over us by means of the body and its possessions. Permit us to show them that they have no power over any man. And I on my part would say: Friends, wait for God: when he shall give the signal and release you from this service, then go to him; but for the present endure to dwell in this place where he has put you. Short indeed is this time of your dwelling here, and easy to bear for those who are so disposed; for what tyrant, or what thief, or what courts of justice are formidable to those who have thus considered as things of no value the body and the possessions of the body? Wait then, do not depart without a reason.

OF CONTENTMENT

With respect to gods, there are some who say that a divine being does not exist; others say that it exists, but is inactive and careless, and takes no forethought about anything; a third class say that such a being exists and exercises forethought, but only about great things and heavenly things, and about nothing on the earth; a fourth class say that a divine being exercises forethought both about things on the earth and heavenly things, but in a general way only, and not about things severally. There is a fifth class to whom

Ulysses and Socrates belong, who say:

I move not without thy knowledge.—Iliad, x., 278.

Before all other things then it is necessary to inquire about each of these opinions, whether it is affirmed truly or not truly. For if there are no gods, how is it our proper end to follow them? And if they exist, but take no care of anything, in this case also how will it be right to follow them? But if indeed they do exist and look after things, still if there is nothing communicated from them to men, nor in fact to myself, how even so is it right (to follow them)? The wise and good man then, after considering all these things, submits his own mind to him who administers the whole, as good citizens do to the law of the state. He who is receiving instruction ought to come to be instructed with this intention, How shall I follow the gods in all things, how shall I be contented with the divine administration, and how can I become free? For he is free to whom everything happens according to his will, and whom no man can hinder. What then, is freedom madness? Certainly not; for madness and freedom do not consist. But, you say, I would have everything result just as I like, and in whatever way I like. You are mad, you are beside yourself. Do you not know that freedom is a noble and valuable thing? But for me inconsiderately to wish for things to happen as I inconsiderately like, this appears to be not only not noble, but even most base. For how do we proceed in the matter of writing? Do I wish to write the name of Dion as I choose? No, but I am taught to choose to write it as it ought to be written. And how with respect to music? In the same manner. And what universally in every art or science? Just the same. If it were not so, it would be of no value to know anything, if knowledge were adapted to every man's whim. Is it then in this alone, in this which is the greatest and the chief thing, I mean freedom, that I am permitted to will inconsiderately? By no means; but to be instructed is this, to learn to wish that everything may happen as it does. And how do things happen? As the disposer has disposed them? And he has appointed summer and winter, and abundance and scarcity, and virtue and vice, and all such opposites for the harmony of the whole; and to each of us he has given a body, and parts of the body, and possessions, and companions.

What then remains, or what method is discovered of holding commerce with them? Is there such a method by which they shall do what seems fit to them, and we not the less shall be in a mood which is conformable to nature? But you are unwilling to endure, and are discontented; and if you are alone, you call it solitude; and if you are with men, you call them knaves and robbers; and you find fault with your own parents and children, and brothers and neighbors. But you ought when you are alone to call this condition by the name of tranquillity and freedom, and to think yourself like to the gods; and when you are with many, you ought not to call it crowd, nor trouble, nor uneasiness, but festival and assembly, and so accept all contentedly.

What then is the punishment of those who do not accept? It is to be what they are. Is any person dissatisfied with being alone? Let him be alone. Is a man dissatisfied with his parents? Let him be a bad son, and lament. Is he dissatisfied with his children? Let him be a bad father. Cast him into prison. What prison? Where he is already, for he is there against his will; and where a man is against his will, there he is in prison. So Socrates was not in prison, for he was there willingly. Must my leg then be lamed? Wretch, do you then on account of one poor leg find fault with the world? Will you not willingly surrender it for the whole? Will you not withdraw from it? Will you not gladly part with it to him who gave it? And will you be vexed and discontented with the things established by Zeus, which he, with the Moirae (fates) who were present and spinning the thread of your generation, defined and put in order? Know you not how small a part you are compared with the whole. I mean with respect to the body, for as to intelligence you are not inferior to the gods nor less; for the magnitude of intelligence is not measured by length nor yet by height, but by thoughts.

HOW EVERYTHING MAY BE DONE ACCEPTABLY TO THE GODS

When some one asked, How may a man eat acceptably to the gods, he answered: If he can eat justly and contentedly, and with equanimity, and temperately, and orderly, will it not be also acceptable to the gods? But when you have asked for warm water and the slave has not heard, or if he did hear has brought only tepid water, or he is not even found to be in the house, then not to be vexed or to burst with passion, is not this acceptable to the gods? How then shall a man endure such persons as this slave? Slave yourself, will you not bear with your own brother, who has Zeus for his progenitor, and is like a son from the same seeds and of the same descent from above? But if you have been put in any such higher place, will you immediately make yourself a tyrant? Will you not remember who you are, and whom you rule? That they are kinsmen, that they are brethren by nature, that they are the offspring of Zeus? But I have purchased them, and they have not purchased me. Do you see in what direction you are looking, that it is towards the earth, towards the pit, that it is towards these wretched laws of dead men? but towards the laws of the gods you are not looking.

WHAT PHILOSOPHY PROMISES

When a man was consulting him how he should persuade his brother to cease being angry with him, Epictetus replied: Philosophy does not propose to secure for a man any external thing. If it did (or if it were not, as I say), philosophy would be allowing something which is not within its province. For as the carpenter's material is wood, and that of the statuary is copper, so the matter of the art of living is each man's life. When then is my brother's? That again belongs to his own art; but with respect to yours, it is one of the external things, like a piece of land, like health, like reputation. But Philosophy promises none of these. In every circumstance I will maintain, she says, the governing part conformable to nature. Whose governing part? His in whom I am, she says.

How then shall my brother cease to be angry with me? Bring him to me and I will tell him. But I have nothing to say to you about his anger.

When the man who was consulting him said, I seek to know this, How, even if my brother is not reconciled to me, shall I maintain myself in a state conformable to nature? Nothing great, said Epictetus, is produced suddenly, since not even the grape or the fig is. If you say to me now that you want a fig, I will answer to you that it requires time: let it flower first, then put forth fruit, and then ripen. Is then the fruit of a fig-tree not perfected suddenly and in one hour, and would you possess the fruit of a man's mind in so short a time and so easily? Do not expect it, even if I tell you.

THAT WE OUGHT NOT TO BE ANGRY WITH THE ERRORS (FAULTS) OF OTHERS

Ought not then this robber and this adulterer to be destroyed? By no means say so, but speak rather in this way: This man who has been mistaken and deceived about the most important things, and blinded, not in the faculty of vision which distinguishes white and black, but in the faculty which distinguishes good and bad, should we not destroy him? If you speak thus you will see how inhuman this is which you say, and that it is just as if you would say, Ought we not to destroy this blind and deaf man? But if the greatest harm is the privation of the greatest things, and the greatest thing in every man is the will or choice such as it ought to be, and a man is deprived of this will, why are you also angry with him? Man, you ought not to be affected contrary to nature by the bad things of another. Pity him rather; drop this readiness to be offended and to hate, and these words which the many utter: "These accursed and odious fellows." How have you been made so wise at once? and how are you so peevish? Why then are we angry? Is it because we value so much the things of which these men rob us? Do not admire your clothes, and then you will not be angry with the thief. Consider this matter thus: you have fine clothes; your neighbor has not; you have a window; you wish to air the clothes. The thief does not know wherein man's good consists, but he thinks that it consist in having fine clothes, the very thing which you also think. Must he not then come and take them away? When you show a cake to greedy persons, and swallow it all yourself, do you expect them not to snatch it from you? Do not provoke them; do not have a window; do not air your clothes. I also lately had an iron lamp placed by the side of my household gods; hearing a noise at the door, I ran down, and found that the lamp had been carried off. I reflected that he who had taken the lamp had done nothing strange. What then? To-morrow, I said, you will find an earthen lamp; for a man only loses that which he has. I have lost my garment. The reason is that you had a garment. I have a pain in my head. Have you any pain in your horns? Why then are you troubled? For we only lose those things, we have only pains about those things, which we possess.

But the tyrant will chain—what? The leg. He will take away—what? The neck. What then will he not chain and not take away? The will. This is why the ancients taught the maxim, Know thyself. Therefore we ought to exercise ourselves in small things, and beginning with them to proceed to the greater. I have pain in the head. Do not say, Alas! I have pain in the ear. Do not say alas! And I do not say that you are not allowed to groan, but do not groan inwardly; and if your slave is slow in bringing a bandage, do not cry out and torment yourself, and say, Every body hates me; for who would not hate such a man? For the future, relying on these opinions, walk about upright, free; not trusting to the size of your body, as an athlete, for a man ought not to be invincible in the way that an ass is.

HOW WE SHOULD BEHAVE TO TYRANTS

If a man possesses any superiority, or thinks that he does when he does not, such a man, if he is uninstructed, will of necessity be puffed up through it. For instance, the tyrant says, I am master of all! And what can you do for me? Can you give me desire which shall have no hindrance? How can you? Have you the infallible power of avoiding what you would avoid? Have you the power of moving towards an object without error? And how do you possess this power? Come, when you are in a ship, do you trust to yourself or to the helmsman? And when you are in a chariot, to whom do you trust but to the driver? And how is it in all other arts? Just the same. In what, then, lies your power? All men pay respect to me. Well, I also pay respect to my platter, and I wash it and wipe it; and for the sake of my oil-flask, I drive a peg into the wall. Well, then, are these things superior to me? No, but they supply some of my wants, and for this reason I take care of them. Well, do I not attend to my ass? Do I not wash his feet? Do I not clean him? Do you not know that every man has regard to himself, and to you just the same as he has regard to his ass? For who has regard to you as a man? Show me. Who wishes to become like you? Who imitates you, as he imitates Socrates? But I can cut off your head. You say right. I had forgotten that I must have regard to you, as I would to a fever and the bile, and raise an altar to you, as there is at Rome an altar to fever. What is it then that disturbs and terrifies the multitude? Is it the tyrant and his guards? (By no means.) I hope that it is not so. It is not possible that what is by nature free can be disturbed by anything else, or hindered by any other thing than by itself. But it is a man's own opinions which disturb him. For when the tyrant says to a man, I will chain your leg, he who values his leg says, Do not; have pity. But he who values his own will says, If it appears more advantageous to you, chain it. Do you not care? I do not care. I will show you that I am master. You cannot do that. Zeus has set me free; do you think that he intended to allow his own son to be enslaved? But you are master of my carcase; take it. So when you approach me, you have no regard to me? No, but I have regard to myself; and if you wish me to say that I have regard to you also, I tell you that I have the same regard to you that I have to my pipkin. What then? When absurd notions about things independent of our will, as if they were good and (or) bad, lie at the bottom of our opinions, we must of necessity pay regard to tyrants: for I wish that men would pay regard to tyrants only, and not also to the bedchamber men. How is it that the man becomes all at once wise, when Cæsar has made him superintendent of the close stool? How is it that we say immediately, Felicion spoke sensibly to me? I wish he were ejected from the bedchamber, that he might again appear to you to be a fool.

Has a man been exalted to the tribuneship? All who meet him offer their congratulations; one kisses his eyes, another the neck, and the slaves kiss his hands. He goes to his house, he finds torches lighted. He ascends the Capitol; he offers a sacrifice on the occasion. Now who ever sacrificed for having had good desires? for having acted conformably to nature? For in fact we thank the gods for those things in which we place our good.

A person was talking to me to-day about the priesthood of Augustus. I say to him: Man, let the thing alone; you will spend much for no purpose. But he replies, Those who draw up agreements will write my name. Do you then stand by those who read them, and say to such persons, It is I whose name is written there? And if you can now be present on all such occasions, what will you do when you are dead? My name will remain. Write it on a stone, and it will remain. But come, what remembrance of you will there be beyond Nicopolis? But I shall wear a crown of gold. If you desire a crown at all, take a crown of roses and put it on, for it will be more elegant in appearance.

AGAINST THOSE WHO WISH TO BE ADMIRED

When a man holds his proper station in life, he does not gape after things beyond it. Man, what do you wish to happen to you? I am satisfied if I desire and avoid conformably to nature, if I employ movements towards and from an object as I am by nature formed to do, and purpose and design and assent. Why then do you strut before us as if you had swallowed a spit? My wish has always been that those who meet me should admire me, and those who follow me should exclaim, O the great philosopher! Who are they by whom you wish to be admired? Are they not those of whom you are used to say that they are mad? Well, then, do you wish to be admired by madmen?

ON PRECOGNITIONS

Precognitions are common to all men, and precognition is not contradictory to precognition. For who of us does not assume that Good is useful and eligible, and in all circumstances that we ought to follow and pursue it? And who of us does not assume that Justice is beautiful and becoming? When then does the contradiction arise? It arises in the adaptation of the præcognitions to the particular cases. When one man says, "He has done well; he is a brave man," and another says, "Not so; but he has acted foolishly," then the disputes arise among men. This is the dispute among the Jews and the Syrians and the Egyptians and the Romans; not whether holiness should be preferred to all things and in all cases should be pursued, but whether it is holy to eat pig's flesh or not holy. You will find this dispute also between Agamemnon and Achilles; for call them forth. What do you say, Agamemnon? ought not that to be done which is proper and right? "Certainly." Well, what do you say, Achilles? do you not admit that what is good ought to be done? "I do most certainly." Adapt your præcognitions then to the present matter. Here the dispute begins. Agamemnon says, "I ought not to give up Chryseis to her father." Achilles says, "You ought." It is certain that one of the two makes a wrong adaptation of the præcognition of "ought" or "duty." Further, Agamemnon says, "Then if I ought to restore Chryseis, it is fit that I take his prize from some of you." Achilles replies, "Would you then take her whom I love?" "Yes, her whom you love." "Must I then be the only man who goes without a prize? and must I be the only man who has no prize?" Thus the dispute begins.

What then is education? Education is the learning how to adapt the natural præcognitions to the particular things conformably to nature; and then to distinguish that of things some are in our power, but others are not. In our power are will and all acts which depend on the will; things not in our power are the body, the parts of the body, possessions, parents, brothers, children, country, and, generally, all with whom we live in society. In what then should we place the good? To what kind of things ([Greek: ousia]) shall we adapt it? To the things which are in our power? Is not health then a good thing, and soundness of limb, and life, and are not children and parents and country? Who will tolerate you if you deny this?

Let us then transfer the notion of good to these things. Is it possible, then, when a man sustains damage and does not obtain good things, that he can be happy? It is not possible. And can he maintain towards society a proper behavior? He can not. For I am naturally formed to look after my own interest. If it is my interest to have an estate in land, it is my interest also to take it from my neighbor. If it is my interest to have a garment, it is my interest also to steal it from the bath. This is the origin of wars, civil commotions, tyrannies, conspiracies. And how shall I be still able to maintain my duty towards Zeus? For if I sustain damage and am unlucky, he takes no care of me. And what is he to me if he cannot help me? And further, what is he to me if he allows me to be in the condition in which I am? I now begin to hate him. Why then do we build temples, why setup statues to Zeus, as well as to evil demons, such as to Fever; and how is Zeus the Saviour, and how the giver of rain, and the giver of fruits? And in truth if we place the nature of Good in any such things, all this follows.

What should we do then? This is the inquiry of the true philosopher who is in labor. Now I do not see what the good is nor the bad. Am I not mad? Yes. But suppose that I place the good somewhere among the things which depend on the will; all will laugh at me. There will come some greyhead wearing many gold rings on his fingers, and he will shake his head and say: "Hear, my child. It is right that you should philosophize; but you ought to have some brains also; all this that you are doing is silly. You learn the syllogism from philosophers; but you know how to act better than philosophers do." Man why then do you blame me, if I know? What shall I say to this slave? If I am silent, he will burst.

I must speak in this way: "Excuse me, as you would excuse lovers; I am not my own master; I am mad."

HOW WE SHOULD STRUGGLE WITH CIRCUMSTANCES

It is circumstances (difficulties) which show what men are. Therefore when a difficulty falls upon you, remember that God, like a trainer of wrestlers, has matched you with a rough young man. For what purpose? you may say. Why, that you may become an Olympic conqueror; but it is not accomplished without sweat. In my opinion no man has had a more profitable difficulty than you have had, if you choose to make use of it as an athlete would deal with a young antagonist. We are now sending a scout to Rome; but no man sends a cowardly scout, who, if he only hears a noise and sees a shadow anywhere, comes running back in terror and reports that the enemy is close at hand. So now if you should come and tell us: "Fearful is the state of affairs at Rome; terrible is death; terrible is exile; terrible is calumny; terrible is poverty; fly, my friends, the enemy is near," we shall answer: "Begone, prophesy for yourself; we have committed only one fault, that we sent such a scout."
Diogenes, who was sent as a scout before you, made a different report to us. He says that death is no evil, for neither is it base; he says that fame (reputation) is the noise of madmen. And what has this spy said about pain, about pleasure, and about poverty? He says that to be naked is better than any purple robe, and to sleep on the bare ground is the softest bed; and he gives as a proof of each thing that he affirms his own courage, his tranquillity, his freedom, and the healthy appearance and compactness of his body. There is no enemy near, he says; all is peace. How so, Diogenes? "See," he replies, "if I am struck, if I have been wounded, if I have fled from any man." This is what a scout ought to be. But you come to us and tell us one thing after another. Will you not go back, and you will see clearer when you have laid aside fear?

ON THE SAME

If these things are true, and if we are not silly, and are not acting hypocritically when we say that the good of man is in the will, and the evil too, and that everything else does not concern us, why are we still disturbed, why are we still afraid? The things about which we have been busied are in no man's power; and the things which are in the power of others, we care not for. What kind of trouble have we still?
But give me directions. Why should I give you directions? Has not Zeus given you directions? Has he not given to you what is your own free from hindrance and free from impediment, and what is not your own subject to hindrance and impediment? What directions then, what kind of orders did you bring when you came from him? Keep by every means what is your own; do not desire what belongs to others. Fidelity (integrity) is your own, virtuous shame is your own; who then can take these things from you? who else than yourself will hinder you from using them? But how do you act? When you seek what is not your own, you lose that which is your own. Having such promptings and

commands from Zeus, what kind do you still ask from me? Am I more powerful than he, am I more worthy of confidence? But if you observe these, do you want any others besides? "Well, but he has not given these orders," you will say. Produce your prcognitions ([Greek: prolaepseis]), produce these proofs of philosophers, produce what you have often heard, and produce what you have said yourself, produce what you have read, produce what you have meditated on; and you will then see that all these things are from God.

If I have set my admiration on the poor body, I have given myself up to be a slave; if on my poor possessions, I also make myself a slave. For I immediately make it plain with what I may be caught; as if the snake draws in his head, I tell you to strike that part of him which he guards; and do you be assured that whatever part you choose to guard, that part your master will attack. Remembering this, whom will you still flatter or fear?

But I should like to sit where the Senators sit. Do you see that you are putting yourself in straits, you are squeezing yourself? How then shall I see well in any other way in the amphitheatre? Man, do not be a spectator at all, and you will not be squeezed. Why do you give yourself trouble? Or wait a little, and when the spectacle is over, seat yourself in the place reserved for the Senators and sun yourself. For remember this general truth, that it is we who squeeze ourselves, who put ourselves in straits; that is, our opinions squeeze us and put us in straits. For what is it to be reviled? Stand by a stone and revile it, and what will you gain? If then a man listens like a stone, what profit is there to the reviler? But if the reviler has as a stepping-stone (or ladder) the weakness of him who is reviled, then he accomplishes something. Strip him. What do you mean by him? Lay hold of his garment, strip it off. I have insulted you. Much good may it do you.

This was the practice of Socrates; this was the reason why he always had one face. But we choose to practise and study anything rather than the means by which we shall be unimpeded and free. You say: "Philosophers talk paradoxes." But are there no paradoxes in the other arts? And what is more paradoxical than to puncture a man's eye in order that he may see? If any one said this to a man ignorant of the surgical art, would he not ridicule the speaker? Where is the wonder, then, if in philosophy also many things which are true appear paradoxical to the inexperienced?

IN HOW MANY WAYS APPEARANCES EXIST, AND WHAT AIDS WE SHOULD PROVIDE AGAINST THEM

Appearances are to us in four ways. For either things appear as they are; or they are not, and do not even appear to be; or they are, and do not appear to be; or they are not, and yet appear to be. Further, in all these cases to form a right judgment (to hit the mark) is the office of an educated man. But whatever it is that annoys (troubles) us, to that we ought to apply a remedy. If the sophisms of Pyrrho and of the Academics are what annoys (troubles), we must apply the remedy to them. If it is the persuasion of appearances, by which some things appear to be good, when they are not good, let us seek a remedy for this. If it is habit which annoys us, we must try to seek aid against habit. What aid, then, can we find against habit? The contrary habit. You hear the ignorant say: "That unfortunate person is dead; his father and mother are overpowered with sorrow; he was cut off by an untimely death and in a foreign land." Hear the contrary way of speaking. Tear yourself from these expressions; oppose to one habit the contrary habit; to sophistry oppose reason, and the exercise and discipline of reason; against persuasive (deceitful) appearances we ought to have manifest præcognitions ([Greek: prolaepseis]), cleared of all impurities and ready to hand.

When death appears an evil, we ought to have this rule in readiness, that it is fit to avoid evil things, and that death is a necessary thing. For what shall I do, and where shall I escape it? Suppose that I am not Sarpedon, the son of Zeus, nor able to speak in this noble way. I will go and I am resolved either to behave bravely myself or to give to another the opportunity of doing so; if I cannot succeed in doing anything myself, I will not grudge another the doing of something noble. Suppose that it is above our power to act thus; is it not in our power to reason thus? Tell me where I can escape death; discover for me the country, show me the men to whom I must go, whom death does not visit. Discover to me a charm against death. If I have not one, what do you wish me to do? I cannot escape from death. Shall I not escape from the fear of death, but shall I die lamenting and trembling? For the origin of perturbation is this, to wish for something, and that this should not happen. Therefore if I am able to change externals according to my wish, I change them; but if I cannot, I am ready to tear out the eyes of him who hinders me. For the nature of man is not to endure to be deprived of the good, and not to endure the falling into the evil. Then at last, when I am neither able to change circumstances nor to tear out the eyes of him who hinders me, I sit down and groan, and abuse whom I can, Zeus and the rest of the gods. For if they do not care for me, what are they to me? Yes, but you will be an impious man. In what respect, then, will it be worse for me than it is now? To sum up, remember that unless piety and your interest be in the same thing, piety cannot be maintained in any man. Do not these things seem necessary (true)?

THAT WE OUGHT NOT TO BE ANGRY WITH MEN; AND WHAT ARE THE SMALL AND THE GREAT THINGS AMONG MEN

What is the cause of assenting to anything? The fact that it appears to be true. It is not possible then to assent to that which appears not to be true. Why? Because this is the nature of the understanding, to incline to the true, to be dissatisfied with the false, and in matters uncertain to withhold assent. What is the proof of this? Imagine (persuade yourself), if you can, that it is now night. It is not possible. Take away your persuasion that it is day. It is not possible. Persuade yourself or take away your persuasion that the stars are even in number. It is impossible. When then any man assents to that which is false, be assured that he did not intend to assent to it as false, for every soul is unwillingly deprived of the truth, as Plato says; but the falsity seemed to him to be true. Well, in acts what have we of the like kind as we have here truth or falsehood? We have the fit and the not fit (duty and not duty), the profitable and the unprofitable, that which is suitable to a person and that which is not, and whatever is like these. Can then a man think that a thing is useful to him and not choose it? He cannot. How says Medea?

"'Tis true I know what evil I shall do,
But passion overpowers the better counsel."

She thought that to indulge her passion and take vengeance on her husband was more profitable than to spare her children. It was so; but she was deceived. Show her plainly that she is deceived, and she will not do it; but so long as you do not show it, what can she follow except that which appears to herself (her opinion)? Nothing else. Why then are you angry with the unhappy woman that she has been bewildered about the most important things, and is become a viper instead of a human creature? And why not, if it is possible, rather pity, as we pity the blind and the lame, so those who are blinded and maimed in the faculties which are supreme?

Whoever then clearly remembers this, that to man the measure of every act is the appearance (the opinion), whether the thing appears good or bad. If good, he is free from blame; if bad, himself suffers the penalty, for it is impossible that he who is deceived can be one person, and he who suffers another person—whoever remembers this will not be angry with any man, will not be vexed at any man, will not revile or blame any man, nor hate, nor quarrel with any man.

So then all these great and dreadful deeds have this origin, in the appearance (opinion)? Yes, this origin and no other. The Iliad is nothing else than appearance and the use of appearances. It appeared to Alexander to carry off the wife of Menelaus. It appeared to Helene to follow him. If then it had appeared to Menelaus to feel that it was a gain to be deprived of such a wife, what would have happened? Not only would the Iliad have been lost, but the Odyssey also. On so small a matter then did such great things depend? But what do you mean by such great things? Wars and civil commotions, and the destruction of many men and cities. And what great matter is this? Is it nothing? But what great matter is the death of many oxen, and many sheep, and many nests of swallows or storks being burnt or destroyed? Are these things then like those? Very like. Bodies of men are destroyed, and the bodies of oxen and sheep; the dwellings of men are burnt, and the nests of storks. What is there in this great or dreadful? Or show me what is the difference between a man's house and a stork's nest, as far as each is a dwelling; except that man builds his little houses of beams and tiles and bricks, and the stork builds them of sticks and mud. Are a stork and a man then like things? What say you? In body they are very much alike.

Does a man then differ in no respect from a stork? Don't suppose that I say so; but there is no difference in these matters (which I have mentioned). In what then is the difference? Seek and you will find that there is a difference in another matter. See whether it is not in a man the understanding of what he does, see if it is not in social community, in fidelity, in modesty, in steadfastness, in intelligence. Where then is the great good and evil in men? It is where the difference is. If the difference is preserved and remains fenced round, and neither modesty is destroyed, nor fidelity, nor intelligence, then the man also is preserved; but if any of these things is destroyed and stormed like a city, then the man too perishes: and in this consist the great things. Alexander, you say, sustained great damage then when the Hellenes invaded and when they ravaged Troy, and when his brothers perished. By no means; for no man is damaged by an action which is not his own; but what happened at that time was only the destruction of stork's nests. Now the ruin of Alexander was when he lost the character of modesty, fidelity, regard to hospitality, and to decency. When was Achilles ruined? Was it when Patroclus died? Not so. But it happened when he began to be angry, when he wept for a girl, when he forgot that he was at Troy not to get mistresses, but to fight. These things are the ruin of men, this is being besieged, this is the destruction of cities, when right opinions are destroyed, when they are corrupted.

ON CONSTANCY (OR FIRMNESS)

The being (nature) of the good is a certain will; the being of the bad is a certain kind of will. What, then, are externals? Materials for the will, about which the will being conversant shall obtain its own good or evil. How shall it obtain the good? If it does not admire (over-value) the materials; for the opinions about the materials, if the opinions are right, make the will good: but perverse and distorted opinions make the will bad. God has fixed this law, and says, "If you would have anything good, receive it from yourself." You say, No, but I will have it from another. Do not so: but receive it from yourself. Therefore when the tyrant threatens and calls me, I say, Whom do you threaten? If he says, I will put you in chains, I say, You threaten my hands and my feet. If he says, I will cut off your head, I reply, You threaten my head. If he says, I will throw you into prison, I say, You threaten the whole of this poor body. If he threatens me with banishment, I say the same. Does he then not threaten you at all? If I feel that all these things do not concern me, he does not threaten me at all; but if I fear any of them, it is I whom he threatens. Whom then do I fear? the master of what? The master of things which are in my own power? There is no such master. Do I fear the master of things which are not in my power? And what are these things to me?

Do you philosophers then teach us to despise kings? I hope not. Who among us teaches to claim against them the power over things which they possess? Take my poor body, take my property, take my reputation, take those who are about me. If I advise any persons to claim these things, they may truly accuse me. Yes, but I intend to command your opinions also. And who has given you this power? How can you conquer the opinion of another man? By applying terror to it, he replies, I will conquer it. Do you not know that opinion conquers itself, and is not conquered by another? But nothing else can conquer will except the will itself. For this reason too the law of God is most powerful and most just, which is this: Let the stronger always be superior to the weaker. Ten are stronger than one. For what? For putting in chains, for killing, for dragging whither they choose, for taking away what a man has. The ten therefore conquer the one in this in which they are stronger. In what then are the ten weaker? If the one possesses right opinions and the others do not. Well then, can the ten conquer in this matter? How is it possible? If we were placed in the scales, must not the heavier draw down the scale in which it is.

How strange then that Socrates should have been so treated by the Athenians. Slave, why do you say Socrates? Speak of the thing as it is: how strange that the poor body of Socrates should have been carried off and dragged to prison by stronger men, and that anyone should have given hemlock to the poor body of Socrates, and that it should breathe out the life. Do these things seem strange, do they seem unjust, do you on account of these things blame God? Had Socrates then no equivalent for these things? Where then for him was the nature of good? Whom shall we listen to, you or him? And what does Socrates say? "Anytus and Melitus can kill me, but they cannot hurt me." And further, he says, "If it so pleases God, so let it be."

But show me that he who has the inferior principles overpowers him who is superior in principles. You will never show this, nor come near showing it; for this is the law of nature and of God that the superior shall always overpower the inferior. In what? In that in which it is superior. One body is stronger than another: many are stronger than one: the thief is stronger than he who is not a thief. This is the reason why I also lost my lamp, because in wakefulness the thief was superior to me. But the man bought the lamp at this price: for a lamp he became a thief, a faithless fellow, and like a wild beast. This seemed to him a good bargain. Be it so. But a man has seized me by the cloak, and is drawing me to the public place: then others bawl out, Philosopher, what has been the use of your opinions? see, you are dragged to prison, you are going to be beheaded. And what system of philosophy ([Greek: eisagogaen)] could I have made so that, if a stronger man should have laid hold of my cloak, I should not be dragged off; that if ten men should have laid hold of me and cast me into prison, I should not be cast in? Have I learned nothing else then? I have learned to see that everything which happens, if it be independent of my will, is nothing to me. I may ask, if you have not gained by this. Why then do you seek advantage in anything else than in that in which you have learned that advantage is?

Will you not leave the small arguments ([Greek: logaria]) about these matters to others, to lazy fellows, that they may sit in a corner and receive their sorry pay, or grumble that no one gives them anything; and will you not come forward and make use of what you have learned? For it is not these small arguments that are wanted now; the writings of the Stoics are full of them. What then is the thing which is wanted? A man who shall apply them, one who by his acts shall bear testimony to his words. Assume, I intreat you, this character, that we may no longer use in the schools the examples of the ancients, but may have some example of our own.

To whom then does the contemplation of these matters (philosophical inquiries) belong? To him who has leisure, for man is an animal that loves contemplation. But it is shameful to contemplate these things as runaway slaves do; we should sit, as in a theatre, free from distraction, and listen at one time to the tragic actor, at another time to the lute-player; and not do as slaves do. As soon as the slave has taken his station he praises the actor and at the same time looks round; then if any one calls out his master's name, the slave is immediately frightened and disturbed. It is shameful for philosophers thus to contemplate the works of nature. For what is a master? Man is not the master of man; but death is, and life and pleasure and pain; for if he comes without these things, bring Caesar to me and you will see how firm I am. But when he shall come with these things, thundering and lightning, and when I am afraid of them, what do I do then except to recognize my master like the runaway slave? But so long as I have any respite from these terrors, as a runaway slave stands in the theatre, so do I. I bathe, I drink, I sing; but all this I do with terror and uneasiness. But if I shall release myself from my masters, that is from those things by means of which masters are formidable, what further trouble have I, what master have I still?

What then, ought we to publish these things to all men? No, but we ought to accommodate ourselves to the ignorant ([Greek: tois idiotais]) and to say: "This man recommends to me that which he thinks good for himself. I excuse him." For Socrates also excused the jailer who had the charge of him in prison and was weeping when Socrates was going to drink the poison, and said, "How generously he laments over us." Does he then say to the jailer that for this reason we have sent away the women? No, but he says it to his friends who were able to hear (understand) it; and he treats the jailer as a child.

THAT CONFIDENCE (COURAGE) IS NOT INCONSISTENT WITH CAUTION

The opinion of the philosophers perhaps seem to some to be a paradox; but still let us examine as well as we can, if it is true that it is possible to do everything both with caution and with confidence. For caution seems to be in a manner contrary to confidence, and contraries are in no way consistent. That which seems to many to be a paradox in the matter under consideration in my opinion is of this kind; if we asserted that we ought to employ caution and confidence in the same things, men might justly accuse us of bringing together things which cannot be united. But now where is the difficulty in what is said? for if these things are true, which have been often said and often proved, that the nature of good is in the use of appearances, and the nature of evil likewise, and that things independent of our will do not admit either the nature of evil or of good, what paradox do the philosophers assert if they say that where things are not dependent on the will, there you should employ confidence, but where they are dependent on the will, there you should employ caution? For if the bad consists in the bad exercise of the will, caution ought only to be used where things are dependent on the will. But if things independent of the will and not in our power are nothing to us, with respect to these we must employ confidence; and thus we shall both be cautious and confident, and indeed confident because of our caution. For by employing caution towards things which are really bad, it will result that we shall have confidence with respect to things which are not so.

We are then in the condition of deer; when they flee from the huntsmen's feathers in fright, whither do they turn and in what do they seek refuge as safe? They turn to the nets, and thus they perish by confounding things which are objects of fear with things that they ought not to fear. Thus we also act: in what cases do we fear? In things which are independent of the will. In what cases on the contrary do we behave with confidence, as if there were no danger? In things dependent on the will. To be deceived then, or to act rashly, or shamelessly, or with base desire to seek something, does not concern us at all, if we only hit the mark in things which are independent of our will. But where there is death or exile or pain or infamy, there we attempt to run away, there we are struck with terror. Therefore, as we may expect it to happen with those who err in the greatest matters, we convert natural confidence (that is, according to nature) into audacity, desperation, rashness, shamelessness; and we convert natural caution and modesty into cowardice and meanness, which are full of fear and confusion. For if a man should transfer caution to those things in which the will may be exercised and the acts of the will, he will immediately by willing to be cautious have also the power of avoiding what he chooses; but if he transfer it to the things which are not in his power and will, and attempt to avoid the things which are in the power of others, he will of necessity fear, he will be unstable, he will be disturbed; for death or pain is not formidable, but the fear of pain or death. For this reason we commend the poet, who said:

"Not death is evil, but a shameful death."

Confidence (courage) then ought to be employed against death, and caution against the fear of death. But now we do the contrary, and employ against death the attempt to escape; and to our opinion about it we employ carelessness, rashness, and indifference. These things Socrates properly used to call tragic masks; for as to children masks appear terrible and fearful from inexperience, we also are affected in like manner by events (the things which happen in life) for no other reason than children are by masks. For what is a child? Ignorance. What is a child? Want of knowledge. For when a child knows these things, he is in no way inferior to us. What is death? A tragic mask. Turn it and examine it. See, it does not bite. The poor body must be separated from the spirit either now or later as it was separated from it before. Why then are you troubled if it be separated now? for if it is not separated now, it will be separated afterwards. Why? That the period of the universe may be completed, for it has need of the present, and of the future, and of the past. What is pain? A mask. Turn it and examine it. The poor flesh is moved roughly, then on the contrary smoothly. If this does not satisfy (please) you, the door is open; if it does, bear (with things). For the door ought to be open for all occasions; and so we have no trouble.

What then is the fruit of these opinions? It is that which ought to be the most noble and the most becoming to those who are really educated, release from perturbation, release from fear. Freedom. For in these matters we must not believe the many, who say that free persons only ought to be educated, but we should rather believe the philosophers who say that the educated only are free. How is this? In this manner: Is freedom anything else than the power of living as we choose? Nothing else. Tell me then, ye men, do you wish to live in error? We do not. No one then who lives in error is free. Do you wish to live in fear? Do you wish to live in sorrow? Do you wish to live in perturbation? By no means. No one then who is in a state of fear or sorrow or perturbation is free; but whoever is delivered from sorrows and fears and perturbations, he is at the same time also delivered from servitude. How then can we continue to believe you, most dear legislators, when you say, We only allow free persons to be educated? For philosophers say we allow none to be free except the educated; that is, God does not allow it. When then a man has turned round before the prætor his own slave, has he done nothing? He has done something. What? He has turned round his own slave before the prætor. Has he done nothing more? Yes: he is also bound to pay for him the tax called the twentieth. Well then, is not the man who has gone through this ceremony become free? No more than he is become free from perturbations. Have you who are able to turn round (free) others no master? is not money your master, or a girl or a boy, or some tyrant or some friend of the tyrant? Why do you trouble then when you are going off to any trial (danger) of this kind? It is for this reason that I often say, study and hold in readiness these principles by which you may determine what those things are with reference to which you ought to be cautious, courageous in that which does not depend on your will, cautious in that which does depend on it.

OF TRANQUILLITY (FREEDOM FROM PERTURBATION)

Consider, you who are going into court, what you wish to maintain and what you wish to succeed in. For if you wish to maintain a will conformable to nature, you have every security, every facility, you have no troubles. For if you wish to maintain what is in your own power and is naturally free, and if you are content with these, what else do you care for? For who is the master of such things? Who can take them away? If you choose to be modest and faithful, who shall not allow you to be so? If you choose not to be restrained or compelled, who shall compel you to desire what you think that you ought not to desire? who shall compel you to avoid what you do not think fit to avoid? But what do you say? The judge will determine against you something that appears formidable; but that you should also suffer in trying to avoid it, how can he do that? When then the pursuit of objects and the avoiding of them are in your power, what else do you care for? Let this be your preface, this your narrative, this your confirmation, this your victory, this your peroration, this your applause (or the approbation which you will receive).

Therefore Socrates said to one who was reminding him to prepare for his trial, Do you not think then that I have been preparing for it all my life? By what kind of preparation? I have maintained that which was in my own power. How then? I have never done anything unjust either in my private or in my public life.

But if you wish to maintain externals also, your poor body, your little property, and your little estimation, I advise you to make from this moment all possible preparation, and then consider both the nature of your judge and your adversary. If it is necessary to embrace his knees, embrace his knees; if to weep, weep; if to groan, groan. For when you have subjected to externals what is your own, then be a slave and do not resist, and do not sometimes choose to be a slave, and sometimes not choose, but with all your mind be one or the other, either free or a slave, either instructed or uninstructed, either a well-bred cock or a mean one, either endure to be beaten until you die or yield at once; and let it not happen to you to receive many stripes and then to yield. But if these things are base, determine immediately. Where is the nature of evil and good? It is where truth is: where truth is and where nature is, there is caution: where truth is, there is courage where nature is.

For this reason also it is ridiculous to say, Suggest something to me (tell me what to do). What should I suggest to you? Well, form my mind so as to accommodate itself to any event. Why that is just the same as if a man who is ignorant of letters should say, Tell me what to write when any name is proposed to me. For if I should tell him to write Dion, and then another should come and propose to him not the name of Dion but that of Theon, what will be done? what will he write? But if you have practised writing, you are also prepared to write (or to do) anything that is required. If you are not, what can I now suggest? For if circumstances require something else, what will you say, or what will you do? Remember then this general precept and you will need no suggestion. But if you gape after externals, you must of necessity ramble up and down in obedience to the will of your master. And who is the master? He who has the power over the things which you seek to gain or try to avoid.

HOW MAGNANIMITY IS CONSISTENT WITH CARE

Things themselves (materials) are indifferent; but the use of them is not indifferent. How then shall a man preserve firmness and tranquillity, and at the same time be careful and neither rash nor negligent? If he imitates those who play at dice. The counters are indifferent; the dice are indifferent. How do I know what the cast will be? But to use carefully and dexterously the cast of the dice, this is my business. Thus then in life also the chief business is this: distinguish and separate things, and say: Externals are not in my power: will is in my power. Where shall I seek the good and the bad? Within, in the things which are my own. But in what does not belong to you call nothing either good or bad, or profit or damage or anything of the kind.

What then? Should we use such things carelessly? In no way: for this on the other hand is bad for the faculty of the will, and consequently against nature; but we should act carefully because the use is not indifferent, and we should also act with firmness and freedom from perturbations because the material is indifferent. For where the material is not indifferent, there no man can hinder me or compel me. Where I can be hindered and compelled, the obtaining of those things is not in my power, nor is it good or bad; but the use is either bad or good, and the use is in my power. But it is difficult to mingle and to bring together these two things—the carefulness of him who is affected by the matter (or things about him), and the firmness of him who has no regard for it; but it is not impossible: and if it is, happiness is impossible. But we should act as we do in the case of a voyage. What can I do? I can choose the master of the ship, the sailors, the day, the opportunity. Then comes a storm. What more have I to care for? for my part is done. The business belongs to another, the master. But the ship is sinking—what then have I to do? I do the only thing that I can, not to be drowned full of fear, nor screaming nor blaming God, but knowing that what has been produced must also perish: for I am not an immortal being, but a man, a part of the whole, as an hour is a part of the day: I must be present like the hour, and past like the hour. What difference then does it make to me how I pass away, whether by being suffocated or by a fever, for I must pass through some such means.

How then is it said that some external things are according to nature and others contrary to nature? It is said as it might be said if we were separated from union (or society): for to the foot I shall say that it is according to nature for it to be clean; but if you take it as a foot and as a thing not detached (independent), it will befit it both to step into the mud and tread on thorns, and sometimes to be cut off for the good of the whole body; otherwise it is no longer a foot. We should think in some such way about ourselves also. What are you? A man. If you consider yourself as detached from other men, it is according to nature to live to old age, to be rich, to be healthy. But if you consider yourself as a man and a part of a certain whole, it is for the sake of that whole that at one time you should be sick, at another time take a voyage and run into danger, and at another time be in want, and in some cases die prematurely. Why then are you troubled? Do you not know, that as a foot is no longer a foot if it is detached from the body, so you are no longer a man if you are separated from other men. For what is a man? A part of a state, of that first which consists of gods and of men; then of that which is called next to it, which is a small image of the universal state. What then must I be brought to trial; must another have a fever, another sail on the sea, another die, and another be condemned? Yes, for it is impossible in such a universe of things, among so many living together, that such things should not happen, some to one and others to others. It is your duty then since you are come here, to say what you ought, to arrange these things as it is fit. Then some one says, "I shall charge you with doing me wrong." Much good may it do you: I have done my part; but whether you also have done yours, you must look to that; for there is some danger of this too, that it may escape your notice.

OF INDIFFERENCE

The hypothetical proposition is indifferent: the judgment about it is not indifferent, but it is either knowledge or opinion or error. Thus life is indifferent: the use is not indifferent. When any man then tells you that these things also are indifferent, do not become negligent; and when a man invites you to be careful (about such things), do not become abject and struck with admiration of material things. And it is good for you to know your own preparation and power, that in those matters where you have not been prepared, you may keep quiet, and not be vexed, if others have the advantage over you. For you too in syllogisms will claim to have the advantage over them; and if others should be vexed at this, you will console them by saying, "I have learned them, and you have not." Thus also where there is need of any practice, seek not that which is acquired from the need (of such practice), but yield in that matter to those who have had practice, and be yourself content with firmness of mind.

Go and salute a certain person. How? Not meanly. But I have been shut out, for I have not learned to make my way through the window; and when I have found the door shut, I must either come back or enter through the window. But still speak to him. In what way? Not meanly. But suppose that you have not got what you wanted. Was this your business, and not his? Why then do you claim that which belongs to another? Always remember what is your own, and what belongs to another; and you will not be disturbed. Chrysippus therefore said well, So long as future things are uncertain, I always cling to those which are more adapted to the conservation of that which is according to nature; for God himself has given me the faculty of such choice. But if I knew that it was fated (in the order of things) for me to be sick, I would even move towards it; for the foot also, if it had intelligence, would move to go into the mud. For why are ears of corn produced? Is it not that they may become dry? And do they not become dry that they may be reaped? for they are not separated from communion with other things. If then they had perception, ought they to wish never to be reaped? But this is a curse upon ears of corn to be never reaped. So we must know that in the case of men too it is a curse not to die, just the same as not to be ripened and not to be reaped. But since we must be reaped, and we also know that we are reaped, we are vexed at it; for we neither know what we are nor have we studied what belongs to man, as those who have studied horses know what belongs to horses. But Chrysantas when he was going to strike the enemy checked himself when he heard the trumpet sounding a retreat: so it seemed better to him to obey the general's command than to follow his own inclination. But not one of us chooses, even when necessity summons, readily to obey it, but weeping and groaning we suffer what we do suffer, and we call them "circumstances." What kind of circumstances, man? If you give the name of circumstances to the things which are around you, all things are circumstances; but if you call hardships by this name, what hardship is there in the dying of that which has been produced? But that which destroys is either a sword, or a wheel, or the sea, or a tile, or a tyrant. Why do you care about the way of going down to Hades? All ways are equal. But if you will listen to the truth, the way which the tyrant sends you is shorter. A tyrant never killed a man in six months: but a fever is often a year about it. All these things are only sound and the noise of empty names.

HOW WE OUGHT TO USE DIVINATION

Through an unreasonable regard to divination many of us omit many duties. For what more can the diviner see than death or danger or disease, or generally things of that kind? If then I must expose myself to danger for a friend, and if it is my duty even to die for him, what need have I then for divination? Have I not within me a diviner who has told me the nature of good and of evil, and has explained to me the signs (or marks) of both? What need have I then to consult the viscera of victims or the flight of birds, and why do I submit when he says, It is for your interest? For does he know what is for my interest, does he know what is good; and as he has learned the signs of the viscera, has he also learned the signs of good and evil? For if he knows the signs of these, he knows the signs both of the beautiful and of the ugly, and of the just and of the unjust. Do you tell me, man, what is the thing which is signified for me: is it life or death, poverty or wealth? But whether these things are for my interest or whether they are not, I do not intend to ask you. Why don't you give your opinion on matters of grammar, and why do you give it here about things on which we are all in error and disputing with one another?

What then leads us to frequent use of divination? Cowardice, the dread of what will happen. This is the reason why we flatter the diviners. Pray, master, shall I succeed to the property of my father? Let us see: let us sacrifice on the occasion. Yes, master, as fortune chooses. When he has said, You shall succeed to the inheritance, we thank him as if we received the inheritance from him. The consequence is that they play upon us.

Will you not then seek the nature of good in the rational animal? for if it is not there, you will not choose to say that it exists in any other thing (plant or animal). What then? are not plants and animals also the works of God? They are; but they are not superior things, nor yet parts of the gods. But you are a superior thing; you are a portion separated from the Deity; you have in yourself a certain portion of him. Why then are you ignorant of your own noble descent? Why do you not know whence you came? will you not remember when you are eating who you are who eat and whom you feed? When you are in social intercourse, when you are exercising yourself, when you are engaged in discussion, know you not that you are nourishing a god, that you are exercising a god? Wretch, you are carrying about a god with you, and you know it not. Do you think that I mean some god of silver or of gold, and external? You carry him within yourself, and you perceive not that you are polluting him by impure thoughts and dirty deeds. And if an image of God were present, you would not dare to do any of the things which you are doing; but when God himself is present within and sees all and hears all, you are not ashamed of thinking such things and doing such things, ignorant as you are of your own nature and subject to the anger of God. Then why do we fear when we are sending a young man from the school into active life, lest he should do anything improperly, eat improperly, have improper intercourse with women; and lest the rags in which he is wrapped should debase him, lest fine garments should make him proud. This youth (if he acts thus) does not know his own God; he knows not with whom he sets out (into the world). But can we endure when he says, "I wish I had you (God) with me." Have you not God with you? and do you seek for any other when you have him? or will God tell you anything else than this? If you were a statue of Phidias, either Athena or Zeus, you would think both of yourself and of the artist, and if you had any understanding (power of perception) you would try to do nothing unworthy of him who made you or of yourself, and try not to appear in an unbecoming dress (attitude) to those who look upon you. But now because Zeus has made you, for this reason do you care not how you shall appear? And yet is the artist (in the one case) like the artist in the other? or the work in the one case like the other? And what work of an artist, for instance, has in itself the faculties, which the artist shows in making it? Is it not marble or bronze, or gold or ivory? and the Athena of Phidias, when she has once extended the hand and received in it the figure of Victory, stands in that attitude for ever. But the works of God have power of motion, they breathe, they have the faculty of using the appearances of things and the power of examining them. Being the work of such an artist do you dishonor him? And what shall I say, not only that he made you, but also entrusted you to yourself and made you a deposit to yourself? Will you not think of this too, but do you also dishonor your guardianship? But if God had entrusted an orphan to you, would you thus neglect him? He has delivered yourself to your own care, and says: "I had no one fitter to entrust him to than yourself; keep him for me such as he is by nature, modest, faithful, erect, unterrified, free from passion and perturbation." And then you do not keep him such.

But some will say, Whence has this fellow got the arrogance which he displays and these supercilious looks? I have not yet so much gravity as befits a philosopher; for I do not yet feel confidence in what I have learned and in what I have assented to. I still fear my own weakness. Let me get confidence and then you shall see a countenance such as I ought to have and an attitude such as I ought to have; then I will show to you the statue, when it is perfected, when it is polished. What do you expect? a supercilious countenance? Does the Zeus at Olympia lift up his brow? No, his look is fixed as becomes him who is ready to say:

Irrevocable is my word and shall not fail.—Iliad, i., 526.

Such will I show myself to you, faithful, modest, noble, free from perturbation. What, and immortal, too, except from old age, and from sickness? No, but dying as becomes a god, sickening as becomes a god. This power I possess; this I can do. But the rest I do not possess, nor can I do. I will show the nerves (strength) of a philosopher. What nerves are these? A desire never disappointed, an aversion which never falls on that which it would avoid, a proper pursuit ([Greek: hormaen]), a diligent purpose, an assent which is not rash. These you shall see.

THAT WHEN WE CANNOT FULFIL THAT WHICH THE CHARACTER OF A MAN PROMISES, WE ASSUME THE CHARACTER OF A PHILOSOPHER

It is no common (easy) thing to do this only, to fulfil the promise of a man's nature. For what is a man? The answer is, A rational and mortal being. Then by the rational faculty from whom are we separated? From wild beasts. And from what others? From sheep and like animals. Take care then to do nothing like a wild beast; but if you do, you have lost the character of a man; you have not fulfilled your promise. See that you do nothing like a sheep; but if you do, in this case also the man is lost. What then do we do as sheep? When we act gluttonously, when we act lewdly, when we act rashly, filthily, inconsiderately, to what have we declined? To sheep. What have we lost? The rational faculty. When we act contentiously and harmfully and passionately and violently, to what have we declined? To wild beasts. Consequently some of us are great wild beasts, and others little beasts, of a bad disposition and small, whence we may say, Let me be eaten by a lion. But in all these ways the promise of a man acting as a man is destroyed. For when is a conjunctive (complex) proposition maintained? When it fulfils what its nature promises; so that the preservation of a complex proposition is when it is a conjunction of truths. When is a disjunctive maintained? When it fulfils what it promises. When are flutes, a lyre, a horse, a dog, preserved? (When they severally keep their promise.) What is the wonder then if man also in like manner is preserved, and in like manner is lost? Each man is improved and preserved by corresponding acts, the carpenter by acts of carpentry, the grammarian by acts of grammar. But if a man accustoms himself to write ungrammatically, of necessity his art will be corrupted and destroyed. Thus modest actions preserve the modest man, and immodest actions destroy him; and actions of fidelity preserve the faithful man, and the contrary actions destroy him. And on the other hand contrary actions strengthen contrary characters: shamelessness strengthens the shameless man, faithlessness the faithless man, abusive words the abusive man, anger the man of an angry temper, and unequal receiving and giving make the avaricious man more avaricious.

For this reason philosophers admonish us not to be satisfied with learning only, but also to add study, and then practice. For we have long been accustomed to do contrary things, and we put in practice opinions which are contrary to true opinions. If then we shall not also put in practice right opinions, we shall be nothing more than the expositors of the opinions of others. For now who among us is not able to discourse according to the rules of art about good and evil things (in this fashion)? That of things some are good, and some are bad, and some are indifferent: the good then are virtues, and the things which participate in virtues; and the bad are the contrary; and the indifferent are wealth, health, reputation. Then, if in the midst of our talk there should happen some greater noise than usual, or some of those who are present should laugh at us, we are disturbed. Philosopher, where are the things which you were talking about? Whence did you produce and utter them? From the lips, and thence only. Why then do you corrupt the aids provided by others? Why do you treat the weightiest matters as if you were playing a game of dice? For it is one thing to lay up bread and wine as in a storehouse, and another thing to eat. That which has been eaten, is digested, distributed, and is become sinews, flesh, bones, blood, healthy color, healthy breath. Whatever is stored up, when you choose you can readily take and show it; but you have no other advantage from it except so far as to appear to possess it. For what is the difference between explaining these doctrines and those of men who have different opinions? Sit down now and explain according to the rules of art the opinions of Epicurus, and perhaps you will explain his opinions in a more useful manner than Epicurus himself. Why then do you call yourself a Stoic? Why do you deceive the many? Why do you act the part of a Jew, when you are a Greek? Do you not see how (why) each is called a Jew, or a Syrian, or an Egyptian? and when we see a man inclining to two sides, we are accustomed to say, This man is not a Jew, but he acts as one. But when he has assumed the affects of one who has been imbued with Jewish doctrine and has adopted that sect, then he is in fact and he is named a Jew.

HOW WE MAY DISCOVER THE DUTIES OF LIFE FROM NAMES

Consider who you are. In the first place, you are a man; and this is one who has nothing superior to the faculty of the will, but all other things subjected to it; and the faculty itself he possesses unenslaved and free from subjection. Consider then from what things you have been separated by reason. You have been separated from wild beasts; you have been separated from domestic animals ([Greek: probaton]). Further, you are a citizen of the world, and a part of it, not one of the subservient (serving), but one of the principal (ruling) parts, for you are capable of comprehending the divine administration and of considering the connection of things. What then does the character of a citizen promise (profess)? To hold nothing as profitable to himself; to deliberate about nothing as if he were detached from the community, but to act as the hand or foot would do, if they had reason and understood the constitution of nature, for they would never put themselves in motion nor desire anything otherwise than with reference to the whole. Therefore, the philosophers say well, that if the good man had foreknowledge of what would happen, he would co-operate towards his own sickness and death and mutilation, since he knows that these things are assigned to him according to the universal arrangement, and that the whole is superior to the part, and the state to the citizen. But now because we do not know the future, it is our duty to stick to the things which are in their nature more suitable for our choice, for we were made among other things for this.

After this, remember that you are a son. What does this character promise? To consider that everything which is the son's belongs to the father, to obey him in all things, never to blame him to another, nor to say or do anything which does him injury, to yield to him in all things and give way, co-operating with him as far as you can. After this know that you are a brother also, and that to this character it is due to make concessions; to be easily persuaded, to speak good of your brother, never to claim in opposition to him any of the things which are independent of the will, but readily to give them up, that you may have the larger share in what is dependent on the will. For see what a thing it is, in place of a lettuce, if it should so happen, or a seat, to gain for yourself goodness of disposition. How great is the advantage.

Next to this, if you are a senator of any state, remember that you are a senator; if a youth, that you are a youth; if an old man, that you are an old man; for each of such names, if it comes to be examined, marks out the proper duties.

162

But if you go and blame your brother, I say to you, You have forgotten who you are and what is your name. In the next place, if you were a smith and made a wrong use of the hammer, you would have forgotten the smith; and if you have forgotten the brother and instead of a brother have become an enemy, would you appear not to have changed one thing for another in that case? And if instead of a man, who is a tame animal and social, you are become a mischievous wild beast, treacherous, and biting, have you lost nothing? But (I suppose) you must lose a bit of money that you may suffer damage? And does the loss of nothing else do a man damage? If you had lost the art of grammar or music, would you think the loss of it a damage? and if you shall lose modesty, moderation ([Greek: chtastolaen]) and gentleness, do you think the loss nothing? And yet the things first mentioned are lost by some cause external and independent of the will, and the second by our own fault; and as to the first neither to have them nor to lose them is shameful; but as to the second, not to have them and to lose them is shameful and matter of reproach and a misfortune.

What then? shall I not hurt him who has hurt me? In the first place consider what hurt ([Greek: blabae]) is, and remember what you have heard from the philosophers. For if the good consists in the will (purpose, intention, [Greek: proaireeis]), and the evil also in the will, see if what you say is not this: What then, since that man has hurt himself by doing an unjust act to me, shall I not hurt myself by doing some unjust act to him? Why do we not imagine to ourselves (mentally think of) something of this kind? But where there is any detriment to the body or to our possession, there is harm there; and where the same thing happens to the faculty of the will, there is (you suppose) no harm; for he who has been deceived or he who has done an unjust act neither suffers in the head nor in the eye nor in the hip, nor does he lose his estate; and we wish for nothing else than (security to) these things. But whether we shall have the will modest and faithful or shameless and faithless, we care not the least, except only in the school so far as a few words are concerned. Therefore our proficiency is limited to these few words; but beyond them it does not exist even in the slightest degree.

WHAT THE BEGINNING OF PHILOSOPHY IS

The beginning of philosophy, to him at least who enters on it in the right way and by the door is a consciousness of his own weakness and inability about necessary things; for we come into the world with no natural notion of a right-angled triangle, or of a diesis (a quarter tone), or of a half-tone; but we learn each of these things by a certain transmission according to art; and for this reason those who do not know them do not think that they know them. But as to good and evil, and beautiful and ugly, and becoming and unbecoming, and happiness and misfortune, and proper and improper, and what we ought to do and what we ought not to do, who ever came into the world without having an innate idea of them? Wherefore we all use these names, and we endeavor to fit the preconceptions to the several cases (things) thus: he has done well; he has not done well; he has done as he ought, not as he ought; he has been unfortunate, he has been fortunate; he is unjust, he is just; who does not use these names? who among us defers the use of them till he has learned them, as he defers the use of the words about lines (geometrical figures) or sounds? And the cause of this is that we come into the world already taught as it were by nature some things on this matter ([Greek: topon]), and proceeding from these we have added to them self-conceit ([Greek: oiaesin]). For why, a man says, do I not know the beautiful and the ugly? Have I not the notion of it? You have. Do I not adapt it to particulars? You do. Do I not then adapt it properly? In that lies the whole question; and conceit is added here; for beginning from these things which are admitted men proceed to that which is matter of dispute by means of unsuitable adaptation; for if they possessed this power of adaptation in addition to those things, what would hinder them from being perfect? But now since you think that you properly adapt the preconceptions to the particulars, tell me whence you derive this (assume that you do so). Because I think so. But it does not seem so to another, and he thinks that he also makes a proper adaptation; or does he not think so? He does think so. Is it possible then that both of you can properly apply the preconceptions to things about which you have contrary opinions? It is not possible. Can you then show us anything better towards adapting the preconceptions beyond your thinking that you do? Does the madman do any other things than the things which seem to him right? Is then this criterion sufficient for him also? It is not sufficient. Come then to something which is superior to seeming ([Greek: tou dochein]). What is this?

Observe, this is the beginning of philosophy, a perception of the disagreement of men with one another, and an inquiry into the cause of the disagreement, and a condemnation and distrust of that which only "seems," and a certain investigation of that which "seems" whether it "seems" rightly, and a discovery of some rule ([Greek: chanonos]), as we have discovered a balance in the determination of weights, and a carpenter's rule (or square) in the case of straight and crooked things.—This is the beginning of philosophy. Must we say that all things are right which seem so to all? And how is it possible that contradictions can be right?—Not all then, but all which seem to us to be right.—How more to you than those which seem right to the Syrians? why more than what seem right to the Egyptians? why more than what seems right to me or to any other man? Not at all more. What then "seems" to every man is not sufficient for determining what "is"; for neither in the case of weights nor measures are we satisfied with the bare appearance, but in each case we have discovered a certain rule. In this matter then is there no rule superior to what "seems"? And how is it possible that the most necessary things among men should have no sign (mark), and be incapable of being discovered? There is then some rule. And why then do we not seek the rule and discover it, and afterwards use it without varying from it, not even stretching out the finger without it? For this, I think, is that which when it is discovered cures of their madness those who use mere "seeming" as a measure, and misuse it; so that for the future proceeding from certain things (principles) known and made clear we may use in the case of particular things the preconceptions which are distinctly fixed.

What is the matter presented to us about which we are inquiring? Pleasure (for example). Subject it to the rule, throw it into the balance. Ought the good to be such a thing that it is fit that we have confidence in it? Yes. And in which we ought to confide? It ought to be. Is it fit to trust to anything which is insecure? No. Is then pleasure anything secure? No. Take it then and throw it out of the scale, and drive it far away from the place of good things. But if you are not sharp-sighted, and one balance is not enough for you, bring another. Is it fit to be elated over what is good? Yes. Is it proper then to be elated over present pleasure? See that you do not say that it is proper; but if you do, I shall then not think you worthy even of the balance. Thus things are tested and weighed when the rules are ready. And to philosophize is this, to examine and confirm the rules; and then to use them when they are known is the act of a wise and good man.

OF DISPUTATION OR DISCUSSION

What things a man must learn in order to be able to apply the art of disputation, has been accurately shown by our philosophers (the Stoics); but with respect to the proper use of the things, we are entirely without practice. Only give to any of us, whom you please, an illiterate man to discuss with, and he cannot discover how to deal with the man. But when he has moved the man a little, if he answers beside the purpose, he does not know how to treat him, but he then either abuses or ridicules him, and says, He is an illiterate man; it is not possible to do anything with him. Now a guide, when he has found a man out of the road, leads him into the right way; he does not ridicule or abuse him and then leave him. Do you also show the illiterate man the truth, and you will see that he follows. But so long as you do not show him the truth, do not ridicule him, but rather feel your own incapacity.
Now this was the first and chief peculiarity of Socrates, never to be irritated in argument, never to utter anything abusive, anything insulting, but to bear with abusive persons and to put an end to the quarrel. If you would know what great power he had in this way, read the Symposium of Xenophon, and you will see how many quarrels he put an end to. Hence with good reason in the poets also this power is most highly praised:

Quickly with skill he settles great disputes.
-       Hesiod, Theogony, v. 87.

ON ANXIETY (SOLICITUDE)

When I see a man anxious, I say, What does this man want? If he did not want something which is not in his power, how could he be anxious? For this reason a lute player when he is singing by himself has no anxiety, but when he enters the theatre, he is anxious, even if he has a good voice and plays well on the lute; for he not only wishes to sing well, but also to obtain applause: but this is not in his power. Accordingly, where he has skill, there he has confidence.

Bring any single person who knows nothing of music, and the musician does not care for him. But in the matter where a man knows nothing and has not been practised, there he is anxious. What matter is this? He knows not what a crowd is or what the praise of a crowd is. However, he has learned to strike the lowest chord and the highest; but what the praise of the many is, and what power it has in life, he neither knows nor has he thought about it. Hence he must of necessity tremble and grow pale. Is any man then afraid about things which are not evils? No. Is he afraid about things which are evils, but still so far within his power that they may not happen? Certainly he is not. If then the things which are independent of the will are neither good nor bad, and all things which do depend on the will are within our power, and no man can either take them from us or give them to us, if we do not choose, where is room left for anxiety? But we are anxious about our poor body, our little property, about the will of Caesar; but not anxious about things internal. Are we anxious about not forming a false opinion? No, for this is in my power. About not exerting our movements contrary to nature? No, not even about this. When then you see a man pale, as the physician says, judging from the complexion, this man's spleen is disordered, that man's liver; so also say, this man's desire and aversion are disordered, he is not in the right way, he is in a fever. For nothing else changes the color, or causes trembling or chattering of the teeth, or causes a man to

Sink in his knees and shift from foot to foot.
Iliad, xiii., 281.

For this reason, when Zeno was going to meet Antigonus, he was not anxious, for Antigonus had no power over any of the things which Zeno admired; and Zeno did not care for those things over which Antigonus had power. But Antigonus was anxious when he was going to meet Zeno, for he wished to please Zeno; but this was a thing external (out of his power). But Zeno did not want to please Antigonus; for no man who is skilled in any art wishes to please one who has no such skill.

Should I try to please you? Why? I suppose, you know the measure by which one man is estimated by another. Have you taken pains to learn what is a good man and what is a bad man, and how a man becomes one or the other? Why then are you not good yourself? How, he replies, am I not good? Because no good man laments or groans or weeps, no good man is pale and trembles, or says, How will he receive me, how will he listen to me? Slave, just as it pleases him. Why do you care about what belongs to others? Is it now his fault if he receives badly what proceeds from you? Certainly. And is it possible that a fault should be one man's, and the evil in another? No. Why then are you anxious about that which belongs to others? Your question is reasonable; but I am anxious how I shall speak to him. Cannot you then speak to him as you choose? But I fear that I may be disconcerted? If you are going to write the name of Dion, are you afraid that you would be disconcerted? By no means. Why? is it not because you have practised writing the name? Certainly. Well, if you were going to read the name, would you not feel the same? and why?

Because every art has a certain strength and confidence in the things which belong to it. Have you then not practised speaking? and what else did you learn in the school? Syllogisms and sophistical propositions? For what purpose? was it not for the purpose of discoursing skilfully? and is not discoursing skilfully the same as discoursing seasonably and cautiously and with intelligence, and also without making mistakes and without hindrance, and besides all this with confidence? Yes. When then you are mounted on a horse and go into a plain, are you anxious at being matched against a man who is on foot, and anxious in a matter in which you are practised, and he is not? Yes, but that person (to whom I am going to speak) has power to kill me. Speak the truth, then, unhappy man, and do not brag, nor claim to be a philosopher, nor refuse to acknowledge your masters, but so long as you present this handle in your body, follow every man who is stronger than yourself. Socrates used to practice speaking, he who talked as he did to the tyrants, to the dicasts (judges), he who talked in his prison. Diogenes had practised speaking, he who spoke as he did to Alexander, to the pirates, to the person who bought him. These men were confident in the things which they practised. But do you walk off to your own affairs and never leave them: go and sit in a corner, and weave syllogisms, and propose them to another. There is not in you the man who can rule a state.

TO NASO

When a certain Roman entered with his son and listened to one reading, Epictetus said, This is the method of instruction; and he stopped. When the Roman asked him to go on, Epictetus said, Every art when it is taught causes labor to him who is unacquainted with it and is unskilled in it, and indeed the things which proceed from the arts immediately show their use in the purpose for which they were made; and most of them contain something attractive and pleasing. For indeed to be present and to observe how a shoemaker learns is not a pleasant thing; but the shoe is useful and also not disagreeable to look at. And the discipline of a smith when he is learning is very disagreeable to one who chances to be present and is a stranger to the art: but the work shows the use of the art. But you will see this much more in music; for if you are present while a person is learning, the discipline will appear most disagreeable; and yet the results of music are pleasing and delightful to those who know nothing of music. And here we conceive the work of a philosopher to be something of this kind: he must adapt his wish ([Greek: boulaesin]) to what is going on, so that neither any of the things which are taking place shall take place contrary to our wish, nor any of the things which do not take place shall not take place when we wish that they should. From this the result is to those who have so arranged the work of philosophy, not to fail in the desire, nor to fall in with that which they would avoid; without uneasiness, without fear, without perturbation to pass through life themselves, together with their associates maintaining the relations both natural and acquired, as the relation of son, of father, of brother, of citizen, of man, of wife, of neighbor, of fellow-traveller, of ruler, of ruled. The work of a philosopher we conceive to be something like this. It remains next to inquire how this must be accomplished.

We see then that the carpenter ([Greek: techton]) when he has learned certain things becomes a carpenter; the pilot by learning certain things becomes a pilot. May it not then in philosophy also not be sufficient to wish to be wise and good, and that there is also a necessity to learn certain things? We inquire then what these things are. The philosophers say that we ought first to learn that there is a God and that he provides for all things; also that it is not possible to conceal from him our acts, or even our intentions and thoughts. The next thing is to learn what is the nature of the gods; for such as they are discovered to be, he, who would please and obey them, must try with all his power to be like them. If the divine is faithful, man also must be faithful; if it is free, man also must be free; if beneficent, man also must be beneficent; if magnanimous, man also must be magnanimous; as being then an imitator of God he must do and say everything consistently with this fact.

TO OR AGAINST THOSE WHO OBSTINATELY PERSIST IN WHAT THEY HAVE DETERMINED

When some persons have heard these words, that a man ought to be constant (firm), and that the will is naturally free and not subject to compulsion, but that all other things are subject to hindrance, to slavery, and are in the power of others, they suppose that they ought without deviation to abide by everything which they have determined. But in the first place that which has been determined ought to be sound (true). I require tone (sinews) in the body, but such as exists in a healthy body, in an athletic body; but if it is plain to me that you have the tone of a frenzied man and you boast of it, I shall say to you, Man, seek the physician; this is not tone, but atony (deficiency in right tone). In a different way something of the same kind is felt by those who listen to these discourses in a wrong manner; which was the case with one of my companions, who for no reason resolved to starve himself to death. I heard of it when it was the third day of his abstinence from food, and I went to inquire what had happened. "I have resolved," he said. "But still tell me what it was which induced you to resolve; for if you have resolved rightly, we shall sit with you and assist you to depart, but if you have made an unreasonable resolution, change your mind." "We ought to keep to our determinations." "What are you doing, man? We ought to keep not to all our determinations, but to those which are right; for if you are now persuaded that it is right, do not change your mind, if you think fit, but persist and say, We ought to abide by our determinations. Will you not make the beginning and lay the foundation in an inquiry whether the determination is sound or not sound, and so then build on it firmness and security? But if you lay a rotten and ruinous foundation, will not your miserable little building fall down the sooner, the more and the stronger are the materials which you shall lay on it? Without any reason would you withdraw from us out of life a man who is a friend and a companion, a citizen of the same city, both the great and the small city? Then while you are committing murder and destroying a man who has done no wrong, do you say that you ought to abide by your determinations? And if it ever in any way came into your head to kill me, ought you to abide by your determinations?"

Now this man was with difficulty persuaded to change his mind. But it is impossible to convince some persons at present; so that I seem now to know what I did not know before, the meaning of the common saying, that you can neither persuade nor break a fool. May it never be my lot to have a wise fool for my friend; nothing is more untractable. "I am determined," the man says. Madmen are also, but the more firmly they form a judgment on things which do not exist, the more hellebore they require. Will you not act like a sick man and call in the physician?—I am sick, master, help me; consider what I must do: it is my duty to obey you. So it is here also: I know not what I ought to do, but I am come to learn.—Not so; but speak to me about other things: upon this I have determined.—What other things? for what is greater and more useful than for you to be persuaded that it is not sufficient to have made your determination and not to change it. This is the tone (energy) of madness, not of health.—I will die, if you compel me to this.—Why, man? What has happened?—I have determined—I have had a lucky escape that you have not determined to kill me—I take no money. Why?—I have determined—Be assured that with the very tone (energy) which you now use in refusing to take, there is nothing to hinder you at some time from inclining without reason to take money, and then saying, I have determined. As in a distempered body, subject to defluxions, the humor inclines sometimes to these parts, and then to those, so too a sickly soul knows not which way to incline; but if to this inclination and movement there is added a tone (obstinate resolution), then the evil becomes past help and cure.

THAT WE DO NOT STRIVE TO USE OUR OPINIONS ABOUT GOOD AND EVIL

Where is the good? In the will. Where is the evil? In the will. Where is neither of them? In those things which are independent of the will. Well then? Does any one among us think of these lessons out of the schools? Does any one meditate (strive) by himself to give an answer to things as in the case of questions?—Is it day?—Yes.—Is it night?—No.—Well, is the number of stars even?—I cannot say.—When money is shown (offered) to you, have you studied to make the proper answer, that money is not a good thing? Have you practised yourself in these answers, or only against sophisms? Why do you wonder then if in the cases which you have studied, in those you have improved; but in those which you have not studied, in those you remain the same? When the rhetorician knows that he has written well, that he has committed to memory what he has written, and brings an agreeable voice, why is he still anxious? Because he is not satisfied with having studied. What then does he want? To be praised by the audience? For the purpose then of being able to practise declamation he has been disciplined; but with respect to praise and blame he has not been disciplined. For when did he hear from any one what praise is, what blame is, what the nature of each is, what kind of praise should be sought, or what kind of blame should be shunned? And when did he practise this discipline which follows these words (things)? Why then do you still wonder, if in the matters which a man has learned, there he surpasses others, and in those in which he has not been disciplined, there he is the same with the many. So the lute player knows how to play, sings well, and has a fine dress, and yet he trembles when he enters on the stage; for these matters he understands, but he does not know what a crowd is, nor the shouts of a crowd, nor what ridicule is. Neither does he know what anxiety is, whether it is our work or the work of another, whether it is possible to stop it or not. For this reason if he has been praised, he leaves the theatre puffed up, but if he has been ridiculed, the swollen bladder has been punctured and subsides.

This is the case also with ourselves. What do we admire? Externals. About what things are we busy? Externals. And have we any doubt then why we fear or why we are anxious? What then happens when we think the things, which are coming on us, to be evils? It is not in our power not to be afraid, it is not in our power not to be anxious. Then we say, Lord God, how shall I not be anxious? Fool, have you not hands, did not God make them for you? Sit down now and pray that your nose may not run. Wipe yourself rather and do not blame him. Well then, has he given to you nothing in the present case? Has he not given to you endurance? Has he not given to you magnanimity? Has he not given to you manliness? When you have such hands do you still look for one who shall wipe your nose? But we neither study these things nor care for them. Give me a man who cares how he shall do anything, not for the obtaining of a thing, but who cares about his own energy. What man, when he is walking about, cares for his own energy? Who, when he is deliberating, cares about his own deliberation, and not about obtaining that about which he deliberates? And if he succeeds, he is elated and says, How well we have deliberated; did I not tell you, brother, that it is impossible, when we have thought about anything, that it should not turn out thus? But if the thing should turn out otherwise, the wretched man is humbled; he knows not even what to say about what has taken place. Who among us for the sake of this matter has consulted a seer? Who among us as to his actions has not slept in indifference? Who? Give (name) to me one that I may see the man whom I have long been looking for, who is truly noble and ingenuous, whether young or old; name him.

What then are the things which are heavy on us and disturb us? What else than opinions? What else than opinions lies heavy upon him who goes away and leaves his companions and friends and places and habits of life? Now little children, for instance, when they cry on the nurse leaving them for a short time, forget their sorrow if they receive a small cake. Do you choose then that we should compare you to little children? No, by Zeus, for I do not wish to be pacified by a small cake, but by right opinions. And what are these? Such as a man ought to study all day, and not to be affected by anything that is not his own, neither by companion nor place nor gymnasia, and not even by his own body, but to remember the law and to have it before his eyes. And what is the divine law? To keep a man's own, not to claim that which belongs to others, but to use what is given, and when it is not given, not to desire it; and when a thing is taken away, to give it up readily and immediately, and to be thankful for the time that a man has had the use of it, if you would not cry for your nurse and mamma. For what matter does it make by what thing a man is subdued, and on what he depends? In what respect are you better than he who cries for a girl, if you grieve for a little gymnasium, and little porticos, and young men, and such places of amusement? Another comes and laments that he shall no longer drink the water of Dirce. Is the Marcian water worse than that of Dirce? But I was used to the water of Dirce. And you in turn will be used to the other. Then if you become attached to this also, cry for this too, and try to make a verse like the verse of Euripides,

The hot baths of Nero and the Marcian water.

See how tragedy is made when common things happen to silly men.

When then shall I see Athens again and the Acropolis? Wretch, are you not content with what you see daily? Have you anything better or greater to see than the sun, the moon, the stars, the whole earth, the sea? But if indeed you comprehend Him who administers the whole, and carry him about in yourself, do you still desire small stones and a beautiful rock?

HOW WE MUST ADAPT PRECONCEPTIONS TO PARTICULAR CASES

What is the first business of him who philosophizes? To throw away self-conceit ([Greek: oiaesis]). For it is impossible for a man to begin to learn that which he thinks that he knows. As to things then which ought to be done and ought not to be done, and good and bad, and beautiful and ugly, all of us talking of them at random go to the philosophers; and on these matters we praise, we censure, we accuse, we blame, we judge and determine about principles honorable and dishonorable. But why do we go to the philosophers? Because we wish to learn what we do not think that we know. And what is this? Theorems. For we wish to learn what philosophers say as being something elegant and acute; and some wish to learn that they may get profit from what they learn. It is ridiculous then to think that a person wishes to learn one thing, and will learn another; or further, that a man will make proficiency in that which he does not learn. But the many are deceived by this which deceived also the rhetorician Theopompus, when he blames even Plato for wishing everything to be defined. For what does he say? Did none of us before you use the words good or just, or do we utter the sounds in an unmeaning and empty way without understanding what they severally signify? Now who tells you, Theopompus, that we had not natural notions of each of these things and preconceptions ([Greek: prolaepseis])? But it is not possible to adapt preconceptions to their correspondent objects if we have not distinguished (analyzed) them, and inquired what object must be subjected to each preconception. You may make the same charge against physicians also. For who among us did not use the words healthy and unhealthy before

171

Hippocrates lived, or did we utter these words as empty sounds? For we have also a certain preconception of health, but we are not able to adapt it. For this reason one says, Abstain from food; another says, Give food; another says, Bleed; and another says, Use cupping. What is the reason? is it any other than that a man cannot properly adapt the preconceptions of health to particulars?

HOW WE SHOULD STRUGGLE AGAINST APPEARANCES

Every habit and faculty is maintained and increased by the corresponding actions: the habit of walking by walking, the habit of running by running. If you would be a good reader, read; if a writer, write. But when you shall not have read for thirty days in succession, but have done something else, you will know the consequence. In the same way, if you shall have lain down ten days, get up and attempt to make a long walk, and you will see how your legs are weakened. Generally then if you would make anything a habit, do it; if you would not make it a habit, do not do it, but accustom yourself to do something else in place of it.

So it is with respect to the affections of the soul: when you have been angry, you must know that not only has this evil befallen you, but that you have also increased the habit, and in a manner thrown fuel upon fire.

In this manner certainly, as philosophers say, also diseases of the mind grow up. For when you have once desired money, if reason be applied to lead to a perception of the evil, the desire is stopped, and the ruling faculty of our mind is restored to the original authority. But if you apply no means of cure, it no longer returns to the same state, but being again excited by the corresponding appearance, it is inflamed to desire quicker than before: and when this takes place continually, it is henceforth hardened (made callous), and the disease of the mind confirms the love of money. For he who has had a fever, and has been relieved from it, is not in the same state that he was before, unless he has been completely cured. Something of the kind happens also in diseases of the soul. Certain traces and blisters are left in it, and unless a man shall completely efface them, when he is again lashed on the same places, the lash will produce not blisters (weals) but sores. If then you wish not to be of an angry temper, do not feed the habit: throw nothing on it which will increase it: at first keep quiet, and count the days on which you have not been angry. I used to be in passion every day; now every second day; then every third, then every fourth. But if you have intermitted thirty days, make a sacrifice to God. For the habit at first begins to be weakened, and then is completely destroyed. "I have not been vexed to-day, nor the day after, nor yet on any succeeding day during two or three months; but I took care when some exciting things happened." Be assured that you are in a good way.

How then shall this be done? Be willing at length to be approved by yourself, be willing to appear beautiful to God, desire to be in purity with your own pure self and with God. Then when any such appearance visits you, Plato says, Have recourse to expiations, go a suppliant to the temples of the averting deities. It is even sufficient if you resort to the society of noble and just men, and compare yourself with them, whether you find one who is living or dead.

But in the first place, be not hurried away by the rapidity of the appearance, but say, Appearances, wait for me a little; let me see who you are, and what you are about; let me put you to the test. And then do not allow the appearance to lead you on and draw lively pictures of the things which will follow; for if you do, it will carry you off wherever it pleases. But rather bring in to oppose it some other beautiful and noble appearance, and cast out this base appearance. And if you are accustomed to be exercised in this way, you will see what shoulders, what sinews, what strength you have. But now it is only trifling words, and nothing more.

This is the true athlete, the man who exercises himself against such appearances. Stay, wretch, do not be carried away. Great is the combat, divine is the work; it is for kingship, for freedom, for happiness, for freedom from perturbation. Remember God; call on him as a helper and protector, as men at sea call on the Dioscuri in a storm. For what is a greater storm than that which comes from appearances which are violent and drive away the reason? For the storm itself, what else is it but an appearance? For take away the fear of death, and suppose as many thunders and lightnings as you please, and you will know what calm and serenity there is in the ruling faculty. But if you have once been defeated and say that you will conquer hereafter, and then say the same again, be assured that you will at last be in so wretched a condition and so weak that you will not even know afterwards that you are doing wrong, but you will even begin to make apologies (defences) for your wrong-doing, and then you will confirm the saying of Hesiod to be true,

With constant ills the dilatory strives.

OF INCONSISTENCY

Some things men readily confess, and other things they do not. No one then will confess that he is a fool or without understanding; but quite the contrary you will hear all men saying, I wish that I had fortune equal to my understanding. But men readily confess that they are timid, and they say: I am rather timid, I confess; but as to other respects you will not find me to be foolish. A man will not readily confess that he is intemperate; and that he is unjust, he will not confess at all. He will by no means confess that he is envious or a busybody. Most men will confess that they are compassionate. What then is the reason?

The chief thing (the ruling thing) is inconsistency and confusion in the things which relate to good and evil. But different men have different reasons; and generally what they imagine to be base, they do not confess at all. But they suppose timidity to be a characteristic of a good disposition, and compassion also; but silliness to be the absolute characteristic of a slave. And they do not at all admit (confess) the things which are offences against society. But in the case of most errors for this reason chiefly they are induced to confess them, because they imagine that there is something involuntary in them as in timidity and compassion; and if a man confess that he is in any respect intemperate, he alleges love (or passion) as an excuse for what is involuntary. But men do not imagine injustice to be at all involuntary. There is also in jealousy, as they suppose, something involuntary; and for this reason they confess to jealousy also.

Living then among such men, who are so confused, so ignorant of what they say, and of the evils which they have or have not, and why they have them, or how they shall be relieved of them, I think it is worth the trouble for a man to watch constantly (and to ask) whether I also am one of them, what imagination I have about myself, how I conduct myself, whether I conduct myself as a prudent man, whether I conduct myself as a temperate man, whether I ever say this, that I have been taught to be prepared for everything that may happen. Have I the consciousness, which a man who knows nothing ought to have, that I know nothing? Do I go to my teacher as men go to oracles, prepared to obey? or do I like a snivelling boy go to my school to learn history and understand the books which I did not understand before, and, if it should happen so, to explain them also to others? Man, you have had a fight in the house with a poor slave, you have turned the family upside down, you have frightened the neighbors, and you come to me as if you were a wise man, and you take your seat and judge how I have explained some word, and how I have babbled whatever came into my head. You come full of envy, and humbled, because you bring nothing from home; and you sit during the discussion thinking of nothing else than how your father is disposed towards you and your brother. What are they saying about me there? now they think that I am improving, and are saying, He will return with all knowledge. I wish I could learn everything before I return; but much labor is necessary, and no one sends me anything, and the baths at Nicopolis are dirty; everything is bad at home, and bad here.

ON FRIENDSHIP

What a man applies himself to earnestly, that he naturally loves. Do men then apply themselves earnestly to the things which are bad? By no means. Well, do they apply themselves to things which in no way concern themselves? Not to these either. It remains then that they employ themselves earnestly only about things which are good; and if they are earnestly employed about things, they love such things also. Whoever then understands what is good can also know how to love; but he who cannot distinguish good from bad, and things which are neither good nor bad from both, how can he possess the power of loving? To love, then, is only in the power of the wise.

For universally, be not deceived, every animal is attached to nothing so much as to its own interests. Whatever then appears to it an impediment to this interest, whether this be a brother, or a father, or a child, or beloved, or lover, it hates, spurns, curses; for its nature is to love nothing so much as its own interests: this is father, and brother, and kinsman, and country, and God. When then the gods appear to us to be an impediment to this, we abuse them and throw down their statues and burn their temples, as Alexander ordered the temples of Aesculapius to be burned when his dear friend died.

For this reason, if a man put in the same place his interest, sanctity, goodness, and country, and parents, and friends, all these are secured: but if he puts in one place his interest, in another his friends, and his country and his kinsmen and justice itself, all these give way, being borne down by the weight of interest. For where the I and the Mine are placed, to that place of necessity the animal inclines; if in the flesh, there is the ruling power; if in the will, it is there; and if it is in externals, it is there. If then I am there where my will is, then only shall I be a friend such as I ought to be, and son, and father; for this will be my interest, to maintain the character of fidelity, of modesty, of patience, of abstinence, of active co-operation, of observing my relations (towards all). But if I put myself in one place, and honesty in another, then the doctrine of Epicurus becomes strong, which asserts either that there is no honesty or it is that which opinion holds to be honest (virtuous).

It was through this ignorance that the Athenians and the Lacedaemonians quarrelled, and the Thebans with both; and the great king quarrelled with Hellas, and the Macedonians with both: and the Romans with the Getae. And still earlier the Trojan war happened for these reasons. Alexander was the guest of Menelaus, and if any man had seen their friendly disposition, he would not have believed any one who said that they were not friends. But there was cast between them (as between dogs) a bit of meat, a handsome woman, and about her war arose. And now when you see brothers to be friends appearing to have one mind, do not conclude from this anything about their friendship, not even if they swear it and say that it is impossible for them to be separated from one another. For the ruling principle of a bad man cannot be trusted; it is insecure, has no certain rule by which it is directed, and is overpowered at different times by different appearances. But examine, not what other men examine, if they are born of the same parents and brought up together, and under the same pedagogue; but examine this only, wherein they place their interest, whether in externals or in the will. If in externals, do not name them friends, no more than name them trustworthy or constant, or brave or free; do not name them even men, if you have any judgment. For that is not a principle of human nature which makes them bite one another, and abuse one another, and occupy deserted places or public places, as if they were mountains, and in the courts of justice display the acts of robbers; nor yet that which makes them intemperate and adulterers and corrupters, nor that which makes them do whatever else men do against one another through this one opinion only, that of placing themselves and their interests in the things which are not within the power of their will. But if you hear that in truth these men think the good to be only there, where will is, and where there is a right use of appearances, no longer trouble yourself whether they are father or son, or brothers, or have associated a long time and are companions, but when you have ascertained this only, confidently declare that they are friends, as you declare that they are faithful, that they are just. For where else is friendship than where there is fidelity, and modesty, where there is a communion of honest things and of nothing else.

But you may say, Such a one treated me with regard so long; and did he not love me? How do you know, slave, if he did not regard you in the same way as he wipes his shoes with a sponge, or as he takes care of his beast? How do you know, when you have ceased to be useful as a vessel, he will not throw you away like a broken platter? But this woman is my wife, and we have lived together so long. And how long did Eriphyle live with Amphiaraus, and was the mother of children and of many? But a necklace came between them: and what is a necklace? It is the opinion about such things. That was the bestial principle, that was the thing which broke asunder the friendship between husband and wife, that which did not allow the woman to be a wife nor the mother to be a mother. And let every man among you who has seriously resolved either to be a friend himself or to have another for his friend, cut out these opinions, hate them, drive them from his soul. And thus first of all he will not reproach himself, he will not be at variance with himself, he will not change his mind, he will not torture himself. In the next place, to another also, who is like himself, he will be altogether and completely a friend. But he will bear with the man who is unlike himself, he will be kind to him, gentle, ready to pardon on account of his ignorance, on account of his being mistaken in things of the greatest importance; but he will be harsh to no man, being well convinced of Plato's doctrine that every mind is deprived of truth unwillingly. If you cannot do this, yet you can do in all other respects as friends do, drink together, and lodge together, and sail together, and you may be born of the same parents, for snakes also are: but neither will they be friends, nor you, so long as you retain these bestial and cursed opinions.

ON THE POWER OF SPEAKING

Every man will read a book with more pleasure or even with more ease, if it is written in fairer characters. Therefore every man will also listen more readily to what is spoken, if it is signified by appropriate and becoming words. We must not say then that there is no faculty of expression: for this affirmation is the characteristic of an impious and also of a timid man. Of an impious man, because he undervalues the gifts which come from God, just as if he would take away the commodity of the power of vision, or hearing, or of seeing. Has then God given you eyes to no purpose? and to no purpose has he infused into them a spirit so strong and of such skilful contrivance as to reach a long way and to fashion the forms of things which are seen? What messenger is so swift and vigilant? And to no purpose has he made the interjacent atmosphere so efficacious and elastic that the vision penetrates through the atmosphere which is in a manner moved? And to no purpose has he made light, without the presence of which there would be no use in any other thing?
Man, be neither ungrateful for these gifts nor yet forget the things which are superior to them. But indeed for the power of seeing and hearing, and indeed for life itself, and for the things which contribute to support it, for the fruits which are dry, and for wine and oil give thanks to God: but remember that he has given you something else better than all these, I mean the power of using them, proving them, and estimating the value of each. For what is that which gives information about each of these powers, what each of them is worth? Is it each faculty itself? Did you ever hear the faculty of vision saying anything

about itself? or the faculty of hearing? or wheat, or barley, or a horse, or a dog? No; but they are appointed as ministers and slaves to serve the faculty which has the power of making use of the appearances of things. And if you inquire what is the value of each thing, of whom do you inquire? who answers you? How then can any other faculty be more powerful than this, which uses the rest as ministers and itself proves each and pronounces about them? for which of them knows what itself is, and what is its own value? which of them knows when it ought to employ itself and when not? what faculty is it which opens and closes the eyes, and turns them away from objects to which it ought not to apply them and does apply them to other objects? Is it the faculty of vision? No, but it is the faculty of the will. What is that faculty which closes and opens the ears? what is that by which they are curious and inquisitive, or on the contrary unmoved by what is said? is it the faculty of hearing? It is no other than the faculty of the will. Will this faculty then, seeing that it is amidst all the other faculties which are blind and dumb and unable to see anything else except the very acts for which they are appointed in order to minister to this (faculty) and serve it, but this faculty alone sees sharp and sees what is the value of each of the rest; will this faculty declare to us that anything else is the best, or that itself is? And what else does the eye do when it is opened than see? But whether we ought to look on the wife of a certain person, and in what manner, who tells us? The faculty of the will. And whether we ought to believe what is said or not to believe it, and if we do believe, whether we ought to be moved by it or not, who tells us? Is it not the faculty of the will?

But if you ask me what then is the most excellent of all things, what must I say? I cannot say the power of speaking, but the power of the will, when it is right ([Greek: orthae]). For it is this which uses the other (the power of speaking), and all the other faculties both small and great. For when this faculty of the will is set right, a man who is not good becomes good: but when it fails, a man becomes bad. It is through this that we are unfortunate, that we are fortunate, that we blame one another, are pleased with one another. In a word, it is this which if we neglect it makes unhappiness, and if we carefully look after it, makes happiness.

What then is usually done? Men generally act as a traveller would do on his way to his own country, when he enters a good inn, and being pleased with it should remain there. Man, you have forgotten your purpose: you were not travelling to this inn, but you were passing through it. But this is a pleasant inn. And how many other inns are pleasant? and how many meadows are pleasant? yet only for passing through. But your purpose is this, to return to your country, to relieve your kinsmen of anxiety, to discharge the duties of a citizen, to marry, to beget children, to fill the usual magistracies. For you are not come to select more pleasant places, but to live in these where you were born and of which you were made a citizen. Something of the kind takes place in the matter which we are considering. Since by the aid of speech and such communication as you receive here you must advance to perfection, and purge your will and correct the faculty which makes use of the appearances of things; and since it is necessary also for the teaching (delivery) of theorems to be effected by a certain mode of expression and with a certain variety and sharpness, some persons captivated by these very things abide in them, one captivated by the expression, another by syllogisms, another again by sophisms, and still another by some other inn ([Greek: paudocheiou]) of the kind; and there they stay and waste away as they were among sirens.

Man, your purpose (business) was to make yourself capable of using conformably to nature the appearances presented to you, in your desires not to be frustrated, in your aversion from things not to fall into that which you would avoid, never to have no luck (as one may say), nor ever to have bad luck, to be free, not hindered, not compelled, conforming yourself to the administration of Zeus, obeying it, well satisfied with this, blaming no one, charging no one with fault, able from your whole soul to utter these verses:
Lead me, O Zeus, and thou too Destiny.

TO (OR AGAINST) A PERSON WHO WAS ONE OF THOSE WHO WERE NOT VALUED (ESTEEMED) BY HIM

A certain person said to him (Epictetus): Frequently I desired to hear you and came to you, and you never gave me any answer; and now, if it is possible, I entreat you to say something to me. Do you think, said Epictetus, that as there is an art in anything else, so there is also an art in speaking, and that he who has the art, will speak skilfully, and he who has not, will speak unskilfully?—I do think so.—He then who by speaking receives benefit himself, and is able to benefit others, will speak skilfully; but he who is rather damaged by speaking and does damage to others, will he be unskilled in this art of speaking? And you may find that some are damaged and others benefited by speaking. And are all who hear benefited by what they hear? Or will you find that among them also some are benefited and some damaged? There are both among these also, he said. In this case also then those who hear skilfully are benefited, and those who hear unskilfully are damaged? He admitted this. Is there then a skill in hearing also, as there is in speaking? It seems so. If you choose, consider the matter in this way also. The practice of music, to whom does it belong? To a musician. And the proper making of a statue, to whom do you think that it belongs? To a statuary. And the looking at a statue skilfully, does this appear to you to require the aid of no art? This also requires the aid of art. Then if speaking properly is the business of the skilful man, do you see that to hear also with benefit is the business of the skilful man? Now as to speaking and hearing perfectly, and usefully, let us for the present, if you please, say no more, for both of us are a long way from everything of the kind. But I think that every man will allow this, that he who is going to hear philosophers requires some amount of practice in hearing. Is it not so?

Why then do you say nothing to me? I can only say this to you, that he who knows not who he is, and for what purpose he exists, and what is this world, and with whom he is associated, and what things are the good and the bad, and the beautiful and the ugly, and who neither understands discourse nor demonstration, nor what is true nor what is false, and who is not able to distinguish them, will neither desire according to nature nor turn away nor move towards, nor intend (to act), nor assent, nor dissent, nor suspend his judgment: to say all in a few words, he will go about dumb and blind, thinking that he is somebody, but being nobody. Is this so now for the first time? Is it not the fact that ever since the human race existed, all errors and misfortunes have arisen through this ignorance?

This is all that I have to say to you; and I say even this not willingly. Why? Because you have not roused me. For what must I look to in order to be roused, as men who are expert in riding are roused by generous horses? Must I look to your body? You treat it disgracefully. To your dress? That is luxurious. To your behavior, to your look? That is the same as nothing. When you would listen to a philosopher, do not say to him, You tell me nothing; but only show yourself worthy of hearing or fit for hearing; and you will see how you will move the speaker.

THAT LOGIC IS NECESSARY

When one of those who were present said, Persuade me that logic is necessary, he replied, Do you wish me to prove this to you? The answer was, Yes. Then I must use a demonstrative form of speech. This was granted. How then will you know if I am cheating you by my argument? The man was silent. Do you see, said Epictetus, that you yourself are admitting that logic is necessary, if without it you cannot know so much as this, whether logic is necessary or not necessary?

OF FINERY IN DRESS

A certain young man, a rhetorician, came to see Epictetus, with his hair dressed more carefully than was usual and his attire in an ornamental style; whereupon Epictetus said, Tell me if you do not think that some dogs are beautiful and some horses, and so of all other animals. I do think so, the youth replied. Are not then some men also beautiful and others ugly? Certainly. Do we then for the same reason call each of them in the same kind beautiful, or each beautiful for something peculiar? And you will judge of this matter thus. Since we see a dog naturally formed for one thing, and a horse for another, and for another still, as an example, a nightingale, we may generally and not improperly declare each of them to be beautiful then when it is most excellent according to its nature; but since the nature of each is different, each of them seems to me to be beautiful in a different way. Is it not so? He admitted that it was. That then which makes a dog beautiful, makes a horse ugly; and that which makes a horse beautiful, makes a dog ugly, if it is true that their natures are different. It seems to be so. For I think that what makes a Pancratiast beautiful, makes a wrestler to be not good, and a runner to be most ridiculous; and he who is beautiful for the Pentathlon, is very ugly for wrestling. It is so, said he. What then makes a man beautiful? Is it that which in its kind makes both a dog and a horse beautiful? It is, he said. What then makes a dog beautiful? The possession of the excellence of a dog. And what makes a horse beautiful? The possession of the excellence of a horse. What then makes a man beautiful? Is it not the possession of the excellence of a man? And do you then, if you wish to be beautiful, young man, labor at this, the acquisition of human excellence? But what is this? Observe whom you yourself praise, when you praise many persons without partiality: do you praise the just or the unjust? The just. Whether do you praise the moderate or the immoderate? The moderate. And the temperate or the intemperate? The temperate. If then you make yourself such a person, you will know that you will make yourself beautiful; but so long as you neglect these things, you must be ugly ([Greek: aischron]), even though you contrive all you can to appear beautiful.

IN WHAT A MAN OUGHT TO BE EXERCISED WHO HAS MADE PROFICIENCY; AND THAT WE NEGLECT THE CHIEF THINGS

There are three things (topics, [Greek: topoi]) in which a man ought to exercise himself who would be wise and good. The first concerns the desires and the aversions, that a man may not fail to get what he desires, and that he may not fall into that which he does not desire. The second concerns the movements towards an object and the movements from an object, and generally in doing what a man ought to do, that he may act according to order, to reason, and not carelessly. The third thing concerns freedom from deception and rashness in judgment, and generally it concerns the assents ([Greek: sugchatatheseis]). Of these topics the chief and the most urgent is that which relates to the affects ([Greek: ta pathae] perturbations); for an affect is produced in no other way than by a failing to obtain that which a man desires or falling into that which a man would wish to avoid. This is that which brings in perturbations, disorders, bad fortune, misfortunes, sorrows, lamentations, and envy; that which makes men envious and jealous; and by these causes we are unable even to listen to the precepts of reason. The second topic concerns the duties of a man; for I ought not to be free from affects ([Greek: apathae]) like a statue, but I ought to maintain the relations ([Greek: scheseis]) natural and acquired, as a pious man, as a son, as a father, as a citizen.

The third topic is that which immediately concerns those who are making proficiency, that which concerns the security of the other two, so that not even in sleep any appearance unexamined may surprise us, nor in intoxication, nor in melancholy. This, it may be said, is above our power. But the present philosophers neglecting the first topic and the second (the affects and duties), employ themselves on the third, using sophistical arguments ([Greek: metapiptontas]), making conclusions from questioning, employing hypotheses, lying. For a man must, it is said, when employed on these matters, take care that he is not deceived. Who must? The wise and good man. This then is all that is wanting to you. Have you successfully worked out the rest? Are you free from deception in the matter of money? If you see a beautiful girl do you resist the appearance? If your neighbor obtains an estate by will, are you not vexed? Now is there nothing else wanting to you except unchangeable firmness of mind ([Greek: ametaptosia])? Wretch, you hear these very things with fear and anxiety that some person may despise you, and with inquiries about what any person may say about you. And if a man come and tell you that in a certain conversation in which the question was, Who is the best philosopher, a man who was present said that a certain person was the chief philosopher, your little soul which was only a finger's length stretches out to two cubits. But if another who is present says, You are mistaken; it is not worth while to listen to a certain person, for what does he know? he has only the first principles, and no more? then you are confounded, you grow pale, you cry out immediately, I will show him who I am, that I am a great philosopher. It is seen by these very things: why do you wish to show it by others? Do you not know that Diogenes pointed out one of the sophists in this way by stretching out his middle finger? And then when the man was wild with rage, This, he said, is the certain person: I have pointed him out to you. For a man is not shown by the finger, as a stone or a piece of wood; but when any person shows the man's principles, then he shows him as a man.

Let us look at your principles also. For is it not plain that you value not at all your own will ([Greek: proairesis]), but you look externally to things which are independent of your will? For instance, what will a certain person say? and what will people think of you? Will you be considered a man of learning; have you read Chrysippus or Antipater? for if you have read Archedamus also, you have every thing (that you can desire). Why you are still uneasy lest you should not show us who you are? Would you let me tell you what manner of man you have shown us that you are? You have exhibited yourself to us as a mean fellow, querulous, passionate, cowardly, finding fault with everything, blaming everybody, never quiet, vain: this is what you have exhibited to us. Go away now and read Archedamus; then if a mouse should leap down and make a noise, you are a dead man. For such a death awaits you as it did—what was the man's name—Crinis; and he too was proud, because he understood Archedamus. Wretch, will you not dismiss these things that do not concern you at all? These things are suitable to those who are able to learn them without perturbation, to those who can say: "I am not subject to anger, to grief, to envy: I am not hindered, I am not restrained. What remains for me? I have leisure, I am tranquil: let us see how we must deal with sophistical arguments; let us see how when a man has accepted an hypothesis he shall not be led away to any thing absurd." To them such things belong. To those who are happy it is appropriate to light a fire, to dine; if they choose, both to sing and to dance. But when the vessel is sinking, you come to me and hoist the sails.

WHAT IS THE MATTER ON WHICH A GOOD MAN SHOULD BE EMPLOYED, AND IN WHAT WE OUGHT CHIEFLY TO PRACTISE OURSELVES

The material for the wise and good man is his own ruling faculty: and the body is the material for the physician and the aliptes (the man who oils persons); the land is the matter for the husbandman. The business of the wise and good man is to use appearances conformably to nature: and as it is the nature of every soul to assent to the truth, to dissent from the false, and to remain in suspense as to that which is uncertain; so it is its nature to be moved towards the desire for the good, and to aversion from the evil; and with respect to that which is neither good nor bad it feels indifferent. For as the money-changer (banker) is not allowed to reject Caesar's coin, nor the seller of herbs, but if you show the coin, whether he chooses or not, he must give up what is sold for the coin; so it is also in the matter of the soul. When the good appears, it immediately attracts to itself; the evil repels from itself. But the soul will never reject the manifest appearance of the good, any more than persons will reject Caesar's coin. On this principle depends every movement both of man and God.

Against (or with respect to) this kind of thing chiefly a man should exercise himself. As soon as you go out in the morning, examine every man whom you see, every man whom you hear; answer as to a question, What have you seen? A handsome man or woman? Apply the rule. Is this independent of the will, or dependent? Independent. Take it away. What have you seen? A man lamenting over the death of a child. Apply the rule. Death is a thing independent of the will. Take it away. Has the proconsul met you? Apply the rule. What kind of a thing is a proconsul's office? Independent of the will or dependent on it? Independent. Take this away also; it does not stand examination; cast it away; it is nothing to you.

If we practised this and exercised ourselves in it daily from morning to night, something indeed would be done. But now we are forthwith caught half asleep by every appearance, and it is only, if ever, that in the school we are roused a little. Then when we go out, if we see a man lamenting, we say, He is undone. If we see a consul, we say, He is happy. If we see an exiled man, we say, He is miserable. If we see a poor man, we say, He is wretched; he has nothing to eat. We ought then to eradicate these bad opinions, and to this end we should direct all our efforts. For what is weeping and lamenting? Opinion. What is bad fortune? Opinion. What is civil sedition, what is divided opinion, what is blame, what is accusation, what is impiety, what is trifling? All these things are opinions, and nothing more, and opinions about things independent of the will, as if they were good and bad. Let a man transfer these opinions to things dependent on the will, and I engage for him that he will be firm and constant, whatever may be the state of things around him. Such as is a dish of water, such is the soul. Such as is the ray of light which falls on the water, such are the appearances. When the water is moved, the ray also seems to be moved, yet it is not moved. And when then a man is seized with giddiness, it is not the arts and the virtues which are confounded, but the spirit (the nervous power) on which they are impressed; but if the spirit be restored to its settled state, those things also are restored.

MISCELLANEOUS

When some person asked him how it happened that since reason has been more cultivated by the men of the present age, the progress made in former times was greater. In what respect, he answered, has it been more cultivated now, and in what respect was the progress greater then? For in that in which it has now been more cultivated, in that also the progress will now be found. At present it has been cultivated for the purpose of resolving syllogisms, and progress is made. But in former times it was cultivated for the purpose of maintaining the governing faculty in a condition conformable to nature, and progress was made. Do not then mix things which are different, and do not expect, when you are laboring at one thing to make progress in another. But see if any man among us when he is intent upon this, the keeping himself in a state conformable to nature and living so always, does not make progress. For you will not find such a man.

It is not easy to exhort weak young men; for neither is it easy to hold (soft) cheese with a hook. But those who have a good natural disposition, even if you try to turn them aside, cling still more to reason.

TO THE ADMINISTRATOR OF THE FREE CITIES WHO WAS AN EPICUREAN

When the administrator came to visit him, and the man was an Epicurean, Epictetus said, It is proper for us who are not philosophers to inquire of you who are philosophers, as those who come to a strange city inquire of the citizens and those who are acquainted with it, what is the best thing in the world, in order that we also after inquiry may go in quest of that which is best and look at it, as strangers do with the things in cities. For that there are three things which relate to man—soul, body, and things external, scarcely any man denies. It remains for you philosophers to answer what is the best. What shall we say to men? Is the flesh the best? and was it for this that Maximus sailed as far as Cassiope in winter (or bad weather) with his son, and accompanied him that he might be gratified in the flesh? When the man said that it was not, and added, Far be that from him. Is it not fit then, Epictetus said, to be actively employed about the best? It is certainly of all things the most fit. What then do we possess which is better than the flesh? The soul, he replied. And the good things of the best, are they better, or the good things of the worse? The good things of the best. And are the good things of the best within the power of the will or not within the power of the will? They are within the power of the will. Is then the pleasure of the soul a thing within the power of the will? It is, he replied. And on what shall this pleasure depend? On itself? But that cannot be conceived; for there must first exist a certain substance or nature ([Greek: ousia]) of good, by obtaining which we shall have pleasure in the soul. He assented to this also. On what then shall we depend for this pleasure of the soul? for if it shall depend on things of the soul, the substance (nature) of the good is discovered; for good cannot be one thing, and that at which we are rationally delighted another thing; nor if that which precedes is not good, can that which comes after be good, for in order that the thing which comes after may be good, that which precedes must be good. But you would not affirm this, if you are in your right mind, for you would then say what is inconsistent both with Epicurus and the rest of your doctrines. It remains then that the pleasure of the soul is in the pleasure from things of the body; and again that those bodily things must be the things which precede and the substance (nature) of the good.

Seek for doctrines which are consistent with what I say, and by making them your guide you will with pleasure abstain from things which have such persuasive power to lead us and overpower us. But if to the persuasive power of these things, we also devise such a philosophy as this which helps to push us on towards them and strengthens us to this end, what will be the consequence? In a piece of toreutic art which is the best part? the silver or the workmanship? The substance of the hand is the flesh; but the work of the hand is the principal part (that which precedes and leads the rest). The duties then are also three: those which are directed towards the existence of a thing; those which are directed towards its existence in a particular kind; and third, the chief or leading things themselves. So also in man we ought not to value the material, the poor flesh, but the principal (leading things, [Greek: ta proaegoumena]). What are these? Engaging in public business, marrying, begetting children, venerating God, taking care of parents, and generally, having desires, aversions ([Greek: echchlinein]), pursuits of things and avoidances, in the way in which we ought to do these things, and according to our nature. And how are we constituted by nature? Free, noble, modest; for what other animal blushes? what other is capable of receiving the appearance (the impression) of shame? and we are so constituted by nature as to subject pleasure to these things, as a minister, a servant, in order that it may call forth our activity, in order that it may keep us constant in acts which are conformable to nature.

HOW WE MUST EXERCISE OURSELVES AGAINST APPEARANCES

As we exercise ourselves against sophistical questions, so we ought to exercise ourselves daily against appearances; for these appearances also propose questions to us. A certain person's son is dead. Answer; the thing is not within the power of the will: it is not an evil. A father has disinherited a certain son. What do you think of it? It is a thing beyond the power of the will, not an evil. Cæsar has condemned a person. It is a thing beyond the power of the will, not an evil. The man is afflicted at this. Affliction is a thing which depends on the will: it is an evil. He has borne the condemnation bravely. That is a thing within the power of the will: it is a good. If we train ourselves in this manner, we shall make progress; for we shall never assent to anything of which there is not an appearance capable of being comprehended. Your son is dead. What has happened? Your son is dead. Nothing more? Nothing. Your ship is lost. What has happened? Your ship is lost. A man has been led to prison. What has happened? He has been led to prison. But that herein he has fared badly, every man adds from his own opinion. But Zeus, you say, does not do right in these matters. Why? because he has made you capable of endurance? because he has made you magnanimous? because he has taken from that which befalls you the power of being evils? because it is in your power to be happy while you are

184

suffering what you suffer? because he has opened the door to you, when things do not please you? Man, go out and do not complain!

Hear how the Romans feel towards philosophers, if you would like to know. Italicus, who was the most in repute of the philosophers, once when I was present, being vexed with his own friends and as if he was suffering something intolerable, said: "I cannot bear it, you are killing me; you will make me such as that man is," pointing to me.

TO A CERTAIN RHETORICIAN WHO WAS GOING UP TO ROME ON A SUIT

When a certain person came to him, who was going up to Rome on account of a suit which had regard to his rank, Epictetus inquired the reason of his going to Rome, and the man then asked what he thought about the matter. Epictetus replied: If you ask me what you will do in Rome, whether you will succeed or fail, I have no rule ([Greek: theoraema]) about this. But if you ask me how you will fare, I can tell you: if you have right opinions ([Greek: dogmata]), you will fare well; if they are false, you will fare ill. For to every man the cause of his acting is opinion. For what is the reason why you desired to be elected governor of the Cnossians? Your opinion. What is the reason that you are now going up to Rome? Your opinion. And going in winter, and with danger and expense? I must go. What tells you this? Your opinion. Then if opinions are the causes of all actions, and a man has bad opinions, such as the cause may be, such also is the effect! Have we then all sound opinions, both you and your adversary? And how do you differ? But have you sounder opinions than your adversary? Why? You think so. And so does he think that his opinions are better; and so do madmen. This is a bad criterion. But show to me that you have made some inquiry into your opinions and have taken some pains about them. And as now you are sailing to Rome in order to become governor of the Cnossians, and you are not content to stay at home with the honors which you had, but you desire something greater and more conspicuous, so when did you ever make a voyage for the purpose of examining your own opinions, and casting them out, if you have any that are bad? Whom have you approached for this purpose? What time have you fixed for it? What age? Go over the times of your life by yourself, if you are ashamed of me (knowing the fact) when you were a boy, did you examine your own opinions? and did you not then, as you do all things now, do as you did do? and when you were become a youth and attended the rhetoricians, and yourself practised rhetoric, what did you imagine that you were deficient in? And when you were a young man and engaged in public matters, and pleaded causes yourself, and were gaining reputation, who then seemed your equal? And when would you have submitted to any man examining and showing that your opinions are bad? What then do you wish me to say to you? Help me in this matter. I have no theorem (rule) for this. Nor have you, if you came to me for this purpose, come to me as a philosopher, but as to a seller of vegetables or a shoemaker. For what purpose then have philosophers theorems? For this purpose, that whatever may happen, our ruling faculty may be and continue to be conformable to nature. Does this seem to you a small thing? No; but the greatest. What then? does it need only a short time? and is it possible to seize it as you pass by? If you can, seize it.

Then you will say, I met with Epictetus as I should meet with a stone or a statue: for you saw me and nothing more. But he meets with a man as a man, who learns his opinions, and in his turn shows his own. Learn my opinions: show me yours; and then say that you have visited me. Let us examine one another: if I have any bad opinion, take it away; if you have any, show it. This is the meaning of meeting with a philosopher. Not so (you say): but this is only a passing visit, and while we are hiring the vessel, we can also see Epictetus. Let us see what he says. Then you go away and say: Epictetus was nothing; he used solecisms and spoke in a barbarous way. For of what else do you come as judges? Well, but a man may say to me, if I attend to such matters (as you do), I shall have no land as you have none; I shall have no silver cups as you have none, nor fine beasts as you have none. In answer to this it is perhaps sufficient to say: I have no need of such things; but if you possess many things you have need of others: whether you choose or not, you are poorer than I am. What then have I need of? Of that which you have not? of firmness, of a mind which is conformable to nature, of being free from perturbation.

IN WHAT MANNER WE OUGHT TO BEAR SICKNESS

When the need of each opinion comes, we ought to have it in readiness: on the occasion of breakfast, such opinions as relate to breakfast; in the bath, those that concern the bath; in bed, those that concern bed.

Let sleep not come upon thy languid eyes
Before each daily action thou hast scann'd;
What's done amiss, what done, what left undone;
From first to last examine all, and then
Blame what is wrong, in what is right rejoice.

And we ought to retain these verses in such way that we may use them, not that we may utter them aloud, as when we exclaim, "Paean Apollo." Again in fever we should have ready such opinions as concern a fever; and we ought not, as soon as the fever begins, to lose and forget all. A man who has a fever may say: If I philosophize any longer, may I be hanged: wherever I go, I must take care of the poor body, that a fever may not come. But what is philosophizing? Is it not a preparation against events which may happen? Do you not understand that you are saying something of this kind? "If I shall still prepare myself to bear with patience what happens, may I be hanged." But this is just as if a man after receiving blows should give up the Pancratium. In the Pancratium it is in our power to desist and not to receive blows.

But in the other matter if we give up philosophy, what shall we gain? What then should a man say on the occasion of each painful thing? It was for this that I exercised myself, for this I disciplined myself. God says to you: Give me a proof that you have duly practised athletics, that you have eaten what you ought, that you have been exercised, that you have obeyed the aliptes (the oiler and rubber). Then do you show yourself weak when the time for action comes? Now is the time for the fever. Let it be borne well. Now is the time for thirst, bear it well. Now is the time for hunger, bear it well. Is it not in your power? Who shall hinder you? The physician will hinder you from drinking; but he cannot prevent you from bearing thirst well: and he will hinder you from eating; but he cannot prevent you from bearing hunger well.

But I cannot attend to my philosophical studies. And for what purpose do you follow them? Slave, is it not that you may be happy, that you may be constant, is it not that you may be in a state conformable to nature and live so? What hinders you when you have a fever from having your ruling faculty conformable to nature? Here is the proof of the thing, here is the test of the philosopher. For this also is a part of life, like walking, like sailing, like journeying by land, so also is fever. Do you read when you are walking? No. Nor do you when you have a fever. But if you walk about well, you have all that belongs to a man who walks. If you bear a fever well, you have all that belongs to a man in a fever. What is it to bear a fever well? Not to blame God or man; not to be afflicted at that which happens, to expect death well and nobly, to do what must be done: when the physician comes in, not to be frightened at what he says; nor if he says you are doing well, to be overjoyed. For what good has he told you? and when you were in health, what good was that to you? And even if he says you are in a bad way, do not despond. For what is it to be ill? is it that you are near the severance of the soul and the body? what harm is there in this? If you are not near now, will you not afterwards be near? Is the world going to be turned upside down when you are dead? Why then do you flatter the physician? Why do you say if you please, master, I shall be well? Why do you give him an opportunity of raising his eyebrows (being proud; or showing his importance)? Do you not value a physician, as you do a shoemaker when he is measuring your foot, or a carpenter when he is building your house, and so treat the physician as to the body which is not yours, but by nature dead? He who has a fever has an opportunity of doing this: if he does these things, he has what belongs to him. For it is not the business of a philosopher to look after these externals, neither his wine nor his oil nor his poor body, but his own ruling power. But as to externals how must he act? so far as not to be careless about them. Where then is there reason for fear? where is there then still reason for anger, and of fear about what belongs to others, about things which are of no value? For we ought to have these two principles in readiness, that except the will nothing is good nor bad; and that we ought not to lead events, but to follow them. My brother ought not to have behaved thus to me. No, but he will see to that; and, however he may behave, I will conduct myself towards him as I ought. For this is my own business; that belongs to another: no man can prevent this, the other thing can be hindered.

ABOUT EXERCISE

We ought not to make our exercises consist in means contrary to nature and adapted to cause admiration, for if we do so, we who call ourselves philosophers, shall not differ at all from jugglers. For it is difficult even to walk on a rope; and not only difficult, but it is also dangerous. Ought we for this reason to practice walking on a rope, or setting up a palm-tree, or embracing statues? By no means. Every thing which is difficult and dangerous is not suitable for practice; but that is suitable which conduces to the working out of that which is proposed to us. And what is that which is proposed to us as a thing to be worked out? To live with desire and aversion (avoidance of certain things) free from restraint. And what is this? Neither to be disappointed in that which you desire, nor to fall into anything which you would avoid. Towards this object then exercise (practice) ought to tend. For since it is not possible to have your desire not disappointed and your aversion free from falling into that which you would avoid, without great and constant practice, you must know that if you allow your desire and aversion to turn to things which are not within the power of the will, you will neither have your desire capable of attaining your object, nor your aversion free from the power of avoiding that which you would avoid. And since strong habit leads (prevails), and we are accustomed to employ desire and aversion only to things which are not within the power of our will, we ought to oppose to this habit a contrary habit, and where there is great slipperiness in the appearances, there to oppose the habit of exercise. Then at last, if occasion presents itself, for the purpose of trying yourself at a proper time you will descend into the arena to know if appearances overpower you as they did formerly. But at first fly far from that which is stronger than yourself; the contest is unequal between a charming young girl and a beginner in philosophy. The earthen pitcher, as the saying is, and the rock do not agree.

WHAT SOLITUDE IS, AND WHAT KIND OF PERSON A SOLITARY MAN IS

Solitude is a certain condition of a helpless man. For because a man is alone, he is not for that reason also solitary; just as though a man is among numbers, he is not therefore not solitary. When then we have lost either a brother, or a son, or a friend on whom we were accustomed to repose, we say that we are left solitary, though we are often in Rome, though such a crowd meet us, though so many live in the same place, and sometimes we have a great number of slaves. For the man who is solitary, as it is conceived, is considered to be a helpless person and exposed to those who wish to harm him. For this reason when we travel, then especially do we say that we are lonely when we fall among robbers, for it is not the sight of a human creature which removes us from solitude, but the sight of one who is faithful and modest and helpful to us. For if being alone is enough to make solitude, you may say that even Zeus is solitary in the conflagration and bewails himself saying, Unhappy that I am who have neither Hera, nor Athena, nor Apollo, nor brother, nor son, nor descendant, nor kinsman. This is what some say that he does when he is alone at the conflagration. For they do not understand how a man passes his life when he is alone, because they set out from a certain natural principle, from the natural desire of community and mutual love and from the pleasure of conversation among men. But none the less a man ought to be prepared in a manner for this also (being alone), to be able to be sufficient for himself and to be his own companion. For as Zeus dwells with himself, and is tranquil by himself, and thinks of his own administration and of its nature, and is employed in thoughts suitable to himself; so ought we also to be able to talk with ourselves, not to feel the want of others also, not to be unprovided with the means of passing our time; to observe the divine administration, and the relation of ourselves to everything else; to consider how we formerly were affected towards things that happened and how at present; what are still the things which give us pain; how these also can be cured and how removed; if any things require improvement, to improve them according to reason.

Well then, if some man should come upon me when I am alone and murder me? Fool, not murder You, but your poor body.

What kind of solitude then remains? what want? why do we make ourselves worse than children; and what do children do when they are left alone? They take up shells and ashes, and they build something, then pull it down, and build something else, and so they never want the means of passing the time. Shall I then, if you sail away, sit down and weep, because I have been left alone and solitary? Shall I then have no shells, no ashes? But children do what they do through want of thought (or deficiency in knowledge), and we through knowledge are unhappy.

Every great power (faculty) is dangerous to beginners. You must then bear such things as you are able, but conformably to nature: but not ... Practise sometimes a way of living like a person out of health that you may at some time live like a man in health.

CERTAIN MISCELLANEOUS MATTERS

As bad tragic actors cannot sing alone, but in company with many, so some persons cannot walk about alone. Man, if you are anything, both walk alone and talk to yourself, and do not hide yourself in the chorus. Examine a little at last, look around, stir yourself up, that you may know who you are.

You must root out of men these two things, arrogance (pride) and distrust. Arrogance then is the opinion that you want nothing (are deficient in nothing); but distrust is the opinion that you cannot be happy when so many circumstances surround you. Arrogance is removed by confutation; and Socrates was the first who practised this. And (to know) that the thing is not impossible inquire and seek. This search will do you no harm; and in a manner this is philosophizing, to seek how it is possible to employ desire and aversion ([Greek: echchlisis]) without impediment.

I am superior to you, for my father is a man of consular rank. Another says, I have been a tribune, but you have not. If we were horses, would you say, My father was swifter? I have much barley and fodder, or elegant neck ornaments. If then you were saying this, I said, Be it so: let us run then. Well, is there nothing in a man such as running in a horse, by which it will be known which is superior and inferior? Is there not modesty ([Greek: aidos]), fidelity, justice? Show yourself superior in these, that you may be superior as a man. If you tell me that you can kick violently, I also will say to you, that you are proud of that which is the act of an ass.

THAT WE OUGHT TO PROCEED WITH CIRCUMSPECTION TO EVERYTHING

In every act consider what precedes and what follows, and then proceed to the act. If you do not consider, you will at first begin with spirit, since you have not thought at all of the things which follow; but afterwards when some consequences have shown themselves, you will basely desist (from that which you have begun).—I wish to conquer at the Olympic games.—(And I too, by the gods; for it is a fine thing.) But consider here what precedes and what follows; and then, if it is for your good, undertake the thing. You must act according to rules, follow strict diet, abstain from delicacies, exercise yourself by compulsion at fixed times, in heat, in cold; drink no cold water, nor wine, when there is opportunity of drinking it. In a word, you must surrender yourself to the trainer, as you do to a physician. Next in the contest, you must be covered with sand, sometimes dislocate a hand, sprain an ankle, swallow a quantity of dust, be scourged with the whip; and after undergoing all this, you must sometimes be conquered. After reckoning all these things, if you have still an inclination, go to the athletic practice. If you do not reckon them, observe you will behave like children who at one time play as wrestlers, then as gladiators, then blow a trumpet, then act a tragedy, when they have seen and admired such things. So you also do: you are at one time a wrestler (athlete), then a gladiator, then a philosopher, then a rhetorician; but with your whole soul you are nothing: like the ape you imitate all that you see; and always one thing after another pleases you, but that which becomes familiar displeases you. For you have never undertaken anything after consideration, nor after having explored the whole matter and put it to a strict examination; but you have undertaken it at hazard and with a cold desire. Thus some persons having seen a philosopher and having heard one speak like Euphrates—and yet who can speak like him?—wish to be philosophers themselves.

Man, consider first what the matter is (which you propose to do), then your own nature also, what it is able to bear. If you are a wrestler, look at your shoulders, your thighs, your loins: for different men are naturally formed for different things. Do you think that, if you do (what you are doing daily), you can be a philosopher? Do you think that you can eat as you do now, drink as you do now, and in the same way be angry and out of humor? You must watch, labor, conquer certain desires, you must depart from your kinsmen, be despised by your slaves, laughed at by those who meet you, in everything you must be in an inferior condition, as to magisterial office, in honors, in courts of justice. When you have considered all these things completely, then, if you think proper, approach to philosophy, if you would gain in exchange for these things freedom from perturbations, liberty, tranquillity. If you have not considered these things, do not approach philosophy: do not act like children, at one time a philosopher, then a tax collector, then a rhetorician, then a procurator (officer) of Cæsar. These things are not consistent. You must be one man either good or bad; you must either labor at your own ruling faculty or at external things; you must either labor at things within or at external things; that is, you must either occupy the place of a philosopher or that of one of the vulgar.

A person said to Rufus when Galba was murdered: Is the world now governed by Providence? But Rufus replied: Did I ever incidentally form an argument from Galba that the world is governed by Providence?

THAT WE OUGHT WITH CAUTION TO ENTER INTO FAMILIAR INTERCOURSE WITH MEN

If a man has frequent intercourse with others either for talk, or drinking together, or generally for social purposes, he must either become like them, or change them to his own fashion. For if a man places a piece of quenched charcoal close to a piece that is burning, either the quenched charcoal will quench the other, or the burning charcoal will light that which is quenched. Since then the danger is so great, we must cautiously enter into such intimacies with those of the common sort, and remember that it is impossible that a man can keep company with one who is covered with soot without being partaker of the soot himself. For what will you do if a man speaks about gladiators, about horses, about athletes, or what is worse about men? Such a person is bad, such a person is good; this was well done, this was done badly. Further, if he scoff, or ridicule, or show an ill-natured disposition? Is any man among us prepared like a lute-player when he takes a lute, so that as soon as he has touched the strings, he discovers which are discordant, and tunes the instrument? Such a power as Socrates had who in all his social intercourse could lead his companions to his own purpose? How should you have this power? It is therefore a necessary consequence that you are carried about by the common kind of people.

Why then are they more powerful than you? Because they utter these useless words from their real opinions; but you utter your elegant words only from your lips; for this reason they are without strength and dead, and it is nauseous to listen to your exhortations and your miserable virtue, which is talked of everywhere (up and down). In this way the vulgar have the advantage over you; for every opinion ([Greek: dogma]) is strong and invincible. Until then the good ([Greek: chompsai]) sentiments ([Greek: hupolaepseis]) are fixed in you, and you shall have acquired a certain power for your security, I advise you to be careful in your association with common persons; if you are not, every day like wax in the sun there will be melted away whatever you inscribe on your minds in the school. Withdraw then yourselves far from the sun so long as you have these waxen sentiments. For this reason also philosophers advise men to leave their native country, because ancient habits distract them and do not allow a beginning to be made of a different habit; nor can we tolerate those who meet us and say: See such a one is now a philosopher, who was once so and so. Thus also physicians send those who have lingering diseases to a different country and a different air; and they do right. Do you also introduce other habits than those which you have; fix you opinions and exercise yourselves in them. But you do not so; you go hence to a spectacle, to a show of gladiators, to a place of exercise ([Greek: chuston]), to a circus; then you come back hither, and again from this place you go to those places, and still the same persons. And there is no pleasing (good) habit, nor attention, nor care about self and observation of this kind. How shall I use the appearances presented to me? according to nature, or contrary to nature? how do I answer to them? as I ought, or as I ought not? Do I say to those things which are independent of the will, that they do not concern me? For if you are not yet in this state, fly from your former habits, fly from the common sort, if you intend ever to begin to be something.

ON PROVIDENCE

When you make any charge against Providence, consider, and you will learn that the thing has happened according to reason. Yes, but the unjust man has the advantage. In what? In money. Yes, for he is superior to you in this, that he flatters, is free from shame, and is watchful. What is the wonder? But see if he has the advantage over you in being faithful, in being modest; for you will not find it to be so; but wherein you are superior, there you will find that you have the advantage. And I once said to a man who was vexed because Philostorgus was fortunate: Would you choose to lie with Sura? May it never happen, he replied, that this day should come? Why then are you vexed, if he receives something in return for that which he sells; or how can you consider him happy who acquires those things by such means as you abominate; or what wrong does Providence, if he gives the better things to the better men? Is it not better to be modest than to be rich? He admitted this. Why are you vexed then, man, when you possess the better thing? Remember then always and have in readiness the truth, that this is a law of nature, that the superior has an advantage over the inferior in that in which he is superior; and you will never be vexed.

But my wife treats me badly. Well, if any man asks you what this is, say, my wife treats me badly. Is there then nothing more? Nothing. My father gives me nothing. (What is this? my father gives me nothing. Is there nothing else then? Nothing); but to say that this is an evil is something which must be added to it externally, and falsely added. For this reason we must not get rid of poverty, but of the opinion about poverty, and then we shall be happy.

ABOUT CYNICISM

When one of his pupils inquired of Epictetus, and he was a person who appeared to be inclined to Cynicism, what kind of person a Cynic ought to be, and what was the notion ([Greek: prolaepsis]) of the thing, we will inquire, said Epictetus, at leisure; but I have so much to say to you that he who without God attempts so great a matter, is hateful to God, and has no other purpose than to act indecently in public.

In the first place, in the things which relate to yourself, you must not be in any respect like what you do now; you must not blame God or man; you must take away desire altogether, you must transfer avoidance ([Greek: echchlisis]) only to the things which are within the power of the will; you must not feel anger nor resentment or envy nor pity; a girl must not appear handsome to you, nor must you love a little reputation, nor be pleased with a boy or a cake. For you ought to know that the rest of men throw walls around them and houses and darkness when they do any such things, and they have many means of concealment. A man shuts the door, he sets somebody before the chamber; if a person comes, say that he is out, he is not at leisure. But the Cynic instead of all these things must use modesty as his protection; if he does not, he will be indecent in his nakedness and under the open sky. This is his house, his door; this is the slave before his bedchamber; this is his darkness. For he ought not to wish to hide anything that he does; and if he does, he is gone, he has lost the character of a Cynic, of a man who lives under the open sky, of a free man; he has begun to fear some external thing, he has begun to have need of concealment, nor can he get concealment when he chooses. For where shall he hide himself and how? And if by chance this public instructor shall be detected, this pædagogue, what kind of things will he be compelled to suffer? when then a man fears these things, is it possible for him to be bold with his whole soul to superintend men? It cannot be: it is impossible.

In the first place then you must make your ruling faculty pure, and this mode of life also. Now (you should say), to me the matter to work on is my understanding, as wood is to the carpenter, as hides to the shoemaker; and my business is the right use of appearances. But the body is nothing to me: the parts of it are nothing to me. Death? Let it come when it chooses, either death of the whole or of a part. Fly, you say. And whither; can any man eject me out of the world? He cannot. But wherever I go, there is the sun, there is the moon, there are the stars, dreams, omens, and the conversation ([Greek: omilia]) with gods.

Then, if he is thus prepared, the true Cynic cannot be satisfied with this; but he must know that he is sent a messenger from Zeus to men about good and bad things, to show them that they have wandered and are seeking the substance of good and evil where it is not, but where it is, they never think; and that he is a spy, as Diogenes was carried off to Philip after the battle of Chaeroneia as a spy. For in fact a Cynic is a spy of the things which are good for men and which are evil, and it is his duty to examine carefully and to come and report truly, and not to be struck with terror so as to point out as enemies those who are not enemies, nor in any other way to be perturbed by appearances nor confounded.

It is his duty then to be able with a loud voice, if the occasion should arise, and appearing on the tragic stage to say like Socrates: Men, whither are you hurrying, what are you doing, wretches? like blind people you are wandering up and down; you are going by another road, and have left the true road; you seek for prosperity and happiness where they are not, and if another shows you where they are, you do not believe him. Why do you seek it without? In the body? It is not there. If you doubt, look at Myro, look at Ophellius. In possessions? It is not there. But if you do not believe me, look at Croesus: look at those who are now rich, with what lamentations their life is filled. In power? It is not there. If it is, those must be happy who have been twice and thrice consuls; but they are not. Whom shall we believe in these matters? You who from without see their affairs and are dazzled by an appearance, or the men themselves? What do they say? Hear them when they groan, when they grieve, when on account of these very consulships and glory and splendor they think that they are more wretched and in greater danger. Is it in royal power? It is not: if it were, Nero would have been happy, and Sardanapalus. But neither was Agamemnon happy, though he was a better man than Sardanapalus and Nero; but while others are snoring, what is he doing?

"Much from his head he tore his rooted hair." Iliad, x., 15.

and what does he say himself?

"I am perplexed," he says, "and disturb'd I am," and "my heart out of my bosom Is leaping."
Iliad, x., 91.

Wretch, which of your affairs goes badly? Your possessions? No. Your body? No. But you are rich in gold and copper. What then is the matter with you?

That part of you, whatever it is, has been neglected by you and is corrupted, the part with which we desire, with which we avoid, with which we move towards and move from things. How neglected? He knows not the nature of good for which he is made by nature and the nature of evil; and what is his own, and what belongs to another; and when anything that belongs to others goes badly, he says, Woe to me, for the Hellenes are in danger. Wretched is his ruling faculty, and alone neglected and uncared for. The Hellenes are going to die destroyed by the Trojans. And if the Trojans do not kill them, will they not die? Yes; but not all at once. What difference then does it make? For if death is an evil, whether men die altogether, or if they die singly, it is equally an evil. Is anything else then going to happen than the separation of the soul and the body? Nothing. And if the Hellenes perish, is the door closed, and is it not in your power to die? It is. Why then do you lament (and say), Oh, you are a king and have the sceptre of Zeus? An unhappy king does not exist more than an unhappy god. What then art thou? In truth a shepherd: for you weep as shepherds do, when a wolf has carried off one of their sheep: and these who are governed by you are sheep. And why did you come hither? Was your desire in any danger? was your aversion ([Greek: echchlisis])? was your movement (pursuits)? was your avoidance of things? He replies, No; but the wife of my brother was carried off. Was it not then a great gain to be deprived of an adulterous wife? Shall we be despised then by the Trojans? What kind of people are the Trojans, wise or foolish? If they are wise, why do you fight with them? If they are fools, why do you care about them?

Do you possess the body then free or is it in servile condition? We do not know. Do you not know that it is the slave of fever, of gout, ophthalmia, dysentery, of a tyrant, of fire, of iron, of everything which is stronger? Yes, it is a slave. How then is it possible that anything which belongs to the body can be free from hindrance? and how is a thing great or valuable which is naturally dead, or earth, or mud? Well then, do you possess nothing which is free? Perhaps nothing. And who is able to compel you to assent to that which appears false? No man. And who can compel you not to assent to that which appears true? No man. By this then you see that there is something in you naturally free. But to desire or to be averse from, or to move towards an object or to move from it, or to prepare yourself, or to propose to do anything, which of you can do this, unless he has received an impression of the appearance of that which is profitable or a duty? No man. You have then in these things also something which is not hindered and is free. Wretched men, work out this, take care of this, seek for good here.

THAT WE OUGHT NOT TO BE MOVED BY A DESIRE OF THOSE THINGS WHICH ARE NOT IN OUR POWER

Let not that which in another is contrary to nature be an evil to you; for you are not formed by nature to be depressed with others nor to be unhappy with others, but to be happy with them. If a man is unhappy, remember that his unhappiness is his own fault; for God has made all men to be happy, to be free from perturbations. For this purpose he has given means to them, some things to each person as his own, and other things not as his own; some things subject to hindrance and compulsion and deprivation; and these things are not a man's own; but the things which are not subject to hindrances, are his own; and the nature of good and evil, as it was fit to be done by him who takes care of us and protects us like a father, he has made our own. But you say, I have parted from a certain person, and he is grieved. Why did he consider as his own that which belongs to another? why, when he looked on you and was rejoiced, did he not also reckon that you are a mortal, that it is natural for you to part from him for a foreign country? Therefore he suffers the consequences of his own folly. But why do you or for what purpose bewail yourself? Is it that you also have not thought of these things? but like poor women who are good for nothing, you have enjoyed all things in which you took pleasure, as if you would always enjoy them, both places and men and conversation; and now you sit and weep because you do not see the same persons and do not live in the same places. Indeed you deserve this, to be more wretched than crows and ravens who have the power of flying where they please and changing their nests for others, and crossing the seas without lamenting or regretting their former condition. Yes, but this happens to them because they are irrational creatures. Was reason then given to us by the gods for the purpose of unhappiness and misery, that we may pass our lives in wretchedness and lamentation? Must all persons be immortal and must no man go abroad, and must we ourselves not go abroad, but remain rooted like plants; and if any of our familiar friends goes abroad, must we sit and weep; and on the contrary, when he returns, must we dance and clap our hands like children?

But my mother laments when she does not see me. Why has she not learned these principles? and I do not say this, that we should not take care that she may not lament, but I say that we ought not to desire in every way what is not our own. And the sorrow of another is another's sorrow; but my sorrow is my own. I then will stop my own sorrow by every means, for it is in my power; and the sorrow of another I will endeavor to stop as far as I can; but I will not attempt to do it by every means; for if I do, I shall be fighting against God, I shall be opposing Zeus and shall be placing myself against him in the administration of the universe; and the reward (the punishment) of this fighting against God and of this disobedience not only will the children of my children pay, but I also shall myself, both by day and by night, startled by dreams, perturbed, trembling at every piece of news, and having my tranquillity depending on the letters of others. Some person has arrived from Rome. I only hope there is no harm. But what harm can happen to you, where you are not? From Hellas (Greece) some one is come; I hope that there is no harm. In this way every place may be the cause of misfortune to you. Is it not enough for you to be unfortunate there where you are, and must you be so even beyond sea, and by the report of letters? Is this the way in which your affairs are in a state of security? Well then suppose that my friends have died in the places which are far from me. What else have they suffered than that which is the condition of mortals? Or how are you desirous at the same time to live to old age, and at the same time not to see the death of any person whom you love? Know you not that in the course of a long time many and various kinds of things must happen; that a fever shall overpower one, a robber another, and a third a tyrant? Such is the condition of things around us, such are those who live with us in the world; cold and heat, and unsuitable ways of living, and journeys by land, and voyages by sea, and winds, and various circumstances which surround us, destroy one man, and banish another, and throw one upon an embassy and another into an army. Sit down then in a flutter at all these things, lamenting, unhappy, unfortunate, dependent on another, and dependent not on one or two, but on ten thousands upon ten thousands.

Did you hear this when you were with the philosophers? did you learn this? do you not know that human life is a warfare? that one man must keep watch, another must go out as a spy, and a third must fight? and it is not possible that all should be in one place, nor is it better that it should be so. But you neglecting to do the commands of the general complain when anything more hard than usual is imposed on you, and you do not observe what you make the army become as far as it is in your power; that if all imitate you, no man will dig a trench, no man will put a rampart round, nor keep watch, nor expose himself to danger, but will appear to be useless for the purposes of an army. Again, in a vessel if you go as a sailor, keep to one place and stick to it. And if you are ordered to climb the mast, refuse; if to run to the head of the ship, refuse; and what master of a ship will endure you? and will he not pitch you overboard as a useless thing, an impediment only and bad example to the other sailors? And so it is here also: every man's life is a kind of warfare, and it is long and diversified. You must observe the duty of a soldier and do every thing at the nod of the general; if it is possible, divining what his wishes are; for there is no resemblance between that general and this, neither in strength nor in superiority of character. Know you not that a good man does nothing for the sake of appearance, but for the sake of doing right? What advantage is it then to him to have done right? And what advantage is it to a man who writes the name of Dion to write it as he ought? The advantage is to have written it. Is there no reward then? Do you seek a reward for a good man greater than doing what is good and just? At Olympia you wish for nothing more, but it seems to you enough to be crowned at the games. Does it seem to you so small and worthless a thing to be good and happy? For these purposes being introduced by the gods into this city (the world), and it being now your duty to undertake the work of a man, do you still want nurses also and a mamma, and do foolish women by their weeping move you and make you effeminate? Will you thus never cease to be a foolish child? know you not that he who does the acts of a child, the older he is, the more ridiculous he is?

So in this matter also: if you kiss your own child, or your brother or friend, never give full license to the appearance ([Greek: phantasian]), and allow not your pleasure to go as far as it chooses; but check it, and curb it as those who stand behind men in their triumphs and remind them that they are mortal. Do you also remind yourself in like manner, that he whom you love is mortal, and that what you love is nothing of your own; it has been given to you for the present, not that it should not be taken from you, nor has it been given to you for all time, but as a fig is given to you or a bunch of grapes at the appointed season of the year. But if you wish for these things in winter, you are a fool. So if you wish for your son or friend when it is not allowed to you, you must know that you are wishing for a fig in winter. For such as winter is to a fig, such is every event which happens from the universe to the things which are taken away according to its nature. And further, at the times when you are delighted with a thing, place before yourself the contrary appearances. What harm is it while you are kissing your child to say with a lisping voice: To-morrow you will die; and to a friend also: To-morrow you will go away or I shall, and never shall we see one another again? But these are words of bad omen—and some incantations also are of bad omen; but because they are useful, I don't care for this; only let them be useful. But do you call things to be of bad omen except those which are significant of some evil? Cowardice is a word of bad omen, and meanness of spirit, and sorrow, and grief, and shamelessness. These words are of bad omen; and yet we ought not to hesitate to utter them in order to protect ourselves against the things. Do you tell me that a name which is significant of any natural thing is of evil omen? say that even for the ears of corn to be reaped is of bad omen, for it signifies the destruction of the ears, but not of the world. Say that the falling of the leaves also is of bad omen, and for the dried fig to take the place of the green fig, and for raisins to be made from the grapes. For all these things are changes from a former state into other states; not a destruction, but a certain fixed economy and administration. Such is going away from home and a small change: such is death, a greater change, not from the state which now is to that which is not, but to that which is not now. Shall I then no longer exist? You will not exist, but you will be something else, of which the world now has need; for you also came into existence not when you chose, but when the world had need of you. Let these thoughts be ready to hand by night and by day; these you should write, these you should read; about these you should talk to yourself and to others. Ask a man: Can you help me at all for this purpose? and further, go to another and to another. Then if anything that is said be contrary to your wish, this reflection first will immediately relieve you, that it is not unexpected. For it is a great thing in all cases to say: I knew that I begot a son who is mortal. For so you also will say: I knew that I am mortal, I knew that I may leave my home, I knew that I may be ejected from it, I knew that I may be led to prison. Then if you turn round and look to yourself, and seek the place from which comes that which has happened, you will forthwith recollect that it comes from the place of things which are out of the power of the will, and of things which are not my own. What then is it to me? Then, you will ask, and this is the chief thing: And who is it that sent it? The leader, or the general, the state, the law of the state. Give it me then, for I must always obey the law in everything. Then, when the appearance (of things) pains you, for it is not in your power to prevent this, contend against it by the aid of reason, conquer it: do not allow it to gain strength nor to lead you to the consequences by raising images such as it pleases and as it pleases. If you be in Gyara, do not imagine the mode of living at Rome, and how many pleasures there were for him who lived there and how many there would be for him who returned to Rome; but fix your mind on this matter, how a man who lives in Gyara ought to live in Gyara like a man of courage. And if you be in Rome, do not imagine what the life in Athens is, but think only of the life in Rome.

Then in the place of all other delights substitute this, that of being conscious that you are obeying God, that not in word, but in deed you are performing the acts of a wise and good man. For what a thing it is for a man to be able to say to himself: Now whatever the rest may say in solemn manner in the schools and may be judged to be saying in a way contrary to common opinion (or in a strange way), this I am doing; and they are sitting and are discoursing of my virtues and inquiring about me and praising me; and of this Zeus has willed that I shall receive from myself a demonstration, and shall myself know if he has a soldier such as he ought to have, a citizen such as he ought to have, and if he has chosen to produce me to the rest of mankind as a witness of the things which are independent of the will: See that you fear without reason, that you foolishly desire what you do desire; seek not the good in things external; seek it in yourselves: if you do not, you will not find it. For this purpose he leads me at one time hither, at another time sends me thither, shows me to men as poor, without authority, and sick; sends me to Gyara, leads me into prison, not because he hates me—far from him be such a meaning, for who hates the best of his servants? nor yet because he cares not for me, for he does not neglect any even of the smallest things; but he does this for the purpose of exercising me and making use of me as a witness to others. Being appointed to such a service, do I still care about the place in which I am, or with whom I am, or what men say about me? and do I not entirely direct my thoughts to God and to his instructions and commands?

Having these things (or thoughts) always in hand, and exercising them by yourself, and keeping them in readiness, you will never be in want of one to comfort you and strengthen you. For it is not shameful to be without something to eat, but not to have reason sufficient for keeping away fear and sorrow. But if once you have gained exemption from sorrow and fear, will there any longer be a tyrant for you, or a tyrant's guard, or attendants on Cæsar? Or shall any appointment to offices at court cause you pain, or shall those who sacrifice in the Capitol on the occasion of being named to certain functions, cause pain to you who have received so great authority from Zeus? Only do not make a proud display of it, nor boast of it; but show it by your acts; and if no man perceives it, be satisfied that you are yourself in a healthy state and happy.

TO THOSE WHO FALL OFF (DESIST) FROM THEIR PURPOSE

Consider as to the things which you proposed to yourself at first, which you have secured, and which you have not; and how you are pleased when you recall to memory the one, and are pained about the other; and if it is possible, recover the things wherein you failed. For we must not shrink when we are engaged in the greatest combat, but we must even take blows. For the combat before us is not in wrestling and the Pancration, in which both the successful and the unsuccessful may have the greatest merit, or may have little, and in truth may be very fortunate or very unfortunate; but the combat is for good fortune and happiness themselves. Well then, even if we have renounced the contest in this matter (for good fortune and happiness), no man hinders us from renewing the combat again, and we are not compelled to wait for another four years that the games at Olympia may come again; but as soon as you have recovered and restored yourself, and employ the same zeal, you may renew the combat again; and if again you renounce it, you may again renew it; and if you once gain the victory, you are like him who has never renounced the combat. Only do not through a habit of doing the same thing (renouncing the combat), begin to do it with pleasure, and then like a bad athlete go about after being conquered in all the circuit of the games like quails who have run away.

TO THOSE WHO FEAR WANT

Are you not ashamed at being more cowardly and more mean than fugitive slaves? How do they when they run away leave their masters? on what estates do they depend, and what domestics do they rely on? Do they not after stealing a little, which is enough for the first days, then afterwards move on through land or through sea, contriving one method after another for maintaining their lives? And what fugitive slave ever died of hunger? But you are afraid lest necessary things should fail you, and are sleepless by night. Wretch, are you so blind, and don't you see the road to which the want of necessaries leads?—Well, where does it lead?—to the same place to which a fever leads, or a stone that falls on you, to death. Have you not often said this yourself to your companions? have you not read much of this kind, and written much? and how often have you boasted that you were easy as to death? Learn then first what are the things which are shameful, and then tell us that you are a philosopher: but at present do not, even if any other man calls you so, allow it.

Is that shameful to you which is not your own act, that of which you are not the cause, that which has come to you by accident, as a headache, as a fever? If your parents were poor, and left their property to others, and if while they live, they do not help you at all, is this shameful to you? Is this what you learned with the philosophers? Did you never hear that the thing which is shameful ought to be blamed, and that which is blamable is worthy of blame? Whom do you blame for an act which is not his own, which he did not do himself? Did you then make your father such as he is, or is it in your power to improve him? Is this power given to you? Well then, ought you to wish the things which are not given to you, or to be ashamed if you do not obtain them? And have you also been accustomed while you were studying philosophy to look to others and to hope for nothing from yourself? Lament then and groan and eat with fear that you may not have food to-morrow. Tremble about your poor slaves lest they steal, lest they run away, lest they die. So live, and continue to live, you who in name only have approached philosophy, and have disgraced its theorems as far as you can by showing them to be useless and unprofitable to those who take them up; you, who have never sought constancy, freedom from perturbation, and from passions; you who have not sought any person for the sake of this object, but many for the sake of syllogisms; you who have

200

never thoroughly examined any of these appearances by yourself, Am I able to bear, or am I not able to bear? What remains for me to do? But as if all your affairs were well and secure, you have been resting on the third topic, that of things being unchanged, in order that you may possess unchanged—what? cowardice, mean spirit, the admiration of the rich, desire without attaining any end, and avoidance ([Greek: echchlisin]) which fails in the attempt? About security in these things you have been anxious.

Ought you not to have gained something in addition from reason, and then to have protected this with security? And whom did you ever see building a battlement all around and encircling it with a wall? And what doorkeeper is placed with no door to watch? But you practise in order to be able to prove— what? You practise that you may not be tossed as on the sea through sophisms, and tossed about from what? Show me first what you hold, what you measure, or what you weigh; and show me the scales or the medimnus (the measure); or how long will you go on measuring the dust? Ought you not to demonstrate those things which make men happy, which make things go on for them in the way as they wish, and why we ought to blame no man, accuse no man, and acquiesce in the administration of the universe?

ABOUT FREEDOM

He is free who lives as he wishes to live; who is neither subject to compulsion nor to hindrance, nor to force; whose movements to action ([Greek: hormai]) are not impeded, whose desires attain their purpose, and who does not fall into that which he would avoid ([Greek: echchliseis aperiptotoi]). Who then chooses to live in error? No man. Who chooses to live deceived, liable to mistake, unjust, unrestrained, discontented, mean? No man. Not one then of the bad lives as he wishes; nor is he then free. And who chooses to live in sorrow, fear, envy, pity, desiring and failing in his desires, attempting to avoid something and falling into it? Not one. Do we then find any of the bad free from sorrow, free from fear, who does not fall into that which he would avoid, and does not obtain that which he wishes? Not one; nor then do we find any bad man free.

Further, then, answer me this question, also: does freedom seem to you to be something great and noble and valuable? How should it not seem so? Is it possible then when a man obtains anything so great and valuable and noble to be mean? It is not possible. When then you see any man subject to another or flattering him contrary to his own opinion, confidently affirm that this man also is not free; and not only if he do this for a bit of supper, but also if he does it for a government (province) or a consulship; and call these men little slaves who for the sake of little matters do these things, and those who do so for the sake of great things call great slaves, as they deserve to be. This is admitted also. Do you think that freedom is a thing independent and self-governing? Certainly. Whomsoever then it is in the power of another to hinder and compel, declare that he is not free. And do not look, I entreat you, after his grandfathers and great-grandfathers, or inquire about his being bought or sold, but if you hear him saying from his heart and with feeling, "Master," even if the twelve fasces precede him (as consul), call him a slave. And if you hear him say, "Wretch that I am, how much I suffer," call him a slave. If, finally, you see him lamenting, complaining, unhappy, call him a slave, though he wears a praetexta. If, then, he is doing nothing of this kind do not yet say that he is free, but learn his opinions, whether they are subject to compulsion, or may produce hindrance, or to bad fortune, and if you find him such, call him a slave who has a holiday in the Saturnalia; say that his master is from home; he will return soon, and you will know what he suffers.

What then is that which makes a man free from hindrance and makes him his own master? For wealth does not do it, nor consulship, nor provincial government, nor royal power; but something else must be discovered. What then is that which when we write makes us free from hindrance and unimpeded? The knowledge of the art of writing. What then is it in playing the lute? The science of playing the lute. Therefore in life also it is the science of life. You have then heard in a general way; but examine the thing also in the several parts. Is it possible that he who desires any of the things which depend on others can be free from hindrance? No. Is it possible for him to be unimpeded? No. Therefore he cannot be free. Consider then, whether we have nothing which is in our own power only, or whether we have all things, or whether some things are in our own power, and others in the power of others. What do you mean? When you wish the body to be entire (sound) is it in your power or not? It is not in my power. When you wish it to be healthy? Neither is this in my power. When you wish it to be handsome? Nor is this. Life or death? Neither is this in my power. Your body then is another's, subject to every man who is stronger than yourself. It is. But your estate is it in your power to have it when you please, and as long as you please, and such as you please? No. And your slaves? No. And your clothes? No. And your house? No. And your horses? Not one of these things. And if you wish by all means your children to live, or your wife, or your brother, or your friends, is it in your power? This also is not in my power.

Whether then have you nothing which is in your own power, which depends on yourself only and cannot be taken from you, or have you anything of the kind? I know not. Look at the thing then thus, and examine it. Is any man able to make you assent to that which is false? No man. In the matter of assent then you are free from hindrance and obstruction. Granted. Well; and can a man force you to desire to move towards that to which you do not choose? He can, for when he threatens me with death or bonds he compels me to desire to move towards it. If then you despise death and bonds, do you still pay any regard to him? No. Is then the despising of death an act of your own or is it not yours? It is my act.

When you have made this preparation, and have practised this discipline, to distinguish that which belongs to another from that which is your own, the things which are subject to hindrance from those which are not, to consider the things free from hindrance to concern yourself, and those which are not free not to concern yourself, to keep your desire steadily fixed to the things which do concern yourself, and turned from the things which do not concern yourself; do you still fear any man? No one. For about what will you be afraid?

About the things which are your own, in which consists the nature of good and evil? and who has power over these things? who can take them away? who can impede them? No man can, no more than he can impede God. But will you be afraid about your body and your possessions, about things which are not yours, about things which in no way concern you? and what else have you been studying from the beginning than to distinguish between your own and not your own, the things which are in your power and not in your power, the things subject to hindrance and not subject? and why have you come to the philosophers? was it that you may nevertheless be unfortunate and unhappy? You will then in this way, as I have supposed you to have done, be without fear and disturbance. And what is grief to you? for fear comes from what you expect, but grief from that which is present. But what further will you desire? For of the things which are within the power of the will, as being good and present, you have a proper and regulated desire; but of the things which are not in the power of the will you do not desire any one, and so you do not allow any place to that which is irrational, and impatient, and above measure hasty.

Then after receiving everything from another and even yourself, are you angry and do you blame the giver if he takes anything from you? Who are you, and for what purpose did you come into the world? Did not he (God) introduce you here, did he not show you the light, did he not give you fellow-workers, and perceptions and reason? and as whom did he introduce you here? did he not introduce you as subject to death, and as one to live on the earth with a little flesh, and to observe his administration, and to join with him in the spectacle and the festival for a short time? Will you not then, as long as you have been permitted, after seeing the spectacle and the solemnity, when he leads you out, go with adoration of him and thanks for what you have heard and seen? No; but I would still enjoy the feast. The initiated too would wish to be longer in the initiation; and perhaps also those at Olympia to see other athletes. But the solemnity is ended; go away like a grateful and modest man; make room for others; others also must be born, as you were, and, being born, they must have a place, and houses, and necessary things. And if the first do not retire, what remains? Why are you insatiable? Why are you not content? why do you contract the world? Yes, but I would have my little children with me and my wife. What, are they yours? do they not belong to the giver, and to him who made you? then will you not give up what belongs to others? will you not give way to him who is superior? Why then did he introduce me into the world on these conditions? And if the conditions do not suit you, depart. He has no need of a spectator who is not satisfied. He wants those who join in the festival, those who take part in the chorus, that they may rather applaud, admire, and celebrate with hymns the solemnity. But those who can bear no trouble, and the cowardly, he will not unwillingly see absent from the great assembly ([Greek: panaeguris]) for they did not when they were present behave as they ought to do at a festival nor fill up their place properly, but they lamented, found fault with the deity, fortune, their companions; not seeing both what they had, and their own powers, which they received for contrary purposes, the powers of magnanimity, of a generous mind, manly spirit, and what we are now inquiring about, freedom. For what purpose then have I received these things? To use them. How long? So long as he who has lent them chooses. What if they are necessary to me? Do not attach yourself to them and they will not be necessary; do not say to yourself that they are necessary, and then they are not necessary.

You then, a man may say, are you free? I wish, by the gods, and pray to be free; but I am not yet able to face my masters, I still value my poor body, I value greatly the preservation of it entire, though I do not possess it entire. But I can point out to you a free man, that you may no longer seek an example. Diogenes was free. How was he free? Not because he was born of free parents, but because he was himself free, because he had cast off all the handles of slavery, and it was not possible for any man to approach him, nor had any man the means of laying hold of him to enslave him. He had everything easily loosed, everything only hanging to him. If you laid hold of his property, he would have rather let it go and be yours, than he would have followed you for it; if you had laid hold of his leg, he would have let go his leg; if of all his body, all his poor body; his intimates, friends, country, just the same. For he knew from whence he had them, and from whom, and on what conditions. His true parents indeed, the gods, and his real country he would never have deserted, nor would he have yielded to any man in obedience to them and to their orders, nor would any man have died for his country more readily. For he was not used to inquire when he should be considered to have done anything on behalf of the whole of things (the universe, or all the world), but he remembered that everything which is done comes from thence and is done on behalf of that country and is commanded by him who administers it. Therefore see what Diogenes himself says and writes: "For this reason," he says, "Diogenes, it is in your power to speak both with the King of the Persians and with Archidamus the King of the Lacedaemonians, as you please." Was it because he was born of free parents? I suppose all the Athenians and all the Lacedaemonians, because they were born of slaves, could not talk with them (these kings) as they wished, but feared and paid court to them. Why then does he say that it is in his power? Because I do not consider the poor body to be my own, because I want nothing, because law is everything to me, and nothing else is. These were the things which permitted him to be free.

Think of these things, these opinions, these words; look to these examples, if you would be free, if you desire the thing according to its worth. And what is the wonder if you buy so great a thing at the price of things so many and so great? For the sake of this which is called liberty, some hang themselves, others throw themselves down precipices, and sometimes even whole cities have perished; and will you not for the sake of the true and unassailable and secure liberty give back to God when he demands them the things which he has given? Will you not, as Plato says, study not to die only, but also to endure torture, and exile, and scourging, and, in a word, to give up all which is not your own? If you will not, you will be a slave among slaves, even if you be ten thousand times a consul; and if you make your way up to the palace (Caesar's residence), you will no less be a slave; and you will feel that perhaps philosophers utter words which are contrary to common opinion (paradoxes), as Cleanthes also said, but not words contrary to reason. For you will know by experience that the words are true, and that there is no profit from the things which are valued and eagerly sought to those who have obtained them; and to those who have not yet obtained them there is an imagination ([Greek: phantasia]), that when these things are come, all that is good will come with them; then, when they are come, the feverish feeling is the same, the tossing to and fro is the same, the satiety, the desire of things, which are not present; for freedom is acquired not by the full possession of the things which are desired, but by removing the desire. And that you may know that this is true, as you have labored for those things, so transfer your labor to these: be vigilant for the purpose of acquiring an opinion which will make you free; pay court to a philosopher instead of to a rich old man; be seen about a philosopher's doors; you will not disgrace yourself by being seen; you will not go away empty nor without profit, if you go to the philosopher as you ought, and if not (if you do not succeed), try at least; the trial (attempt) is not disgraceful.

ON FAMILIAR INTIMACY

To this matter before all you must attend, that you be never so closely connected with any of your former intimates or friends as to come down to the same acts as he does. If you do not observe this rule, you will ruin yourself. But if the thought arises in your mind, "I shall seem disobliging to him and he will not have the same feeling towards me," remember that nothing is done without cost, nor is it possible for a man if he does not do the same things to be the same man that he was. Choose then which of the two you will have, to be equally loved by those by whom you were formerly loved, being the same with your former self; or, being superior, not to obtain from your friends the same that you did before.

WHAT THINGS WE SHOULD EXCHANGE FOR OTHER THINGS

Keep this thought in readiness, when you lose anything external, what you acquire in place of it; and if it be worth more, never say, I have had a loss; neither if you have got a horse in place of an ass, or an ox in place of a sheep, nor a good action in place of a bit of money, nor in place of idle talk such tranquillity as befits a man, nor in place of lewd talk if you have acquired modesty. If you remember this, you will always maintain your character such as it ought to be. But if you do not, consider that the times of opportunity are perishing, and that whatever pains you take about yourself, you are going to waste them all and overturn them. And it needs only a few things for the loss and overturning of all—namely, a small deviation from reason. For the steerer of a ship to upset it, he has no need of the same means as he has need of for saving it; but if he turns it a little to the wind, it is lost; and if he does not do this purposely, but has been neglecting his duty a little, the ship is lost. Something of the kind happens in this case also; if you only fall a nodding a little, all that you have up to this time collected is gone. Attend therefore to the appearances of things, and watch over them; for that which you have to preserve is no small matter, but it is modesty and fidelity and constancy, freedom from the affects, a state of mind undisturbed, freedom from fear, tranquillity, in a word liberty. For what will you sell these things? See what is the value of the things which you will obtain in exchange for these.—But shall I not obtain any such thing for it?—See, and if you do in return get that, see what you receive in place of it. I possess decency, he possesses a tribuneship: he possesses a prætorship, I possess modesty. But I do not make acclamations where it is not becoming: I will not stand up where I ought not; for I am free, and a friend of God. and so I obey him willingly. But I must not claim (seek) anything else, neither body nor possession, nor magistracy, nor good report, nor in fact anything. For he (God) does not allow me to claim (seek) them, for if he had chosen, he would have made them good for me; but he has not done so, and for this reason I cannot transgress his commands. Preserve that which is your own good in everything; and as to every other thing, as it is permitted, and so far as to behave consistently with reason in respect to them, content with this only. If you do not, you will be unfortunate, you will fail in all things, you will be hindered, you will be impeded. These are the laws which have been sent from thence (from God); these are the orders. Of these laws a man ought to be an expositor, to these he ought to submit, not to those of Masurius and Cassius.

TO THOSE WHO ARE DESIROUS OF PASSING LIFE IN TRANQUILLITY

Remember that not only the desire of power and of riches makes us mean and subject to others, but even the desire of tranquillity, and of leisure, and of travelling abroad, and of learning. For, to speak plainly, whatever the external thing may be, the value which we set upon it places us in subjection to others. What then is the difference between desiring to be a senator or not desiring to be one; what is the difference between desiring power or being content with a private station; what is the difference between saying, I am unhappy, I have nothing to do, but I am bound to my books as a corpse; or saying, I am unhappy, I have no leisure for reading? For as salutations and power are things external and independent of the will, so is a book. For what purpose do you choose to read? Tell me. For if you only direct your purpose to being amused or learning something, you are a silly fellow and incapable of enduring labor. But if you refer reading to the proper end, what else is this than a tranquil and happy life ([Greek: eusoia])? But if reading does not secure for you a happy and tranquil life, what is the use of it? But it does secure this, the man replies, and for this reason I am vexed that I am deprived of it.—And what is this tranquil and happy life, which any man can impede, I do not say Caesar or Caesar's friend, but a crow, a piper, a fever, and thirty thousand other things? But a tranquil and happy life contains nothing so sure as continuity and freedom from obstacle. Now I am called to do something: I will go then with the purpose of observing the measures (rules) which I must keep, of acting with modesty, steadiness, without desire and aversion to things external; and then that I may attend to men, what they say, how they are moved; and this not with any bad disposition, or that I may have something to blame or to ridicule; but I turn to myself, and ask if I also commit the same faults. How then shall I cease to commit them? Formerly I also acted wrong, but now I do not: thanks to God.

What then is the reason of this? The reason is that we have never read for this purpose, we have never written for this purpose, so that we may in our actions use in a way conformable to nature the appearances presented to us; but we terminate in this, in learning what is said, and in being able to expound it to another, in resolving a syllogism, and in handling the hypothetical syllogism. For this reason where our study (purpose) is, there alone is the impediment. Would you have by all means the things which are not in your power? Be prevented then, be hindered, fail in your purpose. But if we read what is written about action (efforts, [Greek: hormae]), not that we may see what is said about action, but that we may act well; if we read what is said about desire and aversion (avoiding things), in order that we may neither fail in our desires, nor fall into that which we try to avoid; if we read what is said about duty (officium), in order that remembering the relations (of things to one another) we may do nothing irrationally nor contrary to these relations; we should not be vexed, in being hindered as to our readings, but we should be satisfied with doing the acts which are conformable (to the relations), and we should be reckoning not what so far we have been accustomed to reckon: To-day I have read so many verses, I have written so many; but (we should say), To-day I have employed my action as it is taught by the philosophers; I have not employed my desire; I have used avoidance ([Greek: echchlisei]) only with respect to things which are within the power of my will; I have not been afraid of such a person, I have not been prevailed upon by the entreaties of another; I have exercised my patience, my abstinence, my co-operation with others; and so we should thank God for what we ought to thank him.

There is only one way to happiness, and let this rule be ready both in the morning and during the day and by night: the rule is not to look towards things which are out of the power of our will, to think that nothing is our own, to give up all things to the Divinity, to Fortune; to make them the superintendents of these things, whom Zeus also has made so; for a man to observe that only which is his own, that which cannot be hindered; and when we read, to refer our reading to this only, and our writing and our listening. For this reason I cannot call the man industrious, if I hear this only, that he reads and writes; and even if a man adds that he reads all night, I cannot say so, if he knows not to what he should refer his reading. For neither do you say that a man is industrious if he keeps awake for a girl, nor do I. But if he does it (reads and writes) for reputation, I say that he is a lover of reputation. And if he does it for money, I say that he is a lover of money, not a lover of labor; and if he does it through love of learning, I say that he is a lover of learning. But if he refers his labor to his own ruling power that he may keep it in a state conformable to nature and pass his life in that state, then only do I say that he is industrious. For never commend a man on account of these things which are common to all, but on account of his opinions (principles); for these are the things which belong to each man, which make his actions bad or good. Remembering these rules, rejoice in that which is present, and be content with the things which come in season. If you see anything which you have learned and inquired about occurring to you in your course of life (or opportunely applied by you to the acts of life), be delighted at it. If you have laid aside or have lessened bad disposition and a habit of reviling; if you have done so with rash temper, obscene words, hastiness, sluggishness; if you are not moved by what you formerly were, and not in the same way as you once were, you can celebrate a festival daily, to-day because you have behaved well in one act, and to-morrow because you have behaved well in another. How much greater is this a reason for making sacrifices than a consulship or the government of a province? These things come to you from yourself and from the gods. Remember this, who gives these things and to whom, and for what purpose. If you cherish yourself in these thoughts, do you still think that it makes any difference where you shall be happy, where you shall please God? Are not the gods equally distant from all places? Do they not see from all places alike that which is going on?

AGAINST THE QUARRELSOME AND FEROCIOUS

The wise and good man neither himself fights with any person, nor does he allow another, so far as he can prevent it. And an example of this as well as of all other things is proposed to us in the life of Socrates, who not only himself on all occasions avoided fights (quarrels), but would not allow even others to quarrel. See in Xenophon's Symposium how many quarrels he settled, how further he endured Thrasymachus and Polus and Callicles; how he tolerated his wife, and how he tolerated his son who attempted to confute him and to cavil with him. For he remembered well that no man has in his power another man's ruling principle. He wished therefore for nothing else than that which was his own. And what is this? Not that this or that man may act according to nature, for that is a thing which belongs to another; but that while others are doing their own acts, as they choose, he may nevertheless be in a condition conformable to nature and live in it, only doing what is his own to the end that others also may be in a state conformable to nature. For this is the object always set before him by the wise and good man. Is it to be commander (a praetor) of an army? No; but if it is permitted him, his object is in this matter to maintain his own ruling principle. Is it to marry? No; but if marriage is allowed to him, in this matter his object is to maintain himself in a condition conformable to nature. But if he would have his son not to do wrong or his wife, he would have what belongs to another not to belong to another: and to be instructed is this, to learn what things are a man's own and what belongs to another.

How then is there left any place for fighting (quarrelling) to a man who has this opinion (which he ought to have)? Is he surprised at any thing which happens, and does it appear new to him? Does he not expect that which comes from the bad to be worse and more grievous than that what actually befalls him? And does he not reckon as pure gain whatever they (the bad) may do which falls short of extreme wickedness? Such a person has reviled you. Great thanks to him for not having struck you. But he has struck me also. Great thanks that he did not wound you. But he wounded me also. Great thanks that he did not kill you. For when did he learn or in what school that man is a tame animal, that men love one another, that an act of injustice is a great harm to him who does it. Since then he has not learned this and is not convinced of it, why shall he not follow that which seems to be for his own interest? Your neighbor has thrown stones. Have you then done anything wrong? But the things in the house have been broken. Are you then a utensil? No; but a free power of will. What then is given to you (to do) in answer to this? If you are like a wolf, you must bite in return, and throw more stones. But, if you consider what is proper for a man, examine your storehouse, see with what faculties you came into the world. Have you the disposition of a wild beast, have you the disposition of revenge for an injury? When is a horse wretched? When he is deprived of his natural faculties, not when he cannot crow like a cock, but when he cannot run. When is a dog wretched? Not when he cannot fly, but when he cannot track his game. Is then a man also unhappy in this way, not because he cannot strangle lions or embrace statues, for he did not come into the world in the possession of certain powers from nature for this purpose, but because he has lost his probity and his fidelity? People ought to meet and lament such a man for the misfortunes into which he has fallen; not indeed to lament because a man has been born or has died, but because it has happened to him in his lifetime to have lost the things which are his own, not that which he received from his father, not his land and house, and his inn, and his slaves; for not one of these things is a man's own, but all belong to others, are servile, and subject to account ([Greek: hupeithuna]), at different times given to different persons by those who have them in their power: but I mean the things which belong to him as a man, the marks (stamps) in his mind with which he came into the world, such as we seek also on coins, and if we find them we approve of the coins, and if we do not find the marks we reject them. What is the stamp on this sestertius? The stamp of Trajan. Present it. It is the stamp of Nero. Throw it away; it cannot be accepted, it is counterfeit. So also in this case: What is the stamp of his opinions? It is gentleness, a sociable disposition, a tolerant temper, a disposition to mutual affections. Produce these qualities. I accept them: I consider this man a citizen, I accept him as a neighbor, a companion in my voyages. Only see that he has not Nero's stamp. Is he passionate, is he full of resentment, is he fault-finding? If the whim seizes him, does he break the heads of those who come in his way? (If so), why then did you say that he is a man? Is everything judged (determined) by the bare form? If that is so, say that the form in wax is an apple and has the smell and the taste of an apple. But the external figure is not enough: neither then is the nose enough and the eyes to make the man, but he must have the opinions of a man. Here is a man who does not listen to reason, who does not know when he is refuted: he is an ass; in another man the sense of shame is become dead: he is good for nothing, he is anything rather than a man. This man seeks whom he may meet and kick or bite, so that he is not even a sheep or an ass, but a kind of wild beast.

What then? would you have me to be despised?—By whom? by those who

209

know you? and how shall those who know you despise a man who is gentle and modest? Perhaps you mean by those who do not know you? What is that to you? For no other artisan cares for the opinion of those who know not his art. But they will be more hostile to me for this reason. Why do you say "me"? Can any man injure your will, or prevent you from using in a natural way the appearances which are presented to you? In no way can he. Why then are you still disturbed and why do you choose to show yourself afraid? And why do you not come forth and proclaim that you are at peace with all men whatever they may do, and laugh at those chiefly who think that they can harm you? These slaves, you can say, know not either who I am, nor where lies my good or my evil, because they have no access to the things which are mine.

In this way also those who occupy a strong city mock the besiegers (and say): What trouble these men are now taking for nothing; our wall is secure, we have food for a very long time, and all other resources. These are the things which make a city strong and impregnable; but nothing else than his opinions makes a man's soul impregnable. For what wall is so strong, or what body is so hard, or what possession is so safe, or what honor (rank, character) so free from assault (as a man's opinions)? All (other) things everywhere are perishable, easily taken by assault, and if any man in any way is attached to them, he must be disturbed, except what is bad, he must fear, lament, find his desires disappointed, and fall into things which he would avoid. Then do we not choose to make secure the only means of safety which are offered to us, and do we not choose to withdraw ourselves from that which is perishable and servile and to labor at the things which are imperishable and by nature free; and do we not remember that no man either hurts another or does good to another, but that a man's opinions about each thing, is that which hurts him, is that which overturns him; this is fighting, this is civil discord, this is war? That which made Eteocles and Polynices enemies was nothing else than this opinion which they had about royal power, their opinion about exile, that the one is the extreme of evils, the other the greatest good. Now this is the nature of every man to seek the good, to avoid the bad; to consider him who deprives us of the one and involves us in the other an enemy and treacherous, even if he be a brother, or a son, or a father. For nothing is more akin to us than the good; therefore, if these things (externals) are good and evil, neither is a father a friend to sons, nor a brother to a brother, but all the world is everywhere full of enemies, treacherous men, and sycophants. But if the will ([Greek: proairesis], the purpose, the intention) being what it ought to be, is the only good; and if the will being such as it ought not to be, is the only evil, where is there any strife, where is there reviling? about what? about the things which do not concern us? and strife with whom? with the ignorant, the unhappy, with those who are deceived about the chief things?

Remembering this Socrates managed his own house and endured a very ill-tempered wife and a foolish (ungrateful?) son.

AGAINST THOSE WHO LAMENT OVER BEING PITIED

I am grieved, a man says, at being pitied. Whether then is the fact of your being pitied a thing which concerns you or those who pity you? Well, is it in your power to stop this pity? It is in my power, if I show them that I do not require pity. And whether then are you in the condition of not deserving (requiring) pity, or are you not in that condition? I think that I am not; but these persons do not pity me, for the things for which, if they ought to pity me, it would be proper, I mean, for my faults; but they pity me for my poverty, for not possessing honorable offices, for diseases and deaths and other such things. Whether then are you prepared to convince the many, that not one of these things is an evil, but that it is possible for a man who is poor and has no office ([Greek: anarchonti)] and enjoys no honor to be happy; or to show yourself to them as rich and in power? For the second of these things belong to a man who is boastful, silly, and good for nothing. And consider by what means the pretence must be supported. It will be necessary for you to hire slaves and to possess a few silver vessels, and to exhibit them in public, if it is possible, though they are often the same, and to attempt to conceal the fact that they are the same, and to have splendid garments, and all other things for display, and to show that you are a man honored by the great, and to try to sup at their houses, or to be supposed to sup there, and as to your person to employ some mean arts, that you may appear to be more handsome and nobler than you are. These things you must contrive, if you choose to go by the second path in order not to be pitied. But the first way is both impracticable and long, to attempt the very thing which Zeus has not been able to do, to convince all men what things are good and bad. Is this power given to you? This only is given to you, to convince yourself; and you have not convinced yourself. Then I ask you, do you attempt to persuade other men? and who has lived so long with you as you with yourself? and who has so much power of convincing you as you have of convincing yourself; and who is better disposed and nearer to you than you are to yourself? How then have you not yet convinced yourself in order to learn? At present are not things upside down? Is this what you have been earnest about doing, to learn to be free from grief and free from disturbance, and not to be humbled (abject), and to be free? Have you not heard then that there is only one way which leads to this end, to give up (dismiss) the things which do not depend on the will, to withdraw from them, and to admit that they belong to others? For another man then to have an opinion about you, of what kind is it? It is a thing independent of the will— Then is it nothing to you? It is nothing. When then you are still vexed at this and disturbed, do you think that you are convinced about good and evil?

ON FREEDOM FROM FEAR

What makes the tyrant formidable? The guards, you say, and their swords, and the men of the bedchamber, and those who exclude them who would enter. Why then if you bring a boy (child) to the tyrant when he is with his guards, is he not afraid; or is it because the child does not understand these things? If then any man does understand what guards are and that they have swords, and comes to the tyrant for this very purpose because he wishes to die on account of some circumstance and seeks to die easily by the hand of another, is he afraid of the guards? No, for he wishes for the thing which makes the guards formidable. If then any man neither wishing to die nor to live by all means, but only as it may be permitted, approaches the tyrant what hinders him from approaching the tyrant without fear? Nothing. If then a man has the same opinion about his property as the man whom I have instanced has about his body; and also about his children and his wife, and in a word is so affected by some madness or despair that he cares not whether he possesses them or not, but like children who are playing with shells (quarrel) about the play, but do not trouble themselves about the shells, so he too has set no value on the materials (things), but values the pleasure that he has with them and the occupation, what tyrant is then formidable to him, or what guards or what swords?

What hinders a man, who has clearly separated (comprehended) these things, from living with a light heart and bearing easily the reins, quietly expecting everything which can happen, and enduring that which has already happened? Would you have me to bear poverty? Come and you will know what poverty is when it has found one who can act well the part of a poor man. Would you have me to possess power? Let me have power, and also the trouble of it. Well, banishment? Wherever I shall go, there it will be well with me; for here also where I am, it was not because of the place that it was well with me, but because of my opinions which I shall carry off with me, for neither can any man deprive me of them; but my opinions alone are mine and they cannot be taken from me, and I am satisfied while I have them, wherever I may be and whatever I am doing. But now it is time to die. Why do you say to die? Make no tragedy show of the thing, but speak of it as it is. It is now time for the matter (of the body) to be resolved into the things out of which it was composed. And what is the formidable thing here? what is going to perish of the things which are in the universe? what new thing or wondrous is going to happen? Is it for this reason that a tyrant is formidable? Is it for this reason that the guards appear to have swords which are large and sharp? Say this to others; but I have considered about all these things; no man has power over me. I have been made free; I know his commands, no man can now lead me as a slave. I have a proper person to assert my freedom; I have proper judges. (I say) are you not the master of my body? What then is that to me? Are you not the master of my property? What then is that to me? Are you not the master of my exile or of my chains? Well, from all these things and all the poor body itself I depart at your bidding, when you please. Make trial of your power, and you will know how far it reaches.

Whom then can I still fear? Those who are over the bedchamber? Lest they should do, what? Shut me out? If they find that I wish to enter, let them shut me out. Why then do you go to the doors? Because I think it befits me, while the play (sport) lasts, to join in it. How then are you not shut out? Because unless some one allows me to go in, I do not choose to go in, but am always content with that which happens; for I think that what God chooses is better than what I choose. I will attach myself as a minister and follower to him; I have the same movements (pursuits) as he has, I have the same desires; in a word, I have the same will ([Greek: sunthelo]). There is no shutting out for me, but for those who would force their way in. Why then do not I force my way in? Because I know that nothing good is distributed within to those who enter. But when I hear any man called fortunate because he is honored by Cæsar, I say what does he happen to get? A province (the government of a province). Does he also obtain an opinion such as he ought? The office of a Prefect. Does he also obtain the power of using his office well? Why do I still strive to enter (Caesar's chamber)? A man scatters dried figs and nuts: the children seize them, and fight with one another; men do not, for they think them to be a small matter. But if a man should throw about shells, even the children do not seize them. Provinces are distributed: let children look to that. Money is distributed; let children look to that. Prætorships, consulships, are distributed; let children scramble for them, let them be shut out, beaten, kiss the hands of the giver, of the slaves: but to me these are only dried figs and nuts. What then? If you fail to get them, while Cæsar is scattering them about, do not be troubled; if a dried fig come into your lap, take it and eat it; for so far you may value even a fig. But if I shall stoop down and turn another over, or be turned over by another, and shall flatter those who have got into (Caesar's) chamber, neither is a dried fig worth the trouble, nor anything else of the things which are not good, which the philosophers have persuaded me not to think good.

TO A PERSON WHO HAD BEEN CHANGED TO A CHARACTER OF SHAMELESSNESS

When you see another man in the possession of power (magistracy), set against this the fact that you have not the want (desire) of power; when you see another rich, see what you possess in place of riches: for if you possess nothing in place of them, you are miserable; but if you have not the want of riches, know that you possess more than this man possesses and what is worth much more.

WHAT THINGS WE OUGHT TO DESPISE AND WHAT THINGS WE OUGHT TO VALUE

The difficulties of all men are about external things, their helplessness is about external. What shall I do? how will it be? how will it turn out? will this happen? will that? All these are the words of those who are turning themselves to things which are not within the power of the will. For who says, How shall I not assent to that which is false? how shall I not turn away from the truth? If a man be of such a good disposition as to be anxious about these things I will remind him of this: Why are you anxious? The thing is in your own power, be assured; do not be precipitate in assenting before you apply the natural rule. On the other side, if a man is anxious (uneasy) about desire, lest it fail in its purpose and miss its end, and with respect to the avoidance of things, lest he should fall into that which he would avoid, I will first kiss (love) him, because he throws away the things about which others are in a flutter (others desire) and their fears, and employs his thoughts about his own affairs and his own condition. Then I shall say to him: If you do not choose to desire that which you will fail to obtain nor to attempt to avoid that into which you will fall, desire nothing which belongs to (which is in the power of) others, nor try to avoid any of the things which are not in your power. If you do not observe this rule, you must of necessity fail in your desires and fall into that which you would avoid. What is the difficulty here? where is there room for the words How will it be? and How will it turn out? and Will this happen or that?

Now is not that which will happen independent of the will? Yes. And the nature of good and of evil, is it not in the things which are within the power of the will? Yes. Is it in your power then to treat according to nature everything which happens? Can any person hinder you? No man. No longer then say to me, How will it be? For, however it may be, you will dispose of it well, and the result to you will be a fortunate one. What would Hercules have been if he said: How shall a great lion not appear to me, or a great boar, or savage men? And what do you care for that? If a great boar appear, you will fight a greater fight; if bad men appear, you will relieve the earth of the bad. Suppose then that I lose my life in this way. You will die a good man, doing a noble act. For since he must certainly die, of necessity a man must be found doing something, either following the employment of a husbandman, or digging, or trading, or serving in a consulship, or suffering from indigestion or from diarrhoea. What then do you wish to be doing when you are found by death? I, for my part, would wish to be found doing something which belongs to a man, beneficent, suitable to the general interest, noble. But if I cannot be found doing things so great, I would be found doing at least that which I cannot be hindered from doing, that which is permitted me to do, correcting myself, cultivating the faculty which makes use of appearances, laboring at freedom from the affects (laboring at tranquillity of mind); rendering to the relations of life their due. If I succeed so far, also (I would be found) touching on (advancing to) the third topic (or head) safety in forming judgments about things. If death surprises me when I am busy about these things, it is enough for me if I can stretch out my hands to God and say: The means which I have received from thee for seeing thy administration (of the world) and following it I have not neglected; I have not dishonored thee by my acts; see how I have used my perceptions, see how I have used my preconceptions; have I ever blamed thee? have I been discontented with anything that happens, or wished it to be otherwise? have I wished to transgress the (established) relations (of things)? That thou hast given me life, I thank thee for what thou hast given. So long as I have used the things which are thine I am content. Take them back and place them wherever thou mayest choose, for thine were all things, thou gavest them to me. Is it not enough to depart in this state of mind? and what life is better and more becoming than that of a man who is in this state of mind? and what end is more happy?

ABOUT PURITY (CLEANLINESS)

Some persons raise a question whether the social feeling is contained in the nature of man; and yet I think that these same persons would have no doubt that love of purity is certainly contained in it, and that if man is distinguished from other animals by anything, he is distinguished by this. When then we see any other animal cleaning itself, we are accustomed to speak of the act with surprise, and to add that the animal is acting like a man; and on the other hand, if a man blames an animal for being dirty, straightway, as if we were making an excuse for it, we say that of course the animal is not a human creature. So we suppose that there is something superior in man, and that we first receive it from the gods. For since the gods by their nature are pure and free from corruption, so far as men approach them by reason, so far do they cling to purity and to a love (habit) of purity. But since it is impossible that man's nature ([Greek: ousia]) can be altogether pure, being mixed (composed) of such materials, reason is applied, as far as it is possible, and reason endeavors to make human nature love purity.

The first then and highest purity is that which is in the soul; and we say the same of impurity. Now you could not discover the impurity of the soul as you could discover that of the body; but as to the soul, what else could you find in it than that which makes it filthy in respect to the acts which are her own? Now the acts of the soul are movement towards an object or movement from it, desire, aversion, preparation, design (purpose), assent. What then is it which in these acts makes the soul filthy and impure? Nothing else than her own bad judgments ([Greek: chrimata]). Consequently the impurity of the soul is the soul's bad opinions; and the purification of the soul is the planting in it of proper opinions; and the soul is pure which has proper opinions, for the soul alone in her own acts is free from perturbation and pollution.

For we ought not even by the appearance of the body to deter the multitude from philosophy; but as in other things, a philosopher should show himself cheerful and tranquil, so also he should in the things that relate to the body. See, ye men, that I have nothing, that I want nothing; see how I am without a house, and without a city, and an exile, if it happens to be so, and without a hearth I live more free from trouble and more happily than all of noble birth and than the rich. But look at my poor body also and observe that it is not injured by my hard way of living. But if a man says this to me, who has the appearance (dress) and face of a condemned man, what god shall persuade me to approach philosophy, if it makes men such persons? Far from it; I would not choose to do so, even if I were going to become a wise man. I indeed would rather that a young man, who is making his first movements towards philosophy, should come to me with his hair carefully trimmed than with it dirty and rough, for there is seen in him a certain notion (appearance) of beauty and a desire of (attempt at) that which is becoming; and where he supposes it to be, there also he strives that it shall be. It is only necessary to show him (what it is), and to say: Young man, you seek beauty, and you do well; you must know then that it (is produced) grows in that part of you where you have the rational faculty; seek it there where you have the movements towards and movements from things, where you have the desires towards and the aversion from things; for this is what you have in yourself of a superior kind; but the poor body is naturally only earth; why do you labor about it to no purpose? if you shall learn nothing else, you will learn from time that the body is nothing. But if a man comes to me daubed with filth, dirty, with a moustache down to his knees, what can I say to him, by what kind of resemblance can I lead him on? For about what has he busied himself which resembles beauty, that I may be able to change him and say, Beauty is not in this, but in that? Would you have me to tell him, that beauty consists not in being daubed with muck, but that it lies in the rational part? Has he any desire of beauty? has he any form of it in his mind? Go and talk to a hog, and tell him not to roll in the mud.

ON ATTENTION

When you have remitted your attention for a short time, do not imagine this, that you will recover it when you choose; but let this thought be present to you, that in consequence of the fault committed today your affairs must be in a worse condition for all that follows. For first, and what causes most trouble, a habit of not attending is formed in you; then a habit of deferring your attention. And continually from time to time you drive away by deferring it the happiness of life, proper behavior, the being and living conformably to nature. If then the procrastination of attention is profitable, the complete omission of attention is more profitable; but if it is not profitable, why do you not maintain your attention constant? Today I choose to play. Well then, ought you not to play with attention? I choose to sing. What then hinders you from doing so with attention? Is there any part of life excepted, to which attention does not extend? For will you do it (anything in life) worse by using attention, and better by not attending at all? And what else of the things in life is done better by those who do not use attention? Does he who works in wood work better by not attending to it? Does the captain of a ship manage it better by not attending? and are any of the smaller acts done better by inattention? Do you not see that when you have let your mind loose, it is no longer in your power to recall it, either to propriety, or to modesty, or to moderation; but you do everything that comes into your mind in obedience to your inclinations.

First then we ought to have these (rules) in readiness, and to do nothing without them, and we ought to keep the soul directed to this mark, to pursue nothing external, and nothing which belongs to others (or is in the power of others), but to do as he has appointed who has the power; we ought to pursue altogether the things which are in the power of the will, and all other things as it is permitted. Next to this we ought to remember who we are, and what is our name, and to endeavor to direct our duties towards the character (nature) of our several relations (in life) in this manner: what is the season for singing, what is the season for play, and in whose presence; what will be the consequence of the act; whether our associates will despise us, whether we shall despise them; when to jeer ([Greek: schopsai]), and whom to ridicule; and on what occasion to comply and with whom; and finally, in complying how to maintain our own character. But wherever you have deviated from any of these rules, there is damage immediately, not from anything external, but from the action itself.

What then? is it possible to be free from faults (if you do all this)? It is not possible; but this is possible, to direct your efforts incessantly to being faultless. For we must be content if by never remitting this attention we shall escape at least a few errors. But now when you have said, Tomorrow I will begin to attend, you must be told that you are saying this, Today I will be shameless, disregardful of time and place, mean; it will be in the power of others to give me pain; today I will be passionate and envious. See how many evil things you are permitting yourself to do. If it is good to use attention tomorrow, how much better is it to do so today? if tomorrow it is in your interest to attend, much more is it today, that you may be able to do so tomorrow also, and may not defer it again to the third day.

AGAINST OR TO THOSE WHO READILY TELL THEIR OWN AFFAIRS

When a man has seemed to us to have talked with simplicity (candor) about his own affairs, how is it that at last we are ourselves also induced to discover to him our own secrets and we think this to be candid behavior? In the first place, because it seems unfair for a man to have listened to the affairs of his neighbor, and not to communicate to him also in turn our own affairs; next, because we think that we shall not present to them the appearance of candid men when we are silent about our own affairs. Indeed, men are often accustomed to say, I have told you all my affairs, will you tell me nothing of your own? where is this done? Besides, we have also this opinion that we can safely trust him who has already told us his own affairs; for the notion rises in our mind that this man could never divulge our affairs because he would be cautious that we also should not divulge his. In this way also the incautious are caught by the soldiers at Rome. A soldier sits by you in a common dress and begins to speak ill of Caesar; then you, as if you had received a pledge of his fidelity by his having begun the abuse, utter yourself also what you think, and then you are carried off in chains.

Something of this kind happens to us also generally. Now as this man has confidently intrusted his affairs to me, shall I also do so to any man whom I meet? (No), for when I have heard, I keep silence, if I am of such a disposition; but he goes forth and tells all men what he has heard. Then, if I hear what has been done, if I be a man like him, I resolve to be revenged, I divulge what he has told me; I both disturb others, and am disturbed myself. But if I remember that one man does not injure another, and that every man's acts injure and profit him, I secure this, that I do not anything like him, but still I suffer what I do suffer through my own silly talk.

True, but it is unfair when you have heard the secrets of your neighbor for you in your turn to communicate nothing to him. Did I ask you for your secrets, my man? did you communicate your affairs on certain terms, that you should in return hear mine also? If you are a babbler and think that all who meet you are friends, do you wish me also to be like you? But why, if you did well in intrusting your affairs to me, and it is not well for me to intrust mine to you, do you wish me to be so rash? It is just the same as if I had a cask which is water-tight, and you one with a hole in it, and you should come and deposit with me your wine that I might put it into my cask, and then should complain that I also did not intrust my wine to you, for you have a cask with a hole in it. How then is there any equality here? You intrusted your affairs to a man who is faithful and modest, to a man who thinks that his own actions alone are injurious and (or) useful, and that nothing external is. Would you have me intrust mine to you, a man who has dishonored his own faculty of will, and who wishes to gain some small bit of money or some office or promotion in the court (emperor's palace), even if you should be going to murder your own children, like Medea? Where (in what) is this equality (fairness)? But show yourself to me to be faithful, modest, and steady; show me that you have friendly opinions; show that your cask has no hole in it; and you will see how I shall not wait for you to trust me with your own affairs, but I myself shall come to you and ask you to hear mine. For who does not choose to make use of a good vessel? Who does not value a benevolent and faithful adviser? Who will not willingly receive a man who is ready to bear a share, as we may say, of the difficulty of his circumstances, and by this very act to ease the burden, by taking a part of it.

LETTERS FROM A STOIC

Epistulae Morales AD Lucilium

All Three Volumes

By Lucius Annaeus Seneca

Letter I - On Saving Time

Greetings from Seneca to his friend Lucilius.

Continue to act thus, my dear Lucilius — set yourself free for your own sake; gather and save your time, which till lately has been forced from you, or filched away, or has merely slipped from your hands. Make yourself believe the truth of my words, — that certain moments are torn from us, that some are gently removed, and that others glide beyond our reach. The most disgraceful kind of loss, however, is that due to carelessness. Furthermore, if you will pay close heed to the problem, you will find that the largest portion of our life passes while we are doing ill, a goodly share while we are doing nothing, and the whole while we are doing that which is not to the purpose. What man can you show me who places any value on his time, who reckons the worth of each day, who understands that he is dying daily? For we are mistaken when we look forward to death; the major portion of death has already passed. Whatever years be behind us are in death's hands.

Therefore, Lucilius, do as you write me that you are doing: hold every hour in your grasp. Lay hold of to-day's task, and you will not need to depend so much upon to-morrow's. While we are postponing, life speeds by. Nothing, Lucilius, is ours, except time. We were entrusted by nature with the ownership of this single thing, so fleeting and slippery that anyone who will can oust us from possession. What fools these mortals be! They allow the cheapest and most useless things, which can easily be replaced, to be charged in the reckoning, after they have acquired them; but they never regard themselves as in debt when they have received some of that precious commodity, — time! And yet time is the one loan which even a grateful recipient cannot repay.

You may desire to know how I, who preach to you so freely, am practising. I confess frankly: my expense account balances, as you would expect from one who is free-handed but careful. I cannot boast that I waste nothing, but I can at least tell you what I am wasting, and the cause and manner of the loss; I can give you the reasons why I am a poor man. My situation, however, is the same as that of many who are reduced to slender means through no fault of their own: every one forgives them, but no one comes to their rescue.

What is the state of things, then? It is this: I do not regard a man as poor, if the little which remains is enough for him. I advise you, however, to keep what is really yours; and you cannot begin too early. For, as our ancestors believed, it is too late to spare when you reach the dregs of the cask. Of that which remains at the bottom, the amount is slight, and the quality is vile. Farewell.

Letter II - On Discursiveness in Reading

Judging by what you write me, and by what I hear, I am forming a good opinion regarding your future. You do not run hither and thither and distract yourself by changing your abode; for such restlessness is the sign of a disordered spirit. The primary indication, to my thinking, of a well-ordered mind is a man's ability to remain in one place and linger in his own company. Be careful, however, lest this reading of many authors and books of every sort may tend to make you discursive and unsteady. You must linger among a limited number of master thinkers, and digest their works, if you would derive ideas which shall win firm hold in your mind. Everywhere means nowhere. When a person spends all his time in foreign travel, he ends by having many acquaintances, but no friends. And the same thing must hold true of men who seek intimate acquaintance with no single author, but visit them all in a hasty and hurried manner. Food does no good and is not assimilated into the body if it leaves the stomach as soon as it is eaten; nothing hinders a cure so much as frequent change of medicine; no wound will heal when one salve is tried after another; a plant which is often moved can never grow strong. There is nothing so efficacious that it can be helpful while it is being shifted about. And in reading of many books is distraction.

Accordingly, since you cannot read all the books which you may possess, it is enough to possess only as many books as you can read. "But," you reply, "I wish to dip first into one book and then into another." I tell you that it is the sign of an overnice appetite to toy with many dishes; for when they are manifold and varied, they cloy but do not nourish. So you should always read standard authors; and when you crave a change, fall back upon those whom you read before. Each day acquire something that will fortify you against poverty, against death, indeed against other misfortunes as well; and after you have run over many thoughts, select one to be thoroughly digested that day. This is my own custom; from the many things which I have read, I claim some one part for myself.

The thought for today is one which I discovered in Epicurus; for I am wont to cross over even into the enemy's camp, – not as a deserter, but as a scout. He says: "Contented poverty is an honourable estate." Indeed, if it be contented, it is not poverty at all. It is not the man who has too little, but the man who craves more, that is poor. What does it matter how much a man has laid up in his safe, or in his warehouse, how large are his flocks and how fat his dividends, if he covets his neighbour's property, and reckons, not his past gains, but his hopes of gains to come? Do you ask what is the proper limit to wealth? It is, first, to have what is necessary, and, second, to have what is enough. Farewell.

Letter III - On True and False Friendship

You have sent a letter to me through the hand of a "friend" of yours, as you call him. And in your very next sentence you warn me not to discuss with him all the matters that concern you, saying that even you yourself are not accustomed to do this; in other words, you have in the same letter affirmed and denied that he is your friend. Now if you used this word of ours in the popular sense, and called him "friend" in the same way in which we speak of all candidates for election as "honourable gentlemen," and as we greet all men whom we meet casually, if their names slip us for the moment, with the salutation "my dear sir," – so be it. But if you consider any man a friend whom you do not trust as you trust yourself, you are mightily mistaken and you do not sufficiently understand what true friendship means. Indeed, I would have you discuss everything with a friend; but first of all discuss the man himself. When friendship is settled, you must trust; before friendship is formed, you must pass judgment. Those persons indeed put last first and confound their duties, who, violating the rules of Theophrastus, judge a man after they have made him their friend, instead of making him their friend after they have judged him. Ponder for a long time whether you shall admit a given person to your friendship; but when you have decided to admit him, welcome him with all your heart and soul. Speak as boldly with him as with yourself. As to yourself, although you should live in such a way that you trust your own self with nothing which you could not entrust even to your enemy, yet, since certain matters occur which convention keeps secret, you should share with a friend at least all your worries and reflections. Regard him as loyal, and you will make him loyal. Some, for example, fearing to be deceived, have taught men to deceive; by their suspicions they have given their friend the right to do wrong. Why need I keep back any words in the presence of my friend? Why should I not regard myself as alone when in his company?

There is a class of men who communicate, to anyone whom they meet, matters which should be revealed to friends alone, and unload upon the chance listener whatever irks them. Others, again, fear to confide in their closest intimates; and if it were possible, they would not trust even themselves, burying their secrets deep in their hearts. But we should do neither. It is equally faulty to trust everyone and to trust no one. Yet the former fault is, I should say, the more ingenuous, the latter the more safe. In like manner you should rebuke these two kinds of men, – both those who always lack repose, and those who are always in repose. For love of bustle is not industry, – it is only the restlessness of a hunted mind. And true repose does not consist in condemning all motion as merely vexation; that kind of repose is slackness and inertia. Therefore, you should note the following saying, taken from my reading in Pomponius: "Some men shrink into dark corners, to such a degree that they see darkly by day." No, men should combine these tendencies, and he who reposes should act and he who acts should take repose. Discuss the problem with Nature; she will tell you that she has created both day and night. Farewell.

Letter IV - On the Terrors of Death

Keep on as you have begun, and make all possible haste, so that you may have longer enjoyment of an improved mind, one that is at peace with itself. Doubtless you will derive enjoyment during the time when you are improving your mind and setting it at peace with itself; but quite different is the pleasure which comes from contemplation when one's mind is so cleansed from every stain that it shines. You remember, of course, what joy you felt when you laid aside the garments of boyhood and donned the man's toga, and were escorted to the forum; nevertheless, you may look for a still greater joy when you have laid aside the mind of boyhood and when wisdom has enrolled you among men. For it is not boyhood that still stays with us, but something worse, – boyishness. And this condition is all the more serious because we possess the authority of old age, together with the follies of boyhood, yea, even the follies of infancy. Boys fear trifles, children fear shadows, we fear both.

All you need to do is to advance; you will thus understand that some things are less to be dreaded, precisely because they inspire us with great fear. No evil is great which is the last evil of all. Death arrives; it would be a thing to dread, if it could remain with you. But death must either not come at all, or else must come and pass away.

"It is difficult, however," you say, "to bring the mind to a point where it can scorn life." But do you not see what trifling reasons impel men to scorn life? One hangs himself before the door of his mistress; another hurls himself from the house-top that he may no longer be compelled to bear the taunts of a bad-tempered master; a third, to be saved from arrest after running away, drives a sword into his vitals. Do you not suppose that virtue will be as efficacious as excessive fear? No man can have a peaceful life who thinks too much about lengthening it, or believes that living through many consulships is a great blessing. Rehearse this thought every day, that you may be able to depart from life contentedly; for many men clutch and cling to life, even as those who are carried down a rushing stream clutch and cling to briars and sharp rocks.

Most men ebb and flow in wretchedness between the fear of death and the hardships of life; they are unwilling to live, and yet they do not know how to die. For this reason, make life as a whole agreeable to yourself by banishing all worry about it. No good thing renders its possessor happy, unless his mind is reconciled to the possibility of loss; nothing, however, is lost with less discomfort than that which, when lost, cannot be missed. Therefore, encourage and toughen your spirit against the mishaps that afflict even the most powerful. For example, the fate of Pompey was settled by a boy and a eunuch, that of Crassus by a cruel and insolent Parthian. Gaius Caesar ordered Lepidus to bare his neck for the axe of the tribune Dexter; and he himself offered his own throat to Chaerea. No man has ever been so far advanced by Fortune that she did not threaten him as greatly as she had previously indulged him. Do not trust her seeming calm; in a moment the sea is moved to its depths. The very day the ships have made a brave show in the games, they are engulfed. Reflect that a highwayman or an enemy may cut your throat; and, though he is not your master, every slave wields the power of life and death over you. Therefore I declare to you: he is lord of your life that scorns his own. Think of those who have perished through plots in their own home, slain either openly or by guile; you will that just as many have been killed by angry slaves as by angry kings. What matter, therefore, how powerful he be whom you fear, when every one possesses the power which inspires your fear? "But," you will say, "if you should chance to fall into the hands of the enemy, the conqueror will command that you be led away," – yes, whither you are already being led. Why do you voluntarily deceive yourself and require to be told now for the first time what fate it is that you have long been labouring under? Take my word for it: since the day you were born you are being led thither. We must ponder this thought, and thoughts of the like nature, if we desire to be calm as we await that last hour, the fear of which makes all previous hours uneasy.

But I must end my letter. Let me share with you the saying which pleased me to-day. It, too, is culled from another man's Garden: "Poverty brought into conformity with the law of nature, is great wealth." Do you know what limits that law of nature ordains for us? Merely to avert hunger, thirst, and cold. In order to banish hunger and thirst, it is not necessary for you to pay court at the doors of the purse-proud, or to submit to the stern frown, or to the kindness that humiliates; nor is it necessary for you to scour the seas, or go campaigning; nature's needs are easily provided and ready to hand. It is the superfluous things for which men sweat, – the superfluous things that wear our togas threadbare, that force us to grow old in camp, that dash us upon foreign shores. That which is enough is ready to our hands. He who has made a fair compact with poverty is rich. Farewell.

Letter V - On the Philosopher's Mean

I commend you and rejoice in the fact that you are persistent in your studies, and that, putting all else aside, you make it each day your endeavour to become a better man. I do not merely exhort you to keep at it; I actually beg you to do so. I warn you, however, not to act after the fashion of those who desire to be conspicuous rather than to improve, by doing things which will rouse comment as regards your dress or general way of living. Repellent attire, unkempt hair, slovenly beard, open scorn of silver dishes, a couch on the bare earth, and any other perverted forms of self-display, are to be avoided. The mere name of philosophy, however quietly pursued, is an object of sufficient scorn; and what would happen if we should begin to separate ourselves from the customs of our fellow-men? Inwardly, we ought to be different in all respects, but our exterior should conform to society. Do not wear too fine, nor yet too frowzy, a toga. One needs no silver plate, encrusted and embossed in solid gold; but we should not believe the lack of silver and gold to be proof of the simple life. Let us try to maintain a higher standard of life than that of the multitude, but not a contrary standard; otherwise, we shall frighten away and repel the very persons whom we are trying to improve. We also bring it about that they are unwilling to imitate us in anything, because they are afraid lest they might be compelled to imitate us in everything.

The first thing which philosophy undertakes to give is fellow-feeling with all men; in other words, sympathy and sociability. We part company with our promise if we are unlike other men. We must see to it that the means by which we wish to draw admiration be not absurd and odious. Our motto, as you know, is "Live according to Nature"; but it is quite contrary to nature to torture the body, to hate unlaboured elegance, to be dirty on purpose, to eat food that is not only plain, but disgusting and forbidding. Just as it is a sign of luxury to seek out dainties, so it is madness to avoid that which is customary and can be purchased at no great price. Philosophy calls for plain living, but not for penance; and we may perfectly well be plain and neat at the same time. This is the mean of which I approve; our life should observe a happy medium between the ways of a sage and the ways of the world at large; all men should admire it, but they should understand it also.

"Well then, shall we act like other men? Shall there be no distinction between ourselves and the world?" Yes, a very great one; let men find that we are unlike the common herd, if they look closely. If they visit us at home, they should admire us, rather than our household appointments. He is a great man who uses earthenware dishes as if they were silver; but he is equally great who uses silver as if it were earthenware. It is the sign of an unstable mind not to be able to endure riches.

But I wish to share with you to-day's profit also. I find in the writings of our Hecato that the limiting of desires helps also to cure fears: "Cease to hope," he says, "and you will cease to fear." "But how," you will reply, "can things so different go side by side?" In this way, my dear Lucilius: though they do seem at variance, yet they are really united. Just as the same chain fastens the prisoner and the soldier who guards him, so hope and fear, dissimilar as they are, keep step together; fear follows hope. I am not surprised that they proceed in this way; each alike belongs to a mind that is in suspense, a mind that is fretted by looking forward to the future. But the chief cause of both these ills is that we do not adapt ourselves to the present, but send our thoughts a long way ahead. And so foresight, the noblest blessing of the human race, becomes perverted. Beasts avoid the dangers which they see, and when they have escaped them are free from care; but we men torment ourselves over that which is to come as well as over that which is past. Many of our blessings bring bane to us; for memory recalls the tortures of fear, while foresight anticipates them. The present alone can make no man wretched. Farewell.

Letter VI - On Sharing Knowledge

I feel, my dear Lucilius, that I am being not only reformed, but transformed. I do not yet, however, assure myself, or indulge the hope, that there are no elements left in me which need to be changed. Of course there are many that should be made more compact, or made thinner, or be brought into greater prominence. And indeed this very fact is proof that my spirit is altered into something better, – that it can see its own faults, of which it was previously ignorant. In certain cases sick men are congratulated because they themselves have perceived that they are sick.

I therefore wish to impart to you this sudden change in myself; I should then begin to place a surer trust in our friendship, – the true friendship which hope and fear and self-interest cannot sever, the friendship in which and for the sake of which men meet death.

I can show you many who have lacked, not a friend, but a friendship; this, however, cannot possibly happen when souls are drawn together by identical inclinations into an alliance of honourable desires. And why can it not happen? Because in such cases men know that they have all things in common, especially their troubles.

You cannot conceive what distinct progress I notice that each day brings to me. And when you say: "Give me also a share in these gifts which you have found so helpful," I reply that I am anxious to heap all these privileges upon you, and that I am glad to learn in order that I may teach. Nothing will ever please me, no matter how excellent or beneficial, if I must retain the knowledge of it to myself. And if wisdom were given me under the express condition that it must be kept hidden and not uttered, I should refuse it. No good thing is pleasant to possess, without friends to share it.

I shall therefore send to you the actual books; and in order that you may not waste time in searching here and there for profitable topics, I shall mark certain passages, so that you can turn at once to those which I approve and admire. Of course, however, the living voice and the intimacy of a common life will help you more than the written word. You must go to the scene of action, first, because men put more faith in their eyes than in their ears, and second, because the way is long if one follows precepts, but short and helpful, if one follows patterns.

Cleanthes could not have been the express image of Zeno, if he had merely heard his lectures; he shared in his life, saw into his hidden purposes, and watched him to see whether he lived according to his own rules. Plato, Aristotle, and the whole throng of sages who were destined to go each his different way, derived more benefit from the character than from the words of Socrates. It was not the class-room of Epicurus, but living together under the same roof, that made great men of Metrodorus, Hermarchus, and Polyaenus. Therefore I summon you, not merely that you may derive benefit, but that you may confer benefit; for we can assist each other greatly.

Meanwhile, I owe you my little daily contribution; you shall be told what pleased me to-day in the writings of Hecato; it is these words: "What progress, you ask, have I made? I have begun to be a friend to myself." That was indeed a great benefit; such a person can never be alone. You may be sure that such a man is a friend to all mankind. Farewell.

Letter VII - On Crowds

Do you ask me what you should regard as especially to be avoided? I say, crowds; for as yet you cannot trust yourself to them with safety. I shall admit my own weakness, at any rate; for I never bring back home the same character that I took abroad with me. Something of that which I have forced to be calm within me is disturbed; some of the foes that I have routed return again. Just as the sick man, who has been weak for a long time, is in such a condition that he cannot be taken out of the house without suffering a relapse, so we ourselves are affected when our souls are recovering from a lingering disease. To consort with the crowd is harmful; there is no person who does not make some vice attractive to us, or stamp it upon us, or taint us unconsciously therewith. Certainly, the greater the mob with which we mingle, the greater the danger.

But nothing is so damaging to good character as the habit of lounging at the games; for then it is that vice steals subtly upon one through the avenue of pleasure. What do you think I mean? I mean that I come home more greedy, more ambitious, more voluptuous, and even more cruel and inhuman, because I have been among human beings. By chance I attended a mid-day exhibition, expecting some fun, wit, and relaxation, – an exhibition at which men's eyes have respite from the slaughter of their fellow-men. But it was quite the reverse. The previous combats were the essence of compassion; but now all the trifling is put aside and it is pure murder. The men have no defensive armour. They are exposed to blows at all points, and no one ever strikes in vain. Many persons prefer this programme to the usual pairs and to the bouts "by request." Of course they do; there is no helmet or shield to deflect the weapon. What is the need of defensive armour, or of skill? All these mean delaying death. In the morning they throw men to the lions and the bears; at noon, they throw them to the spectators. The spectators demand that the slayer shall face the man who is to slay him in his turn; and they always reserve the latest conqueror for another butchering. The outcome of every fight is death, and the means are fire and sword. This sort of thing goes on while the arena is empty. You may retort: "But he was a highway robber; he killed a man!" And what of it? Granted that, as a murderer, he deserved this punishment, what crime have you committed, poor fellow, that you should deserve to sit and see this show? In the morning they cried "Kill him! Lash him! Burn him! Why does he meet the sword in so cowardly a way? Why does he strike so feebly? Why doesn't he die game? Whip him to meet his wounds! Let them receive blow for blow, with chests bare and exposed to the stroke!" And when the games stop for the intermission, they announce: "A little throat-cutting in the meantime, so that there may still be something going on!"

Come now; do you not understand even this truth, that a bad example reacts on the agent? Thank the immortal gods that you are teaching cruelty to a person who cannot learn to be cruel. The young character, which cannot hold fast to righteousness, must be rescued from the mob; it is too easy to side with the majority. Even Socrates, Cato, and Laelius might have been shaken in their moral strength by a crowd that was unlike them; so true it is that none of us, no matter how much he cultivates his abilities, can withstand the shock of faults that approach, as it were, with so great a retinue. Much harm is done by a single case of indulgence or greed; the familiar friend, if he be luxurious, weakens and softens us imperceptibly; the neighbour, if he be rich, rouses our covetousness; the companion, if he be slanderous, rubs off some of his rust upon us, even though we be spotless and sincere. What then do you think the effect will be on character, when the world at large assaults it! You must either imitate or loathe the world.

But both courses are to be avoided; you should not copy the bad simply because they are many, nor should you hate the many because they are unlike you. Withdraw into yourself, as far as you can. Associate with those who will make a better man of you. Welcome those whom you yourself can improve. The process is mutual; for men learn while they teach. There is no reason why pride in advertising your abilities should lure you into publicity, so that you should desire to recite or harangue before the general public. Of course I should be willing for you to do so if you had a stock-in-trade that suited such a mob; as it is, there is not a man of them who can understand you. One or two individuals will perhaps come in your way, but even these will have to be moulded and trained by you so that they will understand you. You may say: "For what purpose did I learn all these things?" But you need not fear that you have wasted your efforts; it was for yourself that you learned them.

In order, however, that I may not to-day have learned exclusively for myself, I shall share with you three excellent sayings, of the same general purport, which have come to my attention. This letter will give you one of them as payment of my debt; the other two you may accept as a contribution in advance. Democritus says: "One man means as much to me as a multitude, and a multitude only as much as one man." The following also was nobly spoken by someone or other, for it is doubtful who the author was; they asked him what was the object of all this study applied to an art that would reach but very few. He replied: "I am content with few, content with one, content with none at all." The third saying – and a noteworthy one, too – is by Epicurus, written to one of the partners of his studies: "I write this not for the many, but for you; each of us is enough of an audience for the other." Lay these words to heart, Lucilius, that you may scorn the pleasure which comes from the applause of the majority. Many men praise you; but have you any reason for being pleased with yourself, if you are a person whom the many can understand? Your good qualities should face inwards. Farewell.

Letter VIII - On the Philosopher's Seclusion

"Do you bid me," you say, "shun the throng, and withdraw from men, and be content with my own conscience? Where are the counsels of your school, which order a man to die in the midst of active work?" As to the course which I seem to you to be urging on you now and then, my object in shutting myself up and locking the door is to be able to help a greater number. I never spend a day in idleness; I appropriate even a part of the night for study. I do not allow time for sleep but yield to it when I must, and when my eyes are wearied with waking and ready to fall shut, I keep them at their task. I have withdrawn not only from men, but from affairs, especially from my own affairs; I am working for later generations, writing down some ideas that may be of assistance to them. There are certain wholesome counsels, which may be compared to prescriptions of useful drugs; these I am putting into writing; for I have found them helpful in ministering to my own sores, which, if not wholly cured, have at any rate ceased to spread.

I point other men to the right path, which I have found late in life, when wearied with wandering. I cry out to them: "Avoid whatever pleases the throng: avoid the gifts of Chance! Halt before every good which Chance brings to you, in a spirit of doubt and fear; for it is the dumb animals and fish that are deceived by tempting hopes. Do you call these things the 'gifts' of Fortune? They are snares. And any man among you who wishes to live a life of safety will avoid, to the utmost of his power, these limed twigs of her favour, by which we mortals, most wretched in this respect also, are deceived; for we think that we hold them in our grasp, but they hold us in theirs. Such a career leads us into precipitous ways, and life on such heights ends in a fall. Moreover, we cannot even stand up against prosperity when she begins to drive us to leeward; nor can we go down, either, 'with the ship at least on her course,' or once for all; Fortune does not capsize us, – she plunges our bows under and dashes us on the rocks.

"Hold fast, then, to this sound and wholesome rule of life – that you indulge the body only so far as is needful for good health. The body should be treated more rigorously, that it may not be disobedient to the mind. Eat merely to relieve your hunger; drink merely to quench your thirst; dress merely to keep out the cold; house yourself merely as a protection against personal discomfort. It matters little whether the house be built of turf, or of variously coloured imported marble; understand that a man is sheltered just as well by a thatch as by a roof of gold. Despise everything that useless toil creates as an ornament and an object of beauty. And reflect that nothing except the soul is worthy of wonder; for to the soul, if it be great, naught is great."

When I commune in such terms with myself and with future generations, do you not think that I am doing more good than when I appear as counsel in court, or stamp my seal upon a will, or lend my assistance in the senate, by word or action, to a candidate? Believe me, those who seem to be busied with nothing are busied with the greater tasks; they are dealing at the same time with things mortal and things immortal.

But I must stop, and pay my customary contribution, to balance this letter. The payment shall not be made from my own property; for I am still conning Epicurus. I read to-day, in his works, the following sentence: "If you would enjoy real freedom, you must be the slave of Philosophy." The man who submits and surrenders himself to her is not kept waiting; he is emancipated on the spot. For the very service of Philosophy is freedom.

It is likely that you will ask me why I quote so many of Epicurus's noble words instead of words taken from our own school. But is there any reason why you should regard them as sayings of Epicurus and not common property? How many poets give forth ideas that have been uttered, or may be uttered, by philosophers! I need not touch upon the tragedians and our writers of national drama; for these last are also somewhat serious, and stand half-way between comedy and tragedy. What a quantity of sagacious verses lie buried in the mime! How many of Publilius's lines are worthy of being spoken by buskin-clad actors, as well as by wearers of the slipper! I shall quote one verse of his, which concerns philosophy, and particularly that phase of it which we were discussing a moment ago, wherein he says that the gifts of Chance are not to be regarded as part of our possessions:

Still alien is whatever you have gained/By coveting

I recall that you yourself expressed this idea much more happily and concisely:

What Chance has made yours is not really yours.

And a third, spoken by you still more happily, shall not be omitted:

The good that could be given, can be removed.

I shall not charge this up to the expense account, because I have given it to you from your own stock. Farewell.

Letter IX - On Philosophy and Friendship

You desire to know whether Epicurus is right when, in one of his letters, he rebukes those who hold that the wise man is self-sufficient and for that reason does not stand in need of friendships. This is the objection raised by Epicurus against Stilbo and those who believe that the Supreme Good is a soul which is insensible to feeling.

We are bound to meet with a double meaning if we try to express the Greek term "lack of feeling" summarily, in a single word, rendering it by the Latin word impatientia. For it may be understood in the meaning the opposite to that which we wish it to have. What we mean to express is, a soul which rejects any sensation of evil; but people will interpret the idea as that of a soul which can endure no evil. Consider, therefore, whether it is not better to say "a soul that cannot be harmed," or "a soul entirely beyond the realm of suffering." There is this difference between ourselves and the other school: our ideal wise man feels his troubles, but overcomes them; their wise man does not even feel them. But we and they alike hold this idea, – that the wise man is self-sufficient. Nevertheless, he desires friends, neighbours, and associates, no matter how much he is sufficient unto himself. And mark how self-sufficient he is; for on occasion he can be content with a part of himself. If he lose a hand through disease or war, or if some accident puts out one or both of his eyes, he will be satisfied with what is left, taking as much pleasure in his impaired and maimed body as he took when it was sound. But while he does not pine for these parts if they are missing, he prefers not to lose them. In this sense the wise man is self-sufficient, that he can do without friends, not that he desires to do without them. When I say "can," I mean this: he endures the loss of a friend with equanimity.

But he need never lack friends, for it lies in his own control how soon he shall make good a loss. Just as Phidias, if he lose a statue, can straightway carve another, even so our master in the art of making friendships can fill the place of a friend he has lost. If you ask how one can make oneself a friend quickly, I will tell you, provided we are agreed that I may pay my debt at once and square the account, so far as this letter is concerned. Hecato, says: "I can show you a philtre, compounded without drugs, herbs, or any witch's incantation: 'If you would be loved, love.'" Now there is great pleasure, not only in maintaining old and established friendships, but also in beginning and acquiring new ones. There is the same difference between winning a new friend and having already won him, as there is between the farmer who sows and the farmer who reaps.

The philosopher Attalus used to say: "It is more pleasant to make than to keep a friend, as it is more pleasant to the artist to paint than to have finished painting." When one is busy and absorbed in one's work, the very absorption affords great delight; but when one has withdrawn one's hand from the completed masterpiece, the pleasure is not so keen. Henceforth it is the fruits of his art that he enjoys; it was the art itself that he enjoyed while he was painting. In the case of our children, their young manhood yields the more abundant fruits, but their infancy was sweeter.

Let us now return to the question. The wise man, I say, self-sufficient though he be, nevertheless desires friends if only for the purpose of practising friendship, in order that his noble qualities may not lie dormant. Not, however, for the purpose mentioned by Epicurus in the letter quoted above: "That there may be someone to sit by him when he is ill, to help him when he is in prison or in want;" but that he may have someone by whose sick-bed he himself may sit, someone a prisoner in hostile hands whom he himself may set free. He who regards himself only, and enters upon friendships for this reason, reckons wrongly. The end will be like the beginning: he has made friends with one who might assist him out of bondage; at the first rattle of the chain such a friend will desert him. These are the so-called "fair-weather" friendships; one who is chosen for the sake of utility will be satisfactory only so long as he is useful. Hence prosperous men are blockaded by troops of friends; but those who have failed stand amid vast loneliness their friends fleeing from the very crisis which is to test their worth. Hence, also, we notice those many shameful cases of persons who, through fear, desert or betray. The beginning and the end cannot but harmonize. He who begins to be your friend because it pays will also cease because it pays. A man will be attracted by some reward offered in exchange for his friendship, if he be attracted by aught in friendship other than friendship itself.

For what purpose, then, do I make a man my friend? In order to have someone for whom I may die, whom I may follow into exile, against whose death I may stake my own life, and pay the pledge, too. The friendship which you portray is a bargain and not a friendship; it regards convenience only, and looks to the results. Beyond question the feeling of a lover has in it something akin to friendship; one might call it friendship run mad. But, though this is true, does anyone love for the sake of gain, or promotion, or renown? Pure love, careless of all other things, kindles the soul with desire for the beautiful object, not without the hope of a return of the affection. What then? Can a cause which is more honourable produce a passion that is base? You may retort: "We are now discussing the question whether friendship is to be cultivated for its own sake." On the contrary, nothing more urgently requires demonstration; for if friendship is to be sought for its own sake, he may seek it who is self-sufficient. "How, then," you ask, "does he seek it?" Precisely as he seeks an object of great beauty, not attracted to it by desire for gain, nor yet frightened by the instability of Fortune. One who seeks friendship for favourable occasions, strips it of all its nobility.

"The wise man is self-sufficient." This phrase, my dear Lucilius, is incorrectly explained by many; for they withdraw the wise man from the world, and force him to dwell within his own skin. But we must mark with care what this sentence signifies and how far it applies; the wise man is sufficient unto himself for a happy existence, but not for mere existence. For he needs many helps towards mere existence; but for a happy existence he needs only a sound and upright soul, one that despises Fortune.

I should like also to state to you one of the distinctions of Chrysippus, who declares that the wise man is in want of nothing, and yet needs many things. "On the other hand," he says, "nothing is needed by the fool, for he does not understand how to use anything, but he is in want of everything." The wise man needs hands, eyes, and many things that are necessary for his daily use; but he is in want of nothing. For want implies a necessity, and nothing is necessary to the wise man. Therefore, although he is self-sufficient, yet he has need of friends. He craves as many friends as possible, not, however, that he may live happily; for he will live happily even without friends. The Supreme Good calls for no practical aids from outside; it is developed at home, and arises entirely within itself. If the good seeks any portion of itself from without, it begins to be subject to the play of Fortune.

People may say: "But what sort of existence will the wise man have, if he be left friendless when thrown into prison, or when stranded in some foreign nation, or when delayed on a long voyage, or when out upon a lonely shore?" His life will be like that of Jupiter, who, amid the dissolution of the world, when the gods are confounded together and Nature rests for a space from her work, can retire into himself and give himself over to his own thoughts. In some such way as this the sage will act; he will retreat into himself, and live with himself. As long as he is allowed to order his affairs according to his judgment, he is self-sufficient – and marries a wife; he is self-sufficient – and brings up children; he is self-sufficient – and yet could not live if he had to live without the society of man. Natural promptings, and not his own selfish needs, draw him into Friendships. For just as other things have for us an inherent attractiveness, so has friendship. As we hate solitude and crave society, as nature draws men to each other, so in this matter also there is an attraction which makes us desirous of friendship. Nevertheless, though the sage may love his friends dearly, often comparing them with himself, and putting them ahead of himself, yet all the good will be limited to his own being, and he will speak the words which were spoken by the very Stilbo whom Epicurus criticizes in his letter. For Stilbo, after his country was captured and his children and his wife lost, as he emerged from the general desolation alone and yet happy, spoke as follows to Demetrius, called Sacker of Cities because of the destruction he brought upon them, in answer to the question whether he had lost anything: "I have all my goods with me!" There is a brave and stout-hearted man for you! The enemy conquered, but Stilbo conquered his conqueror. "I have lost nothing!" Aye, he forced Demetrius to wonder whether he himself had conquered after all. "My goods are all with me!" In other words, he deemed nothing that might be taken from him to be a good.

We marvel at certain animals because they can pass through fire and suffer no bodily harm; but how much more marvellous is a man who has marched forth unhurt and unscathed through fire and sword and devastation!

Do you understand now how much easier it is to conquer a whole tribe than to conquer one man? This saying of Stilbo makes common ground with Stoicism; the Stoic also can carry his goods unimpaired through cities that have been burned to ashes; for he is self-sufficient. Such are the bounds which he sets to his own happiness.

But you must not think that our school alone can utter noble words; Epicurus himself, the reviler of Stilbo, spoke similar language; put it down to my credit, though I have already wiped out my debt for the present day. He says: "Whoever does not regard what he has as most ample wealth, is unhappy, though he be master of the whole world." Or, if the following seems to you a more suitable phrase, – for we must try to render the meaning and not the mere words: "A man may rule the world and still be unhappy, if he does not feel that he is supremely happy." In order, however, that you may know that these sentiments are universal, suggested, of course, by Nature, you will find in one of the comic poets this verse;

Unblest is he who thinks himself unblest.

or what does your condition matter, if it is bad in your own eyes? You may say; "What then? If yonder man, rich by base means, and yonder man, lord of many but slave of more, shall call themselves happy, will their own opinion make them happy?" It matters not what one says, but what one feels; also, not how one feels on one particular day, but how one feels at all times. There is no reason, however, why you should fear that this great privilege will fall into unworthy hands; only the wise man is pleased with his own. Folly is ever troubled with weariness of itself. Farewell.

Letter X - On Living to Oneself

Yes, I do not change my opinion: avoid the many, avoid the few, avoid even the individual. I know of no one with whom I should be willing to have you shared. And see what an opinion of you I have; for I dare to trust you with your own self. Crates, they say, the disciple of the very Stilbo whom I mentioned in a former letter, noticed a young man walking by himself, and asked him what he was doing all alone. "I am communing with myself," replied the youth. "Pray be careful, then," said Crates, "and take good heed; you are communing with a bad man!"

When persons are in mourning, or fearful about something, we are accustomed to watch them that we may prevent them from making a wrong use of their loneliness. No thoughtless person ought to be left alone; in such cases he only plans folly, and heaps up future dangers for himself or for others; he brings into play his base desires; the mind displays what fear or shame used to repress; it whets his boldness, stirs his passions, and goads his anger. And finally, the only benefit that solitude confers, – the habit of trusting no man, and of fearing no witnesses, – is lost to the fool; for he betrays himself.

Mark therefore what my hopes are for you, – nay, rather, what I am promising myself, inasmuch as hope is merely the title of an uncertain blessing:

I do not know any person with whom I should prefer you to associate rather than yourself. I remember in what a great-souled way you hurled forth certain phrases, and how full of strength they were! I immediately congratulated myself and said: "These words did not come from the edge of the lips; these utterances have a solid foundation. This man is not one of the many; he has regard for his real welfare." Speak, and live, in this way; see to it that nothing keeps you down. As for your former prayers, you may dispense the gods from answering them; offer new prayers; pray for a sound mind and for good health, first of soul and then of body. And of course you should offer those prayers frequently. Call boldly upon God; you will not be asking him for that which belongs to another.

But I must, as is my custom, send a little gift along with this letter. It is a true saying which I have found in Athenodorus: "Know that thou art freed from all desires when thou hast reached such a point that thou prayest to God for nothing except what thou canst pray for openly." But how foolish men are now! They whisper the basest of prayers to heaven; but if anyone listens, they are silent at once. That which they are unwilling for men to know, they communicate to God. Do you not think, then, that some such wholesome advice as this could be given you: "Live among men as if God beheld you; speak with God as if men were listening"? Farewell.

Letter XI - On the Blush of Modesty

Your friend and I have had a conversation. He is a man of ability; his very first words showed what spirit and understanding he possesses, and what progress he has already made. He gave me a foretaste, and he will not fail to answer thereto. For he spoke not from forethought, but was suddenly caught off his guard. When he tried to collect himself, he could scarcely banish that hue of modesty, which is a good sign in a young man; the blush that spread over his face seemed so to rise from the depths. And I feel sure that his habit of blushing will stay with him after he has strengthened his character, stripped off all his faults, and become wise. For by no wisdom can natural weaknesses of the body be removed. That which is implanted and inborn can be toned down by training, but not overcome. The steadiest speaker, when before the public, often breaks into a perspiration, as if he had wearied or over-heated himself; some tremble in the knees when they rise to speak; I know of some whose teeth chatter, whose tongues falter, whose lips quiver. Training and experience can never shake off this habit; nature exerts her own power and through such a weakness makes her presence known even to the strongest. I know that the blush, too, is a habit of this sort, spreading suddenly over the faces of the most dignified men. It is, indeed more prevalent in youth, because of the warmer blood and the sensitive countenance; nevertheless, both seasoned men and aged men are affected by it. Some are most dangerous when they redden, as if they were letting all their sense of shame escape. Sulla, when the blood mantled his cheeks, was in his fiercest mood. Pompey had the most sensitive cast of countenance; he always blushed in the presence of a gathering, and especially at a public assembly. Fabianus also, I remember, reddened when he appeared as a witness before the senate; and his embarrassment became him to a remarkable degree. Such a habit is not due to mental weakness, but to the novelty of a situation; an inexperienced person is not necessarily confused, but is usually affected, because he slips into this habit by natural tendency of the body. Just as certain men are full-blooded, so others are of a quick and mobile blood, that rushes to the face at once.

As I remarked, Wisdom can never remove this habit; for if she could rub out all our faults, she would be mistress of the universe. Whatever is assigned to us by the terms of our birth and the blend in our constitutions, will stick with us, no matter how hard or how long the soul may have tried to master itself. And we cannot forbid these feelings any more than we can summon them. Actors in the theatre, who imitate the emotions, who portray fear and nervousness, who depict sorrow, imitate bashfulness by hanging their heads, lowering their voices, and keeping their eyes fixed and rooted upon the ground. They cannot, however, muster a blush; for the blush cannot be prevented or acquired. Wisdom will not assure us of a remedy, or give us help against it; it comes or goes unbidden, and is a law unto itself.

But my letter calls for its closing sentence. Hear and take to heart this useful and wholesome motto: "Cherish some man of high character, and keep him ever before your eyes, living as if he were watching you, and ordering all your actions as if he beheld them." Such, my dear Lucilius, is the counsel of Epicurus; he has quite properly given us a guardian and an attendant. We can get rid of most sins, if we have a witness who stands near us when we are likely to go wrong. The soul should have someone whom it can respect, – one by whose authority it may make even its inner shrine more hallowed. Happy is the man who can make others better, not merely when he is in their company, but even when he is in their thoughts! And happy also is he who can so revere a man as to calm and regulate himself by calling him to mind! One who can so revere another, will soon be himself worthy of reverence. Choose therefore a Cato; or, if Cato seems too severe a model, choose some Laelius, a gentler spirit. Choose a master whose life, conversation, and soul-expressing face have satisfied you; picture him always to yourself as your protector or your pattern. For we must indeed have someone according to whom we may regulate our characters; you can never straighten that which is crooked unless you use a ruler. Farewell.

Letter XII - On Old Age

Wherever I turn, I see evidences of my advancing years. I visited lately my country-place, and protested against the money which was spent on the tumble-down building. My bailiff maintained that the flaws were not due to his own carelessness; "he was doing everything possible, but the house was old." And this was the house which grew under my own hands! What has the future in store for me, if stones of my own age are already crumbling? I was angry, and I embraced the first opportunity to vent my spleen in the bailiff's presence. "It is clear," I cried, "that these plane-trees are neglected; they have no leaves.

Their branches are so gnarled and shrivelled; the boles are so rough and unkempt! This would not happen, if someone loosened the earth at their feet, and watered them." The bailiff swore by my protecting deity that "he was doing everything possible, and never relaxed his efforts, but those trees were old." Between you and me, I had planted those trees myself, I had seen them in their first leaf. Then I turned to the door and asked: "Who is that broken-down dotard? You have done well to place him at the entrance; for he is outward bound. Where did you get him? What pleasure did it give you to take up for burial some other man's dead?" But the slave said: "Don't you know me, sir? I am Felicio; you used to bring me little images. My father was Philositus the steward, and I am your pet slave." "The man is clean crazy," I remarked. "Has my pet slave become a little boy again? But it is quite possible; his teeth are just dropping out."

I owe it to my country-place that my old age became apparent whithersoever I turned. Let us cherish and love old age; for it is full of pleasure if one knows how to use it. Fruits are most welcome when almost over; youth is most charming at its close; the last drink delights the toper, the glass which souses him and puts the finishing touch on his drunkenness. Each pleasure reserves to the end the greatest delights which it contains. Life is most delightful when it is on the downward slope, but has not yet reached the abrupt decline. And I myself believe that the period which stands, so to speak, on the edge of the roof, possesses pleasures of its own. Or else the very fact of our not wanting pleasures has taken the place of the pleasures themselves. How comforting it is to have tired out one's appetites, and to have done with them! "But," you say, "it is a nuisance to be looking death in the face!" Death, however, should be looked in the face by young and old alike. We are not summoned according to our rating on the censor's list. Moreover, no one is so old that it would be improper for him to hope for another day of existence. And one day, mind you, is a stage on life's journey.

Our span of life is divided into parts; it consists of large circles enclosing smaller. One circle embraces and bounds the rest; it reaches from birth to the last day of existence. The next circle limits the period of our young manhood. The third confines all of childhood in its circumference. Again, there is, in a class by itself, the year; it contains within itself all the divisions of time by the multiplication of which we get the total of life. The month is bounded by a narrower ring. The smallest circle of all is the day; but even a day has its beginning and its ending, its sunrise and its sunset. Hence Heraclitus, whose obscure style gave him his surname, remarked: "One day is equal to every day." Different persons have interpreted the saying in different ways. Some hold that days are equal in number of hours, and this is true; for if by "day" we mean twenty-four hours' time, all days must be equal, inasmuch as the night acquires what the day loses. But others maintain that one day is equal to all days through resemblance, because the very longest space of time possesses no element which cannot be found in a single day, – namely, light and darkness, – and even to eternity day makes these alternations more numerous, not different when it is shorter and different again when it is longer. Hence, every day ought to be regulated as if it closed the series, as if it rounded out and completed our existence.

Pacuvius, who by long occupancy made Syria his own, used to hold a regular burial sacrifice in his own honour, with wine and the usual funeral feasting, and then would have himself carried from the dining-room to his chamber, while eunuchs applauded and sang in Greek to a musical accompaniment: "He has lived his life, he has lived his life!" Thus Pacuvius had himself carried out to burial every day. Let us, however, do from a good motive what he used to do from a debased motive; let us go to our sleep with joy and gladness; let us say:

I have lived; the course which Fortune set for me/Is finished.

And if God is pleased to add another day, we should welcome it with glad hearts. That man is happiest, and is secure in his own possession of himself, who can await the morrow without apprehension. When a man has said: "I have lived!", every morning he arises he receives a bonus.

But now I ought to close my letter. "What?" you say; "shall it come to me without any little offering? "Be not afraid; it brings something, – nay, more than something, a great deal. For what is more noble than the following saying of which I make this letter the bearer: "It is wrong to live under constraint; but no man is constrained to live under constraint." Of course not. On all sides lie many short and simple paths to freedom; and let us thank God that no man can be kept in life. We may spurn the very constraints that hold us. "Epicurus," you reply, "uttered these words; what are you doing with another's property?" Any truth, I maintain, is my own property. And I shall continue to heap quotations from Epicurus upon you, so that all persons who swear by the words of another, and put a value upon the speaker and not upon the thing spoken, may understand that the best ideas are common property. Farewell.

Letter XIII - On Groundless Fears

I know that you have plenty of spirit; for even before you began to equip yourself with maxims which were wholesome and potent to overcome obstacles, you were taking pride in your contest with Fortune; and this is all the more true, now that you have grappled with Fortune and tested your powers. For our powers can never inspire in us implicit faith in ourselves except when many difficulties have confronted us on this side and on that, and have occasionally even come to close quarters with us. It is only in this way that the true spirit can be tested, – the spirit that will never consent to come under the jurisdiction of things external to ourselves. This is the touchstone of such a spirit; no prizefighter can go with high spirits into the strife if he has never been beaten black and blue; the only contestant who can confidently enter the lists is the man who has seen his own blood, who has felt his teeth rattle beneath his opponent's fist, who has been tripped and felt the full force of his adversary's charge, who has been downed in body but not in spirit, one who, as often as he falls, rises again with greater defiance than ever. So then, to keep up my figure, Fortune has often in the past got the upper hand of you, and yet you have not surrendered, but have leaped up and stood your ground still more eagerly. For manliness gains much strength by being challenged; nevertheless, if you approve, allow me to offer some additional safeguards by which you may fortify yourself.

There are more things, Lucilius, likely to frighten us than there are to crush us; we suffer more often in imagination than in reality. I am not speaking with you in the Stoic strain but in my milder style. For it is our Stoic fashion to speak of all those things, which provoke cries and groans, as unimportant and beneath notice; but you and I must drop such great-sounding words, although, heaven knows, they are true enough. What I advise you to do is, not to be unhappy before the crisis comes; since it may be that the dangers before which you paled as if they were threatening you, will never come upon you; they certainly have not yet come. Accordingly, some things torment us more than they ought; some torment us before they ought; and some torment us when they ought not to torment us at all. We are in the habit of exaggerating, or imagining, or anticipating, sorrow.

The first of these three faults may be postponed for the present, because the subject is under discussion and the case is still in court, so to speak. That which I should call trifling, you will maintain to be most serious; for of course I know that some men laugh while being flogged, and that others wince at a box on the ear. We shall consider later whether these evils derive their power from their own strength, or from our own weakness.

Do me the favour, when men surround you and try to talk you into believing that you are unhappy, to consider not what you hear but what you yourself feel, and to take counsel with your feelings and question yourself independently, because you know your own affairs better than anyone else does. Ask: "Is there any reason why these persons should condole with me? Why should they be worried or even fear some infection from me, as if troubles could be transmitted? Is there any evil involved, or is it a matter merely of ill report, rather than an evil?" Put the question voluntarily to yourself: "Am I tormented without sufficient reason, am I morose, and do I convert what is not an evil into what is an evil?" You may retort with the question: "How am I to know whether my sufferings are real or imaginary?" Here is the rule for such matters: we are tormented either by things present, or by things to come, or by both. As to things present, the decision is easy. Suppose that your person enjoys freedom and health, and that you do not suffer from any external injury. As to what may happen to it in the future, we shall see later on. To-day there is nothing wrong with it. "But," you say, "something will happen to it." First of all, consider whether your proofs of future trouble are sure. For it is more often the case that we are troubled by our apprehensions, and that we are mocked by that mocker, rumour, which is wont to settle wars, but much more often settles individuals. Yes, my dear Lucilius; we agree too quickly with what people say. We do not put to the test those things which cause our fear; we do not examine into them; we blench and retreat just like soldiers who are forced to abandon their camp because of a dust-cloud raised by stampeding cattle, or are thrown into a panic by the spreading of some unauthenticated rumour. And somehow or other it is the idle report that disturbs us most. For truth has its own definite boundaries, but that which arises from uncertainty is delivered over to guesswork and the irresponsible license of a frightened mind. That is why no fear is so ruinous and so uncontrollable as panic fear. For other fears are groundless, but this fear is witless.

Let us, then, look carefully into the matter. It is likely that some troubles will befall us; but it is not a present fact. How often has the unexpected happened! How often has the expected never come to pass! And even though it is ordained to be, what does it avail to run out to meet your suffering? You will suffer soon enough, when it arrives; so look forward meanwhile to better things. What shall you gain by doing this? Time. There will be many happenings meanwhile which will serve to postpone, or end, or pass on to another person, the trials which are near or even in your very presence. A fire has opened the way to flight. Men have been let down softly by a catastrophe. Sometimes the sword has been checked even at the victim's throat. Men have survived their own executioners. Even bad fortune is fickle. Perhaps it will come, perhaps not; in the meantime it is not. So look forward to better things.

The mind at times fashions for itself false shapes of evil when there are no signs that point to any evil; it twists into the worst construction some word of doubtful meaning; or it fancies some personal grudge to be more serious than it really is, considering not how angry the enemy is, but to what lengths he may go if he is angry. But life is not worth living, and there is no limit to our sorrows, if we indulge our fears to the greatest possible extent; in this matter, let prudence help you, and contemn with a resolute spirit even when it is in plain sight. If you cannot do this, counter one weakness with another, and temper your fear with hope. There is nothing so certain among these objects of fear that it is not more certain still that things we dread sink into nothing and that things we hope for mock us.

Accordingly, weigh carefully your hopes as well as your fears, and whenever all the elements are in doubt, decide in your own favour; believe what you prefer. And if fear wins a majority of the votes, incline in the other direction anyhow, and cease to harass your soul, reflecting continually that most mortals, even when no troubles are actually at hand or are certainly to be expected in the future, become excited and disquieted. No one calls a halt on himself, when he begins to be urged ahead; nor does he regulate his alarm according to the truth. No one says; "The author of the story is a fool, and he who has believed it is a fool, as well as he who fabricated it." We let ourselves drift with every breeze; we are frightened at uncertainties, just as if they were certain. We observe no moderation. The slightest thing turns the scales and throws us forthwith into a panic.

But I am ashamed either to admonish you sternly or to try to beguile you with such mild remedies. Let another say. "Perhaps the worst will not happen." You yourself must say. "Well, what if it does happen? Let us see who wins! Perhaps it happens for my best interests; it may be that such a death will shed credit upon my life." Socrates was ennobled by the hemlock draught. Wrench from Cato's hand his sword, the vindicator of liberty, and you deprive him of the greatest share of his glory. I am exhorting you far too long, since you need reminding rather than exhortation. The path on which I am leading you is not different from that on which your nature leads you; you were born to such conduct as I describe. Hence there is all the more reason why you should increase and beautify the good that is in you.

But now, to close my letter, I have only to stamp the usual seal upon it, in other words, to commit thereto some noble message to be delivered to you: "The fool, with all his other faults, has this also, he is always getting ready to live." Reflect, my esteemed Lucilius, what this saying means, and you will see how revolting is the fickleness of men who lay down every day new foundations of life, and begin to build up fresh hopes even at the brink of the grave. Look within your own mind for individual instances; you will think of old men who are preparing themselves at that very hour for a political career, or for travel, or for business. And what is baser than getting ready to live when you are already old? I should not name the author of this motto, except that it is somewhat unknown to fame and is not one of those popular sayings of Epicurus which I have allowed myself to praise and to appropriate. Farewell.

Letter XIV - On the Reasons for Withdrawing from the World

I confess that we all have an inborn affection for our body; I confess that we are entrusted with its guardianship. I do not maintain that the body is not to be indulged at all; but I maintain that we must not be slaves to it. He will have many masters who makes his body his master, who is over-fearful in its behalf, who judges everything according to the body. We should conduct ourselves not as if we ought to live for the body, but as if we could not live without it. Our too great love for it makes us restless with fears, burdens us with cares, and exposes us to insults. Virtue is held too cheap by the man who counts his body too dear. We should cherish the body with the greatest care; but we should also be prepared, when reason, self-respect, and duty demand the sacrifice, to deliver it even to the flames.

Let us, however, in so far as we can, avoid discomforts as well as dangers, and withdraw to safe ground, by thinking continually how we may repel all objects of fear. If I am not mistaken, there are three main classes of these: we fear want, we fear sickness, and we fear the troubles which result from the violence of the stronger. And of all these, that which shakes us most is the dread which hangs over us from our neighbour's ascendancy; for it is accompanied by great outcry and uproar. But the natural evils which I have mentioned, – want and sickness, steal upon us silently with no shock of terror to the eye or to the ear. The other kind of evil comes, so to speak, in the form of a huge parade. Surrounding it is a retinue of swords and fire and chains and a mob of beasts to be let loose upon the disembowelled entrails of men. Picture to yourself under this head the prison, the cross, the rack, the hook, and the stake which they drive straight through a man until it protrudes from his throat. Think of human limbs torn apart by chariots driven in opposite directions, of the terrible shirt smeared and interwoven with inflammable materials, and of all the other contrivances devised by cruelty, in addition to those which I have mentioned! It is not surprising, then, if our greatest terror is of such a fate; for it comes in many shapes and its paraphernalia are terrifying. For just as the torturer accomplishes more in proportion to the number of instruments which he displays, – indeed, the spectacle overcomes those who would have patiently withstood the suffering, – similarly, of all the agencies which coerce and master our minds, the most effective are those which can make a display. Those other troubles are of course not less serious; I mean hunger, thirst, ulcers of the stomach, and fever that parches our very bowels. They are, however, secret; they have no bluster and no heralding; but these, like huge arrays of war, prevail by virtue of their display and their equipment.

Let us, therefore, see to it that we abstain from giving offence. It is sometimes the people that we ought to fear; or sometimes a body of influential oligarchs in the Senate, if the method of governing the State is such that most of the business is done by that body; and sometimes individuals equipped with power by the people and against the people. It is burdensome to keep the friendship of all such persons; it is enough not to make enemies of them. So the wise man will never provoke the anger of those in power; nay, he will even turn his course, precisely as he would turn from a storm if he were steering a ship. When you travelled to Sicily, you crossed the Straits. The reckless pilot scorned the blustering South Wind, – the wind which roughens the Sicilian Sea and forces it into choppy currents; he sought not the shore on the left, but the strand hard by the place where Charybdis throws the seas into confusion. Your more careful pilot, however, questions those who know the locality as to the tides and the meaning of the clouds; he holds his course far from that region notorious for its swirling waters. Our wise man does the same he shuns a strong man who may be injurious to him, making a point of not seeming to avoid him, because an important part of one's safety lies in not seeking safety openly; for what one avoids, one condemns,

We should therefore look about us, and see how we may protect ourselves from the mob. And first of all, we should have no cravings like theirs; for rivalry results in strife. Again, let us possess nothing that can be snatched from us to the great profit of a plotting foe. Let there be as little booty as possible on your person. No one sets out to shed the blood of his fellow-men for the sake of bloodshed, – at any rate very few. More murderers speculate on their profits than give vent to hatred. If you are empty-handed, the highwayman passes you by: even along an infested road, the poor may travel in peace. Next, we must follow the old adage and avoid three things with special care: hatred, jealousy, and scorn. And wisdom alone can show you how this may be done. It is hard to observe a mean; we must be chary of letting the fear of jealousy lead us into becoming objects of scorn, lest, when we choose not to stamp others down, we let them think that they can stamp us down. The power to inspire fear has caused many men to be in fear. Let us withdraw ourselves in every way; for it is as harmful to be scorned as to be admired.

One must therefore take refuge in philosophy; this pursuit, not only in the eyes of good men, but also in the eyes of those who are even moderately bad, is a sort of protecting emblem. For speechmaking at the bar, or any other pursuit that claims the people's attention, wins enemies for a man; but philosophy is peaceful and minds her own business. Men cannot scorn her; she is honoured by every profession, even the vilest among them. Evil can never grow so strong, and nobility of character can never be so plotted against, that the name of philosophy shall cease to be worshipful and sacred.

Philosophy itself, however should be practised with calmness and moderation. "Very well, then," you retort, "do you regard the philosophy of Marcus Cato as moderate? Cato's voice strove to check a civil war. Cato parted the swords of maddened chieftains. When some fell foul of Pompey and others fell foul of Caesar, Cato defied both parties at once!" Nevertheless, one may well question whether, in those days, a wise man ought to have taken any part in public affairs, and ask: "What do you mean, Marcus Cato? It is not now a question of freedom; long since has freedom gone to rack and ruin. The question is, whether it is Caesar or Pompey who controls the State. Why, Cato, should you take sides in that dispute? It is no business of yours; a tyrant is being selected. What does it concern you who conquers? The better man may win; but the winner is bound to be the worse man." I have referred to Cato's final role. But even in previous years the wise man was not permitted to intervene in such plundering of the state; for what could Cato do but raise his voice and utter unavailing words? At one time he was "bustled" by the mob and spat upon and forcibly removed from the forum and marked for exile; at another, he was taken straight to prison from the senate-chamber.

However, we shall consider later whether the wise man ought to give his attention to politics; meanwhile, I beg you to consider those Stoics who, shut out from public life, have withdrawn into privacy for the purpose of improving men's existence and framing laws for the human race without incurring the displeasure of those in power. The wise man will not upset the customs of the people, nor will he invite the attention of the populace by any novel ways of living.

"What then? Can one who follows out this Plan be safe in any case?" I cannot guarantee you this any more than I can guarantee good health in the case of a man who observes moderation; although, as a matter of fact, good health results from such moderation. Sometimes a vessel perishes in harbour; but what do you think happens on the open sea? And how much more beset with danger that man would be, who even in his leisure is not secure, if he were busily working at many things! Innocent persons sometimes perish; who would deny that? But the guilty perish more frequently. A soldier's skill is not at fault if he receives the death-blow through his armour. And finally, the wise man regards the reason for all his actions, but not the results. The beginning is in our own power; fortune decides the issue, but I do not allow her to pass sentence upon myself. You may say: "But she can inflict a measure of suffering and of trouble." The highwayman does not pass sentence when he slays.

Now you are stretching forth your hand for the daily gift. Golden indeed will be the gift with which I shall load you; and, inasmuch as we have mentioned gold, let me tell you how its use and enjoyment may bring you greater pleasure. "He who needs riches least, enjoys riches most." "Author's name, please!" you say. Now, to show you how generous I am, it is my intent to praise the dicta of other schools. The phrase belongs to Epicurus, or Metrodorus, or some one of that particular thinking-shop. But what difference does it make who spoke the words? They were uttered for the world. He who craves riches feels fear on their account. No man, however, enjoys a blessing that brings anxiety; he is always trying to add a little more. While he puzzles over increasing his wealth, he forgets how to use it. He collects his accounts, he wears out the pavement in the forum, he turns over his ledger, – in short, he ceases to be master and becomes a steward. Farewell.

Letter XV - On Brawn and Brains

The old Romans had a custom which survived even into my lifetime. They would add to the opening words of a letter: "If you are well, it is well; I also am well." Persons like ourselves would do well to say. "If you are studying philosophy, it is well." For this is just what "being well" means. Without philosophy the mind is sickly, and the body, too, though it may be very powerful, is strong only as that of a madman or a lunatic is strong. This, then, is the sort of health you should primarily cultivate; the other kind of health comes second, and will involve little effort, if you wish to be well physically. It is indeed foolish, my dear Lucilius, and very unsuitable for a cultivated man, to work hard over developing the muscles and broadening the shoulders and strengthening the lungs. For although your heavy feeding produce good results and your sinews grow solid, you can never be a match, either in strength or in weight, for a first-class bull. Besides, by overloading the body with food you strangle the soul and render it less active. Accordingly, limit the flesh as much as possible, and allow free play to the spirit. Many inconveniences beset those who devote themselves to such pursuits. In the first place, they have their exercises, at which they must work and waste their life-force and render it less fit to bear a strain or the severer studies. Second, their keen edge is dulled by heavy eating. Besides, they must take orders from slaves of the vilest stamp, – men who alternate between the oil-flask and the flagon, whose day passes satisfactorily if they have got up a good perspiration and quaffed, to make good what they have lost in sweat, huge draughts of liquor which will sink deeper because of their fasting. Drinking and sweating, – it's the life of a dyspeptic!

Now there are short and simple exercises which tire the body rapidly, and so save our time; and time is something of which we ought to keep strict account. These exercises are running, brandishing weights, and jumping, – high-jumping or broad-jumping, or the kind which I may call, "the Priest's dance," or, in slighting terms, "the clothes-cleaner's jump." Select for practice any one of these, and you will find it plain and easy. But whatever you do, come back soon from body to mind. The mind must be exercised both day and night, for it is nourished by moderate labour. and this form of exercise need not be hampered by cold or hot weather, or even by old age. Cultivate that good which improves with the years. Of course I do not command you to be always bending over your books and your writing materials; the mind must have a change, – but a change of such a kind that it is not unnerved, but merely unbent. Riding in a litter shakes up the body, and does not interfere with study: one may read, dictate, converse, or listen to another; nor does walking prevent any of these things.

You need not scorn voice-culture; but I forbid you to practise raising and lowering your voice by scales and specific intonations. What if you should next propose to take lessons in walking! If you consult the sort of person whom starvation has taught new tricks, you will have someone to regulate your steps, watch every mouthful as you eat, and go to such lengths as you yourself, by enduring him and believing in him, have encouraged his effrontery to go. "What, then?" you will ask; "is my voice to begin at the outset with shouting and straining the lungs to the utmost?" No; the natural thing is that it be aroused to such a pitch by easy stages, just as persons who are wrangling begin with ordinary conversational tones and then pass to shouting at the top of their lungs. No speaker cries "Help me, citizens!" at the outset of his speech. Therefore, whenever your spirit's impulse prompts you, raise a hubbub, now in louder now in milder tones, according as your voice, as well as your spirit, shall suggest to you, when you are moved to such a performance. Then let your voice, when you rein it in and call it back to earth, come down gently, not collapse; it should trail off in tones half way between high and low, and should not abruptly drop from its raving in the uncouth manner of countrymen. For our purpose is, not to give the voice exercise, but to make it give us exercise.

You see, I have relieved you of no slight bother; and I shall throw in a little complementary present, – it is Greek, too. Here is the proverb; it is an excellent one: "The fool's life is empty of gratitude and full of fears; its course lies wholly toward the future." "Who uttered these words?" you say. The same writer whom I mentioned before. And what sort of life do you think is meant by the fool's life? That of Baba and Isio? No; he means our own, for we are plunged by our blind desires into ventures which will harm us, but certainly will never satisfy us; for if we could be satisfied with anything, we should have been satisfied long ago; nor do we reflect how pleasant it is to demand nothing, how noble it is to be contented and not to be dependent upon Fortune. Therefore continually remind yourself, Lucilius, how many ambitions you have attained. When you see many ahead of you, think how many are behind! If you would thank the gods, and be grateful for your past life, you should contemplate how many men you have outstripped. But what have you to do with the others? You have outstripped yourself.

Fix a limit which you will not even desire to pass, should you have the power. At last, then, away with all these treacherous goods! They look better to those who hope for them than to those who have attained them. If there were anything substantial in them, they would sooner or later satisfy you; as it is, they merely rouse the drinkers' thirst. Away with fripperies which only serve for show! As to what the future's uncertain lot has in store, why should I demand of Fortune that she give rather than demand of myself that I should not crave? And why should I crave? Shall I heap up my winnings, and forget that man's lot is unsubstantial? For what end should I toil? Lo, to-day is the last; if not, it is near the last. Farewell.

Letter XVI - On Philosophy, the Guide of Life

It is clear to you, I am sure, Lucilius, that no man can live a happy life, or even a supportable life, without the study of wisdom; you know also that a happy life is reached when our wisdom is brought to completion, but that life is at least endurable even when our wisdom is only begun. This idea, however, clear though it is, must be strengthened and implanted more deeply by daily reflection; it is more important for you to keep the resolutions you have already made than to go on and make noble ones. You must persevere, must develop new strength by continuous study, until that which is only a good inclination becomes a good settled purpose. Hence you no longer need to come to me with much talk and protestations; I know that you have made great progress. I understand the feelings which prompt your words; they are not feigned or specious words. Nevertheless I shall tell you what I think, – that at present I have hopes for you, but not yet perfect trust. And I wish that you would adopt the same attitude towards yourself; there is no reason why you should put confidence in yourself too quickly and readily. Examine yourself; scrutinize and observe yourself in divers ways; but mark, before all else, whether it is in philosophy or merely in life itself that you have made progress. Philosophy is no trick to catch the public; it is not devised for show. It is a matter, not of words, but of facts. It is not pursued in order that the day may yield some amusement before it is spent, or that our leisure may be relieved of a tedium that irks us. It moulds and constructs the soul; it orders our life, guides our conduct, shows us what we should do and what we should leave undone; it sits at the helm and directs our course as we waver amid uncertainties. Without it, no one can live fearlessly or in peace of mind. Countless things that happen every hour call for advice; and such advice is to be sought in philosophy.

Perhaps someone will say: "How can philosophy help me, if Fate exists? Of what avail is philosophy, if God rules the universe? Of what avail is it, if Chance governs everything? For not only is it impossible to change things that are determined, but it is also impossible to plan beforehand against what is undetermined; either God has forestalled my plans, and decided what I am to do, or else Fortune gives no free play to my plans." Whether the truth, Lucilius, lies in one or in all of these views, we must be philosophers; whether Fate binds us down by an inexorable law, or whether God as arbiter of the universe has arranged everything, or whether Chance drives and tosses human affairs without method, philosophy ought to be our defence. She will encourage us to obey God cheerfully, but Fortune defiantly; she will teach us to follow God and endure Chance. But it is not my purpose now to be led into a discussion as to what is within our own control, – if foreknowledge is supreme, or if a chain of fated events drags us along in its clutches, or if the sudden and the unexpected play the tyrant over us; I return now to my warning and my exhortation, that you should not allow the impulse of your spirit to weaken and grow cold. Hold fast to it and establish it firmly, in order that what is now impulse may become a habit of the mind.

If I know you well, you have already been trying to find out, from the very beginning of my letter, what little contribution it brings to you. Sift the letter, and you will find it. You need not wonder at any genius of mine; for as yet I am lavish only with other men's property. – But why did I say "other men"? Whatever is well said by anyone is mine. This also is a saying of Epicurus: "If you live according to nature, you will never be poor; if you live according to opinion, you will never be rich." Nature's wants are slight; the demands of opinion are boundless. Suppose that the property of many millionaires is heaped up in your possession. Assume that fortune carries you far beyond the limits of a private income, decks you with gold, clothes you in purple, and brings you to such a degree of luxury and wealth that you can bury the earth under your marble floors; that you may not only possess, but tread upon, riches. Add statues, paintings, and whatever any art has devised for the luxury; you will only learn from such things to crave still greater.

Natural desires are limited; but those which spring from false opinion can have no stopping-point. The false has no limits. When you are travelling on a road, there must be an end; but when astray, your wanderings are limitless. Recall your steps, therefore, from idle things, and when you would know whether that which you seek is based upon a natural or upon a misleading desire, consider whether it can stop at any definite point. If you find, after having travelled far, that there is a more distant goal always in view, you may be sure that this condition is contrary to nature. Farewell.

Letter XVII - On Philosophy and Riches

Cast away everything of that sort, if you are wise; nay, rather that you may be wise; strive toward a sound mind at top speed and with your whole strength. If any bond holds you back, untie it, or sever it. "But," you say, "my estate delays me; I wish to make such disposition of it that it may suffice for me when I have nothing to do, lest either poverty be a burden to me, or I myself a burden to others." You do not seem, when you say this, to know the strength and power of that good which you are considering. You do indeed grasp the all important thing, the great benefit which philosophy confers, but you do not yet discern accurately its various functions, nor do you yet know how great is the help we receive from philosophy in everything, everywhere, – how, (to use Cicero's language,) it not only succours us in the greatest matters but also descends to the smallest. Take my advice; call wisdom into consultation; she will advise you not to sit for ever at your ledger. Doubtless, your object, what you wish to attain by such postponement of your studies, is that poverty may not have to be feared by you. But what if it is something to be desired? Riches have shut off many a man from the attainment of wisdom; poverty is unburdened and free from care. When the trumpet sounds, the poor man knows that he is not being attacked; when there is a cry of "Fire,"he only seeks a way of escape, and does not ask what he can save; if the poor man must go to sea, the harbour does not resound, nor do the wharves bustle with the retinue of one individual. No throng of slaves surrounds the poor man, – slaves for whose mouths the master must covet the fertile crops of regions beyond the sea. It is easy to fill a few stomachs, when they are well trained and crave nothing else but to be filled. Hunger costs but little; squeamishness costs much. Poverty is contented with fulfilling pressing needs.

Why, then, should you reject Philosophy as a comrade? Even the rich man copies her ways when he is in his senses. If you wish to have leisure for your mind, either be a poor man, or resemble a poor man. Study cannot be helpful unless you take pains to live simply; and living simply is voluntary poverty. Away, then, with all excuses like: "I have not yet enough; when I have gained the desired amount, then I shall devote myself wholly to philosophy." And yet this ideal, which you are putting off and placing second to other interests, should be secured first of all; you should begin with it. You retort: "I wish to acquire something to live on." Yes, but learn while you are acquiring it; for if anything forbids you to live nobly, nothing forbids you to die nobly. There is no reason why poverty should call us away from philosophy, – no, nor even actual want. For when hastening after wisdom, we must endure even hunger. Men have endured hunger when their towns were besieged, and what other reward for their endurance did they obtain than that they did not fall under the conqueror's power? How much greater is the promise of the prize of everlasting liberty, and the assurance that we need fear neither God nor man! Even though we starve, we must reach that goal. Armies have endured all manner of want, have lived on roots, and have resisted hunger by means of food too revolting to mention. All this they have suffered to gain a kingdom, and, – what is more marvellous, – to gain a kingdom that will be another's. Will any man hesitate to endure poverty, in order that he may free his mind from madness?

Therefore one should not seek to lay up riches first; one may attain to philosophy, however, even without money for the journey. It is indeed so. After you have come to possess all other things, shall you then wish to possess wisdom also? Is philosophy to be the last requisite in life, – a sort of supplement? Nay, your plan should be this: be a philosopher now, whether you have anything or not, – for if you have anything, how do you know that you have not too much already? – but if you have nothing, seek understanding first, before anything else. "But," you say, "I shall lack the necessities of life." In the first place, you cannot lack them; because nature demands but little, and the wise man suits his needs to nature. But if the utmost pinch of need arrives, he will quickly take leave of life and cease being a trouble to himself. If, however, his means of existence are meagre and scanty, he will make the best of them, without being anxious or worried about anything more than the bare necessities; he will do justice to his belly and his shoulders; with free and happy spirit he will laugh at the bustling of rich men, and the flurried ways of those who are hastening after wealth, and say: "Why of your own accord postpone your real life to the distant future? Shall you wait for some interest to fall due, or for some income on your merchandise, or for a place in the will of some wealthy old man, when you can be rich here and now. Wisdom offers wealth in ready money, and pays it over to those in whose eyes she has made wealth superfluous." These remarks refer to other men; you are nearer the rich class. Change the age in which you live, and you have too much. But in every age, what is enough remains the same.

I might close my letter at this point, if I had not got you into bad habits. One cannot greet Parthian royalty without bringing a gift; and in your case I cannot say farewell without paying a price. But what of it? I shall borrow from Epicurus: "The acquisition of riches has been for many men, not an end, but a change, of troubles." I do not wonder. For the fault is not in the wealth, but in the mind itself. That which had made poverty a burden to us, has made riches also a burden. Just as it matters little whether you lay a sick man on a wooden or on a golden bed, for whithersoever he be moved he will carry his malady with him; so one need not care whether the diseased mind is bestowed upon riches or upon poverty. His malady goes with the man. Farewell,

Letter XVIII - On Festivals and Fasting

It is the month of December, and yet the city is at this very moment in a sweat. License is given to the general merrymaking. Everything resounds with mighty preparations, – as if the Saturnalia differed at all from the usual business day! So true it is that the difference is nil, that I regard as correct the remark of the man who said: "Once December was a month; now it is a year."

If I had you with me, I should be glad to consult you and find out what you think should be done, – whether we ought to make no change in our daily routine, or whether, in order not to be out of sympathy with the ways of the public, we should dine in gayer fashion and doff the toga. As it is now, we Romans have changed our dress for the sake of pleasure and holiday-making, though in former times that was only customary when the State was disturbed and had fallen on evil days. I am sure that, if I know you aright, playing the part of an umpire you would have wished that we should be neither like the liberty-capped throng in all ways, nor in all ways unlike them; unless, perhaps, this is just the season when we ought to lay down the law to the soul, and bid it be alone in refraining from pleasures just when the whole mob has let itself go in pleasures; for this is the surest proof which a man can get of his own constancy, if he neither seeks the things which are seductive and allure him to luxury, nor is led into them. It shows much more courage to remain dry and sober when the mob is drunk and vomiting; but it shows greater self-control to refuse to withdraw oneself and to do what the crowd does, but in a different way, – thus neither making oneself conspicuous nor becoming one of the crowd. For one may keep holiday without extravagance.

I am so firmly determined, however, to test the constancy of your mind that, drawing from the teachings of great men, I shall give you also a lesson: Set aside a certain number of days, during which you shall be content with the scantiest and cheapest fare, with coarse and rough dress, saying to yourself the while: "Is this the condition that I feared?" It is precisely in times of immunity from care that the soul should toughen itself beforehand for occasions of greater stress, and it is while Fortune is kind that it should fortify itself against her violence. In days of peace the soldier performs manoeuvres, throws up earthworks with no enemy in sight, and wearies himself by gratuitous toil, in order that he may be equal to unavoidable toil. If you would not have a man flinch when the crisis comes, train him before it comes. Such is the course which those men have followed who, in their imitation of poverty, have every month come almost to want, that they might never recoil from what they had so often rehearsed.

You need not suppose that I mean meals like Timon's, or "paupers' huts," or any other device which luxurious millionaires use to beguile the tedium of their lives. Let the pallet be a real one, and the coarse cloak; let the bread be hard and grimy. Endure all this for three or four days at a time, sometimes for more, so that it may be a test of yourself instead of a mere hobby. Then, I assure you, my dear Lucilius, you will leap for joy when filled with a pennyworth of food, and you will understand that a man's peace of mind does not depend upon Fortune; for, even when angry she grants enough for our needs.

There is no reason, however, why you should think that you are doing anything great; for you will merely be doing what many thousands of slaves and many thousands of poor men are doing every day. But you may credit yourself with this item, – that you will not be doing it under compulsion, and that it will be as easy for you to endure it permanently as to make the experiment from time to time. Let us practise our strokes on the "dummy"; let us become intimate with poverty, so that Fortune may not catch us off our guard. We shall be rich with all the more comfort, if we once learn how far poverty is from being a burden.

Even Epicurus, the teacher of pleasure, used to observe stated intervals, during which he satisfied his hunger in niggardly fashion; he wished to see whether he thereby fell short of full and complete happiness, and, if so, by what amount he fell short, and whether this amount was worth purchasing at the price of great effort. At any rate, he makes such a statement in the well known letter written to Polyaenus in the archonship of Charinus. Indeed, he boasts that he himself lived on less than a penny, but that Metrodorus, whose progress was not yet so great, needed a whole penny. Do you think that there can be fullness on such fare? Yes, and there is pleasure also, – not that shifty and fleeting Pleasure which needs a fillip now and then, but a pleasure that is steadfast and sure. For though water, barley-meal, and crusts of barley-bread, are not a cheerful diet, yet it is the highest kind of Pleasure to be able to derive pleasure from this sort of food, and to have reduced one's needs to that modicum which no unfairness of Fortune can snatch away. Even prison fare is more generous; and those who have been set apart for capital punishment are not so meanly fed by the man who is to execute them. Therefore, what a noble soul must one have, to descend of one's own free will to a diet which even those who have been sentenced to death have not to fear! This is indeed forestalling the spear thrusts of Fortune.

So begin, my dear Lucilius, to follow the custom of these men, and set apart certain days on which you shall withdraw from your business and make yourself at home with the scantiest fare. Establish business relations with poverty.

Dare, O my friend, to scorn the sight of wealth,
And mould thyself to kinship with thy God.

For he alone is in kinship with God who has scorned wealth. Of course I do not forbid you to possess it, but I would have you reach the point at which you possess it dauntlessly; this can be accomplished only by persuading yourself that you can live happily without it as well as with it, and by regarding riches always as likely to elude you.

But now I must begin to fold up my letter. "Settle your debts first," you cry. Here is a draft on Epicurus; he will pay down the sum: "Ungoverned anger begets madness." You cannot help knowing the truth of these words, since you have had not only slaves, but also enemies. But indeed this emotion blazes out against all sorts of persons; it springs from love as much as from hate, and shows itself not less in serious matters than in jest and sport. And it makes no difference how important the provocation may be, but into what kind of soul it penetrates. Similarly with fire; it does not matter how great is the flame, but what it falls upon. For solid timbers have repelled a very great fire; conversely, dry and easily inflammable stuff nourishes the slightest spark into a conflagration. So it is with anger, my dear Lucilius; the outcome of a mighty anger is madness, and hence anger should be avoided, not merely that we may escape excess, but that we may have a healthy mind. Farewell.

Letter XIX - On Worldliness and Retirement

I leap for joy whenever I receive letters from you. For they fill me with hope; they are now not mere assurances concerning you, but guarantees. And I beg and pray you to proceed in this course; for what better request could I make of a friend than one which is to be made for his own sake? If possible, withdraw yourself from all the business of which you speak; and if you cannot do this, tear yourself away. We have dissipated enough of our time already – let us in old age begin to pack up our baggage. Surely there is nothing in this that men can begrudge us. We have spent our lives on the high seas; let us die in harbour. Not that I would advise you to try to win fame by your retirement; one's retirement should neither be paraded nor concealed. Not concealed, I say, for I shall not go so far in urging you as to expect you to condemn all men as mad and then seek out for yourself a hiding-place and oblivion; rather make this your business, that your retirement be not conspicuous, though it should be obvious. In the second place, while those whose choice is unhampered from the start will deliberate on that other question, whether they wish to pass their lives in obscurity, in your case there is not a free choice. Your ability and energy have thrust you into the work of the world; so have the charm of your writings and the friendships you have made with famous and notable men. Renown has already taken you by storm. You may sink yourself into the depths of obscurity and utterly hide yourself; yet your earlier acts will reveal you. You cannot keep lurking in the dark; much of the old gleam will follow you wherever you fly.

Peace you can claim for yourself without being disliked by anyone, without any sense of loss, and without any pangs of spirit. For what will you leave behind you that you can imagine yourself reluctant to leave? Your clients? But none of these men courts you for yourself; they merely court something from you. People used to hunt friends, but now they hunt pelf; if a lonely old man changes his will, the morning-caller transfers himself to another door. Great things cannot be bought for small sums; so reckon up whether it is preferable to leave your own true self, or merely some of your belongings. Would that you had had the privilege of growing old amid the limited circumstances of your origin, and that fortune had not raised you to such heights! You were removed far from the sight of wholesome living by your swift rise to prosperity, by your province, by your position as procurator, and by all that such things promise; you will next acquire more important duties and after them still more. And what will be the result? Why wait until there is nothing left for you to crave? That time will never come. We hold that there is a succession of causes, from which fate is woven; similarly, you may be sure, there is a succession in our desires; for one begins where its predecessor ends. You have been thrust into an existence which will never of itself put an end to your wretchedness and your slavery. Withdraw your chafed neck from the yoke; it is better that it should be cut off once for all, than galled for ever. If you retreat to privacy, everything will be on a smaller scale, but you will be satisfied abundantly; in your present condition, however, there is no satisfaction in the plenty which is heaped upon you on all sides. Would you rather be poor and sated, or rich and hungry? Prosperity is not only greedy, but it also lies exposed to the greed of others. And as long as nothing satisfies you, you yourself cannot satisfy others.

"But," you say, "how can I take my leave?" Any way you please. Reflect how many hazards you have ventured for the sake of money, and how much toil you have undertaken for a title! You must dare something to gain leisure, also, – or else grow old amid the worries of procuratorships abroad and subsequently of civil duties at home, living in turmoil and in ever fresh floods of responsibilities, which no man has ever succeeded in avoiding by unobtrusiveness or by seclusion of life. For what bearing on the case has your personal desire for a secluded life? Your position in the world desires the opposite! What if, even now, you allow that position to grow greater? But all that is added to your successes will be added to your fears. At this point I should like to quote a saying of Maecenas, who spoke the truth when he stood on the very summit: "There's thunder even on the loftiest peaks." If you ask me in what book these words are found, they occur in the volume entitled Prometheus. He simply meant to say that these lofty peaks have their tops surrounded with thunder-storms. But is any power worth so high a price that a man like you would ever, in order to obtain it, adopt a style so debauched as that? Maecenas was indeed a man of parts, who would have left a great pattern for Roman oratory to follow, had his good fortune not made him effeminate, – nay, had it not emasculated him! An end like his awaits you also, unless you forthwith shorten sail and, – as Maecenas was not willing to do until it was too late, – hug the shore!

This saying of Maecenas's might have squared my account with you; but I feel sure, knowing you, that you will get out an injunction against me, and that you will be unwilling to accept payment of my debt in such crude and debased currency. However that may be, I shall draw on the account of Epicurus. He says: "You must reflect carefully beforehand with whom you are to eat and drink, rather than what you are to eat and drink. For a dinner of meats without the company of a friend is like the life of a lion or a wolf." This privilege will not be yours unless you withdraw from the world; otherwise, you will have as guests only those whom your slave-secretary sorts out from the throng of callers. It is, however, a mistake to select your friend in the reception-hall or to test him at the dinner-table. The most serious misfortune for a busy man who is overwhelmed by his possessions is, that he believes men to be his friends when he himself is not a friend to them, and that he deems his favours to be effective in winning friends, although, in the case of certain men, the more they owe, the more they hate. A trifling debt makes a man your debtor; a large one makes him an enemy. "What," you say, "do not kindnesses establish friendships?" They do, if one has had the privilege of choosing those who are to receive them, and if they are placed judiciously, instead of being scattered broadcast.

Therefore, while you are beginning to call your mind your own, meantime apply this maxim of the wise: consider that it is more important who receives a thing, than what it is he receives. Farewell.

Letter XX - On Practising what you Preach

If you are in good health and if you think yourself worthy of becoming at last your own master, I am glad. For the credit will be mine, if I can drag you from the floods in which you are being buffeted without hope of emerging. This, however, my dear Lucilius, I ask and beg of you, on your part, that you let wisdom sink into your soul, and test your progress, not by mere speech or writings, but by stoutness of heart and decrease of desire. Prove your words by your deeds.

Far different is the purpose of those who are speech-making and trying to win the approbation of a throng of hearers, far different that of those who allure the ears of young men and idlers by many-sided or fluent argumentation; philosophy teaches us to act, not to speak; it exacts of every man that he should live according to his own standards, that his life should not be out of harmony with his words, and that, further, his inner life should be of one hue and not out of harmony with all his activities. This, I say, is the highest duty and the highest proof of wisdom, — that deed and word should be in accord, that a man should be equal to himself under all conditions, and always the same.

"But," you reply, "who can maintain this standard?" Very few, to be sure; but there are some. It is indeed a hard undertaking, and I do not say that the philosopher can always keep the same pace. But he can always travel the same path. Observe yourself, then, and see whether your dress and your house are inconsistent, whether you treat yourself lavishly and your family meanly, whether you eat frugal dinners and yet build luxurious houses. You should lay hold, once for all, upon a single norm to live by, and should regulate your whole life according to this norm. Some men restrict themselves at home, but strut with swelling port before the public; such discordance is a fault, and it indicates a wavering mind which cannot yet keep its balance. And I can tell you, further, whence arise this unsteadiness and disagreement of action and purpose; it is because no man resolves upon what he wishes, and, even if he has done so, he does not persist in it, but jumps the track; not only does he change, but he returns and slips back to the conduct which he has abandoned and abjured. Therefore, to omit the ancient definitions of wisdom and to include the whole manner of human life, I can be satisfied with the following: "What is wisdom? Always desiring the same things, and always refusing the same things." You may be excused from adding the little proviso, – that what you wish, should be right; since no man can always be satisfied with the same thing, unless it is right.

For this reason men do not know what they wish, except at the actual moment of wishing; no man ever decided once and for all to desire or to refuse. Judgment varies from day to day, and changes to the opposite, making many a man pass his life in a kind of game. Press on, therefore, as you have begun; perhaps you will be led to perfection, or to a point which you alone understand is still short of perfection.

"But what," you say, "will become of my crowded household without a household income?" If you stop supporting that crowd, it will support itself; or perhaps you will learn by the bounty of poverty what you cannot learn by your own bounty. Poverty will keep for you your true and tried friends; you will be rid of the men who were not seeking you for yourself, but for something which you have. Is it not true, however, that you should love poverty, if only for this single reason, – that it will show you those by whom you are loved? O when will that time come, when no one shall tell lies to compliment you! Accordingly, let your thoughts, your efforts, your desires, help to make you content with your own self and with the goods that spring from yourself; and commit all your other prayers to God's keeping! What happiness could come closer home to you? Bring yourself down to humble conditions, from which you cannot be ejected and in order that you may do so with greater alacrity, the contribution contained in this letter shall refer to that subject; I shall bestow it upon you forthwith.

Although you may look askance, Epicurus will once again be glad to settle my indebtedness: "Believe me, your words will be more imposing if you sleep on a cot and wear rags. For in that case you will not be merely saying them; you will be demonstrating their truth." I, at any rate, listen in a different spirit to the utterances of our friend Demetrius, after I have seen him reclining without even a cloak to cover him, and, more than this, without rugs to lie upon. He is not only a teacher of the truth, but a witness to the truth. "May not a man, however, despise wealth when it lies in his very pocket?" Of course; he also is great-souled, who sees riches heaped up round him and, after wondering long and deeply because they have come into his possession, smiles, and hears rather than feels that they are his. It means much not to be spoiled by intimacy with riches; and he is truly great who is poor amidst riches. "Yes, but I do not know," you say, "how the man you speak of will endure poverty, if he falls into it suddenly." Nor do I, Epicurus, know whether the poor man you speak of will despise riches, should he suddenly fall into them; accordingly, in the case of both, it is the mind that must be appraised, and we must investigate whether your man is pleased with his poverty, and whether my man is displeased with his riches. Otherwise, the cot-bed and the rags are slight proof of his good intentions, if it has not been made clear that the person concerned endures these trials not from necessity but from preference.

It is the mark, however, of a noble spirit not to precipitate oneself into such things on the ground that they are better, but to practise for them on the ground that they are thus easy to endure. And they are easy to endure, Lucilius; when, however, you come to them after long rehearsal, they are even pleasant; for they contain a sense of freedom from care, – and without this nothing is pleasant. I hold it essential, therefore, to do as I have told you in a letter that great men have often done: to reserve a few days in which we may prepare ourselves for real poverty by means of fancied poverty. There is all the more reason for doing this, because we have been steeped in luxury and regard all duties as hard and onerous. Rather let the soul be roused from its sleep and be prodded, and let it be reminded that nature has prescribed very little for us. No man is born rich. Every man, when he first sees light, is commanded to be content with milk and rags. Such is our beginning, and yet kingdoms are all too small for us! Farewell.

Letter XXI - On the Renown which my Writings will Bring you

Do you conclude that you are having difficulties with those men about whom you wrote to me? Your greatest difficulty is with yourself; for you are your own stumbling-block. You do not know what you want. You are better at approving the right course than at following it out. You see where the true happiness lies, but you have not the courage to attain it. Let me tell you what it is that hinders you, inasmuch as you do not of yourself discern it.

You think that this condition, which you are to abandon, is one of importance, and after resolving upon that ideal state of calm into which you hope to pass, you are held back by the lustre of your present life, from which it is your intention to depart, just as if you were about to fall into a state of filth and darkness. This is a mistake, Lucilius; to go from your present life into the other is a promotion. There is the same difference between these two lives as there is between mere brightness and real light; the latter has a definite source within itself, the other borrows its radiance; the one is called forth by an illumination coming from the outside, and anyone who stands between the source and the object immediately turns the latter into a dense shadow; but the other has a glow that comes from within.

It is your own studies that will make you shine and will render you eminent, Allow me to mention the case of Epicurus. He was writing to Idomeneus and trying to recall him from a showy existence to sure and steadfast renown. Idomeneus was at that time a minister of state who exercised a rigorous authority and had important affairs in hand. "If," said Epicurus, "you are attracted by fame, my letters will make you more renowned than all the things which you cherish and which make you cherished." Did Epicurus speak falsely? Who would have known of Idomeneus, had not the philosopher thus engraved his name in those letters of his? All the grandees and satraps, even the king himself, who was petitioned for the title which Idomeneus sought, are sunk in deep oblivion. Cicero's letters keep the name of Atticus from perishing. It would have profited Atticus nothing to have an Agrippa for a son-in-law, a Tiberius for the husband of his grand-daughter, and a Drusus Caesar for a great-grandson; amid these mighty names his name would never be spoken, had not Cicero bound him to himself. The deep flood of time will roll over us; some few great men will raise their heads above it, and, though destined at the last to depart into the same realms of silence, will battle against oblivion and maintain their ground for long.

That which Epicurus could promise his friend, this I promise you, Lucilius. I shall find favour among later generations; I can take with me names that will endure as long as mine. Our poet Vergil promised an eternal name to two heroes, and is keeping his promise:

> Blest heroes twain! If power my song possess,
> The record of your names shall never be
> Erased from out the book of Time, while yet
> Aeneas' tribe shall keep the Capitol,
> That rock immovable, and Roman sire
> Shall empire hold.

Whenever men have been thrust forward by fortune, whenever they have become part and parcel of another's influence, they have found abundant favour, their houses have been thronged, only so long as they themselves have kept their position; when they themselves have left it, they have slipped at once from the memory of men. But in the case of innate ability, the respect in which it is held increases, and not only does honour accrue to the man himself, but whatever has attached itself to his memory is passed on from one to another.

In order that Idomeneus may not be introduced free of charge into my letter, he shall make up the indebtedness from his own account. It was to him that Epicurus addressed the well-known saying urging him to make Pythocles rich, but not rich in the vulgar and equivocal way. "If you wish," said he, "to make Pythocles rich, do not add to his store of money, but subtract from his desires." This idea is too clear to need explanation, and too clever to need reinforcement. There is, however, one point on which I would warn you, – not to consider that this statement applies only to riches; its value will be the same, no matter how you apply it. "If you wish to make Pythocles honourable, do not add to his honours, but subtract from his desires"; "if you wish Pythocles to have pleasure for ever, do not add to his pleasures, but subtract from his desires"; "if you wish to make Pythocles an old man, filling his life to the full, do not add to his years, but subtract from his desires." There is no reason why you should hold that these words belong to Epicurus alone; they are public property. I think we ought to do in philosophy as they are wont to do in the Senate: when someone has made a motion, of which I approve to a certain extent, I ask him to make his motion in two parts, and I vote for the part which I approve. So I am all the more glad to repeat the distinguished words of Epicurus, in order that I may prove to those who have recourse to him through a bad motive, thinking that they will have in him a screen for their own vices, that they must live honourably, no matter what school they follow.

Go to his Garden and read the motto carved there:
"Stranger, here you will do well to tarry; here our highest good is pleasure."

The care-taker of that abode, a kindly host, will be ready for you; he will welcome you with barley-meal and serve you water also in abundance, with these words: "Have you not been well entertained?" "This garden," he says, "does not whet your appetite; it quenches it. Nor does it make you more thirsty with every drink; it slakes the thirst by a natural cure, a cure that demands no fee. This is the 'pleasure' in which I have grown old."

In speaking with you, however, I refer to those desires which refuse alleviation, which must be bribed to cease. For in regard to the exceptional desires, which may be postponed, which may be chastened and checked, I have this one thought to share with you: a pleasure of that sort is according to our nature, but it is not according to our needs; one owes nothing to it; whatever is expended upon it is a free gift. The belly will not listen to advice; it makes demands, it importunes. And yet it is not a troublesome creditor; you can send it away at small cost, provided only that you give it what you owe, not merely all you are able to give. Farewell.

Letter XXII - On the Futility of Half-Way Measures

You understand by this time that you must withdraw yourself from those showy and depraved pursuits; but you still wish to know how this may be accomplished. There are certain things which can be pointed out only by someone who is present. The physician cannot prescribe by letter the proper time for eating or bathing; he must feel the pulse. There is an old adage about gladiators, – that they plan their fight in the ring; as they intently watch, something in the adversary's glance, some movement of his hand, even some slight bending of his body, gives a warning. We can formulate general rules and commit them to writing, as to what is usually done, or ought to be done; such advice may be given, not only to our absent friends, but also to succeeding generations. In regard, however, to that second question, – when or how your plan is to be carried out, – no one will advise at long range; we must take counsel in the presence of the actual situation. You must be not only present in the body, but watchful in mind, if you would avail yourself of the fleeting opportunity. Accordingly, look about you for the opportunity; if you see it, grasp it, and with all your energy and with all your strength devote yourself to this task – to rid yourself of those business duties.

Now listen carefully to the opinion which I shall offer; it is my opinion that you should withdraw either from that kind of existence, or else from existence altogether. But I likewise maintain that you should take a gentle path, that you may loosen rather than cut the knot which you have bungled so badly in tying, – provided that if there shall be no other way of loosening it, you may actually cut it. No man is so faint-hearted that he would rather hang in suspense for ever than drop once for all. Meanwhile, – and this is of first importance, – do not hamper yourself; be content with the business into which you have lowered yourself, or, as you prefer to have people think, have tumbled. There is no reason why you should be struggling on to something further; if you do, you will lose all grounds of excuse, and men will see that it was not a tumble. The usual explanation which men offer is wrong: "I was compelled to do it. Suppose it was against my will; I had to do it." But no one is compelled to pursue prosperity at top speed; it means something to call a halt, – even if one does not offer resistance, – instead of pressing eagerly after favouring fortune. Shall you then be put out with me, if I not only come to advise you, but also call in others to advise you, – wiser heads than my own, men before whom I am wont to lay any problem upon which l am pondering? Read the letter of Epicurus which appears on this matter; it is addressed to Idomeneus. The writer asks him to hasten as fast as he can, and beat a retreat before some stronger influence comes between and takes from him the liberty to withdraw. But he also adds that one should attempt nothing except at the time when it can be attempted suitably and seasonably. Then, when the long-sought occasion comes, let him be up and doing. Epicurus forbids us to doze when we are meditating escape; he bids us hope for a safe release from even the hardest trials, provided that we are not in too great a hurry before the time, nor too dilatory when the time arrives.

Now, I suppose, you are looking for a Stoic motto also. There is really no reason why anyone should slander that school to you on the ground of its rashness; as a matter of fact, its caution is greater than its courage. You are perhaps expecting the sect to utter such words as these: "It is base to flinch under a burden. Wrestle with the duties which you have once undertaken. No man is brave and earnest if he avoids danger, if his spirit does not grow with the very difficulty of his task." Words like these will indeed be spoken to you, if only your perseverance shall have an object that is worth while, if only you will not have to do or to suffer anything unworthy of a good man; besides, a good man will not waste himself upon mean and discreditable work or be busy merely for the sake of being busy. Neither will he, as you imagine, become so involved in ambitious schemes that he will have continually to endure their ebb and flow. Nay, when he sees the dangers, uncertainties, and hazards in which he was formerly tossed about, he will withdraw, – not turning his back to the foe, but falling back little by little to a safe position. From business, however, my dear Lucilius, it is easy to escape, if only you will despise the rewards of business. We are held back and kept from escaping by thoughts like these: "What then? Shall I leave behind me these great prospects? Shall I depart at the very time of harvest? Shall I have no slaves at my side? no retinue for my litter? no crowd in my reception room?"

Hence men leave such advantages as these with reluctance; they love the reward of their hardships, but curse the hardships themselves. Men complain about their ambitions as they complain about their mistresses; in other words, if you penetrate their real feelings, you will find, not hatred, but bickering.

Search the minds of those who cry down what they have desired, who talk about escaping from things which they are unable to do without; you will comprehend that they are lingering of their own free will in a situation which they declare they find it hard and wretched to endure. It is so, my dear Lucilius; there are a few men whom slavery holds fast, but there are many more who hold fast to slavery.

If, however, you intend to be rid of this slavery; if freedom is genuinely pleasing in your eyes; and if you seek counsel for this one purpose, – that you may have the good fortune to accomplish this purpose without perpetual annoyance, – how can the whole company of Stoic thinkers fail to approve your course? Zeno, Chrysippus, and all their kind will give you advice that is temperate, honourable, and suitable. But if you keep turning round and looking about, in order to see how much you may carry away with you, and how much money you may keep to equip yourself for the life of leisure, you will never find a way out. No man can swim ashore and take his baggage with him. Rise to a higher life, with the favour of the gods; but let it not be favour of such a kind as the gods give to men when with kind and genial faces they bestow magnificent ills, justified in so doing by the one fact that the things which irritate and torture have been bestowed in answer to prayer.

I was just putting the seal upon this letter; but it must be broken again, in order that it may go to you with its customary contribution, bearing with it some noble word. And lo, here is one that occurs to my mind; I do not know whether its truth or its nobility of utterance is the greater. "Spoken by whom?" you ask. By Epicurus; for I am still appropriating other men's belongings. The words are: "Everyone goes out of life just as if he had but lately entered it." Take anyone off his guard, young, old, or middle-aged; you will find that all are equally afraid of death, and equally ignorant of life. No one has anything finished, because we have kept putting off into the future all our undertakings. No thought in the quotation given above pleases me more than that it taunts old men with being infants. "No one," he says, "leaves this world in a different manner from one who has just been born." That is not true; for we are worse when we die than when we were born; but it is our fault, and not that of Nature. Nature should scold us, saying: "What does this mean? I brought you into the world without desires or fears, free from superstition, treachery and the other curses. Go forth as you were when you entered!"

A man has caught the message of wisdom, if he can die as free from care as he was at birth; but as it is we are all a-flutter at the approach of the dreaded end. Our courage fails us, our cheeks blanch; our tears fall, though they are unavailing. But what is baser than to fret at the very threshold of peace? The reason, however is, that we are stripped of all our goods, we have jettisoned our cargo of life and are in distress; for no part of it has been packed in the hold; it has all been heaved overboard and has drifted away. Men do not care how nobly they live, but only how long, although it is within the reach of every man to live nobly, but within no man's power to live long. Farewell.

Letter XXIII - On the True Joy which Comes from Philosophy

Do you suppose that I shall write you how kindly the winter season has dealt with us, – a short season and a mild one, – or what a nasty spring we are having, – cold weather out of season, – and all the other trivialities which people write when they are at a loss for topics of conversation? No; I shall communicate something which may help both you and myself. And what shall this "something" be, if not an exhortation to soundness of mind? Do you ask what is the foundation of a sound mind? It is, not to find joy in useless things. I said that it was the foundation; it is really the pinnacle. We have reached the heights if we know what it is that we find joy in and if we have not placed our happiness in the control of externals. The man who is goaded ahead by hope of anything, though it be within reach, though it be easy of access, and though his ambitions have never played him false, is troubled and unsure of himself. Above all, my dear Lucilius, make this your business: learn how to feel joy.

Do you think that I am now robbing you of many pleasures when I try to do away with the gifts of chance, when I counsel the avoidance of hope, the sweetest thing that gladdens our hearts? Quite the contrary; I do not wish you ever to be deprived of gladness. I would have it born in your house; and it is born there, if only it be inside of you. Other objects of cheer do not fill a man's bosom; they merely smooth his brow and are inconstant, – unless perhaps you believe that he who laughs has joy. The very soul must be happy and confident, lifted above every circumstance.

Real joy, believe me, is a stern matter. Can one, do you think, despise death with a care-free countenance, or with a "blithe and gay" expression, as our young dandies are accustomed to say? Or can one thus open his door to poverty, or hold the curb on his pleasures, or contemplate the endurance of pain? He who ponders these things in his heart is indeed full of joy; but it is not a cheerful joy. It is just this joy, however, of which I would have you become the owner; for it will never fail you when once you have found its source. The yield of poor mines is on the surface; those are really rich whose veins lurk deep, and they will make more bountiful returns to him who delves unceasingly. So too those baubles which delight the common crowd afford but a thin pleasure, laid on as a coating, and even joy that is only plated lacks a real basis. But the joy of which I speak, that to which I am endeavouring to lead you, is something solid, disclosing itself the more fully as you penetrate into it. Therefore I pray you, my dearest Lucilius, do the one thing that can render you really happy: cast aside and trample under foot all the things that glitter outwardly and are held out to you by another or as obtainable from another; look toward the true good, and rejoice only in that which comes from your own store. And what do I mean by "from your own store"? I mean from your very self, that which is the best part of you. The frail body, also, even though we can accomplish nothing without it, is to be regarded as necessary rather than as important; it involves us in vain pleasures, short-lived, and soon to be regretted, which, unless they are reined in by extreme self-control, will be transformed into the opposite. This is what I mean: pleasure, unless it has been kept within bounds, tends to rush headlong into the abyss of sorrow.

But it is hard to keep within bounds in that which you believe to be good. The real good may be coveted with safety. Do you ask me what this real good is, and whence it derives? I will tell you: it comes from a good conscience, from honourable purposes, from right actions, from contempt of the gifts of chance, from an even and calm way of living which treads but one path. For men who leap from one purpose to another, or do not even leap but are carried over by a sort of hazard, – how can such wavering and unstable persons possess any good that is fixed and lasting? There are only a few who control themselves and their affairs by a guiding purpose; the rest do not proceed; they are merely swept along, like objects afloat in a river. And of these objects, some are held back by sluggish waters and are transported gently; others are torn along by a more violent current; some, which are nearest the bank, are left there as the current slackens; and others are carried out to sea by the onrush of the stream. Therefore, we should decide what we wish, and abide by the decision.

Now is the time for me to pay my debt. I can give you a saying of your friend Epicurus and thus clear this letter of its obligation. "It is bothersome always to be beginning life." Or another, which will perhaps express the meaning better: "They live ill who are always beginning to live." You are right in asking why; the saying certainly stands in need of a commentary. It is because the life of such persons is always incomplete. But a man cannot stand prepared for the approach of death if he has just begun to live. We must make it our aim already to have lived long enough. No one deems that he has done so, if he is just on the point of planning his life. You need not think that there are few of this kind; practically everyone is of such a stamp. Some men, indeed, only begin to live when it is time for them to leave off living. And if this seems surprising to you, I shall add that which will surprise you still more: Some men have left off living before they have begun. Farewell.

Letter XXIV - On Despising Death

You write me that you are anxious about the result of a lawsuit, with which an angry opponent is threatening you; and you expect me to advise you to picture to yourself a happier issue, and to rest in the allurements of hope. Why, indeed, is it necessary to summon trouble, – which must be endured soon enough when it has once arrived, or to anticipate trouble and ruin the present through fear of the future? It is indeed foolish to be unhappy now because you may be unhappy at some future time. But I shall conduct you to peace of mind by another route: if you would put off all worry, assume that what you fear may happen will certainly happen in any event; whatever the trouble may be, measure it in your own mind, and estimate the amount of your fear. You will thus understand that what you fear is either insignificant or short-lived. And you need not spend a long time in gathering illustrations which will strengthen you; every epoch has produced them. Let your thoughts travel into any era of Roman or foreign history, and there will throng before you notable examples of high achievement or of high endeavour.

If you lose this case, can anything more severe happen to you than being sent into exile or led to prison? Is there a worse fate that any man may fear than being burned or being killed? Name such penalties one by one, and mention the men who have scorned them; one does not need to hunt for them, – it is simply a matter of selection. Sentence of conviction was borne by Rutilius as if the injustice of the decision were the only thing which annoyed him. Exile was endured by Metellus with courage, by Rutilius even with gladness; for the former consented to come back only because his country called him; the latter refused to return when Sulla summoned him, – and nobody in those days said "No" to Sulla! Socrates in prison discoursed, and declined to flee when certain persons gave him the opportunity; he remained there, in order to free mankind from the fear of two most grievous things, death and imprisonment. Mucius put his hand into the fire. It is painful to be burned; but how much more painful to inflict such suffering upon oneself! Here was a man of no learning, not primed to face death and pain by any words of wisdom, and equipped only with the courage of a soldier, who punished himself for his fruitless daring; he stood and watched his own right hand falling away piecemeal on the enemy's brazier, nor did he withdraw the dissolving limb, with its uncovered bones, until his foe removed the fire. He might have accomplished something more successful in that camp, but never anything more brave. See how much keener a brave man is to lay hold of danger than a cruel man is to inflict it: Porsenna was more ready to pardon Mucius for wishing to slay him than Mucius to pardon himself for failing to slay Porsenna!

"Oh," say you, "those stories have been droned to death in all the schools; pretty soon, when you reach the topic 'On Despising Death,' you will be telling me about Cato." But why should I not tell you about Cato, how he read Plato's book on that last glorious night, with a sword laid at his pillow? He had provided these two requisites for his last moments, – the first, that he might have the will to die, and the second, that he might have the means. So he put his affairs in order, – as well as one could put in order that which was ruined and near its end, – and thought that he ought to see to it that no one should have the power to slay or the good fortune to save Cato. Drawing the sword, – which he had kept unstained from all bloodshed against the final day, he cried: "Fortune, you have accomplished nothing by resisting all my endeavours. I have fought, till now, for my country's freedom, and not for my own, I did not strive so doggedly to be free, but only to live among the free. Now, since the affairs of mankind are beyond hope, let Cato be withdrawn to safety." So saying, he inflicted a mortal wound upon his body. After the physicians had bound it up, Cato had less blood and less strength, but no less courage; angered now not only at Caesar but also at himself, he rallied his unarmed hands against his wound, and expelled, rather than dismissed, that noble soul which had been so defiant of all worldly power.

I am not now heaping up these illustrations for the purpose of exercising my wit, but for the purpose of encouraging you to face that which is thought to be most terrible. And I shall encourage you all the more easily by showing that not only resolute men have despised that moment when the soul breathes its last, but that certain persons, who were craven in other respects, have equalled in this regard the courage of the bravest. Take, for example, Scipio, the father-in-law of Gnaeus Pompeius: he was driven back upon the African coast by a head-wind and saw his ship in the power of the enemy. He therefore pierced his body with a sword; and when they asked where the commander was, he replied: "All is well with the commander." These words brought him up to the level of his ancestors and suffered not the glory which fate gave to the Scipios in Africa to lose its continuity. It was a great deed to conquer Carthage, but a greater deed to conquer death. "All is well with the commander!" Ought a general to die otherwise, especially one of Cato's generals? I shall not refer you to history, or collect examples of those men who throughout the ages have despised death; for they are very many. Consider these times of ours, whose enervation and over-refinement call forth our complaints; they nevertheless will include men of every rank, of every lot in life, and of every age, who have cut short their misfortunes by death.

Believe me, Lucilius; death is so little to be feared that through its good offices nothing is to be feared. Therefore, when your enemy threatens, listen unconcernedly. Although your conscience makes you confident, yet, since many things have weight which are outside your case, both hope for that which is utterly just, and prepare yourself against that which is utterly unjust. Remember, however, before all else, to strip things of all that disturbs and confuses, and to see what each is at bottom; you will then comprehend that they contain nothing fearful except the actual fear. That you see happening to boys happens also to ourselves, who are only slightly bigger boys: when those whom they love, with whom they daily associate, with whom they play, appear with masks on, the boys are frightened out of their wits. We should strip the mask, not only from men, but from things, and restore to each object its own aspect.

"Why dost thou hold up before my eyes swords, fires, and a throng of executioners raging about thee? Take away all that vain show, behind which thou lurkest and scarest fools! Ah! thou art naught but Death, whom only yesterday a manservant of mine and a maid-servant did despise! Why dost thou again unfold and spread before me, with all that great display, the whip and the rack? Why are those engines of torture made ready, one for each several member of the body, and all the other innumerable machines for tearing a man apart piecemeal? Away with all such stuff, which makes us numb with terror! And thou, silence the groans the cries, and the bitter shrieks ground out of the victim as he is torn on the rack! Forsooth thou are naught but Pain, scorned by yonder gout-ridden wretch, endured by yonder dyspeptic in the midst of his dainties, borne bravely by the girl in travail. Slight thou art, if I can bear thee; short thou art if I cannot bear thee!"

Ponder these words which you have often heard and often uttered. Moreover, prove by the result whether that which you have heard and uttered is true. For there is a very disgraceful charge often brought against our school, – that we deal with the words, and not with the deeds, of philosophy.

What, have you only at this moment learned that death is hanging over your head, at this moment exile, at this moment grief? You were born to these perils. Let us think of everything that can happen as something which will happen. I know that you have really done what I advise you to do; I now warn you not to drown your soul in these petty anxieties of yours; if you do, the soul will be dulled and will have too little vigour left when the time comes for it to arise. Remove the mind from this case of yours to the case of men in general. Say to yourself that our petty bodies are mortal and frail; pain can reach them from other sources than from wrong or the might of the stronger. Our pleasures themselves become torments; banquets bring indigestion, carousals paralysis of the muscles and palsy, sensual habits affect the feet, the hands, and every joint of the body.

I may become a poor man; I shall then be one among many. I may be exiled; I shall then regard myself as born in the place to which I shall be sent. They may put me in chains. What then? Am I free from bonds now? Behold this clogging burden of a body, to which nature has fettered me! "I shall die," you say; you mean to say "I shall cease to run the risk of sickness; I shall cease to run the risk of imprisonment; I shall cease to run the risk of death." I am not so foolish as to go through at this juncture the arguments which Epicurus harps upon, and say that the terrors of the world below are idle, – that Ixion does not whirl round on his wheel, that Sisyphus does not shoulder his stone uphill, that a man's entrails cannot be restored and devoured every day; no one is so childish as to fear Cerberus, or the shadows, or the spectral garb of those who are held together by naught but their unfleshed bones. Death either annihilates us or strips us bare. If we are then released, there remains the better part, after the burden has been withdrawn; if we are annihilated, nothing remains; good and bad are alike removed.

Allow me at this point to quote a verse of yours, first suggesting that, when you wrote it, you meant it for yourself no less than for others. It is ignoble to say one thing and mean another; and how much more ignoble to write one thing and mean another! I remember one day you were handling the well-known commonplace, – that we do not suddenly fall on death, but advance towards it by slight degrees; we die every day. For every day a little of our life is taken from us; even when we are growing, our life is on the wane. We lose our childhood, then our boyhood, and then our youth. Counting even yesterday, all past time is lost time; the very day which we are now spending is shared between ourselves and death. It is not the last drop that empties the water-clock, but all that which previously has flowed out; similarly, the final hour when we cease to exist does not of itself bring death; it merely of itself completes the death-process. We reach death at that moment, but we have been a long time on the way. In describing this situation, you said in your customary, style (for you are always impressive, but never more pungent than when you are putting the truth in appropriate words):

Not single is the death which comes; the death
Which takes us off is but the last of all.

I prefer that you should read your own words rather than my letter; for then it will be clear to you that this death, of which we are afraid, is the last but not the only death. I see what you are looking for; you are asking what I have packed into my letter, what inspiriting saying from some master-mind, what useful precept. So I shall send you something dealing with this very subject which has been under discussion. Epicurus upbraids those who crave, as much as those who shrink from, death: "It is absurd," he says, "to run towards death because you are tired of life, when it is your manner of life that has made you run towards death." And in another passage: "What is so absurd as to seek death, when it is through fear of death that you have robbed your life of peace?" And you may add a third statement, of the same stamp: "Men are so thoughtless, nay, so mad, that some, through fear of death, force themselves to die."

Whichever of these ideas you ponder, you will strengthen your mind for the endurance alike of death and of life. For we need to be warned and strengthened in both directions, – not to love or to hate life overmuch; even when reason advises us to make an end of it, the impulse is not to be adopted without reflection or at headlong speed. The grave and wise man should not beat a hasty retreat from life; he should make a becoming exit. And above all, he should avoid the weakness which has taken possession of so many, – the lust for death. For just as there is an unreflecting tendency of the mind towards other things, so, my dear Lucilius, there is an unreflecting tendency towards death; this often seizes upon the noblest and most spirited men, as well as upon the craven and the abject. The former despise life; the latter find it irksome.

Others also are moved by a satiety of doing and seeing the same things, and not so much by a hatred of life as because they are cloyed with it. We slip into this condition, while philosophy itself pushes us on, and we say; "How long must I endure the same things? Shall I continue to wake and sleep, be hungry and be cloyed, shiver and perspire? There is an end to nothing; all things are connected in a sort of circle; they flee and they are pursued. Night is close at the heels of day, day at the heels of night; summer ends in autumn, winter rushes after autumn, and winter softens into spring; all nature in this way passes, only to return. I do nothing new; I see nothing new; sooner or later one sickens of this, also." There are many who think that living is not painful, but superfluous. Farewell.

Letter XXV - On Reformation

With regard to these two friends of ours, we must proceed along different lines; the faults of the one are to be corrected, the other's are to be crushed out. I shall take every liberty; for I do not love this one if I am unwilling to hurt his feelings. "What," you say, "do you expect to keep a forty-year-old ward under your tutelage? Consider his age, how hardened it now is, and past handling! Such a man cannot be re-shaped; only young minds are moulded." I do not know whether I shall make progress; but I should prefer to lack success rather than to lack faith. You need not despair of curing sick men even when the disease is chronic, if only you hold out against excess and force them to do and submit to many things against their will. As regards our other friend I am not sufficiently confident, either, except for the fact that he still has sense of shame enough to blush for his sins. This modesty should be fostered; so long as it endures in his soul, there is some room for hope. But as for this veteran of yours, I think we should deal more carefully with him, that he may not become desperate about himself. There is no better time to approach him than now, when he has an interval of rest and seems like one who has corrected his faults. Others have been cheated by this interval of virtue on his part, but he does not cheat me. I feel sure that these faults will return, as it were, with compound interest, for just now, I am certain, they are in abeyance but not absent. I shall devote some time to the matter, and try to see whether or not something can be done.

But do you yourself, as indeed you are doing, show me that you are stout-hearted; lighten your baggage for the march. None of our possessions is essential. Let us return to the law of nature; for then riches are laid up for us. The things which we actually need are free for all, or else cheap; nature craves only bread and water. No one is poor according to this standard; when a man has limited his desires within these bounds, he can challenge the happiness of Jove himself, as Epicurus says. I must insert in this letter one or two more of his sayings: "Do everything as if Epicurus were watching you." There is no real doubt that it is good for one to have appointed a guardian over oneself, and to have someone whom you may look up to, someone whom you may regard as a witness of your thoughts. It is, indeed, nobler by far to live as you would live under the eyes of some good man, always at your side; but nevertheless I am content if you only act, in whatever you do, as you would act if anyone at all were looking on; because solitude prompts us to all kinds of evil. And when you have progressed so far that you have also respect for yourself, you may send away your attendant; but until then, set as a guard over yourself the authority of some man, whether your choice be the great Cato or Scipio, or Laelius, – or any man in whose presence even abandoned wretches would check their bad impulses. Meantime, you are engaged in making of yourself the sort of person in whose company you would not dare to sin. When this aim has been accomplished and you begin to hold yourself in some esteem, I shall gradually allow you to do what Epicurus, in another passage, suggests: "The time when you should most of all withdraw into yourself is when you are forced to be in a crowd."

You ought to make yourself of a different stamp from the multitude. Therefore, while it is not yet safe to withdraw into solitude, seek out certain individuals; for everyone is better off in the company of somebody or other, – no matter who, – than in his own company alone. "The time when you should most of all withdraw into yourself is when you are forced to be in a crowd." Yes, provided that you are a good, tranquil, and self-restrained man; otherwise, you had better withdraw into a crowd in order to get away from your self. Alone, you are too close to a rascal. Farewell.

Letter XXVI - On Old Age and Death

I was just lately telling you that I was within sight of old age. I am now afraid that I have left old age behind me. For some other word would now apply to my years, or at any rate to my body; since old age means a time of life that is weary rather than crushed. You may rate me in the worn-out class, – of those who are nearing the end.

Nevertheless, I offer thanks to myself, with you as witness; for I feel that age has done no damage to my mind, though I feel its effects on my constitution. Only my vices, and the outward aids to these vices, have reached senility; my mind is strong and rejoices that it has but slight connexion with the body. It has laid aside the greater part of its load. It is alert; it takes issue with me on the subject of old age; it declares that old age is its time of bloom. Let me take it at its word, and let it make the most of the advantages it possesses. The mind bids me do some thinking and consider how much of this peace of spirit and moderation of character I owe to wisdom and how much to my time of life; it bids me distinguish carefully what I cannot do and what I do not want to do. For why should one complain or regard it as a disadvantage, if powers which ought to come to an end have failed? "But," you say, "it is the greatest possible disadvantage to be worn out and to die off, or rather, if I may speak literally, to melt away! For we are not suddenly smitten and laid low; we are worn away, and every day reduces our powers to a certain extent."

But is there any better end to it all than to glide off to one's proper haven, when nature slips the cable? Not that there is anything painful in a shock and a sudden departure from existence; it is merely because this other way of departure is easy, – a gradual withdrawal. I, at any rate, as if the test were at hand and the day were come which is to pronounce its decision concerning all the years of my life, watch over myself and commune thus with myself: "The showing which we have made up to the present time, in word or deed, counts for nothing. All this is but a trifling and deceitful pledge of our spirit, and is wrapped in much charlatanism. I shall leave it to Death to determine what progress I have made. Therefore with no faint heart I am making ready for the day when, putting aside all stage artifice and actor's rouge, I am to pass judgment upon myself, – whether I am merely declaiming brave sentiments, or whether I really feel them; whether all the bold threats I have uttered against fortune are a pretence and a farce. Put aside the opinion of the world; it is always wavering and always takes both sides. Put aside the studies which you have pursued throughout your life; Death will deliver the final judgment in your case. This is what I mean: your debates and learned talks, your maxims gathered from the teachings of the wise, your cultured conversation, – all these afford no proof of the real strength of your soul. Even the most timid man can deliver a bold speech. What you have done in the past will be manifest only at the time when you draw your last breath. I accept the terms; I do not shrink from the decision." This is what I say to myself, but I would have you think that I have said it to you also. You are younger; but what does that matter? There is no fixed count of our years. You do not know where death awaits you; so be ready for it everywhere.

I was just intending to stop, and my hand was making ready for the closing sentence; but the rites are still to be performed and the travelling money for the letter disbursed. And just assume that I am not telling where I intend to borrow the necessary sum; you know upon whose coffers I depend. Wait for me but a moment, and I will pay you from my own account; meanwhile, Epicurus will oblige me with these words: "Think on death," or rather, if you prefer the phrase, on "migration to heaven." The meaning is clear, – that it is a wonderful thing to learn thoroughly how to die. You may deem it superfluous to learn a text that can be used only once; but that is just the reason why we ought to think on a thing. When we can never prove whether we really know a thing, we must always be learning it. "Think on death." In saying this, he bids us think on freedom. He who has learned to die has unlearned slavery; he is above any external power, or, at any rate, he is beyond it. What terrors have prisons and bonds and bars for him? His way out is clear. There is only one chain which binds us to life, and that is the love of life. The chain may not be cast off, but it may be rubbed away, so that, when necessity shall demand, nothing may retard or hinder us from being ready to do at once that which at some time we are bound to do. Farewell.

Letter XXVII - On the Good which Abides

"What," say you, "are you giving me advice? Indeed, have you already advised yourself, already corrected your own faults? Is this the reason why you have leisure to reform other men?" No, I am not so shameless as to undertake to cure my fellow-men when I am ill myself. I am, however, discussing with you troubles which concern us both, and sharing the remedy with you, just as if we were lying ill in the same hospital. Listen to me, therefore, as you would if I were talking to myself. I am admitting you to my inmost thoughts, and am having it out with myself, merely making use of you as my pretext. I keep crying out to myself: "Count your years, and you will be ashamed to desire and pursue the same things you desired in your boyhood days. Of this one thing make sure against your dying day, – let your faults die before you die. Away with those disordered pleasures, which must be dearly paid for; it is not only those which are to come that harm me, but also those which have come and gone. Just as crimes, even if they have not been detected when they were committed, do not allow anxiety to end with them; so with guilty pleasures, regret remains even after the pleasures are over. They are not substantial, they are not trustworthy; even if they do not harm us, they are fleeting. Cast about rather for some good which will abide. But there can be no such good except as the soul discovers it for itself within itself. Virtue alone affords everlasting and peace-giving joy; even if some obstacle arise, it is but like an intervening cloud, which floats beneath the sun but never prevails against it."

When will it be your lot to attain this joy? Thus far, you have indeed not been sluggish, but you must quicken your pace. Much toil remains; to confront it, you must yourself lavish all your waking hours, and all your efforts, if you wish the result to be accomplished. This matter cannot be delegated to someone else. The other kind of literary activity admits of outside assistance. Within our own time there was a certain rich man named Calvisius Sabinus; he had the bank-account and the brains of a freedman. I never saw a man whose good fortune was a greater offence against propriety. His memory was so faulty that he would sometimes forget the name of Ulysses, or Achilles, or Priam, – names which we know as well as we know those of our own attendants. No major-domo in his dotage, who cannot give men their right names, but is compelled to invent names for them, – no such man, I say, calls off the names of his master's tribesmen so atrociously as Sabinus used to call off the Trojan and Achaean heroes. But none the less did he desire to appear learned. So he devised this short cut to learning: he paid fabulous prices for slaves, – one to know Homer by heart and another to know Hesiod; he also delegated a special slave to each of the nine lyric poets. You need not wonder that he paid high prices for these slaves; if he did not find them ready to hand he had them made to order. After collecting this retinue, he began to make life miserable for his guests; he would keep these fellows at the foot of his couch, and ask them from time to time for verses which he might repeat, and then frequently break down in the middle of a word. Satellius Quadratus, a feeder, and consequently a fawner, upon addle-pated millionaires, and also (for this quality goes with the other two) a flouter of them, suggested to Sabinus that he should have philologists to gather up the bits. Sabinus remarked that each slave cost him one hundred thousand sesterces; Satellius replied: "You might have bought as many book-cases for a smaller sum." But Sabinus held to the opinion that what any member of his household knew, he himself knew also. This same Satellius began to advise Sabinus to take wrestling lessons, – sickly, pale, and thin as he was, Sabinus answered: "How can I? I can scarcely stay alive now." "Don't say that, I implore you," replied the other, "consider how many perfectly healthy slaves you have!" No man is able to borrow or buy a sound mind; in fact, as it seems to me, even though sound minds were for sale, they would not find buyers. Depraved minds, however, are bought and sold every day.

But let me pay off my debt and say farewell: "Real wealth is poverty adjusted to the law of Nature." Epicurus has this saying in various ways and contexts; but it can never be repeated too often, since it can never be learned too well. For some persons the remedy should be merely prescribed; in the case of others, it should be forced down their throats. Farewell.

Letter XXVIII - On Travel as a Cure for Discontent

Do you suppose that you alone have had this experience? Are you surprised, as if it were a novelty, that after such long travel and so many changes of scene you have not been able to shake off the gloom and heaviness of your mind? You need a change of soul rather than a change of climate. Though you may cross vast spaces of sea, and though, as our Vergil remarks,

Lands and cities are left astern

your faults will follow you whithersoever you travel. Socrates made the same remark to one who complained; he said: "Why do you wonder that globe-trotting does not help you, seeing that you always take yourself with you? The reason which set you wandering is ever at your heels." What pleasure is there in seeing new lands? Or in surveying cities and spots of interest? All your bustle is useless. Do you ask why such flight does not help you? It is because you flee along with yourself. You must lay aside the burdens of the mind; until you do this, no place will satisfy you. Reflect that your present behaviour is like that of the prophetess whom Vergil describes: she is excited and goaded into fury, and contains within herself much inspiration that is not her own:

> *The priestess raves, if haply she may shake*
> *The great god from her heart.*

You wander hither and yon, to rid yourself of the burden that rests upon you, though it becomes more troublesome by reason of your very restlessness, just as in a ship the cargo when stationary makes no trouble, but when it shifts to this side or that, it causes the vessel to heel more quickly in the direction where it has settled. Anything you do tells against you, and you hurt yourself by your very unrest; for you are shaking up a sick man.

That trouble once removed, all change of scene will become pleasant; though you may be driven to the uttermost ends of the earth, in whatever corner of a savage land you may find yourself, that place, however forbidding, will be to you a hospitable abode. The person you are matters more than the place to which you go; for that reason we should not make the mind a bondsman to any one place. Live in this belief: "I am not born for any one corner of the universe; this whole world is my country." If you saw this fact clearly, you would not be surprised at getting no benefit from the fresh scenes to which you roam each time through weariness of the old scenes. For the first would have pleased you in each case, had you believed it wholly yours. As it is, however, you are not journeying; you are drifting and being driven, only exchanging one place for another, although that which you seek, – to live well, – is found everywhere. Can there be any spot so full of confusion as the Forum? Yet you can live quietly even there, if necessary. Of course, if one were allowed to make one's own arrangements, I should flee far from the very sight and neighbourhood of the Forum. For just as pestilential places assail even the strongest constitution, so there are some places which are also unwholesome for a healthy mind which is not yet quite sound, though recovering from its ailment. I disagree with those who strike out into the midst of the billows and, welcoming a stormy existence, wrestle daily in hardihood of soul with life's problems. The wise man will endure all that, but will not choose it; he will prefer to be at peace rather than at war. It helps little to have cast out your own faults if you must quarrel with those of others. Says one: "There were thirty tyrants surrounding Socrates, and yet they could not break his spirit"; but what does it matter how many masters a man has? "Slavery" has no plural; and he who has scorned it is free, – no matter amid how large a mob of over-lords he stands.

It is time to stop, but not before I have paid duty. "The knowledge of sin is the beginning of salvation." This saying of Epicurus seems to me to be a noble one. For he who does not know that he has sinned does not desire correction; you must discover yourself in the wrong before you can reform yourself. Some boast of their faults. Do you think that the man has any thought of mending his ways who counts over his vices as if they were virtues? Therefore, as far as possible, prove yourself guilty, hunt up charges against yourself; play the part, first of accuser, then of judge, last of intercessor. At times be harsh with yourself. Farewell.

Letter XXIX - On the Critical Condition of Marcellinus

You have been inquiring about our friend Marcellinus and you desire to know how he is getting along. He seldom comes to see me, for no other reason than that he is afraid to hear the truth, and at present he is removed from my danger of hearing it; for one must not talk to a man unless he is willing to listen. That is why it is often doubted whether Diogenes and the other Cynics, who employed an undiscriminating freedom of speech and offered advice to any who came in their way, ought to have pursued such a plan. For what if one should chide the deaf or those who are speechless from birth or by illness? But you answer: "Why should I spare words? They cost nothing. I cannot know whether I shall help the man to whom I give advice; but I know well that I shall help someone if I advise many. I must scatter this advice by the handful. It is impossible that one who tries often should not sometime succeed."

This very thing, my dear Lucilius, is, I believe, exactly what a great-souled man ought not to do; his influence is weakened; it has too little effect upon those whom it might have set right if it had not grown so stale. The archer ought not to hit the mark only sometimes; he ought to miss it only sometimes. That which takes effect by chance is not an art. Now wisdom is an art; it should have a definite aim, choosing only those who will make progress, but withdrawing from those whom it has come to regard as hopeless, – yet not abandoning them too soon, and just when the case is becoming hopeless trying drastic remedies.

As to our friend Marcellinus, I have not yet lost hope. He can still be saved, but the helping hand must be offered soon. There is indeed danger that he may pull his helper down; for there is in him a native character of great vigour, though it is already inclining to wickedness. Nevertheless I shall brave this danger and be bold enough to show him his faults. He will act in his usual way; he will have recourse to his wit, – the wit that can call forth smiles even from mourners. He will turn the jest, first against himself, and then against me. He will forestall every word which I am about to utter. He will quiz our philosophic systems; he will accuse philosophers of accepting doles, keeping mistresses, and indulging their appetites.

He will point out to me one philosopher who has been caught in adultery, another who haunts the cafes, and another who appears at court. He will bring to my notice Aristo, the philosopher of Marcus Lepidus, who used to hold discussions in his carriage; for that was the time which he had taken for editing his researches, so that Scaurus said of him when asked to what school he belonged: "At any rate, he isn't one of the Walking Philosophers." Julius Graecinus, too, a man of distinction, when asked for an opinion on the same point, replied: "I cannot tell you; for I don't know what he does when dismounted," as if the query referred to a chariot-gladiator. It is mountebanks of that sort, for whom it would be more creditable to have left philosophy alone than to traffic in her, whom Marcellinus will throw in my teeth. But I have decided to put up with taunts; he may stir my laughter, but I perchance shall stir him to tears; or, if he persist in his jokes, I shall rejoice, so to speak, in the midst of sorrow, because he is blessed with such a merry sort of lunacy. But that kind of merriment does not last long. Observe such men, and you will note that within a short space of time they laugh to excess and rage to excess. It is my plan to approach him and to show him how much greater was his worth when many thought it less. Even though I shall not root out his faults, I shall put a check upon them; they will not cease, but they will stop for a time; and perhaps they will even cease, if they get the habit of stopping. This is a thing not to be despised, since to men who are seriously stricken the blessing of relief is a substitute for health. So while I prepare myself to deal with Marcellinus, do you in the meantime, who are able, and who understand whence and whither you have made your way, and who for that reason have an inkling of the distance yet to go, regulate your character, rouse your courage, and stand firm in the face of things which have terrified you. Do not count the number of those who inspire fear in you. Would you not regard as foolish one who was afraid of a multitude in a place where only one at a time could pass? Just so, there are not many who have access to you to slay you, though there are many who threaten you with death. Nature has so ordered it that, as only one has given you life, so only one will take it away.

If you had any shame, you would have let me off from paying the last instalment. Still, I shall not be niggardly either, but shall discharge my debts to the last penny and force upon you what I still owe: "I have never wished to cater to the crowd; for what I know, they do not approve, and what they approve, I do not know." "Who said this?" you ask, as if you were ignorant whom I am pressing into service; it is Epicurus. But this same watchword rings in your ears from every sect, – Peripatetic, Academic, Stoic, Cynic. For who that is pleased by virtue can please the crowd? It takes trickery to win popular approval; and you must needs make yourself like unto them; they will withhold their approval if they do not recognise you as one of themselves. However, what you think of yourself is much more to the point than what others think of you. The favour of ignoble men can be won only by ignoble means. What benefit, then, will that vaunted philosophy confer, whose praises we sing, and which, we are told, is to be preferred to every art and every possession? Assuredly, it will make you prefer to please yourself rather than the populace, it will make you weigh, and not merely count, men's judgments, it will make you live without fear of gods or men, it will make you either overcome evils or end them. Otherwise, if I see you applauded by popular acclamation, if your entrance upon the scene is greeted by a roar of cheering and clapping, marks of distinction meet only for actors, – if the whole state, even the women and children, sing your praises, how can I help pitying you? For I know what pathway leads to such popularity. Farewell.

Letter XXX - On Conquering the Conqueror

I have beheld Aufidius Bassus, that noble man, shattered in health and wrestling with his years. But they already bear upon him so heavily that he cannot be raised up; old age has settled down upon him with great, – yes, with its entire, weight. You know that his body was always delicate and sapless. For a long time he has kept it in hand, or, to speak more correctly, has kept it together; of a sudden it has collapsed. Just as in a ship that springs a leak, you can always stop the first or the second fissure, but when many holes begin to open and let in water, the gaping hull cannot be saved; similarly, in an old man's body, there is a certain limit up to which you can sustain and prop its weakness. But when it comes to resemble a decrepit building, when every joint begins to spread and while one is being repaired another falls apart, – then it is time for a man to look about him and consider how he may get out.

But the mind of our friend Bassus is active. Philosophy bestows this boon upon us; it makes us joyful in the very sight of death, strong and brave no matter in what state the body may be, cheerful and never failing though the body fail us. A great pilot can sail even when his canvas is rent; if his ship be dismantled, he can yet put in trim what remains of her hull and hold her to her course. This is what our friend Bassus is doing; and he contemplates his own end with the courage and countenance which you would regard as undue indifference in a man who so contemplated another's.

This is a great accomplishment, Lucilius, and one which needs long practice to learn, – to depart calmly when the inevitable hour arrives. Other kinds of death contain an ingredient of hope: a disease comes to an end; a fire is quenched; falling houses have set down in safety those whom they seemed certain to crush; the sea has cast ashore unharmed those whom it had engulfed, by the same force through which it drew them down; the soldier has drawn back his sword from the very neck of his doomed foe. But those whom old age is leading away to death have nothing to hope for; old age alone grants no reprieve. No ending, to be sure, is more painless; but there is none more lingering.

Our friend Bassus seemed to me to be attending his own funeral, and laying out his own body for burial, and living almost as if he had survived his own death, and bearing with wise resignation his grief at his own departure. For he talks freely about death, trying hard to persuade us that if this process contains any element of discomfort or of fear, it is the fault of the dying person, and not of death itself; also, that there is no more inconvenience at the actual moment than there is after it is over. "And it is just as insane," he adds, "for a man to fear what will not happen to him, as to fear what he will not feel if it does happen." Or does anyone imagine it to be possible that the agency by which feeling is removed can be itself felt? "Therefore," says Bassus, "death stands so far beyond all evil that it is beyond all fear of evils."

I know that all this has often been said and should be often repeated; but neither when I read them were such precepts so effective with me, nor when I heard them from the lips of those who were at a safe distance from the fear of the things which they declared were not to be feared. But this old man had the greatest weight with me when he discussed death and death was near. For I must tell you what I myself think: I hold that one is braver at the very moment of death than when one is approaching death. For death, when it stands near us, gives even to inexperienced men the courage not to seek to avoid the inevitable. So the gladiator, who throughout the fight has been no matter how faint-hearted, offers his throat to his opponent and directs the wavering blade to the vital spot. But an end that is near at hand, and is bound to come, calls for tenacious courage of soul; this is a rarer thing, and none but the wise man can manifest it.

Accordingly, I listened to Bassus with the deepest pleasure; he was casting his vote concerning death and pointing out what sort of a thing it is when it is observed, so to speak, nearer at hand. I suppose that a man would have your confidence in a larger degree, and would have more weight with you, if he had come back to life and should declare from experience that there is no evil in death; and so, regarding the approach of death, those will tell you best what disquiet it brings who have stood in its path, who have seen it coming and have welcomed it. Bassus may be included among these men; and he had no wish to deceive us. He says that it is as foolish to fear death as to fear old age; for death follows old age precisely as old age follows youth. He who does not wish to die cannot have wished to live. For life is granted to us with the reservation that we shall die; to this end our path leads. Therefore, how foolish it is to fear it, since men simply await that which is sure, but fear only that which is uncertain! Death has its fixed rule, – equitable and unavoidable. Who can complain when he is governed by terms which include everyone? The chief part of equity, however, is equality.

But it is superfluous at the present time to plead Nature's cause; for she wishes our laws to be identical with her own; she but resolves that which she has compounded, and compounds again that which she has resolved. Moreover, if it falls to the lot of any man to be set gently adrift by old age, – not suddenly torn from life, but withdrawn bit by bit, oh, verily he should thank the gods, one and all, because, after he has had his fill, he is removed to a rest which is ordained for mankind, a rest that is welcome to the weary. You may observe certain men who crave death even more earnestly than others are wont to beg for life. And I do not know which men give us greater courage, – those who call for death, or those who meet it cheerfully and tranquilly, – for the first attitude is sometimes inspired by madness and sudden anger, the second is the calm which results from fixed judgment. Before now men have gone to meet death in a fit of rage; but when death comes to meet him, no one welcomes it cheerfully, except the man who has long since composed himself for death.

I admit, therefore, that I have visited this dear friend of mine more frequently on many pretexts, but with the purpose of learning whether I should find him always the same, and whether his mental strength was perhaps waning in company with his bodily powers. But it was on the increase, just as the joy of the charioteer is wont to show itself more clearly when he is on the seventh round of the course, and nears the prize. Indeed, he often said, in accord with the counsels of Epicurus: "I hope, first of all, that there is no pain at the moment when a man breathes his last; but if there is, one will find an element of comfort in its very shortness. For no great pain lasts long. And at all events, a man will find relief at the very time when soul and body are being torn asunder, even though the process be accompanied by excruciating pain, in the thought that after this pain is over he can feel no more pain. I am sure, however, that an old man's soul is on his very lips, and that only a little force is necessary to disengage it from the body. A fire which has seized upon a substance that sustains it needs water to quench it, or, sometimes, the destruction of the building itself; but the fire which lacks sustaining fuel dies away of its own accord."

I am glad to hear such words, my dear Lucilius, not as new to me, but as leading me into the presence of an actual fact. And what then? Have I not seen many men break the thread of life? I have indeed seen such men; but those have more weight with me who approach death without any loathing for life, letting death in, so to speak, and not pulling it towards them. Bassus kept saying: "It is due to our own fault that we feel this torture, because we shrink from dying only when we believe that our end is near at hand." But who is not near death? It is ready for us in all places and at all times. "Let us consider," he went on to say, "when some agency of death seems imminent, how much nearer are other varieties of dying which are not feared by us." A man is threatened with death by an enemy, but this form of death is anticipated by an attack of indigestion. And if we are willing to examine critically the various causes of our fear, we shall find that some exist, and others only seem to be. We do not fear death; we fear the thought of death. For death itself is always the same distance from us; wherefore, if it is to be feared at all, it is to be feared always. For what season of our life is exempt from death?

But what I really ought to fear is that you will hate this long letter worse than death itself; so I shall stop. Do you, however, always think on death in order that you may never fear it. Farewell.

Letter XXXI - On Siren Songs

Now I recognize my Lucilius! He is beginning to reveal the character of which he gave promise. Follow up the impulse which prompted you to make for all that is best, treading under your feet that which is approved by the crowd. I would not have you greater or better than you planned; for in your case the mere foundations have covered a large extent of ground; only finish all that you have laid out, and take in hand the plans which you have had in mind. In short, you will be a wise man, if you stop up your ears; nor is it enough to close them with wax; you need a denser stopple than that which they say Ulysses used for his comrades. The song which he feared was alluring, but came not from every side; the song, however, which you have to fear, echoes round you not from a single headland, but from every quarter of the world. Sail, therefore, not past one region which you mistrust because of its treacherous delights, but past every city. Be deaf to those who love you most of all; they pray for bad things with good intentions. And, if you would be happy, entreat the gods that none of their fond desires for you may be brought to pass. What they wish to have heaped upon you are not really good things;

there is only one good, the cause and the support of a happy life, – trust in oneself. But this cannot be attained, unless one has learned to despise toil and to reckon it among the things which are neither good nor bad. For it is not possible that a single thing should be bad at one time and good at another, at times light and to be endured, and at times a cause of dread. Work is not a good. Then what is a good? I say, the scorning of work. That is why I should rebuke men who toil to no purpose. But when, on the other hand, a man is struggling towards honourable things, in proportion as he applies himself more and more, and allows himself less and less to be beaten or to halt, I shall recommend his conduct and shout my encouragement, saying: "By so much you are better! Rise, draw a fresh breath, and surmount that hill, if possible, at a single spurt!"

Work is the sustenance of noble minds. There is, then, no reason why, in accordance with that old vow of your parents, you should pick and choose what fortune you wish should fall to your lot, or what you should pray for; besides, it is base for a man who has already travelled the whole round of highest honours to be still importuning the gods. What need is there of vows? Make yourself happy through your own efforts; you can do this, if once you comprehend that whatever is blended with virtue is good, and that whatever is joined to vice is bad. Just as nothing gleams if it has no light blended with it, and nothing is black unless it contains darkness or draws to itself something of dimness, and as nothing is hot without the aid of fire, and nothing cold without air; so it is the association of virtue and vice that makes things honourable or base.

What then is good? The knowledge of things. What is evil? The lack of knowledge of things. Your wise man, who is also a craftsman, will reject or choose in each case as it suits the occasion; but he does not fear that which he rejects, nor does he admire that which he chooses, if only he has a stout and unconquerable soul. I forbid you to be cast down or depressed. It is not enough if you do not shrink from work; ask for it. "But," you say, "is not trifling and superfluous work, and work that has been inspired by ignoble causes, a bad sort of work?" No; no more than that which is expended upon noble endeavours, since the very quality that endures toil and rouses itself to hard and uphill effort, is of the spirit, which says: "Why do you grow slack? It is not the part of a man to fear sweat." And besides this, in order that virtue may be perfect, there should be an even temperament and a scheme of life that is consistent with itself throughout; and this result cannot be attained without knowledge of things, and without the art which enables us to understand things human and things divine. That is the greatest good. If you seize this good, you begin to be the associate of the gods, and not their suppliant.

"But how," you ask, "does one attain that goal?" You do not need to cross the Pennine or Graian hills, or traverse the Candavian waste, or face the Syrtes, or Scylla, or Charybdis, although you have travelled through all these places for the bribe of a petty governorship; the journey for which nature has equipped you is safe and pleasant. She has given you such gifts that you may, if you do not prove false to them, rise level with God. Your money, however, will not place you on a level with God; for God has no property. Your bordered robe will not do this; for God is not clad in raiment; nor will your reputation, nor a display of self, nor a knowledge of your name wide-spread throughout the world; for no one has knowledge of God; many even hold him in low esteem, and do not suffer for so doing. The throng of slaves which carries your litter along the city streets and in foreign places will not help you; for this God of whom I speak, though the highest and most powerful of beings, carries all things on his own shoulders. Neither can beauty or strength make you blessed, for none of these qualities can withstand old age.

What we have to seek for, then, is that which does not each day pass more and more under the control of some power which cannot be withstood. And what is this? It is the soul, – but the soul that is upright, good, and great. What else could you call such a soul than a god dwelling as a guest in a human body? A soul like this may descend into a Roman knight just as well as into a freedman's son or a slave. For what is a Roman knight, or a freedmen's son, or a slave? They are mere titles, born of ambition or of wrong. One may leap to heaven from the very slums. Only rise

And mould thyself to kinship with thy God.

This moulding will not be done in gold or silver; an image that is to be in the likeness of God cannot be fashioned of such materials; remember that the gods, when they were kind unto men, were moulded in clay. Farewell.

Letter XXXII - On Progress

I have been asking about you, and inquiring of everyone who comes from your part of the country, what you are doing, and where you are spending your time, and with whom. You cannot deceive me; for I am with you. Live just as if I were sure to get news of your doings, nay, as if I were sure to behold them. And if you wonder what particularly pleases me that I hear concerning you, it is that I hear nothing, that most of those whom I ask do not know what you are doing.

This is sound practice – to refrain from associating with men of different stamp and different aims. And I am indeed confident that you cannot be warped, that you will stick to your purpose, even though the crowd may surround and seek to distract you. What, then, is on my mind? I am not afraid lest they work a change in you; but I am afraid lest they may hinder your progress. And much harm is done even by one who holds you back, especially since life is so short; and we make it still shorter by our unsteadiness, by making ever fresh beginnings at life, now one and immediately another. We break up life into little bits, and fritter it away. Hasten ahead, then, dearest Lucilius, and reflect how greatly you would quicken your speed if an enemy were at your back, or if you suspected the cavalry were approaching and pressing hard upon your steps as you fled. It is true; the enemy is indeed pressing upon you; you should therefore increase your speed and escape away and reach a safe position, remembering continually what a noble thing it is to round out your life before death comes, and then await in peace the remaining portion of your time, claiming nothing for yourself, since you are in possession of the happy life; for such a life is not made happier for being longer. O when shall you see the time when you shall know that time means nothing to you, when you shall be peaceful and calm, careless of the morrow, because you are enjoying your life to the full?

Would you know what makes men greedy for the future? It is because no one has yet found himself. Your parents, to be sure, asked other blessings for you; but I myself pray rather that you may despise all those things which your parents wished for you in abundance. Their prayers plunder many another person, simply that you may be enriched. Whatever they make over to you must be removed from someone else. I pray that you may get such control over yourself that your mind, now shaken by wandering thoughts, may at last come to rest and be steadfast, that it may be content with itself and, having attained an understanding of what things are truly good, – and they are in our possession as soon as we have this knowledge, – that it may have no need of added years. He has at length passed beyond all necessities – he has won his honourable discharge and is free, – who still lives after his life has been completed. Farewell.

Letter XXXIII - On the Futility of Learning Maxims

You wish me to close these letters also, as I closed my former letters, with certain utterances taken from the chiefs of our school. But they did not interest themselves in choice extracts; the whole texture of their work is full of strength. There is unevenness, you know, when some objects rise conspicuous above others. A single tree is not remarkable if the whole forest rises to the same height. Poetry is crammed with utterances of this sort, and so is history. For this reason I would not have you think that these utterances belong to Epicurus. they are common property and are emphatically our own. They are, however, more noteworthy in Epicurus, because they appear at infrequent intervals and when you do not expect them, and because it is surprising that brave words should be spoken at any time by a man who made a practice of being effeminate. For that is what most persons maintain. In my own opinion, however, Epicurus is really a brave man, even though he did wear long sleeves. Fortitude, energy, and readiness for battle are to be found among the Persians, just as much as among men who have girded themselves up high.

Therefore, you need not call upon me for extracts and quotations; such thoughts as one may extract here and there in the works of other philosophers run through the whole body of our writings. Hence we have no "show-window goods," nor do we deceive the purchaser in such a way that, if he enters our shop, he will find nothing except that which is displayed in the window. We allow the purchasers themselves to get their samples from anywhere they please. Suppose we should desire to sort out each separate motto from the general stock; to whom shall we credit them? To Zeno, Cleanthes, Chrysippus, Panaetius, or Posidonius? We Stoics are not subjects of a despot: each of us lays claim to his own freedom. With them, on the other hand, whatever Hermarchus says or Metrodorus, is ascribed to one source. In that brotherhood, everything that any man utters is spoken under the leadership and commanding authority of one alone. We cannot, I maintain, no matter how we try, pick out anything from so great a multitude of things equally good.

Only the poor man counts his flock.

Wherever you direct your gaze, you will meet with something that might stand out from the rest, if the context in which you read it were not equally notable.

For this reason, give over hoping that you can skim, by means of epitomes, the wisdom of distinguished men. Look into their wisdom as a whole; study it as a whole. They are working out a plan and weaving together, line upon line, a masterpiece, from which nothing can be taken away without injury to the whole. Examine the separate parts, if you like, provided you examine them as parts of the man himself. She is not a beautiful woman whose ankle or arm is praised, but she whose general appearance makes you forget to admire her single attributes.

If you insist, however, I shall not be niggardly with you, but lavish; for there is a huge multitude of these passages; they are scattered about in profusion, – they do not need to be gathered together, but merely to be picked up. They do not drip forth occasionally; they flow continuously. They are unbroken and are closely connected. Doubtless they would be of much benefit to those who are still novices and worshipping outside the shrine; for single maxims sink in more easily when they are marked off and bounded like a line of verse. That is why we give to children a proverb, or that which the Greeks call Chria, to be learned by heart; that sort of thing can be comprehended by the young mind, which cannot as yet hold more. For a man, however, whose progress is definite, to chase after choice extracts and to prop his weakness by the best known and the briefest sayings and to depend upon his memory, is disgraceful; it is time for him to lean on himself. He should make such maxims and not memorize them. For it is disgraceful even for an old man, or one who has sighted old age, to have a note-book knowledge. "This is what Zeno said." But what have you yourself said? "This is the opinion of Cleanthes." But what is your own opinion? How long shall you march under another man's orders? Take command, and utter some word which posterity will remember. Put forth something from your own stock. For this reason I hold that there is nothing of eminence in all such men as these, who never create anything themselves, but always lurk in the shadow of others, playing the role of interpreters, never daring to put once into practice what they have been so long in learning. They have exercised their memories on other men's material. But it is one thing to remember, another to know. Remembering is merely safeguarding something entrusted to the memory; knowing, however, means making everything your own; it means not depending upon the copy and not all the time glancing back at the master. "Thus said Zeno, thus said Cleanthes, indeed!" Let there be a difference between yourself and your book! How long shall you be a learner? From now on be a teacher as well! "But why," one asks, "should I have to continue hearing lectures on what I can read?" "The living voice," one replies, "is a great help." Perhaps, but not the voice which merely makes itself the mouthpiece of another's words, and only performs the duty of a reporter.

Consider this fact also. Those who have never attained their mental independence begin, in the first place, by following the leader in cases where everyone has deserted the leader; then, in the second place, they follow him in matters where the truth is still being investigated. However, the truth will never be discovered if we rest contented with discoveries already made. Besides, he who follows another not only discovers nothing but is not even investigating. What then? Shall I not follow in the footsteps of my predecessors? I shall indeed use the old road, but if I find one that makes a shorter cut and is smoother to travel, I shall open the new road. Men who have made these discoveries before us are not our masters, but our guides. Truth lies open for all; it has not yet been monopolized. And there is plenty of it left even for posterity to discover. Farewell.

Letter XXXIV - On a Promising Pupil

I grow in spirit and leap for joy and shake off my years and my blood runs warm again, whenever I understand, from your actions and your letters, how far you have outdone yourself; for as to the ordinary man, you left him in the rear long ago. If the farmer is pleased when his tree develops so that it bears fruit, if the shepherd takes pleasure in the increase of his flocks, if every man regards his pupil as though he discerned in him his own early manhood, – what, then, do you think are the feelings of those who have trained a mind and moulded a young idea, when they see it suddenly grown to maturity?

I claim you for myself; you are my handiwork. When I saw your abilities, I laid my hand upon you, I exhorted you, I applied the goad and did not permit you to march lazily, but roused you continually. And now I do the same; but by this time I am cheering on one who is in the race and so in turn cheers me on.

"What else do you want of me, then?" you ask; "the will is still mine." Well, the will in this case is almost everything, and not merely the half, as in the proverb "A task once begun is half done." It is more than half, for the matter of which we speak is determined by the soul. Hence it is that the larger part of goodness is the will to become good. You know what I mean by a good man? One who is complete, finished, – whom no constraint or need can render bad. I see such a person in you, if only you go steadily on and bend to your task, and see to it that all your actions and words harmonize and correspond with each other and are stamped in the same mould. If a man's acts are out of harmony, his soul is crooked. Farewell.

Letter XXXV - On the Friendship of Kindred Minds

When I urge you so strongly to your studies, it is my own interest which I am consulting; I want your friendship, and it cannot fall to my lot unless you proceed, as you have begun, with the task of developing yourself. For now, although you love me, you are not yet my friend. "But," you reply, "are these words of different meaning?" Nay, more, they are totally unlike in meaning. A friend loves you, of course; but one who loves you is not in every case your friend. Friendship, accordingly, is always helpful, but love sometimes even does harm. Try to perfect yourself, if for no other reason, in order that you may learn how to love.

Hasten, therefore, in order that, while thus perfecting yourself for my benefit, you may not have learned perfection for the benefit of another. To be sure, I am already deriving some profit by imagining that we two shall be of one mind, and that whatever portion of my strength has yielded to age will return to me from your strength, although there is not so very much difference in our ages. But yet I wish to rejoice in the accomplished fact. We feel a joy over those whom we love, even when separated from them, but such a joy is light and fleeting; the sight of a man, and his presence, and communion with him, afford something of living pleasure; this is true, at any rate, if one not only sees the man one desires, but the sort of man one desires. Give yourself to me, therefore, as a gift of great price, and, that you may strive the more, reflect that you yourself are mortal, and that I am old. Hasten to find me, but hasten to find yourself first. Make progress, and, before all else, endeavour to be consistent with yourself. And when you would find out whether you have accomplished anything, consider whether you desire the same things today that you desired yesterday. A shifting of the will indicates that the mind is at sea, heading in various directions, according to the course of the wind. But that which is settled and solid does not wander from its place. This is the blessed lot of the completely wise man, and also, to a certain extent, of him who is progressing and has made some headway. Now what is the difference between these two classes of men? The one is in motion, to be sure, but does not change its position; it merely tosses up and down where it is; the other is not in motion at all. Farewell.

Letter XXXVI - On the Value of Retirement

Encourage your friend to despise stout-heartedly those who upbraid him because he has sought the shade of retirement and has abdicated his career of honours, and, though he might have attained more, has preferred tranquillity to them all. Let him prove daily to these detractors how wisely he has looked out for his own interests. Those whom men envy will continue to march past him; some will be pushed out of the ranks, and others will fall. Prosperity is a turbulent thing; it torments itself. It stirs the brain in more ways than one, goading men on to various aims, – some to power, and others to high living. Some it puffs up; others it slackens and wholly enervates.

"But," the retort comes, "so-and-so carries his prosperity well." Yes; just as he carries his liquor. So you need not let this class of men persuade you that one who is besieged by the crowd is happy; they run to him as crowds rush for a pool of water, rendering it muddy while they drain it. But you say: "Men call our friend a trifler and a sluggard." There are men, you know, whose speech is awry, who use the contrary terms. They called him happy; what of it? Was he happy? Even the fact that to certain persons he seems a man of a very rough and gloomy cast of mind, does not trouble me. Aristo used to say that he preferred a youth of stern disposition to one who was a jolly fellow and agreeable to the crowd. "For," he added, "wine which, when new, seemed harsh and sour, becomes good wine; but that which tasted well at the vintage cannot stand age." So let them call him stern and a foe to his own advancement, it is just this sternness that will go well when it is aged, provided only that he continues to cherish virtue and to absorb thoroughly the studies which make for culture, – not those with which it is sufficient for a man to sprinkle himself, but those in which the mind should be steeped. Now is the time to learn. "What? Is there any time when a man should not learn?" By no means; but just as it is creditable for every age to study, so it is not creditable for every age to be instructed. An old man learning his A B C is a disgraceful and absurd object; the young man must store up, the old man must use. You will therefore be doing a thing most helpful to yourself if you make this friend of yours as good a man as possible; those kindnesses, they tell us, are to be both sought for and bestowed, which benefit the giver no less than the receiver; and they are unquestionably the best kind.

Finally, he has no longer any freedom in the matter; he has pledged his word. And it is less disgraceful to compound with a creditor than to compound with a promising future. To pay his debt of money, the business man must have a prosperous voyage, the farmer must have fruitful fields and kindly weather; but the debt which your friend owes can be completely paid by mere goodwill. Fortune has no jurisdiction over character. Let him so regulate his character that in perfect peace he may bring to perfection that spirit within him which feels neither loss nor gain, but remains in the same attitude, no matter how things fall out. A spirit like this, if it is heaped with worldly goods, rises superior to its wealth; if, on the other hand, chance has stripped him of a part of his wealth, or even all, it is not impaired.

If your friend had been born in Parthia, he would have begun, when a child, to bend the bow; if in Germany, he would forthwith have been brandishing his slender spear; if he had been born in the days of our forefathers, he would have learned to ride a horse and smite his enemy hand to hand. These are the occupations which the system of each race recommends to the individual, – yes, prescribes for him. To what, then, shall this friend of yours devote his attention? I say, let him learn that which is helpful against all weapons, against every kind of foe, – contempt of death; because no one doubts that death has in it something that inspires terror, so that it shocks even our souls, which nature has so moulded that they love their own existence; for otherwise there would be no need to prepare ourselves, and to whet our courage, to face that towards which we should move with a sort of voluntary instinct, precisely as all men tend to preserve their existence. No man learns a thing in order that, if necessity arises, he may lie down with composure upon a bed of roses; but he steels his courage to this end, that he may not surrender his plighted faith to torture, and that, if need be, he may some day stay out his watch in the trenches, even though wounded, without even leaning on his spear; because sleep is likely to creep over men who support themselves by any prop whatsoever.

In death there is nothing harmful; for there must exist something to which it is harmful. And yet, if you are possessed by so great a craving for a longer life, reflect that none of the objects which vanish from our gaze and are re-absorbed into the world of things, from which they have come forth and are soon to come forth again, is annihilated; they merely end their course and do not perish. And death, which we fear and shrink from, merely interrupts life, but does not steal it away; the time will return when we shall be restored to the light of day; and many men would object to this, were they not brought back in forgetfulness of the past.

But I mean to show you later, with more care, that everything which seems to perish merely changes. Since you are destined to return, you ought to depart with a tranquil mind. Mark how the round of the universe repeats its course; you will see that no star in our firmament is extinguished, but that they all set and rise in alternation. Summer has gone, but another year will bring it again; winter lies low, but will be restored by its own proper months; night has overwhelmed the sun, but day will soon rout the night again. The wandering stars retrace their former courses; a part of the sky is rising unceasingly, and a part is sinking. One word more, and then I shall stop; infants, and boys, and those who have gone mad, have no fear of death, and it is most shameful if reason cannot afford us that peace of mind to which they have been brought by their folly. Farewell.

Letter XXXVII - On Allegiance to Virtue

You have promised to be a good man; you have enlisted under oath; that is the strongest chain which will hold you to a sound understanding. Any man will be but mocking you, if he declares that this is an effeminate and easy kind of soldiering. I will not have you deceived. The word of this most honourable compact are the same as the words of that most disgraceful one, to wit: "Through burning, imprisonment, or death by the sword." From the men who hire out their strength for the arena, who eat and drink what they must pay for with their blood, security is taken that they will endure such trials even though they be unwilling; from you, that you will endure them willingly and with alacrity. The gladiator may lower his weapon and test the pity of the people; but you will neither lower your weapon nor beg for life. You must die erect and unyielding. Moreover, what profit is it to gain a few days or a few years? There is no discharge for us from the moment we are born.

"Then how can I free myself?" you ask. You cannot escape necessities, but you can overcome them

By force a way is made.

And this way will be afforded you by philosophy. Betake yourself therefore to philosophy if you would be safe, untroubled, happy, in fine, if you wish to be, – and that is most important, – free. There is no other way to attain this end. Folly is low, abject, mean, slavish, and exposed to many of the cruellest passions. These passions, which are heavy taskmasters, sometimes ruling by turns, and sometimes together, can be banished from you by wisdom, which is the only real freedom. There is but one path leading thither, and it is a straight path; you will not go astray. Proceed with steady step, and if you would have all things under your control, put yourself under the control of reason; if reason becomes your ruler, you will become ruler over many. You will learn from her what you should undertake, and how it should be done; you will not blunder into things. You can show me no man who knows how he began to crave that which he craves. He has not been led to that pass by forethought; he has been driven to it by impulse. Fortune attacks us as often as we attack Fortune. It is disgraceful, instead of proceeding ahead, to be carried along, and then suddenly, amid the whirlpool of events, to ask in a dazed way: "How did I get into this condition?" Farewell.

Letter XXXVIII - On Quiet Conversation

You are right when you urge that we increase our mutual traffic in letters. But the greatest benefit is to be derived from conversation, because it creeps by degrees into the soul. Lectures prepared beforehand and spouted in the presence of a throng have in them more noise but less intimacy. Philosophy is good advice; and no one can give advice at the top of his lungs. Of course we must sometimes also make use of these harangues, if I may so call them, when a doubting member needs to be spurred on; but when the aim is to make a man learn and not merely to make him wish to learn, we must have recourse to the low-toned words of conversation. They enter more easily, and stick in the memory; for we do not need many words, but, rather, effective words.

Words should be scattered like seed; no matter how small the seed may be, if it has once found favourable ground, it unfolds its strength and from an insignificant thing spreads to its greatest growth. Reason grows in the same way; it is not large to the outward view, but increases as it does its work. Few words are spoken; but if the mind has truly caught them, they come into their strength and spring up. Yes, precepts and seeds have the same quality; they produce much, and yet they are slight things. Only, as I said, let a favourable mind receive and assimilate them. Then of itself the mind also will produce bounteously in its turn, giving back more than it has received. Farewell.

Letter XXXIX - On Noble Aspirations

I shall indeed arrange for you, in careful order and narrow compass, the notes which you request. But consider whether you may not get more help from the customary method than from that which is now commonly called a "breviary," though in the good old days, when real Latin was spoken, it was called a "summary." The former is more necessary to one who is learning a subject, the latter to one who knows it. For the one teaches, the other stirs the memory. But I shall give you abundant opportunity for both. A man like you should not ask me for this authority or that; he who furnishes a voucher for his statements argues himself unknown. I shall therefore write exactly what you wish, but I shall do it in my own way; until then, you have many authors whose works will presumably keep your ideas sufficiently in order. Pick up the list of the philosophers; that very act will compel you to wake up, when you see how many men have been working for your benefit. You will desire eagerly to be one of them yourself, for this is the most excellent quality that the noble soul has within itself, that it can be roused to honourable things.

No man of exalted gifts is pleased with that which is low and mean; the vision of great achievement summons him and uplifts him. Just as the flame springs straight into the air and cannot be cabined or kept down any more than it can repose in quiet, so our soul is always in motion, and the more ardent it is, the greater its motion and activity. But happy is the man who has given it this impulse toward better things! He will place himself beyond the jurisdiction of chance; he will wisely control prosperity; he will lessen adversity, and will despise what others hold in admiration. It is the quality of a great soul to scorn great things and to prefer that which is ordinary rather than that which is too great. For the one condition is useful and life-giving; but the other does harm just because it is excessive. Similarly, too rich a soil makes the grain fall flat, branches break down under too heavy a load, excessive productiveness does not bring fruit to ripeness. This is the case with the soul also; for it is ruined by uncontrolled prosperity, which is used not only to the detriment of others, but also to the detriment of itself. What enemy was ever so insolent to any opponent as are their pleasures to certain men? The only excuse that we can allow for the incontinence and mad lust of these men is the fact that they suffer the evils which they have inflicted upon others. And they are rightly harassed by this madness, because desire must have unbounded space for its excursions, if it transgresses nature's mean. For this has its bounds, but waywardness and the acts that spring from wilful lust are without boundaries. Utility measures our needs; but by what standard can you check the superfluous? It is for this reason that men sink themselves in pleasures, and they cannot do without them when once they have become accustomed to them, and for this reason they are most wretched, because they have reached such a pass that what was once superfluous to them has become indispensable. And so they are the slaves of their pleasures instead of enjoying them; they even love their own ills, – and that is the worst ill of all! Then it is that the height of unhappiness is reached, when men are not only attracted, but even pleased, by shameful things, and when there is no longer any room for a cure, now that those things which once were vices have become habits. Farewell.

Letter XL - On the Proper Style for a Philosopher's Discourse

I thank you for writing to me so often; for you are revealing your real self to me in the only way you can. I never receive a letter from you without being in your company forthwith. If the pictures of our absent friends are pleasing to us, though they only refresh the memory and lighten our longing by a solace that is unreal and unsubstantial, how much more pleasant is a letter, which brings us real traces, real evidences, of an absent friend! For that which is sweetest when we meet face to face is afforded by the impress of a friend's hand upon his letter, – recognition.

You write me that you heard a lecture by the philosopher Serapio, when he landed at your present place of residence. "He is wont," you say, "to wrench up his words with a mighty rush, and he does not let them flow forth one by one, but makes them crowd and dash upon each other. For the words come in such quantity that a single voice is inadequate to utter them." I do not approve of this in a philosopher; his speech, like his life, should be composed; and nothing that rushes headlong and is hurried is well ordered. That is why, in Homer, the rapid style, which sweeps down without a break like a snow-squall, is assigned to the younger speaker; from the old man eloquence flows gently, sweeter than honey.

Therefore, mark my words; that forceful manner of speech, rapid and copious, is more suited to a mountebank than to a man who is discussing and teaching an important and serious subject. But I object just as strongly that he should drip out his words as that he should go at top speed; he should neither keep the ear on the stretch, nor deafen it. For that poverty-stricken and thin-spun style also makes the audience less attentive because they are weary of its stammering slowness; nevertheless, the word which has been long awaited sinks in more easily than the word which flits past us on the wing. Finally, people speak of "handing down" precepts to their pupils; but one is not "handing down" that which eludes the grasp. Besides, speech that deals with the truth should be unadorned and plain. This popular style has nothing to do with the truth; its aim is to impress the common herd, to ravish heedless ears by its speed; it does not offer itself for discussion, but snatches itself away from discussion. But how can that speech govern others which cannot itself be governed? May I not also remark that all speech which is employed for the purpose of healing our minds, ought to sink into us? Remedies do not avail unless they remain in the system.

Besides, this sort of speech contains a great deal of sheer emptiness; it has more sound than power. My terrors should be quieted, my irritations soothed, my illusions shaken off, my indulgences checked, my greed rebuked. And which of these cures can be brought about in a hurry? What physician can heal his patient on a flying visit? May I add that such a jargon of confused and ill-chosen words cannot afford pleasure, either? No; but just as you are well satisfied, in the majority of cases, to have seen through tricks which you did not think could possibly be done, so in the case of these word-gymnasts to have heard them once is amply sufficient. For what can a man desire to learn or to imitate in them? What is he to think of their souls, when their speech is sent into the charge in utter disorder, and cannot be kept in hand? Just as, when you run down hill, you cannot stop at the point where you had decided to stop, but your steps are carried along by the momentum of your body and are borne beyond the place where you wished to halt; so this speed of speech has no control over itself, nor is it seemly for philosophy; since philosophy should carefully place her words, not fling them out, and should proceed step by step.

"What then?" you say; "should not philosophy sometimes take a loftier tone?" Of course she should; but dignity of character should be preserved, and this is stripped away by such violent and excessive force. Let philosophy possess great forces, but kept well under control; let her stream flow unceasingly, but never become a torrent. And I should hardly allow even to an orator a rapidity of speech like this, which cannot be called back, which goes lawlessly ahead; for how could it be followed by jurors, who are often inexperienced and untrained? Even when the orator is carried away by his desire to show off his powers, or by uncontrollable emotion, even then he should not quicken his pace and heap up words to an extent greater than the ear can endure.

You will be acting rightly, therefore, if you do not regard those men who seek how much they may say, rather than how they shall say it, and if for yourself you choose, provided a choice must be made, to speak as Publius Vinicius the stammerer does. When Asellius was asked how Vinicius spoke, he replied: "Gradually"! (It was a remark of Geminus Varius, by the way: "I don't see how you can call that man 'eloquent'; why, he can't get out three words together.") Why, then, should you not choose to speak as Vinicius does? Though of course some wag may cross your path, like the person who said, when Vinicius was dragging out his words one by one, as if he were dictating and not speaking. "Say, haven't you anything to say?" And yet that were the better choice, for the rapidity of Quintus Haterius, the most famous orator of his age, is, in my opinion, to be avoided by a man of sense. Haterius never hesitated, never paused; he made only one start, and only one stop.

However, I suppose that certain styles of speech are more or less suitable to nations also; in a Greek you can put up with the unrestrained style, but we Romans, even when writing, have become accustomed to separate our words. And our compatriot Cicero, with whom Roman oratory sprang into prominence, was also a slow pacer. The Roman language is more inclined to take stock of itself, to weigh, and to offer something worth weighing. Fabianius, a man noteworthy because of his life, his knowledge, and, less important than either of these, his eloquence also, used to discuss a subject with dispatch rather than with haste; hence you might call it ease rather than speed. I approve this quality in the wise man; but I do not demand it; only let his speech proceed unhampered, though I prefer that it should be deliberately uttered rather than spouted.

However, I have this further reason for frightening you away from the latter malady, namely, that you could only be successful in practising this style by losing your sense of modesty; you would have to rub all shame from your countenance, and refuse to hear yourself speak. For that heedless flow will carry with it many expressions which you would wish to criticize. And, I repeat, you could not attain it and at the same time preserve your sense of shame. Moreover, you would need to practise every day, and transfer your attention from subject matter to words. But words, even if they came to you readily and flowed without any exertion on your part, yet would have to be kept under control. For just as a less ostentatious gait becomes a philosopher, so does a restrained style of speech, far removed from boldness. Therefore, the ultimate kernel of my remarks is this: I bid you be slow of speech. Farewell

Letter XLI - On the God within Us

You are doing an excellent thing, one which will be wholesome for you, if, as you write me, you are persisting in your effort to attain sound understanding; it is foolish to pray for this when you can acquire it from yourself. We do not need to uplift our hands towards heaven, or to beg the keeper of a temple to let us approach his idol's ear, as if in this way our prayers were more likely to be heard. God is near you, he is with you, he is within you. This is what I mean, Lucilius: a holy spirit indwells within us, one who marks our good and bad deeds, and is our guardian. As we treat this spirit, so are we treated by it. Indeed, no man can be good without the help of God. Can one rise superior to fortune unless God helps him to rise? He it is that gives noble and upright counsel. In each good man

A god doth dwell, but what god know we not.

If ever you have come upon a grove that is full of ancient trees which have grown to an unusual height, shutting out a view of the sky by a veil of pleached and intertwining branches, then the loftiness of the forest, the seclusion of the spot, and your marvel at the thick unbroken shade in the midst of the open spaces, will prove to you the presence of deity. Or if a cave, made by the deep crumbling of the rocks, holds up a mountain on its arch, a place not built with hands but hollowed out into such spaciousness by natural causes, your soul will be deeply moved by a certain intimation of the existence of God. We worship the sources of mighty rivers; we erect altars at places where great streams burst suddenly from hidden sources; we adore springs of hot water as divine, and consecrate certain pools because of their dark waters or their immeasurable depth. If you see a man who is unterrified in the midst of dangers, untouched by desires, happy in adversity, peaceful amid the storm, who looks down upon men from a higher plane, and views the gods on a footing of equality, will not a feeling of reverence for him steal over you, will you not say: "This quality is too great and too lofty to be regarded as resembling this petty body in which it dwells? A divine power has descended upon that man." When a soul rises superior to other souls, when it is under control, when it passes through every experience as if it were of small account, when it smiles at our fears and at our prayers, it is stirred by a force from heaven. A thing like this cannot stand upright unless it be propped by the divine. Therefore, a greater part of it abides in that place from whence it came down to earth. Just as the rays of the sun do indeed touch the earth, but still abide at the source from which they are sent; even so the great and hallowed soul, which has come down in order that we may have a nearer knowledge of divinity, does indeed associate with us, but still cleaves to its origin; on that source it depends, thither it turns its gaze and strives to go, and it concerns itself with our doings only as a being superior to ourselves.

What, then, is such a soul? One which is resplendent with no external good, but only with its own. For what is more foolish than to praise in a man the qualities which come from without? And what is more insane than to marvel at characteristics which may at the next instant be passed on to someone else? A golden bit does not make a better horse. The lion with gilded mane, in process of being trained and forced by weariness to endure the decoration, is sent into the arena in quite a different way from the wild lion whose spirit is unbroken; the latter, indeed, bold in his attack, as nature wished him to be, impressive because of his wild appearance, – and it is his glory that none can look upon him without fear, – is favoured in preference to the other lion, that languid and gilded brute.

No man ought to glory except in that which is his own. We praise a vine if it makes the shoots teem with increase, if by its weight it bends to the ground the very poles which hold its fruit; would any man prefer to this vine one from which golden grapes and golden leaves hang down? In a vine the virtue peculiarly its own is fertility; in man also we should praise that which is his own. Suppose that he has a retinue of comely slaves and a beautiful house, that his farm is large and large his income; none of these things is in the man himself; they are all on the outside. Praise the quality in him which cannot be given or snatched away, that which is the peculiar property of the man. Do you ask what this is? It is soul, and reason brought to perfection in the soul. For man is a reasoning animal. Therefore, man's highest good is attained, if he has fulfilled the good for which nature designed him at birth. And what is it which this reason demands of him? The easiest thing in the world, – to live in accordance with his own nature. But this is turned into a hard task by the general madness of mankind; we push one another into vice. And how can a man be recalled to salvation, when he has none to restrain him, and all mankind to urge him on? Farewell.

Letter XLII - On Values

Has that friend of yours already made you believe that he is a good man? And yet it is impossible in so short a time for one either to become good or be known as such. Do you know what kind of man I now mean when I speak of "a good man"? I mean one of the second grade, like your friend. For one of the first class perhaps springs into existence, like the phoenix, only once in five hundred years. And it is not surprising, either, that greatness develops only at long intervals; Fortune often brings into being commonplace powers, which are born to please the mob; but she holds up for our approval that which is extraordinary by the very fact that she makes it rare.

This man, however, of whom you spoke, is still far from the state which he professes to have reached. And if he knew what it meant to be "a good man," he would not yet believe himself such; perhaps he would even despair of his ability to become good. "But," you say, "he thinks ill of evil men." Well, so do evil men themselves; and there is no worse penalty for vice than the fact that it is dissatisfied with itself and all its fellows. "But he hates those who make an ungoverned use of great power suddenly acquired." I retort that he will do the same thing as soon as he acquires the same powers. In the case of many men, their vices, being powerless, escape notice; although, as soon as the persons in question have become satisfied with their own strength, the vices will be no less daring than those which prosperity has already disclosed. These men simply lack the means whereby they may unfold their wickedness. Similarly, one can handle even a poisonous snake while it is stiff with cold; the poison is not lacking; it is merely numbed into inaction. In the case of many men, their cruelty, ambition, and indulgence only lack the favour of Fortune to make them dare crimes that would match the worst. That their wishes are the same you will in a moment discover, in this way: give them the power equal to their wishes.

Do you remember how, when you declared that a certain person was under your influence, I pronounced him fickle and a bird of passage, and said that you held him not by the foot but merely by a wing? Was I mistaken? You grasped him only by a feather; he left it in your hands and escaped. You know what an exhibition he afterwards made of himself before you, how many of the things he attempted were to recoil upon his own head. He did not see that in endangering others he was tottering to his own downfall. He did not reflect how burdensome were the objects which he was bent upon attaining, even if they were not superfluous.

Therefore, with regard to the objects which we pursue, and for which we strive with great effort, we should note this truth; either there is nothing desirable in them, or the undesirable is preponderant. Some objects are superfluous; others are not worth the price we pay for them. But we do not see this clearly, and we regard things as free gifts when they really cost us very dear. Our stupidity may be clearly proved by the fact that we hold that "buying" refers only to the objects for which we pay cash, and we regard as free gifts the things for which we spend our very selves. These we should refuse to buy, if we were compelled to give in payment for them our houses or some attractive and profitable estate; but we are eager to attain them at the cost of anxiety, of danger, and of lost honour, personal freedom, and time; so true it is that each man regards nothing as cheaper than himself.

Let us therefore act, in all our plans and conduct, just as we are accustomed to act whenever we approach a huckster who has certain wares for sale; let us see how much we must pay for that which we crave. Very often the things that cost nothing cost us the most heavily; I can show you many objects the quest and acquisition of which have wrested freedom from our hands. We should belong to ourselves, if only these things did not belong to us.

I would therefore have you reflect thus, not only when it is a question of gain, but also when it is a question of loss. "This object is bound to perish." Yes, it was a mere extra; you will live without it just as easily as you have lived before. If you have possessed it for a long time, you lose it after you have had your fill of it; if you have not possessed it long, then you lose it before you have become wedded to it. "You will have less money." Yes, and less trouble. "Less influence." Yes, and less envy. Look about you and note the things that drive us mad, which we lose with a flood of tears; you will perceive that it is not the loss that troubles us with reference to these things, but a notion of loss. No one feels that they have been lost, but his mind tells him that it has been so. He that owns himself has lost nothing. But how few men are blessed with ownership of self! Farewell.

Letter XLIII - On the Relativity of Fame

Do you ask how the news reached me, and who informed me, that you were entertaining this idea, of which you had said nothing to a single soul? It was that most knowing of persons, – gossip. "What," you say, "am I such a great personage that I can stir up gossip?" Now there is no reason why you should measure yourself according to this part of the world; have regard only to the place where you are dwelling. Any point which rises above adjacent points is great, at the spot where it rises. For greatness is not absolute; comparison increases it or lessens it. A ship which looms large in the river seems tiny when on the ocean. A rudder which is large for one vessel, is small for another.

So you in your province are really of importance, though you scorn yourself. Men are asking what you do, how you dine, and how you sleep, and they find out, too; hence there is all the more reason for your living circumspectly. Do not, however, deem yourself truly happy until you find that you can live before men's eyes, until your walls protect but do not hide you; although we are apt to believe that these walls surround us, not to enable us to live more safely, but that we may sin more secretly. I shall mention a fact by which you may weigh the worth of a man's character: you will scarcely find anyone who can live with his door wide open. It is our conscience, not our pride, that has put doorkeepers at our doors; we live in such a fashion that being suddenly disclosed to view is equivalent to being caught in the act. What profits it, however, to hide ourselves away, and to avoid the eyes and ears of men? A good conscience welcomes the crowd, but a bad conscience, even in solitude, is disturbed and troubled. If your deeds are honourable, let everybody know them; if base, what matters it that no one knows them, as long as you yourself know them? How wretched you are if you despise such a witness! Farewell.

Letter XLIV - On Philosophy and Pedigrees

You are again insisting to me that you are a nobody, and saying that nature in the first place, and fortune in the second, have treated you too scurvily, and this in spite of the fact that you have it in your power to separate yourself from the crowd and rise to the highest human happiness! If there is any good in philosophy, it is this, – that it never looks into pedigrees. All men, if traced back to their original source, spring from the gods. You are a Roman knight, and your persistent work promoted you to this class; yet surely there are many to whom the fourteen rows are barred; the senate-chamber is not open to all; the army, too, is scrupulous in choosing those whom it admits to toil and danger. But a noble mind is free to all men; according to this test, we may all gain distinction. Philosophy neither rejects nor selects anyone; its light shines for all. Socrates was no aristocrat. Cleanthes worked at a well and served as a hired man watering a garden. Philosophy did not find Plato already a nobleman; it made him one. Why then should you despair of becoming able to rank with men like these? They are all your ancestors, if you conduct yourself in a manner worthy of them; and you will do so if you convince yourself at the outset that no man outdoes you in real nobility. We have all had the same number of forefathers; there is no man whose first beginning does not transcend memory. Plato says: "Every king springs from a race of slaves, and every slave has had kings among his ancestors." The flight of time, with its vicissitudes, has jumbled all such things together, and Fortune has turned them upside down. Then who is well-born? He who is by nature well fitted for virtue. That is the one point to be considered; otherwise, if you hark back to antiquity, every one traces back to a date before which there is nothing. From the earliest beginnings of the universe to the present time, we have been led forward out of origins that were alternately illustrious and ignoble. A hall full of smoke-begrimed busts does not make the nobleman. No past life has been lived to lend us glory, and that which has existed before us is not ours; the soul alone renders us noble, and it may rise superior to Fortune out of any earlier condition, no matter what that condition has been.

Suppose, then, that you were not that Roman knight, but a freedman, you might nevertheless by your own efforts come to be the only free man amid a throng of gentlemen. "How?" you ask. Simply by distinguishing between good and bad things without patterning your opinion from the populace. You should look, not to the source from which these things come, but to the goal towards which they tend. If there is anything that can make life happy, it is good on its own merits; for it cannot degenerate into evil. Where, then, lies the mistake, since all men crave the happy life? It is that they regard the means for producing happiness as happiness itself, and, while seeking happiness, they are really fleeing from it. For although the sum and substance of the happy life is unalloyed freedom from care, and though the secret of such freedom is unshaken confidence, yet men gather together that which causes worry, and, while travelling life's treacherous road, not only have burdens to bear, but even draw burdens to themselves; hence they recede farther and farther from the achievement of that which they seek, and the more effort they expend, the more they hinder themselves and are set back. This is what happens when you hurry through a maze; the faster you go, the worse you are entangled. Farewell.

Letter XLV - On Sophistical Argumentation

You complain that in your part of the world there is a scant supply of books. But it is quality, rather than quantity, that matters; a limited list of reading benefits; a varied assortment serves only for delight. He who would arrive at the appointed end must follow a single road and not wander through many ways. What you suggest is not travelling; it is mere tramping.

"But," you say, "I should rather have you give me advice than books."

Still, I am ready to send you all the books I have, to ransack the whole storehouse. If it were possible, I should join you there myself; and were it not for the hope that you will soon complete your term of office, I should have imposed upon myself this old man's journey; no Scylla or Charybdis or their storied straits could have frightened me away. I should not only have crossed over, but should have been willing to swim over those waters, provided that I could greet you and judge in your presence how much you had grown in spirit.

Your desire, however, that I should dispatch to you my own writings does not make me think myself learned, any more than a request for my picture would flatter my beauty. I know that it is due to your charity rather than to your judgment. And even if it is the result of judgment, it was charity that forced the judgment upon you. But whatever the quality of my works may be, read them as if I were still seeking, and were not aware of, the truth, and were seeking it obstinately, too. For I have sold myself to no man; I bear the name of no master. I give much credit to the judgment of great men; but I claim something also for my own. For these men, too, have left to us, not positive discoveries, but problems whose solution is still to be sought. They might perhaps have discovered the essentials, had they not sought the superfluous also. They lost much time in quibbling about words and in sophistical argumentation; all that sort of thing exercises the wit to no purpose. We tie knots and bind up words in double meanings, and then try to untie them.

Have we leisure enough for this? Do we already know how to live, or die? We should rather proceed with our whole souls towards the point where it is our duty to take heed lest things, as well as words, deceive us. Why, pray, do you discriminate between similar words, when nobody is ever deceived by them except during the discussion? It is things that lead us astray: it is between things that you must discriminate. We embrace evil instead of good; we pray for something opposite to that which we have prayed for in the past. Our prayers clash with our prayers, our plans with our plans. How closely flattery resembles friendship! It not only apes friendship, but outdoes it, passing it in the race; with wide-open and indulgent ears it is welcomed and sinks to the depths of the heart, and it is pleasing precisely wherein it does harm. Show me how I may be able to see through this resemblance! An enemy comes to me full of compliments, in the guise of a friend. Vices creep into our hearts under the name of virtues, rashness lurks beneath the appellation of bravery, moderation is called sluggishness, and the coward is regarded as prudent; there is great danger if we go astray in these matters. So stamp them with special labels.

Then, too, the man who is asked whether he has horns on his head is not such a fool as to feel for them on his forehead, nor again so silly or dense that you can persuade him by means of argumentation, no matter how subtle, that he does not know the facts. Such quibbles are just as harmlessly deceptive as the juggler's cup and dice, in which it is the very trickery that pleases me. But show me how the trick is done, and I have lost my interest therein. And I hold the same opinion about these tricky word-plays; for by what other name can one call such sophistries? Not to know them does no harm, and mastering them does no good. At any rate, if you wish to sift doubtful meanings of this kind, teach us that the happy man is not he whom the crowd deems happy, namely, he into whose coffers mighty sums have flowed, but he whose possessions are all in his soul, who is upright and exalted, who spurns inconstancy, who sees no man with whom he wishes to change places, who rates men only at their value as men, who takes Nature for his teacher, conforming to her laws and living as she commands, whom no violence can deprive of his possessions, who turns evil into good, is unerring in judgment, unshaken, unafraid, who may be moved by force but never moved to distraction, whom Fortune when she hurls at him with all her might the deadliest missile in her armoury, may graze, though rarely, but never wound. For Fortune's other missiles, with which she vanquishes mankind in general, rebound from such a one, like hail which rattles on the roof with no harm to the dweller therein, and then melts away.

Why do you bore me with that which you yourself call the "liar fallacy,"about which so many books have been written? Come now, suppose that my whole life is a lie; prove that to be wrong and, if you are sharp enough, bring that back to the truth. At present it holds things to be essential of which the greater part is superfluous. And even that which is not superfluous is of no significance in respect to its power of making one fortunate and blest. For if a thing be necessary, it does not follow that it is a good. Else we degrade the meaning of "good," if we apply that name to bread and barley-porridge and other commodities without which we cannot live. The good must in every case be necessary; but that which is necessary is not in every case a good, since certain very paltry things are indeed necessary. No one is to such an extent ignorant of the noble meaning of the word "good," as to debase it to the level of these humdrum utilities.

What, then? Shall you not rather transfer your efforts to making it clear to all men that the search for the superfluous means a great outlay of time, and that many have gone through life merely accumulating the instruments of life? Consider individuals, survey men in general; there is none whose life does not look forward to the morrow. "What harm is there in this," you ask? Infinite harm; for such persons do not live, but are preparing to live. They postpone everything. Even if we paid strict attention, life would soon get ahead of us; but as we are now, life finds us lingering and passes us by as if it belonged to another, and though it ends on the final day, it perishes every day.

But I must not exceed the bounds of a letter, which ought not to fill the reader's left hand. So I shall postpone to another day our case against the hair-splitters, those over-subtle fellows who make argumentation supreme instead of subordinate. Farewell.

Letter XLVI - On a New Book by Lucilius

I received the book of yours which you promised me. I opened it hastily with the idea of glancing over it at leisure; for I meant only to taste the volume. But by its own charm the book coaxed me into traversing it more at length.

You may understand from this fact how eloquent it was; for it seemed to be written in the smooth style, and yet did not resemble your handiwork or mine, but at first sight might have been ascribed to Titus Livius or to Epicurus. Moreover, I was so impressed and carried along by its charm that I finished it without any postponement. The sunlight called to me, hunger warned, and clouds were lowering; but I absorbed the book from beginning to end.

I was not merely pleased; I rejoiced. So full of wit and spirit it was! I should have added "force," had the book contained moments of repose, or had it risen to energy only at intervals. But I found that there was no burst of force, but an even flow, a style that was vigorous and chaste. Nevertheless I noticed from time to time your sweetness, and here and there that mildness of yours. Your style is lofty and noble; I want you to keep to this manner and this direction. Your subject also contributed something; for this reason you should choose productive topics, which will lay hold of the mind and arouse it.

I shall discuss the book more fully after a second perusal; meantime, my judgment is somewhat unsettled, just as if I had heard it read aloud, and had not read it myself. You must allow me to examine it also. You need not be afraid; you shall hear the truth. Lucky fellow, to offer a man no opportunity to tell you lies at such long range! Unless perhaps, even now, when excuses for lying are taken away, custom serves as an excuse for our telling each other lies! Farewell.

Letter XLVII - On Master and Slave

I am glad to learn, through those who come from you, that you live on friendly terms with your slaves. This befits a sensible and well-educated man like yourself. "They are slaves," people declare. Nay, rather they are men. "Slaves!" No, comrades. "Slaves!" No, they are unpretentious friends. "Slaves!" No, they are our fellow-slaves, if one reflects that Fortune has equal rights over slaves and free men alike.

That is why I smile at those who think it degrading for a man to dine with his slave. But why should they think it degrading? It is only because purse-proud etiquette surrounds a householder at his dinner with a mob of standing slaves. The master eats more than he can hold, and with monstrous greed loads his belly until it is stretched and at length ceases to do the work of a belly; so that he is at greater pains to discharge all the food than he was to stuff it down. All this time the poor slaves may not move their lips, even to speak. The slightest murmur is repressed by the rod; even a chance sound, – a cough, a sneeze, or a hiccup, – is visited with the lash. There is a grievous penalty for the slightest breach of silence. All night long they must stand about, hungry and dumb.

The result of it all is that these slaves, who may not talk in their master's presence, talk about their master. But the slaves of former days, who were permitted to converse not only in their master's presence, but actually with him, whose mouths were not stitched up tight, were ready to bare their necks for their master, to bring upon their own heads any danger that threatened him; they spoke at the feast, but kept silence during torture. Finally, the saying, in allusion to this same high-handed treatment, becomes current: "As many enemies as you have slaves." They are not enemies when we acquire them; we make them enemies.

I shall pass over other cruel and inhuman conduct towards them; for we maltreat them, not as if they were men, but as if they were beasts of burden. When we recline at a banquet, one slave mops up the disgorged food, another crouches beneath the table and gathers up the left-overs of the tipsy guests. Another carves the priceless game birds; with unerring strokes and skilled hand he cuts choice morsels along the breast or the rump. Hapless fellow, to live only for the purpose of cutting fat capons correctly – unless, indeed, the other man is still more unhappy than he, who teaches this art for pleasure's sake, rather than he who learns it because he must. Another, who serves the wine, must dress like a woman and wrestle with his advancing years; he cannot get away from his boyhood; he is dragged back to it; and though he has already acquired a soldier's figure, he is kept beardless by having his hair smoothed away or plucked out by the roots, and he must remain awake throughout the night, dividing his time between his master's drunkenness and his lust; in the chamber he must be a man, at the feast a boy. Another, whose duty it is to put a valuation on the guests, must stick to his task, poor fellow, and watch to see whose flattery and whose immodesty, whether of appetite or of language, is to get them an invitation for to-morrow. Think also of the poor purveyors of food, who note their masters' tastes with delicate skill, who know what special flavours will sharpen their appetite, what will please their eyes, what new combinations will rouse their cloyed stomachs, what food will excite their loathing through sheer satiety, and what will stir them to hunger on that particular day. With slaves like these the master cannot bear to dine; he would think it beneath his dignity to associate with his slave at the same table! Heaven forfend!

But how many masters is he creating in these very men! I have seen standing in the line, before the door of Callistus, the former master, of Callistus; I have seen the master himself shut out while others were welcomed, – the master who once fastened the "For Sale" ticket on Callistus and put him in the market along with the good-for-nothing slaves. But he has been paid off by that slave who was shuffled into the first lot of those on whom the crier practises his lungs; the slave, too, in his turn has cut his name from the list and in his turn has adjudged him unfit to enter his house. The master sold Callistus, but how much has Callistus made his master pay for!

Kindly remember that he whom you call your slave sprang from the same stock, is smiled upon by the same skies, and on equal terms with yourself breathes, lives, and dies. It is just as possible for you to see in him a free-born man as for him to see in you a slave. As a result of the massacres in Marius's day, many a man of distinguished birth, who was taking the first steps toward senatorial rank by service in the army, was humbled by fortune, one becoming a shepherd, another a caretaker of a country cottage. Despise, then, if you dare, those to whose estate you may at any time descend, even when you are despising them.

I do not wish to involve myself in too large a question, and to discuss the treatment of slaves, towards whom we Romans are excessively haughty, cruel, and insulting. But this is the kernel of my advice: Treat your inferiors as you would be treated by your betters. And as often as you reflect how much power you have over a slave, remember that your master has just as much power over you. "But I have no master," you say. You are still young; perhaps you will have one. Do you not know at what age Hecuba entered captivity, or Croesus, or the mother of Darius, or Plato, or Diogenes?

Associate with your slave on kindly, even on affable, terms; let him talk with you, plan with you, live with you. I know that at this point all the exquisites will cry out against me in a body; they will say: "There is nothing more debasing, more disgraceful, than this." But these are the very persons whom I sometimes surprise kissing the hands of other men's slaves. Do you not see even this, how our ancestors removed from masters everything invidious, and from slaves everything insulting? They called the master "father of the household," and the slaves "members of the household," a custom which still holds in the mime. They established a holiday on which masters and slaves should eat together, – not as the only day for this custom, but as obligatory on that day in any case. They allowed the slaves to attain honours in the household and to pronounce judgment; they held that a household was a miniature commonwealth.

"Do you mean to say," comes the retort, "that I must seat all my slaves at my own table?" No, not any more than that you should invite all free men to it. You are mistaken if you think that I would bar from my table certain slaves whose duties are more humble, as, for example, yonder muleteer or yonder herdsman; I propose to value them according to their character, and not according to their duties. Each man acquires his character for himself, but accident assigns his duties. Invite some to your table because they deserve the honor, and others that they may come to deserve it. For if there is any slavish quality in them as the result of their low associations, it will be shaken off by intercourse with men of gentler breeding. You need not, my dear Lucilius, hunt for friends only in the forum or in the Senate-house; if you are careful and attentive, you will find them at home also. Good material often stands idle for want of an artist; make the experiment, and you will find it so. As he is a fool who, when purchasing a horse, does not consider the animal's points, but merely his saddle and bridle; so he is doubly a fool who values a man from his clothes or from his rank, which indeed is only a robe that clothes us.

"He is a slave." His soul, however, may be that of a freeman. "He is a slave." But shall that stand in his way? Show me a man who is not a slave; one is a slave to lust, another to greed, another to ambition, and all men are slaves to fear. I will name you an ex-consul who is slave to an old hag, a millionaire who is slave to a serving-maid; I will show you youths of the noblest birth in serfdom to pantomime players! No servitude is more disgraceful than that which is self-imposed.

You should therefore not be deterred by these finicky persons from showing yourself to your slaves as an affable person and not proudly superior to them; they ought to respect you rather than fear you. Some may maintain that I am now offering the liberty-cap to slaves in general and toppling down lords from their high estate, because I bid slaves respect their masters instead of fearing them. They say: "This is what he plainly means: slaves are to pay respect as if they were clients or early-morning callers!" Anyone who holds this opinion forgets that what is enough for a god cannot be too little for a master. Respect means love, and love and fear cannot be mingled. So I hold that you are entirely right in not wishing to be feared by your slaves, and in lashing them merely with the tongue; only dumb animals need the thong.

That which annoys us does not necessarily injure us; but we are driven into wild rage by our luxurious lives, so that whatever does not answer our whims arouses our anger. We don the temper of kings. For they, too, forgetful alike of their own strength and of other men's weakness, grow white-hot with rage, as if they had received an injury, when they are entirely protected from danger of such injury by their exalted station. They are not unaware that this is true, but by finding fault they seize upon opportunities to do harm; they insist that they have received injuries, in order that they may inflict them.

I do not wish to delay you longer; for you need no exhortation. This, among other things, is a mark of good character: it forms its own judgments and abides by them; but badness is fickle and frequently changing, not for the better, but for something different. Farewell.

Letter XLVIII - On Quibbling as Unworthy of the Philosopher

In answer to the letter which you wrote me while travelling, – a letter as long as the journey itself, – I shall reply later. I ought to go into retirement, and consider what sort of advice I should give you. For you yourself, who consult me, also reflected for a long time whether to do so; how much more, then, should I myself reflect, since more deliberation is necessary in settling than in propounding a problem! And this is particularly true when one thing is advantageous to you and another to me. Am I speaking again in the guise of an Epicurean? But the fact is, the same thing is advantageous to me which is advantageous to you; for I am not your friend unless whatever is at issue concerning you is my concern also. Friendship produces between us a partnership in all our interests. There is no such thing as good or bad fortune for the individual; we live in common. And no one can live happily who has regard to himself alone and transforms everything into a question of his own utility; you must live for your neighbour, if you would live for yourself. This fellowship, maintained with scrupulous care, which makes us mingle as men with our fellow-men and holds that the human race have certain rights in common, is also of great help in cherishing the more intimate fellowship which is based on friendship, concerning which I began to speak above. For he that has much in common with a fellow-man will have all things in common with a friend.

And on this point, my excellent Lucilius, I should like to have those subtle dialecticians of yours advise me how I ought to help a friend, or how a fellow man, rather than tell me in how many ways the word "friend" is used, and how many meanings the word "man" possesses. Lo, Wisdom and Folly are taking opposite sides. Which shall I join? Which party would you have me follow? On that side, "man" is the equivalent of "friend"; on the other side, "friend" is not the equivalent of "man." The one wants a friend for his own advantage; the other wants to make himself an advantage to his friend. What you have to offer me is nothing but distortion of words and splitting of syllables. It is clear that unless I can devise some very tricky premises and by false deductions tack on to them a fallacy which springs from the truth, I shall not be able to distinguish between what is desirable and what is to be avoided! I am ashamed! Old men as we are, dealing with a problem so serious, we make play of it!

"'Mouse' is a syllable. Now a mouse eats its cheese; therefore, a syllable eats cheese." Suppose now that I cannot solve this problem; see what peril hangs over my head as a result of such ignorance! What a scrape I shall be in! Without doubt I must beware, or some day I shall be catching syllables in a mousetrap, or, if I grow careless, a book may devour my cheese! Unless, perhaps, the following syllogism is shrewder still: "'Mouse' is a syllable. Now a syllable does not eat cheese. Therefore a mouse does not eat cheese." What childish nonsense! Do we knit our brows over this sort of problem? Do we let our beards grow long for this reason? Is this the matter which we teach with sour and pale faces?

Would you really know what philosophy offers to humanity? Philosophy offers counsel. Death calls away one man, and poverty chafes another; a third is worried either by his neighbour's wealth or by his own. So-and-so is afraid of bad luck; another desires to get away from his own good fortune. Some are ill-treated by men, others by the gods. Why, then, do you frame for me such games as these? It is no occasion for jest; you are retained as counsel for unhappy mankind. You have promised to help those in peril by sea, those in captivity, the sick and the needy, and those whose heads are under the poised axe. Whither are you straying? What are you doing?

This friend, in whose company you are jesting, is in fear. Help him, and take the noose from about his neck. Men are stretching out imploring hands to you on all sides; lives ruined and in danger of ruin are begging for some assistance; men's hopes, men's resources, depend upon you. They ask that you deliver them from all their restlessness, that you reveal to them, scattered and wandering as they are, the clear light of truth. Tell them what nature has made necessary, and what superfluous; tell them how simple are the laws that she has laid down, how pleasant and unimpeded life is for those who follow these laws, but how bitter and perplexed it is for those who have put their trust in opinion rather than in nature.

I should deem your games of logic to be of some avail in relieving men's burdens, if you could first show me what part of these burdens they will relieve. What among these games of yours banishes lust? Or controls it? Would that I could say that they were merely of no profit! They are positively harmful. I can make it perfectly clear to you whenever you wish, that a noble spirit when involved in such subtleties is impaired and weakened. I am ashamed to say what weapons they supply to men who are destined to go to war with fortune, and how poorly they equip them! Is this the path to the greatest good?

Is philosophy to proceed by such claptrap and by quibbles which would be a disgrace and a reproach even for expounders of the law? For what else is it that you men are doing, when you deliberately ensnare the person to whom you are putting questions, than making it appear that the man has lost his case on a technical error? But just as the judge can reinstate those who have lost a suit in this way, so philosophy has reinstated these victims of quibbling to their former condition. Why do you men abandon your mighty promises, and, after having assured me in high-sounding language that you will permit the glitter of gold to dazzle my eyesight no more than the gleam of the sword, and that I shall, with mighty steadfastness, spurn both that which all men crave and that which all men fear, why do you descend to the ABC's of scholastic pedants? What is your answer?

Is this the path to heaven?

For that is exactly what philosophy promises to me, that I shall be made equal to God. For this I have been summoned, for this purpose have I come. Philosophy, keep your promise!

Therefore, my dear Lucilius, withdraw yourself as far as possible from these exceptions and objections of so-called philosophers. Frankness, and simplicity beseem true goodness. Even if there were many years left to you, you would have had to spend them frugally in order to have enough for the necessary things; but as it is, when your time is so scant, what madness it is to learn superfluous things! Farewell.

Letter XLIX - On the Shortness of Life

A man is indeed lazy and careless, my dear Lucilius, if he is reminded of a friend only by seeing some landscape which stirs the memory; and yet there are times when the old familiar haunts stir up a sense of loss that has been stored away in the soul, not bringing back dead memories, but rousing them from their dormant state, just as the sight of a lost friend's favourite slave, or his cloak, or his house, renews the mourner's grief, even though it has been softened by time.

Now, lo and behold, Campania, and especially Naples and your beloved Pompeii, struck me, when I viewed them, with a wonderfully fresh sense of longing for you. You stand in full view before my eyes. I am on the point of parting from you. I see you choking down your tears and resisting without success the emotions that well up at the very moment when you try to check them. I seem to have lost you but a moment ago. For what is not "but a moment ago" when one begins to use the memory? It was but a moment ago that I sat, as a lad, in the school of the philosopher Sotion, but a moment ago that I began to plead in the courts, but a moment ago that I lost the desire to plead, but a moment ago that I lost the ability. Infinitely swift is the flight of time, as those see more clearly who are looking backwards. For when we are intent on the present, we do not notice it, so gentle is the passage of time's headlong flight. Do you ask the reason for this? All past time is in the same place; it all presents the same aspect to us, it lies together. Everything slips into the same abyss. Besides, an event which in its entirety is of brief compass cannot contain long intervals. The time which we spend in living is but a point, nay, even less than a point. But this point of time, infinitesimal as it is, nature has mocked by making it seem outwardly of longer duration; she has taken one portion thereof and made it infancy, another childhood, another youth, another the gradual slope, so to speak, from youth to old age, and old age itself is still another. How many steps for how short a climb! It was but a moment ago that I saw you off on your journey; and yet this "moment ago" makes up a goodly share of our existence, which is so brief, we should reflect, that it will soon come to an end altogether. In other years time did not seem to me to go so swiftly; now, it seems fast beyond belief, perhaps, because I feel that the finish-line is moving closer to me, or it may be that I have begun to take heed and reckon up my losses.

For this reason I am all the more angry that some men claim the major portion of this time for superfluous things, – time which, no matter how carefully it is guarded, cannot suffice even for necessary things. Cicero declared that if the number of his days were doubled, he should not have time to read the lyric poets. And you may rate the dialecticians in the same class; but they are foolish in a more melancholy way. The lyric poets are avowedly frivolous; but the dialecticians believe that they are themselves engaged upon serious business. I do not deny that one must cast a glance at dialectic; but it ought to be a mere glance, a sort of greeting from the threshold, merely that one may not be deceived, or judge these pursuits to contain any hidden matters of great worth.

Why do you torment yourself and lose weight over some problem which it is more clever to have scorned than to solve? When a soldier is undisturbed and travelling at his ease, he can hunt for trifles along his way; but when the enemy is closing in on the rear, and a command is given to quicken the pace, necessity makes him throw away everything which he picked up in moments of peace and leisure. I have no time to investigate disputed inflections of words, or to try my cunning upon them.

> Behold the gathering clans, the fast-shut gates,
> And weapons whetted ready for the war.

I need a stout heart to hear without flinching this din of battle which sounds round about. And all would rightly think me mad if, when graybeards and women were heaping up rocks for the fortifications, when the armour-clad youths inside the gates were awaiting, or even demanding, the order for a sally, when the spears of the foemen were quivering in our gates and the very ground was rocking with mines and subterranean passages, – I say, they would rightly think me mad if I were to sit idle, putting such petty posers as this: "What you have not lost, you have. But you have not lost any horns. Therefore, you have horns," or other tricks constructed after the model of this piece of sheer silliness. And yet I may well seem in your eyes no less mad, if I spend my energies on that sort of thing; for even now I am in a state of siege.

And yet, in the former case it would be merely a peril from the outside that threatened me, and a wall that sundered me from the foe; as it is now, death-dealing perils are in my very presence. I have no time for such nonsense; a mighty undertaking is on my hands. What am I to do? Death is on my trail, and life is fleeting away; teach me something with which to face these troubles. Bring it to pass that I shall cease trying to escape from death, and that life may cease to escape from me. Give me courage to meet hardships; make me calm in the face of the unavoidable. Relax the straitened limits of the time which is allotted me. Show me that the good in life does not depend upon life's length, but upon the use we make of it; also, that it is possible, or rather usual, for a man who has lived long to have lived too little. Say to me when I lie down to sleep: "You may not wake again!" And when I have waked: "You may not go to sleep again!" Say to me when I go forth from my house: "You may not return!" And when I return: "You may never go forth again!" You are mistaken if you think that only on an ocean voyage there is a very slight space between life and death. No, the distance between is just as narrow everywhere. It is not everywhere that death shows himself so near at hand; yet everywhere he is as near at hand.

Rid me of these shadowy terrors; then you will more easily deliver to me the instruction for which I have prepared myself. At our birth nature made us teachable, and gave us reason, not perfect, but capable of being perfected. Discuss for me justice, duty, thrift, and that twofold purity, both the purity which abstains from another's person, and that which takes care of one's own self. If you will only refuse to lead me along by-paths, I shall more easily reach the goal at which I am aiming. For, as the tragic poet says:

The language of truth is simple.

We should not, therefore, make that language intricate; since there is nothing less fitting for a soul of great endeavour than such crafty cleverness. Farewell.

Letter L - On our Blindness and its Cure

I received your letter many months after you had posted it; accordingly, I thought it useless to ask the carrier what you were busied with. He must have a particularly good memory if he can remember that! But I hope by this time you are living in such a way that I can be sure what it is you are busied with, no matter where you may be. For what else are you busied with except improving yourself every day, laying aside some error, and coming to understand that the faults which you attribute to circumstances are in yourself? We are indeed apt to ascribe certain faults to the place or to the time; but those faults will follow us, no matter how we change our place.

You know Harpaste, my wife's female clown; she has remained in my house, a burden incurred from a legacy. I particularly disapprove of these freaks; whenever I wish to enjoy the quips of a clown, I am not compelled to hunt far; I can laugh at myself. Now this clown suddenly became blind. The story sounds incredible, but I assure you that it is true: she does not know that she is blind. She keeps asking her attendant to change her quarters; she says that her apartments are too dark.

You can see clearly that that which makes us smile in the case of Harpaste happens to all the rest of us; nobody understands that he is himself greedy, or that he is covetous. Yet the blind ask for a guide, while we wander without one, saying: "I am not self-seeking; but one cannot live at Rome in any other way. I am not extravagant, but mere living in the city demands a great outlay. It is not my fault that I have a choleric disposition, or that I have not settled down to any definite scheme of life; it is due to my youth." Why do we deceive ourselves? The evil that afflicts us is not external, it is within us, situated in our very vitals; for that reason we attain soundness with all the more difficulty, because we do not know that we are diseased.

Suppose that we have begun the cure; when shall we throw off all these diseases, with all their virulence? At present, we do not even consult the physician, whose work would be easier if he were called in when the complaint was in its early stages. The tender and the inexperienced minds would follow his advice if he pointed out the right way. No man finds it difficult to return to nature, except the man who has deserted nature. We blush to receive instruction in sound sense; but, by Heaven, if we think it base to seek a teacher of this art, we should also abandon any hope that so great a good could be instilled into us by mere chance.

No, we must work. To tell the truth, even the work is not great, if only, as I said, we begin to mould and reconstruct our souls before they are hardened by sin. But I do not despair even of a hardened sinner. There is nothing that will not surrender to persistent treatment, to concentrated and careful attention; however much the timber may be bent, you can make it straight again. Heat unbends curved beams, and wood that grew naturally in another shape is fashioned artificially according to our needs. How much more easily does the soul permit itself to be shaped, pliable as it is and more yielding than any liquid! For what else is the soul than air in a certain state? And you see that air is more adaptable than any other matter, in proportion as it is rarer than any other.

There is nothing, Lucilius, to hinder you from entertaining good hopes about us, just because we are even now in the grip of evil, or because we have long been possessed thereby. There is no man to whom a good mind comes before an evil one. It is the evil mind that gets first hold on all of us. Learning virtue means unlearning vice. We should therefore proceed to the task of freeing ourselves from faults with all the more courage because, when once committed to us, the good is an everlasting possession; virtue is not unlearned. For opposites find difficulty in clinging where they do not belong, therefore they can be driven out and hustled away; but qualities that come to a place which is rightfully theirs abide faithfully. Virtue is according to nature; vice is opposed to it and hostile. But although virtues, when admitted, cannot depart and are easy to guard, yet the first steps in the approach to them are toilsome, because it is characteristic of a weak and diseased mind to fear that which is unfamiliar. The mind must, therefore, be forced to make a beginning; from then on, the medicine is not bitter; for just as soon as it is curing us it begins to give pleasure. One enjoys other cures only after health is restored, but a draught of philosophy is at the same moment wholesome and pleasant. Farewell.

Letter LI - On Baiae and Morals

Every man does the best he can, my dear Lucilius! You over there have Etna, that lofty and most celebrated mountain of Sicily; (although I cannot make out why Messala, – or was it Valgius? for I have been reading in both, – has called it "unique," inasmuch as many regions belch forth fire, not merely the lofty ones where the phenomenon is more frequent, – presumably because fire rises to the greatest possible height, – but low-lying places also.) As for myself, I do the best I can; I have had to be satisfied with Baiae; and I left it the day after I reached it; for Baiae is a place to be avoided, because, though it has certain natural advantages, luxury has claimed it for her own exclusive resort. "What then," you say, "should any place be singled out as an object of aversion?" Not at all. But just as, to the wise and upright man, one style of clothing is more suitable than another, without his having an aversion for any particular colour, but because he thinks that some colours do not befit one who has adopted the simple life; so there are places also, which the wise man or he who is on the way toward wisdom will avoid as foreign to good morals. Therefore, if he is contemplating withdrawal from the world, he will not select Canopus (although Canopus does not keep any man from living simply), nor Baiae either; for both places have begun to be resorts of vice. At Canopus luxury pampers itself to the utmost degree; at Baiae it is even more lax, as if the place itself demanded a certain amount of licence.

We ought to select abodes which are wholesome not only for the body but also for the character. Just as I do not care to live in a place of torture, neither do I care to live in a cafe. To witness persons wandering drunk along the beach, the riotous revelling of sailing parties, the lakes a-din with choral song, and all the other ways in which luxury, when it is, so to speak, released from the restraints of law not merely sins, but blazons its sins abroad, – why must I witness all this? We ought to see to it that we flee to the greatest possible distance from provocations to vice. We should toughen our minds, and remove them far from the allurements of pleasure. A single winter relaxed Hannibal's fibre; his pampering in Campania took the vigour out of that hero who had triumphed over Alpine snows. He conquered with his weapons, but was conquered by his vices. We too have a war to wage, a type of warfare in which there is allowed no rest or furlough. To be conquered, in the first place, are pleasures, which, as you see, have carried off even the sternest characters. If a man has once understood how great is the task which he has entered upon, he will see that there must be no dainty or effeminate conduct. What have I to do with those hot baths or with the sweating-room where they shut in the dry steam which is to drain your strength? Perspiration should flow only after toil.

Suppose we do what Hannibal did, – check the course of events, give up the war, and give over our bodies to be coddled. Every one would rightly blame us for our untimely sloth, a thing fraught with peril even for the victor, to say nothing of one who is only on the way to victory. And we have even less right to do this than those followers of the Carthaginian flag; for our danger is greater than theirs if we slacken, and our toil is greater than theirs even if we press ahead. Fortune is fighting against me, and I shall not carry out her commands. I refuse to submit to the yoke; nay rather, I shake off the yoke that is upon me, – an act which demands even greater courage. The soul is not to be pampered; surrendering to pleasure means also surrendering to pain, surrendering to toil, surrendering to poverty. Both ambition and anger will wish to have the same rights over me as pleasure, and I shall be torn asunder, or rather pulled to pieces, amid all these conflicting passions. I have set freedom before my eyes; and I am striving for that reward. And what is freedom, you ask? It means not being a slave to any circumstance, to any constraint, to any chance; it means compelling Fortune to enter the lists on equal terms. And on the day when I know that I have the upper hand, her power will be naught. When I have death in my own control, shall I take orders from her?

Therefore, a man occupied with such reflections should choose an austere and pure dwelling-place. The spirit is weakened by surroundings that are too pleasant, and without a doubt one's place of residence can contribute towards impairing its vigour. Animals whose hoofs are hardened on rough ground can travel any road; but when they are fattened on soft marshy meadows their hoofs are soon worn out. The bravest soldier comes from rock-ribbed regions; but the town-bred and the home-bred are sluggish in action. The hand which turns from the plough to the sword never objects to toil; but your sleek and well-dressed dandy quails at the first cloud of dust. Being trained in a rugged country strengthens the character and fits it for great undertakings. It was more honourable in Scipio to spend his exile at Liternum, than at Baiae; his downfall did not need a setting so effeminate. Those also into whose hands the rising fortunes of Rome first transferred the wealth of the state, Gaius Marius, Gnaeus Pompey, and Caesar, did indeed build villas near Baiae; but they set them on the very tops of the mountains. This seemed more soldier-like, to look down from a lofty height upon lands spread far and wide below. Note the situation, position, and type of building which they chose; you will see that they were not country-places, – they were camps. Do you suppose that Cato would ever have dwelt in a pleasure-palace, that he might count the lewd women as they sailed past, the many kinds of barges painted in all sorts of colours, the roses which were wafted about the lake, or that he might listen to the nocturnal brawls of serenaders? Would he not have preferred to remain in the shelter of a trench thrown up by his own hands to serve for a single night? Would not anyone who is a man have his slumbers broken by a war-trumpet rather than by a chorus of serenaders?

But I have been haranguing against Baiae long enough; although I never could harangue often enough against vice. Vice, Lucilius, is what I wish you to proceed against, without limit and without end. For it has neither limit nor end. If any vice rend your heart, cast it away from you; and if you cannot be rid of it in any other way, pluck out your heart also. Above all, drive pleasures from your sight. Hate them beyond all other things, for they are like the bandits whom the Egyptians call "lovers," who embrace us only to garrotte us. Farewell.

Letter LII - On Choosing our Teachers

What is this force, Lucilius, that drags us in one direction when we are aiming in another, urging us on to the exact place from which we long to withdraw? What is it that wrestles with our spirit, and does not allow us to desire anything once for all? We veer from plan to plan. None of our wishes is free, none is unqualified, none is lasting. "But it is the fool," you say, "who is inconsistent; nothing suits him for long." But how or when can we tear ourselves away from this folly? No man by himself has sufficient strength to rise above it; he needs a helping hand, and some one to extricate him.

Epicurus remarks that certain men have worked their way to the truth without any one's assistance, carving out their own passage. And he gives special praise to these, for their impulse has come from within, and they have forged to the front by themselves. Again, he says, there are others who need outside help, who will not proceed unless someone leads the way, but who will follow faithfully. Of these, he says, Metrodorus was one; this type of man is also excellent, but belongs to the second grade. We ourselves are not of that first class, either; we shall be well treated if we are admitted into the second. Nor need you despise a man who can gain salvation only with the assistance of another; the will to be saved means a great deal, too.

You will find still another class of man, – and a class not to be despised, – who can be forced and driven into righteousness, who do not need a guide as much as they require someone to encourage and, as it were, to force them along. This is the third variety. If you ask me for a man of this pattern also, Epicurus tells us that Hermarchus was such. And of the two last-named classes, he is more ready to congratulate the one, but he feels more respect for the other; for although both reached the same goal, it is a greater credit to have brought about the same result with the more difficult material upon which to work.

Suppose that two buildings have been erected, unlike as to their foundations, but equal in height and in grandeur. One is built on faultless ground, and the process of erection goes right ahead. In the other case, the foundations have exhausted the building materials, for they have been sunk into soft and shifting ground and much labour has been wasted in reaching the solid rock. As one looks at both of them, one sees clearly what progress the former has made but the larger and more difficult part of the latter is hidden. So with men's dispositions; some are pliable and easy to manage, but others have to be laboriously wrought out by hand, so to speak, and are wholly employed in the making of their own foundations. I should accordingly deem more fortunate the man who has never had any trouble with himself; but the other, I feel, has deserved better of himself, who has won a victory over the meanness of his own nature, and has not gently led himself, but has wrestled his way, to wisdom.

You may be sure that this refractory nature, which demands much toil, has been implanted in us. There are obstacles in our path; so let us fight, and call to our assistance some helpers. "Whom," you say, "shall I call upon? Shall it be this man or that?" There is another choice also open to you; you may go to the ancients; for they have the time to help you. We can get assistance not only from the living, but from those of the past. Let us choose, however, from among the living, not men who pour forth their words with the greatest glibness, turning out commonplaces and holding. as it were, their own little private exhibitions, – not these, I say, but men who teach us by their lives, men who tell us what we ought to do and then prove it by practice, who show us what we should avoid, and then are never caught doing that which they have ordered us to avoid.

Choose as a guide one whom you will admire more when you see him act than when you hear him speak. Of course I would not prevent you from listening also to those philosophers who are wont to hold public meetings and discussions, provided they appear before the people for the express purpose of improving themselves and others, and do not practise their profession for the sake of self-seeking. For what is baser than philosophy courting applause? Does the sick man praise the surgeon while he is operating? In silence and with reverent awe submit to the cure. Even though you cry applause, I shall listen to your cries as if you were groaning when your sores were touched. Do you wish to bear witness that you are attentive, that you are stirred by the grandeur of the subject? You may do this at the proper time; I shall of course allow you to pass judgment and cast a vote as to the better course. Pythagoras made his pupils keep silence for five years; do you think that they had the right on that account to break out immediately into applause?

How mad is he who leaves the lecture-room in a happy frame of mind simply because of applause from the ignorant! Why do you take pleasure in being praised by men whom you yourself cannot praise? Fabianus used to give popular talks, but his audience listened with self-control. Occasionally a loud shout of praise would burst forth, but it was prompted by the greatness of his subject, and not by the sound of oratory that slipped forth pleasantly and softly. There should be a difference between the applause of the theatre and the applause of the school; and there is a certain decency even in bestowing praise. If you mark them carefully, all acts are always significant, and you can gauge character by even the most trifling signs. The lecherous man is revealed by his gait, by a movement of the hand, sometimes by a single answer, by his touching his head with a finger, by the shifting of his eye. The scamp is shown up by his laugh; the madman by his face and general appearance. These qualities become known by certain marks; but you can tell the character of every man when you see how he gives and receives praise. The philosopher's audience, from this corner and that, stretch forth admiring hands, and sometimes the adoring crowd almost hang over the lecturer's head. But, if you really understand, that is not praise; it is merely applause. These outcries should be left for the arts which aim to please the crowd; let philosophy be worshipped in silence. Young men, indeed, must sometimes have free play to follow their impulses, but it should only be at times when they act from impulse, and when they cannot force themselves to be silent. Such praise as that gives a certain kind of encouragement to the hearers themselves, and acts as a spur to the youthful mind. But let them be roused to the matter, and not to the style; otherwise, eloquence does them harm, making them enamoured of itself, and not of the subject.

I shall postpone this topic for the present; it demands a long and special investigation, to show how the public should be addressed, what indulgences should be allowed to a speaker on a public occasion, and what should be allowed to the crowd itself in the presence of the speaker. There can be no doubt that philosophy has suffered a loss, now that she has exposed her charms for sale. But she can still be viewed in her sanctuary, if her exhibitor is a priest and not a pedlar. Farewell.

Letter LIII - On the Faults of the Spirit

You can persuade me into almost anything now, for I was recently persuaded to travel by water. We cast off when the sea was lazily smooth; the sky, to be sure, was heavy with nasty clouds, such as usually break into rain or squalls. Still, I thought that the few miles between Puteoli and your dear Parthenope might be run off in quick time, despite the uncertain and lowering sky. So, in order to get away more quickly, I made straight out to sea for Nesis, with the purpose of cutting across all the inlets. But when we were so far out that it made little difference to me whether I returned or kept on, the calm weather, which had enticed me, came to naught. The storm had not yet begun, but the ground-swell was on, and the waves kept steadily coming faster. I began to ask the pilot to put me ashore somewhere; he replied that the coast was rough and a bad place to land, and that in a storm he feared a lee shore more than anything else. But I was suffering too grievously to think of the danger, since a sluggish seasickness which brought no relief was racking me, the sort that upsets the liver without clearing it. Therefore I laid down the law to my pilot, forcing him to make for the shore, willy-nilly. When we drew near, I did not wait for things to be done in accordance with Vergil's orders, until

Prow faced seawards

or

Anchor plunged from bow

I remembered my profession as a veteran devotee of cold water, and, clad as I was in my cloak, let myself down into the sea, just as a cold-water bather should. What do you think my feelings were, scrambling over the rocks, searching out the path, or making one for myself? I understood that sailors have good reason to fear the land. It is hard to believe what I endured when I could not endure myself; you may be sure that the reason why Ulysses was shipwrecked on every possible occasion was not so much because the sea-god was angry with him from his birth; he was simply subject to seasickness. And in the future I also, if I must go anywhere by sea, shall only reach my destination in the twentieth year.

When I finally calmed my stomach (for you know that one does not escape seasickness by escaping from the sea) and refreshed my body with a rubdown, I began to reflect how completely we forget or ignore our failings, even those that affect the body, which are continually reminding us of their existence, – not to mention those which are more serious in proportion as they are more hidden. A slight ague deceives us; but when it has increased and a genuine fever has begun to burn, it forces even a hardy man, who can endure much suffering, to admit that he is ill. There is pain in the foot, and a tingling sensation in the joints; but we still hide the complaint and announce that we have sprained a joint, or else are tired from over-exercise. Then the ailment, uncertain at first, must be given a name; and when it begins to swell the ankles also, and has made both our feet "right" feet, we are bound to confess that we have the gout. The opposite holds true of diseases of the soul; the worse one is, the less one perceives it. You need not be surprised, my beloved Lucilius. For he whose sleep is light pursues visions during slumber, and sometimes, though asleep, is conscious that he is asleep; but sound slumber annihilates our very dreams and sinks the spirit down so deep that it has no perception of self. Why will no man confess his faults? Because he is still in their grasp; only he who is awake can recount his dream, and similarly a confession of sin is a proof of sound mind.

Let us, therefore, rouse ourselves, that we may be able to correct our mistakes. Philosophy, however, is the only power that can stir us, the only power that can shake off our deep slumber. Devote yourself wholly to philosophy. You are worthy of her; she is worthy of you; greet one another with a loving embrace. Say farewell to all other interests with courage and frankness. Do not study philosophy merely during your spare time.

If you were ill, you would stop caring for your personal concerns, and forget your business duties; you would not think highly enough of any client to take active charge of his case during a slight abatement of your sufferings. You would try your hardest to be rid of the illness as soon as possible. What, then? Shall you not do the same thing now? Throw aside all hindrances and give up your time to getting a sound mind; for no man can attain it if he is engrossed in other matters. Philosophy wields her own authority; she appoints her own time and does not allow it to be appointed for her. She is not a thing to be followed at odd times, but a subject for daily practice; she is mistress, and she commands our attendance. Alexander, when a certain state promised him a part of its territory and half its entire property, replied: "I invaded Asia with the intention, not of accepting what you might give, but of allowing you to keep what I might leave." Philosophy likewise keeps saying to all occupations: "I do not intend to accept the time which you have left over, but I shall allow you to keep what I myself shall leave."

Turn to her, therefore, with all your soul, sit at her feet, cherish her; a great distance will then begin to separate you from other men. You will be far ahead of all mortals, and even the gods will not be far ahead of you. Do you ask what will be the difference between yourself and the gods? They will live longer. But, by my faith, it is the sign of a great artist to have confined a full likeness to the limits of a miniature. The wise man's life spreads out to him over as large a surface as does all eternity to a god. There is one point in which the sage has an advantage over the god; for a god is freed from terrors by the bounty of nature, the wise man by his own bounty. What a wonderful privilege, to have the weaknesses of a man and the serenity of a god! The power of philosophy to blunt the blows of chance is beyond belief. No missile can settle in her body; she is well-protected and impenetrable. She spoils the force of some missiles and wards them off with the loose folds of her gown, as if they had no power to harm; others she dashes aside, and hurls them back with such force that they recoil upon the sender. Farewell.

Letter LIV - On Asthma and Death

My ill-health had allowed me a long furlough, when suddenly it resumed the attack. "What kind of ill-health?" you say. And you surely have a right to ask; for it is true that no kind is unknown to me. But I have been consigned, so to speak, to one special ailment. I do not know why I should call it by its Greek name; for it is well enough described as "shortness of breath." Its attack is of very brief duration, like that of a squall at sea; it usually ends within an hour. Who indeed could breathe his last for long? I have passed through all the ills and dangers of the flesh; but nothing seems to me more troublesome than this. And naturally so; for anything else may be called illness; but this is a sort of continued "last gasp." Hence physicians call it "practising how to die." For some day the breath will succeed in doing what it has so often essayed. Do you think I am writing this letter in a merry spirit, just because I have escaped? It would be absurd to take delight in such supposed restoration to health, as it would be for a defendant to imagine that he had won his case when he had succeeded in postponing his trial. Yet in the midst of my difficult breathing I never ceased to rest secure in cheerful and brave thoughts.

"What?" I say to myself; "does death so often test me? Let it do so; I myself have for a long time tested death." "When?" you ask. Before I was born. Death is non-existence, and I know already what that means. What was before me will happen again after me. If there is any suffering in this state, there must have been such suffering also in the past, before we entered the light of day. As a matter of fact, however, we felt no discomfort then. And I ask you, would you not say that one was the greatest of fools who believed that a lamp was worse off when it was extinguished than before it was lighted? We mortals also are lighted and extinguished; the period of suffering comes in between, but on either side there is a deep peace. For, unless I am very much mistaken, my dear Lucilius, we go astray in thinking that death only follows, when in reality it has both preceded us and will in turn follow us. Whatever condition existed before our birth, is death. For what does it matter whether you do not begin at all, or whether you leave off, inasmuch as the result of both these states is non-existence?

I have never ceased to encourage myself with cheering counsels of this kind, silently, of course, since I had not the power to speak; then little by little this shortness of breath, already reduced to a sort of panting, came on at greater intervals, and then slowed down and finally stopped. Even by this time, although the gasping has ceased, the breath does not come and go normally; I still feel a sort of hesitation and delay in breathing. Let it be as it pleases, provided there be no sigh from the soul. Accept this assurance from me – I shall never be frightened when the last hour comes; I am already prepared and do not plan a whole day ahead. But do you praise and imitate the man whom it does not irk to die, though he takes pleasure in living. For what virtue is there in going away when you are thrust out? And yet there is virtue even in this: I am indeed thrust out, but it is as if I were going away willingly. For that reason the wise man can never be thrust out, because that would mean removal from a place which he was unwilling to leave; and the wise man does nothing unwillingly. He escapes necessity, because he wills to do what necessity is about to force upon him. Farewell.

Letter LV - On Vatia's Villa

I have just returned from a ride in my litter; and I am as weary as if I had walked the distance, instead of being seated. Even to be carried for any length of time is hard work, perhaps all the more so because it is an unnatural exercise; for Nature gave us legs with which to do our own walking, and eyes with which to do our own seeing. Our luxuries have condemned us to weakness; we have ceased to be able to do that which we have long declined to do. Nevertheless, I found it necessary to give my body a shaking up, in order that the bile which had gathered in my throat, if that was my trouble, might be shaken out, or, if the very breath within me had become, for some reason, too thick, that the jolting, which I have felt was a good thing for me, might make it thinner. So I insisted on being carried longer than usual, along an attractive beach, which bends between Cumae and Servilius Vatia's country-house, shut in by the sea on one side and the lake on the other, just like a narrow path. It was packed firm under foot, because of a recent storm; since, as you know, the waves, when they beat upon the beach hard and fast, level it out; but a continuous period of fair weather loosens it, when the sand, which is kept firm by the water, loses its moisture.

As my habit is, I began to look about for something there that might be of service to me, when my eyes fell upon the villa which had once belonged to Vatia. So this was the place where that famous praetorian millionaire passed his old age! He was famed for nothing else than his life of leisure, and he was regarded as lucky only for that reason. For whenever men were ruined by their friendship with Asinius Gallus whenever others were ruined by their hatred of Sejanus, and later by their intimacy with him, – for it was no more dangerous to have offended him than to have loved him, – people used to cry out: "O Vatia, you alone know how to live!" But what he knew was how to hide, not how to live; and it makes a great deal of difference whether your life be one of leisure or one of idleness. So I never drove past his country-place during Vatia's lifetime without saying to myself: "Here lies Vatia!"

But, my dear Lucilius, philosophy is a thing of holiness, something to be worshipped, so much so that the very counterfeit pleases. For the mass of mankind consider that a person is at leisure who has withdrawn from society, is free from care, self-sufficient, and lives for himself; but these privileges can be the reward only of the wise man. Does he who is a victim of anxiety know how to live for himself? What? Does he even know (and that is of first importance) how to live at all? For the man who has fled from affairs and from men, who has been banished to seclusion by the unhappiness which his own desires have brought upon him, who cannot see his neighbour more happy than himself, who through fear has taken to concealment, like a frightened and sluggish animal. – this person is not living for himself he is living for his belly, his sleep, and his lust, – and that is the most shameful thing in the world. He who lives for no one does not necessarily live for himself. Nevertheless, there is so much in steadfastness and adherence to one's purpose that even sluggishness, if stubbornly maintained, assumes an air of authority with us.

I could not describe the villa accurately; for I am familiar only with the front of the house, and with the parts which are in public view and can be seen by the mere passer-by. There are two grottoes, which cost a great deal of labour, as big as the most spacious hall, made by hand. One of these does not admit the rays of the sun, while the other keeps them until the sun sets. There is also a stream running through a grove of plane-trees, which draws for its supply both on the sea and on Lake Acheron; it intersects the grove just like a race-way and is large enough to support fish, although its waters are continually being drawn off. When the sea is calm, however, they do not use the stream, only touching the well-stocked waters when the storms give the fishermen a forced holiday. But the most convenient thing about the villa is the fact that Baiae is next door, it is free from all the inconveniences of that resort, and yet enjoys its pleasures. I myself understand these attractions, and I believe that it is a villa suited to every season of the year. It fronts the west wind, which it intercepts in such a way that Baiae is denied it. So it seems that Vatia was no fool when he selected this place as the best in which to spend his leisure when it was already unfruitful and decrepit.

The place where one lives, however, can contribute little towards tranquillity; it is the mind which must make everything agreeable to itself. I have seen men despondent in a gay and lovely villa, and I have seen them to all appearance full of business in the midst of a solitude. For this reason you should not refuse to believe that your life is well-placed merely because you are not now in Campania. But why are you not there? Just let your thoughts travel, even to this place. You may hold converse with your friends when they are absent, and indeed as often as you wish and for as long as you wish. For we enjoy this, the greatest of pleasures, all the more when we are absent from one another. For the presence of friends makes us fastidious; and because we can at any time talk or sit together, when once we have parted we give not a thought to those whom we have just beheld. And we ought to bear the absence of friends cheerfully, just because everyone is bound to be often absent from his friends even when they are present. Include among such cases, in the first place, the nights spent apart, then the different engagements which each of two friends has, then the private studies of each and their excursions into the country, and you will see that foreign travel does not rob us of much. A friend should be retained in the spirit; such a friend can never be absent. He can see every day whomsoever he desires to see.

I would therefore have you share your studies with me, your meals, and your walks. We should be living within too narrow limits if anything were barred to our thoughts. I see you, my dear Lucilius, and at this very moment I hear you; I am with you to such an extent that I hesitate whether I should not begin to write you notes instead of letters. Farewell.

Letter LVI - On Quiet and Study

Beshrew me if I think anything more requisite than silence for a man who secludes himself in order to study! Imagine what a variety of noises reverberates about my ears! I have lodgings right over a bathing establishment. So picture to yourself the assortment of sounds, which are strong enough to make me hate my very powers of hearing! When your strenuous gentleman, for example, is exercising himself by flourishing leaden weights; when he is working hard, or else pretends to be working hard, I can hear him grunt; and whenever he releases his imprisoned breath, I can hear him panting in wheezy and high-pitched tones. Or perhaps I notice some lazy fellow, content with a cheap rubdown, and hear the crack of the pummelling hand on his shoulder, varying in sound according as the hand is laid on flat or hollow. Then, perhaps, a professional comes along, shouting out the score; that is the finishing touch. Add to this the arresting of an occasional roisterer or pickpocket, the racket of the man who always likes to hear his own voice in the bathroom, or the enthusiast who plunges into the swimming-tank with unconscionable noise and splashing. Besides all those whose voices, if nothing else, are good, imagine the hair-plucker with his penetrating, shrill voice, – for purposes of advertisement, – continually giving it vent and never holding his tongue except when he is plucking the armpits and making his victim yell instead. Then the cakeseller with his varied cries, the sausageman, the confectioner, and all the vendors of food hawking their wares, each with his own distinctive intonation. So you say: "What iron nerves or deadened ears, you must have, if your mind can hold out amid so many noises, so various and so discordant, when our friend Chrysippus is brought to his death by the continual good-morrows that greet him!" But I assure you that this racket means no more to me than the sound of waves or falling water; although you will remind me that a certain tribe once moved their city merely because they could not endure the din of a Nile cataract. Words seem to distract me more than noises; for words demand attention, but noises merely fill the ears and beat upon them. Among the sounds that din round me without distracting, I include passing carriages, a machinist in the same block, a saw-sharpener near by, or some fellow who is demonstrating with little pipes and flutes at the Trickling Fountain, shouting rather than singing.

Furthermore, an intermittent noise upsets me more than a steady one. But by this time I have toughened my nerves against all that sort of thing, so that I can endure even a boatswain marking the time in high-pitched tones for his crew. For I force my mind to concentrate, and keep it from straying to things outside itself; all outdoors may be bedlam, provided that there is no disturbance within, provided that fear is not wrangling with desire in my breast, provided that meanness and lavishness are not at odds, one harassing the other. For of what benefit is a quiet neighbourhood, if our emotions are in an uproar?

'Twas night, and all the world was lulled to rest.

This is not true; for no real rest can be found when reason has not done the lulling. Night brings our troubles to the light, rather than banishes them; it merely changes the form of our worries. For even when we seek slumber, our sleepless moments are as harassing as the daytime. Real tranquillity is the state reached by an unperverted mind when it is relaxed. Think of the unfortunate man who courts sleep by surrendering his spacious mansion to silence, who, that his ear may be disturbed by no sound, bids the whole retinue of his slaves be quiet and that whoever approaches him shall walk on tiptoe; he tosses from this side to that and seeks a fitful slumber amid his frettings! He complains that he has heard sounds, when he has not heard them at all. The reason, you ask? His soul's in an uproar; it must be soothed, and its rebellious murmuring checked. You need not suppose that the soul is at peace when the body is still. Sometimes quiet means disquiet.

We must therefore rouse ourselves to action and busy ourselves with interests that are good, as often as we are in the grasp of an uncontrollable sluggishness. Great generals, when they see that their men are mutinous, check them by some sort of labour or keep them busy with small forays. The much occupied man has no time for wantonness, and it is an obvious commonplace that the evils of leisure can be shaken off by hard work. Although people may often have thought that I sought seclusion because I was disgusted with politics and regretted my hapless and thankless position, yet, in the retreat to which apprehension and weariness have driven me, my ambition sometimes develops afresh. For it is not because my ambition was rooted out that it has abated, but because it was wearied or perhaps even put out of temper by the failure of its plans. And so with luxury, also, which sometimes seems to have departed, and then when we have made a profession of frugality, begins to fret us and, amid our economies, seeks the pleasures which we have merely left but not condemned. Indeed, the more stealthily it comes, the greater is its force. For all unconcealed vices are less serious; a disease also is farther on the road to being cured when it breaks forth from concealment and manifests its power. So with greed, ambition, and the other evils of the mind, – you may be sure that they do most harm when they are hidden behind a pretence of soundness.

Men think that we are in retirement, and yet we are not. For if we have sincerely retired, and have sounded the signal for retreat, and have scorned outward attractions, then, as I remarked above, no outward thing will distract us; no music of men or of birds can interrupt good thoughts, when they have once become steadfast and sure. The mind which starts at words or at chance sounds is unstable and has not yet withdrawn into itself; it contains within itself an element of anxiety and rooted fear, and this makes one a prey to care, as our Vergil says:

> I, whom of yore no dart could cause to flee,
> Nor Greeks, with crowded lines of infantry.
> Now shake at every sound, and fear the air,
> Both for my child and for the load I bear.

This man in his first state is wise; he blenches neither at the brandished spear, nor at the clashing armour of the serried foe, nor at the din of the stricken city. This man in his second state lacks knowledge fearing for his own concerns, he pales at every sound; any cry is taken for the battle-shout and overthrows him; the slightest disturbance renders him breathless with fear. It is the load that makes him afraid. Select anyone you please from among your favourites of Fortune, trailing their many responsibilities, carrying their many burdens, and you will behold a picture of Vergil's hero, "fearing both for his child and for the load he bears."

You may therefore be sure that you are at peace with yourself, when no noise readies you, when no word shakes you out of yourself, whether it be of flattery or of threat, or merely an empty sound buzzing about you with unmeaning din. "What then?" you say, "is it not sometimes a simpler matter just to avoid the uproar?" I admit this. Accordingly, I shall change from my present quarters. I merely wished to test myself and to give myself practice. Why need I be tormented any longer, when Ulysses found so simple a cure for his comrades even against the songs of the Sirens? Farewell.

Letter LVII - On the Trials of Travel

When it was time for me to return to Naples from Baiae, I easily persuaded myself that a storm was raging, that I might avoid another trip by sea; and yet the road was so deep in mud, all the way, that I may be thought none the less to have made a voyage. On that day I had to endure the full fate of an athlete; the anointing with which we began was followed by the sand-sprinkle in the Naples tunnel. No place could be longer than that prison; nothing could be dimmer than those torches, which enabled us, not to see amid the darkness, but to see the darkness. But, even supposing that there was light in the place, the dust, which is an oppressive and disagreeable thing even in the open air, would destroy the light; how much worse the dust is there, where it rolls back upon itself, and, being shut in without ventilation, blows back in the faces of those who set it going! So we endured two inconveniences at the same time, and they were diametrically different: we struggled both with mud and with dust on the same road and on the same day.

The gloom, however, furnished me with some food for thought; I felt a certain mental thrill, and a transformation unaccompanied by fear, due to the novelty and the unpleasantness of an unusual occurrence. Of course I am not speaking to you of myself at this point, because I am far from being a perfect person, or even a man of middling qualities; I refer to one over whom fortune has lost her control. Even such a man's mind will be smitten with a thrill and he will change colour. For there are certain emotions, my dear Lucilius, which no courage can avoid; nature reminds courage how perishable a thing it is. And so he will contract his brow when the prospect is forbidding, will shudder at sudden apparitions, and will become dizzy when he stands at the edge of a high precipice and looks down. This is not fear; it is a natural feeling which reason cannot rout. That is why certain brave men, most willing to shed their own blood, cannot bear to see the blood of others. Some persons collapse and faint at the sight of a freshly inflicted wound; others are affected similarly on handling or viewing an old wound which is festering. And others meet the sword-stroke more readily than they see it dealt.

Accordingly, as I said, I experienced a certain transformation, though it could not be called confusion. Then at the first glimpse of restored daylight my good spirits returned without forethought or command. And I began to muse and think how foolish we are to fear certain objects to a greater or less degree, since all of them end in the same way. For what difference does it make whether a watchtower or a mountain crashes down upon us? No difference at all, you will find. Nevertheless, there will be some men who fear the latter mishap to a greater degree, though both accidents are equally deadly; so true it is that fear looks not to the effect, but to the cause of the effect. Do you suppose that I am now referring to the Stoics, who hold that the soul of a man crushed by a great weight cannot abide, and is scattered forthwith, because it has not had a free opportunity to depart? That is not what I am doing; those who think thus are, in my opinion, wrong. Just as fire cannot be crushed out, since it will escape round the edges of the body which overwhelms it; just as the air cannot be damaged by lashes and blows, or even cut into, but flows back about the object to which it gives place; similarly the soul, which consists of the subtlest particles, cannot be arrested or destroyed inside the body, but, by virtue of its delicate substance, it will rather escape through the very object by which it is being crushed. Just as lightning, no matter how widely it strikes and flashes, makes its return through a narrow opening, so the soul, which is still subtler than fire, has a way of escape through any part of the body. We therefore come to this question, – whether the soul can be immortal. But be sure of this: if the soul survives the body after the body is crushed, the soul can in no wise be crushed out, precisely because it does not perish; for the rule of immortality never admits of exceptions, and nothing can harm that which is everlasting. Farewell.

Letter LVIII - On Being

How scant of words our language is, nay, how poverty-stricken, I have not fully understood until to-day. We happened to be speaking of Plato, and a thousand subjects came up for discussion, which needed names and yet possessed none; and there were certain others which once possessed, but have since lost, their words because we were too nice about their use. But who can endure to be nice in the midst of poverty? There is an insect, called by the Greeks oestrus, which drives cattle wild and scatters them all over their pasturing grounds; it used to be called asilus in our language, as you may believe on the authority of Vergil:-

Near Silarus groves, and eke Alburnus' shades
Of green-clad oak-trees flits an insect, named
Asilus by the Romans; in the Greek
The word is rendered oestrus. With a rough
And strident sound it buzzes and drives wild
The terror-stricken herds throughout the woods.

By which I infer that the word has gone out of use. And, not to keep you waiting too long, there were certain uncompounded words current, like cernere ferro inter se, as will be proved again by Vergil:-

Great heroes, born in various lands, had come
To settle matters mutually with the sword.

This "settling matters" we now express by decernere. The plain word has become obsolete. The ancients used to say iusso, instead of iussero, in conditional clauses. You need not take my word, but you may turn again to Vergil:-

The other soldiers shall conduct the fight
With me, where I shall bid.

It is not in my purpose to show, by this array of examples, how much time I have wasted on the study of language; I merely wish you to understand how many words, that were current in the works of Ennius and Accius, have become mouldy with age; while even in the case of Vergil, whose works are explored daily, some of his words have been filched away from us.

You will say, I suppose: "What is the purpose and meaning of this preamble?" I shall not keep you in the dark; I desire, if possible, to say the word essentia to you and obtain a favourable hearing. If I cannot do this, I shall risk it even though it put you out of humour. I have Cicero, as authority for the use of this word, and I regard him as a powerful authority. If you desire testimony of a later date, I shall cite Fabianus, careful of speech, cultivated, and so polished in style that he will suit even our nice tastes. For what can we do, my dear Lucilius? How otherwise can we find a word for that which the Greeks call οὐσία, something that is indispensable, something that is the natural substratum of everything? I beg you accordingly to allow me to use this word essentia. I shall nevertheless take pains to exercise the privilege, which you have granted me, with as sparing a hand as possible; perhaps I shall be content with the mere right. Yet what good will your indulgence do me, if, lo and behold, I can in no wise express in Latin the meaning of the word which gave me the opportunity to rail at the poverty of our language? And you will condemn our narrow Roman limits even more, when you find out that there is a word of one syllable which I cannot translate. "What is this?" you ask. It is the word ὄν. You think me lacking in facility; you believe that the word is ready to hand, that it might be translated by quod est. I notice, however, a great difference; you are forcing me to render a noun by a verb. But if I must do so, I shall render it by quod est. There are six ways in which Plato expresses this idea, according to a friend of ours, a man of great learning, who mentioned the fact to-day. And I shall explain all of them to you, if I may first point out that there is something called genus and something called species.

For the present, however, we are seeking the primary idea of genus, on which the others, the different species, depend, which is the source of all classification, the term under which universal ideas are embraced. And the idea of genus will be reached if we begin to reckon back from particulars; for in this way we shall be conducted back to the primary notion. Now "man" is a species, as Aristotle says; so is "horse," or "dog." We must therefore discover some common bond for all these terms, one which embraces them and holds them subordinate to itself. And what is this? It is "animal." And so there begins to be a genus "animal," including all these terms, "man," "horse," and "dog." But there are certain things which have life (anima) and yet are not "animals." For it is agreed that plants and trees possess life, and that is why we speak of them as living and dying. Therefore the term "living things" will occupy a still higher place, because both animals and plants are included in this category. Certain objects, however, lack life, – such as rocks. There will therefore be another term to take precedence over "living things," and that is "substance." I shall classify "substance" by saying that all substances are either animate or inanimate. But there is still something superior to "substance"; for we speak of certain things as possessing substance, and certain things as lacking substance. What, then, will be the term from which these things are derived? It is that to which we lately gave an inappropriate name, "that which exists." For by using this term they will be divided into species, so that we can say: that which exists either possesses, or lacks, substance.

This, therefore, is what genus is, – the primary, original, and (to play upon the word) "general." Of course there are the other genera: but they are "special" genera: "man" being, for example, a genus. For "man" comprises species: by nations, – Greek, Roman, Parthian; by colours, – white, black, yellow. The term comprises individuals also: Cato, Cicero, Lucretius. So "man" falls into the category genus, in so far as it includes many kinds; but in so far as it is subordinate to another term, it falls into the category species. But the genus "that which exists" is general, and has no term superior to it. It is the first term in the classification of things, and all things are included under it.

The Stoics would set ahead of this still another genus, even more primary; concerning which I shall immediately speak, after proving that the genus which has been discussed above, has rightly been placed first, being, as it is, capable of including everything. I therefore distribute "that which exists" into these two species, – things with, and things without, substance. There is no third class. And how do I distribute "substance"? By saying that it is either animate or inanimate. And how do I distribute the "animate"? By saying: "Certain things have mind, while others have only life." Or the idea may be

316

expressed as follows: "Certain things have the power of movement, of progress, of change of position, while others are rooted in the ground; they are fed and they grow only through their roots." Again, into what species do I divide "animals"? They are either perishable or imperishable. Certain of the Stoics regard the primary genus as the "something." I shall add the reasons they give for their belief; they say: "in the order of nature some things exist, and other things do not exist. And even the things that do not exist are really part of the order of nature. What these are will readily occur to the mind, for example centaurs, giants, and all other figments of unsound reasoning, which have begun to have a definite shape, although they have no bodily consistency."

But I now return to the subject which I promised to discuss for you, namely, how it is that Plato divides all existing things in six different ways. The first class of "that which exists" cannot be grasped by the sight or by the touch, or by any of the senses; but it can be grasped by the thought. Any generic conception, such as the generic idea "man," does not come within the range of the eyes; but "man" in particular does; as, for example, Cicero, Cato. The term "animal" is not seen; it is grasped by thought alone. A particular animal, however, is seen, for example, a horse, a dog.

The second class of "things which exist," according to Plato, is that which is prominent and stands out above everything else; this, he says, exists in a pre-eminent degree. The word "poet" is used indiscriminately, for this term is applied to all writers of verse; but among the Greeks it has come to be the distinguishing mark of a single individual. You know that Homer is meant when you hear men say "the poet." What, then, is this pre-eminent Being? God, surely, one who is greater and more powerful than anyone else.

The third class is made up of those things which exist in the proper sense of the term; they are countless in number, but are situated beyond our sight. "What are these?" you ask. They are Plato's own furniture, so to speak; he calls them "ideas," and from them all visible things are created, and according to their pattern all things are fashioned. They are immortal, unchangeable, inviolable. And this "idea," or rather, Plato's conception of it, is as follows: "The 'idea' is the everlasting pattern of those things which are created by nature." I shall explain this definition, in order to set the subject before you in a clearer light: Suppose that I wish to make a likeness of you; I possess in your own person the pattern of this picture, wherefrom my mind receives a certain outline, which it is to embody in its own handiwork. That outward appearance, then, which gives me instruction and guidance, this pattern for me to imitate, is the "idea." Such patterns, therefore, nature possesses in infinite number, – of men, fish, trees, according to whose model everything that nature has to create is worked out.

In the fourth place we shall put "form." And if you would know what "form" means, you must pay close attention, calling Plato, and not me, to account for the difficulty of the subject. However, we cannot make fine distinctions without encountering difficulties. A moment ago I made use of the artist as an illustration. When the artist desired to reproduce Vergil in colours he would gaze upon Vergil himself. The "idea" was Vergil's outward appearance, and this was the pattern of the intended work. That which the artist draws from this "idea" and has embodied in his own work, is the "form." Do you ask me where the difference lies? The former is the pattern; while the latter is the shape taken from the pattern and embodied in the work. Our artist follows the one, but the other he creates. A statue has a certain external appearance; this external appearance of the statue is the "form." And the pattern itself has a certain external appearance, by gazing upon which the sculptor has fashioned his statue; this is the "idea." If you desire a further distinction, I will say that the "form" is in the artist's work, the "idea" outside his work, and not only outside it, but prior to it.

The fifth class is made up of the things which exist in the usual sense of the term. These things are the first that have to do with us; here we have all such things as men, cattle, and things. In the sixth class goes all that which has a fictitious existence, like void, or time.

Whatever is concrete to the sight or touch, Plato does not include among the things which he believes to be existent in the strict sense of the term. These things are the first that have to do with us: here we have all such things as men, cattle, and things. For they are in a state of flux, constantly diminishing or increasing. None of us is the same man in old age that he was in youth; nor the same on the morrow as on the day preceding. Our bodies are burned along like flowing waters; every visible object accompanies time in its flight; of the things which we see, nothing is fixed. Even I myself as I comment on this change, am changed myself. This is just what Heraclitus says: "We go down twice into the same river, and yet into a different river." For the stream still keeps the same name, but the water has already flowed past. Of course this is much more evident in rivers than in human beings. Still, we mortals are also carried past in no less speedy a course; and this prompts me to marvel at our madness in cleaving with great affection to such a fleeting thing as the body, and in fearing lest some day we may die, when every instant means the death of our previous condition. Will you not stop fearing lest that may happen once which really happens every day? So much for man, – a substance that flows away and falls, exposed to every influence; but the universe, too, immortal and enduring as it is, changes and never remains the same. For though it has within itself all that it has had, it has it in a different way from that in which it has had it; it keeps changing its arrangement.

. "Very well," say you, "what good shall I get from all this fine reasoning?" None, if you wish me to answer your question. Nevertheless, just as an engraver rests his eyes when they have long been under a strain and are weary, and calls them from their work, and "feasts" them, as the saying is; so we at times should slacken our minds and refresh them with some sort of entertainment. But let even your entertainment be work; and even from these various forms of entertainment you will select, if you have been watchful, something that may prove wholesome. That is my habit, Lucilius: I try to extract and render useful some element from every field of thought, no matter how far removed it may be from philosophy. Now what could be less likely to reform character than the subjects which we have been discussing? And how can I be made a better man by the "ideas" of Plato? What can I draw from them that will put a check on my appetites? Perhaps the very thought, that all these things which minister to our senses, which arouse and excite us, are by Plato denied a place among the things that really exist. Such things are therefore imaginary, and though they for the moment present a certain external appearance, yet they are in no case permanent or substantial; none the less, we crave them as if they were always to exist, or as if we were always to possess them.

We are weak, watery beings standing in the midst of unrealities; therefore let us turn our minds to the things that are everlasting. Let us look up to the ideal outlines of all things, that flit about on high, and to the God who moves among them and plans how he may defend from death that which he could not make imperishable because its substance forbade, and so by reason may overcome the defects of the body. For all things abide, not because they are everlasting, but because they are protected by the care of him who governs all things; but that which was imperishable would need no guardian. The Master Builder keeps them safe, overcoming the weakness of their fabric by his own power. Let us despise everything that is so little an object of value that it makes us doubt whether it exists at all. Let us at the same time reflect, seeing that Providence rescues from its perils the world itself, which is no less mortal than we ourselves, that to some extent our petty bodies can be made to tarry longer upon earth by our own providence, if only we acquire the ability to control and check those pleasures whereby the greater portion of mankind perishes. Plato himself, by taking pains, advanced to old age. To be sure, he was the fortunate possessor of a strong and sound body (his very name was given him because of his broad chest); but his strength was much impaired by sea voyages and desperate adventures. Nevertheless, by frugal living, by setting a limit upon all that rouses the appetites, and by painstaking attention to himself, he reached that advanced age in spite of many hindrances. You know, I am sure, that Plato had the good fortune, thanks to his careful living, to die on his birthday, after exactly completing his eighty-first year. For this reason wise men of the East, who happened to be in Athens at that time, sacrificed to him after his death, believing that his length of days was too full for a mortal man, since he had rounded out the perfect number of nine times nine. I do not doubt that he would have been quite willing to forgo a few days from this total, as well as the sacrifice.

Frugal living can bring one to old age; and to my mind old age is not to be refused any more than is to be craved. There is a pleasure in being in one's own company as long as possible, when a man has made himself worth enjoying. The question, therefore, on which we have to record our judgment is, whether one should shrink from extreme old age and should hasten the end artificially, instead of waiting for it to come. A man who sluggishly awaits his fate is almost a coward, just as he is immoderately given to wine who drains the jar dry and sucks up even the dregs. But we shall ask this question also: "Is the extremity of life the dregs, or is it the clearest and purest part of all, provided only that the mind is unimpaired, and the senses, still sound, give their support to the spirit, and the body is not worn out and dead before its time?" For it makes a great deal of difference whether a man is lengthening his life or his death. But if the body is useless for service, why should one not free the struggling soul? Perhaps one ought to do this a little before the debt is due, lest, when it falls due, he may be unable to perform the act. And since the danger of living in wretchedness is greater than the danger of dying soon, he is a fool who refuses to stake a little time and win a hazard of great gain.

Few have lasted through extreme old age to death without impairment, and many have lain inert, making no use of themselves. How much more cruel, then, do you suppose it really is to have lost a portion of your life, than to have lost your right to end that life? . Do not hear me with reluctance, as if my statement applied directly to you, but weigh what I have to say. It is this, that I shall not abandon old age, if old age preserves me intact for myself, and intact as regards the better part of myself; but if old age begins to shatter my mind, and to pull its various faculties to pieces, if it leaves me, not life, but only the breath of life, I shall rush out of a house that is crumbling and tottering. I shall not avoid illness by seeking death, as long as the illness is curable and does not impede my soul. I shall not lay violent hands upon myself just because I am in pain; for death under such circumstances is defeat. But if I find out that the pain must always be endured, I shall depart, not because of the pain but because it will be a hindrance to me as regards all my reasons for living. He who dies just because he is in pain is a weakling, a coward; but he who lives merely to brave out this pain, is a fool.

But I am running on too long; and, besides, there is matter here to fill a day. And how can a man end his life, if he cannot end a letter? So farewell. This last word you will read with greater pleasure than all my deadly talk about death. Farewell.

Letter LIX - On Pleasure and Joy

I received great pleasure from your letter; kindly allow me to use these words in their everyday meaning, without insisting upon their Stoic import. For we Stoics hold that pleasure is a vice. Very likely it is a vice; but we are accustomed to use the word when we wish to indicate a happy state of mind. I am aware that if we test words by our formula, even pleasure is a thing of ill repute, and joy can be attained only by the wise. For "joy" is an elation of spirit, of a spirit which trusts in the goodness and truth of its own possessions. The common usage, however, is that we derive great "joy" from a friend's position as consul, or from his marriage, or from the birth of his child; but these events, so far from being matters of joy, are more often the beginnings of sorrow to come. No, it is a characteristic of real joy that it never ceases, and never changes into its opposite.

Accordingly, when our Vergil speaks of *the evil joys of the mind*, his words are eloquent, but not strictly appropriate. For no "joy" can be evil. He has given the name "joy" to pleasures, and has thus expressed his meaning. For he has conveyed the idea that men take delight in their own evil. Nevertheless, I was not wrong in saying that I received great "pleasure" from your letter; for although an ignorant man may derive "joy" if the cause be an honourable one, yet, since his emotion is wayward, and is likely soon to take another direction, I call it "pleasure"; for it is inspired by an opinion concerning a spurious good; it exceeds control and is carried to excess.

But, to return to the subject, let me tell you what delighted me in your letter. You have your words under control. You are not carried away by your language, or borne beyond the limits which you have determined upon. Many writers are tempted by the charm of some alluring phrase to some topic other than that which they had set themselves to discuss. But this has not been so in your case; all your words are compact, and suited to the subject, You say all that you wish, and you mean still more than you say. This is a proof of the importance of your subject matter, showing that your mind, as well as your words, contains nothing superfluous or bombastic.

I do, however, find some metaphors, not, indeed, daring ones, but the kind which have stood the test of use. I find similes also; of course, if anyone forbids us to use them, maintaining that poets alone have that privilege, he has not, apparently, read any of our ancient prose writers, who had not yet learned to affect a style that should win applause. For those writers, whose eloquence was simple and directed only towards proving their case, are full of comparisons; and I think that these are necessary, not for the same reason which makes them necessary for the poets, but in order that they may serve as props to our feebleness, to bring both speaker and listener face to face with the subject under discussion. For example, I am at this very moment reading Sextius; he is a keen man, and a philosopher who, though he writes in Greek, has the Roman standard of ethics. One of his similes appealed especially to me, that of an army marching in hollow square, in a place where the enemy might be expected to appear from any quarter, ready for battle. "This," said he, "is just what the wise man ought to do; he should have all his fighting qualities deployed on every side, so that wherever the attack threatens, there his supports may be ready to hand and may obey the captain's command without confusion." This is what we notice in armies which serve under great leaders; we see how all the troops simultaneously understand their general's orders, since they are so arranged that a signal given by one man passes down the ranks of cavalry and infantry at the same moment. This, he declares, is still more necessary for men like ourselves; for soldiers have often feared an enemy without reason, and the march which they thought most dangerous has in fact been most secure; but folly brings no repose, fear haunts it both in the van and in the rear of the column, and both flanks are in a panic. Folly is pursued, and confronted, by peril. It blenches at everything; it is unprepared; it is frightened even by auxiliary troops. But the wise man is fortified against all inroads; he is alert; he will not retreat before the attack of poverty, or of sorrow, or of disgrace, or of pain. He will walk undaunted both against them and among them.

We human beings are fettered and weakened by many vices; we have wallowed in them for a long time and it is hard for us to be cleansed. We are not merely defiled; we are dyed by them. But, to refrain from passing from one figure to another, I will raise this question, which I often consider in my own heart: why is it that folly holds us with such an insistent grasp? It is, primarily, because we do not combat it strongly enough, because we do not struggle towards salvation with all our might; secondly, because we do not put sufficient trust in the discoveries of the wise, and do not drink in their words with open hearts; we approach this great problem in too trifling a spirit. But how can a man learn, in the struggle against his vices, an amount that is enough, if the time which he gives to learning is only the amount left over from his vices? None of us goes deep below the surface. We skim the top only, and we regard the smattering of time spent in the search for wisdom as enough and to spare for a busy man. What hinders us most of all is that we are too readily satisfied with ourselves; if we meet with someone who calls us good men, or sensible men, or holy men, we see ourselves in his description, not content with praise in moderation, we accept everything that shameless flattery heaps upon us, as if it were our due. We agree with those who declare us to be the best and wisest of men, although we know that they are given to much lying. And we are so self-complacent that we desire praise for certain actions when we are especially addicted to the very opposite. Yonder person hears himself called "most gentle" when he is inflicting tortures, or "most generous" when he is engaged in looting, or "most temperate" when he is in the midst of drunkenness and lust. Thus it follows that we are unwilling to be reformed, just because we believe ourselves to be the best of men.

Alexander was roaming as far as India, ravaging tribes that were but little known, even to their neighbours. During the blockade of a certain city, while he was reconnoitring the walls and hunting for the weakest spot in the fortifications, he was wounded by an arrow. Nevertheless, he long continued the siege, intent on finishing what he had begun. The pain of his wound, however, as the surface became dry and as the flow of blood was checked, increased; his leg gradually became numb as he sat his horse; and finally, when he was forced to withdraw, he exclaimed: "All men swear that I am the son of Jupiter, but this wound cries out that I am mortal." Let us also act in the same way. Each man, according to his lot in life, is stultified by flattery. We should say to him who flatters us: "You call me a man of sense, but I understand how many of the things which I crave are useless, and how many of the things which I desire will do me harm. I have not even the knowledge, which satiety teaches to animals, of what should be the measure of my food or my drink. I do not yet know how much I can hold."

I shall now show you how you may know that you are not wise. The wise man is joyful, happy and calm, unshaken, he lives on a plane with the gods. Now go, question yourself; if you are never downcast, if your mind is not harassed by my apprehension, through anticipation of what is to come, if day and night your soul keeps on its even and unswerving course, upright and content with itself, then you have attained to the greatest good that mortals can possess. If, however, you seek pleasures of all kinds in all directions, you must know that you are as far short of wisdom as you are short of joy. Joy is the goal which you desire to reach, but you are wandering from the path, if you expect to reach your goal while you are in the midst of riches and official titles, – in other words, if you seek joy in the midst of cares, these objects for which you strive so eagerly, as if they would give you happiness and pleasure, are merely causes of grief.

All men of this stamp, I maintain, are pressing on in pursuit of joy, but they do not know where they may obtain a joy that is both great and enduring. One person seeks it in feasting and self-indulgence; another, in canvassing for honours and in being surrounded by a throng of clients; another, in his mistress; another, in idle display of culture and in literature that has no power to heal; all these men are led astray by delights which are deceptive and short-lived – like drunkenness for example, which pays for a single hour of hilarious madness by a sickness of many days, or like applause and the popularity of enthusiastic approval which are gained, and atoned for, at the cost of great mental disquietude.

Reflect, therefore, on this, that the effect of wisdom is a joy that is unbroken and continuous. The mind of the wise man is like the ultra-lunar firmament; eternal calm pervades that region. You have, then, a reason for wishing to be wise, if the wise man is never deprived of joy. This joy springs only from the knowledge that you possess the virtues. None but the brave, the just, the self-restrained, can rejoice. And when you query: "What do you mean? Do not the foolish and the wicked also rejoice?" I reply, no more than lions who have caught their prey. When men have wearied themselves with wine and lust, when night fails them before their debauch is done, when the pleasures which they have heaped upon a body that is too small to hold them begin to fester, at such times they utter in their wretchedness those lines of Vergil:

Thou knowest how, amid false-glittering joys,
We spent that last of nights.

Pleasure-lovers spend every night amid false-glittering joys, and just as if it were their last. But the joy which comes to the gods, and to those who imitate the gods, is not broken off, nor does it cease; but it would surely cease were it borrowed from without. Just because it is not in the power of another to bestow, neither is it subject to another's whims. That which Fortune has not given, she cannot take away. Farewell.

Letter LX - On Harmful Prayers

I file a complaint, I enter a suit, I am angry. Do you still desire what your nurse, your guardian, or your mother, have prayed for in your behalf? Do you not yet understand what evil they prayed for? Alas, how hostile to us are the wishes of our own folk! And they are all the more hostile in proportion as they are more completely fulfilled. It is no surprise to me, at my age, that nothing but evil attends us from our early youth; for we have grown up amid the curses invoked by our parents. And may the gods give ear to our cry also, uttered in our own behalf, – one which asks no favours!

How long shall we go on making demands upon the gods, as if we were still unable to support ourselves? How long shall we continue to fill with grain the market-places of our great cities? How long must the people gather it in for us? How long shall many ships convey the requisites for a single meal, bringing them from no single sea? The bull is filled when he feeds over a few acres; and one forest is large enough for a herd of elephants. Man, however, draws sustenance both from the earth and from the sea. What, then? Did nature give us bellies so insatiable, when she gave us these puny bodies, that we should outdo the hugest and most voracious animals in greed? Not at all. How small is the amount which will satisfy nature? A very little will send her away contented. It is not the natural hunger of our bellies that costs us dear, but our solicitous cravings. Therefore those who, as Sallust puts it, "hearken to their bellies," should be numbered among the animals, and not among men; and certain men, indeed, should be numbered, not even among the animals, but among the dead. He really lives who is made use of by many; he really lives who makes use of himself. Those men, however, who creep into a hole and grow torpid are no better off in their homes than if they were in their tombs. Right there on the marble lintel of the house of such a man you may inscribe his name, for he has died before he is dead. Farewell.

Letter LXI - On Meeting Death Cheerfully

Let us cease to desire that which we have been desiring. I, at least, am doing this: in my old age I have ceased to desire what I desired when a boy. To this single end my days and my nights are passed; this is my task, this the object of my thoughts, – to put an end to my chronic ills. I am endeavouring to live every day as if it were a complete life. I do not indeed snatch it up as if it were my last; I do regard it, however, as if it might even be my last. The present letter is written to you with this in mind as if death were about to call me away in the very act of writing. I am ready to depart, and I shall enjoy life just because I am not over-anxious as to the future date of my departure.

Before I became old I tried to live well; now that I am old, I shall try to die well; but dying well means dying gladly. See to it that you never do anything unwillingly. That which is bound to be a necessity if you rebel, is not a necessity if you desire it. This is what I mean: he who takes his orders gladly, escapes the bitterest part of slavery, – doing what one does not want to do. The man who does something under orders is not unhappy; he is unhappy who does something against his will. Let us therefore so set our minds in order that we may desire whatever is demanded of us by circumstances, and above all that we may reflect upon our end without sadness. We must make ready for death before we make ready for life. Life is well enough furnished, but we are too greedy with regard to its furnishings; something always seems to us lacking, and will always seem lacking. To have lived long enough depends neither upon our years nor upon our days, but upon our minds. I have lived, my dear friend Lucilius, long enough. I have had my fill; I await death. Farewell.

Letter LXII - On Good Company

We are deceived by those who would have us believe that a multitude of affairs blocks their pursuit of liberal studies; they make a pretence of their engagements, and multiply them, when their engagements are merely with themselves. As for me, Lucilius, my time is free; it is indeed free, and wherever I am, I am master of myself. For I do not surrender myself to my affairs, but loan myself to them, and I do not hunt out excuses for wasting my time. And wherever I am situated, I carry on my own meditations and ponder in my mind some wholesome thought. When I give myself to my friends, I do not withdraw from my own company, nor do I linger with those who are associated with me through some special occasion or some case which arises from my official position. But I spend my time in the company of all the best; no matter in what lands they may have lived, or in what age, I let my thoughts fly to them. Demetrius, for instance, the best of men, I take about with me, and, leaving the wearers of purple and fine linen, I talk with him, half-naked as he is, and hold him in high esteem. Why should I not hold him in high esteem? I have found that he lacks nothing. It is in the power of any man to despise all things, but of no man to possess all things. The shortest cut to riches is to despise riches. Our friend Demetrius, however, lives not merely as if he has learned to despise all things, but as if he has handed them over for others to possess. Farewell.

Letter LXIII - On Grief for Lost Friends

I am grieved to hear that your friend Flaccus is dead, but I would not have you sorrow more than is fitting. That you should not mourn at all I shall hardly dare to insist; and yet I know that it is the better way. But what man will ever be so blessed with that ideal steadfastness of soul, unless he has already risen far above the reach of Fortune? Even such a man will be stung by an event like this, but it will be only a sting. We, however, may be forgiven for bursting into tears, if only our tears have not flowed to excess, and if we have checked them by our own efforts. Let not the eyes be dry when we have lost a friend, nor let them overflow. We may weep, but we must not wail.

Do you think that the law which I lay down for you is harsh, when the greatest of Greek poets has extended the privilege of weeping to one day only, in the lines where he tells us that even Niobe took thought of food? Do you wish to know the reason for lamentations and excessive weeping? It is because we seek the proofs of our bereavement in our tears, and do not give way to sorrow, but merely parade it. No man goes into mourning for his own sake. Shame on our ill-timed folly! There is an element of self-seeking even in our sorrow.

"What," you say, "am I to forget my friend?" It is surely a short-lived memory that you vouchsafe to him, if it is to endure only as long as your grief; presently that brow of yours will be smoothed out in laughter by some circumstance, however casual. It is to a time no more distant than this that I put off the soothing of every regret, the quieting of even the bitterest grief. As soon as you cease to observe yourself, the picture of sorrow which you have contemplated will fade away; at present you are keeping watch over your own suffering. But even while you keep watch it slips away from you, and the sharper it is, the more speedily it comes to an end.

Let us see to it that the recollection of those whom we have lost becomes a pleasant memory to us. No man reverts with pleasure to any subject which he will not be able to reflect upon without pain. So too it cannot but be that the names of those whom we have loved and lost come back to us with a sort of sting; but there is a pleasure even in this sting. For, as my friend Attalus used to say: "The remembrance of lost friends is pleasant in the same way that certain fruits have an agreeably acid taste, or as in extremely old wines it is their very bitterness that pleases us. Indeed, after a certain lapse of time, every thought that gave pain is quenched, and the pleasure comes to us unalloyed." If we take the word of Attalus for it, "to think of friends who are alive and well is like enjoying a meal of cakes and honey; the recollection of friends who have passed away gives a pleasure that is not without a touch of bitterness. Yet who will deny that even these things, which are bitter and contain an element of sourness, do serve to arouse the stomach?" For my part, I do not agree with him. To me, the thought of my dead friends is sweet and appealing. For I have had them as if I should one day lose them; I have lost them as if I have them still.

Therefore, Lucilius, act as befits your own serenity of mind, and cease to put a wrong interpretation on the gifts of Fortune. Fortune has taken away, but Fortune has given. Let us greedily enjoy our friends, because we do not know how long this privilege will be ours. Let us think how often we shall leave them when we go upon distant journeys, and how often we shall fail to see them when we tarry together in the same place; we shall thus understand that we have lost too much of their time while they were alive. But will you tolerate men who are most careless of their friends, and then mourn them most abjectly, and do not love anyone unless they have lost him? The reason why they lament too unrestrainedly at such times is that they are afraid lest men doubt whether they really have loved; all too late they seek for proofs of their emotions. If we have other friends, we surely deserve ill at their hands and think ill of them, if they are of so little account that they fail to console us for the loss of one. If, on the other hand, we have no other friends, we have injured ourselves more than Fortune has injured us; since Fortune has robbed us of one friend, but we have robbed ourselves of every friend whom we have failed to make. Again, he who has been unable to love more than one, has had none too much love even for that one. If a man who has lost his one and only tunic through robbery chooses to bewail his plight rather than look about him for some way to escape the cold, or for something with which to cover his shoulders, would you not think him an utter fool?

You have buried one whom you loved; look about for someone to love. It is better to replace your friend than to weep for him. What I am about to add is, I know, a very hackneyed remark, but I shall not omit it simply because it is a common phrase: a man ends his grief by the mere passing of time, even if he has not ended it of his own accord. But the most shameful cure for sorrow, in the case of a sensible man, is to grow weary of sorrowing. I should prefer you to abandon grief, rather than have grief abandon you; and you should stop grieving as soon as possible, since, even if you wish to do so, it is impossible to keep it up for a long time. Our forefathers have enacted that, in the case of women, a year should be the limit for mourning; not that they needed to mourn for so long, but that they should mourn no longer. In the case of men, no rules are laid down, because to mourn at all is not regarded as honourable. For all that, what woman can you show me, of all the pathetic females that could scarcely be dragged away from the funeral-pile or torn from the corpse, whose tears have lasted a whole month? Nothing becomes offensive so quickly as grief; when fresh, it finds someone to console it and attracts one or another to itself; but after becoming chronic, it is ridiculed, and rightly. For it is either assumed or foolish.

He who writes these words to you is no other than I, who wept so excessively for my dear friend Annaeus Serenus that, in spite of my wishes, I must be included among the examples of men who have been overcome by grief. To-day, however, I condemn this act of mine, and I understand that the reason why I lamented so greatly was chiefly that I had never imagined it possible for his death to precede mine. The only thought which occurred to my mind was that he was the younger, and much younger, too, – as if the Fates kept to the order of our ages!

Therefore let us continually think as much about our own mortality as about that of all those we love. In former days I ought to have said: "My friend Serenus is younger than I; but what does that matter? He would naturally die after me, but he may precede me." It was just because I did not do this that I was unprepared when Fortune dealt me the sudden blow. Now is the time for you to reflect, not only that all things are mortal, but also that their mortality is subject to no fixed law. Whatever can happen at any time can happen to-day. Let us therefore reflect, my beloved Lucilius, that we shall soon come to the goal which this friend, to our own sorrow, has reached. And perhaps, if only the tale told by wise men is true and there is a bourne to welcome us, then he whom we think we have lost has only been sent on ahead. Farewell.

Letter LXIV - On the Philosopher's Task

Yesterday you were with us. You might complain if I said "yesterday" merely. This is why I have added "with us." For, so far as I am concerned, you are always with me. Certain friends had happened in, on whose account a somewhat brighter fire was laid, – not the kind that generally bursts from the kitchen chimneys of the rich and scares the watch, but the moderate blaze which means that guests have come. Our talk ran on various themes, as is natural at a dinner; it pursued no chain of thought to the end, but jumped from one topic to another. We then had read to us a book by Quintus Sextius the Elder. He is a great man, if you have any confidence in my opinion, and a real Stoic, though he himself denies it. Ye Gods, what strength and spirit one finds in him! This is not the case with all philosophers; there are some men of illustrious name whose writings are sapless. They lay down rules, they argue, and they quibble; they do not infuse spirit simply because they have no spirit. But when you come to read Sextius you will say: "He is alive; he is strong; he is free; he is more than a man; he fills me with a mighty confidence before I close his book." I shall acknowledge to you the state of mind I am in when I read his works: I want to challenge every hazard; I want to cry: "Why keep me waiting,

Fortune? Enter the lists! Behold, I am ready for you!" I assume the spirit of a man who seeks where he may make trial of himself where he may show his worth:

> And fretting 'mid the unwarlike flocks he prays
> Some foam-flecked boar may cross his path, or else
> A tawny lion stalking down the hills.

I want something to overcome, something on which I may test my endurance. For this is another remarkable quality that Sextius possesses: he will show you the grandeur of the happy life and yet will not make you despair of attaining it; you will understand that it is on high, but that it is accessible to him who has the will to seek it.

And virtue herself will have the same effect upon you, of making you admire her and yet hope to attain her. In my own case, at any rate the very contemplation of wisdom takes much of my time; I gaze upon her with bewilderment, just as I sometimes gaze upon the firmament itself, which I often behold as if I saw it for the first time. Hence I worship the discoveries of wisdom and their discoverers; to enter, as it were, into the inheritance of many predecessors is a delight. It was for me that they laid up this treasure; it was for me that they toiled. But we should play the part of a careful householder; we should increase what we have inherited. This inheritance shall pass from me to my descendants larger than before. Much still remains to do, and much will always remain, and he who shall be born a thousand ages hence will not be barred from his opportunity of adding something further. But even if the old masters have discovered everything, one thing will be always new, – the application and the scientific study and classification of the discoveries made by others. Assume that prescriptions have been handed down to us for the healing of the eyes; there is no need of my searching for others in addition; but for all that, these prescriptions must be adapted to the particular disease and to the particular stage of the disease. Use this prescription to relieve granulation of the eyelids, that to reduce the swelling of the lids, this to prevent sudden pain or a rush of tears, that to sharpen the vision. Then compound these several prescriptions, watch for the right time of their application, and supply the proper treatment in each case.

The cures for the spirit also have been discovered by the ancients; but it is our task to learn the method and the time of treatment. Our predecessors have worked much improvement, but have not worked out the problem. They deserve respect, however, and should be worshipped with a divine ritual. Why should I not keep statues of great men to kindle my enthusiasm, and celebrate their birthdays? Why should I not continually greet them with respect and honour? The reverence which I owe to my own teachers I owe in like measure to those teachers of the human race, the source from which the beginnings of such great blessings have flowed. If I meet a consul or a praetor, I shall pay him all the honour which his post of honour is wont to receive: I shall dismount, uncover, and yield the road. What, then? Shall I admit into my soul with less than the highest marks of respect Marcus Cato, the Elder and the

Younger, Laelius the Wise, Socrates and Plato, Zeno and Cleanthes? I worship them in very truth, and always rise to do honour to such noble names. Farewell.

Letter LXV - On the First Cause

I shared my time yesterday with ill health; it claimed for itself all the period before noon; in the afternoon, however, it yielded to me. And so I first tested my spirit by reading; then, when reading was found to be possible, I dared to make more demands upon the spirit, or perhaps I should say, to make more concessions to it. I wrote a little, and indeed with more concentration than usual, for I am struggling with a difficult subject and do not wish to be downed. In the midst of this, some friends visited me, with the purpose of employing force and of restraining me, as if I were a sick man indulging in some excess. So conversation was substituted for writing; and from this conversation I shall communicate to you the topic which is still the subject of debate; for we have appointed you referee. You have more of a task on your hands than you suppose, for the argument is threefold.

Our Stoic philosophers, as you know, declare that there are two things in the universe which are the source of everything, – namely, cause and matter. Matter lies sluggish, a substance ready for any use, but sure to remain unemployed if no one sets it in motion. Cause, however, by which we mean reason, moulds matter and turns it in whatever direction it will, producing thereby various concrete results. Accordingly, there must be, in the case of each thing, that from which it is made, and, next, an agent by which it is made. The former is its material, the latter its cause.

All art is but imitation of nature; therefore, let me apply these statements of general principles to the things which have to be made by man. A statue, for example, has afforded matter which was to undergo treatment at the hands of the artist, and has had an artist who was to give form to the matter. Hence, in the case of the statue, the material was bronze, the cause was the workman. And so it goes with all things, – they consist of that which is made and of the maker. The Stoics believe in one cause only – the maker; but Aristotle thinks that the word "cause" can be used in three ways: "The first cause," he says, "is the actual matter, without which nothing can be created. The second is the workman. The third is the form, which is impressed upon every work, – a statue, for example." This last is what Aristotle calls the idos. "There is, too," says he, "a fourth, – the purpose of the work as a whole." Now I shall show you what this last means. Bronze is the "first cause" of the statue, for it could never have been made unless there had been something from which it could be cast and moulded. The "second cause" is the artist; for without the skilled hands of a workman that bronze could not have been shaped to the outlines of the statue. The "third cause" is the form, inasmuch as our statue could never be called The Lance-Bearer or The Boy Binding his Hair had not this special shape been stamped upon it. The "fourth cause" is the purpose of the work. For if this purpose had not existed, the statue would not have been made.

Now what is this purpose? It is that which attracted the artist which he followed when he made the statue. It may have been money, if he has made it for sale; or renown, if he has worked for reputation; or religion, if he has wrought it as a gift for a temple. Therefore this also is a cause contributing towards the making of the statue; or do you think that we should avoid including, among the causes of a thing which has been made, that element without which the thing in question would not have been made?

To these four Plato adds a fifth cause, – the pattern which he himself calls the "idea"; for it is this that the artist gazed upon when he created the work which he had decided to carry out. Now it makes no difference whether he has this pattern outside himself, that he may direct his glance to it, or within himself, conceived and placed there by himself. God has within himself these patterns of all things, and his mind comprehends the harmonies and the measures of the whole totality of things which are to be carried out; he is filled with these shapes which Plato calls the "ideas," – imperishable, unchangeable, not subject to decay. And therefore, though men die, humanity itself, or the idea of man, according to which man is moulded, lasts on, and though men toil and perish, it suffers no change. Accordingly, there are five causes, as Plato says: the material, the agent, the make-up, the model, and the end in view. Last comes the result of all these. Just as in the case of the statue, – to go back to the figure with which we began, – the material is the bronze, the agent is the artist, the make-up is the form which is adapted to the material, the model is the pattern imitated by the agent, the end in view is the purpose in the maker's mind, and, finally, the result of all these is the statue itself. The universe also, in Plato's opinion, possesses all these elements. The agent is God; the source, matter; the form, the shape and the arrangement of the visible world. The pattern is doubtless the model according to which God has made this great and most beautiful creation. The purpose is his object in so doing. Do you ask what God's purpose is? It is goodness. Plato, at any rate, says: "What was God's reason for creating the world? God is good, and no good person is grudging of anything that is good. Therefore, God made it the best world possible." Hand down your opinion, then, O judge; state who seems to you to say what is truest, and not who says what is absolutely true. For to do that is as far beyond our ken as truth itself.

This throng of causes, defined by Aristotle and by Plato, embraces either too much or too little. For if they regard as "causes" of an object that is to be made everything without which the object cannot be made, they have named too few. Time must be included among the causes; for nothing can be made without time. They must also include place; for if there be no place where a thing can be made, it will not be made. And motion too; nothing is either made or destroyed without motion. There is no art without motion, no change of any kind. Now, however, I am searching for the first, the general cause; this must be simple, inasmuch as matter, too, is simple. Do we ask what cause is? It is surely Creative Reason, – in other words, God. For those elements to which you referred are not a great series of independent causes; they all hinge on one alone, and that will be the creative cause. Do you maintain that form is a cause? This is only what the artist stamps upon his work; it is part of a cause, but not the cause. Neither is the pattern a cause, but an indispensable tool of the cause. His pattern is as indispensable to the artist as the chisel or the file; without these, art can make no progress. But for all that, these things are neither parts of the art, nor causes of it. "Then," perhaps you will say, "the purpose of the artist, that which leads him to undertake to create something, is the cause." It may be a cause; it is not, however, the efficient cause, but only an accessory cause. But there are countless accessory causes; what we are discussing is the general cause. Now the statement of Plato and Aristotle is not in accord with their usual penetration, when they maintain that the whole universe, the perfectly wrought work, is a cause. For there is a great difference between a work and the cause of a work.

Either give your opinion, or, as is easier in cases of this kind, declare that the matter is not clear and call for another hearing. But you will reply: "What pleasure do you get from wasting your time on these problems, which relieve you of none of your emotions, rout none of your desires?" So far as I am concerned, I treat and discuss them as matters which contribute greatly toward calming the spirit, and I search myself first, and then the world about me. And not even now am I, as you think, wasting my time. For all these questions, provided that they be not chopped up and torn apart into such unprofitable refinements, elevate and lighten the soul, which is weighted down by a heavy burden and desires to be freed and to return to the elements of which it was once a part. For this body of ours is a weight upon the soul and its penance; as the load presses down the soul is crushed and is in bondage, unless philosophy has come to its assistance and has bid it take fresh courage by contemplating the universe, and has turned it from things earthly to things divine. There it has its liberty, there it can roam abroad; meantime it escapes the custody in which it is bound, and renews its life in heaven. Just as skilled workmen, who have been engaged upon some delicate piece of work which wearies their eyes with straining, if the light which they have is niggardly or uncertain, go forth into the open air and in some park devoted to the people's recreation delight their eyes in the generous light of day; so the soul, imprisoned as it has been in this gloomy and darkened house, seeks the open sky whenever it can, and in the contemplation of the universe finds rest.

The wise man, the seeker after wisdom, is bound closely, indeed, to his body, but he is an absentee so far as his better self is concerned, and he concentrates his thoughts upon lofty things. Bound, so to speak, to his oath of allegiance, he regards the period of life as his term of service. He is so trained that he neither loves nor hates life; he endures a mortal lot, although he knows that an ampler lot is in store for him. Do you forbid me to contemplate the universe? Do you compel me to withdraw from the whole and restrict me to a part? May I not ask what are the beginnings of all things, who moulded the universe, who took the confused and conglomerate mass of sluggish matter, and separated it into its parts? May I not inquire who is the Master-Builder of this universe, how the mighty bulk was brought under the control of law and order, who gathered together the scattered atoms, who separated the disordered elements and assigned an outward form to elements that lay in one vast shapelessness? Or whence came all the expanse of light? And whether is it fire, or even brighter than fire? Am I not to ask these questions? Must I be ignorant of the heights whence I have descended? Whether I am to see this world but once, or to be born many times? What is my destination afterwards? What abode awaits my soul on its release from the laws of slavery among men? Do you forbid me to have a share in heaven? In other words, do you bid me live with my head bowed down? No, I am above such an existence; I was born to a greater destiny than to be a mere chattel of my body, and I regard this body as nothing but a chain which manacles my freedom. Therefore, I offer it as a sort of buffer to fortune, and shall allow no wound to penetrate through to my soul. For my body is the only part of me which can suffer injury. In this dwelling, which is exposed to peril, my soul lives free. Never shall this flesh drive me to feel fear or to assume any pretence that is unworthy of a good man. Never shall I lie in order to honour this petty body. When it seems proper, I shall sever my connexion with it. And at present, while we are bound together, our alliance shall nevertheless not be one of equality; the soul shall bring all quarrels before its own tribunal. To despise our bodies is sure freedom.

To return to our subject; this freedom will be greatly helped by the contemplation of which we were just speaking. All things are made up of matter and of God; God controls matter, which encompasses him and follows him as its guide and leader. And that which creates, in other words, God, is more powerful and precious than matter, which is acted upon by God. God's place in the universe corresponds to the soul's relation to man. World-matter corresponds to our mortal body; therefore let the lower serve the higher. Let us be brave in the face of hazards. Let us not fear wrongs, or wounds, or bonds, or poverty. And what is death? It is either the end, or a process of change. I have no fear of ceasing to exist; it is the same as not having begun. Nor do I shrink from changing into another state, because I shall, under no conditions, be as cramped as I am now. Farewell.

Letter LXVI - On Various Aspects of Virtue

I have just seen my former school-mate Claranus for the first time in many years. You need not wait for me to add that he is an old man; but I assure you that I found him hale in spirit and sturdy, although he is wrestling with a frail and feeble body. For Nature acted unfairly when she gave him a poor domicile for so rare a soul; or perhaps it was because she wished to prove to us that an absolutely strong and happy mind can lie hidden under any exterior. Be that as it may, Claranus overcomes all these hindrances, and by despising his own body has arrived at a stage where he can despise other things also. The poet who sang

Worth shows more pleasing in a form that's fair

is, in my opinion, mistaken. For virtue needs nothing to set it off; it is its own great glory, and it hallows the body in which it dwells. At any rate, I have begun to regard Claranus in a different light; he seems to me handsome, and as well-setup in body as in mind. A great man can spring from a hovel; so can a beautiful and great soul from an ugly and insignificant body. For this reason Nature seems to me to breed certain men of this stamp with the idea of proving that virtue springs into birth in any place whatever. Had it been possible for her to produce souls by themselves and naked, she would have done so; as it is, Nature does a still greater thing, for she produces certain men who, though hampered in their bodies, none the less break through the obstruction. I think Claranus has been produced as a pattern, that we might be enabled to understand that the soul is not disfigured by the ugliness of the body, but rather the opposite, that the body is beautified by the comeliness of the soul.

Now, though Claranus and I have spent very few days together, we have nevertheless had many conversations, which I will at once pour forth and pass on to you. The first day we investigated this problem: how can goods be equal if they are of three kinds? For certain of them, according to our philosophical tenets, are primary, such as joy, peace, and the welfare of one's country. Others are of the second order, moulded in an unhappy material, such as the endurance of suffering, and self-control during severe illness. We shall pray outright for the goods of the first class; for the second class we shall pray only if the need shall arise. There is still a third variety, as, for example, a modest gait, a calm and honest countenance, and a bearing that suits the man of wisdom. Now how can these things be equal when we compare them, if you grant that we ought to pray for the one and avoid the other? If we would make distinctions among them, we had better return to the First Good, and consider what its nature is: the soul that gazes upon truth, that is skilled in what should be sought and what should be avoided, establishing standards of value not according to opinion, but according to nature, – the soul that penetrates the whole world and directs its contemplating gaze upon all its Phenomena, paying strict attention to thoughts and actions, equally great and forceful, superior alike to hardships and blandishments, yielding itself to neither extreme of fortune, rising above all blessings and tribulations, absolutely beautiful, perfectly equipped with grace as well as with strength, healthy and sinewy, unruffled, undismayed, one which no violence can shatter, one which acts of chance can neither exalt nor depress, – a soul like this is virtue itself. There you have its outward appearance, if it should ever come under a single view and show itself once in all its completeness. But there are many aspects of it. They unfold themselves according as life varies and as actions differ; but virtue itself does not become less or greater. For the Supreme Good cannot diminish, nor may virtue retrograde; rather is it transformed, now into one quality and now into another, shaping itself according to the part which it is to play. Whatever it has touched it brings into likeness with itself, and dyes with its own colour. It adorns our actions, our friendships, and sometimes entire households which it has entered and set in order. Whatever it has handled it forthwith makes lovable, notable, admirable.

Therefore the power and the greatness of virtue cannot rise to greater heights, because increase is denied to that which is superlatively great. You will find nothing straighter than the straight, nothing truer than the truth, and nothing more temperate than that which is temperate. Every virtue is limitless; for limits depend upon definite measurements. Constancy cannot advance further, any more than fidelity, or truthfulness, or loyalty. What can be added to that which is perfect? Nothing otherwise that was not perfect to which something has been added. Nor can anything be added to virtue, either, for if anything can be added thereto, it must have contained a defect. Honour, also, permits of no addition; for it is honourable because of the very qualities which I have mentioned. What then? Do you think that propriety, justice, lawfulness, do not also belong to the same type, and that they are kept within fixed limits? The ability to increase is proof that a thing is still imperfect.

The good, in every instance, is subject to these same laws. The advantage of the state and that of the individual are yoked together; indeed it is as impossible to separate them as to separate the commendable from the desirable. Therefore, virtues are mutually equal; and so are the works of virtue, and all men who are so fortunate as to possess these virtues. But, since the virtues of plants and of animals are perishable, they are also frail and fleeting and uncertain. They spring up, and they sink down again, and for this reason they are not rated at the same value; but to human virtues only one rule applies. For right reason is single and of but one kind. Nothing is more divine than the divine, or more heavenly than the heavenly. Mortal things decay, fall, are worn out, grow up, are exhausted, and replenished. Hence, in their case, in view of the uncertainty of their lot, there is inequality; but of things divine the nature is one. Reason, however, is nothing else than a portion of the divine spirit set in a human body. If reason is divine, and the good in no case lacks reason, then the good in every case is divine. And furthermore, there is no distinction between things divine; hence there is none between goods, either. Therefore it follows that joy and a brave unyielding endurance of torture are equal goods; for in both there is the same greatness of soul relaxed and cheerful in the one case, in the other combative and braced for action. What?

Do you not think that the virtue of him who bravely storms the enemy's stronghold is equal to that of him who endures a siege with the utmost patience? Great is Scipio when he invests Numantia, and constrains and compels the hands of an enemy, whom he could not conquer, to resort to their own destruction. Great also are the souls of the defenders – men who know that, as long as the path to death lies open, the blockade is not complete, men who breathe their last in the arms of liberty. In like manner, the other virtues are also equal as compared with one another: tranquillity, simplicity, generosity, constancy, equanimity, endurance. For underlying them all is a single virtue – that which renders the soul straight and unswerving.

"What then," you say; "is there no difference between joy and unyielding endurance of pain?" None at all, as regards the virtues themselves; very great, however, in the circumstances in which either of these two virtues is displayed. In the one case, there is a natural relaxation and loosening of the soul; in the other there is an unnatural pain. Hence these circumstances, between which a great distinction can be drawn, belong to the category of indifferent things, but the virtue shown in each case is equal. Virtue is not changed by the matter with which it deals; if the matter is hard and stubborn, it does not make the virtue worse; if pleasant and joyous, it does not make it better. Therefore, virtue necessarily remains equal. For, in each case, what is done is done with equal uprightness, with equal wisdom, and with equal honour. Hence the states of goodness involved are equal, and it is impossible for a man to transcend these states of goodness by conducting himself better, either the one man in his joy, or the other amid his suffering. And two goods, neither of which can possibly be better, are equal. For if things which are extrinsic to virtue can either diminish or increase virtue, then that which is honourable ceases to be the only good. If you grant this, honour has wholly perished. And why? Let me tell you: it is because no act is honourable that is done by an unwilling agent, that is compulsory. Every honourable act is voluntary. Alloy it with reluctance, complaints, cowardice, or fear, and it loses its best characteristic – self-approval. That which is not free cannot be honourable; for fear means slavery. The honourable is wholly free from anxiety and is calm; if it ever objects, laments, or regards anything as an evil, it becomes subject to disturbance and begins to flounder about amid great confusion. For on one side the semblance of right calls to it, on the other the suspicion of evil drags it back, therefore, when a man is about to do something honourable, he should not regard any obstacles as evils, even though he regard them as inconvenient, but he should will to do the deed, and do it willingly. For every honourable act is done without commands or compulsion; it is unalloyed and contains no admixture of evil.

I know what you may reply to me at this point: "Are you trying to make us believe that it does not matter whether a man feels joy, or whether he lies upon the rack and tires out his torturer?" I might say in answer: "Epicurus also maintains that the wise man, though he is being burned in the bull of Phalaris, will cry out: 'Tis pleasant, and concerns me not at all.'" Why need you wonder, if I maintain that he who reclines at a banquet and the victim who stoutly withstands torture possess equal goods, when Epicurus maintains a thing that is harder to believe, namely, that it is pleasant to be roasted in this way? But the reply which I do make, is that there is great difference between joy and pain; if I am asked to choose, I shall seek the former and avoid the latter. The former is according to nature, the latter contrary to it. So long as they are rated by this standard, there is a great gulf between; but when it comes to a question of the virtue involved, the virtue in each case is the same, whether it comes through joy or through sorrow. Vexation and pain and other inconveniences are of no consequence, for they are overcome by virtue. Just as the brightness of the sun dims all lesser lights, so virtue, by its own greatness, shatters and overwhelms all pains, annoyances, and wrongs; and wherever its radiance reaches, all lights which shine without the help of virtue are extinguished; and inconveniences, when they come in contact with virtue, play no more important a part than does a storm-cloud at sea.

This can be proved to you by the fact that the good man will hasten unhesitatingly to any noble deed; even though he be confronted by the hangman, the torturer, and the stake, he will persist, regarding not what he must suffer, but what he must do; and he will entrust himself as readily to an honourable deed as he would to a good man; he will consider it advantageous to himself, safe, propitious. And he will hold the same view concerning an honourable deed, even though it be fraught with sorrow and hardship, as concerning a good man who is poor or wasting away in exile. Come now, contrast a good man who is rolling in wealth with a man who has nothing, except that in himself he has all things; they will be equally good, though they experience unequal fortune. This same standard, as I have remarked, is to be applied to things as well as to men; virtue is just as praiseworthy if it dwells in a sound and free body, as in one which is sickly or in bondage. Therefore, as regards your own virtue also, you will not praise it any more, if fortune has favoured it by granting you a sound body, than if fortune has endowed you with a body that is crippled in some member, since that would mean rating a master low because he is dressed like a slave. For all those things over which Chance holds sway are chattels, money, person, position; they are weak, shifting, prone to perish, and of uncertain tenure. On the other hand, the works of virtue are free and unsubdued, neither more worthy to be sought when fortune treats them kindly, nor less worthy when any adversity weighs upon them.

Now friendship in the case of men corresponds to desirability in the case of things. You would not, I fancy, love a good man if he were rich any more than if he were poor, nor would you love a strong and muscular person more than one who was slender and of delicate constitution. Accordingly, neither will you seek or love a good thing that is mirthful and tranquil more than one that is full of perplexity and toil. Or, if you do this, you will, in the case of two equally good men, care more for him who is neat and well-groomed than for him who is dirty and unkempt. You would next go so far as to care more for a good man who is sound in all his limbs and without blemish, than for one who is weak or purblind; and gradually your fastidiousness would reach such a point that, of two equally just and prudent men, you would choose him who has long curling hair! Whenever the virtue in each one is equal, the inequality in

336

their other attributes is not apparent. For all other things are not parts, but merely accessories. Would any man judge his children so unfairly as to care more for a healthy son than for one who was sickly, or for a tall child of unusual stature more than for one who was short or of middling height? Wild beasts show no favouritism among their offspring; they lie down in order to suckle all alike; birds make fair distribution of their food. Ulysses hastens back to the rocks of his Ithaca as eagerly as Agamemnon speeds to the kingly walls of Mycenae. For no man loves his native land because it is great; he loves it because it is his own.

And what is the purpose of all this? That you may know that virtue regards all her works in the same light, as if they were her children, showing equal kindness to all, and still deeper kindness to those which encounter hardships; for even parents lean with more affection towards those of their offspring for whom they feel pity. Virtue, too, does not necessarily love more deeply those of her works which she beholds in trouble and under heavy burdens, but, like good parents, she gives them more of her fostering care.

Why is no good greater than any other good? It is because nothing can be more fitting than that which is fitting, and nothing more level than that which is level. You cannot say that one thing is more equal to a given object than another thing; hence also nothing is more honourable than that which is honourable. Accordingly, if all the virtues are by nature equal, the three varieties of goods are equal. This is what I mean: there is an equality between feeling joy with self-control and suffering pain with self-control. The joy in the one case does not surpass in the other the steadfastness of soul that gulps down the groan when the victim is in the clutches of the torturer; goods of the first kind are desirable, while those of the second are worthy of admiration; and in each case they are none the less equal, because whatever inconvenience attaches to the latter is compensated by the qualities of the good, which is so much greater. Any man who believes them to be unequal is turning away from the virtues themselves and is surveying mere externals; true goods have the same weight and the same width. The spurious sort contain much emptiness; hence, when they are weighed in the balance, they are found wanting, although they look imposing and grand to the gaze.

Yes, my dear Lucilius, the good which true reason approves is solid and everlasting; it strengthens the spirit and exalts it, so that it will always be on the heights; but those things which are thoughtlessly praised, and are goods in the opinion of the mob merely puff us up with empty joy. And again, those things which are feared as if they were evils merely inspire trepidation in men's minds, for the mind is disturbed by the semblance of danger, just as animals are disturbed. Hence it is without reason that both these things distract and sting the spirit; the one is not worthy of joy, nor the other of fear. It is reason alone that is unchangeable, that holds fast to its decisions. For reason is not a slave to the senses, but a ruler over them. Reason is equal to reason, as one straight line to another; therefore virtue also is equal to virtue. Virtue is nothing else than right reason. All virtues are reasons. Reasons are reasons, if they are right reasons. If they are right, they are also equal. As reason is, so also are actions; therefore all actions are equal. For since they resemble reason, they also resemble each other. Moreover, I hold that actions are equal to each other in so far as they are honourable and right actions. There will be, of course, great differences according as the material varies, as it becomes now broader and now narrower, now glorious and now base, now manifold in scope and now limited. However, that which is best in all these cases is equal; they are all honourable. In the same way, all good men, in so far as they are good, are equal. There are, indeed, differences of age, one is older, another younger; of body, – one is comely, another is ugly; of fortune, – this man is rich, that man poor, this one is influential, powerful, and well-known to cities and peoples, that man is unknown to most, and is obscure. But all, in respect of that wherein they are good, are equal. The senses do not decide upon things good and evil; they do not know what is useful and what is not useful. They cannot record their opinion unless they are brought face to face with a fact; they can neither see into the future nor recollect the past; and they do not know what results from what. But it is from such knowledge that a sequence and succession of actions is woven, and a unity of life is created, – a unity which will proceed in a straight course. Reason, therefore, is the judge of good and evil; that which is foreign and external she regards as dross, and that which is neither good nor evil she judges as merely accessory, insignificant and trivial. For all her good resides in the soul.

But there are certain goods which reason regards as primary, to which she addresses herself purposely; these are, for example, victory, good children, and the welfare of one's country. Certain others she regards as secondary; these become manifest only in adversity, – for example, equanimity in enduring severe illness or exile. Certain goods are indifferent; these are no more according to nature than contrary to nature, as, for example, a discreet gait and a sedate posture in a chair. For sitting is an act that is not less according to nature than standing or walking. The two kinds of goods which are of a higher order are different; the primary are according to nature, – such as deriving joy from the dutiful behaviour of one's children and from the well-being of one's country. The secondary are contrary to nature, – such as fortitude in resisting torture or in enduring thirst when illness makes the vitals feverish. "What then," you say; "can anything that is contrary to nature be a good?" Of course not; but that in which this good takes its rise is sometimes contrary to nature. For being wounded, wasting away over a fire, being afflicted with bad health, – such things are contrary to nature; but it is in accordance with nature for a man to preserve an indomitable soul amid such distresses. To explain my thought briefly, the material with which a good is concerned is sometimes contrary to nature, but a good itself never is contrary, since no good is without reason, and reason is in accordance with nature.

"What, then," you ask, "is reason?" It is copying nature. "And what," you say, "is the greatest good that man can possess?" It is to conduct oneself according to what nature wills. "There is no doubt," says the objector, "that peace affords more happiness when it has not been assailed than when it has been recovered at the cost of great slaughter." "There is no doubt also," he continues, "that health which has not been impaired affords more happiness than health which has been restored to soundness by means of force, as it were, and by endurance of suffering, after serious illnesses that threaten life itself. And similarly there will be no doubt that joy is a greater good than a soul's struggle to endure to the bitter end the torments of wounds or burning at the stake." By no means. For things that result from hazard admit of wide distinctions, since they are rated according to their usefulness in the eyes of those who experience them, but with regard to goods, the only point to be considered is that they are in agreement with nature; and this is equal in the case of all goods. When at a meeting of the Senate we vote in favour of someone's motion, it cannot be said, "A. is more in accord with the motion than B." All alike vote for the same motion. I make the same statement with regard to virtues, – they are all in accord with nature; and I make it with regard to goods also, – they are all in accord with nature. One man dies young, another in old age, and still another in infancy, having enjoyed nothing more than a mere glimpse out into life. They have all been equally subject to death, even though death has permitted the one to proceed farther along the pathway of life, has cut off the life of the second in his flower, and has broken off the life of the third at its very beginning. Some get their release at the dinner-table. Others extend their sleep into the sleep of death. Some are blotted out during dissipation. Now contrast with these persons individuals who have been pierced by the sword, or bitten to death by snakes, or crushed in ruins, or tortured piecemeal out of existence by the prolonged twisting of their sinews. Some of these departures may be regarded as better, some as worse; but the act of dying is equal in all. The methods of ending life are different; but the end is one and the same. Death has no degrees of greater or less; for it has the same limit in all instances, – the finishing of life.

The same thing holds true, I assure you, concerning goods; you will find one amid circumstances of pure pleasure, another amid sorrow and bitterness. The one controls the favours of fortune; the other overcomes her onslaughts. Each is equally a good, although the one travels a level and easy road, and the other a rough road. And the end of them all is the same – they are goods, they are worthy of praise, they accompany virtue and reason. Virtue makes all the things that it acknowledges equal to one another. You need not wonder that this is one of our principles; we find mentioned in the works of Epicurus two goods, of which his Supreme Good, or blessedness, is composed, namely, a body free from pain and a soul free from disturbance. These goods, if they are complete, do not increase; for how can that which is complete increase? The body is, let us suppose, free from pain; what increase can there be to this absence of pain? The soul is composed and calm; what increase can there be to this tranquillity? . Just as fair weather, purified into the purest brilliancy, does not admit of a still greater degree of clearness; so, when a man takes care of his body and of his soul, weaving the texture of his good from both, his condition is perfect, and he has found the consummation of his prayers, if there is no commotion in his soul or pain in his body. Whatever delights fall to his lot over and above these two things do not increase his Supreme Good; they merely season it, so to speak, and add spice to it. For the absolute good of man's nature is satisfied with peace in the body and peace in the soul. I can show you at this moment in the writings of Epicurus a graded list of goods just like that of our own school. For there are some things, he declares, which he prefers should fall to his lot, such as bodily rest free from all inconvenience, and relaxation of the soul as it takes delight in the contemplation of its own goods. And there are other things which, though he would prefer that they did not happen, he nevertheless praises and approves, for example, the kind of resignation, in times of ill-health and serious suffering, to which I alluded a moment ago, and which Epicurus displayed on that last and most blessed day of his life. For he tells us that he had to endure excruciating agony from a diseased bladder and from an ulcerated stomach, so acute that it permitted no increase of pain; "and yet," he says, "that day was none the less happy." And no man can spend such a day in happiness unless he possesses the Supreme Good.

We therefore find mentioned, even by Epicurus, those goods which one would prefer not to experience; which, however, because circumstances have decided thus, must be welcomed and approved and placed on a level with the highest goods. We cannot say that the good which has rounded out a happy life, the good for which Epicurus rendered thanks in the last words he uttered, is not equal to the greatest. Allow me, excellent Lucilius, to utter a still bolder word: if any goods could be greater than others, I should prefer those which seem harsh to those which are mild and alluring, and should pronounce them greater. For it is more of an accomplishment to break one's way through difficulties than to keep joy within bounds. It requires the same use of reason, I am fully aware, for a man to endure prosperity well and also to endure misfortune bravely. What man may be just as brave who sleeps in front of the ramparts without fear of danger when no enemy attacks the camp, as the man who, when the tendons of his legs have been severed, holds himself up on his knees and does not let fall his weapons; but it is to the blood-stained soldier returning from the front that men cry: "Well done, thou hero!" And therefore I should bestow greater praise upon those goods that have stood trial and show courage, and have fought it out with fortune. Should I hesitate whether to give greater praise to the maimed and shrivelled hand of Mucius than to the uninjured hand of the bravest man in the world? There stood Mucius, despising the enemy and despising the fire, and watched his hand as it dripped blood over the fire on his enemy's altar, until Porsenna, envying the fame of the hero whose punishment he was advocating, ordered the fire to be removed against the will of the victim.

Why should I not reckon this good among the primary goods, and deem it in so far greater than those other goods which are unattended by danger and have made no trial of fortune, as it is a rarer thing to have overcome a foe with a hand lost than with a hand armed? "What then?" you say; "shall you desire this good for yourself?" Of course I shall. For this is a thing that a man cannot achieve unless he can also desire it. Should I desire, instead, to be allowed to stretch out my limbs for my slaves to massage, or to have a woman, or a man changed into the likeness of a woman, pull my finger-joints? I cannot help believing that Mucius was all the more lucky because he manipulated the flames as calmly as if he were holding out his hand to the manipulator. He had wiped out all his previous mistakes; he finished the war unarmed and maimed;

and with that stump of a hand he conquered two kings. Farewell.

Letter LXVII - On Ill-Health and Endurance of Suffering

If I may begin with a commonplace remark, spring is gradually disclosing itself; but though it is rounding into summer, when you would expect hot weather, it has kept rather cool, and one cannot yet be sure of it. For it often slides back into winter weather. Do you wish to know how uncertain it still is? I do not yet trust myself to a bath which is absolutely cold; even at this time I break its chill. You may say that this is no way to show the endurance either of heat or of cold; very true, dear Lucilius, but at my time of life one is at length contented with the natural chill of the body. I can scarcely thaw out in the middle of summer. Accordingly, I spend most of the time bundled up; and I thank old age for keeping me fastened to my bed. Why should I not thank old age on this account? That which I ought not to wish to do, I lack the ability to do. Most of my converse is with books. Whenever your letters arrive, I imagine that I am with you, and I have the feeling that I am about to speak my answer, instead of writing it. Therefore let us together investigate the nature of this problem of yours, just as if we were conversing with one another.

You ask me whether every good is desirable. You say: "If it is a good to be brave under torture, to go to the stake with a stout heart, to endure illness with resignation, it follows that these things are desirable. But I do not see that any of them is worth praying for. At any rate I have as yet known of no man who has paid a vow by reason of having been cut to pieces by the rod, or twisted out of shape by the gout, or made taller by the rack." My dear Lucilius, you must distinguish between these cases; you will then comprehend that there is something in them that is to be desired. I should prefer to be free from torture; but if the time comes when it must be endured, I shall desire that I may conduct myself therein with bravery, honour, and courage. Of course I prefer that war should not occur; but if war does occur, I shall desire that I may nobly endure the wounds, the starvation, and all that the exigency of war brings. Nor am I so mad as to crave illness; but if I must suffer illness, I shall desire that I may do nothing which shows lack of restraint, and nothing that is unmanly. The conclusion is, not that hardships are desirable, but that virtue is desirable, which enables us patiently to endure hardships.

Certain of our school, think that, of all such qualities, a stout endurance is not desirable, – though not to be deprecated either – because we ought to seek by prayer only the good which is unalloyed, peaceful, and beyond the reach of trouble. Personally, I do not agree with them. And why? First, because it is impossible for anything to be good without being also desirable. Because, again, if virtue is desirable, and if nothing that is good lacks virtue, then everything good is desirable. And, lastly, because a brave endurance even under torture is desirable. At this point I ask you: is not bravery desirable? And yet bravery despises and challenges danger. The most beautiful and most admirable part of bravery is that it does not shrink from the stake, advances to meet wounds, and sometimes does not even avoid the spear, but meets it with opposing breast. If bravery is desirable, so is patient endurance of torture; for this is a part of bravery. Only sift these things, as I have suggested; then there will be nothing which can lead you astray. For it is not mere endurance of torture, but brave endurance, that is desirable. I therefore desire that "brave" endurance; and this is virtue.

"But," you say, "who ever desired such a thing for himself?" Some prayers are open and outspoken, when the requests are offered specifically; other prayers are indirectly expressed, when they include many requests under one title. For example, I desire a life of honour. Now a life of honour includes various kinds of conduct; it may include the chest in which Regulus was confined, or the wound of Cato which was torn open by Cato's own hand, or the exile of Rutilius, or the cup of poison which removed Socrates from gaol to heaven. Accordingly, in praying for a life of honour, I have prayed also for those things without which, on some occasions, life cannot be honourable

> O thrice and four times blest were they
> Who underneath the lofty walls of Troy
> Met happy death before their parents' eyes!

What does it matter whether you offer this prayer for some individual, or admit that it was desirable in the past? Decius sacrificed himself for the State; he set spurs to his horse and rushed into the midst of the foe, seeking death. The second Decius, rivalling his father's valour, reproducing the words which had become sacred and already household words, dashed into the thickest of the fight, anxious only that his sacrifice might bring omen of success, and regarding a noble death as a thing to be desired. Do you doubt, then, whether it is best to die glorious and performing some deed of valour? When one endures torture bravely, one is using all the virtues. Endurance may perhaps be the only virtue that is on view and most manifest; but bravery is there too, and endurance and resignation and long-suffering are its branches. There, too, is foresight; for without foresight no plan can be undertaken; it is foresight that advises one to bear as bravely as possible the things one cannot avoid. There also is steadfastness, which cannot be dislodged from its position, which the wrench of no force can cause to abandon its purpose. There is the whole inseparable company of virtues; every honourable act is the work of one single virtue, but it is in accordance with the judgment of the whole council. And that which is approved by all the virtues, even though it seems to be the work of one alone, is desirable.

What? Do you think that those things only are desirable which come to us amid pleasure and ease, and which we bedeck our doors to welcome? There are certain goods whose features are forbidding. There are certain prayers which are offered by a throng, not of men who rejoice, but of men who bow down reverently and worship. Was it not in this fashion, think you, that Regulus prayed that he might reach Carthage? Clothe yourself with a hero's courage, and withdraw for a little space from the opinions of the common man. Form a proper conception of the image of virtue, a thing of exceeding beauty and grandeur; this image is not to be worshipped by us with incense or garlands, but with sweat and blood. Behold Marcus Cato, laying upon that hallowed breast his unspotted hands, and tearing apart the wounds which had not gone deep enough to kill him! Which, pray, shall you say to him: "I hope all will be as you wish," and "I am grieved," or shall it be "Good fortune in your undertaking!"?

In this connexion I think of our friend Demetrius, who calls an easy existence, untroubled by the attacks of Fortune, a "Dead Sea." If you have nothing to stir you up and rouse you to action, nothing which will test your resolution by its threats and hostilities; if you recline in unshaken comfort, it is not tranquillity; it is merely a flat calm. The Stoic Attalus was wont to say: "I should prefer that Fortune keep me in her camp rather than in the lap of luxury. If I am tortured, but bear it bravely, all is well; if I die, but die bravely, it is also well." Listen to Epicurus; he will tell you that it is actually pleasant. I myself shall never apply an effeminate word to an act so honourable and austere. If I go to the stake, I shall go unbeaten. Why should I not regard this as desirable – not because the fire, burns me, but because it does not overcome me? Nothing is more excellent or more beautiful than virtue; whatever we do in obedience to her orders is both good and desirable. Farewell.

Letter LXVIII - On Wisdom and Retirement

I fall in with your plan; retire and conceal yourself in repose. But at the same time conceal your retirement also. In doing this, you may be sure that you will be following the example of the Stoics, if not their precept. But you will be acting according to their precept also; you will thus satisfy both yourself and any Stoic you please. We Stoics do not urge men to take up public life in every case, or at all times, or without any qualification. Besides, when we have assigned to our wise man that field of public life which is worthy of him, – in other words, the universe, – he is then not apart from public life, even if he withdraws; nay, perhaps he has abandoned only one little corner thereof and has passed over into greater and wider regions; and when he has been set in the heavens, he understands how lowly was the place in which he sat when he mounted the curule chair or the judgment-seat. Lay this to heart, that the wise man is never more active in affairs than when things divine as well as things human have come within his ken.

I now return to the advice which I set out to give you, – that you keep your retirement in the background. There is no need to fasten a placard upon yourself with the words: "Philosopher and Quietist." Give your purpose some other name; call it ill-health and bodily weakness, or mere laziness. To boast of our retirement is but idle self-seeking. Certain animals hide themselves from discovery by confusing the marks of their foot-prints in the neighbourhood of their lairs. You should do the same. Otherwise, there will always be someone dogging your footsteps. Many men pass by that which is visible, and peer after things hidden and concealed; a locked room invites the thief. Things which lie in the open appear cheap; the house-breaker passes by that which is exposed to view. This is the way of the world, and the way of all ignorant men: they crave to burst in upon hidden things. It is therefore best not to vaunt one's retirement. It is, however, a sort of vaunting to make too much of one's concealment and of one's withdrawal from the sight of men. So-and-so has gone into his retreat at Tarentum; that other man has shut himself up at Naples; this third person for many years has not crossed the threshold of his own house. To advertise one's retirement is to collect a crowd. When you withdraw from the world your business is to talk with yourself, not to have men talk about you. But what shall you talk about? Do just what people are fond of doing when they talk about their neighbours, – speak ill of yourself when by yourself; then you will become accustomed both to speak and to hear the truth. Above all, however, ponder that which you come to feel is your greatest weakness. Each man knows best the defects of his own body. And so one relieves his stomach by vomiting, another props it up by frequent eating, another drains and purges his body by periodic fasting. Those whose feet are visited by pain abstain either from wine or from the bath. In general, men who are careless in other respects go out of their way to relieve the disease which frequently afflicts them. So it is with our souls; there are in them certain parts which are, so to speak, on the sick-list, and to these parts the cure must be applied.

What, then, am I myself doing with my leisure? I am trying to cure my own sores. If I were to show you a swollen foot, or an inflamed hand, or some shrivelled sinews in a withered leg, you would permit me to lie quiet in one place and to apply lotions to the diseased member. But my trouble is greater than any of these, and I cannot show it to you. The abscess, or ulcer, is deep within my breast. Pray, pray, do not commend me, do not say: "What a great man! He has learned to despise all things; condemning the madnesses of man's life, he has made his escape!" I have condemned nothing except myself. There is no reason why you should desire to come to me for the sake of making progress. You are mistaken if you think that you will get any assistance from this quarter; it is not a physician that dwells here, but a sick man. I would rather have you say, on leaving my presence: "I used to think him a happy man and a learned one, and I had pricked up my ears to hear him; but I have been defrauded. I have seen nothing, heard nothing which I craved and which I came back to hear." If you feel thus, and speak thus, some progress has been made. I prefer you to pardon rather than envy my retirement.

Then you say: "Is it retirement, Seneca, that you are recommending to me? You will soon be falling back upon the maxims of Epicurus!" I do recommend retirement to you, but only that you may use it for greater and more beautiful activities than those which you have resigned; to knock at the haughty doors of the influential, to make alphabetical lists of childless old men, to wield the highest authority in public life, – this kind of power exposes you to hatred, is short-lived, and, if you rate it at its true value, is tawdry. One man shall be far ahead of me as regards his influence in public life, another in salary as an army officer and in the position which results from this, another in the throng of his clients; but it is worth while to be outdone by all these men, provided that I myself can outdo Fortune. And I am no match for her in the throng; she has the greater backing.

Would that in earlier days you had been minded to follow this purpose! Would that we were not discussing the happy life in plain view of death! But even now let us have no delay. For now we can take the word of experience, which tells us that there are many superfluous and hostile things; for this we should long since have taken the word of reason. Let us do what men are wont to do when they are late in setting forth, and wish to make up for lost time by increasing their speed – let us ply the spur. Our time of life is the best possible for these pursuits; for the period of boiling and foaming is now past. The faults that were uncontrolled in the first fierce heat of youth are now weakened, and but little further effort is needed to extinguish them.

"And when," you ask, "will that profit you which you do not learn until your departure, and how will it profit you?" Precisely in this way, that I shall depart a better man. You need not think, however, that any time of life is more fitted to the attainment of a sound mind than that which has gained the victory over itself by many trials and by long and oft-repeated regret for past mistakes, and, its passions assuaged, has reached a state of health. This is indeed the time to have acquired this good; he who has attained wisdom in his old age, has attained it by his years. Farewell.

Letter LXIX - On Rest and Restlessness

I do not like you to change your headquarters and scurry about from one place to another. My reasons are, – first, that such frequent flitting means an unsteady spirit. And the spirit cannot through retirement grow into unity unless it has ceased from its inquisitiveness and its wanderings. To be able to hold your spirit in check, you must first stop the runaway flight of the body. My second reason is, that the remedies which are most helpful are those which are not interrupted. You should not allow your quiet, or the oblivion to which you have consigned your former life, to be broken into. Give your eyes time to unlearn what they have seen, and your ears to grow accustomed to more wholesome words. Whenever you stir abroad you will meet, even as you pass from one place to another, things that will bring back your old cravings. Just as he who tries to be rid of an old love must avoid every reminder of the person once held dear (for nothing grows again so easily as love), similarly, he who would lay aside his desire for all the things which he used to crave so passionately, must turn away both eyes and ears from the objects which he has abandoned. The emotions soon return to the attack; at every turn they will notice before their eyes an object worth their attention. There is no evil that does not offer inducements. Avarice promises money; luxury, a varied assortment of pleasures; ambition, a purple robe and applause, and the influence which results from applause, and all that influence can do. Vices tempt you by the rewards which they offer; but in the life of which I speak, you must live without being paid. Scarcely will a whole life-time suffice to bring our vices into subjection and to make them accept the yoke, swollen as they are by long-continued indulgence; and still less, if we cut into our brief span by any interruptions. Even constant care and attention can scarcely bring any one undertaking to full completion. If you will give ear to my advice, ponder and practise this, – how to welcome death, or even, if circumstances commend that course, to invite it. There is no difference whether death comes to us, or whether we go to death. Make yourself believe that all ignorant men are wrong when they say: "It is a beautiful thing to die one's own death." But there is no man who does not die his own death. What is more, you may reflect on this thought: No one dies except on his own day. You are throwing away none of your own time; for what you leave behind does not belong to you. Farewell.

Letter LXX - On the Proper Time to Slip the Cable

After a long space of time I have seen your beloved Pompeii. I was thus brought again face to face with the days of my youth. And it seemed to me that I could still do, nay, had only done a short time ago, all the things which I did there when a young man. We have sailed past life, Lucilius, as if we were on a voyage, and just as when at sea, to quote from our poet Vergil,

Lands and towns are left astern,

even so, on this journey where time flies with the greatest speed, we put below the horizon first our boyhood and then our youth, and then the space which lies between young manhood and middle age and borders on both, and next, the best years of old age itself. Last of all, we begin to sight the general bourne of the race of man. Fools that we are, we believe this bourne to be a dangerous reef; but it is the harbour, where we must some day put in, which we may never refuse to enter; and if a man has reached this harbour in his early years, he has no more right to complain than a sailor who has made a quick voyage. For some sailors, as you know, are tricked and held back by sluggish winds, and grow weary and sick of the slow-moving calm; while others are carried quickly home by steady gales.

You may consider that the same thing happens to us: life has carried some men with the greatest rapidity to the harbour, the harbour they were bound to reach even if they tarried on the way, while others it has fretted and harassed. To such a life, as you are aware, one should not always cling. For mere living is not a good, but living well. Accordingly, the wise man will live as long as he ought, not as long as he can. He will mark in what place, with whom, and how he is to conduct his existence, and what he is about to do. He always reflects concerning the quality, and not the quantity, of his life. As soon as there are many events in his life that give him trouble and disturb his peace of mind, he sets himself free. And this privilege is his, not only when the crisis is upon him, but as soon as Fortune seems to be playing him false; then he looks about carefully and sees whether he ought, or ought not, to end his life on that account. He holds that it makes no difference to him whether his taking-off be natural or self-inflicted, whether it comes later or earlier. He does not regard it with fear, as if it were a great loss; for no man can lose very much when but a driblet remains. It is not a question of dying earlier or later, but of dying well or ill. And dying well means escape from the danger of living ill.

That is why I regard the words of the well-known Rhodian as most unmanly. This person was thrown into a cage by his tyrant, and fed there like some wild animal. And when a certain man advised him to end his life by fasting, he replied: "A man may hope for anything while he has life." This may be true; but life is not to be purchased at any price. No matter how great or how well-assured certain rewards may be I shall not strive to attain them at the price of a shameful confession of weakness. Shall I reflect that Fortune has all power over one who lives, rather than reflect that she has no power over one who knows how to die? There are times, nevertheless, when a man, even though certain death impends and he knows that torture is in store for him, will refrain from lending a hand to his own punishment, to himself, however, he would lend a hand. It is folly to die through fear of dying. The executioner is upon you; wait for him. Why anticipate him? Why assume the management of a cruel task that belongs to another? Do you grudge your executioner his privilege, or do you merely relieve him of his task? Socrates might have ended his life by fasting; he might have died by starvation rather than by poison. But instead of this he spent thirty days in prison awaiting death, not with the idea "everything may happen," or "so long an interval has room for many a hope" but in order that he might show himself submissive to the laws and make the last moments of Socrates an edification to his friends. What would have been more foolish than to scorn death, and yet fear poison?

Scribonia, a woman of the stern old type, was an aunt of Drusus Libo. This young man was as stupid as he was well born, with higher ambitions than anyone could have been expected to entertain in that epoch, or a man like himself in any epoch at all. When Libo had been carried away ill from the senate-house in his litter, though certainly with a very scanty train of followers, – for all his kinsfolk undutifully deserted him, when he was no longer a criminal but a corpse, – he began to consider whether he should commit suicide, or await death. Scribonia said to him: "What pleasure do you find in doing another man's work?" But he did not follow her advice; he laid violent hands upon himself. And he was right, after all; for when a man is doomed to die in two or three days at his enemy's pleasure, he is really "doing another man's work" if he continues to live.

No general statement can be made, therefore, with regard to the question whether, when a power beyond our control threatens us with death, we should anticipate death, or await it. For there are many arguments to pull us in either direction. If one death is accompanied by torture, and the other is simple and easy, why not snatch the latter? Just as I shall select my ship when I am about to go on a voyage or my house when I propose to take a residence, so I shall choose my death when I am about to depart from life. Moreover, just as a long-drawn out life does not necessarily mean a better one, so a long-drawn-out death necessarily means a worse one. There is no occasion when the soul should be humoured more than at the moment of death. Let the soul depart as it feels itself impelled to go; whether it seeks the sword, or the halter, or some drought that attacks the veins, let it proceed and burst the bonds of its slavery. Every man ought to make his life acceptable to others besides himself, but his death to himself alone. The best form of death is the one we like. Men are foolish who reflect thus: "One person will say that my conduct was not brave enough; another, that I was too headstrong; a third, that a particular kind of death would have betokened more spirit." What you should really reflect is: "I have under consideration a purpose with which the talk of men has no concern!" Your sole aim should be to escape from Fortune as speedily as possible; otherwise, there will be no lack of persons who will think ill of what you have done.

You can find men who have gone so far as to profess wisdom and yet maintain that one should not offer violence to one's own life, and hold it accursed for a man to be the means of his own destruction; we should wait, say they, for the end decreed by nature. But one who says this does not see that he is shutting off the path to freedom. The best thing which eternal law ever ordained was that it allowed to us one entrance into life, but many exits. Must I await the cruelty either of disease or of man, when I can depart through the midst of torture, and shake off my troubles? This is the one reason why we cannot complain of life; it keeps no one against his will. Humanity is well situated, because no man is unhappy except by his own fault. Live, if you so desire; if not, you may return to the place whence you came. You have often been cupped in order to relieve headaches. You have had veins cut for the purpose of reducing your weight. If you would pierce your heart, a gaping wound is not necessary – a lancet will open the way to that great freedom, and tranquillity can be purchased at the cost of a pin-prick.

What, then, is it which makes us lazy and sluggish? None of us reflects that some day he must depart from this house of life; just so old tenants are kept from moving by fondness for a particular place and by custom, even in spite of ill-treatment. Would you be free from the restraint of your body? Live in it as if you were about to leave it. Keep thinking of the fact that some day you will be deprived of this tenure; then you will be more brave against the necessity of departing. But how will a man take thought of his own end, if he craves all things without end? And yet there is nothing so essential for us to consider. For our training in other things is perhaps superfluous. Our souls have been made ready to meet poverty; but our riches have held out. We have armed ourselves to scorn pain; but we have had the good fortune to possess sound and healthy bodies, and so have never been forced to put this virtue to the test. We have taught ourselves to endure bravely the loss of those we love; but Fortune has preserved to us all whom we loved. It is in this one matter only that the day will come which will require us to test our training.

You need not think that none but great men have had the strength to burst the bonds of human servitude; you need not believe that this cannot be done except by a Cato, – Cato, who with his hand dragged forth the spirit which he had not succeeded in freeing by the sword. Nay, men of the meanest lot in life have by a mighty impulse escaped to safety, and when they were not allowed to die at their own convenience, or to suit themselves in their choice of the instruments of death, they have snatched up whatever was lying ready to hand, and by sheer strength have turned objects which were by nature harmless into weapons of their own. For example, there was lately in a training-school for wild-beast gladiators a German, who was making ready for the morning exhibition; he withdrew in order to relieve himself, – the only thing which he was allowed to do in secret and without the presence of a guard. While so engaged, he seized the stick of wood, tipped with a sponge, which was devoted to the vilest uses, and stuffed it, just as it was, down his throat; thus he blocked up his windpipe, and choked the breath from his body. That was truly to insult death! Yes, indeed; it was not a very elegant or becoming way to die; but what is more foolish than to be over-nice about dying? What a brave fellow! He surely deserved to be allowed to choose his fate! How bravely he would have wielded a sword! With what courage he would have hurled himself into the depths of the sea, or down a precipice! Cut off from resources on every hand, he yet found a way to furnish himself with death, and with a weapon for death. Hence you can understand that nothing but the will need postpone death. Let each man judge the deed of this most zealous fellow as he likes, provided we agree on this point, – that the foulest death is preferable to the fairest slavery.

Inasmuch as I began with an illustration taken from humble life I shall keep on with that sort. For men will make greater demands upon themselves, if they see that death can be despised even by the most despised class of men. The Catos, the Scipios, and the others whose names we are wont to hear with admiration, we regard as beyond the sphere of imitation; but I shall now prove to you that the virtue of which I speak is found as frequently in the gladiators' training-school as among the leaders in a civil war. Lately a gladiator, who had been sent forth to the morning exhibition, was being conveyed in a cart along with the other prisoners; nodding as if he were heavy with sleep, he let his head fall over so far that it was caught in the spokes; then he kept his body in position long enough to break his neck by the revolution of the wheel. So he made his escape by means of the very wagon which was carrying him to his punishment.

When a man desires to burst forth and take his departure, nothing stands in his way. It is an open space in which Nature guards us. When our plight is such as to permit it, we may look about us for an easy exit. If you have many opportunities ready to hand, by means of which you may liberate yourself, you may make a selection and think over the best way of gaining freedom; but if a chance is hard to find, instead of the best, snatch the next best, even though it be something unheard of, something new. If you do not lack the courage, you will not lack the cleverness, to die. See how even the lowest class of slave, when suffering goads him on, is aroused and discovers a way to deceive even the most watchful guards! He is truly great who not only has given himself the order to die, but has also found the means.

I have promised you, however, some more illustrations drawn from the same games. During the second event in a sham sea-fight one of the barbarians sank deep into his own throat a spear which had been given him for use against his foe. "Why, oh why," he said, "have I not long ago escaped from all this torture and all this mockery? Why should I be armed and yet wait for death to come?" This exhibition was all the more striking because of the lesson men learn from it that dying is more honourable than killing.

What then? If such a spirit is possessed by abandoned and dangerous men, shall it not be possessed also by those who have trained themselves to meet such contingencies by long meditation, and by reason, the mistress of all things? It is reason which teaches us that fate has various ways of approach, but the same end, and that it makes no difference at what point the inevitable event begins. Reason, too, advises us to die, if we may, according to our taste; if this cannot be, she advises us to die according to our ability, and to seize upon whatever means shall offer itself for doing violence to ourselves. It is criminal to "live by robbery"; but, on the other hand, it is most noble to "die by robbery." Farewell.

Letter LXXI - On the Supreme Good

You are continually referring special questions to me, forgetting that a vast stretch of sea sunders us. Since, however, the value of advice depends mostly on the time when it is given, it must necessarily result that by the time my opinion on certain matters reaches you, the opposite opinion is the better. For advice conforms to circumstances; and our circumstances are carried along, or rather whirled along. Accordingly, advice should be produced at short notice; and even this is too late; it should "grow while we work," as the saying is. And I propose to show you how you may discover the method.

As often as you wish to know what is to be avoided or what is to be sought, consider its relation to the Supreme Good, to the purpose of your whole life. For whatever we do ought to be in harmony with this; no man can set in order the details unless he has already set before himself the chief purpose of his life. The artist may have his colours all prepared, but he cannot produce a likeness unless he has already made up his mind what he wishes to paint. The reason we make mistakes is because we all consider the parts of life, but never life as a whole. The archer must know what he is seeking to hit; then he must aim and control the weapon by his skill. Our plans miscarry because they have no aim. When a man does not know what harbour he is making for, no wind is the right wind. Chance must necessarily have great influence over our lives, because we live by chance. It is the case with certain men, however, that they do not know that they know certain things. Just as we often go searching for those who stand beside us, so we are apt to forget that the goal of the Supreme Good lies near us.

To infer the nature of this Supreme Good, one does not need many words or any round-about discussion; it should be pointed out with the forefinger, so to speak, and not be dissipated into many parts. For what good is there in breaking it up into tiny bits, when you can say: the Supreme Good is that which is honourable? Besides (and you may be still more surprised at this), that which is honourable is the only good; all other goods are alloyed and debased. If you once convince yourself of this, and if you come to love virtue devotedly (for mere loving is not enough), anything that has been touched by virtue will be fraught with blessing and prosperity for you, no matter how it shall be regarded by others. Torture, if only, as you lie suffering, you are more calm in mind than your very torturer; illness, if only you curse not Fortune and yield not to the disease – in short, all those things which others regard as ills will become manageable and will end in good, if you succeed in rising above them.

Let this once be clear, that there is nothing good except that which is honourable, and all hardships will have a just title to the name of "goods," when once virtue has made them honourable. Many think that we Stoics are holding out expectations greater than our human lot admits of; and they have a right to think so. For they have regard to the body only. But let them turn back to the soul, and they will soon measure man by the standard of God. Rouse yourself, most excellent Lucilius, and leave off all this word-play of the philosophers, who reduce a most glorious subject to a matter of syllables, and lower and wear out the soul by teaching fragments; then you will become like the men who discovered these precepts, instead of those who by their teaching do their best to make philosophy seem difficult rather than great.

Socrates, who recalled the whole of philosophy to rules of conduct, and asserted that the highest wisdom consisted in distinguishing between good and evil, said: "Follow these rules, if my words carry weight with you, in order that you may be happy; and let some men think you even a fool. Allow any man who so desires to insult you and work you wrong; but if only virtue dwells with you, you will suffer nothing. If you wish to be happy, if you would be in good faith a good man let one person or another despise you." No man can accomplish this unless he has come to regard all goods as equal, for the reason that no good exists without that which is honourable, and that which is honourable is in every case equal. You may say: "What then? Is there no difference between Cato's being elected praetor and his failure at the polls? Or whether Cato is conquered or conqueror in the battle-line of Pharsalia? And when Cato could not be defeated, though his party met defeat, was not this goodness of his equal to that which would have been his if he had returned victorious to his native land and arranged a peace?" Of course it was; for it is by the same virtue that evil fortune is overcome and good fortune is controlled. Virtue however, cannot be increased or decreased; its stature is uniform. "But," you will object, "Gnaeus Pompey will lose his army; the patricians, those noblest patterns of the State's creation, and the front-rank men of Pompey's party, a senate under arms, will be routed in a single engagement; the ruins of that great oligarchy will be scattered all over the world; one division will fall in Egypt, another in Africa, and another in Spain! And the poor State will not be allowed even the privilege of being ruined once for all!" Yes, all this may happen; Juba's familiarity with every position in his own kingdom may be of no avail to him, of no avail the resolute bravery of his people when fighting for their king; even the men of Utica, crushed by their troubles, may waver in their allegiance; and the good fortune which ever attended men of the name of Scipio may desert Scipio in Africa. But long ago destiny "saw to it that Cato should come to no harm."

"He was conquered in spite of it all!" Well, you may include this among Cato's "failures"; Cato will bear with an equally stout heart anything that thwarts him of his victory, as he bore that which thwarted him of his praetorship. The day whereon he failed of election, he spent in play; the night wherein he intended to die, he spent in reading. He regarded in the same light both the loss of his praetorship and the loss of his life; he had convinced himself that he ought to endure anything which might happen. Why should he not suffer, bravely and calmly, a change in the government? For what is free from the risk of change? Neither earth, nor sky, nor the whole fabric of our universe, though it be controlled by the hand of God. It will not always preserve its present order; it will be thrown from its course in days to come. All things move in accord with their appointed times; they are destined to be born, to grow, and to be destroyed. The stars which you see moving above us, and this seemingly immovable earth to which we cling and on which we are set, will be consumed and will cease to exist. There is nothing that does not have its old age; the intervals are merely unequal at which Nature sends forth all these things towards the same goal. Whatever is will cease to be, and yet it will not perish, but will be resolved into its elements. To our minds, this process means perishing, for we behold only that which is nearest; our sluggish mind, under allegiance to the body, does not penetrate to bournes beyond. Were it not so, the mind would endure with greater courage its own ending and that of its possessions, if only it could hope that life and death, like the whole universe about us, go by turns, that whatever has been put together is broken up again, that whatever has been broken up is put together again, and that the eternal craftsmanship of God, who controls all things is working at this task.

Therefore the wise man will say just what a Marcus Cato would say, after reviewing his past life: "The whole race of man, both that which is and that which is to be, is condemned to die. Of all the cities that at any time have held sway over the world, and of all that have been the splendid ornaments of empires not their own, men shall some day ask where they were, and they shall be swept away by destructions of various kinds; some shall be ruined by wars, others shall be wasted away by inactivity and by the kind of peace which ends in sloth, or by that vice which is fraught with destruction even for mighty dynasties, – luxury. All these fertile plains shall be buried out of sight by a sudden overflowing of the sea, or a slipping of the soil, as it settles to lower levels, shall draw them suddenly into a yawning chasm. Why then should I be angry or feel sorrow, if I precede the general destruction by a tiny interval of time?" Let great souls comply with God's wishes, and suffer unhesitatingly whatever fate the law of the universe ordains; for the soul at death is either sent forth into a better life, destined to dwell with deity amid greater radiance and calm, or else, at least, without suffering any harm to itself, it will be mingled with nature again, and will return to the universe.

Therefore Cato's honourable death was no less a good than his honourable life, since virtue admits of no stretching. Socrates used to say that verity and virtue were the same. Just as truth does not grow, so neither does virtue grow; for it has its due proportions and is complete. You need not, therefore, wonder that goods are equal, both those which are to be deliberately chosen, and those which circumstances have imposed. For if you once adopt the view that they are unequal, deeming, for instance, a brave endurance of torture as among the lesser goods, you will be including it among the evils also; you will pronounce Socrates unhappy in his prison, Cato unhappy when he reopens his wounds with more courage than he allowed in inflicting them, and

Regulus the most ill-starred of all when he pays the penalty for keeping his word even with his enemies. And yet no man, even the most effeminate person in the world, has ever dared to maintain such an opinion. For though such persons deny that a man like Regulus is happy, yet for all that they also deny that he is wretched. The earlier Academics do indeed admit that a man is happy even amid such tortures, but do not admit that he is completely or fully happy. With this view we cannot in any wise agree; for unless a man is happy, he has not attained the Supreme Good; and the good which is supreme admits of no higher degree, if only virtue exists within this man, and if adversity does not impair his virtue, and if, though the body be injured, the virtue abides unharmed. And it does abide. For I understand virtue to be high-spirited and exalted, so that it is aroused by anything that molests it. This spirit, which young men of noble breeding often assume, when they are so deeply stirred by the beauty of some honourable object that they despise all the gifts of chance, is assuredly infused in us and communicated to us by wisdom. Wisdom will bring the conviction that there is but one good – that which is honourable; that this can neither be shortened nor extended, any more than a carpenter's rule, with which straight lines are tested, can be bent. Any change in the rule means spoiling the straight line. Applying, therefore, this same figure to virtue, we shall say: virtue also is straight, and admits of no bending. What can be made more tense than a thing which is already rigid? Such is virtue, which passes judgment on everything, but nothing passes judgment on virtue. And if this rule, virtue, cannot itself be made more straight, neither can the things created by virtue be in one case straighter and in another less straight. For they must necessarily correspond to virtue; hence they are equal.

"What," you say, "do you call reclining at a banquet and submitting to torture equally good?" Does this seem surprising to you? You may be still more surprised at the following, – that reclining at a banquet is an evil, while reclining on the rack is a good, if the former act is done in a shameful, and the latter in an honourable manner. It is not the material that makes these actions good or bad; it is the virtue. All acts in which virtue has disclosed itself are of the same measure and value. At this moment the man who measures the souls of all men by his own is shaking his fist in my face because I hold that there is a parity between the goods involved in the case of one who passes sentence honourably, and of one who suffers sentence honourably; or because I hold that there is a parity between the goods of one who celebrates a triumph, and of one who, unconquered in spirit, is carried before the victor's chariot. For such critics think that whatever they themselves cannot do, is not done; they pass judgment on virtue in the light of their own weaknesses. Why do you marvel if it helps a man, and on occasion even pleases him, to be burned, wounded, slain, or bound in prison? To a luxurious man, a simple life is a penalty; to a lazy man, work is punishment; the dandy pities the diligent man; to the slothful, studies are torture. Similarly, we regard those things with respect to which we are all infirm of disposition, as hard and beyond endurance, forgetting what a torment it is to many men to abstain from wine or to be routed from their beds at break of day. These actions are not essentially difficult; it is we ourselves that are soft and flabby. We must pass judgment concerning great matters with greatness of soul; otherwise, that which is really our fault will seem to be their fault. So it is that certain objects which are perfectly straight, when sunk in water appear to the onlooker as bent or broken off. It matters not only what you see, but with what eyes you see it; our souls are too dull of vision to perceive the truth. But give me an unspoiled and sturdy-minded young man; he will pronounce more fortunate one who sustains on unbending shoulders the whole weight of adversity, who stands out superior to Fortune. It is not a cause for wonder that one is not tossed about when the weather is calm; reserve your wonderment for cases where a man is lifted up when all others sink, and keeps his footing when all others are prostrate.

What element of evil is there in torture and in the other things which we call hardships? It seems to me that there is this evil, – that the mind sags, and bends, and collapses. But none of these things can happen to the sage; he stands erect under any load. Nothing can subdue him; nothing that must be endured annoys him. For he does not complain that he has been struck by that which can strike any man. He knows his own strength; he knows that he was born to carry burdens. I do not withdraw the wise man from the category of man, nor do I deny to him the sense of pain as though he were a rock that has no feelings at all. I remember that he is made up of two parts: the one part is irrational, – it is this that may be bitten, burned, or hurt; the other part is rational, – it is this which holds resolutely to opinions, is courageous, and unconquerable. In the latter is situated man's Supreme Good. Before this is completely attained, the mind wavers in uncertainty; only when it is fully achieved is the mind fixed and steady. And so when one has just begun, or is on one's way to the heights and is cultivating virtue, or even if one is drawing near the perfect good but has not yet put the finishing touch upon it, one will retrograde at times and there will be a certain slackening of mental effort. For such a man has not yet traversed the doubtful ground; he is still standing in slippery places. But the happy man, whose virtue is complete, loves himself most of all when his bravery has been submitted to the severest test, and when he not only, endures but welcomes that which all other men regard with fear, if it is the price which he must pay for the performance of a duty which honour imposes, and he greatly prefers to have men say of him: "how much more noble!" rather than "how much more lucky!"

And now I have reached the point to which your patient waiting summons me. You must not think that our human virtue transcends nature; the wise man will tremble, will feel pain, will turn pale, For all these are sensations of the body. Where, then, is the abode of utter distress, of that which is truly an evil? In the other part of us, no doubt, if it is the mind that these trials drag down, force to a confession of its servitude, and cause to regret its existence. The wise man, indeed, overcomes Fortune by his virtue, but many who profess wisdom are sometimes frightened by the most unsubstantial threats. And at this stage it is a mistake on our part to make the same demands upon the wise man and upon the learner. I still exhort myself to do that which I recommend; but my exhortations are not yet followed. And even if this were the case, I should not have these principles so ready for practice, or so well trained, that they would rush to my assistance in every crisis. Just as wool takes up certain colours at once, while there are others which it will not absorb unless it is soaked and steeped in them many times; so other systems of doctrine can be immediately applied by men's minds after once being accepted, but this system of which I speak, unless it has gone deep and has sunk in for a long time, and has not merely coloured but thoroughly permeated the soul, does not fulfil any of its promises. The matter can be imparted quickly and in very few words: "Virtue is the only good; at any rate there is no good without virtue; and virtue itself is situated in our nobler part, that is, the rational part." And what will this virtue be? A true and never-swerving judgment. For therefrom will spring all mental impulses, and by its agency every external appearance that stirs our impulses will be clarified. It will be in keeping with this judgment to judge all things that have been coloured by virtue as goods, and as equal goods.

Bodily goods are, to be sure, good for the body; but they are not absolutely good. There will indeed be some value in them; but they will possess no genuine merit, for they will differ greatly; some will be less, others greater. And we are constrained to acknowledge that there are great differences among the very followers of wisdom. One man has already made so much progress that he dares to raise his eyes and look Fortune in the face, but not persistently, for his eyes soon drop, dazzled by her overwhelming splendour; another has made so much progress that he is able to match glances with her, – that is, unless he has already reached the summit and is full of confidence. That which is short of perfection must necessarily be unsteady, at one time progressing, at another slipping or growing faint; and it will surely slip back unless it keeps struggling ahead; for if a man slackens at all in zeal and faithful application, he must retrograde. No one can resume his progress at the point where he left off. Therefore let us press on and persevere. There remains much more of the road than we have put behind us; but the greater part of progress is the desire to progress.

I fully understand what this task is. It is a thing which I desire, and I desire it with all my heart. I see that you also have been aroused and are hastening with great zeal towards infinite beauty. Let us, then, hasten; only on these terms will life be a boon to us; otherwise, there is delay, and indeed disgraceful delay, while we busy ourselves with revolting things. Let us see to it that all time belongs to us. This, however, cannot be unless first of all our own selves begin to belong to us. And when will it be our privilege to despise both kinds of fortune? When will it be our privilege, after all the passions have been subdued and brought under our own control, to utter the words "I have conquered!"? Do you ask me whom I have conquered? Neither the Persians, nor the far-off Medes, nor any warlike race that lies beyond the Dahae; not these, but greed, ambition, and the fear of death that has conquered the conquerors of the world. Farewell.

Letter LXXII - On Business as the Enemy of Philosophy

The subject concerning which you question me was once clear to my mind, and required no thought, so thoroughly had I mastered it. But I have not tested my memory of it for some time, and therefore it does not readily come back to me. I feel that I have suffered the fate of a book whose rolls have stuck together by disuse; my mind needs to be unrolled, and whatever has been stored away there ought to be examined from time to time, so that it may be ready for use when occasion demands. Let us therefore put this subject off for the present; for it demands much labour and much care. As soon as I can hope to stay for any length of time in the same place, I shall then take your question in hand. For there are certain subjects about which you can write even while travelling in a gig, and there are also subjects which need a study-chair, and quiet, and seclusion. Nevertheless I ought to accomplish something even on days like these, – days which are fully employed, and indeed from morning till night. For there is never a moment when fresh employments will not come along; we sow them, and for this reason several spring up from one. Then, too, we keep adjourning our own cases by saying: "As soon as I am done with this, I shall settle down to hard work," or: "If I ever set this troublesome matter in order, I shall devote myself to study."

But the study of philosophy is not to be postponed until you have leisure; everything else is to be neglected in order that we may attend to philosophy, for no amount of time is long enough for it, even though our lives be prolonged from boyhood to the uttermost bounds of time allotted to man. It makes little difference whether you leave philosophy out altogether or study it intermittently; for it does not stay as it was when you dropped it, but, because its continuity has been broken, it goes back to the position in which it was at the beginning, like things which fly apart when they are stretched taut. We must resist the affairs which occupy our time; they must not be untangled, but rather put out of the way. Indeed, there is no time that is unsuitable for helpful studies; and yet many a man fails to study amid the very circumstances which make study necessary. He says: "Something will happen to hinder me." No, not in the case of the man whose spirit, no matter what his business may be, is happy and alert. It is those who are still short of perfection whose happiness can be broken off; the joy of a wise man, on the other hand, is a woven fabric, rent by no chance happening and by no change of fortune; at all times and in all places he is at peace. For his joy depends on nothing external and looks for no boon from man or fortune. His happiness is something within himself; it would depart from his soul if it entered in from the outside; it is born there. Sometimes an external happening reminds him of his mortality, but it is a light blow, and merely grazes the surface of his skin. Some trouble, I repeat, may touch him like a breath of wind, but that Supreme Good of his is unshaken. This is what I mean: there are external disadvantages, like pimples and boils that break out upon a body which is normally strong and sound; but there is no deep-seated malady. The difference, I say, between a man of perfect wisdom and another who is progressing in wisdom is the same as the difference between a healthy man and one who is convalescing from a severe and lingering illness, for whom "health" means only a lighter attack of his disease. If the latter does not take heed, there is an immediate relapse and a return to the same old trouble; but the wise man cannot slip back, or slip into any more illness at all. For health of body is a temporary matter which the physician cannot guarantee, even though he has restored it; nay, he is often roused from his bed to visit the same patient who summoned him before. The mind, however, once healed, is healed for good and all.

I shall tell you what I mean by health: if the mind is content with its own self; if it has confidence in itself; if it understands that all those things for which men pray, all the benefits which are bestowed and sought for, are of no importance in relation to a life of happiness; under such conditions it is sound. For anything that can be added to is imperfect; anything that can suffer loss is not lasting; but let the man whose happiness is to be lasting, rejoice in what is truly his own. Now all that which the crowd gapes after, ebbs and flows. Fortune gives us nothing which we can really own. But even these gifts of Fortune please us when reason has tempered and blended them to our taste; for it is reason which makes acceptable to us even external goods that are disagreeable to use if we absorb them too greedily. Attalus used to employ the following simile: "Did you ever see a dog snapping with wide-open jaws at bits of bread or meat which his master tosses to him? Whatever he catches, he straightway swallows whole, and always opens his jaws in the hope of something more. So it is with ourselves; we stand expectant, and whatever Fortune has thrown to us we forthwith bolt, without any real pleasure, and then stand alert and frantic for something else to snatch." But it is not so with the wise man; he is satisfied. Even if something falls to him, he merely accepts it carelessly and lays it aside. The happiness that he enjoys is supremely great, is lasting, is his own. Assume that a man has good intentions, and has made progress, but is still far from the heights; the result is a series of ups and downs; he is now raised to heaven, now brought down to earth. For those who lack experience and training, there is no limit to the downhill course; such a one falls into the Chaos of Epicurus, – empty and boundless. There is still a third class of men, – those who toy with wisdom, – they have not indeed touched it, but yet are in sight of it, and have it, so to speak, within striking distance. They are not dashed about, nor do they drift back either; they are not on dry land, but are already in port.

Therefore, considering the great difference between those on the heights and those in the depths, and seeing that even those in the middle are pursued by an ebb and flow peculiar to their state and pursued also by an enormous risk of returning to their degenerate ways, we should not give ourselves up to matters which occupy our time. They should be shut out; if they once gain an entrance, they will bring in still others to take their places. Let us resist them in their early stages. It is better that they shall never begin than that they shall be made to cease. Farewell.

Letter LXXIII - On Philosophers and Kings

It seems to me erroneous to believe that those who have loyally dedicated themselves to philosophy are stubborn and rebellious, scorners of magistrates or kings or of those who control the administration of public affairs. For, on the contrary, no class of man is so popular with the philosopher as the ruler is; and rightly so, because rulers bestow upon no men a greater privilege than upon those who are allowed to enjoy peace and leisure. Hence, those who are greatly profited, as regards their purpose of right living, by the security of the State, must needs cherish as a father the author of this good; much more so, at any rate, than those restless persons who are always in the public eye, who owe much to the ruler, but also expect much from him, and are never so generously loaded with favours that their cravings, which grow by being supplied, are thoroughly satisfied. And yet he whose thoughts are of benefits to come has forgotten the benefits received; and there is no greater evil in covetousness than its ingratitude. Besides, no man in public life thinks of the many whom he has outstripped; he thinks rather of those by whom he is outstripped. And these men find it less pleasing to see many behind them than annoying to see anyone ahead of them. That is the trouble with every sort of ambition; it does not look back. Nor is it ambition alone that is fickle, but also every sort of craving, because it always begins where it ought to end.

But that other man, upright and pure, who has left the senate and the bar and all affairs of state, that he may retire to nobler affairs, cherishes those who have made it possible for him to do this in security; he is the only person who returns spontaneous thanks to them, the only person who owes them a great debt without their knowledge. Just as a man honours and reveres his teachers, by whose aid he has found release from his early wanderings, so the sage honours these men, also, under whose guardianship he can put his good theories into practice. But you answer: "Other men too are protected by a king's personal power." Perfectly true. But just as, out of a number of persons who have profited by the same stretch of calm weather, a man deems that his debt to Neptune is greater if his cargo during that voyage has been more extensive and valuable, and just as the vow is paid with more of a will by the merchant than by the passenger, and just as, from among the merchants themselves, heartier thanks are uttered by the dealer in spices, purple fabrics, and objects worth their weight in gold, than by him who has gathered cheap merchandise that will be nothing but ballast for his ship; similarly, the benefits of this peace, which extends to all, are more deeply appreciated by those who make good use of it.

For there are many of our toga-clad citizens to whom peace brings more trouble than war. Or do those, think you, owe as much as we do for the peace they enjoy, who spend it in drunkenness, or in lust, or in other vices which it were worth even a war to interrupt? No, not unless you think that the wise man is so unfair as to believe that as an individual he owes nothing in return for the advantages which he enjoys with all the rest. I owe a great debt to the sun and to the moon; and yet they do not rise for me alone. I am personally beholden to the seasons and to the god who controls them, although in no respect have they been apportioned for my benefit. The foolish greed of mortals makes a distinction between possession and ownership, and believes that it has ownership in nothing in which the general public has a share. But our philosopher considers nothing more truly his own than that which he shares in partnership with all mankind. For these things would not be common property, as indeed they are, unless every individual had his quota; even a joint interest based upon the slightest share makes one a partner. Again, the great and true goods are not divided in such a manner that each has but a slight interest; they belong in their entirety to each individual. At a distribution of grain men receive only the amount that has been promised to each person; the banquet and the meat-dole, or all else that a man can carry away with him, are divided into parts. These goods, however, are indivisible, – I mean peace and liberty, – and they belong in their entirety to all men just as much as they belong to each individual.

Therefore the philosopher thinks of the person who makes it possible for him to use and enjoy these things, of the person who exempts him when the state's dire need summons to arms, to sentry duty, to the defence of the walls, and to the manifold exactions of war; and he gives thanks to the helmsman of his state. This is what philosophy teaches most of all, – honourably to avow the debt of benefits received, and honourably to pay them; sometimes, however, the acknowledgment itself constitutes payment. Our philosopher will therefore acknowledge that he owes a large debt to the ruler who makes it possible, by his management and foresight, for him to enjoy rich leisure, control of his own time, and a tranquillity uninterrupted by public employments.

Shepherd! a god this leisure gave to me,
For he shall be my god eternally.

And if even such leisure as that of our poet owes a great debt to its author, though its greatest boon is this:

As thou canst see,
He let me turn my cattle out to feed,
And play what fancy pleased on rustic reed;

how highly are we to value this leisure of the philosopher, which is spent among the gods, and makes us gods? Yes, this is what I mean, Lucilius; and I invite you to heaven by a short cut.

Sextius used to say that Jupiter had no more power than the good man. Of course, Jupiter has more gifts which he can offer to mankind; but when you are choosing between two good men, the richer is not necessarily the better, any more than, in the case of two pilots of equal skill in managing the tiller, you would call him the better whose ship is larger and more imposing. In what respect is Jupiter superior to our good man? His goodness lasts longer; but the wise man does not set a lower value upon himself, just because his virtues are limited by a briefer span. Or take two wise men; he who has died at a greater age is not happier than he whose virtue has been limited to fewer years: similarly, a god has no advantage over a wise man in point of happiness, even though he has such an advantage in point of years. That virtue is not greater which lasts longer. Jupiter possesses all things, but he has surely given over the possession of them to others; the only use of them which belongs to him is this: he is the cause of their use to all men. The wise man surveys and scorns all the possessions of others as calmly as does Jupiter, and regards himself with the greater esteem because, while Jupiter cannot make use of them, he, the wise man, does not wish to do so. Let us therefore believe Sextius when he shows us the path of perfect beauty, and cries: "This is 'the way to the stars'; this is the way, by observing thrift, self-restraint, and courage!"

The gods are not disdainful or envious; they open the door to you; they lend a hand as you climb. Do you marvel that man goes to the gods? God comes to men; nay, he comes nearer, – he comes into men. No mind that has not God, is good. Divine seeds are scattered throughout our mortal bodies; if a good husbandman receives them, they spring up in the likeness of their source and of a parity with those from which they came. If, however, the husbandman be bad, like a barren or marshy soil, he kills the seeds, and causes tares to grow up instead of wheat. Farewell.

Letter LXXIV - On Virtue as a Refuge from Worldly Distractions

Your letter has given me pleasure, and has roused me from sluggishness. It has also prompted my memory, which has been for some time slack and nerveless.

You are right, of course, my dear Lucilius, in deeming the chief means of attaining the happy life to consist in the belief that the only good lies in that which is honourable. For anyone who deems other things to be good, puts himself in the power of Fortune, and goes under the control of another; but he who has in every case defined the good by the honourable, is happy with an inward happiness.

One man is saddened when his children die; another is anxious when they become ill; a third is embittered when they do something disgraceful, or suffer a taint in their reputation. One man, you will observe, is tortured by passion for his neighbour's wife, another by passion for his own. You will find men who are completely upset by failure to win an election, and others who are actually plagued by the offices which they have won. But the largest throng of unhappy men among the host of mortals are those whom the expectation of death, which threatens them on every hand, drives to despair. For there is no quarter from which death may not approach. Hence, like soldiers scouting in the enemy's country, they must look about in all directions, and turn their heads at every sound; unless the breast be rid of this fear, one lives with a palpitating heart. You will readily recall those who have been driven into exile and dispossessed of their property. You will also recall (and this is the most serious kind of destitution) those who are poor in the midst of their riches. You will recall men who have suffered shipwreck, or those whose sufferings resemble shipwreck; for they were untroubled and at ease, when the anger or perhaps the envy of the populace, – a missile most deadly to those in high places, – dismantled them like a storm which is wont to rise when one is most confident of continued calm, or like a sudden stroke of lightning which even causes the region round about it to tremble. For just as anyone who stands near the bolt is stunned and resembles one who is struck so in these sudden and violent mishaps, although but one person is overwhelmed by the disaster, the rest are overwhelmed by fear, and the possibility that they may suffer makes them as downcast as the actual sufferer.

Every man is troubled in spirit by evils that come suddenly upon his neighbour. Like birds, who cower even at the whirr of an empty sling, we are distracted by mere sounds as well as by blows. No man therefore can be happy if he yields himself up to such foolish fancies. For nothing brings happiness unless it also brings calm; it is a bad sort of existence that is spent in apprehension. Whoever has largely surrendered himself to the power of Fortune has made for himself a huge web of disquietude, from which he cannot get free; if one would win a way to safety, there is but one road, – to despise externals and to be contented with that which is honourable. For those who regard anything as better than virtue, or believe that there is any good except virtue, are spreading their arms to gather in that which Fortune tosses abroad, and are anxiously awaiting her favours. Picture now to yourself that Fortune is holding a festival, and is showering down honours, riches, and influence upon this mob of mortals; some of these gifts have already been torn to pieces in the hands of those who try to snatch them, others have been divided up by treacherous partnerships, and still others have been seized to the great detriment of those into whose possession they have come. Certain of these favours have fallen to men while they were absent-minded; others have been lost to their seekers because they were snatching too eagerly for them, and, just because they are greedily seized upon, have been knocked from their hands. There is not a man among them all, however, – even he who has been lucky in the booty which has fallen to him, – whose joy in his spoil has lasted until the morrow.

The most sensible man, therefore, as soon as he sees the dole being brought in, runs from the theatre; for he knows that one pays a high price for small favours. No one will grapple with him on the way out, or strike him as he departs; the quarrelling takes place where the prizes are. Similarly with the gifts which Fortune tosses down to us; wretches that we are, we become excited, we are torn asunder, we wish that we had many hands, we look back now in this direction and now in that. All too slowly, as it seems, are the gifts thrown in our direction; they merely excite our cravings, since they can reach but few and are awaited by all. We are keen to intercept them as they fall down. We rejoice if we have laid hold of anything; and some have been mocked by the idle hope of laying hold; we have either paid a high price for worthless plunder with some disadvantage to ourselves, or else have been defrauded and are left in the lurch. Let us therefore withdraw from a game like this, and give way to the greedy rabble; let them gaze after such "goods," which hang suspended above them, and be themselves still more in suspense.

Whoever makes up his mind to be happy should conclude that the good consists only in that which is honourable. For if he regards anything else as good, he is, in the first place, passing an unfavourable judgment upon Providence because of the fact that upright men often suffer misfortunes, and that the time which is allotted to us is but short and scanty, if you compare it with the eternity which is allotted to the universe.

It is a result of complaints like these that we are unappreciative in our comments upon the gifts of heaven; we complain because they are not always granted to us, because they are few and unsure and fleeting. Hence we have not the will either to live or to die; we are possessed by hatred of life, by fear of death. Our plans are all at sea, and no amount of prosperity can satisfy us. And the reason for all this is that we have not yet attained to that good which is immeasurable and unsurpassable, in which all wishing on our part must cease, because there is no place beyond the highest. Do you ask why virtue needs nothing? Because it is pleased with what it has, and does not lust after that which it has not. Whatever is enough is abundant in the eyes of virtue.

Dissent from this judgment, and duty and loyalty will not abide. For one who desires to exhibit these two qualities must endure much that the world calls evil; we must sacrifice many things to which we are addicted, thinking them to be goods. Gone is courage, which should be continually testing itself; gone is greatness of soul, which cannot stand out clearly unless it has learned to scorn as trivial everything that the crowd covets as supremely important; and gone is kindness and the repaying of kindness, if we fear toil, if we have acknowledged anything to be more precious than loyalty, if our eyes are fixed upon anything except the best.

But to pass these questions by: either these so-called goods are not goods, or else man is more fortunate than God, because God has no enjoyment of the things which are given to us. For lust pertains not to God, nor do elegant banquets, nor wealth, nor any of the things that allure mankind and lead him on through the influence of degrading pleasure. Therefore, it is, either not incredible that there are goods which God does not possess, or else the very fact that God does not possess them is in itself a proof that these things are not goods. Besides, many things which are wont to be regarded as goods are granted to animals in fuller measure than to men. Animals eat their food with better appetite, are not in the same degree weakened by sexual indulgence, and have a greater and more uniform constancy in their strength. Consequently, they are much more fortunate than man. For there is no wickedness, no injury to themselves, in their way of living. They enjoy their pleasures and they take them more often and more easily, without any of the fear that results from shame or regret.

This being so, you should consider whether one has a right to call anything good in which God is outdone by man. Let us limit the Supreme Good to the soul; it loses its meaning if it is taken from the best part of us and applied to the worst, that is, if it is transferred to the senses; for the senses are more active in dumb beasts. The sum total of our happiness must not be placed in the flesh; the true goods are those which reason bestows, substantial and eternal; they cannot fall away, neither can they grow less or be diminished. Other things are goods according to opinion, and though they are called by the same name as the true goods, the essence of goodness is not in them. Let us therefore call them "advantages," and, to use our technical term, "preferred" things. Let us, however, recognize that they are our chattels, not parts of ourselves; and let us have them in our possession, but take heed to remember that they are outside ourselves. Even though they are in our possession, they are to be reckoned as things subordinate and poor, the possession of which gives no man a right to plume himself. For what is more foolish than being self-complacent about something which one has not accomplished by one's own efforts? Let everything of this nature be added to us, and not stick fast to us, so that, if it is withdrawn, it may come away without tearing off any part of us. Let us use these things, but not boast of them, and let us use them sparingly, as if they were given for safe-keeping and will be withdrawn. Anyone who does not employ reason in his possession of them never keeps them long; for prosperity of itself, if uncontrolled by reason, overwhelms itself. If anyone has put his trust in goods that are most fleeting, he is soon bereft of them, and, to avoid being bereft, he suffers distress. Few men have been permitted to lay aside prosperity gently. The rest all fall, together with the things amid which they have come into eminence, and they are weighted down by the very things which had before exalted them. For this reason foresight must be brought into play, to insist upon a limit or upon frugality in the use of these things, since license overthrows and destroys its own abundance. That which has no limit has never endured, unless reason, which sets limits, has held it in check. The fate of many cities will prove the truth of this; their sway has ceased at the very prime because they were given to luxury, and excess has ruined all that had been won by virtue. We should fortify ourselves against such calamities. But no wall can be erected against Fortune which she cannot take by storm; let us strengthen our inner defences. If the inner part be safe, man can be attacked, but never captured.

Do you wish to know what this weapon of defence is? It is the ability to refrain from chafing over whatever happens to one, of knowing that the very agencies which seem to bring harm are working for the preservation of the world, and are a part of the scheme for bringing to fulfilment the order of the universe and its functions. Let man be pleased with whatever has pleased God; let him marvel at himself and his own resources for this very reason, that he cannot be overcome, that he has the very powers of evil subject to his control, and that he brings into subjection chance and pain and wrong by means of that strongest of powers – reason. Love reason! The love of reason will arm you against the greatest hardships. Wild beasts dash against the hunter's spear through love of their young, and it is their wildness and their unpremeditated onrush that keep them from being tamed; often a desire for glory has stirred the mind of youth to despise both sword and stake; the mere vision and semblance of virtue impel certain men to a self-imposed death. In proportion as reason is stouter and steadier than ally of these emotions, so much the more forcefully will she make her way through the midst of utter terrors and dangers.

Men say to us: "You are mistaken if you maintain that nothing is a good except that which is honourable; a defence like this will not make you safe from Fortune and free from her assaults. For you maintain that dutiful children, and a well-governed country, and good parents, are to be reckoned as goods; but you cannot see these dear objects in danger and be yourself at ease. Your calm will be disturbed by a siege conducted against your country, by the death of your children, or by the enslaving of your parents." I will first state what we Stoics usually reply to these objectors, and then will add what additional answer should, in my opinion, be given.

The situation is entirely different in the case of goods whose loss entails some hardship substituted in their place; for example, when good health is impaired there is a change to ill-health; when the eye is put out, we are visited with blindness; we not only lose our speed when our leg-muscles are cut, but infirmity takes the place of speed. But no such danger is involved in the case of the goods to which we referred a moment ago. And why if I have lost a good friend, I have no false friend whom I must endure in his place; nor if I have buried a dutiful son, must I face in exchange unfilial conduct. In the second place, this does not mean to me the taking-off of a friend or of a child; it is the mere taking-off of their bodies. But a good can be lost in only one way, by changing into what is bad; and this is impossible according to the law of nature, because every virtue, and every work of virtue, abides uncorrupted. Again, even if friends have perished, or children of approved goodness who fulfil their father's prayers for them, there is something that can fill their place. Do you ask what this is? It is that which had made them good in the first place, namely, virtue. Virtue suffers no space in us to be unoccupied; it takes possession of the whole soul and removes all sense of loss. It alone is sufficient; for the strength and beginnings of all goods exist in virtue herself. What does it matter if running water is cut off and flows away, as long as the fountain from which it has flowed is unharmed? You will not maintain that a man's life is more just if his children are unharmed than if they have passed away, nor yet better appointed, nor more intelligent, nor more honourable; therefore, no better, either. The addition of friends does not make one wiser, nor does their taking away make one more foolish; therefore, not happier or more wretched, either. As long is your virtue is unharmed, you will not feel the loss of anything that has been withdrawn from you. You may say, "Come now; is not a man happier when girt about with a large company of friends and children?" Why should this be so? For the Supreme Good is neither impaired nor increased thereby; it abides within its own limits, no matter how Fortune has conducted herself. Whether a long old age falls to one's lot, or whether the end comes on this side of old age – the measure of the Supreme Good is unvaried, in spite of the difference in years.

Whether you draw a larger or a smaller circle, its size affects its area, not its shape. One circle may remain as it is for a long time while you may contract the other forthwith, or even merge it completely with the sand in which it was drawn; yet each circle has had the same shape. That which is straight is not judged by its size, or by its number, or by its duration; it can no more be made longer than it can be made shorter. Scale down the honourable life as much as you like from the full hundred years, and reduce it to a single day; it is equally honourable. Sometimes virtue is widespread, governing kingdoms, cities, and provinces, creating laws, developing friendships, and regulating the duties that hold good between relatives and children; at other times it is limited by the narrow bounds of poverty, exile, or bereavement. But it is no smaller when it is reduced from prouder heights to a private station, from a royal palace to a humble dwelling, or when from a general and broad jurisdiction it is gathered into the narrow limits of a private house or a tiny corner. Virtue is just as great, even when it has retreated within itself and is shut in on all sides. For its spirit is no less great and upright, its sagacity no less complete, its justice no less inflexible. It is, therefore, equally happy. For happiness has its abode in one place only, namely, in the mind itself, and is noble, steadfast, and calm; and this state cannot be attained without a knowledge of things divine and human.

The other answer, which I promised to make to your objection, follows from this reasoning. The wise man is not distressed by the loss of children or of friends. For he endures their death in the same spirit in which he awaits his own. And he fears the one as little as he grieves for the other. For the underlying principle of virtue is conformity; all the works of virtue are in harmony and agreement with virtue itself. But this harmony is lost if the soul, which ought to be uplifted, is cast down by grief or a sense of loss. It is ever a dishonour for a man to be troubled and fretted, to be numbed when there is any call for activity. For that which is honourable is free from care and untrammelled, is unafraid, and stands girt for action. "What," you ask, "will the wise man experience no emotion like disturbance of spirit? Will not his features change colour, his countenance be agitated, and his limbs grow cold? And there are other things which we do, not under the influence of the will, but unconsciously and as the result of a sort of natural impulse." I admit that this is true; but the sage will retain the firm belief that none of these things is evil, or important enough to make a healthy mind break down. Whatever shall remain to be done virtue can do with courage and readiness. For anyone would admit that it is a mark of folly to do in a slothful and rebellious spirit whatever one has to do, or to direct the body in one direction and the mind in another, and thus to be torn between utterly conflicting emotions. For folly is despised precisely because of the things for which she vaunts and admires herself, and she does not do gladly even those things in which she prides herself. But if folly fears some evil, she is burdened by it in the very moment of awaiting it, just as if it had actually come, – already suffering in apprehension whatever she fears she may suffer. Just as in the body symptoms of latent ill-health precede the disease – there is, for example, a certain weak sluggishness, a lassitude which is not the result of any work, a trembling, and a shivering that pervades the limbs, – so the feeble spirit is shaken by its ills a long time before it is overcome by them. It anticipates them, and totters before its time.

But what is greater madness than to be tortured by the future and not to save your strength for the actual suffering, but to invite and bring on wretchedness? If you cannot be rid of it, you ought at least to postpone it. Will you not understand that no man should be tormented by the future? The man who has been told that he will have to endure torture fifty years from now is not disturbed thereby, unless he has leaped over the intervening years, and has projected himself into the trouble that is destined to arrive a generation later. In the same way, souls that enjoy being sick and that seize upon excuses for sorrow are saddened by events long past and effaced from the records. Past and future are both absent; we feel neither of them. But there can be no pain except as the result of what you feel. Farewell.

Letter LXXV - On the Diseases of the Soul

You have been complaining that my letters to you are rather carelessly written. Now who talks carefully unless he also desires to talk affectedly? I prefer that my letters should be just what my conversation would be if you and I were sitting in one another's company or taking walks together, spontaneous and easy; for my letters have nothing strained or artificial about them. If it were possible, I should prefer to show, rather than speak, my feelings. Even if I were arguing a point, I should not stamp my foot, or toss my arms about, or raise my voice; but I should leave that sort of thing to the orator, and should be content to have conveyed my feelings to you without having either embellished them or lowered their dignity. I should like to convince you entirely of this one fact, – that I feel whatever I say, that I not only feel it, but am wedded to it. It is one sort of kiss which a man gives his mistress and another which he gives his children; yet in the father's embrace also, holy and restrained as it is, plenty of affection is disclosed.

I prefer, however, that our conversation on matters so important should not be meagre and dry; for even philosophy does not renounce the company of cleverness. One should not, however, bestow very much attention upon mere words. Let this be the kernel of my idea: let us say what we feel, and feel what we say; let speech harmonize with life. That man has fulfilled his promise who is the same person both when you see him and when you hear him. We shall not fail to see what sort of man he is and how large a man he is, if only he is one and the same. Our words should aim not to please, but to help. If, however, you can attain eloquence without painstaking, and if you either are naturally gifted or can gain eloquence at slight cost, make the most of it and apply it to the noblest uses. But let it be of such a kind that it displays facts rather than itself. It and the other arts are wholly concerned with cleverness; but our business here is the soul.

A sick man does not call in a physician who is eloquent; but if it so happens that the physician who can cure him likewise discourses elegantly about the treatment which is to be followed, the patient will take it in good part. For all that, he will not find any reason to congratulate himself on having discovered a physician who is eloquent. For the case is no different from that of a skilled pilot who is also handsome. Why do you tickle my ears? Why do you entertain me? There is other business at hand; I am to be cauterized, operated upon, or put on a diet. That is why you were summoned to treat me!

You are required to cure a disease that is chronic and serious, – one which affects the general weal. You have as serious a business on hand as a physician has during a plague. Are you concerned about words? Rejoice this instant if you can cope with things. When shall you learn all that there is to learn? When shall you so plant in your mind that which you have learned, that it cannot escape? When shall you put it all into practice? For it is not sufficient merely to commit these things to memory, like other matters; they must be practically tested. He is not happy who only knows them, but he who does them. You reply: "What? Are there no degrees of happiness below your 'happy' man? Is there a sheer descent immediately below wisdom?" I think not. For though he who makes progress is still numbered with the fools, yet he is separated from them by a long interval. Among the very persons who are making progress there are also great spaces intervening. They fall into three classes, as certain philosophers believe. First come those who have not yet attained wisdom but have already gained a place near by. Yet even that which is not far away is still outside. These, if you ask me, are men who have already laid aside all passions and vices, who have learned what things are to be embraced; but their assurance is not yet tested. They have not yet put their good into practice, yet from now on they cannot slip back into the faults which they have escaped. They have already arrived at a point from which there is no slipping back, but they are not yet aware of the fact; as I remember writing in another letter, "They are ignorant of their knowledge." It has now been vouchsafed to them to enjoy their good, but not yet to be sure of it. Some define this class, of which I have been speaking, – a class of men who are making progress, – as having escaped the diseases of the mind, but not yet the passions, and as still standing upon slippery ground; because no one is beyond the dangers of evil except him who has cleared himself of it wholly. But no one has so cleared himself except the man who has adopted wisdom in its stead.

I have often before explained the difference between the diseases of the mind and its passions. And I shall remind you once more: the diseases are hardened and chronic vices, such as greed and ambition; they have enfolded the mind in too close a grip, and have begun to be permanent evils thereof. To give a brief definition: by "disease" we mean a persistent perversion of the judgment, so that things which are mildly desirable are thought to be highly desirable. Or, if you prefer, we may define it thus: to be too zealous in striving for things which are only mildly desirable or not desirable at all, or to value highly things which ought to be valued but slightly or valued not at all. "Passions" are objectionable impulses of the spirit, sudden and vehement; they have come so often, and so little attention has been paid to them, that they have caused a state of disease; just as a catarrh, when there has been but a single attack and the catarrh has not yet become habitual, produces a cough, but causes consumption when it has become regular and chronic. Therefore we may say that those who have made most progress are beyond the reach of the "diseases"; but they still feel the "passions" even when very near perfection.

The second class is composed of those who have laid aside both the greatest ills of the mind and its passions, but yet are not in assured possession of immunity. For they can still slip back into their former state. The third class are beyond the reach of many of the vices and particularly of the great vices, but not beyond the reach of all. They have escaped avarice, for example, but still feel anger; they no longer are troubled by lust, but are still troubled by ambition; they no longer have desire, but they still have fear. And just because they fear, although they are strong enough to withstand certain things, there are certain things to which they yield; they scorn death, but are in terror of pain.

Let us reflect a moment on this topic. It will be well with us if we are admitted to this class. The second stage is gained by great good fortune with regard to our natural gifts and by great and unceasing application to study. But not even the third type is to be despised. Think of the host of evils which you see about you; behold how there is no crime that is not exemplified, how far wickedness advances every day, and how prevalent are sins in home and commonwealth. You will see, therefore, that we are making a considerable gain, if we are not numbered among the basest.

"But as for me," you say, "I hope that it is in me to rise to a higher rank than that!" I should pray, rather than promise, that we may attain this; we have been forestalled. We hasten towards virtue while hampered by vices. I am ashamed to say it; but we worship that which is honourable only in so far as we have time to spare. But what a rich reward awaits us if only we break off the affairs which forestall us and the evils that cling to us with utter tenacity! Then neither desire nor fear shall rout us. Undisturbed by fears, unspoiled by pleasures, we shall be afraid neither of death nor of the gods; we shall know that death is no evil and that the gods are not powers of evil. That which harms has no greater power than that which receives harm, and things which are utterly good have no power at all to harm. There await us, if ever we escape from these low dregs to that sublime and lofty height, peace of mind and, when all error has been driven out, perfect liberty. You ask what this freedom is? It means not fearing either men or gods; it means not craving wickedness or excess; it means possessing supreme power over oneself And it is a priceless good to be master of oneself. Farewell.

Letter LXXVI - On Learning Wisdom in Old Age

You have been threatening me with your enmity, if I do not keep you informed about all my daily actions. But see, now, upon what frank terms you and I live: for I shall confide even the following fact to your ears. I have been hearing the lectures of a philosopher; four days have already passed since I have been attending his school and listening to the harangue, which begins at two o'clock. "A fine time of life for that!" you say. Yes, fine indeed! Now what is more foolish than refusing to learn, simply because one has not been learning for a long time? "What do you mean? Must I follow the fashion set by the fops and youngsters?" But I am pretty well off if this is the only thing that discredits my declining years. Men of all ages are admitted to this class-room. You retort: "Do we grow old merely in order to tag after the youngsters?" But if I, an old man, go to the theatre, and am carried to the races, and allow no duel in the arena to be fought to a finish without my presence, shall I blush to attend a philosopher's lecture?

You should keep learning as long as you are ignorant, – even to the end of your life, if there is anything in the proverb. And the proverb suits the present case as well as any: "As long as you live, keep learning how to live." For all that, there is also something which I can teach in that school. You ask, do you, what I can teach? That even an old man should keep learning. But I am ashamed of mankind, as often as I enter the lecture-hall. On my way to the house of Metronax I am compelled to go, as you know, right past the Neapolitan Theatre. The building is jammed; men are deciding, with tremendous zeal, who is entitled to be called a good flute-player; even the Greek piper and the herald draw their crowds. But in the other place, where the question discussed is: "What is a good man?" and the lesson which we learn is "How to be a good man," very few are in attendance, and the majority think that even these few are engaged in no good business; they have the name of being empty-headed idler. I hope I may be blessed with that kind of mockery; for one should listen in an unruffled spirit to the railings of the ignorant; when one is marching toward the goal of honour, one should scorn scorn itself.

Proceed, then, Lucilius, and hasten, lest you yourself be compelled to learn in your old age, as is the case with me. Nay, you must hasten all the more, because for a long time you have not approached the subject, which is one that you can scarcely learn thoroughly when you are old. "How much progress shall I make?" you ask. Just as much as you try to make. Why do you wait? Wisdom comes haphazard to no man. Money will come of its own accord; titles will be given to you; influence and authority will perhaps be thrust upon you; but virtue will not fall upon you by chance. Either is knowledge thereof to be won by light effort or small toil; but toiling is worth while when one is about to win all goods at a single stroke. For there is but a single good, – namely, that which is honourable; in all those other things of which the general opinion approves, you will find no truth or certainty. Why it is, however, that there is but one good, namely, that which is honourable, I shall now tell you, inasmuch as you judge that in my earlier letter I did not carry the discussion far enough, and think that this theory was commended to you rather than proved. I shall also compress the remarks of other authors into narrow compass.

Everything is estimated by the standard of its own good. The vine is valued for its productiveness and the flavour of its wine, the stag for his speed. We ask, with regard to beasts of burden, how sturdy of back they are; for their only use is to bear burdens. If a dog is to find the trail of a wild beast, keenness of scent is of first importance; if to catch his quarry, swiftness of foot; if to attack and harry it, courage. In each thing that quality should be best for which the thing is brought into being and by which it is judged. And what quality is best in man? It is reason; by virtue of reason he surpasses the animals, and is surpassed only by the gods. Perfect reason is therefore the good peculiar to man; all other qualities he shares in some degree with animals and plants. Man is strong; so is the lion. Man is comely; so is the peacock. Man is swift; so is the horse. I do not say that man is surpassed in all these qualities. I am not seeking to find that which is greatest in him, but that which is peculiarly his own. Man has body; so also have trees. Man has the power to act and to move at will; so have beasts and worms. Man has a voice; but how much louder is the voice of the dog, how much shriller that of the eagle, how much deeper that of the bull, how much sweeter and more melodious that of the nightingale! What then is peculiar to man? Reason. When this is right and has reached perfection, man's felicity is complete. Hence, if everything is praiseworthy and has arrived at the end intended by its nature, when it has brought its peculiar good to perfection, and if man's peculiar good is reason; then, if a man has brought his reason to perfection, he is praiseworthy and has readied the end suited to his nature. This perfect reason is called virtue, and is likewise that which is honourable.

Hence that in man is alone a good which alone belongs to man. For we are not now seeking to discover what is a good, but what good is man's. And if there is no other attribute which belongs peculiarly to man except reason, then reason will be his one peculiar good, but a good that is worth all the rest put together. If any man is bad, he will, I suppose, be regarded with disapproval; if good, I suppose he will be regarded with approval. Therefore, that attribute of man whereby he is approved or disapproved is his chief and only good. You do not doubt whether this is a good; you merely doubt whether it is the sole good. If a man possess all other things, such as health, riches, pedigree, a crowded reception-hall, but is confessedly bad, you will disapprove of him. Likewise, if a man possess none of the things which I have mentioned, and lacks money, or an escort of clients, or rank and a line of grandfathers and great-grandfathers, but is confessedly good, you will approve of him. Hence, this is man's one peculiar good, and the possessor of it is to be praised even if he lacks other things; but he who does not possess it, though he possess everything else in abundance is condemned and rejected. The same thing holds good regarding men as regarding things. A ship is said to be good not when it is decorated with costly colours, nor when its prow is covered with silver or gold or its figure-head embossed in ivory, nor when it is laden with the imperial revenues or with the wealth of kings, but when it is steady and staunch and taut, with seams that keep out the water, stout enough to endure the buffeting of the waves' obedient to its helm, swift and caring naught for the winds. You will speak of a sword as good, not when its sword-belt is of gold, or its scabbard studded with gems, but when its edge is fine for cutting and its point will pierce any armour. Take the carpenter's rule: we do not ask how beautiful it is, but how straight it is. Each thing is praised in regard to that attribute which is taken as its standard, in regard to that which is its peculiar quality.

Therefore in the case of man also, it is not pertinent to the question to know how many acres he ploughs, how much money he has out at interest, how many callers attend his receptions, how costly is the couch on which he lies, how transparent are the cups from which he drinks, but how good he is. He is good, however, if his reason is well-ordered and right and adapted to that which his nature has willed. It is this that is called virtue; this is what we mean by "honourable"; it is man's unique good. For since reason alone brings man to perfection, reason alone, when perfected, makes man happy. This, moreover, is man's only good, the only means by which he is made happy. We do indeed say that those things also are goods which are furthered and brought together by virtue, – that is, all the works of virtue; but virtue itself is for this reason the only good, because there is no good without virtue. If every good is in the soul, then whatever strengthens, uplifts, and enlarges the soul, is a good; virtue, however, does make the soul stronger, loftier, and larger. For all other things, which arouse our desires, depress the soul and weaken it, and when we think that they are uplifting the soul, they are merely puffing it up and cheating it with much emptiness. Therefore, that alone is good which will make the soul better.

All the actions of life, taken as a whole, are controlled by the consideration of what is honourable or base; it is with reference to these two things that our reason is governed in doing or not doing a particular thing. I shall explain what I mean: A good man will do what he thinks it will be honourable for him to do, even if it involves toil; he will do it even if it involves harm to him; he will do it even if it involves peril; again, he will not do that which will be base, even if it brings him money, or pleasure, or power. Nothing will deter him from that which is honourable, and nothing will tempt him into baseness. Therefore, if he is determined invariably to follow that which is honourable, invariably to avoid baseness, and in every act of his life to have regard for these two things, deeming nothing else good except that which is honourable, and nothing else bad except that which is base; if virtue alone is unperverted in him and by itself keeps its even course, then virtue is that man's only good, and nothing can thenceforth happen to it which may make it anything else than good. It has escaped all risk of change; folly may creep upwards towards wisdom, but wisdom never slips back into folly.

You may perhaps remember my saying that the things which have been generally desired and feared have been trampled down by many a man in moments of sudden passion. There have been found men who would place their hands in the flames, men whose smiles could not be stopped by the torturer, men who would shed not a tear at the funeral of their children, men who would meet death unflinchingly. It is love, for example, anger, lust, which have challenged dangers. If a momentary stubbornness can accomplish all this when roused by some goad that pricks the spirit, how much more can be accomplished by virtue, which does not act impulsively or suddenly, but uniformly and with a strength that is lasting! It follows that the things which are often scorned by the men who are moved with a sudden passion, and are always scorned by the wise, are neither goods nor evils. Virtue itself is therefore the only good; she marches proudly between the two extremes of fortune, with great scorn for both.

If, however, you accept the view that there is anything good besides that which is honourable, all the virtues will suffer. For it will never be possible for any virtue to be won and held, if there is anything outside itself which virtue must take into consideration. If there is any such thing, then it is at variance with reason, from which the virtues spring, and with truth also, which cannot exist without reason. Any opinion, however, which is at variance with truth, is wrong. A good man, you will admit, must have the highest sense of duty toward the gods. Hence he will endure with an unruffled spirit whatever happens to him; for he will know that it has happened as a result of the divine law, by which the whole creation moves. This being so, there will be for him one good, and only one, namely, that which is honourable; for one of its dictates is that we shall obey the gods and not blaze forth in anger at sudden misfortunes or deplore our lot, but rather patiently accept fate and obey its commands. If anything except the honourable is good, we shall be hounded by greed for life, and by greed for the things which provide life with its furnishings, – an intolerable state, subject to no limits, unstable. The only good, therefore, is that which is honourable, that which is subject to bounds.

I have declared that man's life would be more blest than that of the gods, if those things which the gods do not enjoy are goods, – such as money and offices of dignity. There is this further consideration: if only it is true that our souls, when released from the body, still abide, a happier condition is in store for them than is theirs while they dwell in the body. And yet, if those things are goods which we make use of for our bodies' sake, our souls will be worse off when set free; and that is contrary to our belief, to say that the soul is happier when it is cabined and confined than when it is free and has betaken itself to the universe. I also said that if those things which dumb animals possess equally with man are goods, then dumb animals also will lead a happy life; which is of course impossible. One must endure all things in defence of that which is honourable; but this would not be necessary if there existed any other good besides that which is honourable.

Although this question was discussed by me pretty extensively in a previous letter, I have discussed it summarily and briefly run through the argument. But an opinion of this kind will never seem true to you unless you exalt your mind and ask yourself whether, at the call of duty, you would be willing to die for your country, and buy the safety of all your fellow-citizens at the price of your own; whether you would offer your neck not only with patience, but also with gladness. If you would do this, there is no other good in your eyes. For you are giving up everything in order to acquire this good. Consider how great is the power of that which is honourable: you will die for your country, even at a moment's notice, when you know that you ought to do so. Sometimes, as a result of noble conduct, one wins great joy even in a very short and fleeting space of time; and though none of the fruits of a deed that has been done will accrue to the doer after he is dead and removed from the sphere of human affairs, yet the mere contemplation of a deed that is to be done is a delight, and the brave and upright man, picturing to himself the guerdons of his death, – guerdons such as the freedom of his country and the deliverance of all those for whom he is paying out his life, – partakes of the greatest pleasure and enjoys the fruit of his own peril. But that man also who is deprived of this joy, the joy which is afforded by the contemplation of some last noble effort, will leap to his death without a moment's hesitation, content to act rightly and dutifully. Moreover, you may confront him with many discouragements; you may say: "Your deed will speedily be forgotten," or "Your fellow-citizens will offer you scant thanks." He will answer: "All these matters lie outside my task. My thoughts are on the deed itself. I know that this is honourable. Therefore, whithersoever I am led and summoned by honour, I will go."

This, therefore, is the only good, and not only is every soul that has reached perfection aware of it, but also every soul that is by nature noble and of right instincts; all other goods are trivial and mutable. For this reason we are harassed if we possess them. Even though, by the kindness of Fortune, they have been heaped together, they weigh heavily upon their owners, always pressing them down and sometimes crushing them. None of those whom you behold clad in purple is happy, any more than one of these actors upon whom the play bestows a sceptre and a cloak while on the stage; they strut their hour before a crowded house, with swelling port and buskined foot; but when once they make their exit the foot-gear is removed and they return to their proper stature. None of those who have been raised to a loftier height by riches and honours is really great. Why then does he seem great to you? It is because you are measuring the pedestal along with the man. A dwarf is not tall, though he stand upon a mountain-top; a colossal statue will still be tall, though you place it in a well. This is the error under which we labour; this is the reason why we are imposed upon: we value no man at what he is, but add to the man himself the trappings in which he is clothed. But when you wish to inquire into a man's true worth, and to know what manner of man he is, look at him when he is naked; make him lay aside his inherited estate, his titles, and the other deceptions of fortune; let him even strip off his body. Consider his soul, its quality and its stature, and thus learn whether its greatness is borrowed, or its own.

If a man can behold with unflinching eyes the flash of a sword, if he knows that it makes no difference to him whether his soul takes flight through his mouth or through a wound in his throat, you may call him happy; you may also call him happy if, when he is threatened with bodily torture, whether it be the result of accident or of the might of the stronger, he can without concern hear talk of chains, or of exile, or of all the idle fears that stir men's minds, and can say:

> "O maiden, no new sudden form of toil
> Springs up before my eyes; within my soul
> I have forestalled and surveyed everything.

To-day it is you who threaten me with these terrors; but I have always threatened myself with them, and have prepared myself as a man to meet man's destiny." If an evil has been pondered beforehand, the blow is gentle when it comes. To the fool, however, and to him who trusts in fortune, each event as it arrives "comes in a new and sudden form," and a large part of evil, to the inexperienced, consists in its novelty. This is proved by the fact that men endure with greater courage, when they have once become accustomed to them, the things which they had at first regarded as hardships. Hence, the wise man accustoms himself to coming trouble, lightening by long reflection the evils which others lighten by long endurance. We sometimes hear the inexperienced say: "I knew that this was in store for me." But the wise man knows that all things are in store for him. Whatever happens, he says: "I knew it." Farewell.

Letter LXXVII - On Taking One's Own Life

Suddenly there came into our view to-day the "Alexandrian" ships, — I mean those which are usually sent ahead to announce the coming of the fleet; they are called "mail-boats." The Campanians are glad to see them; all the rabble of Puteoli stand on the docks, and can recognize the "Alexandrian" boats, no matter how great the crowd of vessels, by the very trim of their sails. For they alone may keep spread their topsails, which all ships use when out at sea, because nothing sends a ship along so well as its upper canvas; that is where most of the speed is obtained. So when the breeze has stiffened and becomes stronger than is comfortable, they set their yards lower; for the wind has less force near the surface of the water. Accordingly, when they have made Capreae and the headland whence

Tall Pallas watches on the stormy peak

all other vessels are bidden to be content with the mainsail, and the topsail stands out conspicuously on the "Alexandrian" mail-boats.

While everybody was bustling about and hurrying to the water-front, I felt great pleasure in my laziness, because, although I was soon to receive letters from my friends, I was in no hurry to know how my affairs were progressing abroad, or what news the letters were bringing; for some time now I have had no losses, nor gains either. Even if I were not an old man, I could not have helped feeling pleasure at this; but as it is, my pleasure was far greater. For, however small my possessions might be, I should still have left over more travelling-money than journey to travel, especially since this journey upon which we have set out is one which need not be followed to the end. An expedition will be incomplete if one stops half-way, or anywhere on this side of one's destination; but life is not incomplete if it is honourable. At whatever point you leave off living, provided you leave off nobly, your life is a whole. Often, however, one must leave off bravely, and our reasons therefore need not be momentous; for neither are the reasons momentous which hold us here.

Tullius Marcellinus, a man whom you knew very well, who in youth was a quiet soul and became old prematurely, fell ill of a disease which was by no means hopeless; but it was protracted and troublesome, and it demanded much attention; hence he began to think about dying. He called many of his friends together. Each one of them gave Marcellinus advice, – the timid friend urging him to do what he had made up his mind to do; the flattering and wheedling friend giving counsel which he supposed would be more pleasing to Marcellinus when he came to think the matter over; but our Stoic friend, a rare man, and, to praise him in language which he deserves, a man of courage and vigour admonished him best of all, as it seems to me. For he began as follows: "Do not torment yourself, my dear Marcellinus, as if the question which you are weighing were a matter of importance. It is not an important matter to live; all your slaves live, and so do all animals; but it is important to die honourably, sensibly, bravely. Reflect how long you have been doing the same thing: food, sleep, lust, – this is one's daily round. The desire to die may be felt, not only by the sensible man or the brave or unhappy man, but even by the man who is merely surfeited."

Marcellinus did not need someone to urge him, but rather someone to help him; his slaves refused to do his bidding. The Stoic therefore removed their fears, showing them that there was no risk involved for the household except when it was uncertain whether the master's death was self-sought or not; besides, it was as bad a practice to kill one's master as it was to prevent

374

him forcibly from killing himself. Then he suggested to Marcellinus himself that it would be a kindly act to distribute gifts to those who had attended him throughout his whole life, when that life was finished, just as, when a banquet is finished, the remaining portion is divided among the attendants who stand about the table. Marcellinus was of a compliant and generous disposition, even when it was a question of his own property; so he distributed little sums among his sorrowing slaves, and comforted them besides. No need had he of sword or of bloodshed; for three days he fasted and had a tent put up in his very bedroom. Then a tub was brought in; he lay in it for a long time, and, as the hot water was continually poured over him, he gradually passed away, not without a feeling of pleasure, as he himself remarked, – such a feeling as a slow dissolution is wont to give. Those of us who have ever fainted know from experience what this feeling is.

This little anecdote into which I have digressed will not be displeasing to you. For you will see that your friend departed neither with difficulty nor with suffering. Though he committed suicide, yet he withdrew most gently, gliding out of life. The anecdote may also be of some use; for often a crisis demands just such examples. There are times when we ought to die and are unwilling; sometimes we die and are unwilling. No one is so ignorant as not to know that we must at some time die; nevertheless, when one draws near death, one turns to flight, trembles, and laments. Would you not think him an utter fool who wept because he was not alive a thousand years ago? And is he not just as much of a fool who weeps because he will not be alive a thousand years from now? It is all the same; you will not be, and you were not. Neither of these periods of time belongs to you. You have been cast upon this point of time; if you would make it longer, how much longer shall you make it? Why weep? Why pray? You are taking pains to no purpose.

> Give over thinking that your prayers can bend
> Divine decrees from their predestined end.

These decrees are unalterable and fixed; they are governed by a mighty and everlasting compulsion. Your goal will be the goal of all things. What is there strange in this to you? You were born to be subject to this law; this fate befell your father, your mother, your ancestors, all who came before you; and it will befall all who shall come after you. A sequence which cannot be broken or altered by any power binds all things together and draws all things in its course. Think of the multitudes of men doomed to death who will come after you, of the multitudes who will go with you! You would die more bravely, I suppose, in the company of many thousands; and yet there are many thousands, both of men and of animals, who at this very moment, while you are irresolute about death, are breathing their last, in their several ways. But you, – did you believe that you would not some day reach the goal towards which you have always been travelling? No journey but has its end.

You think, I suppose, that it is now in order for me to cite some examples of great men. No, I shall cite rather the case of a boy. The story of the Spartan lad has been preserved: taken captive while still a stripling, he kept crying in his Doric dialect, "I will not be a slave!" and he made good his word;

for the very first time he was ordered to perform a menial and degrading service, – and the command was to fetch a chamber-pot, – he dashed out his brains against the wall. So near at hand is freedom, and is anyone still a slave? Would you not rather have your own son die thus than reach old age by weakly yielding? Why therefore are you distressed, when even a boy can die so bravely? Suppose that you refuse to follow him; you will be led. Take into your own control that which is now under the control of another. Will you not borrow that boy's courage, and say: "I am no slave!"? Unhappy fellow, you are a slave to men, you are a slave to your business, you are a slave to life. For life, if courage to die be lacking, is slavery.

Have you anything worth waiting for? Your very pleasures, which cause you to tarry and hold you back, have already been exhausted by you. None of them is a novelty to you, and there is none that has not already become hateful because you are cloyed with it. You know the taste of wine and cordials. It makes no difference whether a hundred or a thousand measures pass through your bladder; you are nothing but a wine-strainer. You are a connoisseur in the flavour of the oyster and of the mullet; your luxury has not left you anything untasted for the years that are to come; and yet these are the things from which you are torn away unwillingly. What else is there which you would regret to have taken from you? Friends? But who can be a friend to you? Country? What? Do you think enough of your country to be late to dinner? The light of the sun? You would extinguish it, if you could; for what have you ever done that was fit to be seen in the light? Confess the truth; it is not because you long for the senate chamber or the forum, or even for the world of nature, that you would fain put off dying; it is because you are loth to leave the fish-market, though you have exhausted its stores.

You are afraid of death; but how can you scorn it in the midst of a mushroom supper? You wish to live; well, do you know how to live? You are afraid to die. But come now: is this life of yours anything but death? Gaius Caesar was passing along the Via Latina, when a man stepped out from the ranks of the prisoners, his grey beard hanging down even to his breast, and begged to be put to death. "What!" said Caesar, "are you alive now?" That is the answer which should be given to men to whom death would come as a relief. "You are afraid to die; what! are you alive now?" "But," says one, "I wish to live, for I am engaged in many honourable pursuits. I am loth to leave life's duties, which I am fulfilling with loyalty and zeal." Surely you are aware that dying is also one of life's duties? You are deserting no duty; for there is no definite number established which you are bound to complete. There is no life that is not short. Compared with the world of nature, even Nestor's life was a short one, or Sattia's, the woman who bade carve on her tombstone that she had lived ninety and nine years. Some persons, you see, boast of their long lives; but who could have endured the old lady if she had had the luck to complete her hundredth year? It is with life as it is with a play, – it matters not how long the action is spun out, but how good the acting is. It makes no difference at what point you stop. Stop whenever you choose; only see to it that the closing period is well turned. Farewell.

Letter LXXVIII - On the Healing Power of the Mind

That you are frequently troubled by the snuffling of catarrh and by short attacks of fever which follow after long and chronic catarrhal seizures, I am sorry to hear; particularly because I have experienced this sort of illness myself, and scorned it in its early stages. For when I was still young, I could put up with hardships and show a bold front to illness. But I finally succumbed, and arrived at such a state that I could do nothing but snuffle, reduced as I was to the extremity of thinness. I often entertained the impulse of ending my life then and there; but the thought of my kind old father kept me back. For I reflected, not how bravely I had the power to die, but how little power he had to bear bravely the loss of me. And so I commanded myself to live. For sometimes it is an act of bravery even to live.

Now I shall tell you what consoled me during those days, stating at the outset that these very aids to my peace of mind were as efficacious as medicine. Honourable consolation results in a cure; and whatever has uplifted the soul helps the body also. My studies were my salvation. I place it to the credit of philosophy that I recovered and regained my strength. I owe my life to philosophy, and that is the least of my obligations! My friends, too, helped me greatly toward good health; I used to be comforted by their cheering words, by the hours they spent at my bedside, and by their conversation. Nothing, my excellent Lucilius, refreshes and aids a sick man so much as the affection of his friends; nothing so steals away the expectation and the fear of death. In fact, I could not believe that, if they survived me, I should be dying at all. Yes, I repeat, it seemed to me that I should continue to live, not with them, but through them. I imagined myself not to be yielding up my soul, but to be making it over to them.

All these things gave me the inclination to succour myself and to endure any torture; besides, it is a most miserable state to have lost one's zest for dying, and to have no zest in living. These, then, are the remedies to which you should have recourse. The physician will prescribe your walks and your exercise; he will warn you not to become addicted to idleness, as is the tendency of the inactive invalid; he will order you to read in a louder voice and to exercise your lungs the passages and cavity of which are affected; or to sail and shake up your bowels by a little mild motion; he will recommend the proper food, and the suitable time for aiding your strength with wine or refraining from it in order to keep your cough from being irritated and hacking. But as for me, my counsel to you is this, – and it is a cure, not merely of this disease of yours, but of your whole life, – "Despise death." There is no sorrow in the world, when we have escaped from the fear of death. There are these three serious elements in every disease: fear of death, bodily pain, and interruption of pleasures. Concerning death enough has been said, and I shall add only a word: this fear is not a fear of disease, but a fear of nature. Disease has often postponed death, and a vision of dying has been many a man's salvation. You will die, not because you are ill, but because you are alive; even when you have been cured, the same end awaits you; when you have recovered, it will be not death, but ill-health, that you have escaped.

Let us now return to the consideration of the characteristic disadvantage of disease: it is accompanied by great suffering. The suffering, however, is rendered endurable by interruptions; for the strain of extreme pain must come to an end. No man can suffer both severely and for a long time; Nature, who loves us most tenderly, has so constituted us as to make pain either endurable or short. The severest pains have their seat in the most slender parts of our body; nerves, joints, and any other of the narrow passages, hurt most cruelly when they have developed trouble within their contracted spaces. But these parts soon become numb, and by reason of the pain itself lose the sensation of pain, whether because the life-force, when checked in its natural course and changed for the worse, loses the peculiar power through which it thrives and through which it warns us, or because the diseased humours of the body, when they cease to have a place into which they may flow, are thrown back upon themselves, and deprive of sensation the parts where they have caused congestion. So gout, both in the feet and in the hands, and all pain in the vertebrae and in the nerves, have their intervals of rest at the times when they have dulled the parts which they before had tortured; the first twinges, in all such cases, are what cause the distress, and their onset is checked by lapse of time, so that there is an end of pain when numbness has set in. Pain in the teeth, eyes, and ears is most acute for the very reason that it begins among the narrow spaces of the body, – no less acute, indeed, than in the head itself. But if it is more violent than usual, it turns to delirium and stupor. This is, accordingly, a consolation for excessive pain, – that you cannot help ceasing to feel it if you feel it to excess. The reason, however, why the inexperienced are impatient when their bodies suffer is, that they have not accustomed themselves to be contented in spirit. They have been closely associated with the body. Therefore a high-minded and sensible man divorces soul from body, and dwells much with the better or divine part, and only as far as he must with this complaining and frail portion.

"But it is a hardship," men say, "to do without our customary pleasures, – to fast, to feel thirst and hunger." These are indeed serious when one first abstains from them. Later the desire dies down, because the appetites themselves which lead to desire are wearied and forsake us; then the stomach becomes petulant, then the food which we craved before becomes hateful. Our very wants die away. But there is no bitterness in doing without that which you have ceased to desire. Moreover, every pain sometimes stops, or at any rate slackens; moreover, one may take precautions against its return, and, when it threatens, may check it by means of remedies. Every variety of pain has its premonitory symptoms; this is true, at any rate, of pain that is habitual and recurrent. One can endure the suffering which disease entails, if one has come to regard its results with scorn. But do not of your own accord make your troubles heavier to bear and burden yourself with complaining. Pain is slight if opinion has added nothing to it; but if, on the other hand, you begin to encourage yourself and say, "It is nothing, – a trifling matter at most; keep a stout heart and it will soon cease"; then in thinking it slight, you will make it slight. Everything depends on opinion; ambition, luxury, greed, hark back to opinion. It is according to opinion that we suffer. A man is as wretched as he has convinced himself that he is. I hold that we should do away with complaint about past sufferings and with all language like this: "None has ever been worse off than I. What sufferings, what evils have I endured! No one has thought that I shall recover. How often have my family bewailed me, and the physicians given me over! Men who are placed on the rack are not torn asunder with such agony!" However, even if all this is true, it is over and gone. What benefit is there in reviewing past sufferings, and in being unhappy, just because once you were unhappy? Besides, every one adds much to his own ills, and tells lies to himself. And that which was bitter to bear is pleasant to have borne; it is natural to rejoice at the ending of one's ills.

Two elements must therefore be rooted out once for all, – the fear of future suffering, and the recollection of past suffering; since the latter no longer concerns me, and the former concerns me not yet. But when set in the very midst of troubles one should say:

Perchance some day the memory of this sorrow
Will even bring delight.

Let such a man fight against them with all his might: if he once gives way, he will be vanquished; but if he strives against his sufferings, he will conquer. As it is, however, what most men do is to drag down upon their own heads a falling ruin which they ought to try to support. If you begin to withdraw your support from that which thrusts toward you and totters and is ready to plunge, it will follow you and lean more heavily upon you; but if you hold your ground and make up your mind to push against it, it will be forced back. What blows do athletes receive on their faces and all over their bodies! Nevertheless, through their desire for fame they endure every torture, and they undergo these things not only because they are fighting but in order to be able to fight. Their very training means torture. So let us also win the way to victory in all our struggles, – for the reward is not a garland or a palm or a trumpeter who calls for silence at the proclamation of our names, but rather virtue, steadfastness of soul, and a peace that is won for all time, if fortune has once been utterly vanquished in any combat. You say, "I feel severe pain." What then; are you relieved from feeling it, if you endure it like a woman? Just as an enemy is more dangerous to a retreating army, so every trouble that fortune brings attacks us all the harder if we yield and turn our backs. "But the trouble is serious." What? Is it for this purpose that we are strong, – that we may have light burdens to bear? Would you have your illness long-drawn-out, or would you have it quick and short? If it is long, it means a respite, allows you a period for resting yourself, bestows upon you the boon of time in plenty; as it arises, so it must also subside. A short and rapid illness will do one of two things: it will quench or be quenched. And what difference does it make whether it is not or I am not? In either case there is an end of pain.

This, too, will help – to turn the mind aside to thoughts of other things and thus to depart from pain. Call to mind what honourable or brave deeds you have done; consider the good side of your own life. Run over in your memory those things which you have particularly admired. Then think of all the brave men who have conquered pain: of him who continued to read his book as he allowed the cutting out of varicose veins; of him who did not cease to smile, though that very smile so enraged his torturers that they tried upon him every instrument of their cruelty. If pain can be conquered by a smile, will it not be conquered by reason? You may tell me now of whatever you like – of colds, bad coughing-spells that bring up parts of our entrails, fever that parches our very vitals, thirst, limbs so twisted that the joints protrude in different directions; yet worse than these are the stake, the rack, the red-hot plates, the instrument that reopens wounds while the wounds themselves are still swollen and that drives their imprint still deeper. Nevertheless there have been men who have not uttered a moan amid these tortures. "More yet!" says the torturer; but the victim has not begged for release. "More yet!" he says again; but no answer has come. "More yet!" the victim has smiled, and heartily, too. Can you not bring yourself, after an example like this, to make a mock at pain?

"But," you object, "my illness does not allow me to be doing anything; it has withdrawn me from all my duties." It is your body that is hampered by ill-health, and not your soul as well. It is for this reason that it clogs the feet of the runner and will hinder the handiwork of the cobbler or the artisan; but if your soul be habitually in practice, you will plead and teach, listen and learn, investigate and meditate. What more is necessary? Do you think that you are doing nothing if you possess self-control in your illness? You will be showing that a disease can be overcome, or at any rate endured. There is, I assure you, a place for virtue even upon a bed of sickness. It is not only the sword and the battle-line that prove the soul alert and unconquered by fear; a man can display bravery even when wrapped in his bed-clothes. You have something to do: wrestle bravely with disease. If it shall compel you to nothing, beguile you to nothing, it is a notable example that you display. O what ample matter were there for renown, if we could have spectators of our sickness! Be your own spectator; seek your own applause.

Again, there are two kinds of pleasures. Disease checks the pleasures of the body, but does not do away with them. Nay, if the truth is to be considered, it serves to excite them; for the thirstier a man is, the more he enjoys a drink; the hungrier he is, the more pleasure he takes in food. Whatever falls to one's lot after a period of abstinence is welcomed with greater zest. The other kind, however, the pleasures of the mind, which are higher and less uncertain, no physician can refuse to the sick man. Whoever seeks these and knows well what they are, scorns all the blandishments of the senses. Men say, "Poor sick fellow!" But why? Is it because he does not mix snow with his wine, or because he does not revive the chill of his drink – mixed as it is in a good-sized bowl – by chipping ice into it? Or because he does not have Lucrine oysters opened fresh at his table? Or because there is no din of cooks about his dining-hall, as they bring in their very cooking apparatus along with their viands? For luxury has already devised this fashion – of having the kitchen accompany the dinner, so that the food may not grow luke-warm, or fail to be hot enough for a palate which has already become hardened. "Poor sick fellow!" – he will eat as much as he can digest. There will be no boar lying before his eyes, banished from the table as if it were a common meat; and on his sideboard there will be heaped together no breast-meat of birds, because it sickens him to see birds served whole. But what evil has been done to you? You will dine like a sick man, nay, sometimes like a sound man.

All these things, however, can be easily endured – gruel, warm water, and anything else that seems insupportable to a fastidious man, to one who is wallowing in luxury, sick in soul rather than in body – if only we cease to shudder at death. And we shall cease, if once we have gained a knowledge of the limits of good and evil; then, and then only, life will not weary us, neither will death make us afraid. For surfeit of self can never seize upon a life that surveys all the things which are manifold, great, divine; only idle leisure is wont to make men hate their lives. To one who roams through the universe, the truth can never pall; it will be the untruths that will cloy. And, on the other hand, if death comes near with its summons, even though it be untimely in its arrival, though it cut one off in one's prime, a man has had a taste of all that the longest life can give. Such a man has in great measure come to understand the universe. He knows that honourable things do not depend on time for their growth; but any life must seem short to those who measure its length by pleasures which are empty and for that reason unbounded.

Refresh yourself with such thoughts as these, and meanwhile reserve some hours for our letters. There will come a time when we shall be united again and brought together; however short this time may be, we shall make it long by knowing how to employ it. For, as Posidonius says: "A single day among the learned lasts longer than the longest life of the ignorant." Meanwhile, hold fast to this thought, and grip it close: yield not to adversity; trust not to prosperity; keep before your eyes the full scope of Fortune's power, as if she would surely do whatever is in her power to do. That which has been long expected comes more gently. Farewell.

Letter LXXIX - On the Rewards of Scientific Discovery

I have been awaiting a letter from you, that you might inform me what new matter was revealed to you during your trip round Sicily, and especially that you might give me further information regarding Charybdis itself. I know very well that Scylla is a rock – and indeed a rock not dreaded by mariners; but with regard to Charybdis I should like to have a full description, in order to see whether it agrees with the accounts in mythology; and, if you have by chance investigated it (for it is indeed worthy of your investigation), please enlighten me concerning the following: Is it lashed into a whirlpool by a wind from only one direction, or do all storms alike serve to disturb its depths? Is it true that objects snatched downwards by the whirlpool in that strait are carried for many miles under water, and then come to the surface on the beach near Tauromenium? If you will write me a full account of these matters, I shall then have the boldness to ask you to perform another task, – also to climb Aetna at my special request. Certain naturalists have inferred that the mountain is wasting away and gradually settling, because sailors used to be able to see it from a greater distance. The reason for this may be, not that the height of the mountain is decreasing, but because the flames have become dim and the eruptions less strong and less copious, and because for the same reason the smoke also is less active by day. However, either of these two things is possible to believe: that on the one hand the mountain is growing smaller because it is consumed from day to day, and that, on the other hand, it remains the same in size because the mountain is not devouring itself, but instead of this the matter which seethes forth collects in some subterranean valley and is fed by other material, finding in the mountain itself not the food which it requires, but simply a passage-way out. There is a well-known place in Lycia – called by the inhabitants "Hephaestion" – where the ground is full of holes in many places and is surrounded by a harmless fire, which does no injury to the plants that grow there. Hence the place is fertile and luxuriant with growth, because the flames do not scorch but merely shine with a force that is mild and feeble.

But let us postpone this discussion, and look into the matter when you have given me a description just how far distant the snow lies from the crater, – I mean the snow which does not melt even in summer, so safe is it from the adjacent fire. But there is no ground for your charging this work to my account; for you were about to gratify your own craze for fine writing, without a commission from anyone at all. Nay, what am I to offer you not merely to describe Aetna in your poem, and not to touch lightly upon a topic which is a matter of ritual for all poets? Ovid could not be prevented from using this theme simply because Vergil had already fully covered it; nor could either of these writers frighten off Cornelius Severus. Besides, the topic has served them all with happy results, and those who have gone before seem to me not to have forestalled all what could be said, but merely to have opened the way.

It makes a great deal of difference whether you approach a subject that has been exhausted, or one where the ground has merely been broken; in the latter case, the topic grows day by day, and what is already discovered does not hinder new discoveries. Besides, he who writes last has the best of the bargain; he finds already at hand words which, when marshalled in a different way, show a new face. And he is not pilfering them, as if they belonged to someone else, when he uses them, for they are common property. Now if Aetna does not make your mouth water, I am mistaken in you. You have for some time been desirous of writing something in the grand style and on the level of the older school. For your modesty does not allow you to set your hopes any higher; this quality of yours is so pronounced that, it sees to me, you are likely to curb the force of your natural ability, if there should be any danger of outdoing others; so greatly do you reverence the old masters. Wisdom has this advantage, among others, – that no man can be outdone by another, except during the climb. But when you have arrived at the top, it is a draw; there is no room for further ascent, the game is over. Can the sun add to his size? Can the moon advance beyond her usual fullness? The seas do not increase in bulk. The universe keeps the same character, the same limits. Things which have reached their full stature cannot grow higher. Men who have attained wisdom will therefore be equal and on the same footing. Each of them will possess his own peculiar gifts – one will be more affable, another more facile, another more ready of speech, a fourth more eloquent; but as regards the quality under discussion, – the element that produces happiness, – it is equal in them all. I do not know whether this Aetna of yours can collapse and fall in ruins, whether this lofty summit, visible for many miles over the deep sea, is wasted by the incessant power of the flames; but I do know that virtue will not be brought down to a lower plane either by flames or by ruins. Hers is the only greatness that knows no lowering; there can be for her no further rising or sinking. Her stature, like that of the stars in the heavens, is fixed. Let us therefore strive to raise ourselves to this altitude.

Already much of the task is accomplished; nay, rather, if I can bring myself to confess the truth, not much. For goodness does not mean merely being better than the lowest. Who that could catch but a mere glimpse of the daylight would boast his powers of vision? One who sees the sun shining through a mist may be contented meanwhile that he has escaped darkness, but he does not yet enjoy the blessing of light. Our souls will not have reason to rejoice in their lot until, freed from this darkness in which they grope, they have not merely glimpsed the brightness with feeble vision, but have absorbed the full light of day and have been restored to their place in the sky, – until, indeed, they have regained the place which they held at the allotment of their birth. The soul is summoned upward by its very origin. And it will reach that goal even before it is released from its prison below, as soon as it has cast off sin and, in purity and lightness, has leaped up into celestial realms of thought.

I am glad, beloved Lucilius, that we are occupied with this ideal, that we pursue it with all our might, even though few know it, or none. Fame is the shadow of virtue; it will attend virtue even against her will. But, as the shadow sometimes precedes and sometimes follows or even lags behind, so fame sometimes goes before us and shows herself in plain sight, and sometimes is in the rear, and is all the greater in proportion as she is late in coming, when once envy has beaten a retreat. How long did men believe Democritus to be mad! Glory barely came to Socrates. And how long did our state remain in ignorance of Cato! They rejected him, and did not know his worth until they had lost him. If Rutilius had not resigned himself to wrong, his innocence and virtue would have escaped notice; the hour of his suffering was the hour of his triumph. Did he not give thanks for his lot, and welcome his exile with open arms? I have mentioned thus far those to whom Fortune has brought renown at the very moment of persecution; but how many there are whose progress toward virtue has come to light only after their death! And how many have been ruined, not rescued, by their reputation? There is Epicurus, for example; mark how greatly he is admired, not only by the more cultured, but also by this ignorant rabble. This man, however, was unknown to Athens itself, near which he had hidden himself away. And so, when he had already survived by many years his friend Metrodorus, he added in a letter these last words, proclaiming with thankful appreciation the friendship that had existed between them: "So greatly blest were Metrodorus and I that it has been no harm to us to be unknown, and almost unheard of, in this well-known land of Greece." Is it not true, therefore, that men did not discover him until after he had ceased to be? Has not his renown shone forth, for all that? Metrodorus also admits this fact in one of his letters: that Epicurus and he were not well known to the public; but he declares that after the lifetime of Epicurus and himself any man who might wish to follow in their footsteps would win great and ready-made renown.

Virtue is never lost to view; and yet to have been lost to view is no loss. There will come a day which will reveal her, though hidden away or suppressed by the spite of her contemporaries. That man is born merely for a few, who thinks only of the people of his own generation. Many thousands of years and many thousands of peoples will come after you; it is to these that you should have regard. Malice may have imposed silence upon the mouths of all who were alive in your day; but there will come men who will judge you without prejudice and without favour. If there is any reward that virtue receives at the hands of fame, not even this can pass away. We ourselves, indeed, shall not be affected by the talk of posterity; nevertheless, posterity will cherish and celebrate us even though we are not conscious thereof. Virtue has never failed to reward a man, both during his life and after his death, provided he has followed her loyally, provided he has not decked himself out or painted himself up, but has been always the same, whether he appeared before men's eyes after being announced, or suddenly and without preparation. Pretence accomplishes nothing. Few are deceived by a mask that is easily drawn over the face. Truth is the same in every part. Things which deceive us have no real substance. Lies are thin stuff; they are transparent, if you examine them with care. Farewell.

Letter LXXX - On Worldly Deceptions

Today I have some free time, thanks not so much to myself as to the games, which have attracted all the bores to the boxing-match. No one will interrupt me or disturb the train of my thoughts, which go ahead more boldly as the result of my very confidence. My door has not been continually creaking on its hinges nor will my curtain be pulled aside; my thoughts may march safely on, – and that is all the more necessary for one who goes independently and follows out his own path. Do I then follow no predecessors? Yes, but I allow myself to discover something new, to alter, to reject. I am not a slave to them, although I give them my approval.

And yet that was a very bold word which I spoke when I assured myself that I should have some quiet, and some uninterrupted retirement. For lo, a great cheer comes from the stadium, and while it does not drive me distracted, yet it shifts my thought to a contrast suggested by this very noise. How many men, I say to myself, train their bodies, and how few train their minds! What crowds flock to the games, spurious as they are and arranged merely for pastime, – and what a solitude reigns where the good arts are taught! How feather-brained are the athletes whose muscles and shoulders we admire! The question which I ponder most of all is this; if the body can be trained to such a degree of endurance that it will stand the blows and kicks of several opponents at once and to such a degree that a man can last out the day and resist the scorching sun in the midst of the burning dust, drenched all the while with his own blood, – if this can be done, how much more easily might the mind be toughened so that it could receive the blows of Fortune and not be conquered, so that it might struggle to its feet again after it has been laid low, after it has been trampled under foot?

For although the body needs many things in order to be strong, yet the mind grows from within, giving to itself nourishment and exercise. Yonder athletes must have copious food, copious drink, copious quantities of oil, and long training besides; but you can acquire virtue without equipment and without expense. All that goes to make you a good man lies within yourself. And what do you need in order to become good? To wish it. But what better thing could you wish for than to break away from this slavery, a slavery that oppresses us all, a slavery which even chattels of the lowest estate, born amid such degradation, strive in every possible way to strip off? In exchange for freedom they pay out the savings which they have scraped together by cheating their own bellies; shall you not be eager to attain liberty at any price, seeing that you claim it as your birthright? Why cast glances toward your strong-box? Liberty cannot be bought. It is therefore useless to enter in your ledger the item of "Freedom," for freedom is possessed neither by those who have bought it, nor by those who have sold it. You must give this good to yourself, and seek it from yourself.

First of all, free yourself from the fear of death, for death puts the yoke about our necks; then free yourself from the fear of poverty. If you would know how little evil there is in poverty, compare the faces of the poor with those of the rich; the poor man smiles more often and more genuinely; his troubles do not go deep down; even if any anxiety comes upon him, it passes like a fitful cloud. But the merriment of those whom men call happy is feigned, while their sadness is heavy and festering, and all the heavier because they may not meanwhile display their grief, but must act the part of happiness in the midst of sorrows that eat out their very hearts. I often feel called upon to use the following illustration, and it seems to me that none expresses more effectively this drama of human life, wherein we are assigned the parts which we are to play so badly. Yonder is the man who stalks upon the stage with swelling port and head thrown back, and says:

Lo, I am he whom Argos hails as lord,
Whom Pelops left the heir of lands that spread
From Hellespont and from th' Ionian sea
E'en to the Isthmian straits.

And who is this fellow? He is but a slave; his wage is five measures of grain and five denarii. Yon other who, proud and wayward and puffed up by confidence in his power, declaims:

Peace, Menelaus, or this hand shall slay thee!

receives a daily pittance and sleeps on rags. You may speak in the same way about all these dandies whom you see riding in litters above the heads of men and above the crowd; in every case their happiness is put on like the actor's mask. Tear it off, and you will scorn them.

When you buy a horse, you order its blanket to be removed; you pull off the garments from slaves that are advertised for sale, so that no bodily flaws may escape your notice; if you judge a man, do you judge him when he is wrapped in a disguise? Slave dealers hide under some sort of finery any defect which may give offence, and for that reason the very trappings arouse the suspicion of the buyer. If you catch sight of a leg or an arm that is bound up in cloths, you demand that it be stripped and that the body itself be revealed to you. Do you see yonder Scythian or Sarmatian king, his head adorned with the badge of his office? If you wish to see what he amounts to, and to know his full worth, take off his diadem; much evil lurks beneath it. But why do I speak of others? If you wish to set a value on yourself, put away your money, your estates, your honours, and look into your own soul. At present, you are taking the word of others for what you are. Farewell.

Letter LXXXI - On Benefits

You complain that you have met with an ungrateful person. If this is your first experience of that sort, you should offer thanks either to your good luck or to your caution. In this case, however, caution can effect nothing but to make you ungenerous. For if you wish to avoid such a danger, you will not confer benefits; and so, that benefits may not be lost with another man, they will be lost to yourself.

It is better, however, to get no return than to confer no benefits. Even after a poor crop one should sow again; for often losses due to continued barrenness of an unproductive soil have been made good by one year's fertility. In order to discover one grateful person, it is worth while to make trial of many ungrateful ones. No man has so unerring a hand when he confers benefits that he is not frequently deceived; it is well for the traveller to wander, that he may again cleave to the path. After a shipwreck, sailors try the sea again. The banker is not frightened away from the forum by the swindler. If one were compelled to drop everything that caused trouble, life would soon grow dull amid sluggish idleness; but in your case this very condition may prompt you to become more charitable. For when the outcome of any undertaking is unsure, you must try again and again, in order to succeed ultimately. I have, however, discussed the matter with sufficient fullness in the volumes which I have written, entitled "On Benefits."

What I think should rather be investigated is this, – a question which I feel has not been made sufficiently clear: "Whether he who has helped us has squared the account and has freed us from our debt, if he has done us harm later." You may add this question also, if you like: "when the harm done later has been more than the help rendered previously." If you are seeking for the formal and just decision of a strict judge, you will find that he checks off one act by the other, and declares: "Though the injuries outweigh the benefits, yet we should credit to the benefits anything that stands over even after the injury." The harm done was indeed greater, but the helpful act was done first. Hence the time also should be taken into account. Other cases are so clear that I need not remind you that you should also look into such points as: How gladly was the help offered, and how reluctantly was the harm done, – since benefits, as well as injuries, depend on the spirit. "I did not wish to confer the benefit; but I was won over by my respect for the man, or by the importunity of his request, or by hope." Our feeling about every obligation depends in each case upon the spirit in which the benefit is conferred; we weigh not the bulk of the gift, but the quality of the good-will which prompted it. So now let us do away with guess-work; the former deed was a benefit, and the latter, which transcended the earlier benefit, is an injury. The good man so arranges the two sides of his ledger that he voluntarily cheats himself by adding to the benefit and subtracting from the injury.

The more indulgent magistrate, however (and I should rather be such a one), will order us to forget the injury and remember the accommodation. "But surely," you say, "it is the part of justice to render to each that which is his due, – thanks in return for a benefit, and retribution, or at any rate ill-will, in return for an injury!" This, I say, will be true when it is one man who has inflicted the injury, and a different man who has conferred the benefit; for if it is the same man, the force of the injury is nullified by the benefit conferred. Indeed, a man who ought to be pardoned, even though there were no good deeds credited to him in the past, should receive something more than mere leniency if he commits a wrong when he has a benefit to his credit. I do not set an equal value on benefits and injuries. I reckon a benefit at a higher rate than an injury. Not all grateful persons know what it involves to be in debt for a benefit; even a thoughtless, crude fellow, one of the common herd, may know, especially soon after he has received the gift; but he does not know how deeply he stands in debt therefor. Only the wise man knows exactly what value should be put upon everything; for the fool whom I just mentioned, no matter how good his intentions may be, either pays less than he owes, or pays it at the wrong time or the wrong place. That for which he should make return he wastes and loses. There is a marvellously accurate phraseology applied to certain subjects, a long-established terminology which indicates certain acts by means of symbols that are most efficient and that serve to outline men's duties. We are, as you know, wont to speak thus: "A. has made a return for the favour bestowed by B." Making a return means handing over of your own accord that which you owe. We do not say, "He has paid back the favour"; for "pay back" is used of a man upon whom a demand for payment is made, of those who pay against their will. Of those who pay under any circumstances whatsoever, and of those who pay through a third party. We do not say, "He has 'restored' the benefit," or 'settled' it; we have never been satisfied with a word which applies properly to a debt of money. Making a return means offering something to him from whom you have received something. The phrase implies a voluntary return; he who has made such a return has served the writ upon himself.

The wise man will inquire in his own mind into all the circumstances: how much he has received, from whom, when, where, how. And so we declare that none but the wise man knows how to make return for a favour; moreover, none but the wise man knows how to confer a benefit, – that man, I mean, who enjoys the giving more than the recipient enjoys the receiving. Now some person will reckon this remark as one of the generally surprising statements such as we Stoics are wont to make and such as the Greeks call "paradoxes," and will say: "Do you maintain, then, that only the wise man knows how to return a favour? Do you maintain that no one else knows how to make restoration to a creditor for a debt? Or, on buying a commodity, to pay full value to the seller?" In order not to bring any odium upon myself, let me tell you that Epicurus says the same thing. At any rate, Metrodorus remarks that only the wise man knows how to return a favour. Again, the objector mentioned above wonders at our saying: "The wise man alone knows how to love, the wise man alone is a real friend." And yet it is a part of love and of friendship to return favours; nay, further, it is an ordinary act, and happens more frequently than real friendship. Again, this same objector wonders at our saying, "There is no loyalty except in the wise man," just as if he himself does not say the same thing! Or do you think that there is any loyalty in him who does not know how to return a favour? These men, accordingly, should cease to discredit us, just as if we were uttering an impossible boast; they should understand that the essence of honour resides in the wise man, while among the crowd we find only the ghost and the semblance of honour. None but the wise man knows how to return a favour. Even a fool can return it in proportion to his knowledge and his power; his fault would be a lack of knowledge rather than a lack of will or desire. To will does not come by teaching.

The wise man will compare all things with one another; for the very same object becomes greater or smaller, according to the time, the place, and the cause. Often the riches that are spent in profusion upon a palace cannot accomplish as much as a thousand denarii given at the right time. Now it makes a great deal of difference whether you give outright, or come to a man's assistance, whether your generosity saves him, or sets him up in life. Often the gift is small, but the consequences great. And what a distinction do you imagine there is between taking something which one lacks, – something which was offered, – and receiving a benefit in order to confer one in return?

But we should not slip back into the subject which we have already sufficiently investigated. In this balancing of benefits and injuries, the good man will, to be sure, judge with the highest degree of fairness, but he will incline towards the side of the benefit; he will turn more readily in this direction. Moreover, in affairs of this kind the person concerned is wont to count for a great deal. Men say: "You conferred a benefit upon me in that matter of the slave, but you did me an injury in the case of my father" or, "You saved my son, but robbed me of a father." Similarly, he will follow up all other matters in which comparisons can be made, and if the difference be very slight, he will pretend not to notice it. Even though the difference be great, yet if the concession can be made without impairment of duty and loyalty, our good man will overlook that is, provided the injury exclusively affects the good man himself. To sum up, the matter stands thus: the good man will be easy-going in striking a balance; he will allow too much to be set against his credit. He will be unwilling to pay a benefit by balancing the injury against it. The side towards which he will lean, the tendency which he will exhibit, is the desire to be under obligations for the favour, and the desire to make return therefor. For anyone who receives a benefit more gladly than he repays it is mistaken. By as much as he who pays is more light-hearted than he who borrows, by so much ought he to be more joyful who unburdens himself of the greatest debt – a benefit received – than he who incurs the greatest obligations. For ungrateful men make mistakes in this respect also: they have to pay their creditors both capital and interest, but they think that benefits are currency which they can use without interest. So the debts grow through postponement, and the later the action is postponed the more remains to be paid. A man is an ingrate if he repays a favour without interest. Therefore, interest also should be allowed for, when you compare your receipts and your expenses. We should try by all means to be as grateful as possible.

For gratitude is a good thing for ourselves, in a sense in which justice, that is commonly supposed to concern other persons, is not; gratitude returns in large measure unto itself. There is not a man who, when he has benefited his neighbour, has not benefited himself, – I do not mean for the reason that he whom you have aided will desire to aid you, or that he whom you have defended will desire to protect you, or that an example of good conduct returns in a circle to benefit the doer, just as examples of bad conduct recoil upon their authors, and as men find no pity if they suffer wrongs which they themselves have demonstrated the possibility of committing; but that the reward for all the virtues lies in the virtues themselves. For they are not practised with a view to recompense; the wages of a good deed is to have done it. I am grateful, not in order that my neighbour, provoked by the earlier act of kindness, may be more ready to benefit me, but simply in order that I may perform a most pleasant and beautiful act; I feel grateful, not because it profits me, but because it pleases me. And, to prove the truth of this to you, I declare that even if I may not be grateful without seeming ungrateful, even if I am able to retain a benefit only by an act which resembles an injury; even so, I shall strive in the utmost calmness of spirit toward the purpose which honour demands, in the very midst of disgrace. No one, I think, rates virtue higher or is more consecrated to virtue than he who has lost his reputation for being a good man in order to keep from losing the approval of his conscience. Thus, as I have said, your being grateful is more conducive to your own good than to your neighbour's good. For while your neighbour has had a common, everyday experience, – namely, receiving back the gift which he had bestowed, – you have had a great experience which is the outcome of an utterly happy condition of soul, – to have felt gratitude. For if wickedness makes men unhappy and virtue makes men blest, and if it is a virtue to be grateful, then the return which you have made is only the customary thing, but the thing to which you have attained is priceless, – the consciousness of gratitude, which comes only to the soul that is divine and blessed. The opposite feeling to this, however, is immediately attended by the greatest unhappiness; no man, if he be ungrateful, will be unhappy in the future. I allow him no day of grace; he is unhappy forthwith.

Let us therefore avoid being ungrateful, not for the sake of others but for our own sakes. When we do wrong, only the least and lightest portion of it flows back upon our neighbour; the worst and, if I may use the term, the densest portion of it stays at home and troubles the owner. My master Attalus used to say: "Evil herself drinks the largest portion of her own poison." The poison which serpents carry for the destruction of others, and secrete without harm to themselves, is not like this poison; for this sort is ruinous to the possessor. The ungrateful man tortures and torments himself; he hates the gifts which he has accepted, because he must make a return for them, and he tries to belittle their value, but he really enlarges and exaggerates the injuries which he has received. And what is more wretched than a man who forgets his benefits and clings to his injuries?

Wisdom, on the other hand, lends grace to every benefit, and of her own free will commends it to her own favour, and delights her soul by continued recollection thereof. Evil men have but one pleasure in benefits, and a very short-lived pleasure at that; it lasts only while they are receiving them. But the wise man derives therefrom an abiding and eternal joy. For he takes delight not so much in receiving the gift as in having received it; and this joy never perishes; it abides with him always. He despises the wrongs done him; he forgets them, not accidentally, but voluntarily. He does not put a wrong construction upon everything, or seek for someone whom he may hold responsible for each happening; he rather ascribes even the sins of men to chance. He will not misinterpret a word or a look; he makes light of all mishaps by interpreting them in a generous way. He does not remember an injury rather than a service. As far as possible, he lets his memory rest upon the earlier and the better deed, never changing his attitude towards those who have deserved well of him, except in climes where the bad deeds far outdistance the good, and the space between them is obvious even to one who closes his eyes to it; even then only to this extent, that he strives, after receiving the preponderant injury, to resume the attitude which he held before he received the benefit. For when the injury merely equals the benefit, a certain amount of kindly feeling is left over. Just as a defendant is acquitted when the votes are equal, and just as the spirit of kindliness always tries to bend every doubtful case toward the better interpretation, so the mind of the wise man, when another's merits merely equal his bad deeds, will, to be sure, cease to feel an obligation, but does not cease to desire to feel it, and acts precisely like the man who pays his debts even after they have been legally cancelled.

But no man can be grateful unless he has learned to scorn the things which drive the common herd to distraction; if you wish to make return for a favour, you must be willing to go into exile, – or to pour forth your blood, or to undergo poverty, or – and this will frequently happen, – even to let your very innocence be stained and exposed to shameful slanders. It is no slight price that a man must pay for being grateful. We hold nothing dearer than a benefit, so long as we are seeking one; we hold nothing cheaper after we have received it. Do you ask what it is that makes us forget benefits received? It is our extreme greed for receiving others. We consider not what we have obtained, but what we are to seek. We are deflected from the right course by riches, titles, power, and everything which is valuable in our opinion but worthless when rated at its real value. We do not know how to weigh matters; we should take counsel regarding them, not with their reputation but with their nature; those things possess no grandeur wherewith to enthral our minds, except the fact that we have become accustomed to marvel at them. For they are not praised because they ought to be desired, but they are desired because they have been praised; and when the error of individuals has once created error on the part of the public, then the public error goes on creating error on the part of individuals.

But just as we take on faith such estimates of values, so let us take on the faith of the people this truth that nothing is more honourable than a grateful heart. This phrase will be echoed by all cities, and by all races, even those from savage countries. Upon this point – good and bad will agree. Some praise pleasure, some prefer toil; some say that pain is the greatest of evils, some say it is no evil at all; some will include riches in the Supreme Good, others will say that their discovery meant harm to the human race, and that none is richer than he to whom Fortune has found nothing to give. Amid all this diversity of opinion all men will yet with one voice, as the saying is, vote "aye" to the proposition that thanks should be returned to those who have deserved well of us. On this question the common herd, rebellious as they are, will all agree, but at present we keep paying back injuries instead of benefits, and the primary reason why a man is ungrateful is that he has found it impossible to be grateful enough. Our madness has gone to such lengths that it is a very dangerous thing to confer great benefits upon a person; for just because he thinks it shameful not to repay, so he would have none left alive whom he should repay. "Keep for yourself what you have received; I do not ask it back – I do not demand it. Let it be safe to have conferred a favour." There is no worse hatred than that which springs from shame at the desecration of a benefit. Farewell.

Letter LXXXII - On the Natural Fear of Death

I have already ceased to be anxious about you. "Whom then of the gods," you ask, "have you found as your voucher?" A god, let me tell you, who deceives no one, – a soul in love with that which is upright and good. The better part of yourself is on safe ground. Fortune can inflict injury upon you; what is more pertinent is that I have no fears lest you do injury to yourself. Proceed as you have begun, and settle yourself in this way of living, not luxuriously, but calmly. I prefer to be in trouble rather than in luxury; and you had better interpret the term "in trouble" as popular usage is wont to interpret it: living a "hard," "rough," "toilsome" life. We are wont to hear the lives of certain men praised as follows, when they are objects of unpopularity: "So-and-So lives luxuriously"; but by this they mean: "He is softened by luxury." For the soul is made womanish by degrees, and is weakened until it matches the ease and laziness in which it lies. Lo, is it not better for one who is really a man even to become hardened? Next, these same dandies fear that which they have made their own lives resemble. Much difference is there between lying idle and lying buried! "But," you say, "is it not better even to lie idle than to whirl round in these eddies of business distraction?" Both extremes are to be deprecated – both tension and sluggishness. I hold that he who lies on a perfumed couch is no less dead than he who is dragged along by the executioner's hook.

Leisure without study is death; it is a tomb for the living man. What then is the advantage of retirement? As if the real causes of our anxieties did not follow us across the seas! What hiding-place is there, where the fear of death does not enter? What peaceful haunts are there, so fortified and so far withdrawn that pain does not fill them with fear? Wherever you hide yourself, human ills will make an uproar all around. There are many external things which compass us about, to deceive us or to weigh upon us; there are many things within which, even amid solitude, fret and ferment.

Therefore, gird yourself about with philosophy, an impregnable wall. Though it be assaulted by many engines, Fortune can find no passage into it. The soul stands on unassailable ground, if it has abandoned external things; it is independent in its own fortress; and every weapon that is hurled falls short of the mark. Fortune has not the long reach with which we credit her; she can seize none except him that clings to her. Let us then recoil from her as far as we are able. This will be possible for us only through knowledge of self and of the world of Nature. The soul should know whither it is going and whence it came, what is good for it and what is evil, what it seeks and what it avoids, and what is that Reason which distinguishes between the desirable and the undesirable, and thereby tames the madness of our desires and calms the violence of our fears.

Some men flatter themselves that they have checked these evils by themselves even without the aid of philosophy; but when some accident catches them off their guard, a tardy confession of error is wrung from them. Their boastful words perish from their lips when the torturer commands them to stretch forth their hands, and when death draws nearer! You might say to such a man: "It was easy for you to challenge evils that were not near-by; but here comes pain, which you declared you could endure; here comes death, against which you uttered many a courageous boast! The whip cracks, the sword flashes:

Ah now, Aeneas, thou must needs be stout
And strong of heart!

This strength of heart, however, will come from constant study, provided that you practise, not with the tongue but with the soul, and provided that you prepare yourself to meet death. To enable yourself to meet death, you may expect no encouragement or cheer from those who try to make you believe, by means of their hair-splitting logic, that death is no evil. For I take pleasure, excellent Lucilius, in poking fun at the absurdities of the Greeks, of which, to my continual surprise, I have not yet succeeded in ridding myself. Our master Zeno uses a syllogism like this: "No evil is glorious; but death is glorious; therefore death is no evil." A cure, Zeno! I have been freed from fear; henceforth I shall not hesitate to bare my neck on the scaffold. Will you not utter sterner words instead of rousing a dying man to laughter? Indeed, Lucilius, I could not easily tell you whether he who thought that he was quenching the fear of death by setting up this syllogism was the more foolish, or he who attempted to refute it, just as if it had anything to do with the matter! For the refuter himself proposed a counter-syllogism, based upon the proposition that we regard death as "indifferent," – one of the things which the Greeks call ἀδιάφορα. "Nothing," he says, "that is indifferent can be glorious; death is glorious; therefore death is not indifferent." You comprehend the tricky fallacy which is contained in this syllogism. – mere death is, in fact, not glorious; but a brave death is glorious. And when you say, "Nothing that is indifferent is glorious," I grant you this much, and declare that nothing is glorious except as it deals with indifferent things. I classify as "indifferent," – that is, neither good nor evil – sickness, pain, poverty, exile, death. None of these things is intrinsically glorious; but nothing can be glorious apart from them. For it is not poverty that we praise, it is the man whom poverty cannot humble or bend. Nor is it exile that we praise, it is the man who withdraws into exile in the spirit in which he would have sent another into exile. It is not pain that we praise, it is the man whom pain has not coerced. One praises not death, but the man whose soul death takes away before it can confound it. All these things are in themselves neither honourable nor glorious; but any one of them that virtue has visited and touched is made honourable and glorious by virtue; they merely lie in between, and the decisive question is only whether wickedness or virtue has laid hold upon them. For instance, the death which in Cato's case is glorious, is in the case of Brutus forthwith base and disgraceful. For this Brutus, condemned to death, was trying to obtain postponement; he withdrew a moment in order to ease himself; when summoned to die and ordered to bare his throat, he exclaimed: "I will bare my throat, if only I may live!" What madness it is to run away, when it is impossible to turn back! "I will bare my throat, if only I may live!" He came very near saying also: "even under Antony!" This fellow deserved indeed to be consigned to life!

But, as I was going on to remark, you see that death in itself is neither an evil nor a good; Cato experienced death most honourably, Brutus most basely. Everything, if you add virtue, assumes a glory which it did not possess before. We speak of a sunny room, even though the same room is pitch-dark at night. It is the day which fills it with light, and the night which steals the light away; thus it is with the things which we call indifferent and "middle,"like riches, strength, beauty, titles, kingship, and their opposites, – death, exile, ill-health, pain, and all such evils, the fear of which upsets us to a greater or less extent; it is the wickedness or the virtue that bestows the name of good or evil. An object is not by its own essence either hot or cold; it is heated when thrown into a furnace, and chilled when dropped into water. Death is honourable when related to that which is honourable; by this I mean virtue and a soul that despises the worst hardships.

Furthermore, there are vast distinctions among these qualities which we call "middle." For example, death is not so indifferent as the question whether your hair should be worn evenly or unevenly. Death belongs among those things which are not indeed evils, but still have in them a semblance of evil; for there are implanted in us love of self, a desire for existence and self-preservation, and also an abhorrence of dissolution, because death seems to rob us of many goods and to withdraw us from the abundance to which we have become accustomed. And there is another element which estranges us from death, we are already familiar with the present, but are ignorant of the future into which we shall transfer ourselves, and we shrink from the unknown. Moreover, it is natural to fear the world of shades, whither death is supposed to lead. Therefore, although death is something indifferent, it is nevertheless not a thing which we can easily ignore. The soul must be hardened by long practice, so that it may learn to endure the sight and the approach of death.

Death ought to be despised more than it is wont to be despised. For we believe too many of the stories about death. Many thinkers have striven hard to increase its ill repute; they have portrayed the prison in the world below and the land overwhelmed by everlasting night, where

> *Within his blood-stained cave Hell's warder huge*
> *Doth sprawl his ugly length on half-crunched bones,*
> *And terrifies the disembodied ghosts*
> *With never-ceasing bark.*

Even if you can win your point and prove that these are mere stories and that nothing is left for the dead to fear, another fear steals upon you. For the fear of going to the underworld is equalled by the fear of going nowhere.

In the face of these notions, which long-standing opinion has dinned in our ears, how can brave endurance of death be anything else than glorious, and fit to rank among the greatest accomplishments of the human mind? For the mind will never rise to virtue if it believes that death is an evil; but it will so rise if it holds that death is a matter of indifference. It is not in the order of nature that a man shall proceed with a great heart to a destiny which he believes to be evil; he will go sluggishly and with reluctance. But nothing glorious can result from unwillingness and cowardice; virtue does nothing under compulsion. Besides, no deed that a man does is honourable unless he has devoted himself thereto and attended to it with all his heart, rebelling against it with no portion of his being. When, however, a man goes to face an evil, either through fear of worse evils or in the hope of goods whose attainment is of sufficient moment to him that he can swallow the one evil which he must endure, – in that case the judgment of the agent is drawn in two directions. On the one side is the motive which bids him carry out his purpose; on the other, the motive which restrains him and makes him flee from something which has aroused his apprehension or leads to danger. Hence he is torn in different directions; and if this happens, the glory of his act is gone. For virtue accomplishes its plans only when the spirit is in harmony with itself. There is no element of fear in any of its actions.

> Yield not to evils, but, still braver, go
> Where'er thy fortune shall allow.

You cannot "still braver go," if you are persuaded that those things are the real evils. Root out this idea from your soul; otherwise your apprehensions will remain undecided and will thus check the impulse to action. You will be pushed into that towards which you ought to advance like a soldier.

Those of our school, it is true, would have men think that Zeno's syllogism is correct, but that the second I mentioned, which is set up against his, is deceptive and wrong. But I for my part decline to reduce such questions to a matter of dialectical rules or to the subtleties of an utterly worn-out system. Away, I say, with all that sort of thing, which makes a man feel, when a question is propounded to him, that he is hemmed in, and forces him to admit a premiss, and then makes him say one thing in his answer when his real opinion is another. When truth is at stake, we must act more frankly; and when fear is to be combated, we must act more bravely. Such questions, which the dialecticians involve in subtleties, I prefer to solve and weigh rationally, with the purpose of winning conviction and not of forcing the judgment.

When a general is about to lead into action an army prepared to meet death for their wives and children, how will he exhort them to battle? I remind you of the Fabii, who took upon a single clan a war which concerned the whole state. I point out to you the Lacedaemonians in position at the very pass of Thermopylae! They have no hope of victory, no hope of returning. The place where they stand is to be their tomb. In what language do you encourage them to bar the way with their bodies and take upon themselves the ruin of their whole tribe, and to retreat from life rather than from their post? Shall you say: "That which is evil is not glorious; but death is glorious; therefore death is not an evil"? What a powerful discourse! After such words, who would hesitate to throw himself upon the serried spears of the foemen, and die in his tracks? But take Leonidas: how bravely did he address his men! He said: "Fellow-soldiers, let us to our breakfast, knowing that we shall sup in Hades!" The food of these men did not grow lumpy in their mouths, or stick in their throats, or slip from their fingers; eagerly did they accept the invitation to breakfast, and to supper also! Think, too, of the famous Roman general; his soldiers had been dispatched to seize a position, and when they were about to make their way through a huge army of the enemy, he addressed them with the words: "You must go now, fellow-soldiers, to yonder place, whence there is no 'must' about your returning!"

You see, then, how straightforward and peremptory virtue is; but what man on earth can your deceptive logic make more courageous or more upright? Rather does it break the spirit, which should never be less straitened or forced to deal with petty and thorny problems than when some great work is being planned. It is not the Three Hundred, – it is all mankind that should be relieved of the fear of death. But how can you prove to all those men that death is no evil? How can you overcome the notions of all our past life, – notions with which we are tinged from our very infancy? What succour can you discover for man's helplessness? What can you say that will make men rush, burning with zeal, into the midst of danger? By what persuasive speech can you turn aside this universal feeling of fear, by what strength of wit can you turn aside the conviction of the human race which steadfastly opposes you? Do you propose to construct catchwords for me, or to string together petty syllogisms? It takes great weapons to strike down great monsters. You recall the fierce serpent in Africa, more frightful to the Roman legions than the war itself, and assailed in vain by arrows and slings; it could not be wounded even by "Pythius," since its huge size, and the toughness which matched its bulk, made spears, or any weapon hurled by the hand of man, glance off. It was finally destroyed by rocks equal in size to millstones. Are you, then, hurling petty weapons like yours even against death? Can you stop a lion's charge by an awl? Your arguments are indeed sharp; but there is nothing sharper than a stalk of grain. And certain arguments are rendered useless and unavailing by their very subtlety. Farewell.

Letter LXXXIII - On Drunkenness

You bid me give you an account of each separate day, and of the whole day too; so you must have a good opinion of me if you think that in these days of mine there is nothing to hide. At any rate, it is thus that we should live, – as if we lived in plain sight of all men; and it is thus that we should think, – as if there were someone who could look into our inmost souls; and there is one who can so look. For what avails it that something is hidden from man? Nothing is shut off from the sight of God. He is witness of our souls, and he comes into the very midst of our thoughts – comes into them, I say, as one who may at any time depart. I shall therefore do as you bid, and shall gladly inform you by letter what I am doing, and in what sequence. I shall keep watching myself continually, and – a most useful habit – shall review each day. For this is what makes us wicked: that no one of us looks back over his own life. Our thoughts are devoted only to what we are about to do. And yet our plans for the future always depend on the past.

To-day has been unbroken; no one has filched the slightest part of it from me. The whole time has been divided between rest and reading. A brief space has been given over to bodily exercise, and on this ground I can thank old age – my exercise costs very little effort; as soon as I stir, I am tired. And weariness is the aim and end of exercise, no matter how strong one is. Do you ask who are my pacemakers? One is enough for me, – the slave Pharius, a pleasant fellow, as you know; but I shall exchange him for another. At my time of life I need one who is of still more tender years. Pharius, at any rate, says that he and I are at the same period of life; for we are both losing our teeth. Yet even now I can scarcely follow his pace as he runs, and within a very short time I shall not be able to follow him at all; so you see what profit we get from daily exercise. Very soon does a wide interval open between two persons who travel different ways. My slave is climbing up at the very moment when I am coming down, and you surely know how much quicker the latter is. Nay, I was wrong; for now my life is not coming down; it is falling outright. Do you ask, for all that, how our race resulted to-day? We raced to a tie, – something which rarely happens in a running contest. After tiring myself out in this way (for I cannot call it exercise), I took a cold bath; this, at my house, means just short of hot. I, the former cold-water enthusiast, who used to celebrate the new year by taking a plunge into the canal, who, just as naturally as I would set out to do some reading or writing, or to compose a speech, used to inaugurate the first of the year with a plunge into the Virgo aqueduct, have changed my allegiance, first to the Tiber, and then to my favourite tank, which is warmed only by the sun, at times when I am most robust and when there is not a flaw in my bodily processes. I have very little energy left for bathing. After the bath, some stale bread and breakfast without a table; no need to wash the hands after such a meal. Then comes a very short nap. You know my habit; I avail myself of a scanty bit of sleep, – unharnessing, as it were. For I am satisfied if I can just stop staying awake. Sometimes I know that I have slept; at other times, I have a mere suspicion.

Lo, now the din of the Races sounds about me! My ears are smitten with sudden and general cheering. But this does not upset my thoughts or even break their continuity. I can endure an uproar with complete resignation. The medley of voices blended in one note sounds to me like the dashing of waves, or like the wind that lashes the tree-tops, or like any other sound which conveys no meaning.

What is it, then, you ask, to which I have been giving my attention? I will tell you, a thought sticks in my mind, left over from yesterday, – namely, what men of the greatest sagacity have meant when they have offered the most trifling and intricate proofs for problems of the greatest importance, – proofs which may be true, but none the less resemble fallacies. Zeno, that greatest of men, the revered founder of our brave and holy school of philosophy, wishes to discourage us from drunkenness. Listen, then, to his arguments proving that the good man will not get drunk: "No one entrusts a secret to a drunken man; but one will entrust a secret to a good man; therefore, the good man will not get drunk." Mark how ridiculous Zeno is made when we set up a similar syllogism in contrast with his. There are many, but one will be enough: "No one entrusts a secret to a man when he is asleep; but one entrusts a secret to a good man; therefore, the good man does not go to sleep." Posidonius pleads the cause of our master Zeno in the only possible way; but it cannot, I hold, be pleaded even in this way. For Posidonius maintains that the word "drunken" is used in two ways, – in the one case of a man who is loaded with wine and has no control over himself; in the other, of a man who is accustomed to get drunk, and is a slave to the habit. Zeno, he says, meant the latter, – the man who is accustomed to get drunk, not the man who is drunk; and no one would entrust to this person any secret, for it might be blabbed out when the man was in his cups. This is a fallacy. For the first syllogism refers to him who is actually drunk and not to him who is about to get drunk. You will surely admit that there is a great difference between a man who is drunk and a drunkard. He who is actually drunk may be in this state for the first time and may not have the habit, while the drunkard is often free from drunkenness. I therefore interpret the word in its usual meaning, especially since the syllogism is set up by a man who makes a business of the careful use of words, and who weighs his language. Moreover, if this is what Zeno meant, and what he wished it to mean to us, he was trying to avail himself of an equivocal word in order to work in a fallacy; and no man ought to do this when truth is the object of inquiry.

But let us admit, indeed, that he meant what Posidonius says; even so, the conclusion is false, that secrets are not entrusted to an habitual drunkard. Think how many soldiers who are not always sober have been entrusted by a general or a captain or a centurion with messages which might not be divulged! With regard to the notorious plot to murder Gaius Caesar, — I mean the Caesar who conquered Pompey and got control of the state, — Tillius Cimber was trusted with it no less than Gaius Cassius. Now Cassius throughout his life drank water; while Tillius Cimber was a sot as well as a brawler. Cimber himself alluded to this fact, saying: "I carry a master? I cannot carry my liquor!" So let each one call to mind those who, to his knowledge, can be ill trusted with wine, but well trusted with the spoken word; and yet one case occurs to my mind, which I shall relate, lest it fall into oblivion. For life should be provided with conspicuous illustrations. Let us not always be harking back to the dim past.

Lucius Piso, the director of Public Safety at Rome, was drunk from the very time of his appointment. He used to spend the greater part of the night at banquets, and would sleep until noon. That was the way he spent his morning hours. Nevertheless, he applied himself most diligently to his official duties, which included the guardianship of the city. Even the sainted Augustus trusted him with secret orders when he placed him in command of Thrace. Piso conquered that country. Tiberius, too, trusted him when he took his holiday in Campania, leaving behind him in the city many a critical matter that aroused both suspicion and hatred. I fancy that it was because Piso's drunkenness turned out well for the Emperor that he appointed to the office of city prefect Cossus, a man of authority and balance, but so soaked and steeped in drink that once, at a meeting of the Senate, whither he had come after banqueting, he was overcome by a slumber from which he could not be roused, and had to be carried home. It was to this man that Tiberius sent many orders, written in his own hand, — orders which he believed he ought not to trust even to the officials of his household. Cossus never let a single secret slip out, whether personal or public.

So let us abolish all such harangues as this: "No man in the bonds of drunkenness has power over his soul. As the very vats are burst by new wine, and as the dregs at the bottom are raised to the surface by the strength of the fermentation; so, when the wine effervesces, whatever lies hidden below is brought up and made visible. As a man overcome by liquor cannot keep down his food when he has over-indulged in wine, so he cannot keep back a secret either. He pours forth impartially both his own secrets and those of other persons." This, of course, is what commonly happens, but so does this, — that we take counsel on serious subjects with those whom we know to be in the habit of drinking freely. Therefore this proposition, which is laid down in the guise of a defence of Zeno's syllogism, is false, — that secrets are not entrusted to the habitual drunkard.

How much better it is to arraign drunkenness frankly and to expose its vices! For even the middling good man avoids them, not to mention the perfect sage, who is satisfied with slaking his thirst; the sage, even if now and then he is led on by good cheer which, for a friend's sake, is carried somewhat too far, yet always stops short of drunkenness. We shall investigate later the question whether the mind of the sage is upset by too much wine and commits follies like those of the toper; but meanwhile, if you wish to prove that a good man ought not to get drunk, why work it out by logic? Show how base it is to pour down more liquor than one can carry, and not to know the capacity of one's own stomach; show how often the drunkard does things which make him blush when he is sober; state that drunkenness is nothing but a condition of insanity purposely assumed. Prolong the drunkard's condition to several days; will you have any doubt about his madness? Even as it is, the madness is no less; it merely lasts a shorter time. Think of Alexander of Macedon, who stabbed Clitus, his dearest and most loyal friend, at a banquet; after Alexander understood what he had done, he wished to die, and assuredly he ought to have died.

Drunkenness kindles and discloses every kind of vice, and removes the sense of shame that veils our evil undertakings. For more men abstain from forbidden actions because they are ashamed of sinning than because their inclinations are good. When the strength of wine has become too great and has gained control over the mind, every lurking evil comes forth from its hiding-place. Drunkenness does not create vice, it merely brings it into view; at such times the lustful man does not wait even for the privacy of a bedroom, but without postponement gives free play to the demands of his passions; at such times the unchaste man proclaims and publishes his malady; at such times your cross-grained fellow does not restrain his tongue or his hand. The haughty man increases his arrogance, the ruthless man his cruelty, the slanderer his spitefulness. Every vice is given free play and comes to the front. Besides, we forget who we are, we utter words that are halting and poorly enunciated, the glance is unsteady, the step falters, the head is dizzy, the very ceiling moves about as if a cyclone were whirling the whole house, and the stomach suffers torture when the wine generates gas and causes our very bowels to swell. However, at the time, these troubles can be endured, so long as the man retains his natural strength; but what can he do when sleep impairs his powers, and when that which was drunkenness becomes indigestion?

Think of the calamities caused by drunkenness in a nation! This evil has betrayed to their enemies the most spirited and warlike races; this evil has made breaches in walls defended by the stubborn warfare of many years; this evil has forced under alien sway peoples who were utterly unyielding and defiant of the yoke; this evil has conquered by the wine-cup those who in the field were invincible. Alexander, whom I have just mentioned, passed through his many marches, his many battles, his many winter campaigns (through which he worked his way by overcoming disadvantages of time or place), the many rivers which flowed from unknown sources, and the many seas, all in safety; it was intemperance in drinking that laid him low, and the famous death-dealing bowl of Hercules.

What glory is there in carrying much liquor? When you have won the prize, and the other banqueters, sprawling asleep or vomiting, have declined your challenge to still other toasts; when you are the last survivor of the revels; when you have vanquished every one by your magnificent show of prowess and there is no man who has proved himself of so great capacity as you, you are vanquished by the cask. Mark Antony was a great man, a man of distinguished ability; but what ruined him and drove him into foreign habits and un-Roman vices, if it was not drunkenness and – no less potent than wine – love of Cleopatra? This it was that made him an enemy of the state; this it was that rendered him no match for his enemies; this it was that made him cruel, when as he sat at table the heads of the leaders of the state were brought in; when amid the most elaborate feasts and royal luxury he would identify the faces and hands of men whom he had proscribed; when, though heavy with wine, he yet thirsted for blood. It was intolerable that he was getting drunk while he did such things; how much more intolerable that he did these things while actually drunk! Cruelty usually follows wine-bibbing; for a man's soundness of mind is corrupted and made savage. Just as a lingering illness makes men querulous and irritable and drives them wild at the least crossing of their desires, so continued bouts of drunkenness bestialize the soul. For when people are often beside themselves, the habit of madness lasts on, and the vices which liquor generated retain their power even when the liquor is gone.

Therefore you should state why the wise man ought not to get drunk. Explain by facts, and not by mere words, the hideousness of the thing, and its haunting evils. Do that which is easiest of all – namely, demonstrate that what men call pleasures are punishments as soon as they have exceeded due bounds. For if you try to prove that the wise man can souse himself with much wine and yet keep his course straight, even though he be in his cups, you may go on to infer by syllogisms that he will not die if he swallows poison, that he will not sleep if he takes a sleeping-potion, that he will not vomit and reject the matter which clogs his stomach when you give him hellebore. But, when a man's feet totter and his tongue is unsteady, what reason have you for believing that he is half sober and half drunk? Farewell.

Letter LXXXIV - On Gathering Ideas

The journeys to which you refer – journeys that shake the laziness out of my system – I hold to be profitable both for my health and for my studies. You see why they benefit my health: since my passion for literature makes me lazy and careless about my body, I can take exercise by deputy; as for my studies, I shall show you why my journeys help them, for I have not stopped my reading in the slightest degree. And reading, I hold, is indispensable – primarily, to keep me from being satisfied with myself alone, and besides, after I have learned what others have found out by their studies, to enable me to pass judgment on their discoveries and reflect upon discoveries that remain to be made. Reading nourishes the mind and refreshes it when it is wearied with study; nevertheless, this refreshment is not obtained without study. We ought not to confine ourselves either to writing or to reading; the one, continuous writing, will cast a gloom over our strength, and exhaust it; the other will make our strength flabby and watery. It is better to have recourse to them alternately, and to blend one with the other, so that the fruits of one's reading may be reduced to concrete form by the pen.

We should follow, men say, the example of the bees, who flit about and cull the flowers that are suitable for producing honey, and then arrange and assort in their cells all that they have brought in; these bees, as our Vergil says,

pack close the flowing honey,
And swell their cells with nectar sweet.

It is not certain whether the juice which they obtain from the flowers forms at once into honey, or whether they change that which they have gathered into this delicious object by blending something therewith and by a certain property of their breath. For some authorities believe that bees do not possess the art of making honey, but only of gathering it; and they say that in India honey has been found on the leaves of certain reeds, produced by a dew peculiar to that climate, or by the juice of the reed itself, which has an unusual sweetness, and richness. And in our own grasses too, they say, the same quality exists, although less clear and less evident; and a creature born to fulfil such a function could hunt it out and collect it. Certain others maintain that the materials which the bees have culled from the most delicate of blooming and flowering plants is transformed into this peculiar substance by a process of preserving and careful storing away, aided by what might be called fermentation, – whereby separate elements are united into one substance.

But I must not be led astray into another subject than that which we are discussing. We also, I say, ought to copy these bees, and sift whatever we have gathered from a varied course of reading, for such things are better preserved if they are kept separate; then, by applying the supervising care with which our nature has endowed us, – in other words, our natural gifts, – we should so blend those several flavours into one delicious compound that, even though it betrays its origin, yet it nevertheless is clearly a different thing from that whence it came. This is what we see nature doing in our own bodies without any labour on our part; the food we have eaten, as long as it retains its original quality and floats, in our stomachs as an undiluted mass, is a burden; but it passes into tissue and blood only when it has been changed from its original form. So it is with the food which nourishes our higher nature, – we should see to it that whatever we have absorbed should not be allowed to remain unchanged, or it will be no part of us. We must digest it; otherwise it will merely enter the memory and not the reasoning power. Let us loyally welcome such foods and make them our own, so that something that is one may be formed out of many elements, just as one number is formed of several elements whenever, by our reckoning, lesser sums, each different from the others, are brought together. This is what our mind should do: it should hide away all the materials by which it has been aided, and bring to light only what it has made of them. Even if there shall appear in you a likeness to him who, by reason of your admiration, has left a deep impress upon you, I would have you resemble him as a child resembles his father, and not as a picture resembles its original; for a picture is a lifeless thing.

"What," you say, "will it not be seen whose style you are imitating, whose method of reasoning, whose pungent sayings?" I think that sometimes it is impossible for it to be seen who is being imitated, if the copy is a true one; for a true copy stamps its own form upon all the features which it has drawn from what we may call the original, in such a way that they are combined into a unity. Do you not see how many voices there are in a chorus? Yet out of the many only one voice results. In that chorus one voice takes the tenor another the bass, another the baritone. There are women, too, as well as men, and the flute is mingled with them. In that chorus the voices of the individual singers are hidden; what we hear is the voices of all together. To be sure, I am referring to the chorus which the old-time philosophers knew; in our present-day exhibitions we have a larger number of singers than there used to be spectators in the theatres of old. All the aisles are filled with rows of singers; brass instruments surround the auditorium; the stage resounds with flutes and instruments of every description; and yet from the discordant sounds a harmony is produced.

I would have my mind of such a quality as this; it should be equipped with many arts, many precepts, and patterns of conduct taken from many epochs of history; but all should blend harmoniously into one. "How," you ask, "can this be accomplished?" By constant effort, and by doing nothing without the approval of reason. And if you are willing to hear her voice, she will say to you: "Abandon those pursuits which heretofore have caused you to run hither and thither. Abandon riches, which are either a danger or a burden to the possessor. Abandon the pleasures of the body and of the mind; they only soften and weaken you. Abandon your quest for office; it is a swollen, idle, and empty thing, a thing that has no goal, as anxious to see no one outstrip it as to see no one at its heels. It is afflicted with envy, and in truth with a twofold envy; and you see how wretched a man's plight is if he who is the object of envy feels envy also."

Do you behold yonder homes of the great, yonder thresholds uproarious with the brawling of those who would pay their respects? They have many an insult for you as you enter the door, and still more after you have entered. Pass by the steps that mount to rich men's houses, and the porches rendered hazardous by the huge throng; for there you will be standing, not merely on the edge of a precipice but also on slippery ground. Instead of this, direct your course hither to wisdom, and seek her ways, which are ways of surpassing peace and plenty. Whatever seems conspicuous in the affairs of men – however petty it may really be and prominent only by contrast with the lowest objects – is nevertheless approached by a difficult and toilsome pathway. It is a rough road that leads to the heights of greatness; but if you desire to scale this peak, which lies far above the range of Fortune, you will indeed look down from above upon all that men regard as most lofty, but none the less you can proceed to the top over level ground. Farewell.

Letter LXXXV - On Some Vain Syllogisms

I had been inclined to spare you, and had omitted any knotty problems that still remained undiscussed; I was satisfied to give you a sort of taste of the views held by the men of our school, who desire to prove that virtue is of itself sufficiently capable of rounding out the happy life. But now you bid me include the entire bulk either of our own syllogisms or of those which have been devised by other schools for the purpose of belittling us. If I shall be willing to do this, the result will be a book, instead of a letter. And I declare again and again that I take no pleasure in such proofs. I am ashamed to enter the arena and undertake battle on behalf of gods and men armed only with an awl.

"He that possesses prudence is also self-restrained; he that possesses self-restraint is also unwavering; he that is unwavering is unperturbed; he that is unperturbed is free from sadness; he that is free from sadness is happy. Therefore, the prudent man is happy, and prudence is sufficient to constitute the happy life."

Certain of the Peripatetics reply to this syllogism by interpreting "unperturbed," "unwavering," and "free from sadness" in such a way as to make "unperturbed" mean one who is rarely perturbed and only to a moderate degree, and not one who is never perturbed. Likewise, they say that a person is called "free from sadness" who is not subject to sadness, one who falls into this objectionable state not often nor in too great a degree. It is not, they say, the way of human nature that a man's spirit should be exempt from sadness, or that the wise man is not overcome by grief but is merely touched by it, and other arguments of this sort, all in accordance with the teachings of their school. They do not abolish the passions in this way; they only moderate them. But how petty is the superiority which we attribute to the wise man, if he is merely braver than the most craven, happier than the most dejected, more self-controlled than the most unbridled, and greater than the lowliest! Would Ladas boast his swiftness in running by comparing himself with the halt and the weak?

> For she could skim the topmost blades of corn
> And touch them not, nor bruise the tender ears;
> Or travel over seas, well-poised above
> The swollen floods, nor dip her flying feet
> In ocean's waters.

This is speed estimated by its own standard, not the kind which wins praise by comparison with that which is slowest. Would you call a man well who has a light case of fever? No, for good health does not mean moderate illness. They say, "The wise man is called unperturbed in the sense in which pomegranates are called mellow – not that there is no hardness at all in their seeds, but that the hardness is less than it was before." That view is wrong; for I am not referring to the gradual weeding out of evils in a good man, but to the complete absence of evils; there should be in him no evils at all, not even any small ones. For if there are any, they will grow, and as they grow will hamper him. Just as a large and complete cataract wholly blinds the eyes, so a medium-sized cataract dulls their vision.

If by your definition the wise man has any passions whatever, his reason will be no match for them and will be carried swiftly along, as it were, on a rushing stream, – particularly if you assign to him, not one passion with which he must wrestle, but all the passions. And a throng of such, even though they be moderate, can affect him more than the violence of one powerful passion. He has a craving for money, although in a moderate degree. He has ambition, but it is not yet fully aroused. He has a hot temper, but it can be appeased. He has inconstancy, but not the kind that is very capricious or easily set in motion. He has lust, but not the violent kind. We could deal better with a person who possessed one full-fledged vice, than with one who possessed all the vices, but none of them in extreme form. Again, it makes no difference how great the passion is; no matter what its size may be, it knows no obedience, and does not welcome advice. Just as no animal, whether wild or tamed and gentle, obeys reason, since nature made it deaf to advice; so the passions do not follow or listen, however slight they are. Tigers and lions never put off their wildness; they sometimes moderate it, and then, when you are least prepared, their softened fierceness is roused to madness. Vices are never genuinely tamed. Again, if reason prevails, the passions will not even get a start; but if they get under way against the will of reason, they will maintain themselves against the will of reason. For it is easier to stop them in the beginning than to control them when they gather force. This half-way ground is accordingly misleading and useless; it is to be regarded just as the declaration that we ought to be "moderately" insane, or "moderately" ill. Virtue alone possesses moderation; the evils that afflict the mind do not admit of moderation. You can more easily remove than control them. Can one doubt that the vices of the human mind, when they have become chronic and callous ("diseases" we call them), are beyond control, as, for example, greed, cruelty, and wantonness? Therefore the passions also are beyond control; for it is from the passions that we pass over to the vices. Again, if you grant any privileges to sadness, fear, desire, and all the other wrong impulses, they will cease to lie within our jurisdiction. And why? Simply because the means of arousing them lie outside our own power. They will accordingly increase in proportion as the causes by which they are stirred up are greater or less. Fear will grow to greater proportions, if that which causes the terror is seen to be of greater magnitude or in closer proximity; and desire will grow keener in proportion as the hope of a greater gain has summoned it to action. If the existence of the passions is not in our own control, neither is the extent of their power; for if you once permit them to get a start, they will increase along with their causes, and they will be of whatever extent they shall grow to be. Moreover, no matter how small these vices are, they grow greater. That which is harmful never keeps within bounds. No matter how trifling diseases are at the beginning, they creep on apace; and sometimes the slightest augmentation of disease lays low the enfeebled body! But what folly it is, when the beginnings of certain things are situated outside our control, to believe that their endings are within our control! How have I the power to bring something to a close, when I have not had the power to check it at the beginning? For it is easier to keep a thing out than to keep it under after you have let it in. Some men have made a distinction as follows, saying: "If a man has self-control and wisdom, he is indeed at peace as regards the attitude and habit of his mind, but not as regards the outcome. For, as far as his habit of mind is concerned, he is not perturbed, or saddened, or afraid; but there are many extraneous causes which strike him and bring perturbation upon him." What they mean to say is this: "So-and-so is indeed not a man of an angry disposition, but still he sometimes gives way to anger," and "He is not, indeed, inclined to fear, but still he sometimes experiences fear"; in other words, he is free from the fault, but is not free from the passion of fear. If, however, fear is once given an entrance, it will by frequent use pass over into a vice; and anger, once admitted into the mind, will alter the earlier habit of a mind that was formerly free from anger. Besides, if the wise man, instead of despising all causes that come from without, ever fears anything, when the time arrives for him to go bravely to meet the spear, or the flames, on behalf of his country, his laws, and his liberty, he will go forth reluctantly and with flagging spirit. Such inconsistency of mind, however, does not suit the character of a wise man.

Then, again, we should see to it that two principles which ought to be tested separately should not be confused. For the conclusion is reached independently that that alone is good which is honourable, and again independently the conclusion that virtue is sufficient for the happy life. If that alone is good which is honourable, everyone agrees that virtue is sufficient for the purpose of living happily; but, on the contrary, if virtue alone makes men happy, it will not be conceded that that alone is good which is honourable. Xenocrates and Speusippus hold that a man can become happy even by virtue alone, not, however, that that which is honourable is the only good. Epicurus also decides that one who possesses virtue is happy, but that virtue of itself is not sufficient for the happy life, because the pleasure that results from virtue, and not virtue itself, makes one happy. This is a futile distinction. For the same philosopher declares that virtue never exists without pleasure; and therefore, if virtue is always connected with pleasure and always inseparable therefrom, virtue is of itself sufficient. For virtue keeps pleasure in its company, and does not exist without it, even when alone. But it is absurd to say that a man will be happy by virtue alone, and yet not absolutely happy. I cannot discover how that may be, since the happy life contains in itself a good that is perfect and cannot be excelled, If a man has this good, life is completely happy.

Now if the life of the gods contains nothing greater or better, and the happy life is divine, then there is no further height to which a man can be raised. Also, if the happy life is in want of nothing, then every happy life is perfect; it is happy and at the same time most happy. Have you any doubt that the happy life is the Supreme Good? Accordingly, if it possesses the Supreme Good, it is supremely happy. Just as the Supreme Good does not admit of increase (for what will be superior to that which is supreme?), exactly so the happy life cannot be increased either; for it is not without the Supreme Good. If then you bring in one man who is "happier" than another, you will also bring in one who is "much happier"; you will then be making countless distinctions in the Supreme Good; although I understand the Supreme Good to be that good which admits of no degree above itself. If one person is less happy than another, it follows that he eagerly desires the life of that other and happier man in preference to his own. But the happy man prefers no other man's life to his own. Either of these two things is incredible: that there should be anything left for a happy man to wish for in preference to what is, or that he should not prefer the thing which is better than what he already has. For certainly, the more prudent he is, the more he will strive after the best, and he will desire to attain it by every possible means. But how can one be happy who is still able, or rather who is still bound, to crave something else? I will tell you what is the source of this error: men do not understand that the happy life is a unit; for it is its essence, and not its extent, that establishes such a life on the noblest Plane. Hence there is complete equality between the life that is long and the life that is short, between that which is spread out and that which is confined, between that whose influence is felt in many places and in many directions, and that which is restricted to one interest. Those who reckon life by number, or by measure, or by parts, rob it of its distinctive quality. Now, in the happy life, what is the distinctive quality? It is its fulness. Satiety, I think, is the limit to our eating or drinking. A eats more and B eats less; what difference does it make? Each is now sated. Or A drinks more and B drinks less; what difference does it make? Each is no longer thirsty, Again, A lives for many years and B for fewer; no matter, if only A's many years have brought as much happiness as B's few years. He whom you maintain to be "less happy" is not happy; the word admits of no diminution.

"He who is brave is fearless; he who is fearless is free from sadness; he who is free from sadness is happy." It is our own school which has framed this syllogism; they attempt to refute it by this answer, namely, that we Stoics are assuming as admitted a premiss which is false and distinctly controverted, — that the brave man is fearless. "What!" they say, "will the brave man have no fear of evils that threaten him? That would be the condition of a madman, a lunatic, rather than of a brave man. The brave man will, it is true, feel fear in only a very slight degree; but he is not absolutely free from fear." Now those who assert this are doubling back to their old argument, in that they regard vices of less degree as equivalent to virtues. For indeed the man who does feel fear, though he feels it rather seldom and to a slight degree, is not free from wickedness, but is merely troubled by it in a milder form. "Not so," is the reply, "for I hold that a man is mad if he does not fear evils which hang over his head." What you say is perfectly true, if the things which threaten are really evils; but if he knows that they are not evils and believes that the only evil is baseness, he will be bound to face dangers without anxiety and to despise things which other men cannot help fearing. Or, if it is the characteristic of a fool and a madman not to fear evils, then the wiser a man is the more he will fear such things! "It is the doctrine of you Stoics, then," they reply, "that a brave man will expose himself to dangers." By no means; he will merely not fear them, though he will avoid them. It is proper for him to be careful, but not to be fearful. "What then? Is he not to fear death, imprisonment, burning, and all the other missiles of Fortune?" Not at all; for he knows that they are not evils, but only seem to be. He reckons all these things as the bugbears of man's existence. Paint him a picture of slavery, lashes, chains, want, mutilation by disease or by torture, – or anything else you may care to mention; he will count all such things as terrors caused by the derangement of the mind. These things are only to be feared by those who are fearful. Or do you regard as an evil that to which some day we may be compelled to resort of our own free will?

What then, you ask, is an evil? It is the yielding to those things which are called evils; it is the surrendering of one's liberty into their control, when really we ought to suffer all things in order to preserve this liberty. Liberty is lost unless we despise those things which put the yoke upon our necks. If men knew what bravery was, they would have no doubts as to what a brave man's conduct should be. For bravery is not thoughtless rashness, or love of danger, or the courting of fear-inspiring objects; it is the knowledge which enables us to distinguish between that which is evil and that which is not. Bravery takes the greatest care of itself, and likewise endures with the greatest patience all things which have a false appearance of being evil. "What then?" is the query; "if the sword is brandished over your brave man's neck, if he is pierced in this place and in that continually, if he sees his entrails in his lap, if he is tortured again after being kept waiting in order that he may thus feel the torture more keenly, and if the blood flows afresh out of bowels where it has but lately ceased to flow, has he no fear? Shall you say that he has felt no pain either?" Yes, he has felt pain; for no human virtue can rid itself of feelings. But he has no fear; unconquered he looks down from a lofty height upon his sufferings. Do you ask me what spirit animates him in these circumstances? It is the spirit of one who is comforting a sick friend.

"That which is evil does harm; that which does harm makes a man worse. But pain and poverty do not make a man worse; therefore they are not evils." "Your proposition," says the objector, "is wrong; for what harms one does not necessarily make one worse. The storm and the squall work harm to the pilot, but they do not make a worse pilot of him for all that." Certain of the Stoic school reply to this argument as follows: "The pilot becomes a worse pilot because of storms or squalls, inasmuch as he cannot carry out his purpose and hold to his course; as far as his art is concerned, he becomes no worse a pilot, but in his work he does become worse." To this the Peripatetics retort: "Therefore, poverty will make even the wise man worse, and so will pain, and so will anything else of that sort. For although those things will not rob him of his virtue, yet they will hinder the work of virtue." This would be a correct statement, were it not for the fact that the pilot and the wise man are two different kinds of person. The wise man's purpose in conducting his life is not to accomplish at all hazards what he tries, but to do all things rightly; the pilot's purpose, however, is to bring his ship into port at all hazards. The arts are handmaids; they must accomplish what they promise to do. But wisdom is mistress and ruler. The arts render a slave's service to life; wisdom issues the commands.

For myself, I maintain that a different answer should be given: that the pilot's art is never made worse by the storm, nor the application of his art either. The pilot has promised you, not a prosperous voyage, but a serviceable performance of his task – that is, an expert knowledge of steering a ship. And the more he is hampered by the stress of fortune, so much the more does his knowledge become apparent. He who has been able to say, "Neptune, you shall never sink this ship except on an even keel," has fulfilled the requirements of his art; the storm does not interfere with the pilot's work, but only with his success. "What then," you say, "is not a pilot harmed by any circumstance which does not permit him to make port, frustrates all his efforts, and either carries him out to sea, or holds the ship in irons, or strips her masts?" No, it does not harm him as a pilot, but only as a voyager; otherwise, he is no pilot. It is indeed so far from hindering the pilot's art that it even exhibits the art; for anyone, in the words of the proverb, is a pilot on a calm sea. These mishaps obstruct the voyage but not the steersman qua steersman. A pilot has a double rôle: one he shares with all his fellow-passengers, for he also is a passenger; the other is peculiar to him, for he is the pilot. The storm harms him as a passenger, but not as a pilot. Again, the pilot's art is another's good – it concerns his passengers just as a physician's art concerns his patients. But the wise man's good is a common good – it belongs both to those in whose company he lives, and to himself also. Hence our pilot may perhaps be harmed, since his services, which have been promised to others, are hindered by the storm; . but the wise man is not harmed by poverty, or by pain, or by any other of life's storms. For all his functions are not checked, but only those which pertain to others; he himself is always in action, and is greatest in performance at the very time when fortune has blocked his way. For then he is actually engaged in the business of wisdom; and this wisdom I have declared already to be, both the good of others, and also his own. Besides, he is not prevented from helping others, even at the time when constraining circumstances press him down. Because of his poverty he is prevented from showing how the State should be handled; but he teaches, none the less, how poverty should be handled. His work goes on throughout his whole life.

Thus no fortune, no external circumstance, can shut off the wise man from action. For the very thing which engages his attention prevents him from attending to other things. He is ready for either outcome: if it brings goods, he controls them; if evils, he conquers them. So thoroughly, I mean, has he schooled himself that he makes manifest his virtue in prosperity as well as in adversity, and keeps his eyes on virtue itself, not on the objects with which virtue deals. Hence neither poverty, nor pain, nor anything else that deflects the inexperienced and drives them headlong, restrains him from his course. Do you suppose that he is weighed down by evils? He makes use of them. It was not of ivory only that Phidias knew how to make statues; he also made statues of bronze. If you had given him marble, or a still meaner material, he would have made of it the best statue that the material would permit. So the wise man will develop virtue, if he may, in the midst of wealth, or, if not, in poverty; if possible, in his own country – if not, in exile; if possible, as a commander – if not, as a common soldier; if possible, in sound health – if not, enfeebled. Whatever fortune he finds, he will accomplish therefrom something noteworthy.

Animal-tamers are unerring; they take the most savage animals, which may well terrify those who encounter them, and subdue them to the will of man; not content with having driven out their ferocity, they even tame them so that they dwell in the same abode. The trainer puts his hand into the lion's mouth; the tiger is kissed by his keeper. The tiny Aethiopian orders the elephant to sink down on its knees, or to walk the rope. Similarly, the wise man is a skilled hand at taming evils. Pain, want, disgrace, imprisonment, exile, – these are universally to be feared; but when they encounter the wise man, they are tamed. Farewell.

Letter LXXXVI - On Scipio's Villa

I am resting at the country-house which once belonged to Scipio Africanus himself; and I write to you after doing reverence to his spirit and to an altar which I am inclined to think is the tomb of that great warrior. That his soul has indeed returned to the skies, whence it came, I am convinced, not because he commanded mighty armies – for Cambyses also had mighty armies, and Cambyses was a madman who made successful use of his madness – but because he showed moderation and a sense of duty to a marvellous extent. I regard this trait in him as more admirable after his withdrawal from his native land than while he was defending her; for there was the alternative: Scipio should remain in Rome, or Rome should remain free. "It is my wish," said he, "not to infringe in the least upon our laws, or upon our customs; let all Roman citizens have equal rights. O my country, make the most of the good that I have done, but without me. I have been the cause of your freedom, and I shall also be its proof; I go into exile, if it is true that I have grown beyond what is to your advantage!"

What can I do but admire this magnanimity, which led him to withdraw into voluntary exile and to relieve the state of its burden? Matters had gone so far that either liberty must work harm to Scipio, or Scipio to liberty. Either of these things was wrong in the sight of heaven. So he gave way to the laws and withdrew to Liternum, thinking to make the state a debtor for his own exile no less than for the exile of Hannibal.

I have inspected the house, which is constructed of hewn stone; the wall which encloses a forest; the towers also, buttressed out on both sides for the purpose of defending the house; the well, concealed among buildings and shrubbery, large enough to keep a whole army supplied; and the small bath, buried in darkness according to the old style, for our ancestors did not think that one could have a hot bath except in darkness. It was therefore a great pleasure to me to contrast Scipio's ways with our own. Think, in this tiny recess the "terror of Carthage," to whom Rome should offer thanks because she was not captured more than once, used to bathe a body wearied with work in the fields! For he was accustomed to keep himself busy and to cultivate the soil with his own hands, as the good old Romans were wont to do. Beneath this dingy roof he stood; and this floor, mean as it is, bore his weight.

But who in these days could bear to bathe in such a fashion? We think ourselves poor and mean if our walls are not resplendent with large and costly mirrors; if our marbles from Alexandria are not set off by mosaics of Numidian stone, if their borders are not faced over on all sides with difficult patterns, arranged in many colours like paintings; if our vaulted ceilings are not buried in glass; if our swimming-pools are not lined with Thasian marble, once a rare and wonderful sight in any temple pools into which we let down our bodies after they have been drained weak by abundant perspiration; and finally, if the water has not poured from silver spigots. I have so far been speaking of the ordinary bathing-establishments; what shall I say when I come to those of the freedmen? What a vast number of statues, of columns that support nothing, but are built for decoration, merely in order to spend money! And what masses of water that fall crashing from level to level! We have become so luxurious that we will have nothing but precious stones to walk upon.

In this bath of Scipio's there are tiny chinks – you cannot call them windows – cut out of the stone wall in such a way as to admit light without weakening the fortifications; nowadays, however, people regard baths as fit only for moths if they have not been so arranged that they receive the sun all day long through the widest of windows, if men cannot bathe and get a coat of tan at the same time, and if they cannot look out from their bath-tubs over stretches of land and sea. So it goes; the establishments which had drawn crowds and had won admiration when they were first opened are avoided and put back in the category of venerable antiques as soon as luxury has worked out some new device, to her own ultimate undoing. In the early days, however, there were few baths, and they were not fitted out with any display. For why should men elaborately fit out that which, costs a penny only, and was invented for use, not merely for delight? The bathers of those day did not have water poured over them, nor did it always run fresh as if from a hot spring; and they did not believe that it mattered at all how perfectly pure was the water into which they were to leave their dirt. Ye gods, what a pleasure it is to enter that dark bath, covered with a common sort of roof, knowing that therein your hero Cato, as aedile, or Fabius Maximus, or one of the Cornelia, has warmed the water with his own hands! For this also used to be the duty of the noblest aediles – to enter these places to which the populace resorted, and to demand that they be cleaned and warmed to a heat required by considerations of use and health, not the heat that men have recently made fashionable, as great as a conflagration – so much so, indeed, that a slave condemned for some criminal offence now ought to be bathed alive! It seems to me that nowadays there is no difference between "the bath is on fire," and "the bath is warm."

How some persons nowadays condemn Scipio as a boor because he did not let daylight into his perspiring-room through wide windows, or because he did not roast in the strong sunlight and dawdle about until he could stew in the hot water! "Poor fool," they say, "he did not know how to live! He did not bathe in filtered water; it was often turbid, and after heavy rains almost muddy!" But it did not matter much to Scipio if he had to bathe in that way; he went there to wash off sweat, not ointment. And how do you suppose certain persons will answer me? They will say: "I don't envy Scipio; that was truly an exile's life – to put up with baths like those!" Friend, if you were wiser, you would know that Scipio did not bathe every day. It is stated by those who have reported to us the old-time ways of Rome that the Romans washed only their arms and legs daily – because those were the members which gathered dirt in their daily toil – and bathed all over only once a week. Here someone will retort: "Yes; pretty dirty fellows they evidently were! How they must have smelled!" But they smelled of the camp, the farm, and heroism. Now that spick-and-span bathing establishments have been devised, men are really fouler than of yore. What says Horatius Flaccus, when he wishes to describe a scoundrel, one who is notorious for his extreme luxury? He says. "Buccillus smells of perfume." Show me a Buccillus in these days; his smell would be the veritable goat-smell – he would take the place of the Gargonius with whom Horace in the same passage contrasted him. It is nowadays not enough to use ointment, unless you put on a fresh coat two or three times a day, to keep it from evaporating on the body. But why should a man boast of this perfume as if it were his own?

If what I am saying shall seem to you too pessimistic, charge it up against Scipio's country-house, where I have learned a lesson from Aegialus, a most careful householder and now the owner of this estate; he taught me that a tree can be transplanted, no matter how far gone in years. We old men must learn this precept; for there is none of us who is not planting an olive-yard for his successor. I have seen them bearing fruit in due season after three or four years of unproductiveness. And you too shall be shaded by the tree which

> *Is slow to grow, but bringeth shade to cheer*
> *Your grandsons in the far-off years*

as our poet Vergil says. Vergil sought, however, not what was nearest to the truth, but what was most appropriate, and aimed, not to teach the farmer, but to please the reader. For example, omitting all other errors of his, I will quote the passage in which it was incumbent upon me to-day to detect a fault:

> *In spring sow beans then, too, O clover plant,*
> *Thou'rt welcomed by the crumbling furrows; and*
> *The millet calls for yearly care.*

You may judge by the following incident whether those plants should be set out at the same time, or whether both should be sowed in the spring. It is June at the present writing, and we are well on towards July; and I have seen on this very day farmers harvesting beans and sowing millet.

But to return to our olive-yard again. I saw it planted in two ways. If the trees were large, Aegialus took their trunks and cut off the branches to the length of one foot each; he then transplanted along with the ball, after cutting off the roots, leaving only the thick part from which the roots hang. He smeared this with manure, and inserted it in the hole, not only heaping up the earth about it, but stamping and pressing it down. There is nothing, he says, more effective than this packing process; in other words, it keeps out the cold and the wind. Besides, the trunk is not shaken so much, and for this reason the packing makes it possible for the young roots to come out and get a hold in the soil. These are of necessity still soft; they have but a slight hold, and a very little shaking uproots them. This ball, moreover, Aegialus lops clean before he covers it up. For he maintains that new roots spring from all the parts which have been shorn. Moreover, the trunk itself should not stand more than three or four feet out of the ground. For there will thus be at once a thick growth from the bottom, nor will there be a large stump, all dry and withered, as is the case with old olive-yards. The second way of setting them out was the following: he set out in similar fashion branches that were strong and of soft bark, as those of young saplings are wont to be. These grow a little more slowly, but, since they spring from what is practically a cutting, there is no roughness or ugliness in them.

This too I have seen recently – an aged vine transplanted from its own plantation. In this case, the fibres also should be gathered together, if possible, and then you should cover up the vine-stem more generously, so that roots may spring up even from the stock. I have seen such plantings made not only in February, but at the very end of March; the plants take hold of and embrace alien elms. But all trees, he declares, which are, so to speak, "thick-stemmed,"should be assisted with tank-water; if we have this help, we are our own rain-makers.

I do not intend to tell you any more of these precepts, lest, as Aegialus did with me, I may be training you up to be my competitor. Farewell.

Letter LXXXVII - Some Arguments in Favour of the Simple Life

"I was shipwrecked before I got aboard." I shall not add how that happened, lest you may reckon this also as another of the Stoic paradoxes; and yet I shall, whenever you are willing to listen, nay, even though you be unwilling, prove to you that these words are by no means untrue, nor so surprising as one at first sight would think. Meantime, the journey showed me this: how much we possess that is superfluous; and how easily we can make up our minds to do away with things whose loss, whenever it is necessary to part with them, we do not feel.

My friend Maximus and I have been spending a most happy period of two days, taking with us very few slaves – one carriage-load – and no paraphernalia except what we wore on our persons. The mattress lies on the ground, and I upon the mattress. There are two rugs – one to spread beneath us and one to cover us. Nothing could have been subtracted from our luncheon; it took not more than an hour to prepare, and we were nowhere without dried figs, never without writing tablets. If I have bread, I use figs as a relish; if not, I regard figs as a substitute for bread. Hence they bring me a New Year feast every day, and I make the New Year happy and prosperous by good thoughts and greatness of soul; for the soul is never greater than when it has laid aside all extraneous things, and has secured peace for itself by fearing nothing, and riches by craving no riches. The vehicle in which I have taken my seat is a farmer's cart. Only by walking do the mules show that they are alive. The driver is barefoot, and not because it is summer either. I can scarcely force myself to wish that others shall think this cart mine. My false embarrassment about the truth still holds out, you see; and whenever we meet a more sumptuous party I blush in spite of myself – proof that this conduct which I approve and applaud has not yet gained a firm and steadfast dwelling-place within me. He who blushes at riding in a rattle-trap will boast when he rides in style.

. So my progress is still insufficient. I have not yet the courage openly to acknowledge my thriftiness. Even yet I am bothered by what other travellers think of me. But instead of this, I should really have uttered an opinion counter to that in which mankind believe, saying, "You are mad, you are misled, your admiration devotes itself to superfluous things! You estimate no man at his real worth. When property is concerned, you reckon up in this way with most scrupulous calculation those to whom you shall lend either money or benefits; for by now you enter benefits also as payments in your ledger. You say. 'His estates are wide, but his debts are large.' 'He has a fine house, but he has built it on borrowed capital.' 'No man will display a more brilliant retinue on short notice, but he cannot meet his debts.' 'If he pays off his creditors, he will have nothing left.'" So you will feel bound to do in all other cases as well, – to find out by elimination the amount of every man's actual possessions.

I suppose you call a man rich just because his gold plate goes with him even on his travels, because he farms land in all the provinces, because he unrolls a large account-book, because he owns estates near the city so great that men would grudge his holding them in the waste lands of Apulia. But after you have mentioned all these facts, he is poor. And why? He is in debt. "To what extent?" you ask. For all that he has. Or perchance you think it matters whether one has borrowed from another man or from Fortune. What good is there in mules caparisoned in uniform livery? Or in decorated chariots and

Steeds decked with purple and with tapestry,
With golden harness hanging from their necks,
Champing their yellow bits, all clothed in gold?

Neither master nor mule is improved by such trappings.

Marcus Cato the Censor, whose existence helped the state as much as did Scipio's, – for while Scipio fought against our enemies, Cato fought against our bad morals, – used to ride a donkey, and a donkey, at that, which carried saddle-bags containing the master's necessaries. O how I should love to see him meet today on the road one of our coxcombs, with his outriders and Numidians, and a great cloud of dust before him! Your dandy would no doubt seem refined and well-attended in comparison with Marcus Cato, – your dandy, who, in the midst of all his luxurious paraphernalia, is chiefly concerned whether to turn his hand to the sword or to the hunting-knife. O what a glory to the times in which he lived, for a general who had celebrated a triumph, a censor, and what is most noteworthy of all, a Cato, to be content with a single nag, and with less than a whole nag at that! For part of the animal was pre-empted by the baggage that hung down on either flank. Would you not therefore prefer Cato's steed, that single steed, saddle-worn by Cato himself, to the coxcomb's whole retinue of plump ponies, Spanish cobs, and trotters? I see that there will be no end in dealing with such a theme unless I make an end myself. So I shall now become silent, at least with reference to superfluous things like these; doubtless the man who first called them "hindrances" had a prophetic inkling that they would be the very sort of thing they now are. At present I should like to deliver to you the syllogisms, as yet very few, belonging to our school and bearing upon the question of virtue, which, in our opinion, is sufficient for the happy life.

"That which is good makes men good. For example, that which is good in the art of music makes the musician. But chance events do not make a good man; therefore, chance events are not goods." The Peripatetics reply to this by saying that the premiss is false; that men do not in every case become good by means of that which is good; that in music there is something good, like a flute, a harp, or an organ suited to accompany singing; but that none of these instruments makes the musician. We shall then reply: "You do not understand in what sense we have used the phrase 'that which is good in music.' For we do not mean that which equips the musician, but that which makes the musician; you, however, are referring to the instruments of the art, and not to the art itself. If, however, anything in the art of music is good, that will in every case make the musician." And I should like to put this idea still more clearly. We define the good in the art of music in two ways: first, that by which the performance of the musician is assisted, and second, that by which his art is assisted. Now the musical instruments have to do with his performance, – such as flutes and organs and harps; but they do not have to do with the musician's art itself. For he is an artist even without them; he may perhaps be lacking in the ability to practise his art. But the good in man is not in the same way twofold; for the good of man and the good of life are the same.

"That which can fall to the lot of any man, no matter how base or despised he may be, is not a good. But wealth falls to the lot of the pander and the trainer of gladiators; therefore wealth is not a good." "Another wrong premiss," they say, "for we notice that goods fall to the lot of the very lowest sort of men, not only in the scholar's art, but also in the art of healing or in the art of navigating." These arts, however, make no profession of greatness of soul; they do not rise to any heights nor do they frown upon what fortune may bring. It is virtue that uplifts man and places him Superior to what mortals hold dear; virtue neither craves overmuch nor fears to excess that which is called good or that which is called bad. Chelidon, one of Cleopatra's eunuchs, possessed great wealth; and recently Natalis – a man whose tongue was as shameless as it was dirty, a man whose mouth used to perform the vilest offices – was the heir of many, and also made many his heirs. What then? Was it his money that made him unclean, or did he himself besmirch his money? Money tumbles into the hands of certain men as a shilling tumbles down a sewer. Virtue stands above all such things. It is appraised in coin of its own minting; and it deems none of these random windfalls to be good. But medicine and navigation do not forbid themselves and their followers to marvel at such things. One who is not a good man can nevertheless be a physician, or a pilot or a scholar, – yes just as well as he can be a cook! He to whose lot it falls to possess something which is not of a random sort, cannot be called a random sort of man: a person is of the same sort as that which he possesses. A strong-box is worth just what it holds; or rather, it is a mere accessory of that which it holds. Who ever sets any price upon a full purse except the price established by the count of the money deposited therein? This also applies to the owners of great estates: they are only accessories and incidentals to their possessions.

Why, then, is the wise man great? Because he has a great soul. Accordingly, it is true that that which falls to the lot even of the most despicable person is not a good. Thus, I should never regard inactivity as a good; for even the tree-frog and the flea possess this quality. Nor should I regard rest and freedom from trouble as a good; for what is more at leisure than a worm? Do you ask what it is that produces the wise man? That which produces a god. You must grant that the wise man has in an element of godliness, heavenliness, grandeur. The good does not come to every one, nor does it allow any random person to possess it. Behold:

> *What fruits each country bears, or will not bear;*
> *Here corn, and there the vine, grow richlier.*
> *And elsewhere still the tender tree and grass*
> *Unbidden clothe themselves in green. Seest thou*
> *How Tmolus ships its saffron perfumes forth,*
> *And ivory comes from Ind; soft Sheba sends*
> *Its incense, and the unclad Chalybes*
> *Their iron.*

These products are apportioned to separate countries in order that human beings may be constrained to traffic among themselves, each seeking something from his neighbour in his turn. So the Supreme Good has also its own abode. It does not grow where ivory grows, or iron. Do you ask where the Supreme Good dwells? In the soul. And unless the soul be pure and holy, there is no room in it for God.

"Good does not result from evil. But riches result from greed; therefore, riches are not a good." "It is not true," they say, "that good does not result from evil. For money comes from sacrilege and theft. Accordingly, although sacrilege and theft are evil, yet they are evil only because they work more evil than good. For they bring gain; but the gain is accompanied by fear, anxiety, and torture of mind and body." Whoever says this must perforce admit that sacrilege, though it be an evil because it works much evil, is yet partly good because it accomplishes a certain amount of good. What can be more monstrous than this? We have, to be sure, actually convinced the world that sacrilege, theft, and adultery are to be regarded as among the goods. How many men there are who do not blush at theft, how many who boast of having committed adultery! For petty sacrilege is punished, but sacrilege on a grand scale is honoured by a triumphal procession. Besides, sacrilege, if it is wholly good in some respect, will also be honourable and will be called right conduct; for it is conduct which concerns ourselves. But no human being, on serious consideration, admits this idea.

Therefore, goods cannot spring from evil. For if, as you object, sacrilege is an evil for the single reason that it brings on much evil, if you but absolve

415

sacrilege of its punishment and pledge it immunity, sacrilege will be wholly good. And yet the worst punishment for crime lies in the crime itself. You are mistaken, I maintain, if you propose to reserve your punishments for the hangman or the prison; the crime is punished immediately after it is committed; nay, rather, at the moment when it is committed. Hence, good does not spring from evil, any more than figs grow from olive-trees. Things which grow correspond to their seed; and goods cannot depart from their class. As that which is honourable does not grow from that which is base, so neither does good grow from evil. For the honourable and the good are identical.

Certain of our school oppose this statement as follows: "Let us suppose that money taken from any source whatsoever is a good; even though it is taken by an act of sacrilege, the money does not on that account derive its origin from sacrilege. You may get my meaning through the following illustration: In the same jar there is a piece of gold and there is a serpent. If you take the gold from the jar, it is not just because the serpent is there too, I say, that the jar yields me the gold – because it contains the serpent as well, – but it yields the gold in spite of containing the serpent also. Similarly, gain results from sacrilege, not just because sacrilege is a base and accursed act, but because it contains gain also. As the serpent in the jar is an evil, and not the gold which lies there, beside the serpent; so in an act of sacrilege it is the crime, not the profit, that is evil." But I differ from these men; for the conditions in each case are not at all the same. In the one instance I can take the gold without the serpent, in the other I cannot make the profit without committing the sacrilege. The gain in the latter case does not lie side by side with the crime; it is blended with the crime.

"That which, while we are desiring to attain it, involves us in many evils, is not a good. But while we are desiring to attain riches, we become involved in many evils; therefore, riches are not a good," "Your first premiss," they say, "contains two meanings; one is: we become involved in many evils while we are desiring to attain riches. But we also become involved in many evils while we are desiring to attain virtue. One man, while travelling in order to prosecute his studies, suffers shipwreck, and another is taken captive. The second meaning is as follows: that through which we become involved in evils is not a good. And it will not logically follow from our proposition that we become involved in evils through riches or through pleasure; otherwise, if it is through riches that we become involved in many evils, riches are not only not a good, but they are positively an evil. You, however, maintain merely that they are not a good. Moreover," the objector says, "you grant that riches are of some use. You reckon them among the advantages; and yet on this basis they cannot even be an advantage, for it is through the pursuit of riches that we suffer much disadvantage." Certain men answer this objection as follows: "You are mistaken if you ascribe disadvantages to riches. Riches injure no one; it is a man's own folly, or his neighbour's wickedness, that harms him in each case, just as a sword by itself does not slay; it is merely the weapon used by the slayer. Riches themselves do not harm you, just because it is on account of riches that you suffer harm."

I think that the reasoning of Posidonius is better: he holds that riches are a cause of evil, not because, of themselves, they do any evil, but because they goad men on so that they are ready to do evil. For the efficient cause, which necessarily produces harm at once, is one thing, and the antecedent cause is another. It is this antecedent cause which inheres in riches; they puff up the spirit and beget pride, they bring on unpopularity and unsettle the mind to such an extent that the mere reputation of having wealth, though it is bound to harm us, nevertheless affords delight. All goods, however, ought properly to be free from blame; they are pure, they do not corrupt the spirit, and they do not tempt us. They do, indeed, uplift and broaden the spirit, but without puffing it up. Those things which are goods produce confidence, but riches produce shamelessness. The things which are goods give us greatness of soul, but riches give us arrogance. And arrogance is nothing else than a false show of greatness.

"According to that argument," the objector says, "riches are not only not a good, but are a positive evil." Now they would be an evil if they did harm of themselves, and if, as I remarked, it were the efficient cause which inheres in them; in fact, however, it is the antecedent cause which inheres in riches, and indeed it is that cause which, so far from merely arousing the spirit, actually drags it along by force. Yes, riches shower upon us a semblance of the good, which is like the reality and wins credence in the eyes of many men. The antecedent cause inheres in virtue also; it is this which brings on envy – for many men become unpopular because of their wisdom, and many men because of their justice. But this cause, though it inheres in virtue, is not the result of virtue itself, nor is it a mere semblance of the reality; nay, on the contrary, far more like the reality is that vision which is flashed by virtue upon the spirits of men, summoning them to love it and marvel thereat.

Posidonius thinks that the syllogism should be framed as follows: "Things which bestow upon the soul no greatness or confidence or freedom from care are not goods. But riches and health and similar conditions do none of these things; therefore, riches and health are not goods." This syllogism he then goes on to extend still farther in the following way: "Things which bestow upon the soul no greatness or confidence or freedom from care, but on the other hand create in it arrogance, vanity, and insolence, are evils. But things which are the gift of Fortune drive us into these evil ways. Therefore these things are not goods." "But," says the objector, "by such reasoning, things which are the gift of Fortune will not even be advantages." No, advantages and goods stand each in a different situation. An advantage is that which contains more of usefulness than of annoyance. But a good ought to be unmixed and with no element in it of harmfulness. A thing is not good if it contains more benefit than injury, but only if it contains nothing but benefit. Besides, advantages may be predicated of animals, of men who are less than perfect, and of fools. Hence the advantageous may have an element of disadvantage mingled with it, but the word "advantageous" is used of the compound because it is judged by its predominant element. The good, however, can be predicated of the wise man alone; it is bound to be without alloy,

Be of good cheer; there is only one knot left for you to untangle, though it is a knot for a Hercules: "Good does not result from evil. But riches result from numerous cases of poverty; therefore, riches are not a good." This syllogism is not recognized by our school, but the Peripatetics both concoct it and give its solution. Posidonius, however, remarks that this fallacy, which has been bandied about among all the schools of dialectic, is refuted by Antipater as follows: "The word 'poverty' is used to denote, not the possession of something, but the non-possession or, as the ancients have put it, deprivation, (for the Greeks use the phrase 'by deprivation,' meaning 'negatively'). 'Poverty' states, not what a man has, but what he has not. Consequently there can be no fullness resulting from a multitude of voids; many positive things, and not many deficiencies, make up riches. You have," says he, "a wrong notion of the meaning of what poverty is. For poverty does not mean the possession of little, but the non-possession of much; it is used, therefore, not of what a man has, but of what he lacks." I could express my meaning more easily if there were a Latin word which could translate the Greek word which means "not-possessing." Antipater assigns this quality to poverty, but for my part I cannot see what else poverty is than the possession of little. If ever we have plenty of leisure, we shall investigate the question: what is the essence of riches, and what the essence of poverty; but when the time comes, we shall also consider whether it is not better to try to mitigate poverty, and to relieve wealth of its arrogance, than to quibble about the words as if the question, of the things were already decided.

Let us suppose that we have been summoned to an assembly; an act dealing with the abolition of riches has been brought before the meeting. Shall we be supporting it, or opposing it, if we use these syllogisms? Will these syllogisms help us to bring it about that the Roman people shall demand poverty and praise it – poverty, the foundation and cause of their empire, – and, on the other hand, shall shrink in fear from their present wealth, reflecting that they have found it among the victims of their conquests, that wealth is the source from which office-seeking and bribery and disorder have burst into a city once characterized by the utmost scrupulousness and sobriety, and that because of wealth an exhibition all too lavish is made of the spoils of conquered nations; reflecting, finally, that whatever one people has snatched away from all the rest may still more easily be snatched by all away from one? Nay, it were better to support this law by our conduct and to subdue our desires by direct assault rather than to circumvent them by logic. If we can, let us speak more boldly; if not, let us speak more frankly.

Letter LXXXVIII - On Liberal and Vocational Studies

You have been wishing to know my views with regard to liberal studies. My answer is this: I respect no study, and deem no study good, which results in money-making. Such studies are profit-bringing occupations, useful only in so far as they give the mind a preparation and do not engage it permanently. One should linger upon them only so long as the mind can occupy itself with nothing greater; they are our apprenticeship, not our real work. Hence you see why "liberal studies" are so called; it is because they are studies worthy of a free-born gentleman. But there is only one really liberal study, – that which gives a man his liberty. It is the study of wisdom, and that is lofty, brave, and great-souled. All other studies are puny and puerile. You surely do not believe that there is good in any of the subjects whose teachers are, as you see, men of the most ignoble and base stamp? We ought not to be learning such things; we should have done with learning them.

Certain persons have made up their minds that the point at issue with regard to the liberal studies is whether they make men good; but they do not even profess or aim at a knowledge of this particular subject. The scholar busies himself with investigations into language, and if it be his desire to go farther afield, he works on history, or, if he would extend his range to the farthest limits, on poetry. But which of these paves the way to virtue? Pronouncing syllables, investigating words, memorizing plays, or making rules for the scansion of poetry, what is there in all this that rids one of fear, roots out desire, or bridles the passions? The question is: do such men teach virtue, or not? If they do not teach it, then neither do they transmit it. If they do teach it, they are philosophers. Would you like to know how it happens that they have not taken the chair for the purpose of teaching virtue? See how unlike their subjects are; and yet their subjects would resemble each other if they taught the same thing.

It may be, perhaps, that they make you believe that Homer was a philosopher, although they disprove this by the very arguments through which they seek to prove it. For sometimes they make of him a Stoic, who approves nothing but virtue, avoids pleasures, and refuses to relinquish honour even at the price of immortality; sometimes they make him an Epicurean, praising the condition of a state in repose, which passes its days in feasting and song; sometimes a Peripatetic, classifying goodness in three ways; sometimes an Academic, holding that all things are uncertain. It is clear, however, that no one of these doctrines is to be fathered upon Homer, just because they are all there; for they are irreconcilable with one another. We may admit to these men, indeed, that Homer was a philosopher; yet surely he became a wise man before he had any knowledge of poetry. So let us learn the particular things that made Homer wise.

It is no more to the point, of course, for me to investigate whether Homer or Hesiod was the older poet, than to know why Hecuba, although younger than Helen, showed her years so lamentably. What, in your opinion, I say, would be the point in trying to determine the respective ages of Achilles and Patroclus? Do you raise the question, "Through what regions did Ulysses stray?" instead of trying to prevent ourselves from going astray at all times? We have no leisure to hear lectures on the question whether he was sea-tost between Italy and Sicily, or outside our known world (indeed, so long a wandering could not possibly have taken place within its narrow bounds); we ourselves encounter storms of the spirit, which toss us daily, and our depravity drives us into all the ills which troubled Ulysses. For us there is never lacking the beauty to tempt our eyes, or the enemy to assail us; on this side are savage monsters that delight in human blood, on that side the treacherous allurements of the ear, and yonder is shipwreck and all the varied category of misfortunes. Show me rather, by the example of Ulysses, how I am to love my country, my wife, my father, and how, even after suffering shipwreck, I am to sail toward these ends, honourable as they are. Why try to discover whether Penelope was a pattern of purity, or whether she had the laugh on her contemporaries? Or whether she suspected that the man in her presence was Ulysses, before she knew it was he? Teach me rather what purity is, and how great a good we have in it, and whether it is situated in the body or in the soul.

Now I will transfer my attention to the musician. You, sir, are teaching me how the treble and the bass are in accord with one another, and how, though the strings produce different notes, the result is a harmony; rather bring my soul into harmony with itself, and let not my purposes be out of tune. You are showing me what the doleful keys are; show me rather how, in the midst of adversity, I may keep from uttering a doleful note. The mathematician teaches me how to lay out the dimensions of my estates; but I should rather be taught how to lay out what is enough for a man to own. He teaches me to count, and adapts my fingers to avarice; but I should prefer him to teach me that there is no point in such calculations, and that one is none the happier for tiring out the book-keepers with his possessions – or rather, how useless property is to any man who would find it the greatest misfortune if he should be required to reckon out, by his own wits, the amount of his holdings. What good is there for me in knowing how to parcel out a piece of land, if I know not how to share it with my brother? What good is there in working out to a nicety the dimensions of an acre, and in detecting the error if a piece has so much as escaped my measuring-rod, if I am embittered when an ill-tempered neighbour merely scrapes off a bit of my land? The mathematician teaches me how I may lose none of my boundaries; I, however, seek to learn how to lose them all with a light heart. "But," comes the reply, "I am being driven from the farm which my father and grandfather owned!" Well? Who owned the land before your grandfather? Can you explain what people (I will not say what person) held it originally? You did not enter upon it as a master, but merely as a tenant. And whose tenant are you? If your claim is successful, you are tenant of the heir. The lawyers say that public property cannot be acquired privately by possession; what you hold and call your own is public property – indeed, it belongs to mankind at large. O what marvellous skill! You know how to measure the circle; you find the square of any shape which is set before you; you compute the distances between the stars; there is nothing which does not come within the scope of your calculations. But if you are a real master of your profession, measure me the mind of man! Tell me how great it is, or how puny!

You know what a straight line is; but how does it benefit you if you do not know what is straight in this life of ours?

I come next to the person who boasts his knowledge of the heavenly bodies, who knows
Whither the chilling star of Saturn hides,
And through what orbit Mercury doth stray.

Of what benefit will it be to know this? That I shall be disturbed because Saturn and Mars are in opposition, or when Mercury sets at eventide in plain view of Saturn, rather than learn that those stars, wherever they are, are propitious, and that they are not subject to change? They are driven along by an unending round of destiny, on a course from which they cannot swerve. They return at stated seasons; they either set in motion, or mark the intervals of the whole world's work. But if they are responsible for whatever happens, how will it help you to know the secrets of the immutable? Or if they merely give indications, what good is there in foreseeing what you cannot escape? Whether you know these things or not, they will take place.

Behold the fleeting sun,
The stars that follow in his train, and thou
Shalt never find the morrow play thee false,
Or be misled by nights without a cloud.

It has, however, been sufficiently and fully ordained that I shall be safe from anything that may mislead me. "What," you say, "does the 'morrow never play me false'? Whatever happens without my knowledge plays me false." I, for my part, do not know what is to be, but I do know what may come to be. I shall have no misgivings in this matter; I await the future in its entirety; and if there is any abatement in its severity, I make the most of it. If the morrow treats me kindly, it is a sort of deception; but it does not deceive me even at that. For just as I know that all things can happen, so I know, too, that they will not happen in every case. I am ready for favourable events in every case, but I am prepared for evil.

In this discussion you must bear with me if I do not follow the regular course. For I do not consent to admit painting into the list of liberal arts, any more than sculpture, marble-working, and other helps toward luxury. I also debar from the liberal studies wrestling and all knowledge that is compounded of oil and mud; otherwise, I should be compelled to admit perfumers also, and cooks, and all others who lend their wits to the service of our pleasures. For what "liberal" element is there in these ravenous takers of emetics, whose bodies are fed to fatness while their minds are thin and dull? Or do we really believe that the training which they give is "liberal" for the young men of Rome, who used to be taught by our ancestors to stand straight and hurl a spear, to wield a pike, to guide a horse, and to handle weapons? Our ancestors used to teach their children nothing that could be learned while lying down. But neither the new system nor the old teaches or nourishes virtue. For what good does it do us to guide a horse and control his speed with the curb, and then find that our own passions, utterly uncurbed, bolt with us? Or to beat many opponents in wrestling or boxing, and then to find that we ourselves are beaten by anger?

"What then," you say, "do the liberal studies contribute nothing to our welfare?" Very much in other respects, but nothing at all as regards virtue. For even these arts of which I have spoken, though admittedly of a low grade – depending as they do upon handiwork – contribute greatly toward the equipment of life, but nevertheless have nothing to do with virtue. And if you inquire, "Why, then, do we educate our children in the liberal studies?" it is not because they can bestow virtue, but because they prepare the soul for the reception of virtue. Just as that "primary course," as the ancients called it, in grammar, which gave boys their elementary training, does not teach them the liberal arts, but prepares the ground for their early acquisition of these arts, so the liberal arts do not conduct the soul all the way to virtue, but merely set it going in that direction.

Posidonius divides the arts into four classes: first we have those which are common and low, then those which serve for amusement, then those which refer to the education of boys, and, finally, the liberal arts. The common sort belong to workmen and are mere hand-work; they are concerned with equipping life; there is in them no pretence to beauty or honour. The arts of amusement are those which aim to please the eye and the ear. To this class you may assign the stage-machinists, who invent scaffolding that goes aloft of its own accord, or floors that rise silently into the air, and many other surprising devices, as when objects that fit together then fall apart, or objects which are separate then join together automatically, or objects which stand erect then gradually collapse. The eye of the inexperienced is struck with amazement by these things; for such persons marvel at everything that takes place without warning, because they do not know the causes. The arts which belong to the education of boys, and are somewhat similar to the liberal arts, are those which the Greeks call the "cycle of studies," but which we Romans call the "liberal." However, those alone are really liberal – or rather, to give them a truer name, "free" – whose concern is virtue.

"But," one will say, "just as there is a part of philosophy which has to do with nature, and a part which has to do with ethics, and a part which has to do with reasoning, so this group of liberal arts also claims for itself a place in philosophy. When one approaches questions that deal with nature, a decision is reached by means of a word from the mathematician. Therefore mathematics is a department of that branch which it aids." But many things aid us and yet are not parts of ourselves. Nay, if they were, they would not aid us. Food is an aid to the body, but is not a part of it. We get some help from the service which mathematics renders; and mathematics is as indispensable to philosophy as the carpenter is to the mathematician. But carpentering is not a part of mathematics, nor is mathematics a part of philosophy. Moreover, each has its own limits; for the wise man investigates and learns the causes of natural phenomena, while the mathematician follows up and computes their numbers and their measurements. The wise man knows the laws by which the heavenly bodies persist, what powers belong to them, and what attributes; the astronomer merely notes their comings and goings, the rules which govern their settings and their risings, and the occasional periods during which they seem to stand still, although as a matter of fact no heavenly body can stand still. The wise man will know what causes the reflection in a mirror; but, the mathematician can merely tell you how far the body should be from the reflection, and what shape of mirror will produce a given reflection. The philosopher will demonstrate that the sun is a large body, while the astronomer will compute just how large, progressing in knowledge by his method of trial and experiment; but in order to progress, he must summon to his aid certain principles. No art, however, is sufficient unto itself, if the foundation upon which it rests depends upon mere favour. Now philosophy asks no favours from any other source; it builds everything on its own soil; but the science of numbers is, so to speak, a structure built on another man's land – it builds on everything on alien soil; It accepts first principles, and by their favour arrives at further conclusions. If it could march unassisted to the truth, if it were able to understand the nature of the universe, I should say that it would offer much assistance to our minds; for the mind grows by contact with things heavenly and draws into itself something from on high. There is but one thing that brings the soul to perfection – the unalterable knowledge of good and evil. But there is no other art which investigates good and evil.

I should like to pass in review the several virtues. Bravery is a scorner of things which inspire fear; it looks down upon, challenges, and crushes the powers of terror and all that would drive our freedom under the yoke. But do "liberal studies" strengthen this virtue? Loyalty is the holiest good in the human heart; it is forced into betrayal by no constraint, and it is bribed by no rewards. Loyalty cries: "Burn me, slay me, kill me! I shall not betray my trust; and the more urgently torture shall seek to find my secret, the deeper in my heart will I bury it!" Can the "liberal arts" produce such a spirit within us? Temperance controls our desires; some it hates and routs, others it regulates and restores to a healthy measure, nor does it ever approach our desires for their own sake. Temperance knows that the best measure of the appetites is not what you want to take, but what you ought to take. Kindliness forbids you to be over-bearing towards your associates, and it forbids you to be grasping. In words and in deeds and in feelings it shows itself gentle and courteous to all men. It counts no evil as another's solely. And the reason why it loves its own good is chiefly because it will some day be the good of another. Do "liberal studies" teach a man such character as this? No; no more than they teach simplicity, moderation and self-restraint, thrift and economy, and that kindliness which spares a neighbour's life as if it were one's own and knows that it is not for man to make wasteful use of his fellow-man.

"But," one says, "since you declare that virtue cannot be attained without the 'liberal studies,' how is it that you deny that they offer any assistance to virtue?" Because you cannot attain virtue without food, either; and yet food has nothing to do with virtue. Wood does not offer assistance to a ship, although a ship cannot be built except of wood. There is no reason, I say, why you should think that anything is made by the assistance of that without which it cannot be made. We might even make the statement that it is possible to attain wisdom without the "liberal studies"; for although virtue is a thing that must be learned, yet it is not learned by means of these studies.

What reason have I, however, for supposing that one who is ignorant of letters will never be a wise man, since wisdom is not to be found in letters? Wisdom communicates facts and not words; and it may be true that the memory is more to be depended upon when it has no support outside itself. Wisdom is a large and spacious thing. It needs plenty of free room. One must learn about things divine and human, the past and the future, the ephemeral and the eternal; and one must learn about Time. See how many questions arise concerning time alone: in the first place, whether it is anything in and by itself; in the second place, whether anything exists prior to time and without time; and again, did time begin along with the universe, or, because there was something even before the universe began, did time also exist then? There are countless questions concerning the soul alone: whence it comes, what is its nature, when it begins to exist, and how long it exists; whether it passes from one place to another and changes its habitation, being transferred successively from one animal shape to another, or whether it is a slave but once, roaming the universe after it is set free; whether it is corporeal or not; what will become of it when it ceases to use us as its medium; how it will employ its freedom when it has escaped from this present prison; whether it will forget all its past, and at that moment begin to know itself when, released from the body, it has withdrawn to the skies.

Thus, whatever phase of things human and divine you have apprehended, you will be wearied by the vast number of things to be answered and things to be learned. And in order that these manifold and mighty subjects may have free entertainment in your soul, you must remove therefrom all superfluous things. Virtue will not surrender herself to these narrow bounds of ours; a great subject needs wide space in which to move. Let all other things be driven out, and let the breast be emptied to receive virtue.

"But it is a pleasure to be acquainted with many arts." Therefore let us keep only as much of them as is essential. Do you regard that man as blameworthy who puts superfluous things on the same footing with useful things, and in his house makes a lavish display of costly objects, but do not deem him blameworthy who has allowed himself to become engrossed with the useless furniture of learning? This desire to know more than is sufficient is a sort of intemperance. Why? Because this unseemly pursuit of the liberal arts makes men troublesome, wordy, tactless, self-satisfied bores, who fail to learn the essentials just because they have learned the non-essentials. Didymus the scholar wrote four thousand books. I should feel pity for him if he had only read the same number of superfluous volumes. In these books he investigates Homer's birthplace, who was really the mother of Aeneas, whether Anacreon was more of a rake or more of a drunkard, whether Sappho was a bad lot and other problems the answers to which, if found, were forthwith to be forgotten. Come now, do not tell me that life is long! Nay, when you come to consider our own countrymen also, I can show you many works which ought to be cut down with the axe.

It is at the cost of a vast outlay of time and of vast discomfort to the ears of others that we win such praise as this: "What a learned man you are!" Let us be content with this recommendation, less citified though it be: "What a good man you are!" Do I mean this? Well, would you have me unroll the annals of the world's history and try to find out who first wrote poetry? Or, in the absence of written records, shall I make an estimate of the number of years which lie between Orpheus and Homer? Or shall I make a study of the absurd writings of Aristarchus, wherein he branded the text of other men's verses, and wear my life away upon syllables? Shall I then wallow in the geometrician's dust? Have I so far forgotten that useful saw "Save your time"? Must I know these things? And what may I choose not to know?

Apion, the scholar, who drew crowds to his lectures all over Greece in the days of Gaius Caesar and was acclaimed a Homerid by every state, used to maintain that Homer, when he had finished his two poems, The Iliad and The Odyssey, added a preliminary poem to his work, wherein he embraced the whole Trojan war. The argument which Apion adduced to prove this statement was that Homer had purposely inserted in the opening line two letters which contained a key to the number of his books. A man who wishes to know many things must know such things as these, and must take no thought of all the time which one loses by ill-health, public duties, private duties, daily duties, and sleep. Apply the measure to the years of your life; they have no room for all these things.

I have been speaking so far of liberal studies; but think how much superfluous and unpractical matter the philosophers contain! Of their own accord they also have descended to establishing nice divisions of syllables, to determining the true meaning of conjunctions and prepositions; they have been envious of the scholars, envious of the mathematicians. They have taken over into their own art all the superfluities of these other arts; the result is that they know more about careful speaking than about careful living. Let me tell you what evils are due to over-nice exactness, and what an enemy it is of truth! Protagoras declares that one can take either side on any question and debate it with equal success – even on this very question, whether every subject can be debated from either point of view. Nausiphanes holds that in things which seem to exist, there is no difference between existence and non-existence. Parmenides maintains that nothing exists of all this which seems to exist, except the universe alone. Zeno of Elea removed all the difficulties by removing one; for he declares that nothing exists. The Pyrrhonean, Megarian, Eretrian, and Academic schools are all engaged in practically the same task; they have introduced a new knowledge, non-knowledge. You may sweep all these theories in with the superfluous troops of "liberal" studies; the one class of men give me a knowledge that will be of no use to me, the other class do away with any hope of attaining knowledge. It is better, of course, to know useless things than to know nothing. One set of philosophers offers no light by which I may direct my gaze toward the truth; the other digs out my very eyes and leaves me blind. If I cleave to Protagoras, there is nothing in the scheme of nature that is not doubtful; if I hold with Nausiphanes, I am sure only of this – that everything is unsure; if with Parmenides, there is nothing except the One; if with Zeno, there is not even the One.

What are we, then? What becomes of all these things that surround us, support us, sustain us? The whole universe is then a vain or deceptive shadow. I cannot readily say whether I am more vexed at those who would have it that we know nothing, or with those who would not leave us even this privilege. Farewell.

Letter LXXXIX - On the Parts of Philosophy

It is a useful fact that you wish to know, one which is essential to him who hastens after wisdom – namely, the parts of philosophy and the division of its huge bulk into separate members. For by studying the parts we can be brought more easily to understand the whole. I only wish that philosophy might come before our eyes in all her unity, just as the whole expanse of the firmament is spread out for us to gaze upon! It would be a sight closely resembling that of the firmament. For then surely philosophy would ravish all mortals with love for her; we should abandon all those things which, in our ignorance of what is great, we believe to be great. Inasmuch, however, as this cannot fall to our lot, we must view philosophy just as men gaze upon the secrets of the firmament.

The wise man's mind, to be sure, embraces the whole framework of philosophy, surveying it with no less rapid glance than our mortal eyes survey the heavens; we, however, who must break through the gloom, we whose vision fails even for that which is near at hand, can be shown with greater ease each separate object even though we cannot yet comprehend the universe. I shall therefore comply with your demand, and shall divide philosophy into parts, but not into scraps. For it is useful that philosophy should be divided, but not chopped into bits. Just as it is hard to take in what is indefinitely large, so it is hard to take in what is indefinitely small. The people are divided into tribes, the army into centuries. Whatever has grown to greater size is more easily identified if it is broken up into parts; but the parts, as I have remarked, must not be countless in number and diminutive in size. For over-analysis is faulty in precisely the same way as no analysis at all; whatever you cut so fine that it becomes dust is as good as blended into a mass again.

In the first place, therefore, if you approve, I shall draw the distinction between wisdom and philosophy. Wisdom is the perfect good of the human mind; philosophy is the love of wisdom, and the endeavour to attain it. The latter strives toward the goal which the former has already reached. And it is clear why philosophy was so called. For it acknowledges by its very name the object of its love. Certain persons have defined wisdom as the knowledge of things divine and things human. Still others say: "Wisdom is knowing things divine and things human, and their causes also." This added phrase seems to me to be superfluous, since the causes of things divine and things human are a part of the divine system. Philosophy also has been defined in various ways; some have called it "the study of virtue," others have referred to it as "a study of the way to amend the mind," and some have named it "the search for right reason." One thing is practically settled, that there is some difference between philosophy and wisdom. Nor indeed is it possible that that which is sought and that which seeks are identical. As there is a great difference between avarice and wealth, the one being the subject of the craving and the other its object, so between philosophy and wisdom. For the one is a result and a reward of the other. Philosophy does the going, and wisdom is the goal. Wisdom is that which the Greeks call σοφία. The Romans also were wont to use this word in the sense in which they now use "philosophy" also. This will be proved to your satisfaction by our old national plays, as well as by the epitaph that is carved on the tomb of Dossennus:

Pause, stranger, and read the wisdom of Dossennus.

Certain of our school, however, although philosophy meant to them "the study of virtue," and though virtue was the object sought and philosophy the seeker, have maintained nevertheless that the two cannot be sundered. For philosophy cannot exist without virtue, nor virtue without philosophy. Philosophy is the study of virtue, by means, however, of virtue itself; but neither can virtue exist without the study of itself, nor can the study of virtue exist without virtue itself. For it is not like trying to hit a target at long range, where the shooter and the object to be shot at are in different places. Nor, as roads which lead into a city, are the approaches to virtue situated outside virtue herself; the path by which one reaches virtue leads by way of virtue herself; philosophy and virtue cling closely together.

The greatest authors, and the greatest number of authors, have maintained that there are three divisions of philosophy – moral, natural, and rational. The first keeps the soul in order; the second investigates the universe; the third works out the essential meanings of words, their combinations, and the proofs which keep falsehood from creeping in and displacing truth. But there have also been those who divided philosophy on the one hand into fewer divisions, on the other hand into more. Certain of the Peripatetic school have added a fourth division, "civil philosophy," because it calls for a special sphere of activity and is interested in a different subject matter. Some have added a department for which they use the Greek term "economics," the science of managing one's own household. Still others have made a distinct heading for the various kinds of life. There is no one of these subdivisions, however, which will not be found under the branch called "moral" philosophy.

The Epicureans held that philosophy was twofold, natural and moral; they did away with the rational branch. Then, when they were compelled by the facts themselves to distinguish between equivocal ideas and to expose fallacies that lay hidden under the cloak of truth they themselves also introduced a heading to which they give the name "forensic and regulative," which is merely "rational" under another name, although they hold that this section is accessory to the department of "natural" philosophy. The Cyrenaic school abolished the natural as well as the rational department, and were content with the moral side alone; and yet these philosophers also include under another title that which they have rejected. For they divide moral philosophy into five parts: What to avoid and what to seek, The Passions, Actions, Causes, Proofs. Now the causes of things really belong to the

427

"natural" division, the proofs to the "rational." Aristo of Chios remarked that the natural and the rational were not only superfluous, but were also contradictory. He even limited the "moral," which was all that was left to him; for he abolished that heading which embraced advice, maintaining that it was the business of the pedagogue, and not of the philosopher – as if the wise man were anything else than the pedagogue of the human race!

Since, therefore, philosophy is threefold, let us first begin to set in order the moral side. It has been agreed that this should be divided into three parts. First, we have the speculative part, which assigns to each thing its particular function and weighs the worth of each; it is highest in point of utility. For what is so indispensable as giving to everything its proper value? The second has to do with impulse, the third with actions. For the first duty is to determine severally what things are worth; the second, to conceive with regard to them a regulated and ordered impulse; the third, to make your impulse and your actions harmonize, so that under all these conditions you may be consistent with yourself. If any of the three be defective, there is confusion in the rest also. For what benefit is there in having all things appraised, each in its proper relations, if you go to excess in your impulses? What benefit is there in having checked your impulses and in having your desires in your own control, if when you come to action you are unaware of the proper times and seasons, and if you do not know when, where, and how each action should be carried out? It is one thing to understand the merits and the values of facts, another thing to know the precise moment for action, and still another to curb impulses and to proceed, instead of rushing, toward what is to be done. Hence life is in harmony with itself only when action has not deserted impulse, and when impulse toward an object arises in each case from the worth of the object, being languid or more eager as the case may be, according as the objects which arouse it are worth seeking.

The natural side of philosophy is twofold: bodily and non-bodily. Each is divided into its own grades of importance, so to speak. The topic concerning bodies deals, first, with these two grades: the creative and the created; and the created things are the elements. Now this very topic of the elements, as some writers hold, is integral; as others hold, it is divided into matter, the cause which moves all things, and the elements. It remains for me to divide rational philosophy into its parts. Now all speech is either continuous, or split up between questioner and answerer. It has been agreed upon that the former should be called rhetoric, and the latter dialectic. Rhetoric deals with words, and meanings, and arrangement. Dialectic is divided into two parts: words and their meanings, that is, into things which are said, and the words in which they are said. Then comes a subdivision of each – and it is of vast extent. Therefore I shall stop at this point, and

But treat the climax of the story;

for if I should take a fancy to give the subdivisions, my letter would become a debater's handbook! I am not trying to discourage you, excellent Lucilius, from reading on this subject, provided only that you promptly relate to conduct all that you have read.

It is your conduct that you must hold in check; you must rouse what is languid in you, bind fast what has become relaxed, conquer what is obstinate, persecute your appetites, and the appetites of mankind, as much as you can; and to those who say: "How long will this unending talk go on?" answer with the words: "I ought to be asking you 'How long will these unending sins of yours go on?'" Do you really desire my remedies to stop before your vices? But I shall speak of my remedies all the more, and just because you offer objections I shall keep on talking. Medicine begins to do good at the time when a touch makes the diseased body tingle with pain. I shall utter words that will help men even against their will. At times you should allow words other than compliments to reach your ears, and because as individuals you are unwilling to hear the truth, hear it collectively. How far will you extend the boundaries of your estates? An estate which held a nation is too narrow for a single lord. How far will you push forward your ploughed fields – you who are not content to confine the measure of your farms even within the amplitude of provinces? You have noble rivers flowing down through your private grounds; you have mighty streams – boundaries of mighty nations – under your dominion from source to outlet. This also is too little for you unless you also surround whole seas with your estates, unless your steward holds sway on the other side of the Adriatic, the Ionian, and the Aegean seas, unless the islands, homes of famous chieftains, are reckoned by you as the most paltry of possessions! Spread them as widely as you will, if only you may have as a "farm" what was once called a kingdom; make whatever you can your own, provided only that it is more than your neighbour's!

And now for a word with you, whose luxury spreads itself out as widely as the greed of those to whom I have just referred. To you I say: "Will this custom continue until there is no lake over which the pinnacles of your country-houses do not tower? Until there is no river whose banks are not bordered by your lordly structures? Wherever hot waters shall gush forth in rills, there you will be causing new resorts of luxury to rise. Wherever the shore shall bend into a bay, there will you straightway be laying foundations, and, not content with any land that has not been made by art, you will bring the sea within your boundaries. On every side let your house-tops flash in the sun, now set on mountain peaks where they command an extensive outlook over sea and land, now lifted from the plain to the height of mountains; build your manifold structures, your huge piles, – you are nevertheless but individuals, and puny ones at that! What profit to you are your many bed-chambers? You sleep in one. No place is yours where you yourselves are not." "Next I pass to you, you whose bottomless and insatiable maw explores on the one hand the seas, on the other the earth, with enormous toil hunting down your prey, now with hook, now with snare, now with nets of various kinds; no animal has peace except when you are cloyed with it. And how slight a portion of those banquets of yours, prepared for you by so many hands, do you taste with your pleasure-jaded palate! How slight a portion of all that game, whose taking was fraught with danger, does the master's sick and squeamish stomach relish? How slight a portion of all those shell-fish, imported from so far, slips down that insatiable gullet? Poor wretches, do you not know that your appetites are bigger than your bellies?"

Talk in this way to other men, – provided that while you talk you also listen; write in this way, – provided that while you write you read, remembering that everything you hear or read, is to be applied to conduct, and to the alleviation of passion's fury. Study, not in order to add anything to your knowledge, but to make your knowledge better. Farewell.

Letter XC - On the Part Played by Philosophy in the Progress of Man

Who can doubt, my dear Lucilius, that life is the gift of the immortal gods, but that living well is the gift of philosophy? Hence the idea that our debt to philosophy is greater than our debt to the gods, in proportion as a good life is more of a benefit than mere life, would be regarded as correct, were not philosophy itself a boon which the gods have bestowed upon us. They have given the knowledge thereof to none, but the faculty of acquiring it they have given to all. For if they had made philosophy also a general good, and if we were gifted with understanding at our birth, wisdom would have lost her best attribute – that she is not one of the gifts of fortune. For as it is, the precious and noble characteristic of wisdom is that she does not advance to meet us, that each man is indebted to himself for her, and that we do not seek her at the hands of others.

What would there be in philosophy worthy of your respect, if she were a thing that came by bounty? Her sole function is to discover the truth about things divine and things human. From her side religion never departs, nor duty, nor justice, nor any of the whole company of virtues which cling together in close-united fellowship. Philosophy has taught us to worship that which is divine, to love that which is human; she has told us that with the gods lies dominion, and among men, fellowship. This fellowship remained unspoiled for a long time, until avarice tore the community asunder and became the cause of poverty, even in the case of those whom she herself had most enriched. For men cease to possess all things the moment they desire all things for their own.

But the first men and those who sprang from them, still unspoiled, followed nature, having one man as both their leader and their law, entrusting themselves to the control of one better than themselves. For nature has the habit of subjecting the weaker to the stronger. Even among the dumb animals those which are either biggest or fiercest hold sway. It is no weakling bull that leads the herd; it is one that has beaten the other males by his might and his muscle. In the case of elephants, the tallest goes first; among men, the best is regarded as the highest. That is why it was to the mind that a ruler was assigned; and for that reason the greatest happiness rested with those peoples among whom a man could not be the more powerful unless he were the better. For that man can safely accomplish what he will who thinks he can do nothing except what he ought to do.

Accordingly, in that age which is maintained to be the golden age, Posidonius holds that the government was under the jurisdiction of the wise. They kept their hands under control, and protected the weaker from the stronger. They gave advice, both to do and not to do; they showed what was useful and what was useless. Their forethought provided that their subjects should lack nothing; their bravery warded off dangers; their kindness enriched and adorned their subjects. For them ruling was a service, not an exercise of royalty. No ruler tried his power against those to whom he owed the beginnings of his power; and no one had the inclination, or the excuse, to do wrong, since the ruler ruled well and the subject obeyed well, and the king could utter no greater threat against disobedient subjects than that they should depart from the kingdom.

But when once vice stole in and kingdoms were transformed into tyrannies, a need arose for laws and these very laws were in turn framed by the wise. Solon, who established Athens upon a firm basis by just laws, was one of the seven men renowned for their wisdom. Had Lycurgus lived in the same period, an eighth would have been added to that hallowed number seven. The laws of Zaleucus and Charondas are praised; it was not in the forum or in the offices of skilled counsellors, but in the silent and holy retreat of Pythagoras, that these two men learned the principles of justice which they were to establish in Sicily (which at that time was prosperous) and throughout Grecian Italy.

Up to this point I agree with Posidonius; but that philosophy discovered the arts of which life makes use in its daily round I refuse to admit. Nor will I ascribe to it an artisan's glory. Posidonius says: "When men were scattered over the earth, protected by eaves or by the dug-out shelter of a cliff or by the trunk of a hollow tree, it was philosophy that taught them to build houses." But I, for my part, do not hold that philosophy devised these shrewdly-contrived dwellings of ours which rise story upon story, where city crowds against city, any more than that she invented the fish-preserves, which are enclosed for the purpose of saving men's gluttony from having to run the risk of storms, and in order that, no matter how wildly the sea is raging, luxury may have its safe harbours in which to fatten fancy breeds of fish. What! Was it philosophy that taught the use of keys and bolts? Nay, what was that except giving a hint to avarice? Was it philosophy that erected all these towering tenements, so dangerous to the persons who dwell in them? Was it not enough for man to provide himself a roof of any chance covering, and to contrive for himself some natural retreat without the help of art and without trouble? Believe me, that was a happy age, before the days of architects, before the days of builders! All this sort of thing was born when luxury was being born, – this matter of cutting timbers square and cleaving a beam with unerring hand as the saw made its way over the marked-out line.

The primal man with wedges split his wood.

For they were not preparing a roof for a future banquet-ball; for no such use did they carry the pine trees or the firs along the trembling streets with a long row of drays – merely to fasten thereon panelled ceilings heavy with gold. Forked poles erected at either end propped up their houses. With close-packed branches and with leaves heaped up and laid sloping they contrived a drainage for even the heaviest rains. Beneath such dwellings, they lived, but they lived in peace. A thatched roof once covered free men; under marble and gold dwells slavery.

On another point also I differ from Posidonius, when he holds that mechanical tools were the invention of wise men. For on that basis one might maintain that those were wise who taught the arts

Of setting traps for game, and liming twigs
For birds, and girdling mighty woods with dogs.

It was man's ingenuity, not his wisdom, that discovered all these devices. And I also differ from him when he says that wise men discovered our mines of iron and copper, "when the earth, scorched by forest fires, melted the veins of ore which lay near the surface and caused the metal to gush forth." Nay, the sort of men who discover such things are the sort of men who are busied with them. Nor do I consider this question so subtle as Posidonius thinks, namely, whether the hammer or the tongs came first into use. They were both invented by some man whose mind was nimble and keen, but not great or exalted; and the same holds true of any other discovery which can only be made by means of a bent body and of a mind whose gaze is upon the ground.

The wise man was easy-going in his way of living. And why not? Even in our own times he would prefer to be as little cumbered as possible. How, I ask, can you consistently admire both Diogenes and Daedalus? Which of these two seems to you a wise man – the one who devised the saw, or the one who, on seeing a boy drink water from the hollow of his hand, forthwith took his cup from his wallet and broke it, upbraiding himself with these words: "Fool that I am, to have been carrying superfluous baggage all this time!" and then curled himself up in his tub and lay down to sleep? In these our own times, which man, pray, do you deem the wiser – the one who invents a process for spraying saffron perfumes to a tremendous height from hidden pipes, who fills or empties canals by a sudden rush of waters, who so cleverly constructs a dining-room with a ceiling of movable panels that it presents one pattern after another, the roof changing as often as the courses, – or the one who proves to others, as well as to himself, that nature has laid upon us no stern and difficult law when she tells us that we can live without the marble-cutter and the engineer, that we can clothe ourselves without traffic in silk fabrics, that we can have everything that is indispensable to our use, provided only that we are content with what the earth has placed on its surface? If mankind were willing to listen to this sage, they would know that the cook is as superfluous to them as the soldier. Those were wise men, or at any rate like the wise, who found the care of the body a problem easy to solve. The things that are indispensable require no elaborate pains for their acquisition; it is only the luxuries that call for labour. Follow nature, and you will need no skilled craftsmen.

Nature did not wish us to be harassed. For whatever she forced upon us, she equipped us. "But cold cannot be endured by the naked body." What then? Are there not the skins of wild beasts and other animals, which can protect us well enough, and more than enough, from the cold? Do not many tribes cover their bodies with the bark of trees? Are not the feathers of birds sewn together to serve for clothing? Even at the present day does not a large portion of the Scythian tribe garb itself in the skins of foxes and mice, soft to the touch and impervious to the winds? "For all that, men must have some thicker protection than the skin, in order to keep off the heat of the sun in summer." What then? Has not antiquity produced many retreats which, hollowed out either by the damage wrought by time or by any other occurrence you will, have opened into caverns? What then? Did not the very first-comers take twigs and weave them by hand into wicker mats, smear them with common mud, and then with stubble and other wild grasses construct a roof, and thus pass their winters secure, the rains carried off by means of the sloping gables? What then? Do not the peoples on the edge of the Syrtes dwell in dug-out houses and indeed all the tribes who, because of the too fierce blaze of the sun, possess no protection sufficient to keep off the heat except the parched soil itself?

Nature was not so hostile to man that, when she gave all the other animals an easy role in life, she made it impossible for him alone to live without all these artifices. None of these was imposed upon us by her; none of them had to be painfully sought out that our lives might be prolonged. All things were ready for us at our birth; it is we that have made everything difficult for ourselves, through our disdain for what is easy. Houses, shelter, creature comforts, food, and all that has now become the source of vast trouble, were ready at hand, free to all, and obtainable for trifling pains. For the limit everywhere corresponded to the need; it is we that have made all those things valuable, we that have made them admired, we that have caused them to be sought for by extensive and manifold devices. Nature suffices for what she demands. Luxury has turned her back upon nature; each day she expands herself, in all the ages she has been gathering strength, and by her wit promoting the vices. At first, luxury began to lust for what nature regarded as superfluous, then for that which was contrary to nature; and finally she made the soul a bondsman to the body, and bade it be an utter slave to the body's lusts. All these crafts by which the city is patrolled – or shall I say kept in uproar – are but engaged in the body's business; time was when all things were offered to the body as to a slave, but now they are made ready for it as for a master. Accordingly, hence have come the workshops of the weavers and the carpenters; hence the savoury smells of the professional cooks; hence the wantonness of those who teach wanton postures, and wanton and affected singing. For that moderation which nature prescribes, which limits our desires by resources restricted to our needs, has abandoned the field; it has now come to this – that to want only what is enough is a sign both of boorishness and of utter destitution.

It is hard to believe, my dear Lucilius, how easily the charm of eloquence wins even great men away from the truth. Take, for example, Posidonius – who, in my estimation, is of the number of those who have contributed most to philosophy – when he wishes to describe the art of weaving. He tells how, first, some threads are twisted and some drawn out from the soft, loose mass of wool; next, how the upright warp keeps the threads stretched by means of hanging weights; then, how the inserted thread of the woof, which softens the hard texture of the web which holds it fast on either side, is forced by the batten to make a compact union with the warp. He maintains that even the weaver's art was discovered by wise men, forgetting that the more complicated art which he describes was invented in later days – the art wherein

> *The web is bound to frame; asunder now*
> *The reed doth part the warp. Between the threads*
> *Is shot the woof by pointed shuttles borne;*
> *The broad comb's well-notched teeth then drive it home.*

Suppose he had had the opportunity of seeing the weaving of our own day, which produces the clothing that will conceal nothing, the clothing which affords – I will not say no protection to the body, but none even to modesty!

Posidonius then passes on to the farmer. With no less eloquence he describes the ground which is broken up and crossed again by the plough, so that the earth, thus loosened, may allow freer play to the roots; then the seed is sown, and the weeds plucked out by hand, lest any chance growth or wild plant spring up and spoil the crop. This trade also, he declares, is the creation of the wise, – just as if cultivators of the soil were not even at the present day discovering countless new methods of increasing the soil's fertility! Furthermore, not confining his attention to these arts, he even degrades the wise man by sending him to the mill. For he tells us how the sage, by imitating the processes of nature, began to make bread. "The grain," he says, "once taken into the mouth, is crushed by the flinty teeth, which meet in hostile encounter, and whatever grain slips out the tongue turns back to the selfsame teeth. Then it is blended into a mass, that it may the more easily pass down the slippery throat. When this has readied the stomach, it is digested by the stomach's equable heat; then, and not till then, it is assimilated with the body. Following this pattern," he goes on, "someone placed two rough stones, the one above the other, in imitation of the teeth, one set of which is stationary and awaits the motion of the other set. Then by the rubbing of the one stone against the other, the grain is crushed and brought back again and again, until by frequent rubbing it is reduced to powder. Then this man sprinkled the meal with water, and by continued manipulation subdued the mass and moulded the loaf. This loaf was, at first, baked by hot ashes or by an earthen vessel glowing hot; later on ovens were gradually discovered and the other devices whose heat will render obedience to the sage's will." Posidonius came very near declaring that even the cobbler's trade was the discovery of the wise man.

Reason did indeed devise all these things, but it was not right reason. It was man, but not the wise man, that discovered them; just as they invented ships, in which we cross rivers and seas – ships fitted with sails for the purpose of catching the force of the winds, ships with rudders added at the stern in order to turn the vessel's course in one direction or another. The model followed was the fish, which steers itself by its tail, and by its slightest motion on this side or on that bends its swift course. "But," says Posidonius, "the wise man did indeed discover all these things; they were, however, too petty for him to deal with himself and so he entrusted them to his meaner assistants." Not so; these early inventions were thought out by no other class of men than those who have them in charge to-day. We know that certain devices have come to light only within our own memory – such as the use of windows which admit the clear light through transparent tiles, and such as the vaulted baths, with pipes let into their walls for the purpose of diffusing the heat which maintains an even temperature in their lowest as well as in their highest spaces. Why need I mention the marble with which our temples and our private houses are resplendent? Or the rounded and polished masses of stone by means of which we erect colonnades and buildings roomy enough for nations? Or our signs for whole words, which enable us to take down a speech, however rapidly uttered, matching speed of tongue by speed of hand? All this sort of thing has been devised by the lowest grade of slaves. Wisdom's seat is higher; she trains not the hands, but is mistress of our minds.

Would you know what wisdom has brought forth to light, what she has accomplished? It is not the graceful poses of the body, or the varied notes produced by horn and flute, whereby the breath is received and, as it passes out or through, is transformed into voice. It is not wisdom that contrives arms, or walls, or instruments useful in war; nay, her voice is for peace, and she summons all mankind to concord. It is not she, I maintain, who is the artisan of our indispensable implements of daily use. Why do you assign to her such petty things? You see in her the skilled artisan of life. The other arts, it is true, wisdom has under her control; for he whom life serves is also served by the things which equip life. But wisdom's course is toward the state of happiness; thither she guides us, thither she opens the way for us. She shows us what things are evil and what things are seemingly evil; she strips our minds of vain illusion. She bestows upon us a greatness which is substantial, but she represses the greatness which is inflated, and showy but filled with emptiness; and she does not permit us to be ignorant of the difference between what is great and what is but swollen; nay, she delivers to us the knowledge of the whole of nature and of her own nature. She discloses to us what the gods are and of what sort they are; what are the nether gods, the household deities, and the protecting spirits; what are the souls which have been endowed with lasting life and have been admitted to the second class of divinities, where is their abode and what their activities, powers, and will.

Such are wisdom's rites of initiation, by means of which is unlocked, not a village shrine, but the vast temple of all the gods – the universe itself, whose true apparitions and true aspects she offers to the gaze of our minds. For the vision of our eyes is too dull for sights so great. Then she goes back to the beginnings of things, to the eternal Reason which was imparted to the whole, and to the force which inheres in all the seeds of things, giving them the power to fashion each thing according to its kind. Then wisdom begins to inquire about the soul, whence it comes, where it dwells, how long it abides, into how many divisions it falls. Finally, she has turned her attention from the corporeal to the incorporeal, and has closely examined truth and the marks whereby truth is known, inquiring next how that which is equivocal can be distinguished from the truth, whether in life or in language; for in both are elements of the false mingled with the true.

It is my opinion that the wise man has not withdrawn himself, as Posidonius thinks, from those arts which we were discussing, but that he never

435

took them up at all. For he would have judged that nothing was worth discovering that he would not afterwards judge to be worth using always. He would not take up things which would have to be laid aside.

"But Anacharsis," says Posidonius, "invented the potter's wheel, whose whirling gives shape to vessels." Then because the potter's wheel is mentioned in Homer, people prefer to believe that Homer's verses are false rather than the story of Posidonius! But I maintain that Anacharsis was not the creator of this wheel; and even if he was, although he was a wise man when he invented it, yet he did not invent it qua "wise man" – just as there are a great many things which wise men do as men, not as wise men. Suppose, for example, that a wise man is exceedingly fleet of foot; he will outstrip all the runners in the race by virtue of being fleet, not by virtue of his wisdom. I should like to show Posidonius some glass-blower who by his breath moulds the glass into manifold shapes which could scarcely be fashioned by the most skilful hand. Nay, these discoveries have been made since we men have ceased to discover wisdom.

But Posidonius again remarks. "Democritus is said to have discovered the arch, whose effect was that the curving line of stones, which gradually lean toward each other, is bound together by the keystone." I am inclined to pronounce this statement false. For there must have been, before Democritus, bridges and gateways in which the curvature did not begin until about the top. It seems to have quite slipped your memory that this same Democritus discovered how ivory could be softened, how, by boiling, a pebble could be transformed into an emerald, – the same process used even to-day for colouring stones which are found to be amenable to this treatment! It may have been a wise man who discovered all such things, but he did not discover them by virtue of being a wise man; for he does many things which we see done just as well, or even more skilfully and dexterously, by men who are utterly lacking in sagacity.

Do you ask what, then, the wise man has found out and what he has brought to light? First of all there is truth, and nature; and nature he has not followed as the other animals do, with eyes too dull to perceive the divine in it. In the second place, there is the law of life, and life he has made to conform to universal principles; and he has taught us, not merely to know the gods, but to follow them, and to welcome the gifts of chance precisely as if they were divine commands. He has forbidden us to give heed to false opinions, and has weighed the value of each thing by a true standard of appraisement. He has condemned those pleasures with which remorse is intermingled, and has praised those goods which will always satisfy; and he has published the truth abroad that he is most happy who has no need of happiness, and that he is most powerful who has power over himself.

I am not speaking of that philosophy which has placed the citizen outside his country and the gods outside the universe, and which has bestowed virtue upon pleasure, but rather of that philosophy which counts nothing good except what is honourable, – one which cannot be cajoled by the gifts either of man or fortune, one whose value is that it cannot be bought for any value. That this philosophy existed in such a rude age, when the arts and crafts were still unknown and when useful things could only be learned by use, – this I refuse to believe.

Next there came the fortune-favoured period when the bounties of nature lay open to all, for men's indiscriminate use, before avarice and luxury had broken the bonds which held mortals together, and they, abandoning their communal existence, had separated and turned to plunder. The men of the second age were not wise men, even though they did what wise men should do. Indeed, there is no other condition of the human race that anyone would regard more highly; and if God should commission a man to fashion earthly creatures and to bestow institutions upon peoples, this man would approve of no other system than that which obtained among the men of that age, when

> No ploughman tilled the soil, nor was it right
> To portion off or bound one's property.
> Men shared their gains, and earth more freely gave
> Her riches to her sons who sought them not.

What race of men was ever more blest than that race? They enjoyed all nature in partnership. Nature sufficed for them, now the guardian, as before she was the parent, of all; and this her gift consisted of the assured possession by each man of the common resources. Why should I not even call that race the richest among mortals, since you could not find a poor person among them?

But avarice broke in upon a condition so happily ordained, and, by its eagerness to lay something away and to turn it to its own private use, made all things the property of others, and reduced itself from boundless wealth to straitened need. It was avarice that introduced poverty and, by craving much, lost all. And so, although she now tries to make good her loss, although she adds one estate to another, evicting a neighbour either by buying him out or by wronging him, although she extends her country-seats to the size of provinces and defines ownership as meaning extensive travel through one's own property, – in spite of all these efforts of hers no enlargement of our boundaries will bring us back to the condition from which we have departed.

When there is no more that we can do, we shall possess much; but we once possessed the whole world! The very soil was more productive when untilled, and yielded more than enough for peoples who refrained from despoiling one another. Whatever gift nature had produced, men found as much pleasure in revealing it to another as in having discovered it. It was possible for no man either to surpass another or to fall short of him; what there was, was divided among unquarrelling friends. Not yet had the stronger begun to lay hands upon the weaker; not yet had the miser, by hiding away what lay before him, begun to shut off his neighbour from even the necessities of life; each cared as much for his neighbour as for himself. Armour lay unused, and the hand, unstained by human blood, had turned all its hatred against wild beasts. The men of that day, who had found in some dense grove protection against the sun, and security against the severity of winter or of rain in their mean hiding-places, spent their lives under the branches of the trees and passed tranquil nights without a sigh. Care vexes us in our purple, and routs us from our beds with the sharpest of goads; but how soft was the sleep the hard earth bestowed upon the men of that day! . No fretted and panelled ceilings hung over them, but as they lay beneath the open sky the stars glided quietly above them, and the firmament, night's noble pageant, marched swiftly by, conducting its mighty task in silence. For them by day, as well as by night, the visions of this most glorious abode were free and open. It was their joy to watch the constellations as they sank from mid-heaven and others, again, as they rose from their hidden abodes. What else but joy could it be to wander among the marvels which dotted the heavens far and wide? But you of the present day shudder at every sound your houses make, and as you sit among your frescoes the slightest creak makes you shrink in terror. They had no houses as big as cities. The air, the breezes blowing free through the open spaces, the flitting shade of crag or tree, springs crystal-clear and streams not spoiled by man's work, whether by water-pipe or by any confinement of the channel, but running at will, and meadows beautiful without the use of art, – amid such scenes were their rude homes, adorned with rustic hand. Such a dwelling was in accordance with nature; therein it was a joy to live, fearing neither the dwelling itself nor for its safety. In these days, however, our houses constitute a large portion of our dread.

But no matter how excellent and guileless was the life of the men of that age, they were not wise men; for that title is reserved for the highest achievement. Still, I would not deny that they were men of lofty spirit and – I may use the phrase – fresh from the gods. For there is no doubt that the world produced a better progeny before it was yet worn out. However, not all were endowed with mental faculties of highest perfection, though in all cases their native powers were more sturdy than ours and more fitted for toil. For nature does not bestow virtue; it is an art to become good. They, at least, searched not in the lowest dregs of the earth for gold, nor yet for silver or transparent stones; and they still were merciful even to the dumb animals – so far removed was that epoch from the custom of slaying man by man, not in anger or through fear, but just to make a show! They had as yet no embroidered garments nor did they weave cloth of gold; gold was not yet even mined.

What, then, is the conclusion of the matter? It was by reason of their ignorance of things that the men of those days were innocent; and it makes a great deal of difference whether one wills not to sin or has not the knowledge to sin. Justice was unknown to them, unknown prudence, unknown also self-control and bravery; but their rude life possessed certain qualities akin to all these virtues. Virtue is not vouchsafed to a soul unless that soul has been trained and taught, and by unremitting practice brought to perfection. For the attainment of this boon, but not in the possession of it, were we born; and even in the best of men, before you refine them by instruction, there is but the stuff of virtue, not virtue itself. Farewell.

Letter XCI - On the Lesson to be Drawn from the Burning of Lyons

Our friend Liberalis is now downcast; for he has just heard of the fire which has wiped out the colony of Lyons. Such a calamity might upset anyone at all, not to speak of a man who dearly loves his country. But this incident has served to make him inquire about the strength of his own character, which he has trained, I suppose, just to meet situations that he thought might cause him fear. I do not wonder, however, that he was free from apprehension touching an evil so unexpected and practically unheard of as this, since it is without precedent. For fire has damaged many a city, but has annihilated none. Even when fire has been hurled against the walls by the hand of a foe, the flame dies out in many places, and although continually renewed, rarely devours so wholly as to leave nothing for the sword. Even an earthquake has scarcely ever been so violent and destructive as to overthrow whole cities. Finally, no conflagration has ever before blazed forth so savagely in any town that nothing was left for a second. So many beautiful buildings, any single one of which would make a single town famous, were wrecked in one night. In time of such deep peace an event has taken place worse than men can possibly fear even in time of war. Who can believe it? When weapons are everywhere at rest and when peace prevails throughout the world, Lyons, the pride of Gaul, is missing!

Fortune has usually allowed all men, when she has assailed them collectively, to have a foreboding of that which they were destined to suffer. Every great creation has had granted to it a period of reprieve before its fall; but in this case, only a single night elapsed between the city at its greatest and the city non-existent. In short, it takes me longer to tell you it has perished than it took for the city to perish.

All this has affected our friend Liberalis, bending his will, which is usually so steadfast and erect in the face of his own trials. And not without reason has he been shaken; for it is the unexpected that puts the heaviest load upon us. Strangeness adds to the weight of calamities, and every mortal feels the greater pain as a result of that which also brings surprise.

Therefore, nothing ought to be unexpected by us. Our minds should be sent forward in advance to meet all problems, and we should consider, not what is wont to happen, but what can happen. For what is there in existence that Fortune, when she has so willed, does not drag down from the very height of its prosperity? And what is there that she does not the more violently assail the more brilliantly it shines? What is laborious or difficult for her? She does not always attack in one way or even with her full strength; at one time she summons our own hands against us; at another time, content with her own powers, she makes use of no agent in devising perils for us. No time is exempt; in the midst of our very pleasures there spring up causes of suffering. War arises in the midst of peace, and that which we depended upon for protection is transformed into a cause of fear; friend becomes enemy, ally becomes foeman. The summer calm is stirred into sudden storms, wilder than the storms of winter. With no foe in sight we are victims of such fates as foes inflict, and if other causes of disaster fail, excessive good fortune finds them for itself. The most temperate are assailed by illness, the strongest by wasting disease, the most innocent by chastisement, the most secluded by the noisy mob.

Chance chooses some new weapon by which to bring her strength to bear against us, thinking we have forgotten her. Whatever structure has been reared by a long sequence of years, at the cost of great toil and through the great kindness of the gods, is scattered and dispersed by a single day. Nay, he who has said "a day" has granted too long a postponement to swift-coming misfortune; an hour, an instant of time, suffices for the overthrow of empires! It would be some consolation for the feebleness of our selves and our works, if all things should perish as slowly as they come into being; but as it is, increases are of sluggish growth, but the way to ruin is rapid. Nothing, whether public or private, is stable; the destinies of men, no less than those of cities, are in a whirl. Amid the greatest calm terror arises, and though no external agencies stir up commotion, yet evils burst forth from sources whence they were least expected. Thrones which have stood the shock of civil and foreign wars crash to the ground though no one sets them tottering. How few the states which have carried their good fortune through to the end!

We should therefore reflect upon all contingencies, and should fortify our minds against the evils which may possibly come. Exile, the torture of disease, wars, shipwreck, – we must think on these. Chance may tear you from your country or your country from you, or may banish you to the desert; this very place, where throngs are stifling, may become a desert. Let us place before our eyes in its entirety the nature of man's lot, and if we would not be overwhelmed, or even dazed, by those unwonted evils, as if they were novel, let us summon to our minds beforehand, not as great an evil as oftentimes happens, but the very greatest evil that possibly can happen. We must reflect upon fortune fully and completely.

How often have cities in Asia, how often in Achaia, been laid low by a single shock of earthquake! How many towns in Syria, how many in Macedonia, have been swallowed up! How often has this kind of devastation laid Cyprus in ruins! How often has Paphos collapsed! Not infrequently are tidings brought to us of the utter destruction of entire cities; yet how small a part of the world are we, to whom such tidings often come!

Let us rise, therefore, to confront the operations of Fortune, and whatever happens, let us have the assurance that it is not so great as rumour advertises it to be. A rich city has been laid in ashes, the jewel of the provinces, counted as one of them and yet not included with them; rich though it was, nevertheless it was set upon a single hill, and that not very large in extent. But of all those cities, of whose magnificence and grandeur you hear today, the very traces will be blotted out by time. Do you not see how, in Achaia, the foundations of the most famous cities have already crumbled to nothing, so that no trace is left to show that they ever even existed? Not only does that which has been made with hands totter to the ground, not only is that which has been set in place by man's art and man's efforts overthrown by the passing days; nay, the peaks of mountains dissolve, whole tracts have settled, and places which once stood far from the sight of the sea are now covered by the waves. The mighty power of fires has eaten away the hills through whose sides they used to glow, and has levelled to the ground peaks which were once most lofty – the sailor's solace and his beacon. The works of nature herself are harassed; hence we ought to bear with untroubled minds the destruction of cities. They stand but to fall! This doom awaits them, one and all; it may be that some internal force, and blasts of violence which are tremendous because their way is blocked, will throw off the weight which holds then down; or that a whirlpool of raging currents, mightier because they are hidden in the bosom of the earth, will break through that which resists its power; or that the vehemence of flames will burst asunder the framework of the earth's crust; or that time, from which nothing is safe, will reduce them little by little; or that a pestilential climate will drive their inhabitants away and the mould will corrode their deserted walls. It would be tedious to recount all the ways by which fate may come; but this one thing I know: all the works of mortal man have been doomed to mortality, and in the midst of things which have been destined to die, we live!

Hence it is thoughts like these, and of this kind, which I am offering as consolation to our friend Liberalis, who burns with a love for his country that is beyond belief. Perhaps its destruction has been brought about only that it may be raised up again to a better destiny. Oftentimes a reverse has but made room for more prosperous fortune. Many structures have fallen only to rise to a greater height. Timagenes, who had a grudge against Rome and her prosperity, used to say that the only reason he was grieved when conflagrations occurred in Rome was his knowledge that better buildings would arise than those which had gone down in the flames. And probably in this city of Lyons, too, all its citizens will earnestly strive that everything shall be rebuilt better in size and security than what they have lost. May it be built to endure and, under happier auspices, for a longer existence! This is indeed but the hundredth year since this colony was founded – not the limit even of a man's lifetime. Led forth by Plancus, the natural advantages of its site have caused it to wax strong and reach the numbers which it contains to-day; and yet how many calamities of the greatest severity has it endured within the space of an old man's life!

Therefore let the mind be disciplined to understand and to endure its own lot, and let it have the knowledge that there is nothing which fortune does not dare – that she has the same jurisdiction over empires as over emperors, the same power over cities as over the citizens who dwell therein. We must not cry out at any of these calamities. Into such a world have we entered, and under such laws do we live. If you like it, obey; if not, depart whithersoever you wish. Cry out in anger if any unfair measures are taken with reference to you individually; but if this inevitable law is binding upon the highest and the lowest alike, be reconciled to fate, by which all things are dissolved. You should not estimate our worth by our funeral mounds or by these monuments of unequal size which line the road; their ashes level all men! We are unequal at birth, but are equal in death. What I say about cities I say also about their inhabitants. Ardea was captured as well as Rome. The great founder of human law has not made distinctions between us on the basis of high lineage or of illustrious names, except while we live. When, however, we come to the end which awaits mortals, he says: "Depart, ambition! To all creatures that burden the earth let one and the same law apply!" For enduring all things, we are equal; no one is more frail than another, no one more certain of his own life on the morrow.

441

Alexander, king of Macedon, began to study geometry; unhappy man, because he would thereby learn how puny was that earth of which he had seized but a fraction! Unhappy man, I repeat, because he was bound to understand that he was bearing a false title. For who can be "great" in that which is puny? The lessons which were being taught him were intricate and could be learned only by assiduous application; they were not the kind to be comprehended by a madman, who let his thoughts range beyond the ocean. "Teach me something easy!" he cries; but his teacher answers: "These things are the same for all, as hard for one as for another." Imagine that nature is saying to us: "Those things of which you complain are the same for all. I cannot give anything easier to any man, but whoever wishes will make things easier for himself." In what way? By equanimity. You must suffer pain, and thirst, and hunger, and old age too, if a longer stay among men shall be granted you; you must be sick, and you must suffer loss and death. Nevertheless, you should not believe those whose noisy clamour surrounds you; none of these things is an evil, none is beyond your power to bear, or is burdensome. It is only by common opinion that there is anything formidable in them. Your fearing death is therefore like your fear of gossip. But what is more foolish than a man afraid of words? Our friend Demetrius is wont to put it cleverly when he says: "For me the talk of ignorant men is like the rumblings which issue from the belly. For," he adds, "what difference does it make to me whether such rumblings come from above or from below?" What madness it is to be afraid of disrepute in the judgment of the disreputable! Just as you have had no cause for shrinking in terror from the talk of men, so you have no cause now to shrink from these things, which you would never fear had not their talk forced fear upon you. Does it do any harm to a good man to be besmirched by unjust gossip? . Then let not this sort of thing damage death, either, in our estimation; death also is in bad odour. But no one of those who malign death has made trial of it.

Meanwhile it is foolhardy to condemn that of which you are ignorant. This one thing, however, you do know – that death is helpful to many, that it sets many free from tortures, want, ailments, sufferings, and weariness. We are in the power of nothing when once we have death in our own power! Farewell.

Letter XCII - On the Happy Life

You and I will agree, I think, that outward things are sought for the satisfaction of the body, that the body is cherished out of regard for the soul, and that in the soul there are certain parts which minister to us, enabling us to move and to sustain life, bestowed upon us just for the sake of the primary part of us. In this primary part there is something irrational, and something rational. The former obeys the latter, while the latter is the only thing that is not referred back to another, but rather refers all things to itself. For the divine reason also is set in supreme command over all things, and is itself subject to none; and even this reason which we possess is the same, because it is derived from the divine reason. Now if we are agreed on this point, it is natural that we shall be agreed on the following also – namely, that the happy life depends upon this and this alone: our attainment of perfect reason. For it is naught but this that keeps the soul from being bowed down, that stands its ground against Fortune; whatever the condition of their affairs may be, it keeps men untroubled. And that alone is a good which is never subject to impairment. That man, I declare, is happy whom nothing makes less strong than he is; he keeps to the heights, leaning upon none but himself; for one who sustains himself by any prop may fall. If the case is otherwise, then things which do not pertain to us will begin to have great influence over us. But who desires Fortune to have the upper hand, or what sensible man prides himself upon that which is not his own?

What is the happy life? It is peace of mind, and lasting tranquillity. This will be yours if you possess greatness of soul; it will be yours if you possess the steadfastness that resolutely clings to a good judgment just reached. How does a man reach this condition? By gaining a complete view of truth, by maintaining, in all that he does, order, measure, fitness, and a will that is inoffensive and kindly, that is intent upon reason and never departs therefrom, that commands at the same time love and admiration. In short, to give you the principle in brief compass, the wise man's soul ought to be such as would be proper for a god. What more can one desire who possesses all honourable things? For if dishonourable things can contribute to the best estate, then there will be the possibility of a happy life under conditions which do not include an honourable life. And what is more base or foolish than to connect the good of a rational soul with things irrational? Yet there are certain philosophers who hold that the Supreme Good admits of increase because it is hardly complete when the gifts of fortune are adverse. Even Antipater, one of the great leaders of this school, admits that he ascribes some influence to externals, though only a very slight influence. You see, however, what absurdity lies in not being content with the daylight unless it is increased by a tiny fire. What importance can a spark have in the midst of this clear sunlight? If you are not contented with only that which is honourable, it must follow that you desire in addition either the kind of quiet which the Greeks call "undisturbedness," or else pleasure. But the former may be attained in any case. For the mind is free from disturbance when it is fully free to contemplate the universe, and nothing distracts it from the contemplation of nature. The second, pleasure, is simply the good of cattle. We are but adding the irrational to the rational, the dishonourable to the honourable. A pleasant physical sensation affects this life of ours; why, therefore, do you hesitate to say that all is well with a man just because all is well with his appetite? And do you rate, I will not say among heroes, but among men, the person whose Supreme Good is a matter of flavours and colours and sounds? Nay, let him withdraw from the ranks of this, the noblest class of living beings, second only to the gods; let him herd with the dumb brutes – an animal whose delight is in fodder!

The irrational part of the soul is twofold: the one part is spirited, ambitious, uncontrolled; its seat is in the passions; the other is lowly, sluggish, and devoted to pleasure. Philosophers have neglected the former, which, though unbridled, is yet better, and is certainly more courageous and more

443

worthy of a man, and have regarded the latter, which is nerveless and ignoble, as indispensable to the happy life. They have ordered reason to serve this latter; they have made the Supreme Good of the noblest living being an abject and mean affair, and a monstrous hybrid, too, composed of various members which harmonize but ill. For as our Vergil, describing Scylla, says

> *Above, a human face and maiden's breast,*
> *A beauteous breast, – below, a monster huge*
> *Of bulk and shapeless, with a dolphin's tail*
> *Joined to a wolf-like belly.*

And yet to this Scylla are tacked on the forms of wild animals, dreadful and swift; but from what monstrous shapes have these wiseacres compounded wisdom! Man's primary art is virtue itself; there is joined to this the useless and fleeting flesh, fitted only for the reception of food, as Posidonius remarks. This divine virtue ends in foulness, and to the higher parts, which are worshipful and heavenly, there is fastened a sluggish and flabby animal. As for the second desideratum, – quiet, – although it would indeed not of itself be of any benefit to the soul, yet it would relieve the soul of hindrances; pleasure, on the contrary, actually destroys the soul and softens all its vigour. What elements so inharmonious as these can be found united? To that which is most vigorous is joined that which is most sluggish, to that which is austere that which is far from serious, to that which is most holy that which is unrestrained even to the point of impurity. "What, then," comes the retort, "if good health, rest, and freedom from pain are not likely to hinder virtue, shall you not seek all these?" Of course I shall seek them, but not because they are goods, – I shall seek them because they are according to nature and because they will be acquired through the exercise of good judgment on my part. What, then, will be good in them? This alone, – that it is a good thing to choose them. For when I don suitable attire, or walk as I should, or dine as I ought to dine, it is not my dinner, or my walk, or my dress that are goods, but the deliberate choice which I show in regard to them, as I observe, in each thing I do, a mean that conforms with reason. Let me also add that the choice of neat clothing is a fitting object of a man's efforts; for man is by nature a neat and well-groomed animal. Hence the choice of neat attire, and not neat attire in itself, is a good; since the good is not in the thing selected, but in the quality of the selection. Our actions are honourable, but not the actual things which we do. And you may assume that what I have said about dress applies also to the body. For nature has surrounded our soul with the body as with a sort of garment; the body is its cloak. But who has ever reckoned the value of clothes by the wardrobe which contained them? The scabbard does not make the sword good or bad. Therefore, with regard to the body I shall return the same answer to you, – that, if I have the choice, I shall choose health and strength, but that the good involved will be my judgment regarding these things, and not the things themselves.

Another retort is: "Granted that the wise man is happy; nevertheless, he does not attain the Supreme Good which we have defined, unless the means also which nature provides for its attainment are at his call. So, while one who possesses virtue cannot be unhappy, yet one cannot be perfectly happy if one lacks such natural gifts as health, or soundness of limb." . But in saying this, you grant the alternative which seems the more difficult to believe, – that the man who is in the midst of unremitting and extreme pain is not wretched, nay, is even happy; and you deny that which is much less serious, – that he is completely happy. And yet, if virtue can keep a man from being wretched, it will be an easier task for it to render him completely happy. For the difference between happiness and complete happiness is less than that between wretchedness and happiness. Can it be possible that a thing which is so powerful as to snatch a man from disaster, and place him among the happy, cannot also accomplish what remains, and render him supremely happy? Does its strength fail at the very top of the climb? . There are in life things which are advantageous and disadvantageous, – both beyond our control. If a good man, in spite of being weighed down by all kinds of disadvantages, is not wretched, how is he not supremely happy, no matter if he does lack certain advantages? For as he is not weighted down to wretchedness by his burden of disadvantages, so he is not withdrawn from supreme happiness through lack of any advantages; nay, he is just as supremely happy without the advantages as he is free from wretchedness though under the load of his disadvantages. Otherwise, if his good can be impaired, it can be snatched from him altogether.

A short space above, I remarked that a tiny fire does not add to the sun's light. For by reason of the sun's brightness any light that shines apart from the sunlight is blotted out. "But," one may say, "there are certain objects that stand in the way even of the sunlight." The sun, however, is unimpaired even in the midst of obstacles, and, though an object may intervene and cut off our view thereof, the sun sticks to his work and goes on his course. Whenever he shines forth from amid the clouds, he is no smaller, nor less punctual either, than when he is free from clouds; since it makes a great deal of difference whether there is merely something in the way of his light or something which interferes with his shining. Similarly, obstacles take nothing away from virtue; it is no smaller, but merely shines with less brilliancy. In our eyes, it may perhaps be less visible and less luminous than before; but as regards itself it is the same and, like the sun when he is eclipsed, is still, though in secret, putting forth its strength. Disasters, therefore, and losses, and wrongs, have only the same power over virtue that a cloud has over the sun.

We meet with one person who maintains that a wise man who has met with bodily misfortune is neither wretched nor happy. But he also is in error, for he is putting the results of chance upon a parity with the virtues, and is attributing only the same influence to things that are honourable as to things that are devoid of honour. But what is more detestable and more unworthy than to put contemptible things in the same class with things worthy of reverence! For reverence is due to justice, duty, loyalty, bravery, and prudence; on the contrary, those attributes are worthless with which the most worthless men are often blessed in fuller measure, – such as a sturdy leg, strong shoulders, good teeth, and healthy and solid muscles. Again, if the wise man whose body is a trial to him shall be regarded as neither wretched nor happy, but shall be left in a sort of half-way position, his life also will be neither desirable nor undesirable. But what is so foolish as to say that the wise man's life is not desirable? And what is so far beyond the bounds of credence as the opinion that any life is neither desirable nor undesirable? Again, if bodily ills do not make a man wretched, they consequently allow him to be happy. For things which have no power to change his condition for the worse, have not the power, either, to disturb that condition when it is at its best.

"But," someone will say, "we know what is cold and what is hot; a lukewarm temperature lies between. Similarly, A is happy, and B is wretched, and C is neither happy nor wretched." I wish to examine this figure, which is brought into play against us. If I add to your lukewarm water a larger quantity of cold water, the result will be cold water. But if I pour in a larger quantity of hot water, the water will finally become hot. In the case, however, of your man who is neither wretched nor happy, no matter how much I add to his troubles, he will not be unhappy, according to your argument; hence your figure offers no analogy. Again, suppose that I set before you a man who is neither miserable nor happy. I add blindness to his misfortunes; he is not rendered unhappy. I cripple him; he is not rendered unhappy. I add afflictions which are unceasing and severe; he is not rendered unhappy. Therefore, one whose life is not changed to misery by all these ills is not dragged by them, either, from his life of happiness. Then if, as you say, the wise man cannot fall from happiness to wretchedness, he cannot fall into non-happiness. For how, if one has begun to slip, can one stop at any particular place? That which prevents him from rolling to the bottom, keeps him at the summit. Why, you urge, may not a happy life possibly be destroyed? It cannot even be disjointed; and for that reason virtue is itself of itself sufficient for the happy life.

"But," it is said, "is not the wise man happier if he has lived longer and has been distracted by no pain, than one who has always been compelled to grapple with evil fortune?" Answer me now, – is he any better or more honourable? If he is not, then he is not happier either. In order to live more happily, he must live more rightly; if he cannot do that, then he cannot live more happily either. Virtue cannot be strained tighter, and therefore neither can the happy life, which depends on virtue. For virtue is so great a good that it is not affected by such insignificant assaults upon it as shortness of life, pain, and the various bodily vexations. For pleasure does not deserve that. virtue should even glance at it. Now what is the chief thing in virtue? It is the quality of not needing a single day beyond the present, and of not reckoning up the days that are ours; in the slightest possible moment of time virtue completes an eternity of good. These goods seem to us incredible and transcending man's nature; for we measure its grandeur by the standard of our own weakness, and we call our vices by the name of virtue. Furthermore, does it not seem just as incredible that any man in the midst of extreme suffering should say, "I am happy"? And yet this utterance was heard in the very factory of pleasure, when Epicurus said: "To-day and one other day have been the happiest of all!" although in the one case he was tortured by strangury, and in the other by the incurable pain of an ulcerated stomach. Why, then, should those goods which virtue bestows be incredible in the sight of us, who cultivate virtue, when they are found even in those who acknowledge pleasure as their mistress? These also, ignoble and base-minded as they are, declare that even in the midst of excessive pain and misfortune the wise man will be neither wretched nor happy. And yet this also is incredible, – nay, still more incredible, than the other case. For I do not understand how, if virtue falls from her heights, she can help being hurled all the way to the bottom. She either must preserve one in happiness, or, if driven from this position, she will not prevent us from becoming unhappy. If virtue only stands her ground, she cannot be driven from the field; she must either conquer or be conquered.

But some say: "Only to the immortal gods is given virtue and the happy life; we can attain but the shadow, as it were, and semblance of such goods as theirs. We approach them, but we never reach them." Reason, however, is a common attribute of both gods and men; in the gods it is already perfected, in us it is capable of being perfected. But it is our vices that bring us to despair; for the second class of rational being, man, is of an inferior order, – a guardian, as it were, who is too unstable to hold fast to what is best, his judgment still wavering and uncertain. He may require the faculties of sight and hearing, good health, a bodily exterior that is not loathsome, and, besides, greater length of days conjoined with an unimpaired constitution. Though by means of reason he can lead a life which will not bring regrets, yet there resides in this imperfect creature, man, a certain power that makes for badness, because he possesses a mind which is easily moved to perversity. Suppose, however, the badness which is in full view, and has previously been stirred to activity, to be removed; the man is still not a good man, but he is being moulded to goodness. One, however, in whom there is lacking any quality that makes for goodness, is bad. But

He in whose body virtue dwells, and spirit
E'er present

is equal to the gods; mindful of his origin, he strives to return thither. No man does wrong in attempting to regain the heights from which he once came down. And why should you not believe that something of divinity exists in one who is a part of God? All this universe which encompasses us is one, and it is God; we are associates of God; we are his members. Our soul has capabilities, and is carried thither, if vices do not hold it down. Just as it is the nature of our bodies to stand erect and look upward to the sky, so the soul, which may reach out as far as it will, was framed by nature to this end, that it should desire equality with the gods. And if it makes use of its powers and stretches upward into its proper region it is by no alien path that it struggles toward the heights. t would be a great task to journey heavenwards; the soul but returns thither. When once it has found the road, it boldly marches on, scornful of all things. It casts, no backward glance at wealth; gold and silver – things which are fully worthy of the gloom in which they once lay – it values not by the sheen which smites the eyes of the ignorant, but by the mire of ancient days, whence our greed first detached and dug them out.

The soul, I affirm, knows that riches are stored elsewhere than in men's heaped-up treasure-houses; that it is the soul, and not the strong-box, which should be filled. It is the soul that men may set in dominion over all things, and may install as owner of the universe, so that it may limit its riches only by the boundaries of East and West, and, like the gods, may possess all things; and that it may, with its own vast resources, look down from on high upon the wealthy, no one of whom rejoices as much in his own wealth as he resents the wealth of another. When the soul has transported itself to this lofty height, it regards the body also, since it is a burden which must be borne, not as a thing to love, but as a thing to oversee; nor is it subservient to that over which it is set in mastery. For no man is free who is a slave to his body. Indeed, omitting all the other masters which are brought into being by excessive care for the body, the sway which the body itself exercises is captious and fastidious. Forth from this body the soul issues, now with unruffled spirit, now with exultation, and, when once it has gone forth, asks not what shall be the end of the deserted day. No; just as we do not take thought for the clippings of the hair and the beard, even so that divine soul, when it is about to issue forth from the mortal man, regards the destination of its earthly vessel – whether it be consumed by fire, or shut in by a stone, or buried in the earth, or torn by wild beasts – as being of no more concern to itself than is the afterbirth to a child just born. And whether this body shall be cast out and plucked to pieces by birds, or devoured when *thrown to the sea-dogs as prey* how does that concern him who is nothing? Nay even when it is among the living, the soul fears nothing that may happen to the body after death; for though such things may have been threats, they were not enough to terrify the soul previous to the moment of death. It says; "I am not frightened by the executioner's hook, nor by the revolting mutilation of the corpse which is exposed to the scorn of those who would witness the spectacle. I ask no man to perform the last rites for me; I entrust my remains to none. Nature has made provision that none shall go unburied. Time will lay away one whom cruelty has cast forth." Those were eloquent words which Maecenas uttered:

I want no tomb; for Nature doth provide
For outcast bodies burial.

You would imagine that this was the saying of a man of strict principles. He was indeed a man of noble and robust native gifts, but in prosperity he impaired these gifts by laxness. Farewell.

Letter XCIII - On the Quality, as Contrasted with the Length, of Life

While reading the letter in which you were lamenting the death of the philosopher Metronax as if he might have, and indeed ought to have, lived longer, I missed the spirit of fairness which abounds in all your discussions concerning men and things, but is lacking when you approach one single subject, – as is indeed the case with us all. In other words, I have noticed many who deal fairly with their fellow-men, but none who deals fairly with the gods. We rail every day at Fate, saying "Why has A been carried off in the very middle of his career? Why is not B. carried off instead? Why should he prolong his old age, which is a burden to himself as well as to others?"

But tell me, pray, do you consider it fairer that you should obey Nature, or that Nature should obey you? And what difference does it make how soon you depart from a place which you must depart from sooner or later? We should strive, not to live long, but to live rightly; for to achieve long life you have need of Fate only, but for right living you need the soul. A life is really long if it is a full life; but fullness is not attained until the soul has rendered to itself its proper Good, that is, until it has assumed control over itself. What benefit does this older man derive from the eighty years he has spent in idleness? A person like him has not lived; he has merely tarried awhile in life. Nor has he died late in life; he has simply been a long time dying. He has lived eighty years, has he? That depends upon the date from which you reckon his death! Your other friend, however, departed in the bloom of his manhood. But he had fulfilled all the duties of a good citizen, a good friend, a good son; in no respect had he fallen short. His age may have been incomplete, but his life was complete. The other man has lived eighty years, has he? Nay, he has existed eighty years, unless perchance you mean by "he has lived" what we mean when we say that a tree "lives."

Pray, let us see to it, my dear Lucilius, that our lives, like jewels of great price, be noteworthy not because of their width but because of their weight. Let us measure them by their performance, not by their duration. Would you know wherein lies the difference between this hardy man who, despising Fortune, has served through every campaign of life and has attained to life's Supreme Good, and that other person over whose head many years have passed? The former exists even after his death; the latter has died even before he was dead.

We should therefore praise, and number in the company of the blest, that man who has invested well the portion of time, however little, that has been allotted to him; for such a one has seen the true light. He has not been one of the common herd. He has not only lived, but flourished. Sometimes he enjoyed fair skies; sometimes, as often happens, it was only through the clouds that there flashed to him the radiance of the mighty star. Why do you ask: "How long did he live?" He still lives! At one bound he has passed over into posterity and has consigned himself to the guardianship of memory.

. And yet I would not on that account decline for myself a few additional years; although, if my life's space be shortened, I shall not say that I have lacked aught that is essential to a happy life. For I have not planned to live up to the very last day that my greedy hopes had promised me; nay, I have looked upon every day as if it were my last. Why ask the date of my birth, or whether I am still enrolled on the register of the younger men? What I have is my own. Just as one of small stature can be a perfect man, so a life of small compass can be a perfect life. Age ranks among the external things. How long I am to exist is not mine to decide, but how long I shall go on existing in my present way is in my own control. This is the only thing you have the right to require of me, – that I shall cease to measure out an inglorious age as it were in darkness, and devote myself to living instead of being carried along past life.

And what, you ask, is the fullest span of life? It is living until you possess wisdom. He who has attained wisdom has reached, not the furthermost, but the most important, goal. Such a one may indeed exult boldly and give thanks to the gods – aye, and to himself also – and he may count himself Nature's creditor for having lived. He will indeed have the right to do so, for he has paid her back a better life than he has received. He has set up the pattern of a good man, showing the quality and the greatness of a good man. Had another year been added, it would merely have been like the past.

And yet how long are we to keep living? We have had the joy of learning the truth about the universe. We know from what beginnings Nature arises; how she orders the course of the heavens; by what successive changes she summons back the year; how she has brought to an end all things that ever have been, and has established herself as the only end of her own being. We know that the stars move by their own motion, and that nothing except the earth stands still, while all the other bodies run on with uninterrupted swiftness. We know how the moon outstrips the sun; why it is that the slower leaves the swifter behind; in what manner she receives her light, or loses it again; what brings on the night, and what brings back the day. To that place you must go where you are to have a closer view of all these things. "And yet," says the wise man, "I do not depart more valiantly because of this hope – because I judge the path lies clear before me to my own gods. I have indeed earned admission to their presence, and in fact have already been in their company; I have sent my soul to them as they had previously sent theirs to me. But suppose that I am utterly annihilated, and that after death nothing mortal remains; I have no less courage, even if, when I depart, my course leads – nowhere."

"But," you say, "he has not lived as many years as he might have lived." There are books which contain very few lines, admirable and useful in spite of their size; and there are also the Annals of Tanusius – you know how bulky the book is, and what men say of it. This is the case with the long life of certain persons, – a state which resembles the Annals of Tanusius! . Do you regard as more fortunate the fighter who is slain on the last day of the games than one who goes to his death in the middle of the festivities? Do you believe that anyone is so foolishly covetous of life that he would rather have his throat cut in the dressing-room than in the amphitheatre? It is by no longer an interval than this that we precede one another. Death visits each and all; the slayer soon follows the slain. It is an insignificant trifle, after all, that people discuss with so much concern. And anyhow, what does it matter for how long a time you avoid that which you cannot escape? Farewell.

Letter XCIV - On the Value of Advice

That department of philosophy which supplies precepts appropriate to the individual case, instead of framing them for mankind at large – which, for instance, advises how a husband should conduct himself towards his wife, or how a father should bring up his children, or how a master should rule his slaves – this department of philosophy, I say, is accepted by some as the only significant part, while the other departments are rejected on the ground that they stray beyond the sphere of practical needs – as if any man could give advice concerning a portion of life without having first gained a knowledge of the sum of life as a whole!

But Aristo the Stoic, on the contrary, believes the above-mentioned department to be of slight import – he holds that it does not sink into the mind, having in it nothing but old wives' precepts, and that the greatest benefit is derived from the actual dogmas of philosophy and from the definition of the Supreme Good. When a man has gained a complete understanding of this definition and has thoroughly learned it, he can frame for himself a precept directing what is to be done in a given case. Just as the student of javelin-throwing keeps aiming at a fixed target and thus trains the hand to give direction to the missile, and when, by instruction and practice, he has gained the desired ability he can then employ it against any target he wishes (having learned to strike not any random object, but precisely the object at which he has aimed), – he who has equipped himself for the whole of life does not need to be advised concerning each separate item, because he is now trained to meet his problem as a whole; for he knows not merely how he should live with his wife or his son, but how he should live aright. In this knowledge there is also included the proper way of living with wife and children.

Cleanthes holds that this department of wisdom is indeed useful, but that it is a feeble thing unless it is derived from general principles – that is, unless it is based upon a knowledge of the actual dogmas of philosophy and its main headings. This subject is therefore twofold, leading to two separate lines of inquiry: first, Is it useful or useless? and, and second, can it of itself produce a good man? – in other words, Is it superfluous, or does it render all other departments superfluous?

Those who urge the view that this department is superfluous argue as follows: "If an object that is held in front of the eyes interferes with the vision, it must be removed. For just as long as it is in the way, it is a waste of time to offer such precepts as these: 'Walk thus and so; extend your hand in that direction.' Similarly, when something blinds a man's soul and hinders it from seeing a line of duty clearly, there is no use in advising him: 'Live thus and so with your father, thus and so with your wife.' For precepts will be of no avail while the mind is clouded with error; only when the cloud is dispersed will it be clear what one's duty is in each case. Otherwise, you will merely be showing the sick man what he ought to do if he were well, instead of making him well. Suppose you are trying to reveal to the poor man the art of 'acting rich'; how can the thing be accomplished as long as his poverty is unaltered? You are trying to make clear to a starveling in what manner he is to act the part of one with a well-filled stomach; the first requisite, however, is to relieve him of the hunger that grips his vitals.

"The same thing, I assure you, holds good of all faults; the faults themselves must be removed, and precepts should not be given which cannot possibly be carried out while the faults remain. Unless you drive out the false opinions under which we suffer, the miser will never receive instruction as to the proper use of his money, nor the coward regarding the way to scorn danger. You must make the miser know that money is neither a good nor an evil; show him men of wealth who are miserable to the last degree. You must make the coward know that the things which generally frighten us out of our wits are less to be feared than rumour advertises them to be, whether the object of fear be suffering or death; that when death comes – fixed by law for us all to suffer – it is often a great solace to reflect that it can never come again; that in the midst of suffering resoluteness of soul will be as good as a cure, for the soul renders lighter any burden that it endures with stubborn defiance. Remember that pain has this most excellent quality: if prolonged it cannot be severe, and if severe it cannot be prolonged; and that we should bravely accept whatever commands the inevitable laws of the universe lay upon us.

"When by means of such doctrines you have brought the erring man to a sense of his own condition, when he has learned that the happy life is not that which conforms to pleasure, but that which conforms to Nature, when he has fallen deeply in love with virtue as man's sole good and has avoided baseness as man's sole evil, and when he knows that all other things – riches, office, health, strength, dominion – fall in between and are not to be reckoned either among goods or among evils, then he will not need a monitor for every separate action, to say to him: 'Walk thus and so, eat thus and so. This is the conduct proper for a man and that for a woman; this for a married man and that for a bachelor.' Indeed, the persons who take the greatest pains to proffer such advice are themselves unable to put it into practice. It is thus that the pedagogue advises the boy, and the grandmother her grandson; it is the hottest-tempered schoolmaster who contends that one should never lose one's temper. Go into an elementary school, and you will learn that just such pronouncements, emanating from high-browed philosophers, are to be found in the lesson-book for boys!

"Shall you then offer precepts that are clear, or precepts that are doubtful? Those which are clear need no counsellor, and doubtful precepts gain no credence; so the giving of precepts is superfluous. Indeed you should study the problem in this way: if you are counselling someone on a matter which is of doubtful clearness and doubtful meaning, you must supplement your precepts by proofs; and if you must resort to proofs, your means of proof are more effective and more satisfactory in themselves. 'It is thus that you must treat your friend, thus your fellow citizen, thus your associate.' And why? 'Because it is just.' Yet I can find all that material included under the head of Justice. I find there that fair play is desirable in itself, that we are not forced into it by fear nor hired to that end for pay, and that no man is just who is attracted by anything in this virtue other than the virtue itself. After convincing myself of this view and thoroughly absorbing it, what good can I obtain from such precepts, which only teach one who is already trained? To one who knows, it is superfluous to give precepts; to one who does not know, it is insufficient. For he must be told, not only what he is being instructed to do, but also why. I repeat, are such precepts useful to him who has correct ideas about good and evil, or to one who has them not? The latter will receive no benefit from you; for some idea that clashes with your counsel has already monopolized his attention. He who has made a careful decision as to what should be sought and what should be avoided knows what he ought to do, without a single word from you. Therefore, that whole department of philosophy may be abolished.

"There are two reasons why we go astray: either there is in the soul an evil quality which has been brought about by wrong opinions, or, even if not possessed by false ideas, the soul is prone to falsehood and rapidly corrupted by some outward appearance which attracts it in the wrong direction. For this reason it is our duty either to treat carefully the diseased mind and free it from faults, or to take possession of the mind when it is still unoccupied and yet inclined to what is evil. Both these results can be attained by the main doctrines of philosophy; therefore the giving of such precepts is of no use. Besides, if we give forth precepts to each individual, the task is stupendous. For one class of advice should be given to the financier, another to the farmer, another to the business man, another to one who cultivates the good graces of royalty, another to him who will seek the friendship of his equals, another to him who will court those of lower rank. In the case of marriage, you will advise one person how he should conduct himself with a wife who before her marriage was a maiden, and another how he should behave with a woman who had previously been wedded to another; how the husband of a rich woman should act, or another man with a dowerless spouse. Or do you not think that there is some difference between a barren woman and one who bears children, between one advanced in years and a mere girl, between a mother and a step-mother? We cannot include all the types, and yet each type requires separate treatment; but the laws of philosophy are concise and are binding in all cases. Moreover, the precepts of wisdom should be definite and certain: when things cannot be defined, they are outside the sphere of wisdom; for wisdom knows the proper limits of things.

"We should therefore do away with this department of precepts, because it cannot afford to all what it promises only to a few; wisdom, however, embraces all. Between the insanity of people in general and the insanity which is subject to medical treatment there is no difference, except that the latter is suffering from disease and the former from false opinions. In the one case, the symptoms of madness may be traced to ill-health; the other is the ill-health of the mind. If one should offer precepts to a madman – how he ought to speak, how he ought to walk, how he ought to conduct himself in public and private, he would be more of a lunatic than the person whom he was advising. What is really necessary is to treat the black bile and remove the essential cause of the madness. And this is what should also be done in the other case – that of the mind diseased. The madness itself must be shaken off; otherwise, your words of advice will vanish into thin air."

This is what Aristo says; and I shall answer his arguments one by one. First, in opposition to what he says about one's obligation to remove that which blocks the eye and hinders the vision. I admit that such a person does not need precepts in order to see, but that he needs treatment for the curing of his eyesight and the getting rid of the hindrance that handicaps him. For it is Nature that gives us our eyesight; and he who removes obstacles restores to Nature her proper function. But Nature does not teach us our duty in every case. Again, if a man's cataract is cured, he cannot, immediately after his recovery, give back their eyesight to other men also; but when we are freed from evil we can free others also. There is no need of encouragement, or even of counsel, for the eye to be able to distinguish different colours; black and white can be differentiated without prompting from another. The mind, on the other hand, needs many precepts in order to see what it should do in life; although in eye-treatment also the physician not only accomplishes the cure, but gives advice into the bargain. He says: "There is no reason why you should at once expose your weak vision to a dangerous glare; begin with darkness, and then go into half-lights, and finally be more bold, accustoming yourself gradually to the bright light of day. There is no reason why you should study immediately after eating; there is no reason why you should impose hard tasks upon your eyes when they are swollen and inflamed; avoid winds and strong blasts of cold air that blow into your face," – and other suggestions of the same sort, which are just as valuable as drugs themselves. The physician's art supplements remedies by advice.

"But," comes the reply, "error is the source of sin; precepts do not remove error, nor do they rout our false opinions on the subject of Good and Evil." I admit that precepts alone are not effective in overthrowing the mind's mistaken beliefs; but they do not on that account fail to be of service when they accompany other measures also. In the first place, they refresh the memory; in the second place, when sorted into their proper classes, the matters which showed themselves in a jumbled mass when considered as a whole, can be considered in this with greater care. According to our opponent's theory, you might even say that consolation, and exhortation were superfluous. Yet they are not superfluous; neither, therefore, is counsel.

"But it is folly," they retort, "to prescribe what a sick man ought to do, just as if he were well, when you should really restore his health; for without health precepts are not worth a jot." But have not sick men and sound men something in common, concerning which they need continual advice? For example, not to grasp greedily after food, and to avoid getting over-tired. Poor and rich have certain precepts which fit them both. "Cure their greed, then," people say, "and you will not need to lecture either the poor or the rich, provided that in the case of each of them the craving has subsided." But is it not one thing to be free from lust for money, and another thing to know how to use this money? Misers do not know the proper limits in money matters, but even those who are not misers fail to comprehend its use. Then comes the reply: "Do away with error, and your precepts become unnecessary." That is wrong; for suppose that avarice is slackened, that luxury is confined, that rashness is reined in, and that laziness is pricked by the spur; even after vices are removed, we must continue to learn what we ought to do, and how we ought to do it.

"Nothing," it is said, "will be accomplished by applying advice to the more serious faults." No; and not even medicine can master incurable diseases; it is nevertheless used in some cases as a remedy, in others as a relief. Not even the power of universal philosophy, though it summon all its strength for the purpose, will remove from the soul what is now a stubborn and chronic disease. But Wisdom, merely because she cannot cure everything, is not incapable of making cures. People say: "What good does it do to point out the obvious?" A great deal of good; for we sometimes know facts without paying attention to them. Advice is not teaching; it merely engages the attention and rouses us, and concentrates the memory, and keeps it from losing grip. We miss much that is set before our very eyes. Advice is, in fact, a sort of exhortation. The mind often tries not to notice even that which lies before our eyes; we must therefore force upon it the knowledge of things that are perfectly well known. One might repeat here the saying of Calvus about Vatinius: "You all know that bribery has been going on, and everyone knows that you know it." You know that friendship should be scrupulously honoured, and yet you do not hold it in honour. You know that a man does wrong in requiring chastity of his wife while he himself is intriguing with the wives of other men; you know that, as your wife should have no dealings with a lover, neither should you yourself with a mistress; and yet you do not act accordingly. Hence, you must be continually brought to remember these facts; for they should not be in storage, but ready for use. And whatever is wholesome should be often discussed and often brought before the mind, so that it may be not only familiar to us, but also ready to hand. And remember, too, that in this way what is clear often becomes clearer.

"But if," comes the answer, "your precepts are not obvious, you will be bound to add proofs; hence the proofs, and not the precepts, will be helpful." But cannot the influence of the monitor avail even without proofs? It is like the opinions of a legal expert, which hold good even though the reasons for them are not delivered. Moreover, the precepts which are given are of great weight in themselves, whether they be woven into the fabric of song, or condensed into prose proverbs, like the famous Wisdom of Cato "Buy not what you need, but what you must have. That which you do not need, is dear even at a farthing." Or those oracular or oracular-like replies, such as . "Be thrifty with time!" "Know thyself!" Shall you need to be told the meaning when someone repeats to you lines like these:

> Forgetting trouble is the way to cure it.
> Fortune favours the brave, but the coward is foiled by his faint heart.

Such maxims need no special pleader; they go straight to our emotions, and help us simply because Nature is exercising her proper function. The soul carries within itself the seed of everything that is honourable, and this seed is stirred to growth by advice, as a spark that is fanned by a gentle breeze develops its natural fire. Virtue is aroused by a touch, a shock. Moreover, there are certain things which, though in the mind, yet are not ready to hand but begin to function easily as soon as they are put into words. Certain things lie scattered about in various places, and it is impossible for the unpractised mind to arrange them in order. Therefore, we should bring them into unity, and join them, so that they may be more powerful and more of an uplift to the soul. Or, if precepts do not avail at all, then every method of instruction should be abolished, and we should be content with Nature alone.

Those who maintain this view do not understand that one man is lively and alert of wit, another sluggish and dull, while certainly some men have more intelligence than others. The strength of the wit is nourished and kept growing by precepts; it adds new points of view to those which are inborn and corrects depraved ideas. "But suppose," people retort, "that a man is not the possessor of sound dogmas, how can advice help him when he is chained down by vicious dogmas?" In this, assuredly, that he is freed there-from; for his natural disposition has not been crushed, but over-shadowed and kept down. Even so it goes on endeavouring to rise again, struggling against the influences that make for evil; but when it wins support and receives the aid of precepts, it grows stronger, provided only that the chronic trouble has not corrupted or annihilated the natural man. For in such a case, not even the training that comes from philosophy, striving with all its might, will make restoration. What difference, indeed, – is there between the dogmas of philosophy and precepts, unless it be this – that the former are general and the latter special? Both deal with advice – the one through the universal, the other through the particular.

Some say: "If one is familiar with upright and honourable dogmas, it will be superfluous to advise him." By no means; for this person has indeed learned to do things which he ought to do; but he does not see with sufficient clearness what these things are. For we are hindered from accomplishing praiseworthy deeds not only by our emotions, but also by want of practice in discovering the demands of a particular situation. Our minds are often under good control, and yet at the same time are inactive and untrained in finding the path of duty, – and advice makes this clear. Again, it is written: "Cast out all false opinions concerning Good and Evil, but replace them with true opinions; then advice will have no function to perform." Order in the soul can doubtless be established in this way; but these are not the only ways. For although we may infer by proofs just what Good and Evil are, nevertheless precepts have their proper role. Prudence and justice consist of certain duties; and duties are set in order by precepts. Moreover, judgment as to Good and Evil is itself strengthened by following up our duties, and precepts conduct us to this end. For both are in accord with each other; nor can precepts take the lead unless the duties follow. They observe their natural order; hence precepts clearly come first.

"Precepts," it is said "are numberless." Wrong again! For they are not numberless so far as concerns important and essential things. Of course there are slight distinctions, due to the time, or the place, or the person; but even in these cases, precepts are given which have a general application. "No one, however," it is said, "cures madness by precepts, and therefore not wickedness either." There is a distinction; for if you rid a man of insanity, he becomes sane again, but if we have removed false opinions, insight into practical conduct does not at once follow. Even though it follows, counsel will none the less confirm one's right opinion concerning Good and Evil. And it is also wrong to believe that precepts are of no use to madmen. For though, by themselves, they are of no avail, yet they are a help towards the cure. Both scolding and chastening rein in a lunatic. Note that I here refer to lunatics whose wits are disturbed but not hopelessly gone.

"Still," it is objected, "laws do not always make us do what we ought to do; and what else are laws than precepts mingled with threats?" Now first of all, the laws do not persuade just because they threaten; precepts, however, instead of coercing, correct men by pleading. Again, laws frighten one out of communicating crime, while precepts urge a man on to his duty. Besides, the laws also are of assistance towards good conduct, at any rate if they instruct as well as command. On this point I disagree with Posidonius, who says: "I do not think that Plato's Laws should have the preambles added to them. For a law should be brief, in order that the uninitiated may grasp it all the more easily. It should be a voice, as it were, sent down from heaven; it should command, not discuss. Nothing seems to me more dull or more foolish than a law with a preamble. Warn me, tell me what you wish me to do; I am not learning but obeying." But laws framed in this way are helpful; hence you will notice that a state with defective laws will have defective morals. "But," it is said, "they are not of avail in every case." Well neither is philosophy; and yet philosophy is not on that account ineffectual and useless in the training of the soul. Furthermore, is not philosophy the Law of Life? Grant, if we will, that the laws do not avail; it does not necessarily follow that advice also should not avail. On this ground, you ought to say that consolation does not avail, and warning, and exhortation, and scolding, and praising; since they are all varieties of advice. It is by such methods that we arrive at a perfect condition of mind. Nothing is more successful in bringing honourable influences to bear upon the mind, or in straightening out the wavering spirit that is prone to evil, than association with good men. For the frequent seeing, the frequent hearing of them little by little sinks into the heart and acquires the force of precepts.

We are indeed uplifted merely by meeting wise men; and one can be helped by a great man even when he is silent. I could not easily tell you how it helps us, though I am certain of the fact that I have received help in that way. Phaedo says: "Certain tiny animals do not leave any pain when they sting us; so subtle is their power, so deceptive for purposes of harm. The bite is disclosed by a swelling, and even in the swelling there is no visible wound." That will also be your experience when dealing with wise men, you will not discover how or when the benefit comes to you, but you will discover that you have received it. "What is the point of this remark?" you ask. It is, that good precepts, often welcomed within you, will benefit you just as much as good examples. Pythagoras declares that our souls experience a change when we enter a temple and behold the images of the gods face to face, and await the utterances of an oracle. Moreover, who can deny that even the most inexperienced are effectively struck by the force of certain precepts? For example, by such brief but weighty saws as: "Nothing in excess," "The greedy mind is satisfied by no gains," "You must expect to be treated by others as you yourself have treated them."We receive a sort if shock when we hear such sayings; no one ever thinks of doubting them or of asking "Why?" So strongly, indeed, does mere truth, unaccompanied by reason, attract us. If reverence reins in the soul and checks vice, why cannot counsel do the same? Also, if rebuke gives one a sense of shame, why has not counsel the same power, even though it does use bare precepts? The counsel which assists suggestion by reason – which adds the motive for doing a given thing and the reward which awaits one who carries out and obeys such precepts is – more effective and settles deeper into the heart. If commands are helpful, so is advice. But one is helped by commands; therefore one is helped also by advice.

Virtue is divided into two parts – into contemplation of truth, and conduct. Training teaches contemplation, and admonition teaches conduct. And right conduct both practises and reveals virtue. But if, when a man is about to act, he is helped by advice, he is also helped by admonition. Therefore, if right conduct is necessary to virtue, and if, moreover, admonition makes clear right conduct, then admonition also is an indispensable thing. There are two strong supports to the soul – trust in the truth and confidence; both are the result of admonition. For men believe it, and when belief is established, the soul receives great inspiration and is filled with confidence. Therefore, admonition is not superfluous.

Marcus Agrippa, a great-souled man, the only person among those whom the civil wars raised to fame and power whose prosperity helped the state, used to say that he was greatly indebted to the proverb "Harmony makes small things grow; lack of harmony makes great things decay." He held that he himself became the best of brothers and the best of friends by virtue of this saying. And if proverbs of such a kind, when welcomed intimately into the soul, can mould this very soul, why cannot the department of philosophy which consists of such proverbs possess equal influence? Virtue depends partly upon training and partly upon practice; you must learn first, and then strengthen your learning by action. If this be true, not only do the doctrines of wisdom help us but the precepts also, which check and banish our emotions by a sort of official decree.

It is said: "Philosophy is divided into knowledge and state of mind. For one who has learned and understood what he should do and avoid, is not a wise man until his mind is metamorphosed into the shape of that which he has learned. This third department – that of precept – is compounded from both the others, from dogmas of philosophy and state of mind. Hence it is superfluous as far as the perfecting of virtue is concerned; the other two parts are enough for the purpose." On that basis, therefore, even consolation would be superfluous, since this also is a combination of the other two, as likewise are exhortation, persuasion, and even proof itself. For proof also originates from a well-ordered and firm mental attitude. But, although these things result from a sound state of mind, yet the sound state of mind also results from them; it is both creative of them and resultant from them. Furthermore, that which you mention is the mark of an already perfect man, of one who has attained the height of human happiness. But the approach to these qualities is slow, and in the meantime in practical matters, the path should be pointed out for the benefit of one who is still short of perfection, but is making progress. Wisdom by her own agency may perhaps show herself this path without the help of admonition; for she has brought the soul to a stage where it can be impelled only in the right direction. Weaker characters, however, need someone to precede them, to say: "Avoid this," or "Do that." Moreover, if one awaits the time when one can know of oneself what the best line of action is, one will sometimes go astray and by going astray will be hindered from arriving at the point where it is possible to be content with oneself. The soul should accordingly be guided at the very moment when it is becoming able to guide itself. Boys study according to direction. Their fingers are held and guided by others so that they may follow the outlines of the letters; next, they are ordered to imitate a copy and base thereon a style of penmanship. Similarly, the mind is helped if it is taught according to direction. Such facts as these prove that this department of philosophy is not superfluous.

The question next arises whether this part alone is sufficient to make men wise. The problem shall be treated at the proper time; but at present, omitting all arguments, is it not clear that we need someone whom we may call upon as our preceptor in opposition to the precepts of men in general? There is no word which reaches our ears without doing us harm; we are injured both by good wishes and by curses. The angry prayers of our enemies instil false fears in us; and the affection of our friends spoils us through their kindly wishes. For this affection sets us a-groping after goods that are far away, unsure, and wavering, when we really might open the store of happiness at home. We are not allowed, I maintain, to travel a straight road. Our parents and our slaves draw us into wrong. Nobody confines his mistakes to himself; people sprinkle folly among their neighbours, and receive it from them in turn. For this reason, in an individual, you find the vices of nations, because the nation has given them to the individual. Each man, in corrupting others, corrupts himself; he imbibes, and then imparts, badness the result is a vast mass of wickedness, because the worst in every separate person is concentrated in one mass.

We should, therefore, have a guardian, as it were, to pluck us continually by the ear and dispel rumours and protest against popular enthusiasms. For you are mistaken if you suppose that our faults are inborn in us; they have come from without, have been heaped upon us. Hence, by receiving frequent admonitions, we can reject the opinions which din about our ears. Nature does not ally us with any vice; she produced us in health and freedom. She put before our eyes no object which might stir in us the itch of greed. She placed gold and silver beneath our feet, and bade those feet stamp down and crush everything that causes us to be stamped down and crushed. Nature elevated our gaze towards the sky and willed that we should look upward to behold her glorious and wonderful works. She gave us the rising and the setting sun, the whirling course of the on-rushing world which discloses the things of earth by day and the heavenly bodies by night, the movements of the stars, which are slow if you compare them with the universe, but most rapid if you reflect on the size of the orbits which they describe with unslackened speed; she showed us the successive eclipses of sun and moon, and other phenomena, wonderful because they occur regularly or because, through sudden causes they help into view – such as nightly trails of fire, or flashes in the open heavens unaccompanied by stroke or sound of thunder, or columns and beams and the various phenomena of flames. She ordained that all these bodies should proceed above our heads; but gold and silver, with the iron which, because of the gold and silver, never brings peace, she has hidden away, as if they were dangerous things to trust to our keeping. It is we ourselves that have dragged them into the light of day to the end that we might fight over them; it is we ourselves who, tearing away the superincumbent earth, have dug out the causes and tools of our own destruction; it is we ourselves who have attributed our own misdeeds to Fortune, and do not blush to regard as the loftiest objects those which once lay in the depths of earth. Do you wish to know how false is the gleam that has deceived your eyes? There is really nothing fouler or more involved in darkness than these things of earth, sunk and covered for so long a time in the mud where they belong. Of course they are foul; they have been hauled out through a long and murky mine-shaft. There is nothing uglier than these metals during the process of refinement and separation from the ore. Furthermore, watch the very workmen who must handle and sift the barren grade of dirt, the sort which comes from the bottom; see how soot-besmeared they are! . And yet the stuff they handle soils the soul more than the body, and there is more foulness in the owner than in the workman.

It is therefore indispensable that we be admonished, that we have some advocate with upright mind, and, amid all the uproar and jangle of falsehood, hear one voice only. But what voice shall this be? Surely a voice which, amid all the tumult of self-seeking, shall whisper wholesome words into the deafened ear, saying: "You need not be envious of those whom the people call great and fortunate; applause need not disturb your composed attitude and your sanity of mind; you need not become disgusted with your calm spirit because you see a great man, clothed in purple, protected by the well-known symbols of authority; you need not judge the magistrate for whom the road is cleared to be any happier than yourself, whom his officer pushes from the road. If you would wield a command that is profitable to yourself, and injurious to nobody, clear your own faults out of the way. There are many who set fire to cities, who storm garrisons that have remained impregnable for generations and safe for numerous ages, who raise mounds as high as the walls they are besieging, who with battering-rams and engines shatter towers that have been reared to a wondrous height. There are many who can send their columns ahead and press destructively upon the rear of the foe, who can reach the Great Sea dripping with the blood of nations; but even these men, before they could conquer their foe, were conquered by their own greed. No one withstood their attack; but they themselves could not withstand desire for power and the impulse to cruelty; at the time when they seemed to be hounding others, they were themselves being hounded. Alexander was hounded into misfortune and dispatched to unknown countries by a mad desire to lay waste other men's territory. Do you believe that the man was in his senses who could begin by devastating Greece, the land where he received his education? One who snatched away the dearest guerdon of each nation, bidding Spartans be slaves, and Athenians hold their tongues? Not content with the ruin of all the states which Philip had either conquered or bribed into bondage, he overthrew various commonwealths in various places and carried his weapons all over the world; his cruelty was tired, but it never ceased – like a wild beast that tears to pieces more than its hunger demands. Already he has joined many kingdoms into one kingdom; already Greeks and Persians fear the same lord; already nations Darius had left free submit to the yoke: yet he passes beyond the Ocean and the Sun, deeming it shame that he should shift his course of victory from the paths which Hercules and Bacchus had trod; he threatens violence to

Nature herself. He does not wish to go; but he cannot stay; he is like a weight that falls headlong, its course ending only when it lies motionless.

It was not virtue or reason which persuaded Gnaeus Pompeius to take part in foreign and civil warfare; it was his mad craving for unreal glory. Now he attacked Spain and the faction of Sertorius; now he fared forth to enchain the pirates and subdue the seas. These were merely excuses and pretexts for extending his power. What drew him into Africa, into the North, against Mithridates, into Armenia and all the corners of Asia? Assuredly it was his boundless desire to grow bigger; for only in his own eyes was he not great enough. And what impelled Gaius Caesar to the combined ruin of himself and of the state? Renown, self-seeking, and the setting no limit to pre-eminence over all other men. He could not allow a single person to outrank him, although the state allowed two men to stand at its head. Do you think that Gaius Marius, who was once consul (he received this office on one occasion, and stole it on all the others) courted all his perils by the inspiration of virtue when he was slaughtering the Teutons and the Cimbri, and pursuing Jugurtha through the wilds of Africa? Marius commanded armies, ambition Marius.

When such men as these were disturbing the world, they were themselves disturbed – like cyclones that whirl together what they have seized, but which are first whirled themselves and can for this reason rush on with all the greater force, having no control over themselves; hence, after causing such destruction to others, they feel in their own body the ruinous force which has enabled them to cause havoc to many. You need never believe that a man can become happy through the unhappiness of another. We must unravel all such cases as are forced before our eyes and crammed into our ears; we must clear out our hearts, for they are full of evil talk. Virtue must be conducted into the place these have seized, – a kind of virtue which may root out falsehood and doctrines which contravene the truth, or may sunder us from the throng, in which we put too great trust, and may restore us to the possession of sound opinions. For this is wisdom – a return to Nature and a restoration to the condition from which man's errors have driven us. It is a great part of health to have forsaken the counsellors of madness and to have fled far from a companionship that is mutually baneful.

That you may know the truth of my remark, see how different is each individual's life before the public from that of his inner self. A quiet life does not of itself give lessons in upright conduct; the countryside does not of itself teach plain living; no, but when witnesses and onlookers are removed, faults which ripen in publicity and display sink into the background. Who puts on the purple robe for the sake of flaunting it in no man's eyes? Who uses gold plate when he dines alone? Who, as he flings himself down beneath the shadow of some rustic tree, displays in solitude the splendour of his luxury? No one makes himself elegant only for his own beholding, or even for the admiration of a few friends or relatives. Rather does he spread out his well-appointed vices in proportion to the size of the admiring crowd. It is so: claqueurs and witnesses are irritants of all our mad foibles. You can make us cease to crave, if you only make us cease to display. Ambition, luxury, and waywardness need a stage to act upon; you will cure all those ills if you seek retirement.

461

Therefore, if our dwelling is situated amid the din of a city, there should be an adviser standing near us. When men praise great incomes, he should praise the person who can be rich with a slender estate and measures his wealth by the use he makes of it. In the face of those who glorify influence and power, he should of his own volition recommend a leisure devoted to study, and a soul which has left the external and found itself. He should point out persons, happy in the popular estimation, who totter on their envied heights of power, who are dismayed and hold a far different opinion of themselves from what others hold of them. That which others think elevated, is to them a sheer precipice. Hence they are frightened and in a flutter whenever they look down the abrupt steep of their greatness. For they reflect that there are various ways of falling and that the topmost point is the most slippery. Then they fear that for which they strove, and the good fortune which made them weighty in the eyes of others weighs more heavily upon themselves. Then they praise easy leisure and independence; they hate the glamour and try to escape while their fortunes are still unimpaired. Then at last you may see them studying philosophy amid their fear, and hunting sound advice when their fortunes go awry. For these two things are, as it were, at opposite poles – good fortune and good sense; that is why we are wiser when in the midst of adversity. It is prosperity that takes away righteousness. Farewell.

Letter XCV - On the Usefulness of Basic Principles

You keep asking me to explain without postponement a topic which I once remarked should be put off until the proper time, and to inform you by letter whether this department of philosophy which the Greeks call paraenetic, and we Romans call the "preceptorial," is enough to give us perfect wisdom. Now I know that you will take it in good part if I refuse to do so. But I accept your request all the more willingly, and refuse to let the common saying lose its point:

Don't ask for what you'll wish you hadn't got.

For sometimes we seek with effort that which we should decline if offered voluntarily. Call that fickleness or call it pettishness, – we must punish the habit by ready compliance. There are many things that we would have men think that we wish, but that we really do not wish. A lecturer sometimes brings upon the platform a huge work of research, written in the tiniest hand and very closely folded; after reading off a large portion, he says: "I shall stop, if you wish;" and a shout arises: "Read on, read on!" from the lips of those who are anxious for the speaker to hold his peace then and there. We often want one thing and pray for another, not telling the truth even to the gods, while the gods either do not hearken, or else take pity on us. But I shall without pity avenge myself and shall load a huge letter upon your shoulders; for your part, if you read it with reluctance, you may say: "I brought this burden upon myself," and may class yourself among those men whose too ambitious wives drive them frantic, or those whom riches harass, earned by extreme sweat of

462

the brow, or those who are tortured with the titles which they have sought by every sort of device and toil, and all others who are responsible for their own misfortunes.

But I must stop this preamble and approach the problem under consideration. Men say: "The happy life consists in upright conduct; precepts guide one to upright conduct; therefore precepts are sufficient for attaining the happy life." But they do not always guide us to upright conduct; this occurs only when the will is receptive; and sometimes they are applied in vain, when wrong opinions obsess the soul. Furthermore, a man may act rightly without knowing that he is acting rightly. For nobody, except he be trained from the start and equipped with complete reason, can develop to perfect proportions, understanding when he should do certain things, and to what extent, and in whose company, and how, and why. Without such training a man cannot strive with all his heart after that which is honourable, or even with steadiness or gladness, but will ever be looking back and wavering.

It is also said: "If honourable conduct results from precepts, then precepts are amply sufficient for the happy life; but the first of these statements is true; therefore the second is true also." We shall reply to these words that honourable conduct is, to be sure, brought about by precepts, but not by precepts alone. "Then," comes the reply, "if the other arts are content with precepts, wisdom will also be content therewith; for wisdom itself is an art of living. And yet the pilot is made by precepts which tell him thus and so to turn the tiller, set his sails, make use of a fair wind, tack, make the best of shifting and variable breezes – all in the proper manner. Other craftsmen also are drilled by precepts; hence precepts will be able to accomplish the same result in the case of our craftsman in the art of living." . Now all these arts are concerned with the tools of life, but not with life as a whole. Hence there is much to clog these arts from without and to complicate them – such as hope, greed, fear. But that art which professes to teach the art of life cannot be forbidden by any circumstance from exercising its functions; for it shakes off complications and pierces through obstacles. Would you like to know how unlike its status is to the other arts? In the case of the latter, it is more pardonable to err voluntarily rather than by accident; but in the case of wisdom the worst fault is to commit sin wilfully. I mean something like this: A scholar will blush for shame, not if he makes a grammatical blunder intentionally, but if he makes it unintentionally; if a physician does not recognize that his patient is failing, he is a much poorer practitioner than if he recognizes the fact and conceals his knowledge. But in this art of living a voluntary mistake is the more shameful.

Furthermore, many arts, aye and the most liberal of them all, have their special doctrine, and not mere precepts of advice – the medical profession, for example. There are the different schools of Hippocrates, of Asclepiades, of Themison. And besides, no art that concerns itself with theories can exist without its own doctrines; the Greeks call them dogmas, while we Romans may use the term "doctrines," or "tenets," or "adopted principles," – such as you will find in geometry or astronomy. But philosophy is both theoretic and practical; it contemplates and at the same time acts. You are indeed mistaken if you think that philosophy offers you nothing but worldly assistance; her aspirations are loftier than that. She cries: "I investigate the whole universe, nor am I content, keeping myself within a mortal dwelling, to give you favourable or unfavourable advice. Great matters invite and such as are set far above you. In the words of Lucretius:

> *To thee shall I reveal the ways of heaven*
> *And the gods, spreading before thine eyes*
> *The atoms, – whence all things are brought to birth,*
> *Increased, and fostered by creative power,*
> *And eke their end when Nature casts them off.*

Philosophy, therefore, being theoretic, must have her doctrines. And why? Because no man can duly perform right actions except one who has been entrusted with reason, which will enable him, in all cases, to fulfil all the categories of duty. These categories he cannot observe unless he receives precepts for every occasion, and not for the present alone. Precepts by themselves are weak and, so to speak, rootless if they be assigned to the parts and not to the whole. It is the doctrines which will strengthen and support us in peace and calm, which will include simultaneously the whole of life and the universe in its completeness. There is the same difference between philosophical doctrines and precepts as there is between elements and members; the latter depend upon the former, while the former are the source both of the latter and of all things.

People say: "The old-style wisdom advised only what one should do and avoid; and yet the men of former days were better men by far. When savants have appeared, sages have become rare. For that frank, simple virtue has changed into hidden and crafty knowledge; we are taught how to debate, not how to live." Of course, as you say, the old-fashioned wisdom, especially in its beginnings, was crude; but so were the other arts, in which dexterity developed with progress. Nor indeed in those days was there yet any need for carefully-planned cures. Wickedness had not yet reached such a high point, or scattered itself so broadcast. Plain vices could be treated by plain cures; now, however, we need defences erected with all the greater care, because of the stronger powers by which we are attacked. Medicine once consisted of the knowledge of a few simples, to stop the flow of blood, or to heal wounds; then by degrees it reached its present stage of complicated variety. No wonder that in early days medicine had less to do! Men's bodies were still sound and strong; their food was light and not spoiled by art and luxury, whereas when they began to seek dishes not for the sake of removing, but of rousing, the appetite, and devised countless sauces to whet their gluttony, – then what before was nourishment to a hungry man became a burden to the full stomach. Thence come paleness, and a trembling of wine-sodden muscles, and a repulsive thinness, due rather to indigestion than to hunger. Thence weak tottering steps, and a reeling gait just like that of drunkenness. Thence dropsy, spreading under the entire skin, and the belly growing to a paunch through an ill habit of taking more than it can hold. Thence yellow jaundice, discoloured countenances, and bodies that rot inwardly, and fingers that grow knotty when the joints stiffen, and muscles that are numbed and without power of feeling, and palpitation of the heart with its ceaseless pounding. Why need I mention dizziness? Or speak of pain in the eye and in the ear, itching and aching in the fevered brain, and internal ulcers throughout the digestive system? Besides these, there are countless kinds of fever, some acute in their malignity, others creeping upon us with subtle damage, and still others which approach us with chills and severe ague. Why should I mention the other innumerable diseases, the tortures that result from high living?

Men used to be free from such ills, because they had not yet slackened their strength by indulgence, because they had control over themselves, and supplied their own needs. They toughened their bodies by work and real toil, tiring themselves out by running or hunting or tilling the earth. They were refreshed by food in which only a hungry man could take pleasure. Hence, there was no need for all our mighty medical paraphernalia, for so many instruments and pill-boxes. For plain reasons they enjoyed plain health; it took elaborate courses to produce elaborate diseases. Mark the number of things – all to pass down a single throat – that luxury mixes together, after ravaging land and sea. So many different dishes must surely disagree; they are bolted with difficulty and are digested with difficulty, each jostling against the other. And no wonder, that diseases which result from ill-assorted food are variable and manifold; there must be an overflow when so many unnatural combinations are jumbled together. Hence there are as many ways of being ill as there are of living. The illustrious founder of the guild and profession of medicine remarked that women never lost their hair or suffered from pain in the feet; and yet nowadays they run short of hair and are afflicted with gout. This does not mean that woman's physique has changed, but that it has been conquered; in rivalling male indulgences they have also rivalled the ills to which men are heirs. They keep just as late hours, and drink just as much liquor; they challenge men in wrestling and carousing; they are no less given to vomiting from distended stomachs and to thus discharging all their wine again; nor are they behind the men in gnawing ice, as a relief to their fevered digestions. And they even match the men in their passions, although they were created to feel love passively (may the gods and goddesses confound them!). They devise the most impossible varieties of unchastity, and in the company of men they play the part of men. What wonder, then, that we can trip up the statement of the greatest and most skilled physician, when so many women are gouty and bald! Because of their vices, women have ceased to deserve the privileges of their sex; they have put off their womanly nature and are therefore condemned to suffer the diseases of men.

Physicians of old time knew nothing about prescribing frequent nourishment and propping the feeble pulse with wine; they did not understand the practice of blood-letting and of easing chronic complaints with sweat-baths; they did not understand how, by bandaging ankles and arms, to recall to the outward parts the hidden strength which had taken refuge in the centre. They were not compelled to seek many varieties of relief, because the varieties of suffering were very few in number. Nowadays, however, to what a stage have the evils of ill-health advanced! This is the interest which we pay on pleasures which we have coveted beyond what is reasonable and right. You need not wonder that diseases are beyond counting: count the cooks! All intellectual interests are in abeyance; those who follow culture lecture to empty rooms, in out-of-the-way places. The halls of the professor and the philosopher are deserted; but what a crowd there is in the cafés! How many young fellows besiege the kitchens of their gluttonous friends! I shall not mention the troops of luckless boys who must put up with other shameful treatment after the banquet is over. I shall not mention the troops of catamites, rated according to nation and colour, who must all have the same smooth skin, and the same amount of youthful down on their cheeks, and the same way of dressing their hair, so that no boy with straight locks may get among the curly-heads. Nor shall I mention the medley of bakers, and the numbers of waiters who at a given signal scurry to carry in the courses. Ye gods! How many men are kept busy to humour a single belly! What? Do you imagine that those mushrooms, the epicure's poison, work no evil results in secret, even though they have had no immediate effect? What? Do you suppose that your summer snow does not harden the tissue of the liver? What? Do you suppose that those oysters, a sluggish food fattened on slime, do not weigh one down with mud-begotten heaviness? What? Do you not think that the so-called "Sauce from the Provinces," the costly extract of poisonous fish, burns up the stomach with its salted putrefaction? What? Do you judge that the corrupted dishes which a man swallows almost burning from the kitchen fire, are quenched in the digestive system without doing harm? How repulsive, then, and how unhealthy are their belchings, and how disgusted men are with themselves when they breathe forth the fumes of yesterday's debauch! You may be sure that their food is not being digested, but is rotting.

I remember once hearing gossip about a notorious dish into which everything over which epicures love to dally had been heaped together by a cookshop that was fast rushing into bankruptcy; there were two kinds of mussels, and oysters trimmed round at the line where they are edible, set off at intervals by sea-urchins; the whole was flanked by mullets cut up and served without the bones. In these days we are ashamed of separate foods; people mix many flavours into one. The dinner table does work which the stomach ought to do. I look forward next to food being served masticated! And how little we are from it already when we pick out shells and bones and the cook performs the office of the teeth!

They say: "It is too much trouble to take our luxuries one by one; let us have everything served at the same time and blended into the same flavour. Why should I help myself to a single dish? Let us have many coming to the table at once; the dainties of various courses should be combined and confounded. Those who used to declare that this was done for display and notoriety should understand that it is not done for show, but that it is an oblation to our sense of duty! Let us have at one time, drenched in the same sauce, the dishes that are usually served separately. Let there be no difference: let oysters, sea-urchins, shell-fish, and mullets be mixed together and cooked in the same dish." No vomited food could be jumbled up more helter-skelter. And as the food itself is complicated, so the resulting diseases are complex, unaccountable, manifold, variegated; medicine has begun to campaign against them in many ways and by many rules of treatment.

Now I declare to you that the same statement applies to philosophy. It was once more simple because men's sins were on a smaller scale, and could be cured with but slight trouble; in the face, however, of all this moral topsy-turvy men must leave no remedy untried. And would that this pest might so at last be overcome! . We are mad, not only individually, but nationally. We check manslaughter and isolated murders; but what of war and the much-vaunted crime of slaughtering whole peoples? There are no limits to our greed, none to our cruelty. And as long as such crimes are committed by stealth and by individuals, they are less harmful and less portentous; but cruelties are practised in accordance with acts of senate and popular assembly, and the public is bidden to do that which is forbidden to the individual. Deeds that would be punished by loss of life when committed in secret, are praised by us because uniformed generals have carried them out. Man, naturally the gentlest class of being, is not ashamed to revel in the blood of others, to wage war, and to entrust the waging of war to his sons, when even dumb beasts and wild beasts keep the peace with one another. Against this overmastering and widespread madness philosophy has become a matter of greater effort, and has taken on strength in proportion to the strength which is gained by the opposition forces.

It used to be easy to scold men who were slaves to drink and who sought out more luxurious food; it did not require a mighty effort to bring the spirit back to the simplicity from which it had departed only slightly. But now

> One needs the rapid hand, the master-craft.

Men seek pleasure from every source. No vice remains within its limits; luxury is precipitated into greed. We are overwhelmed with forgetfulness of that which is honourable. Nothing that has an attractive value, is base. Man, an object of reverence in the eyes of man, is now slaughtered for jest and sport; and those whom it used to be unholy to train for the purpose of inflicting and enduring wounds, are thrust forth exposed and defenceless; and it is a satisfying spectacle to see a man made a corpse.

. Amid this upset condition of morals, something stronger than usual is needed, – something which will shake off these chronic ills; in order to root out a deep-seated belief in wrong ideas, conduct must be regulated by doctrines. It is only when we add precepts, consolation, and encouragement to these, that they can prevail; by themselves they are ineffective. If we would hold men firmly bound and tear them away from the ills which clutch them fast, they must learn what is evil and what is good. They must know that everything except virtue changes its name and becomes now good and now bad. Just as the soldier's primary bond of union is his oath of allegiance and his love for the flag, and a horror of desertion, and just as, after this stage, other duties can easily be demanded of him, and trusts given to him when once the oath has been administered; so it is with those whom you would bring to the happy life: the first foundations must be laid, and virtue worked into these men. Let them be held by a sort of superstitious worship of virtue; let them love her; let them desire to live with her, and refuse to live without her.

"But what, then," people say, "have not certain persons won their way to excellence without complicated training? Have they not made great progress by obeying bare precepts alone?" Very true; but their temperaments were propitious, and they snatched salvation as it were by the way. For just as the immortal gods did not learn virtue having been born with virtue complete, and containing in their nature the essence of goodness – even so certain men are fitted with unusual qualities and reach without a long apprenticeship that which is ordinarily a matter of teaching, welcoming honourable things as soon as they hear them. Hence come the choice minds which seize quickly upon virtue, or else produce it from within themselves. But your dull, sluggish fellow, who is hampered by his evil habits, must have this soul-rust incessantly rubbed off. Now, as the former sort, who are inclined towards the good, can be raised to the heights more quickly: so the weaker spirits will be assisted and freed from their evil opinions if we entrust to them the accepted principles of philosophy; and you may understand how essential these principles are in the following way. Certain things sink into us, rendering us sluggish in some ways, and hasty in others. These two qualities, the one of recklessness and the other of sloth, cannot be respectively checked or roused unless we remove their causes, which are mistaken admiration and mistaken fear. As long as we are obsessed by such feelings, you may say to us: "You owe this duty to your father, this to your children, this to your friends, this to your guests"; but greed will always hold us back, no matter how we try. A man may know that he should fight for his country, but fear will dissuade him. A man may know that he should sweat forth his last drop of energy on behalf of his friends, but luxury will forbid. A man may know that keeping a mistress is the worst kind of insult to his wife, but lust will drive him in the opposite direction. It will therefore be of no avail to give precepts unless you first remove the conditions that are likely to stand in the way of precepts; it will do no more good than to place weapons by your side and bring yourself near the foe without having your hands free to use those weapons. The soul, in order to deal with the precepts which we offer, must first be set free. Suppose that a man is acting as he should; he cannot keep it up continuously or consistently, since he will not know the reason for so acting. Some of his conduct will result rightly because of luck or practice; but there will be in his hand no rule by which he may regulate his acts, and which he may trust to tell him whether that which he has done is right. One who is good through mere chance will not give promise of retaining such a character for ever. Furthermore, precepts will perhaps help you to do what should be done; but they will not help you to do it in the proper way; and if they do not help you to this end, they do not conduct you to virtue. I grant you that, if warned, a man will do what he should; but that is not enough, since the credit lies, not in the actual deed, but in the way it is done. What is more shameful than a costly meal which eats away the income even of a knight? Or what so worthy of the censor's condemnation as to be always indulging oneself and one's "inner man," if I may speak as the gluttons do? And yet often has an inaugural dinner cost the most careful man a cool million! The very sum that is called disgraceful if spent on the appetite, is beyond reproach if spent for official purposes! For it is not luxury but an expenditure sanctioned by custom.

A mullet of monstrous size was presented to the Emperor Tiberius. They say it weighed four and one half pounds (and why should I not tickle the palates of certain epicures by mentioning its weight?). Tiberius ordered it to be sent to the fish-market and put up for sale, remarking: "I shall be taken entirely by surprise, my friends, if either Apicius or P. Octavius does not buy that mullet." The guess came true beyond his expectation: the two men bid, and Octavius won, thereby acquiring a great reputation among his intimates because he had bought for five thousand sesterces a fish which the Emperor had sold, and which even Apicius did not succeed in buying. To pay such a price was disgraceful for Octavius, but not for the individual who purchased the fish in order to present it to Tiberius, – though I should be inclined to blame the latter as well; but at any rate he admired a gift of which he thought Caesar worthy.

When people sit by the bedsides of their sick friends, we honour their motives. But when people do this for the purpose of attaining a legacy, they are like vultures waiting for carrion. The same act may be either shameful or honourable: the purpose and the manner make all the difference. Now each of our acts will be honourable if we declare allegiance to honour and judge honour and its results to be the only good that can fall to man's lot; for other things are only temporarily good. I think, then, that there should be deeply implanted a firm belief which will apply to life as a whole: this is what I call a "doctrine." And as this belief is, so will be our acts and our thoughts. As our acts and our thoughts are, so will our lives be. It is not enough, when a man is arranging his existence as a whole, to give him advice about details. Marcus Brutus, in the book which he has entitled Concerning Duty, gives many precepts to parents, children, and brothers; but no one will do his duty as he ought, unless he has some principle to which he may refer his conduct. We must set before our eyes the goal of the Supreme Good, towards which we may strive, and to which all our acts and words may have reference – just as sailors must guide their course according to a certain star. Life without ideals is erratic: as soon as an ideal is to be set up, doctrines begin to be necessary. I am sure you will admit that there is nothing more shameful than uncertain and wavering conduct, than the habit of timorous retreat. This will be our experience in all cases unless we remove that which checks the spirit and clogs it, and keeps it from making an attempt and trying with all its might.

Precepts are commonly given as to how the gods should be worshipped. But let us forbid lamps to be lighted on the Sabbath, since the gods do not need light, neither do men take pleasure in soot. Let us forbid men to offer morning salutation and to throng the doors of temples; mortal ambitions are attracted by such ceremonies, but God is worshipped by those who truly know Him. Let us forbid bringing towels and flesh-scrapers to Jupiter, and proffering mirrors to Juno; for God seeks no servants. Of course not; he himself does service to mankind, everywhere and to all he is at hand to help. Although a man hear what limit he should observe in sacrifice, and how far he should

469

recoil from burdensome superstitions, he will never make sufficient progress until he has conceived a right idea of God, – regarding Him as one who possesses all things, and allots all things, and bestows them without price. And what reason have the Gods for doing deeds of kindness? It is their nature. One who thinks that they are unwilling to do harm, is wrong; they cannot do harm. They cannot receive or inflict injury; for doing harm is in the same category as suffering harm. The universal nature, all-glorious and all-beautiful, has rendered incapable of inflicting ill those whom it has removed from the danger of ill.

The first way to worship the gods is to believe in the gods; the next to acknowledge their majesty, to acknowledge their goodness without which there is no majesty. Also, to know that they are supreme commanders in the universe, controlling all things by their power and acting as guardians of the human race, even though they are sometimes unmindful of the individual. They neither give nor have evil but they do chasten and restrain certain persons and impose penalties, and sometimes punish by bestowing that which seems good outwardly. Would you win over the gods? Then be a good man. Whoever imitates them, is worshipping them sufficiently. Then comes the second problem, – how to deal with men. What is our purpose? What precepts do we offer? Should we bid them refrain from bloodshed? What a little thing it is not to harm one whom you ought to help! It is indeed worthy of great praise, when man treats man with kindness! Shall we advise stretching forth the hand to the shipwrecked sailor, or pointing out the way to the wanderer, or sharing a crust with the starving? Yes, if I can only tell you first everything which ought to be afforded or withheld; meantime, I can lay down for mankind a rule, in short compass, for our duties in human relationships: . all that you behold, that which comprises both god and man, is one – we are the parts of one great body. Nature produced us related to one another, since she created us from the same source and to the same end. She engendered in us mutual affection, and made us prone to friendships. She established fairness and justice; according to her ruling, it is more wretched to commit than to suffer injury. Through her orders, let our hands be ready for all that needs to be helped. Let this verse be in your heart and on your lips:

I am a man; and nothing in man's lot
Do I deem foreign to me.

Let us possess things in common; for birth is ours in common. Our relations with one another are like a stone arch, which would collapse if the stones did not mutually support each other, and which is upheld in this very way.

Next, after considering gods and men, let us see how we should make use of things. It is useless for us to have mouthed out precepts, unless we begin by reflecting what opinion we ought to hold concerning everything – concerning poverty, riches, renown, disgrace, citizenship, exile. Let us banish rumour and set a value upon each thing, asking what it is and not what it is called.

Now let us turn to a consideration of the virtues. Some persons will advise us to rate prudence very high, to cherish bravery, and to cleave more closely, if possible, to justice than to all other qualities. But this will do us no good if we do not know what virtue is, whether it is simple or compound, whether it is one or more than one, whether its parts are separate or interwoven with one another; whether he who has one virtue possesses the other virtues also; and just what are the distinctions between them. The carpenter does not need to inquire about his art in the light of its origin or of its function, any more than a pantomime need inquire about the art of dancing; if these arts understand themselves, nothing is lacking, for they do not refer to life as a whole. But virtue means the knowledge of other things besides herself: if we would learn virtue we must learn all about virtue. Conduct will not be right unless the will to act is right; for this is the source of conduct. Nor, again, can the will be right without a right attitude of mind; for this is the source of the will. Furthermore, such an attitude of mind will not be found even in the best of men unless he has learned the laws of life as a whole and has worked out a proper judgment about everything, and unless he has reduced facts to a standard of truth. Peace of mind is enjoyed only by those who have attained a fixed and unchanging standard of judgment; the rest of mankind continually ebb and flow in their decisions, floating in a condition where they alternately reject things and seek them. And what is the reason for this tossing to and fro? It is because nothing is clear to them, because they make use of a most unsure criterion – rumour. If you would always desire the same things, you must desire the truth. But one cannot attain the truth without doctrines; for doctrines embrace the whole of life. Things good and evil, honourable and disgraceful, just and unjust, dutiful and undutiful, the virtues and their practice, the possession of comforts, worth and respect, health, strength, beauty, keenness of the senses – all these qualities call for one who is able to appraise them. One should be allowed to know at what value every object is to be rated on the list; for sometimes you are deceived and believe that certain things are worth more than their real value; in fact, so badly are you deceived that you will find you should value at a mere pennyworth those things which we men regard as worth most of all – for example, riches, influence, and power.

You will never understand this unless you have investigated the actual standard by which such conditions are relatively rated. As leaves cannot flourish by their own efforts, but need a branch to which they may cling and from which they may draw sap, so your precepts, when taken alone, wither away; they must be grafted upon a school of philosophy. Moreover, those who do away with doctrines do not understand that these doctrines are proved by the very arguments through which they seem to disprove them. For what are these men saying? They are saying that precepts are sufficient to develop life, and that the doctrines of wisdom (in other words, dogmas) are superfluous. And yet this very utterance of theirs is a doctrine just as if I should now remark that one must dispense with precepts on the ground that they are superfluous, that one must make use of doctrines, and that our studies should be directed solely towards this end; thus, by my very statement that precepts should not be taken seriously, I should be uttering a precept. There are certain matters in philosophy which need admonition; there are others which need proof, and a great deal of proof, too, because they are complicated and can scarcely be made clear with the greatest care and the greatest dialectic skill. If proofs are necessary, so are doctrines; for doctrines deduce the truth by reasoning. Some matters are clear, and others are vague: those which the senses and the memory can embrace are clear; those which are outside their scope are vague.

But reason is not satisfied by obvious facts; its higher and nobler function is to deal with hidden things. Hidden things need proof; proof cannot come without doctrines; therefore, doctrines are necessary. That which leads to a general agreement, and likewise to a perfect one, is an assured belief in certain facts; but if, lacking this assurance, all things are adrift in our minds, then doctrines are indispensable; for they give to our minds the means of unswerving decision. Furthermore, when we advise a man to regard his friends as highly as himself, to reflect that an enemy may become a friend, to stimulate love in the friend, and to check hatred in the enemy, we add: "This is just and honourable." Now the just and honourable element in our doctrines is embraced by reason; hence reason is necessary; for without it the doctrines cannot exist, either. But let us unite the two. For indeed branches are useless without their roots, and the roots themselves are strengthened by the growths which they have produced. Everyone can understand how useful the hands are; they obviously help us. But the heart, the source of the hands growth and power and motion, is hidden. And I can say the same thing about precepts: they are manifest, while the doctrines of wisdom are concealed. And as only the initiated know the more hallowed portion of the rites, so in philosophy the hidden truths are revealed only to those who are members and have been admitted to the sacred rites. But precepts and other such matters are familiar even to the uninitiated.

Posidonius holds that not only precept-giving (there is nothing to prevent my using this word), but even persuasion, consolation, and encouragement, are necessary. To these he adds the investigation of causes (but I fail to see why I should not dare to call it aetiology, since the scholars who mount guard over the Latin language thus use the term as having the right to do so). He remarks that it will also be useful to illustrate each particular virtue; this science Posidonius calls ethology, while others call it characterization. It gives the signs and marks which belong to each virtue and vice, so that by them distinction may be drawn between like things. Its function is the same as that of precept. For he who utters precepts says: "If you would have self-control, act thus and so!" He who illustrates, says "The man who acts thus and so, and refrains from certain other things, possesses self-control." If you ask what the difference here is, I say that the one gives the precepts of virtue, the other its embodiment. These illustrations, or, to use a commercial term, these samples, have, I confess, a certain utility; just put them up for exhibition well recommended, and you will find men to copy them. Would you, for instance, deem it a useful thing to have evidence given you by which you may recognize a thoroughbred horse, and not be cheated in your purchase or waste your time over a low-bred animal? But how much more useful it is to know the marks of a surpassingly fine soul – marks which one may appropriate from another for oneself!

Straightway the foal of the high-bred drove, nursed up in the pastures,
Marches with spirited step, and treads with a delicate motion;
First on the dangerous pathway and into the threatening river,
Trusting himself to the unknown bridge, without fear at its creakings,
Neck thrown high in the air, and clear-cut head, and a belly
Spare, back rounded, and breast abounding in courage and muscle.
He, when the clashing of weapons is heard to resound in the distance,
Leaps from his place, and pricks up his ears, and all in a tremble
Pours forth the pent-up fire that lay close-shut in his nostrils.

Vergil's description, though referring to something else, might perfectly well be the portrayal of a brave man; at any rate, I myself should select no other simile for a hero. If I had to describe Cato, who was unterrified amid the din of civil war, who was first to attack the armies that were already making for the Alps, who plunged face-forward into the civil conflict, this is exactly the sort of expression and attitude which I should give him. Surely none could "march with more spirited step" than one who rose against Caesar and Pompey at the same time and, when some were supporting Caesar's party and others that of Pompey, issued a challenge to both leaders, thus showing that the republic also had some backers. For it is not enough to say of Cato "without fear at its creakings." Of course he is not afraid! He does not quail before real and imminent noises; in the face of ten legions, Gallic auxiliaries, and a motley host of citizens and foreigners, he utters words fraught with freedom, encouraging the Republic not to fail in the struggle for freedom, but to try all hazards; he declares that it is more honourable to fall into servitude than to fall in line with it. What force and energy are his! What confidence he displays amid the general panic! He knows that he is the only one whose standing is not in question, and that men do not ask whether Cato is free, but whether he is still among the free. Hence his contempt for danger and the sword. What a pleasure it is to say, in admiration of the unflinching steadiness of a hero who did not totter when the whole state was in ruins:

A breast abounding in courage and muscle!

It will be helpful not only to state what is the usual quality of good men, and to outline their figures and features, but also to relate and set forth what men there have been of this kind. We might picture that last and bravest wound of Cato's, through which Freedom breathed her last; or the wise Laelius and his harmonious life with his friend Scipio; or the noble deeds of the Elder Cato at home and abroad; or the wooden couches of Tubero, spread at a public feast, goatskins instead of tapestry, and vessels of earthenware set out for the banquet before the very shrine of Jupiter! What else was this except consecrating poverty on the Capitol? Though I know no other deed of his for which to rank him with the Catos, is this one not enough? It was a censorship, not a banquet. How lamentably do those who covet glory fail to understand what glory is, or in what way it should be sought! On that day the Roman populace viewed the furniture of many men; it marvelled only at that of one! The gold and silver of all the others has been broken up and melted down times without number; but Tubero's earthenware will endure throughout eternity. Farewell.

Letter XCVI - On Facing Hardships

Spite of all do you still chafe and complain, not understanding that, in all the evils to which you refer, there is really only one – the fact that you do chafe and complain? If you ask me, I think that for a man there is no misery unless there be something in the universe which he thinks miserable. I shall not endure myself on that day when I find anything unendurable.

I am ill; but that is a part of my lot. My slaves have fallen sick, my income has gone off, my house is rickety, I have been assailed by losses, accidents, toil, and fear; this is a common thing. Nay, that was an understatement; it was an inevitable thing. Such affairs come by order, and not by accident. If you will believe me, it is my inmost emotions that I am just now disclosing to you: when everything seems to go hard and uphill, I have trained myself not merely to obey God, but to agree with His decisions. I follow Him because my soul wills it, and not because I must. Nothing will ever happen to me that I shall receive with ill humour or with a wry face. I shall pay up all my taxes willingly. Now all the things which cause us to groan or recoil, are part of the tax of life – things, my dear Lucilius, which you should never hope and never seek to escape.

It was disease of the bladder that made you apprehensive; downcast letters came from you; you were continually getting worse; I will touch the truth more closely, and say that you feared for your life. But come, did you not know, when you prayed for long life, that this was what you were praying for? A long life includes all these troubles, just as a long journey includes dust and mud and rain. "But," you cry, "I wished to live, and at the same time to be immune from all ills." Such a womanish cry does no credit to a man. Consider in what attitude you shall receive this prayer of mine (I offer it not only in a good, but in a noble spirit): "May gods and goddesses alike forbid that Fortune keep you in luxury!" Ask yourself voluntarily which you would choose if some god gave you the choice – a life in a café or life in a camp.

And yet life, Lucilius, is really a battle. For this reason those who are tossed about at sea, who proceed uphill and downhill over toilsome crags and heights, who go on campaigns that bring the greatest danger, are heroes and front-rank fighters; but persons who live in rotten luxury and ease while others toil, are mere turtle-doves safe only because men despise them. Farewell.

Letter XCVII - On the Degeneracy of the Age

You are mistaken, my dear Lucilius, if you think that luxury, neglect of good manners, and other vices of which each man accuses the age in which he lives, are especially characteristic of our own epoch; no, they are the vices of mankind and not of the times. No era in history has ever been free from blame. Moreover, if you once begin to take account of the irregularities belonging to any particular era, you will find – to man's shame be it spoken –

that sin never stalked abroad more openly than in Cato's very presence. Would anyone believe that money changed hands in the trial when Clodius was defendant on the charge of secret adultery with Caesar's wife, when he violated the ritual of that sacrifice which is said to be offered on behalf of the people when all males are so rigorously removed outside the precinct, that even pictures of all male creatures are covered up? And yet, money was given to the jury, and, baser even than such a bargain, sexual crimes were demanded of married women and noble youths as a sort of additional contribution. The charge involved less sin than the acquittal; for the defendant on a charge of adultery parcelled out the adulteries, and was not sure of his own safety until he had made the jury criminals like himself. All this was done at the trial in which Cato gave evidence, although that was his sole part therein.

I shall quote Cicero's actual words, because the facts are so bad as to pass belief: "He made assignations, promises, pleas, and gifts. And more than this (merciful Heavens, what an abandoned state of affairs!) upon several of the jury, to round out their reward, he even bestowed the enjoyment of certain women and meetings with noble youths." It is superfluous to be shocked at the bribe; the additions to the bribe were worse. "Will you have the wife of that prig, A.? Very good. Or of B., the millionaire? I will guarantee that you shall lie with her. If you fail to commit adultery, condemn Clodius. That beauty whom you desire shall visit you. I assure you a night in that woman's company without delay; my promise shall be carried out faithfully within the legal time of postponement." It means more to parcel out such crimes than to commit them; it means blackmailing dignified matrons. These jurymen in the Clodius trial had asked the Senate for a guard – a favour which would have been necessary only for a jury about to convict the accused; and their request had been granted. Hence the witty remark of Catulus after the defendant had been acquitted: "Why did you ask us for the guard? Were you afraid of having your money stolen from you?" And yet, amid jests like these he got off unpunished who before the trial was an adulterer, during the trial a pander, and who escaped conviction more vilely than he deserved it.

Do you believe that anything could be more disgraceful than such moral standards – when lust could not keep its hands either from religious worship or from the courts of law, when, in the very inquiry which was held in special session by order of the Senate, more crime was committed than investigated? The question at issue was whether one could be safe after committing adultery; it was shown that one could not be safe without committing adultery! All this bargaining took place in the presence of Pompey and Caesar, of Cicero and Cato, – yes, that very Cato whose presence, it is said, caused the people to refrain from demanding the usual quips and cranks of naked actresses at the Floralia, – if you can believe that men were stricter in their conduct at a festival than in a court-room! Such things will be done in the future, as they have been done in the past; and the licentiousness of cities will sometimes abate through discipline and fear, never of itself.

Therefore, you need not believe that it is we who have yielded most to lust and least to law. For young men of to-day live far more simple lives than those of an epoch when a defendant would plead not guilty to an adultery charge before his judges, and his judges admit it before the defendant, when debauchery was practised to secure a verdict, and when Clodius, befriended by the very vices of which he was guilty, played the procurer during the actual hearing of the case. Could one believe this? He to whom one adultery brought condemnation was acquitted because of many. All ages will produce men like Clodius, but not all ages men like Cato. We degenerate easily, because we lack neither guides nor associates in our wickedness, and the wickedness goes on of itself, even without guides or associates. The road to vice is not only downhill, but steep; and many men are rendered incorrigible by the fact that, while in all other crafts errors bring shame to good craftsmen and cause vexation to those who go astray, the errors of life are a positive source of pleasure. The pilot is not glad when his ship is thrown on her beam-ends; the physician is not glad when he buries his patient; the orator is not glad when the defendant loses a case through the fault of his advocate; but on the other hand every man enjoys his own crimes. A. delights in an intrigue – for it was the very difficulty which attracted him thereto. B. delights in forgery and theft, and is only displeased with his sin when his sin has failed to hit the mark. And all this is the result of perverted habits.

Conversely, however, in order that you may know that there is an idea of good conduct present subconsciously in souls which have been led even into the most depraved ways, and that men are not ignorant of what evil is but indifferent – I say that all men hide their sins, and, even though the issue be successful, enjoy the results while concealing the sins themselves. A good conscience, however, wishes to come forth and be seen of men; wickedness fears the very shadows. Hence I hold Epicurus's saying to be most apt: "That the guilty may haply remain hidden is possible, that he should be sure of remaining hidden is not possible," or, if you think that the meaning can be made more clear in this way: "The reason that it is no advantage to wrong-doers to remain hidden is that even though they have the good fortune they have not the assurance of remaining so." This is what I mean: crimes can be well guarded; free from anxiety they cannot be.

This view, I maintain, is not at variance with the principles of our school, if it be so explained. And why? Because the first and worst penalty of sin is to have committed sin; and crime, though Fortune deck it out with her favours, though she protect and take it in her charge, can never go unpunished; since the punishment of crime lies in the crime itself. But none the less do these second penalties press close upon the heels of the first – constant fear, constant terror, and distrust in one's own security.

Why, then, should I set wickedness free from such a punishment? Why should I not always leave it trembling in the balance? Let us disagree with Epicurus on the one point, when he declares that there is no natural justice, and that crime should be avoided because one cannot escape the fear which results therefrom; let us agree with him on the other – that bad deeds are lashed by the whip of conscience, and that conscience is tortured to the greatest degree because unending anxiety drives and whips it on, and it cannot rely upon the guarantors of its own peace of mind. For this, Epicurus, is the very proof that we are by nature reluctant to commit crime, because even in circumstances of safety there is no one who does not feel fear. Good luck frees many men from punishment, but no man from fear. And why should this be if it were not that we have engrained in us a loathing for that which Nature has condemned? Hence even men who hide their sins can never count upon remaining hidden; for their conscience convicts them and reveals them to themselves. But it is the property of guilt to be in fear. It had gone ill with us, owing to the many crimes which escape the vengeance of the law and the prescribed punishments, were it not that those grievous offences against nature must pay the penalty in ready money, and that in place of suffering the punishment comes fear. Farewell.

Letter XCVIII - On the Fickleness of Fortune

You need never believe that anyone who depends upon happiness is happy! It is a fragile support – this delight in adventitious things; the joy which entered from without will some day depart. But that joy which springs wholly from oneself is leal and sound; it increases and attends us to the last; while all other things which provoke the admiration of the crowd are but temporary Goods. You may reply: "What do you mean? Cannot such things serve both for utility and for delight?" Of course. But only if they depend on us, and not we on them. All things that Fortune looks upon become productive and pleasant, only if he who possesses them is in possession also of himself, and is not in the power of that which belongs to him. For men make a mistake, my dear Lucilius, if they hold that anything good, or evil either, is bestowed upon us by Fortune; it is simply the raw material of Goods and Ills that she gives to us – the sources of things which, in our keeping, will develop into good or ill. For the soul is more powerful than any sort of Fortune; by its own agency it guides its affairs in either direction, and of its own power it can produce a happy life, or a wretched one.

A bad man makes everything bad – even things which had come with the appearance of what is best; but the upright and honest man corrects the wrongs of Fortune, and softens hardship and bitterness because he knows how to endure them; he likewise accepts prosperity with appreciation and moderation, and stands up against trouble with steadiness and courage. Though a man be prudent, though he conduct all his interests with well-balanced judgment, though he attempt nothing beyond his strength, he will not attain the Good which is unalloyed and beyond the reach of threats, unless he is sure in dealing with that which is unsure. For whether you prefer to observe other men (and it is easier to make up one's mind when judging the affairs of others), or whether you observe yourself, with all prejudice laid aside, you will perceive and acknowledge that there is no utility in all these desirable and beloved things, unless you equip yourself in opposition to the fickleness of chance and its consequences, and unless you repeat to yourself often and uncomplainingly, at every mishap, the words: "Heaven decreed it otherwise!" Nay rather, to adopt a phrase which is braver and nearer the truth – one on which you may more safely prop your spirit – say to yourself, whenever things turn out contrary to your expectation: "Heaven decreed better!"

If you are thus poised, nothing will affect you and a man will be thus poised if he reflects on the possible ups and downs in human affairs before he feels their force, and if he comes to regard children, or wife, or property, with the idea that he will not necessarily possess them always and that he will not be any more wretched just because he ceases to possess them. It is tragic for the soul to be apprehensive of the future and wretched in anticipation of wretchedness, consumed with an anxious desire that the objects which give pleasure may remain in its possession to the very end. For such a soul will never be at rest; in waiting for the future it will lose the present blessings which it might enjoy. And there is no difference between grief for something lost and the fear of losing it.

But I do not for this reason advise you to be indifferent. Rather do you turn aside from you whatever may cause fear. Be sure to foresee whatever can be foreseen by planning. Observe and avoid, long before it happens, anything that is likely to do you harm. To effect this your best assistance will be a spirit of confidence and a mind strongly resolved to endure all things. He who can bear Fortune, can also beware of Fortune. At any rate, there is no dashing of billows when the sea is calm. And there is nothing more wretched or foolish than premature fear. What madness it is to anticipate one's troubles! . In fine, to express my thoughts in brief compass and portray to you those busybodies and self-tormentors – they are as uncontrolled in the midst of their troubles as they are before them. He suffers more than is necessary, who suffers before it is necessary; such men do not weigh the amount of their suffering, by reason of the same failing which prevents them from being ready for it; and with the same lack of restraint they fondly imagine that their luck will last for ever, and fondly imagine that their gains are bound to increase as well as merely continue. They forget this spring-board on which mortal things are tossed, and they guarantee for themselves exclusively a steady continuance of the gifts of chance.

For this very reason I regard as excellent the saying of Metrodorus, in a letter of consolation to his sister on the loss of her son, a lad of great promise: "All the Good of mortals is mortal." He is referring to those Goods towards which men rush in shoals. For the real Good does not perish; it is certain and lasting and it consists of wisdom and virtue; it is the only immortal thing that falls to mortal lot. But men are so wayward, and so forgetful of their goal and of the point toward which every day jostles them, that they are surprised at losing anything, although some day they are bound to lose everything. Anything of which you are entitled the owner is in your possession but is not your own; for there is no strength in that which is weak, nor anything lasting and invincible in that which is frail. We must lose our lives as surely as we lose our property, and this, if we understand the truth, is itself a consolation. Lose it with equanimity; for you must lose your life also.

What resource do we find, then, in the face of these losses? Simply this – to keep in memory the things we have lost, and not to suffer the enjoyment which we have derived from them to pass away along with them. To have may be taken from us, to have had, never. A man is thankless in the highest degree if, after losing something, he feels no obligation for having received it. Chance robs us of the thing, but leaves us its use and its enjoyment – and we have lost this if we are so unfair as to regret. Just say to yourself: "Of all these experiences that seem so frightful, none is insuperable. Separate trials have been overcome by many: fire by Mucius, crucifixion by Regulus, poison by Socrates, exile by Rutilius, and a sword-inflicted death by Cato; therefore, let us also overcome something." Again, those objects which attract the crowd under the appearance of beauty and happiness, have been scorned by many men and on many occasions. Fabricius when he was general refused riches, and when he was censor branded them with disapproval. Tubero deemed poverty worthy both of himself and of the deity on the Capitol when, by the use of earthenware dishes at a public festival, he showed that man should be satisfied with that which the gods could still use. The elder Sextius rejected the honours of office; he was born with an obligation to take part in public affairs, and yet would not accept the broad stripe even when the deified Julius offered it to him. For he understood that what can be given can also be taken away.

Let us also, therefore, carry out some courageous act of our own accord; let us be included among the ideal types of history. Why have we been slack? Why do we lose heart? That which could be done, can be done, if only we purify our souls and follow Nature; for when one strays away from Nature one is compelled to crave, and fear, and be a slave to the things of chance. We may return to the true path; we may be restored to our proper state; let us therefore be so, in order that we may be able to endure pain, in whatever form it attacks our bodies, and say to Fortune: "You have to deal with a man; seek someone whom you can conquer!"

By these words, and words of a like kind, the malignity of the ulcer is quieted down; and I hope indeed that it can be reduced, and either cured or brought to a stop, and grow old along with the patient himself. I am, however, comfortable in my mind regarding him; what we are now discussing is our own loss – the taking-off of a most excellent old man. For he himself has lived a full life, and anything additional may be craved by him, not for his own sake, but for the sake of those who need his services. In continuing to live, he deals generously. Some other person might have put an end to these sufferings; but our friend considers it no less base to flee from death than to flee towards death. "But," comes the answer, "if circumstances warrant, shall he not take his departure?" Of course, if he can no longer be of service to anyone, if all his business will be to deal with pain. This, my dear Lucilius, is what we mean by studying philosophy while applying it, by practising it on truth – note what courage a prudent man possesses against death, or against pain, when the one approaches and the other weighs heavily. What ought to be done must be learned from one who does it. Up to now we have dealt with arguments – whether any man can resist pain, or whether the approach of death can cast down even great souls. Why discuss it further? Here is an immediate fact for us to tackle – death does not make our friend braver to face pain, nor pain to face death. Rather does he trust himself in the face of both; he does not suffer with resignation because he hopes for death, nor does he die gladly because he is tired of suffering. Pain he endures, death he awaits. Farewell.

Letter XCIX - On Consolation to the Bereaved

I enclose a copy of the letter which I wrote to Marullus at the time when he had lost his little son and was reported to be rather womanish in his grief – a letter in which I have not observed the usual form of condolence: for I did not believe that he should be handled gently, since in my opinion he deserved criticism rather than consolation. When a man is stricken and is finding it most difficult to endure a grievous wound, one must humour him for a while; let him satisfy his grief or at any rate work off the first shock; . but those who have assumed an indulgence in grief should be rebuked forthwith, and should learn that there are certain follies even in tears.

"Is it solace that you look for? Let me give you a scolding instead! You are like a woman in the way you take your son's death; what would you do if you had lost an intimate friend? A son, a little child of unknown promise, is dead; a fragment of time has been lost. We hunt out excuses for grief; we would even utter unfair complaints about Fortune, as if Fortune would never give us just reason for complaining! But I had really thought that you possessed spirit enough to deal with concrete troubles, to say nothing of the shadowy troubles over which men make moan through force of habit. Had you lost a friend (which is the greatest blow of all), you would have had to endeavour rather to rejoice because you had possessed him than to mourn because you had lost him.

"But many men fail to count up how manifold their gains have been, how great their rejoicings. Grief like yours has this among other evils: it is not only useless, but thankless. Has it then all been for nothing that you have had such a friend? During so many years, amid such close associations, after such intimate communion of personal interests, has nothing been accomplished? Do you bury friendship along with a friend? And why lament having lost him, if it be of no avail to have possessed him? Believe me, a great part of those we have loved, though chance has removed their persons, still abides with us. The past is ours, and there is nothing more secure for us than that which has been. We are ungrateful for past gains, because we hope for the future, as if the future – if so be that any future is ours – will not be quickly blended with the past. People set a narrow limit to their enjoyments if they take pleasure only in the present; both the future and the past serve for our delight – the one with anticipation, and the other with memories but the one is contingent and may not come to pass, while the other must have been.

"What madness it is, therefore, to lose our grip on that which is the surest thing of all? Let us rest content with the pleasures we have quaffed in past days, if only, while we quaffed them, the soul was not pierced like a sieve, only to lose again whatever it had received. There are countless cases of men who have without tears buried sons in the prime of manhood – men who have returned from the funeral pyre to the Senate chamber, or to any other official duties, and have straightway busied themselves with something else. And rightly; for in the first place it is idle to grieve if you get no help from grief. In the second place, it is unfair to complain about what has happened to one man but is in store for all. Again, it is foolish to lament one's loss, when there is such a slight interval between the lost and the loser. Hence we should be more resigned in spirit, because we follow closely those whom we have lost.

"Note the rapidity of Time – that swiftest of things; consider the shortness of the course along which we hasten at top speed; mark this throng of humanity all straining toward the same point with briefest intervals between them – even when they seem longest; he whom you count as passed away has simply posted on ahead. And what is more irrational than to bewail your predecessor, when you yourself must travel on the same journey? Does a man bewail an event which he knew would take place? Or, if he did not think of death as man's lot, he has but cheated himself. Does a man bewail an event which he has been admitting to be unavoidable? Whoever complains about the death of anyone, is complaining that he was a man. Everyone is bound by the same terms: he who is privileged to be born, is destined to die. Periods of time separate us, but death levels us. The period which lies between our first day and our last is shifting and uncertain: if you reckon it by its troubles, it is long even to a lad, if by its speed, it is scanty even to a greybeard. Everything is slippery, treacherous, and more shifting than any weather. All things are tossed about and shift into their opposites at the bidding of Fortune; amid such a turmoil of mortal affairs nothing but death is surely in store for anyone. And yet all men complain about the one thing wherein none of them is deceived. 'But he died in boyhood.' I am not yet prepared to say that he who quickly comes to the end of his life has the better of the bargain; let us turn to consider the case of him who has grown to old age. How very little is he superior to the child! Place before your mind's eye the vast spread of time's abyss, and consider the universe; and then contrast our so-called human life with infinity: you will then see how scant is that for which we pray, and which we seek to lengthen. How much of this time is taken up with weeping, how much with worry! How much with prayers for death before death arrives, how much with our health, how much with our fears! How much is occupied by our years of inexperience or of useless endeavour! And half of all this time is wasted in sleeping. Add, besides, our toils, our griefs, our dangers – and you will comprehend that even in the longest life real living is the least portion thereof. Nevertheless, who will make such an admission as: 'A man is not better off who is allowed to return home quickly, whose journey is accomplished before he is wearied out'? Life is neither a Good nor an Evil; it is simply the place where good and evil exist. Hence this little boy has lost nothing except a hazard where loss was more assured than gain. He might have turned out temperate and prudent; he might, with your fostering care, have been moulded to a better standard; but (and this fear is more reasonable) he might have become just like the many. Note the youths of the noblest lineage whose extravagance has flung them into the arena; note those men who cater to the passions of themselves and others in mutual lust, whose days never pass without drunkenness or some signal act of shame; it will thus be clear to you that there was more to fear than to hope for.

"For this reason you ought not to invite excuses for grief or aggravate slight burdens by getting indignant. I am not exhorting you to make an effort and rise to great heights; for my opinion of you is not so low as to make me think that it is necessary for you to summon every bit of your virtue to face this trouble. Yours is not pain; it is a mere sting – and it is you yourself who are turning it into pain.

"Of a surety philosophy has done you much service if you can bear courageously the loss of a boy who was as yet better known to his nurse than to his father! . And what, then? Now, at this time, am I advising you to be hard-hearted, desiring you to keep your countenance unmoved at the very funeral ceremony, and not allowing your soul even to feel the pinch of pain? By no means. That would mean lack of feeling rather than virtue – to behold the burial ceremonies of those near and dear to you with the same expression as you beheld their living forms, and to show no emotion over the first bereavement in your family. But suppose that I forbade you to show emotion; there are certain feelings which claim their own rights. Tears fall, no matter how we try to check them, and by being shed they ease the soul. What, then, shall we do? Let us allow them to fall, but let us not command them do so; let us according as emotion floods our eyes, but not as as mere imitation shall demand. Let us, indeed, add nothing to natural grief, nor augment it by following the example of others. The display of grief makes more demands than grief itself: how few men are sad in their own company! They lament the louder for being heard; persons who are reserved and silent when alone are stirred to new paroxysms of tears when they behold others near them! At such times they lay violent hands upon their own persons, – though they might have done this more easily if no one were present to check them; at such times they pray for death; at such times they toss themselves from their couches. But their grief slackens with the departure of onlookers. In this matter, as in others also, we are obsessed by this fault – conforming to the pattern of the many, and regarding convention rather than duty. We abandon nature and surrender to the mob – who are never good advisers in anything, and in this respect as in all others are most inconsistent. People see a man who bears his grief bravely: they call him undutiful and savage-hearted; they see a man who collapses and clings to his dead: they call him womanish and weak. Everything, therefore, should be referred to reason. But nothing is more foolish than to court a reputation for sadness and to sanction tears; for I hold that with a wise man some tears fall by consent, others by their own force.

"I shall explain the difference as follows: When the first news of some bitter loss has shocked us, when we embrace the form that will soon pass from our arms to the funeral flames – then tears are wrung from us by the necessity of Nature, and the life-force, smitten by the stroke of grief, shakes both the whole body, and the eyes also, from which it presses out and causes to flow the moisture that lies within. Tears like these fall by a forcing-out process, against our will; but different are the tears which we allow to escape when we muse in memory upon those whom we have lost. And there is in them a certain sweet sadness when we remember the sound of a pleasant voice, a genial conversation, and the busy duties of yore; at such a time the eyes are loosened, as it were, with joy. This sort of weeping we indulge; the former sort overcomes us.

"There is, then, no reason why, just because a group of persons is standing in your presence or sitting at your side, you should either check or pour forth your tears; whether restrained or outpoured, they are never so disgraceful as when feigned. Let them flow naturally. But it is possible for tears to flow from the eyes of those who are quiet and at peace. They often flow without impairing the influence of the wise man – with such restraint that they show no want either of feeling or of self-respect. We may, I assure you, obey Nature and yet maintain our dignity. I have seen men worthy of reverence, during the burial of those near and dear, with countenances upon which love was written clear even after the whole apparatus of mourning was removed, and who showed no other conduct than that which was allowed to genuine emotion. There is a comeliness even in grief. This should be cultivated by the wise man; even in tears, just as in other matters also, there is a certain sufficiency; it is with the unwise that sorrows, like joys, gush over.

"Accept in an unruffled spirit that which is inevitable. What can happen that is beyond belief? Or what that is new? How many men at this very moment are making arrangements for funerals! How many are purchasing grave-clothes! How many are mourning, when you yourself have finished mourning! As often as you reflect that your boy has ceased to be, reflect also upon man, who has no sure promise of anything, whom Fortune does not inevitably escort to the confines of old age, but lets him go at whatever point she sees fit. You may, however, speak often concerning the departed, and cherish his memory to the extent of your power. This memory will return to you all the more often if you welcome its coming without bitterness; for no man enjoys converse with one who is sorrowful, much less with sorrow itself. And whatever words, whatever jests of his, no matter how much of a child he was, may have given you pleasure to hear – these I would have you recall again and again; assure yourself confidently that he might have fulfilled the hopes which you, his father, had entertained. Indeed, to forget the beloved dead, to bury their memory along with their bodies, to bewail them bounteously and afterwards think of them but scantily – this is the mark of a soul below that of man. For that is the way in which birds and beasts love their young; their affection is quickly roused and almost reaches madness, but it cools away entirely when its object dies. This quality does not befit a man of sense; he should continue to remember, but should cease to mourn. And in no wise do I approve of the remark of Metrodorus – that there is a certain pleasure akin to sadness, and that one should give chase thereto at such times as these. I am quoting the actual words of Metrodorus. I have no doubt what your feelings will be in these matters; for what is baser than to 'chase after' pleasure in the very midst of mourning – nay rather by means of mourning – and even amid one's tears to hunt out that which will give pleasure? These are the men who accuse us of too great strictness, slandering our precepts because of supposed harshness – because (say they) we declare that grief should either not be given place in the soul at all, or else should be driven out forthwith. But which is the more incredible or inhuman – to feel no grief at the loss of one's friend, or to go a-hawking after pleasure in the midst of grief? That which we Stoics advise, is honourable; when emotion has prompted a moderate flow of tears, and has, so to speak, ceased to effervesce, the soul should not be surrendered to grief.

But what do you mean, Metrodorus, by saying that with our very grief there should be a blending of pleasure? That is the sweetmeat method of pacifying children; that is the way we still the cries of infants, by pouring milk down their throats!

"Even at the moment when your son's body is on the pyre, or your friend breathing his last, will you not suffer your pleasure to cease, rather than tickle your very grief with pleasure? Which is the more honourable – to remove grief from your soul, or to admit pleasure even into the company of grief? Did I say 'admit'? Nay, I mean 'chase after,' and from the hands, too, of grief itself. Metrodorus says: 'There is a certain pleasure which is related to sadness.' We Stoics may say that, but you may not. The only Good which you recognize, is pleasure, and the only Evil, pain; and what relationship can there be between a Good and an Evil? But suppose that such a relationship does exist; now, of all times, is it to be rooted out? Shall we examine grief also, and see with what elements of delight and pleasure it is surrounded? Certain remedies, which are beneficial for some parts of the body, cannot be applied to other parts because these are, in a way, revolting and unfit; and that which in certain cases would work to a good purpose without any loss to one's self-respect, may become unseemly because of the situation of the wound. Are you not, similarly, ashamed to cure sorrow by pleasure? No, this sore spot must be treated in a more drastic way. This is what you should preferably advise: that no sensation of evil can reach one who is dead; for if it can reach him, he is not dead. And I say that nothing can hurt him who is as naught; for if a man can be hurt, he is alive. Do you think him to be badly off because he is no more, or because he still exists as somebody? And yet no torment can come to him from the fact that he is no more – for what feeling can belong to one who does not exist? – nor from the fact that he exists; for he has escaped the greatest disadvantage that death has in it – namely, non-existence.

"Let us say this also to him who mourns and misses the untimely dead: that all of us, whether young or old, live, in comparison with eternity, on the same level as regards our shortness of life. For out of all time there comes to us less than what any one could call least, since 'least' is at any rate some part; but this life of ours is next to nothing, and yet (fools that we are!), we marshal it in broad array!

"These words I have written to you, not with the idea that you should expect a cure from me at such a late date – for it is clear to me that you have told yourself everything that you will read in my letter – but with the idea that I should rebuke you even for the slight delay during which you lapsed from your true self, and should encourage you for the future, to rouse your spirit against Fortune and to be on the watch for all her missiles, not as if they might possibly come, but as if they were bound to come." Farewell.

Letter C - On the Writings of Fabianus

You write me that you have read with the greatest eagerness the work by Fabianus Papirius entitled The Duties of a Citizen, and that it did not come up to your expectations; then, forgetting that you are dealing with a philosopher, you proceed to criticize his style.

Suppose, now, that your statement is true – that he pours forth rather than places his words; let me, however, tell you at the start that this trait of which you speak has a peculiar charm, and that it is a grace appropriate to a smoothly-gliding style. For, I maintain, it matters a great deal whether it tumbles forth, or flows along. Moreover, there is a deal of deference in this regard also – as I shall make clear to you: Fabianus seems to me to have not so much an "efflux" as a "flow" of words: so copious is it, without confusion, and yet not without speed. This is indeed what his style declares and announces – that he has not spent a long time in working his matter over and twisting it into shape. But even supposing the facts are as you would have them; the man was building up character rather than words, and was writing those words for the mind rather than for the ear. Besides, had he been speaking them in his own person, you would not have had time to consider the details – the whole work would have so swept you along. For as a rule that which pleases by its swiftness is of less value when taken in hand for reading.

Nevertheless, this very quality, too, of attracting at first sight is a great advantage, no matter whether careful investigation may discover something to criticize. If you ask me, I should say that he who has forced approval is greater than he who has earned it; and yet I know that the latter is safer, I know that he can give more confident guarantees for the future. A meticulous manner of writing does not suit the philosopher; if he is timid as to words, when will he ever be brave and steadfast, when will he ever really show his worth? . Fabianus's style was not careless, it was assured. That is why you will find nothing shoddy in his work: his words are well chosen and yet not hunted for; they are not unnaturally inserted and inverted, according to the present-day fashion; but they possess distinction, even though they are taken from ordinary speech. There you have honourable and splendid ideas, not fettered into aphorisms, but spoken with greater freedom. We shall of course notice passages that are not sufficiently pruned, not constructed with sufficient care, and lacking the polish which is in vogue nowadays; but after regarding the whole, you will see that there are no futile subtleties of argument. There may, doubtless, be no variety of marbles, no water-supply which flows from one apartment to another, no "pauper-rooms," or any other device that luxury adds when ill content with simple charms; but, in the vulgar phrase, it is "a good house to live in."

Furthermore, opinions vary with regard to the style. Some wish it to be polished down from all roughness; and some take so great a pleasure in the abrupt manner that they would intentionally break up any passage which may by chance spread itself out more smoothly, scattering the closing words in such a way that the sentences may result unexpectedly. Read Cicero: his style has unity; it moves with a modulated pace, and is gentle without being degenerate. The style of Asinius Pollio, on the other hand, is "bumpy," jerky, leaving off when you least expect it. And finally, Cicero always stops gradually; while Pollio breaks off, except in the very few cases where he cleaves to a definite rhythm and a single pattern.

In addition to this, you say that everything in Fabianus seems to you commonplace and lacking in elevation; but I myself hold that he is free from such a fault. For that style of his is not commonplace, but simply calm and adjusted to his peaceful and well-ordered mind – not on a low level but on an even plane. There is lacking the verve and spur of the orator (for which you are looking), and a sudden shock of epigrams. But look, please, at the whole work, how well-ordered it is: there is a distinction in it. His style does not possess, but will suggest, dignity.

Mention someone whom you may rank ahead of Fabianus. Cicero, let us say, whose books on philosophy are almost as numerous as those of Fabianus. I will concede this point; but it is no slight thing to be less than the greatest. Or Asinius Pollio, let us say. I will yield again, and content myself by replying: "It is a distinction to be third in so great a field." You may also include Livy; for Livy wrote both dialogues (which should be ranked as history no less than as philosophy), and works which professedly deal with philosophy. I shall yield in the case of Livy also. But consider how many writers Fabianus outranks, if he is surpassed by three only – and those three the greatest masters of eloquence!

But, it may be said, he does not offer everything: though his style is elevated, it is not strong; though it flows forth copiously, it lacks force and sweep; it is not translucent, but it is lucid. "One would fail," you urge, "to find therein any rugged denunciation of vice, any courageous words in the face of danger, any proud defiance of Fortune, any scornful threats against self-seeking. I wish to see luxury rebuked, lust condemned, waywardness crushed out. Let him show us the keenness of oratory, the loftiness of tragedy, the subtlety of comedy." You wish him to rely on that pettiest of things, phraseology; but he has sworn allegiance to the greatness of his subject and draws eloquence after him as a sort of shadow, but not of set purpose.

Our author will doubtless not investigate every detail, nor subject it to analysis, nor inspect and emphasize each separate word. This I admit. Many phrases will fall short, or will fail to strike home, and at times the style will slip along indolently; but there will be plenty of light throughout the work; there will be long stretches which will not weary the reader. And, finally, he will offer this quality of making it clear to you that he meant what he wrote. You will understand that his aim was to have you know what pleased him, rather than that he should please you. All his work makes for progress and for sanity, without any search for applause.

I do not doubt that his writings are of the kind I have described, although I am harking back to him rather than retaining a sure memory of him, and although the general tone of his writings remains in my mind, not from a careful and recent perusal, but in outline, as is natural after an acquaintance of long ago. But certainly, whenever I heard him lecture, such did his work seem to me – not solid but full, the kind which would inspire young men of promise and rouse their ambition to become like him, without making them hopeless of surpassing him; and this method of encouragement seems to me the most helpful of all. For it is disheartening to inspire in a man the desire, and to take away from him the hope, of emulation. At any rate, his language was fluent, and though one might not approve every detail, the general effect was noble.

Farewell.

Letter CI - On the Futility of Planning Ahead

Every day and every hour reveal to us what a nothing we are, and remind us with some fresh evidence that we have forgotten our weakness; then, as we plan for eternity, they compel us to look over our shoulders at Death.

Do you ask me what this preamble means? It refers to Cornelius Senecio, a distinguished and capable Roman knight, whom you knew: from humble beginnings he had advanced himself to fortune, and the rest of the path already lay downhill before him. For it is easier to grow in dignity than to make a start; and money is very slow to come where there is poverty; until it can creep out of that, it goes halting. Senecio was already bordering upon wealth, helped in that direction by two very powerful assets – knowing how to make money and how to keep it also; either one of these gifts might have made him a rich man. Here was a person who lived most simply, careful of health and wealth alike. He had, as usual, called upon me early in the morning, and had then spent the whole day, even up to nightfall, at the bedside of a friend who was seriously and hopelessly ill. After a comfortable dinner, he was suddenly seized with an acute attack of quinsy, and, with the breath clogged tightly in his swollen throat, barely lived until daybreak. So within a very few hours after the time when he had been performing all the duties of a sound and healthy man, he passed away. He who was venturing investments by land and sea, who had also entered public life and left no type of business untried, during the very realization of financial success and during the very onrush of the money that flowed into his coffers, was snatched from the world!

Graft now thy pears, Meliboeus, and set out thy vines in their order!

But how foolish it is to set out one's life, when one is not even owner of the morrow! O what madness it is to plot out far-reaching hopes! To say: "I will buy and build, loan and call in money, win titles of honour, and then, old and full of years, I will surrender myself to a life of ease." Believe me when I say that everything is doubtful, even for those who are prosperous. No one has any right to draw for himself upon the future. The very thing that we grasp slips through our hands, and chance cuts into the actual hour which we are crowding so full. Time does indeed roll along by fixed law, but as in darkness; and what is it to me whether Nature's course is sure, when my own is unsure?

We plan distant voyages and long-postponed home-comings after roaming over foreign shores, we plan for military service and the slow rewards of hard campaigns, we canvass for governorships and the promotions of one office after another – and all the while death stands at our side; but since we never think of it except as it affects our neighbour, instances of mortality press upon us day by day, to remain in our minds only as long as they stir our wonder.

Yet what is more foolish than to wonder that something which may happen every day has happened on any one day? There is indeed a limit fixed for us, just where the remorseless law of Fate has fixed it; but none of us knows how near he is to this limit. Therefore, let us so order our minds as if we had come to the very end. Let us postpone nothing. Let us balance life's account every day. The greatest flaw in life is that it is always imperfect, and that a certain part of it is postponed. One who daily puts the finishing touches to his life is never in want of time. And yet, from this want arise fear and a craving for the future which eats away the mind. There is nothing more wretched than worry over the outcome of future events; as to the amount or the nature of that which remains, our troubled minds are set aflutter with unaccountable fear.

How, then, shall we avoid this vacillation? In one way only, – if there be no reaching forward in our life, if it is withdrawn into itself. For he only is anxious about the future, to whom the present is unprofitable. But when I have paid my soul its due, when a soundly-balanced mind knows that a day differs not a whit from eternity – whatever days or problems the future may bring – then the soul looks forth from lofty heights and laughs heartily to itself when it thinks upon the ceaseless succession of the ages. For what disturbance can result from the changes and the instability of Chance, if you are sure in the face of that which is unsure?

Therefore, my dear Lucilius, begin at once to live, and count each separate day as a separate life. He who has thus prepared himself, he whose daily life has been a rounded whole, is easy in his mind; but those who live for hope alone find that the immediate future always slips from their grasp and that greed steals along in its place, and the fear of death, a curse which lays a curse upon everything else. Thence came that most debased of prayers, in which Maecenas does not refuse to suffer weakness, deformity, and as a climax the pain of crucifixion provided only that he may prolong the breath of life amid these sufferings:

Fashion me with a palsied hand,
Weak of foot, and a cripple;
Build upon me a crook-backed hump;
Shake my teeth till they rattle;
All is well, if my life remains.
Save, oh, save it, I pray you,
Though I sit on the piercing cross!

There he is, praying for that which, if it had befallen him, would be the most pitiable thing in the world! And seeking a postponement of suffering, as if he were asking for life! I should deem him most despicable had he wished to live up to the very time of crucifixion: "Nay," he cries, "you may weaken my body if you will only leave the breath of life in my battered and ineffective carcass! Maim me if you will, but allow me, misshapen and deformed as I may be, just a little more time in the world! You may nail me up and set my seat upon the piercing cross!" Is it worth while to weigh down upon one's own wound, and hang impaled upon a gibbet, that one may but postpone something which is the balm of troubles, the end of punishment? Is it worth all this to possess the breath of life only to give it up? What would you ask for

Maecenas but the indulgence of Heaven? What does he mean by such womanish and indecent verse? What does he mean by making terms with panic fear? What does he mean by begging so vilely for life? He cannot ever have heard Vergil read the words:

Tell me, is Death so wretched as that?

He asks for the climax of suffering, and – what is still harder to bear – prolongation and extension of suffering; and what does he gain thereby? Merely the boon of a longer existence. But what sort of life is a lingering death? . Can anyone be found who would prefer wasting away in pain, dying limb by limb, or letting out his life drop by drop, rather than expiring once for all? Can any man be found willing to be fastened to the accursed tree, long sickly, already deformed, swelling with ugly tumours on chest and shoulders, and draw the breath of life amid long-drawn-out agony? I think he would have many excuses for dying even before mounting the cross!

Deny, now, if you can, that Nature is very generous in making death inevitable. Many men have been prepared to enter upon still more shameful bargains: to betray friends in order to live longer themselves, or voluntarily to debase their children and so enjoy the light of day which is witness of all their sins. We must get rid of this craving for life, and learn that it makes no difference when your suffering comes, because at some time you are bound to suffer. The point is, not how long you live, but how nobly you live. And often this living nobly means that you cannot live long. Farewell.

Letter CII - On the Intimations of Our Immortality

Just as a man is annoying when he rouses a dreamer of pleasant dreams (for he is spoiling a pleasure which may be unreal but nevertheless has the appearance of reality), even so your letter has done me an injury. For it brought me back abruptly, absorbed as I was in agreeable meditation and ready to proceed still further if it had been permitted me. I was taking pleasure in investigating the immortality of souls, nay, in believing that doctrine. For I was lending a ready ear to the opinions of the great authors, who not only approve but promise this most pleasing condition. I was giving myself over to such a noble hope; for I was already weary of myself, beginning already to despise the fragments of my shattered existence, and feeling that I was destined to pass over into that infinity of time and the heritage of eternity, when I was suddenly awakened by the receipt of your letter, and lost my lovely dream. But, if I can once dispose of you, I shall reseek and rescue it.

There was a remark, at the beginning of your letter, that I had not explained the whole problem wherein I was endeavouring to prove one of the beliefs of our school, that the renown which falls to one's lot after death is a good; for I had not solved the problem with which we are usually confronted: "No good can consist of things that are distinct and separate; yet renown consists of such things." What you are asking about, my dear Lucilius, belongs to another topic of the same subject, and that is why I had postponed the arguments, not only on this one topic, but on other topics which also covered the same ground. For, as you know, certain logical questions are mingled with ethical ones. Accordingly, I handled the essential part of my subject which has to do with conduct – as to whether it is foolish and useless to be concerned with what lies beyond our last day, or whether our goods die with us and there is nothing left of him who is no more, or whether any profit can be attained or attempted beforehand out of that which, when it comes, we shall not be capable of feeling.

All these things have a view to conduct, and therefore they have been inserted under the proper topic. But the remarks of dialecticians in opposition to this idea had to be sifted out, and were accordingly laid aside. Now that you demand an answer to them all, I shall examine all their statements, and then refute them singly. Unless, however, I make a preliminary remark, it will be impossible to understand my rebuttals. And what is that preliminary remark? Simply this: there are certain continuous bodies, such as a man; there are certain composite bodies, – as ships, houses, and everything which is the result of joining separate parts into one sum total: there are certain others made up of things that are distinct, each member remaining separate – like an army, a populace, or a senate. For the persons who go to make up such bodies are united by virtue of law or function; but by their nature they are distinct and individual. Well, what further prefatory remarks do I still wish to make? Simply this: we believe that nothing is a good, if it be composed of things that are distinct. For a single good should be checked and controlled by a single soul; and the essential quality of each single good should be single. This can be proved of itself whenever you desire; in the meanwhile, however, it had to be laid aside, because our own weapons are being hurled at us.

Opponents speak thus: "You say, do you, that no good can be made up of things that are distinct? Yet this renown, of which you speak, is simply the favourable opinion of good men. For just as reputation does not consist of one person's remarks, and as ill repute does not consist of one person's disapproval, so renown does not mean that we have merely pleased one good person. In order to constitute renown, the agreement of many distinguished and praiseworthy men is necessary. But this results from the decision of a number – in other words, of persons who are distinct. Therefore, it is not a good. You say, again, that renown is the praise rendered to a good man by good men. Praise means speech: now speech is utterance with a particular meaning; and utterance, even from the lips of good men, is not a good in itself. For any act of a good man is not necessarily a good; he shouts his applause and hisses his disapproval, but one does not call the shouting or the hissing good – although his entire conduct may be admired and praised – any more than one would applaud a sneeze or a cough. Therefore, renown is not a good. Finally, tell us whether the good belongs to him who praises, or to him who is praised: if you say that the good belongs to him who is praised, you are on as foolish a quest as if you were to maintain that my neighbour's good health is my own. But to praise worthy men is an honourable action; thus the good is exclusively that of the man who does the praising, of the man who performs the action, and not of us, who are being praised. And yet this was the question under discussion."

I shall now answer the separate objections hurriedly. The first question still is, whether any good can consist of things that are distinct – and there are votes cast on both sides. Again, does renown need many votes? Renown can be satisfied with the decision of one good man: it is one good man who decides that we are good. Then the retort is: "What! Would you define reputation as the esteem of one individual, and ill-repute as the rancorous chatter of one man? Glory, too, we take to be more widespread, for it demands the agreement of many men." But the position of the "many" is different from that of "the one." And why? Because, if the good man thinks well of me, it practically amounts to my being thought well of by all good men; for they will all think the same, if they know me. Their judgment is alike and identical; the effect of truth on it is equal. They cannot disagree, which means that they would all hold the same view, being unable to hold different views. "One man's opinion," you say, "is not enough to create glory or reputation." In the former case, one judgment is a universal judgment, because all, if they were asked, would hold one opinion; in the other case, however, men of dissimilar character give divergent judgments. You will find perplexing emotions – everything doubtful, inconstant, untrustworthy. And can you suppose that all men are able to hold one opinion? Even an individual does not hold to a single opinion. With the good man it is truth that causes belief, and truth has but one function and one likeness; while among the second class of which I spoke, the ideas with which they agree are unsound. Moreover, those who are false are never steadfast: they are irregular and discordant. "But praise," says the objector, "is nothing but an utterance, and an utterance is not a good." When they say that renown is praise bestowed on the good by the good, what they refer to is not an utterance but a judgment. For a good man may remain silent; but if he decides that a certain person is worthy, of praise, that person is the object of praise. Besides, praise is one thing, and the giving of praise another; the latter demands utterance also. Hence no one speaks of "a funeral praise," but says "praise-giving" – for its function depends upon speech. And when we say that a man is worthy of praise, we assure human kindness to him, not in words, but in judgment. So the good opinion, even of one who in silence feels inward approval of a good man, is praise.

Again, as I have said, praise is a matter of the mind rather than of the speech; for speech brings out the praise that the mind has conceived, and publishes it forth to the attention of the many. To judge a man worthy of praise, is to praise him. And when our tragic poet sings to us that it is wonderful "to be praised by a well-praised hero," he means, "by one who is worthy of praise." Again, when an equally venerable bard says: "Praise nurtureth the arts," he does not mean the giving of praise, for that spoils the arts. Nothing has corrupted oratory and all other studies that depend on hearing so much as popular approval. Reputation necessarily demands words, but renown can be content with men's judgments, and suffice without the spoken word. It is satisfied not only amid silent approval, but even in the face of open protest. There is, in my opinion, this difference between renown and glory – the latter depends upon the judgments of the many; but renown on the judgments of good men. The retort comes: "But whose good is this renown, this praise rendered to a good man by good men? Is it of the one praised, or of the one who praises?" Of both, I say. It is my own good, in that I am praised, because I am naturally born to love all men, and I rejoice in having done good deeds and congratulate myself on having found men who express their ideas of my virtues with gratitude; that they are grateful, is a good to the many, but it is a good to me also. For my spirit is so ordered that I can regard the good of other men as my own – in any case those of whose good I am myself the cause. This good is also the good of those who render the praise, for it is applied by means of virtue; and every act of virtue is a good. My friends could not have found this blessing if I had not been a man of the right stamp. It is therefore a good belonging to both sides – this being praised when one deserves it – just as truly as a good decision is the good of him who makes the decision and also of him in whose favour the decision was given. Do you doubt that justice is a blessing to its possessor, as well as to the man to whom the just due was paid? To praise the deserving is justice; therefore, the good belongs to both sides.

This will be a sufficient answer to such dealers in subtleties. But it should not be our purpose to discuss things cleverly and to drag Philosophy down from her majesty to such petty quibbles. How much better it is to follow the open and direct road, rather than to map out for yourself a circuitous route which you must retrace with infinite trouble! For such argumentation is nothing else than the sport of men who are skilfully juggling with each other. Tell me rather how closely in accord with nature it is to let one's mind reach out into the boundless universe! The human soul is a great and noble thing; it permits of no limits except those which can be shared even by the gods. First of all, it does not consent to a lowly birthplace, like Ephesus or Alexandria, or any land that is even more thickly populated than these, and more richly spread with dwellings. The soul's homeland is the whole space that encircles the, height and breadth of the firmament, the whole rounded dome within which lie land and sea, within which the upper air that sunders the human from the divine also unites them, and where all the sentinel stars are taking their turn on duty. Again, the soul will not put up with a narrow span of existence. "All the years," says the soul, "are mine; no epoch is closed to great minds; all Time is open for the progress of thought. When the day comes to separate the heavenly from its earthly blend, I shall leave the body here where I found it, and shall of my own volition betake myself to the gods. I am not apart from them now, but am merely detained in a heavy and earthly prison." These delays of mortal existence are a prelude to the longer and better life. As the mother's womb holds us for ten months, making us ready, not for the womb itself, but for the existence into which we seem to be sent forth when at last we are fitted to draw breath and live in the open; just so, throughout the years extending between infancy and old age, we are making ourselves ready for another birth. A different beginning, a different condition, await us. We cannot yet, except at rare intervals, endure the light of heaven; therefore, look forward without fearing to that appointed hour, – the last hour of the body but not of the soul. Survey everything that lies about you, as if it were luggage in a guest-chamber:

you must travel on. Nature strips you as bare at your departure as at your entrance. You may take away no more than you brought in; what is more, you must throw away the major portion of that which you brought with you into life: you will be stripped of the very skin which covers you – that which has been your last protection; you will be stripped of the flesh, and lose the blood which is suffuses and circulated through your body; you will be stripped of bones and sinews, the framework of these transitory and feeble parts.

That day, which you fear as being the end of all things, is the birthday of your eternity. Lay aside your burden – why delay? – just as if you had not previously left the body which was your hiding-place! You cling to your burden, you struggle; at your birth also great effort was necessary on your mother's part to set you free. You weep and wail; and yet this very weeping happens at birth also; but then it was to be excused – for you came into the world wholly ignorant and inexperienced. When you left the warm and cherishing protection of your mother's womb, a freer air breathed into your face; then you winced at the touch of a rough hand, and you looked in amaze at unfamiliar objects, still delicate and ignorant of all things.

But now it is no new thing for you to be sundered from that of which you have previously been a part; let go your already useless limbs with resignation and dispense with that body in which you have dwelt for so long. It will be torn asunder, buried out of sight, and wasted away. Why be downcast? This is what ordinarily happens: when we are born, the afterbirth always perishes. Why love such a thing as if it were your own possession? It was merely your covering. The day will come which will tear you forth and lead you away from the company of the foul and noisome womb. Withdraw from it now too as much as you can, and withdraw from pleasure, except such as may be bound up with essential and important things; estrange yourself from it even now, and ponder on something nobler and loftier. Some day the secrets of nature shall be disclosed to you, the haze will be shaken from your eyes, and the bright light will stream in upon you from all sides.

Picture to yourself how great is the glow when all the stars mingle their fires; no shadows will disturb the clear sky. The whole expanse of heaven will shine evenly; for day and night are interchanged only in the lowest atmosphere. Then you will say that you have lived in darkness, after you have seen, in your perfect state, the perfect light – that light which now you behold darkly with vision that is cramped to the last degree. And yet, far off as it is, you already look upon it in wonder; what do you think the heavenly light will be when you have seen it in its proper sphere?

Such thoughts permit nothing mean to settle in the soul, nothing low, nothing cruel. They maintain that the gods are witnesses of everything. They order us to meet the gods' approval, to prepare ourselves to join them at some future time, and to plan for immortality. He that has grasped this idea shrinks from no attacking army, is not terrified by the trumpet-blast, and is intimidated by no threats. How should it not be that a man feels no fear, if he looks forward to death? He also who believes that the soul abides only as long as it is fettered in the body, scatters it abroad forthwith when dissolved, so that it may be useful even after death. For though he is taken from men's sight, still

Often our thoughts run back to the hero, and often the glory
Won by his race recurs to the mind.

Consider how much we are helped by good example; you will thus understand that the presence of a noble man is of no less service than his memory. Farewell.

Letter CIII - On the Dangers of Association with our Fellow-Men

Why are you looking about for troubles which may perhaps come your way, but which may indeed not come your way at all? I mean fires, falling buildings, and other accidents of the sort that are mere events rather than plots against us. Rather beware and shun those troubles which dog our steps and reach out their hands against us. Accidents, though they may be serious, are few – such as being shipwrecked or thrown from one's carriage; but it is from his fellow-man that a man's everyday danger comes. Equip yourself against that; watch that with an attentive eye. There is no evil more frequent, no evil more persistent, no evil more insinuating. Even the storm, before it gathers, gives a warning; houses crack before they crash; and smoke is the forerunner of fire. But damage from man is instantaneous, and the nearer it comes the more carefully it is concealed.

You are wrong to trust the countenances of those you meet. They have the aspect of men, but the souls of brutes; the difference is that only beasts damage you at the first encounter; those whom they have passed by they do not pursue. For nothing ever goads them to do harm except when need compels them: it is hunger or fear that forces them into a fight. But man delights to ruin man.

You must, however, reflect thus what danger you run at the hand of man, in order that you may deduce what is the duty of man. Try, in your dealings with others, to harm not, in order that you be not harmed. You should rejoice with all in their joys and sympathize with them in their troubles, remembering what you should offer and what you should withhold. And what may you attain by living such a life? Not necessarily freedom from harm at their hands, but at least freedom from deceit. In so far, however, as you are able, take refuge with philosophy: she will cherish you in her bosom, and in her sanctuary you shall be safe, or, at any rate, safer than before. People collide only when they are travelling the same path. But this very philosophy must never be vaunted by you; for philosophy when employed with insolence and arrogance has been perilous to many. Let her strip off your faults, rather than assist you to decry the faults of others. Let her not hold aloof from the customs of mankind, nor make it her business to condemn whatever she herself does not do. A man may be wise without parade and without arousing enmity. Farewell.

Letter CIV - On Care of Health and Peace of Mind

I have run off to my villa at Nomentum, for what purpose, do you suppose? To escape the city? No; to shake off a fever which was surely working its way into my system. It had already got a grip upon me. My physician kept insisting that when the circulation was upset and irregular, disturbing the natural poise, the disease was under way. I therefore ordered my carriage to be made ready at once, and insisted on departing in spite of my wife Paulina's efforts to stop me; for I remembered master Gallio's words, when he began to develop a fever in Achaia and took ship at once, insisting that the disease was not of the body but of the place. That is what I remarked to my dear Paulina, who always urges me to take care of my health. I know that her very life-breath comes and goes with my own, and I am beginning, in my solicitude for her, to be solicitous for myself. And although old age has made me braver to bear many things, I am gradually losing this boon that old age bestows. For it comes into my mind that in this old man there is a youth also, and youth needs tenderness. Therefore, since I cannot prevail upon her to love me any more heroically, she prevails upon me to cherish myself more carefully. For one must indulge genuine emotions; sometimes, even in spite of weighty reasons, the breath of life must be called back and kept at our very lips even at the price of great suffering, for the sake of those whom we hold dear; because the good man should not live as long as it pleases him, but as long as he ought. He who does not value his wife, or his friend, highly enough to linger longer in life – he who obstinately persists in dying is a voluptuary.

The soul should also enforce this command upon itself whenever the needs of one's relatives require; it should pause and humour those near and dear, not only when it desires, but even when it has begun, to die. It gives proof of a great heart to return to life for the sake of others; and noble men have often done this. But this procedure also, I believe, indicates the highest type of kindness: that although the greatest advantage of old age is the opportunity to be more negligent regarding self-preservation and to use life more adventurously, one should watch over one's old age with still greater care if one knows that such action is pleasing, useful, or desirable in the eyes of a person whom one holds dear. This is also a source of no mean joy and profit; for what is sweeter than to be so valued by one's wife that one becomes more valuable to oneself for this reason? Hence my dear Paulina is able to make me responsible, not only for her fears, but also for my own.

So you are curious to know the outcome of this prescription of travel? As soon as I escaped from the oppressive atmosphere of the city, and from that awful odour of reeking kitchens which, when in use, pour forth a ruinous mess of steam and soot, I perceived at once that my health was mending. And how much stronger do you think I felt when I reached my vineyards! Being, so to speak, let out to pasture, I regularly walked into my meals! So I am my old self again, feeling now no wavering languor in my system, and no sluggishness in my brain. I am beginning to work with all my energy.

But the mere place avails little for this purpose, unless the mind is fully master of itself, and can, at its pleasure, find seclusion even in the midst of business; the man, however, who is always selecting resorts and hunting for leisure, will find something to distract his mind in every place. Socrates is reported to have replied, when a certain person complained of having received no benefit from his travels: "It serves you right! You travelled in your own company!" O what a blessing it would be for some men to wander away from themselves! As it is, they cause themselves vexation, worry, demoralization, and fear! What profit is there in crossing the sea and in going from one city to another? If you would escape your troubles, you need not another place but another personality. Perhaps you have reached Athens, or perhaps Rhodes; choose any state you fancy, how does it matter what its character may be? You will be bringing to it your own.

Suppose that you hold wealth to be a good: poverty will then distress you, and, – which is most pitiable, – it will be an imaginary poverty. For you may be rich, and nevertheless, because your neighbour is richer, you suppose yourself to be poor exactly by the same amount in which you fall short of your neighbour. You may deem official position a good; you will be vexed at another's appointment or re-appointment to the consulship; you will be jealous whenever you see a name several times in the state records. Your ambition will be so frenzied that you will regard yourself last in the race if there is anyone in front of you. Or you may rate death as the worst of evils, although there is really no evil therein except that which precedes death's coming – fear. You will be frightened out of your wits, not only by real, but by fancied dangers, and will be tossed for ever on the sea of illusion. What benefit will it be to

Have threaded all the towns of Argolis,
A fugitive through midmost press of foes?

For peace itself will furnish further apprehension. Even in the midst of safety you will have no confidence if your mind has once been given a shock; once it has acquired the habit of blind panic, it is incapable of providing even for its own safety. For it does not avoid danger, but runs away. Yet we are more exposed to danger when we turn our backs.

You may judge it the most grievous of ills to lose any of those you love; while all the same this would be no less foolish than weeping because the trees which charm your eye and adorn your home lose their foliage. Regard everything that pleases you as if it were a flourishing plant; make the most of it while it is in leaf, for different plants at different seasons must fall and die. But just as the loss of leaves is a light thing, because they are born afresh, so it is with the loss of those whom you love and regard as the delight of your life; for they can be replaced even though they cannot be born afresh. "New friends, however, will not be the same." No, nor will you yourself remain the same; you change with every day and every hour. But in other men you more readily see what time plunders; in your own case the change is hidden, because it will not take place visibly. Others are snatched from sight; we ourselves are being stealthily filched away from ourselves. You will not think about any of these problems, nor will you apply remedies to these wounds. You will of your own volition be sowing a crop of trouble by alternate hoping and despairing. If you are wise, mingle these two elements: do not hope without despair, or despair without hope.

What benefit has travel of itself ever been able to give anyone? No restraint upon pleasure, no bridling of desire, no checking of bad temper, no crushing of the wild assaults of passion, no opportunity to rid the soul of evil. Travelling cannot give us judgment, or shake off our errors; it merely holds our attention for a moment by a certain novelty, as children pause to wonder at something unfamiliar. Besides, it irritates us, through the wavering of a mind which is suffering from an acute attack of sickness; the very motion makes it more fitful and nervous. Hence the spots we had sought most eagerly we quit still more eagerly, like birds that flit and are off as soon as they have alighted. What travel will give is familiarity with other nations: it will reveal to you mountains of strange shape, or unfamiliar tracts of plain, or valleys that are watered by everflowing springs, or the characteristics of some river that comes to our attention. We observe how the Nile rises and swells in summer, or how the Tigris disappears, runs underground through hidden spaces, and then appears with unabated sweep; or how the Maeander, that oft-rehearsed theme and plaything of the poets, turns in frequent bendings, and often in winding comes close to its own channel before resuming its course. But this sort of information will not make better or sounder men of us.

We ought rather to spend our time in study, and to cultivate those who are masters of wisdom, learning something which has been investigated, but not settled; by this means the mind can be relieved of a most wretched serfdom, and won over to freedom. Indeed, as long as you are ignorant of what you should avoid or seek, or of what is necessary or superfluous, or of what is right or wrong, you will not be travelling, but merely wandering. There will be no benefit to you in this hurrying to and fro; for you are travelling with your emotions and are followed by your afflictions. Would that they were indeed following you! In that case, they would be farther away; as it is, you are carrying and not leading them. Hence they press about you on all sides, continually chafing and annoying you. It is medicine, not scenery, for which the sick man must go a-searching. Suppose that someone has broken a leg or dislocated a joint: he does not take carriage or ship for other regions, but he calls in the physician to set the fractured limb, or to move it back to its proper place in the socket. What then? When the spirit is broken or wrenched in so many places, do you think that change of place can heal it? The complaint is too deep-seated to be cured by a journey. Travel does not make a physician or an orator; no art is acquired by merely living in a certain place.

Where lies the truth, then? Can wisdom, the greatest of all the arts, be picked up on a journey? I assure you, travel as far as you like, you can never establish yourself beyond the reach of desire, beyond the reach of bad temper, or beyond the reach of fear; had it been so, the human race would long ago have banded together and made a pilgrimage to the spot. Such ills, as long as you carry with you their causes, will load you down and worry you to skin and bone in your wanderings over land and sea. Do you wonder that it is of no use to run away from them? That from which you are running, is within you. Accordingly, reform your own self, get the burden off your own shoulders, and keep within safe limits the cravings which ought to be removed. Wipe out from your soul all trace of sin. If you would enjoy your travels, make healthy the companion of your travels. As long as this companion is avaricious and mean, greed will stick to you; and while you consort with an overbearing man, your puffed-up ways will also stick close. Live with a hangman, and you will never be rid of your cruelty. If an adulterer be your club-mate, he will kindle the baser passions. If you would be stripped of your faults leave far behind you the patterns of the faults. The miser, the swindler, the bully, the cheat, who will do you much harm merely by being near you, are within you.

Change therefore to better associations: live with the Catos, with Laelius, with Tubero. Or, if you enjoy living with Greeks also, spend your time with Socrates and with Zeno: the former will show you how to die if it be necessary; the latter how to die before it is necessary. Live with Chrysippus, with Posidonius: they will make you acquainted with things earthly and things heavenly; they will bid you work hard over something more than neat turns of language and phrases mouthed forth for the entertainment of listeners; they will bid you be stout of heart and rise superior to threats. The only harbour safe from the seething storms of this life is scorn of the future, a firm stand, a readiness to receive Fortune's missiles full in the breast, neither skulking nor turning the back. Nature has brought us forth brave of spirit, and, as she has implanted in certain animals a spirit of ferocity, in others craft, in others terror, so she has gifted us with an aspiring and lofty spirit, which prompts us to seek a life of the greatest honour, and not of the greatest security, that most resembles the soul of the universe, which it follows and imitates as far as our mortal steps permit. This spirit thrusts itself forward, confident of commendation and esteem. It is superior to all, monarch of all it surveys; hence it should be subservient to nothing, finding no task too heavy, and nothing strong enough to weigh down the shoulders of a man.

Shapes dread to look upon, of toil or death

are not in the least dreadful, if one is able to look upon them with unflinching gaze, and is able to pierce the shadows. Many a sight that is held a terror in the night-time, is turned to ridicule by day. "Shapes dread to look upon, of toil or death": our Vergil has excellently said that these shapes are dread, not in reality, but only "to look upon" – in other words, they seem terrible, but are not. And in these visions what is there, I say, as fear-inspiring as rumour has proclaimed? Why, pray, my dear Lucilius, should a man fear toil, or a mortal death? Countless cases occur to my mind of men who think that what they themselves are unable to do is impossible, who maintain that we utter words which are too big for man's nature to carry out. But how much more highly do I think of these men! They can do these things, but decline to do them. To whom that ever tried have these tasks proved false? To what man did they not seem easier in the doing? Our lack of confidence is not the result of difficulty. The difficulty comes from our lack of confidence.

If, however, you desire a pattern, take Socrates, a long-suffering old man, who was sea-tossed amid every hardship and yet was unconquered both by poverty (which his troubles at home made more burdensome) and by toil, including the drudgery of military service. He was much tried at home, whether we think of his wife, a woman of rough manners and shrewish tongue, or of the children whose intractability showed them to be more like their mother than their father. And if you consider the facts, he lived either in time of war, or under tyrants, or under a democracy, which is more cruel than wars and tyrants. The war lasted for twenty-seven years; then the state became the victim of the Thirty Tyrants, of whom many were his personal enemies. At the last came that climax of condemnation under the gravest of charges: they accused him of disturbing the state religion and corrupting the youth, for they declared that he had influenced the youth to defy the gods, to defy the council, and to defy the state in general. Next came the prison, and the cup of poison. But all these measures changed the soul of Socrates so little that they did not even change his features. What wonderful and rare distinction! He maintained this attitude up to the very end, and no man ever saw Socrates too much elated or too much depressed. Amid all the disturbance of Fortune, he was undisturbed.

Do you desire another case? Take that of the younger Marcus Cato, with whom Fortune dealt in a more hostile and more persistent fashion. But he withstood her, on all occasions, and in his last moments, at the point of death, showed that a brave man can live in spite of Fortune, can die in spite of her. His whole life was passed either in civil warfare, or under a political regime which was soon to breed civil war. And you may say that he, just as much as Socrates, declared allegiance to liberty in the midst of slavery – unless perchance you think that Pompey, Caesar, and Crassus were the allies of liberty! No one ever saw Cato change, no matter how often the state changed: he kept himself the same in all circumstances – in the praetorship, in defeat, under accusation, in his province, on the platform, in the army, in death. Furthermore, when the republic was in a crisis of terror, when Caesar was on one side with ten embattled legions at his call, aided by so many foreign nations. and when Pompey was on the other, satisfied to stand alone against all comers, and when the citizens were leaning towards either Caesar or Pompey, Cato alone established a definite party for the Republic. If you would obtain a mental picture of that period, you may imagine on one side the people and the whole proletariat eager for revolution – on the other the senators and knights, the chosen and honoured men of the commonwealth; and there were left between them but these two – the Republic and Cato.

> I tell you, you will marvel when you see
> Atreus' son, and Priam, and Achilles, wroth at both.

Like Achilles, he scorns and disarms each faction. And this is the vote which he casts concerning them both: "If Caesar wins, I slay myself; if Pompey, I go into exile." What was there for a man to fear who, whether in defeat or in victory, had assigned to himself a doom which might have been assigned to him by his enemies in their utmost rage? So he died by his own decision.

You see that man can endure toil: Cato, on foot, led an army through African deserts. You see that thirst can be endured: he marched over sun-baked hills, dragging the remains of a beaten army and with no train of supplies, undergoing lack of water and wearing a heavy suit of armour; always the last to drink of the few springs which they chanced to find. You see that honour, and dishonour too, can be despised: for they report that on the very day when Cato was defeated at the elections, he played a game of ball. You see also that man can be free from fear of those above him in rank: for Cato attacked Caesar and Pompey simultaneously, at a time when none dared fall foul of the one without endeavouring to oblige the other. You see that death can be scorned as well as exile: Cato inflicted exile upon himself and finally death, and war all the while.

And so, if only we are willing to withdraw our necks from the yoke, we can keep as stout a heart against such terrors as these. But first and foremost, we must reject pleasures; they render us weak and womanish; they make great demands upon us, and, moreover, cause us to make great demands upon Fortune. Second, we must spurn wealth: wealth is the diploma of slavery. Abandon gold and silver, and whatever else is a burden upon our richly-furnished homes; liberty cannot be gained for nothing. If you set a high value on liberty, you must set a low value on everything else. Farewell.

Letter CV - On Facing the World with Confidence

I shall now tell you certain things to which you should pay attention in order to live more safely. Do you however, – such is my judgment, – hearken to my precepts just as if I were counselling you to keep safe your health in your country-place at Ardea.

Reflect on the things which goad man into destroying man: you will find that they are hope, envy, hatred, fear, and contempt. Now, of all these, contempt is the least harmful, so much so that many have skulked behind it as a sort of cure. When a man despises you, he works you injury, to be sure, but he passes on; and no one persistently or of set purpose does hurt to a person whom he despises. Even in battle, prostrate soldiers are neglected: men fight with those who stand their ground. And you can avoid the envious hopes of the wicked so long as you have nothing which can stir the evil desires of others, and so long as you possess nothing remarkable. For people crave even little things, if these catch the attention or are of rare occurrence.

You will escape envy if you do not force yourself upon the public view, if you do not boast your possessions, if you understand how to enjoy things privately. Hatred comes either from running foul of others: and this can be avoided by never provoking anyone; or else it is uncalled for: and common-sense will keep you safe from it. Yet it has been dangerous to many; some people have been hated without having had an enemy. As to not being feared, a moderate fortune and an easy disposition will guarantee you that; men should know that you are the sort of person who can be offended without danger; and your reconciliation should be easy and sure. Moreover, it is as troublesome to be feared at home as abroad; it is as bad to be feared by a slave as by a gentleman. For every one has strength enough to do you some harm. Besides, he who is feared, fears also; no one has been able to arouse terror and live in peace of mind.

Contempt remains to be discussed. He who has made this quality an adjunct of his own personality, who is despised because he wishes to be despised and not because he must be despised, has the measure of contempt under his control. Any inconveniences in this respect can be dispelled by honourable occupations and by friendships with men who have influence with an influential person; with these men it will profit you to engage but not to entangle yourself, lest the cure may cost you more than the risk. Nothing, however, will help you so much as keeping still – talking very little with others, and as much as may be with yourself. For there is a sort of charm about conversation, something very subtle and coaxing, which, like intoxication or love, draws secrets from us. No man will keep to himself what he hears. No one will tell another only as much as he has heard. And he who tells tales will tell names, too. Everyone has someone to whom he entrusts exactly what has been entrusted to him. Though he checks his own garrulity, and is content with one hearer, he will bring about him a nation, if that which was a secret shortly before becomes common talk.

The most important contribution to peace of mind is never to do wrong. Those who lack self-control lead disturbed and tumultuous lives; their crimes are balanced by their fears, and they are never at ease. For they tremble after the deed, and they are embarrassed; their consciences do not allow them to busy themselves with other matters, and continually compel them to give an answer. Whoever expects punishment, receives it, but whoever deserves it, expects it. Where there is an evil conscience something may bring safety, but nothing can bring ease; for a man imagines that, even if he is not under arrest, he may soon be arrested. His sleep is troubled; when he speaks of another man's crime, he reflects upon his own, which seems to him not sufficiently blotted out, not sufficiently hidden from view. A wrongdoer sometimes has the luck to escape notice but never the assurance thereof. Farewell.

Letter CVI - On the Corporeality of Virtue

My tardiness in answering your letter was not due to press of business. Do not listen to that sort of excuse; I am at liberty, and so is anyone else who wishes to be at liberty. No man is at the mercy of affairs. He gets entangled in them of his own accord, and then flatters himself that being busy is a proof of happiness. Very well; you no doubt want to know why I did not answer the letter sooner? The matter about which you consulted me was being gathered into the fabric of my volume. For you know that I am planning to cover the whole of moral philosophy and to settle all the problems which concern it. Therefore I hesitated whether to make you wait until the proper time came for this subject, or to pronounce judgment out of the logical order; but it seemed more kindly not to keep waiting one who comes from such a distance. So I propose both to pick this out of the proper sequence of correlated matter, and also to send you, without waiting to be asked, whatever has to do with questions of the same sort.

Do you ask what these are? Questions regarding which knowledge pleases rather than profits; for instance, your question whether the good is corporeal. Now the good is active: for it is beneficial; and what is active is corporeal. The good stimulates the mind and, in a way, moulds and embraces that which is essential to the body. The goods of the body are bodily; so therefore must be the goods of the soul. For the soul, too, is corporeal. Ergo, man's good must be corporeal, since man himself is corporeal. I am sadly astray if the elements which support man and preserve or restore his health, are not bodily; therefore, his good is a body. You will have no doubt, I am sure, that emotions are bodily things (if I may be allowed to wedge in another subject not under immediate discussion), like wrath, love, sternness; unless you doubt whether they change our features, knot our foreheads, relax the countenance, spread blushes, or drive away the blood? What, then? Do you think that such evident marks of the body are stamped upon us by anything else than body? And if emotions are corporeal, so are the diseases of the spirit – such as greed, cruelty, and all the faults which harden in our souls, to such an extent that they get into an incurable state. Therefore evil is also, and all its branches – spite, hatred, pride; . and so also are goods, first because they are opposite poles of the bad, and second because they will manifest to you the same symptoms. Do you not see how a spirit of bravery makes the eye flash? How prudence tends toward concentration? How reverence produces moderation and tranquillity? How joy produces calm? How sternness begets stiffness? How gentleness produces relaxation? These qualities are therefore bodily; for they change the tones and the shapes of substances, exercising their own power in their own kingdoms.

Now all the virtues which I have mentioned are goods, and so are their results. Have you any doubt that whatever can touch is corporeal?

Nothing but body can touch or be touched

as Lucretius says. Moreover, such changes as I have mentioned could not affect the body without touching it. Therefore, they are bodily. Furthermore, any object that has power to move, force, restrain, or control, is corporeal. Come now! Does not fear hold us back? Does not boldness drive us ahead? Bravery spur us on, and give us momentum? Restraint rein us in and call us back? Joy raise our spirits? Sadness cast us down? In short, any act on our part is performed at the bidding of wickedness or virtue. Only a body can control or forcefully affect another body. The good of the body is corporeal; a man's good is related to his bodily good; therefore, it is bodily.

Now that I have humoured your wishes, I shall anticipate your remark, when you say: "What a game of pawns!" We dull our fine edge by such superfluous pursuits; these things make men clever, but not good. Wisdom is a plainer thing than that; nay, it is clearly better to use literature for the improvement of the mind, instead of wasting philosophy itself as we waste other efforts on superfluous things. Just as we suffer from excess in all things, so we suffer from excess in literature; thus we learn our lessons, not for life, but for the lecture-room. Farewell.

Letter CVII - On Obedience to the Universal Will

Where is that common-sense of yours? Where that deftness in examining things? That greatness of soul? Have you come to be tormented by a trifle? Your slaves regarded your absorption in business as an opportunity for them to run away. Well, if your friends deceived you (for by all means let them have the name which we mistakenly bestowed upon them, and so call them, that they may incur more shame by not being such friends) – if your friends, I repeat, deceived you, all your affairs would lack something; as it is, you merely lack men who damaged your own endeavours and considered you burdensome to your neighbours. None of these things is unusual or unexpected. It is as nonsensical to be put out by such events as to complain of being spattered in the street or at getting befouled in the mud. The programme of life is the same as that of a bathing establishment, a crowd, or a journey: sometimes things will be thrown at you, and sometimes they will strike you by accident. Life is not a dainty business. You have started on a long journey; you are bound to slip, collide, fall, become weary, and cry out: "O for Death!" – or in other words, tell lies. At one stage you will leave a comrade behind you, at another you will bury someone, at another you will be apprehensive. It is amid stumblings of this sort that you must travel out this rugged journey.

Does one wish to die? Let the mind be prepared to meet everything; let it know that it has reached the heights round which the thunder plays. Let it know that it has arrived where –

Grief and avenging Care have set their couch,
And pallid sickness dwells, and drear Old Age.

With such messmates must you spend your days. Avoid them you cannot, but despise them you can. And you will despise them, if you often take thought and anticipate the future. Everyone approaches courageously a danger which he has prepared himself to meet long before, and withstands even hardships if he has previously practised how to meet them. But, contrariwise, the unprepared are panic-stricken even at the most trifling things. We must see to it that nothing shall come upon us unforeseen. And since things are all the more serious when they are unfamiliar, continual reflection will give you the power, no matter what the evil may be, not to play the unschooled boy.

"My slaves have run away from me!" Yes, other men have been robbed, blackmailed, slain, betrayed, stamped under foot, attacked by poison or by slander; no matter what trouble you mention, it has happened to many. Again, there are manifold kinds of missiles which are hurled at us. Some are planted in us, some are being brandished and at this very moment are on the way, some which were destined for other men graze us instead. We should not manifest surprise at any sort of condition into which we are born, and which should be lamented by no one, simply because it is equally ordained for all. Yes, I say, equally ordained; for a man might have experienced even that which he has escaped. And an equal law consists, not of that which all have experienced, but of that which is laid down for all. Be sure to prescribe for your mind this sense of equity; we should pay without complaint the tax of our mortality.

Winter brings on cold weather; and we must shiver. Summer returns, with its heat; and we must sweat. Unseasonable weather upsets the health; and we must fall ill. In certain places we may meet with wild beasts, or with men who are more destructive than any beasts. Floods, or fires, will cause us loss. And we cannot change this order of things; but what we can do is to acquire stout hearts, worthy of good men, thereby courageously enduring chance and placing ourselves in harmony with Nature. And Nature moderates this world-kingdom which you see, by her changing seasons: clear weather follows cloudy; after a calm, comes the storm; the winds blow by turns; day succeeds night; some of the heavenly bodies rise, and some set. Eternity consists of opposites.

It is to this law that our souls must adjust themselves, this they should follow, this they should obey. Whatever happens, assume that it was bound to happen, and do not be willing to rail at Nature. That which you cannot reform, it is best to endure, and to attend uncomplainingly upon the God under whose guidance everything progresses; for it is a bad soldier who grumbles when following his commander. For this reason we should welcome our orders with energy and vigour, nor should we cease to follow the natural course of this most beautiful universe, into which all our future sufferings are woven.

Let us address Jupiter, the pilot of this world-mass, as did our great Cleanthes in those most eloquent lines – lines which I shall allow myself to render in Latin, after the example of the eloquent Cicero. If you like them, make the most of them; if they displease you, you will understand that I have simply been following the practise of Cicero:

Lead me, O Master of the lofty heavens,
My Father, whithersoever thou shalt wish.
I shall not falter, but obey with speed.
And though I would not, I shall go, and suffer,
In sin and sorrow what I might have done
In noble virtue. Aye, the willing soul
Fate leads, but the unwilling drags along.

Let us live thus, and speak thus; let Fate find us ready and alert. Here is your great soul – the man who has given himself over to Fate; on the other hand, that man is a weakling and a degenerate who struggles and maligns the order of the universe and would rather reform the gods than reform himself. Farewell.

Letter CVIII - On the Approaches to Philosophy

The topic about which you ask me is one of those where our only concern with knowledge is to have the knowledge. Nevertheless, because it does so far concern us, you are in a hurry; you are not willing to wait for the books which I am at this moment arranging for you, and which embrace the whole department of moral philosophy. I shall send you the books at once; but I shall, before doing that, write and tell you how this eagerness to learn, with which I see you are aflame, should be regulated, so that it may not get in its own way. Things are not to be gathered at random; nor should they be greedily attacked in the mass; one will arrive at a knowledge of the whole by studying the parts. The burden should be suited to your strength, nor should you tackle more than you can adequately handle. Absorb not all that you wish, but all that you can hold. Only be of a sound mind, and then you will be able to hold all that you wish. For the more the mind receives, the more does it expand.

This was the advice, I remember, which Attalus gave me in the days when I practically laid siege to his class-room, the first to arrive and the last to leave. Even as he paced up and down, I would challenge him to various discussions; for he not only kept himself accessible to his pupils, but met them half-way. His words were: "The same purpose should possess both master and scholar – an ambition in the one case to promote, and in the other to progress." He who studies with a philosopher should take away with him some one good thing every day: he should daily return home a sounder man, or in the way to become sounder. And he will thus return; for it is one of the functions of philosophy to help not only those who study her, but those also who associate with her. He that walks in the sun, though he walk not for that purpose, must needs become sunburned. He who frequents the perfumer's shop and lingers even for a short time, will carry with him the scent of the place. And he who follows a philosopher is bound to derive some benefit therefrom, which will help him even though he be remiss. Mark what I say: "remiss," not "recalcitrant."

"What then?" you say, "do we not know certain men who have sat for many years at the feet of a philosopher and yet have not acquired the slightest tinge of wisdom?" Of course I know such men. There are indeed persevering gentlemen who stick at it; I do not call them pupils of the wise, but merely "squatters." Certain of them come to hear and not to learn, just as we are attracted to the theatre to satisfy the pleasures of the ear, whether by a speech, or by a song, or by a play. This class, as you will see, constitutes a large part of the listeners, who regard the philosopher's lecture-room merely as a sort of lounging-place for their leisure. They do not set about to lay aside any faults there, or to receive a rule of life, by which they may test their characters; they merely wish to enjoy to the full the delights of the ear. And yet some arrive even with notebooks, not to take down the matter, but only the words, that they may presently repeat them to others with as little profit to these as they themselves received when they heard them. A certain number are stirred by high-sounding phrases, and adapt themselves to the emotions of the speaker with lively change of face and mind – just like the emasculated Phrygian priests who are wont to be roused by the sound of the flute and go mad to order. But the true hearer is ravished and stirred by the beauty of the subject matter, not by the jingle of empty words. When a bold word has been uttered in defiance of death, or a saucy fling in defiance of Fortune, we take delight in acting straightway upon that which we have heard. Men are impressed by such words, and become what they are bidden to be, should but the impression abide in the mind, and should the populace, who discourage honourable things, not immediately lie in wait to rob them of this noble impulse; only a few can carry home the mental attitude with which they were inspired. It is easy to rouse a listener so that he will crave righteousness; for Nature has laid the foundations and planted the seeds of virtue in us all. And we are all born to these general privileges; hence, when the stimulus is added, the good spirit is stirred as if it were freed from bonds. Have you not noticed how the theatre re-echoes whenever any words are spoken whose truth we appreciate generally and confirm unanimously.

The poor lack much; the greedy man lacks all.
A greedy man does good to none; he does
Most evil to himself.

At such verses as these, your meanest miser claps applause and rejoices to hear his own sins reviled. How much more do you think this holds true, when such things are uttered by a philosopher, when he introduces verses among his wholesome precepts, that he may thus make those verses sink more effectively into the mind of the neophyte! Cleanthes used to say: "As our breath produces a louder sound when it passes through the long and narrow opening of the trumpet and escapes by a hole which widens at the end, even so the fettering rules of poetry clarify our meaning." The very same words are more carelessly received and make less impression upon us, when they are spoken in prose; but when metre is added and when regular prosody has compressed a noble idea, then the selfsame thought comes, as it were, hurtling with a fuller fling. We talk much about despising money, and we give advice on this subject in the lengthiest of speeches, that mankind may believe true riches to exist in the mind and not in one's bank account, and that the man who adapts himself to his slender means and makes himself wealthy on a little sum, is the truly rich man; but our minds are struck more effectively when a verse like this is repeated:

He needs but little who desires but little.

or,

He hath his wish, whose wish includeth naught
Save that which is enough.

When we hear such words as these, we are led towards a confession of the truth.

Even men in whose opinion nothing is enough, wonder and applaud when they hear such words, and swear eternal hatred against money. When you see them thus disposed, strike home, keep at them, and charge them with this duty, dropping all double meanings, syllogisms, hair-splitting, and the other side-shows of ineffective smartness. Preach against greed, preach against high living; and when you notice that you have made progress and impressed the minds of your hearers, lay on still harder. You cannot imagine how much progress can be brought about by an address of that nature, when you are bent on curing your hearers and are absolutely devoted to their best interests. For when the mind is young, it may most easily be won over to desire what is honourable and upright; truth, if she can obtain a suitable pleader, will lay strong hands upon those who can still be taught, those who have been but superficially spoiled.

At any rate, when I used to hear Attalus denouncing sin, error, and the evils of life, I often felt sorry for mankind and regarded Attalus as a noble and majestic being – above our mortal heights. He called himself a king, but I thought him more than a king, because he was entitled to pass judgment on kings. And in truth, when he began to uphold poverty, and to show what a useless and dangerous burden was everything that passed the measure of our need, I often desired to leave his lecture-room a poor man. Whenever he castigated our pleasure-seeking lives, and extolled personal purity, moderation in diet, and a mind free from unnecessary, not to speak of unlawful, pleasures, the desire came upon me to limit my food and drink. And that is why some of these habits have stayed with me, Lucilius. For I had planned my whole life with great resolves. And later, when I returned to the duties of a citizen, I did indeed keep a few of these good resolutions. That is why I have forsaken oysters and mushrooms for ever: since they are not really food, but are relishes to bully the sated stomach into further eating, as is the fancy of gourmands and those who stuff themselves beyond their powers of digestion: down with it quickly, and up with it quickly! That is why I have also throughout my life avoided perfumes; because the best scent for the person is no scent at all. That is why my stomach is unacquainted with wine. That is why throughout my life I have shunned the bath, and have believed that to emaciate the body and sweat it into thinness is at once unprofitable and effeminate. Other resolutions have been broken, but after all in such a way that, in cases where I ceased to practice abstinence, I have observed a limit which is indeed next door to abstinence; perhaps it is even a little more difficult, because it is easier for the will to cut off certain things utterly than to use them with restraint.

Inasmuch as I have begun to explain to you how much greater was my impulse to approach philosophy in my youth than to continue it in my old age, I shall not be ashamed to tell you what ardent zeal Pythagoras inspired in me. Sotion used to tell me why Pythagoras abstained from animal food, and why, in later times, Sextius did also. In each case, the reason was different, but it was in each case a noble reason. Sextius believed that man had enough sustenance without resorting to blood, and that a habit of cruelty is formed whenever butchery is practised for pleasure. Moreover, he thought we should curtail the sources of our luxury; he argued that a varied diet was contrary to the laws of health, and was unsuited to our constitutions. Pythagoras, on the other hand, held that all beings were inter-related, and that there was a system of exchange between souls which transmigrated from one bodily shape into another. If one may believe him, no soul perishes or ceases from its functions at all, except for a tiny interval – when it is being poured from one body into another. We may question at what time and after what seasons of change the soul returns to man, when it has wandered through many a dwelling-place; but meantime, he made men fearful of guilt and parricide, since they might be, without knowing it, attacking the soul of a parent and injuring it with knife or with teeth – if, as is possible, the related spirit be dwelling temporarily in this bit of flesh! When Sotion had set forth this doctrine, supplementing it with his own proofs, he would say: "You do not believe that souls are assigned, first to one body and then to another, and that our so-called death is merely a change of abode? You do not believe that in cattle, or in wild beasts, or in creatures of the deep, the soul of him who was once a man may linger? You do not believe that nothing on this earth is annihilated, but only changes its haunts? And that animals also have cycles of progress and, so to speak, an orbit for their souls, no less than the heavenly bodies, which revolve in fixed circuits? Great men have put faith in this idea; therefore, while holding to your own view, keep the whole question in abeyance in your mind. If the theory is true, it is a mark of purity to refrain from eating flesh; if it be false, it is economy. And what harm does it do to you to give such credence? I am merely depriving you of food which sustains lions and vultures."

I was imbued with this teaching, and began to abstain from animal food; at the end of a year the habit was as pleasant as it was easy. I was beginning to feel that my mind was more active; though I would not to-day positively state whether it really was or not. Do you ask how I came to abandon the practice? It was this way: The days of my youth coincided with the early part of the reign of Tiberius Caesar. Some foreign rites were at that time being inaugurated, and abstinence from certain kinds of animal food was set down as a proof of interest in the strange cult. So at the request of my father, who did not fear prosecution, but who detested philosophy, I returned to my previous habits; and it was no very hard matter to induce me to dine more comfortably.

Attalus used to recommend a pillow which did not give in to the body; and now, old as I am, I use one so hard that it leaves no trace after pressure. I have mentioned all this in order to show you how zealous neophytes are with regard to their first impulses towards the highest ideals, provided that some one does his part in exhorting them and in kindling their ardour. There are indeed mistakes made, through the fault of our advisers, who teach us how to debate and not how to live; there are also mistakes made by the pupils, who come to their teachers to develop, not their souls, but their wits. Thus the study of wisdom has become the study of words.

Now it makes a great deal of difference what you have in mind when you approach a given subject. If a man is to be a scholar, and is examining the works of Vergil, he does not interpret the noble passage

Time flies away, and cannot be restored

in the following sense: "We must wake up; unless we hasten, we shall be left behind. Time rolls swiftly ahead, and rolls us with it. We are hurried along ignorant of our destiny; we arrange all our plans for the future, and on the edge of a precipice are at our ease." Instead of this, he brings to our attention how often Vergil, in speaking of the rapidity of time, uses the word "flies" (fugit).

The choicest days of hapless human life
Fly first; disease and bitter eld succeed,
And toil, till harsh death rudely snatches all.

He who considers these lines in the spirit of a philosopher comments on the words in their proper sense: "Vergil never says, 'Time goes,' but 'Time flies,' because the latter is the quickest kind of movement, and in every case our best days are the first to be snatched away; why, then, do we hesitate to bestir ourselves so that we may be able to keep pace with this swiftest of all swift things?" The good flies past and the bad takes its place. Just as the purest wine flows from the top of the jar and the thickest dregs settle at the bottom; so in our human life, that which is best comes first. Shall we allow other men to quaff the best, and keep the dregs for ourselves? Let this phrase cleave to your soul; you should be satisfied thereby as if it were uttered by an oracle:

> *Each choicest day of hapless human life*
> *Flies first.*

Why "choicest day?" Because what's to come is unsure. Why "choicest day"? Because in our youth we are able to learn; we can bend to nobler purposes minds that are ready and still pliable; because this is the time for work, the time for keeping our minds busied in study and in exercising our bodies with useful effort; for that which remains is more sluggish and lacking in spirit – nearer the end.

Let us therefore strive with all courage, omitting attractions by the way; let us struggle with a single purpose, lest, when we are left behind, we comprehend too late the speed of quick-flying time, whose course we cannot stay. Let every day, as soon as it comes, be welcome as being the choicest, and let it be made our own possession. We must catch that which flees. Now he who scans with a scholar's eye the lines I have just quoted, does not reflect that our first days are the best because disease is approaching and old age weighs upon us and hangs over our heads while we are still thinking about our youth. He thinks rather of Vergil's usual collocation of disease and eld; and indeed rightly. For old age is a disease which we cannot cure. "Besides," he says to himself, "think of the epithet that accompanies eld; Vergil calls it bitter," –

> *Disease and bitter eld succeed.*

And elsewhere Vergil says:

> *There dwelleth pale disease and bitter eld.*

There is no reason why you should marvel that each man can collect from the same source suitable matter for his own studies; for in the same meadow the cow grazes, the dog hunts the hare, and the stork the lizard. When Cicero's book On the State is opened by a philologist, a scholar, or a follower of philosophy, each man pursues his investigation in his own way. The philosopher wonders that so much could have been said therein against justice. The philologist takes up the same book and comments on the text as follows: There were two Roman kings – one without a father and one without a mother. For we cannot settle who was Servius's mother, and Ancus, the grandson of Numa, has no father on record. The philologist also notes that the officer whom we call dictator, and about whom we read in our histories under that title, was named in old times the magister populi; such is the name existing to-day in the augural records, proved by the fact that he whom the dictator

509

chose as second in command was called magister equitum. He will remark, too, that Romulus met his end during an eclipse; that there was an appeal to the people even from the kings (this is so stated in the pontiffs' register and is the opinion of others, including Fenestella). When the scholar unrolls this same volume, he puts down in his notebook the forms of words, noting that reapse, equivalent to re ipsa, is used by Cicero, and sepse just as frequently, which means se ipse. Then he turns his attention to changes in current usage. Cicero, for example, says: "Inasmuch as we are summoned back from the very calx by his interruption." Now the line in the circus which we call the creta was called the calx by men of old time. Again, he puts together some verses by Ennius, especially those which referred to Africanus:

A man to whom nor friend nor foe could give
Due meed for all his efforts and his deed.

From this passage the scholar declares that he infers the word opem to have meant formerly not merely assistance, but efforts. For Ennius must mean that neither friend nor foe could pay Scipio a reward worthy of his efforts. Next, he congratulates himself on finding the source of Vergil's words:

Over whose head the mighty gate of Heaven thunders

remarking that Ennius stole the idea from Homer, and Vergil from Ennius. For there is a couplet by Ennius, preserved in this same book of Cicero's, On the State:

If it be right for a mortal to scale the regions of Heaven,
Then the huge gate of the sky opens in glory to me.

But that I, too, while engaged upon another task, may not slip into the department of the philologist or the scholar, my advice is this – that all study of philosophy and all reading should be applied to the idea of living the happy life, that we should not hunt out archaic or far-fetched words and eccentric metaphors and figures of speech, but that we should seek precepts which will help us, utterances of courage and spirit which may at once be turned into facts. We should so learn them that words may become deeds. And I hold that no man has treated mankind worse than he who has studied philosophy as if it were some marketable trade, who lives in a different manner from that which he advises. For those who are liable to every fault which they castigate advertise themselves as patterns of useless training. A teacher like that can help me no more than a sea-sick pilot can be efficient in a storm. He must hold the tiller when the waves are tossing him; he must wrestle, as it were, with the sea; he must furl his sails when the storm rages; what good is a frightened and vomiting steersman to me? And how much greater, think you, is the storm of life than that which tosses any ship! One must steer, not talk.

All the words that these men utter and juggle before a listening crowd, belong to others. They have been spoken by Plato, spoken by Zeno, spoken by Chrysippus or by Posidonius, and by a whole host of Stoics as numerous as excellent. I shall show you how men can prove their words to be their own: it is by doing what they have been talking about. Since therefore I have given you the message I wished to pass on to you, I shall now satisfy your craving and shall reserve for a new letter a complete answer to your summons; so that you may not approach in a condition of weariness a subject which is thorny and which should be followed with an attentive and painstaking ear. Farewell.

Letter CIX - On the Fellowship of Wise Men

You expressed a wish to know whether a wise man can help a wise man. For we say that the wise man is completely endowed with every good, and has attained perfection; accordingly, the question arises how it is possible for anyone to help a person who possesses the Supreme Good.

Good men are mutually helpful; for each gives practice to the other's virtues and thus maintains wisdom at its proper level. Each needs someone with whom he may make comparisons and investigations. Skilled wrestlers are kept up to the mark by practice; a musician is stirred to action by one of equal proficiency. The wise man also needs to have his virtues kept in action; and as he prompts himself to do things, so is he prompted by another wise man. How can a wise man help another wise man? He can quicken his impulses, and point out to him opportunities for honourable action. Besides, he can develop some of his own ideas; he can impart what he has discovered. For even in the case of the wise man something will always remain to discover, something towards which his mind may make new ventures.

Evil men harm evil men; each debases the other by rousing his wrath, by approving his churlishness, and praising his pleasures; bad men are at their worst stage when their faults are most thoroughly intermingled, and their wickedness has been, so to speak, pooled in partnership. Conversely, therefore, a good man will help another good man. "How?" you ask. Because he will bring joy to the other, he will strengthen his faith, and from the contemplation of their mutual tranquillity the delight of both will be increased. Moreover they will communicate to each other a knowledge of certain facts; for the wise man is not all-knowing. And even if he were all-knowing, someone might be able to devise and point out short cuts, by which the whole matter is more readily disseminated. The wise will help the wise, not, mark you, because of his own strength merely, but because of the strength of the man whom he assists. The latter, it is true, can by himself develop his own parts; nevertheless, even one who is running well is helped by one who cheers him on.

"But the wise man does not really help the wise; he helps himself. Let me tell you this: strip the one of his special powers, and the other will accomplish nothing." You might as well, on that basis, say that sweetness is not in the honey: for it is the person himself who is to eat it, that is so equipped, as to tongue and palate, for tasting this kind of food that the special flavour appeals to him, and anything else displeases. For there are certain men so affected by disease that they regard honey as bitter. Both men should be in good health, that the one may be helpful and the other a proper subject for help. Again they say: "When the highest degree of heat has been attained, it is superfluous to apply more heat; and when the Supreme Good has been attained, it is superfluous to have a helper. Does a completely stocked farmer ask for further supplies from his neighbours? Does a soldier who is sufficiently armed for going well-equipped into action need any more weapons? Very well, neither does the wise man; for he is sufficiently equipped and sufficiently armed for life." My answer to this is, that when one is heated to the highest degree, one must have continued heat to maintain the highest temperature. And if it be objected that heat is self-maintaining, I say that there are great distinctions among the things that you are comparing; for heat is a single thing, but helpfulness is of many kinds. Again, heat is not helped by the addition of further heat, in order to be hot; but the wise man cannot maintain his mental standard without intercourse with friends of his own kind – with whom he may share his goodness. Moreover, there is a sort of mutual friendship among all the virtues. Thus, he who loves the virtues of certain among his peers, and in turn exhibits his own to be loved, is helpful. Like things give pleasure, especially when they are honourable and when men know that there is mutual approval. And besides, none but a wise man can prompt another wise man's soul in an intelligent way, just as man can be prompted in a rational way by man only. As, therefore, reason is necessary for the prompting of reason, so, in order to prompt perfect reason, there is need of perfect reason.

Some say that we are helped even by those who bestow on us the so-called "indifferent" benefits, such as money, influence, security, and all the other valued or essential aids to living. If we argue in this way, the veriest fool will be said to help a wise man. Helping, however, really means prompting the soul in accordance with Nature, both by the prompter's excellence and by the excellence of him who is thus prompted. And this cannot take place without advantage to the helper also. For in training the excellence of another, a man must necessarily train his own. But, to omit from discussion supreme goods or the things which produce them, wise men can none the less be mutually helpful. For the mere discovery of a sage by a sage is in itself a desirable event; since everything good is naturally dear to the good man, and for this reason one feels congenial with a good man as one feels congenial with oneself.

It is necessary for me to pass from this topic to another, in order to prove my point. For the question is asked, whether the wise man will weigh his opinions, or whether he will apply to others for advice. Now he is compelled to do this when he approaches state and home duties – everything, so to speak, that is mortal. He needs outside advice on such matters, as does the physician, the pilot, the attorney, or the pleader of cases. Hence, the wise will sometimes help the wise; for they will persuade each other. But in these matters of great import also, – aye, of divine import, as I have termed them, – the wise man can also be useful by discussing honourable things in common, and by contributing his thoughts and ideas. Moreover, it is in accordance with Nature to show affection for our friends, and to rejoice in their advancement as if it were absolutely our own. For if we have not done this, even virtue, which grows strong only through exercising our perceptions, will not abide with us. Now virtue advises us to arrange the present well, to take thought regarding the future, to deliberate and apply our minds; and one who takes a friend into council with him, can more easily apply his mind and think out his problem.

Therefore he will seek either the perfect wise man or one who has progressed to a point bordering on perfection. The perfect wise man, moreover, will help us if he aids our counsels with ordinary good sense. They say that men see farther in the affairs of others than in their own. A defect of character causes this in those who are blinded by self-love, and whose fear in the hour of peril takes away their clear view of that which is useful; it is when a man is more at ease and freed from fear that he will begin to be wise. Nevertheless, there are certain matters where even wise men see the facts more clearly in the case of others than in their own. Moreover, the wise man will, in company with his fellow sage, confirm the truth of that most sweet and honourable proverb – "always desiring and always refusing the same things": it will be a noble result when they draw the load "with equal yoke."

I have thus answered your demand, although it came under the head of subjects which I include in my volumes On Moral Philosophy. Reflect, as I am often wont to tell you, that there is nothing in such topics for us except mental gymnastics. For I return again and again to the thought: "What good does this do me? Make me more brave now, more just, more restrained! I have not yet the opportunity to make use of my training; for I still need the physician. Why do you ask of me a useless knowledge? You have promised great things; test me, watch me! You assured me that I should be unterrified though swords were flashing round me, though the point of the blade were grazing my throat; you assured me that I should be at ease though fires were blazing round me, or though a sudden whirlwind should snatch up my ship and carry it over all the sea. Now make good for me such a course of treatment that I may despise pleasure and glory. Thereafter you shall teach me to work out complicated problems, to settle doubtful points, to see through that which is not clear; teach me now what it is necessary for me to know!" Farewell.

Letter CX - On True and False Riches

From my villa at Nomentum I send you greeting and bid you keep a sound spirit within you – in other words, gain the blessing of all the gods, for he is assured of their grace and favour who has become a blessing to himself. Lay aside for the present the belief of certain persons – that a god is assigned to each one of us as a sort of attendant – not a god of regular rank, but one of a lower grade – one of those whom Ovid calls "plebeian gods." Yet, while laying aside this belief, I would have you remember that our ancestors, who followed such a creed, have become Stoics; for they have assigned a Genius or a Juno to every individual. Later on we shall investigate whether the gods have enough time on their hands to care for the concerns of private individuals; in the meantime, you must know that whether we are allotted to special guardians, or whether we are neglected and consigned to Fortune, you can curse a man with no heavier curse than to pray that he may be at enmity with himself.

There is no reason, however, why you should ask the gods to be hostile to anyone whom you regard as deserving of punishment; they are hostile to such a person, I maintain, even though he seems to be advanced by their favour. Apply careful investigation, considering how our affairs actually stand, and not what men say of them; you will then understand that evils are more likely to help us than to harm us. For how often has so-called affliction been the source and the beginning of happiness! How often have privileges which we welcomed with deep thanksgiving built steps for themselves to the top of a precipice, still uplifting men who were already distinguished – just as if they had previously stood in a position whence they could fall in safety! But this very fall has in it nothing evil, if you consider the end, after which nature lays no man lower. The universal limit is near; yes, there is near us the point where the prosperous man is upset, and the point where the unfortunate is set free. It is we ourselves that extend both these limits, lengthening them by our hopes and by our fears.

If, however, you are wise, measure all things according to the state of man; restrict at the same time both your joys and your fears. Moreover, it is worth while not to rejoice at anything for long, so that you may not fear anything for long. But why do I confine the scope of this evil? There is no reason why you should suppose that anything is to be feared. All these things which stir us and keep us a-flutter, are empty things. None of us has sifted out the truth; we have passed fear on to one another; none has dared to approach the object which caused his dread, and to understand the nature of his fear – aye, the good behind it. That is why falsehood and vanity still gain credit – because they are not refuted. Let us account it worth while to look closely at the matter; then it will be clear how fleeting, how unsure, and how harmless are the things which we fear. The disturbance in our spirits is similar to that which Lucretius detected:

Like boys who cower frightened in the dark,
So grown-ups in the light of day feel fear.

What, then? Are we not more foolish than any child, we who "in the light of day feel fear"? But you were wrong, Lucretius; we are not afraid in the daylight; we have turned everything into a state of darkness. We see neither what injures nor what profits us; all our lives through we blunder along, neither stopping nor treading more carefully on this account. But you see what madness it is to rush ahead in the dark. Indeed, we are bent on getting ourselves called back from a greater distance; and though we do not know our goal, yet we hasten with wild speed in the direction whither we are straining.

The light, however, may begin to shine, provided we are willing. But such a result can come about only in one way – if we acquire by knowledge this familiarity with things divine and human, if we not only flood ourselves but steep ourselves therein, if a man reviews the same principles even though he understands them and applies them again and again to himself, if he has investigated what is good, what is evil, and what has falsely been so entitled; and, finally, if he has investigated honour and baseness, and Providence. The range of the human intelligence is not confined within these limits; it may also explore outside the universe – its destination and its source, and the ruin towards which all nature hastens so rapidly. We have withdrawn the soul from this divine contemplation and dragged it into mean and lowly tasks, so that it might be a slave to greed, so that it might forsake the universe and its confines, and, under the command of masters who try all possible schemes, pry beneath the earth and seek what evil it can dig up therefrom – discontented with that which was freely offered to it.

Now God, who is the Father of us all, has placed ready to our hands those things which he intended for our own good; he did not wait for any search on our part, and he gave them to us voluntarily. But that which would be injurious, he buried deep in the earth. We can complain of nothing but ourselves; for we have brought to light the materials for our destruction, against the will of Nature, who hid them from us. We have bound over our souls to pleasure, whose service is the source of all evil; we have surrendered ourselves to self-seeking and reputation, and to other aims which are equally idle and useless.

What, then, do I now encourage you to do? Nothing new – we are not trying to find cures for new evils – but this first of all: namely, to see clearly for yourself what is necessary and what is superfluous. What is necessary will meet you everywhere; what is superfluous has always to be hunted-out – and with great endeavour. But there is no reason why you should flatter yourself over-much if you despise gilded couches and jewelled furniture. For what virtue lies in despising useless things? The time to admire your own conduct is when you have come to despise the necessities. You are doing no great thing if you can live without royal pomp, if you feel no craving for boars which weigh a thousand pounds, or for flamingo tongues, or for the other absurdities of a luxury that already wearies of game cooked whole, and chooses different bits from separate animals; I shall admire you only when you have learned to scorn even the common sort of bread, when you have made yourself believe that grass grows for the needs of men as well as of cattle, when you have found out that food from the treetop can fill the belly – into which we cram things of value as if it could keep what it has received. We should satisfy our stomachs without being over-nice. How does it matter what the stomach receives, since it must lose whatever it has received? You enjoy the carefully arranged dainties which are caught on land and sea; some are more pleasing if they are brought fresh to the table, others, if after long feeding and forced fattening they almost melt and can hardly retain their own grease. You like the subtly devised flavour of these dishes. But I assure you that such carefully chosen and variously seasoned dishes, once they have entered the belly, will be overtaken alike by one and the same corruption. Would you despise the pleasures of eating? Then consider its result! I remember some words of Attalus, which elicited general applause:

"Riches long deceived me. I used to be dazed when I caught some gleam of them here and there. I used to think that their hidden influence matched their visible show. But once, at a certain elaborate entertainment, I saw embossed work in silver and gold equalling the wealth of a whole city, and colours and tapestry devised to match objects which surpassed the value of gold or of silver – brought not only from beyond our own borders, but from beyond the borders of our enemies; on one side were slave-boys notable for their training and beauty, on the other were throngs of slave-women, and all the other resources that a prosperous and mighty empire could offer after reviewing its possessions. What else is this, I said to myself, than a stirring-up of man's cravings, which are in themselves provocative of lust? What is the meaning of all this display of money? Did we gather merely to learn what greed was? For my own part I left the place with less craving than I had when I entered. I came to despise riches, not because of their uselessness, but because of their pettiness. Have you noticed how, inside a few hours, that programme, however slow-moving and carefully arranged, was over and done? Has a business filled up this whole life of ours, which could not fill up a whole day?

"I had another thought also: the riches seemed to me to be as useless to the possessors as they were to the onlookers. Accordingly, I say to myself, whenever a show of that sort dazzles my eyes, whenever I see a splendid palace with a well-groomed corps of attendants and beautiful bearers carrying a litter: Why wonder? Why gape in astonishment? It is all show; such things are displayed, not possessed; while they please they pass away. Turn thyself rather to the true riches. Learn to be content with little, and cry out with courage and with greatness of soul: 'We have water, we have porridge; let us compete in happiness with Jupiter himself.' And why not, I pray thee, make this challenge even without porridge and water? For it is base to make the happy life depend upon silver and gold, and just as base to make it depend upon water and porridge. 'But,' some will say, 'what could I do without such things?' Do you ask what is the cure for want? It is to make hunger satisfy hunger; for, all else being equal, what difference is there in the smallness or the largeness of the things that force you to be a slave? What matter how little it is that Fortune can refuse to you? Your very porridge and water can fall under another's jurisdiction; and besides, freedom comes, not to him over whom Fortune has slight power, but to him over whom she has no power at all. This is what I mean: you must crave nothing, if you would vie with Jupiter; for Jupiter craves nothing."

This is what Attalus told us. If you are willing to think often of these things, you will strive not to seem happy, but to be happy, and, in addition, to seem happy to yourself rather than to others. Farewell.

Letter CXI - On the Vanity of Mental Gymnastics

You have asked me to give you a Latin word for the Greek sophismata. Many have tried to define the term, but no name has stuck. This is natural, inasmuch as the thing itself has not been admitted to general use by us; the name, too, has met with opposition. But the word which Cicero used seems to me most suitable: he calls them cavillationes. If a man has surrendered himself to them, he weaves many a tricky subtlety, but makes no progress toward real living; he does not thereby become braver, or more restrained, or loftier of spirit.

He, however, who has practised philosophy to effect his own cure, becomes high-souled, full of confidence, invincible, and greater as you draw near him. This phenomenon is seen in the case of high mountains, which appear less lofty when beheld from afar, but which prove clearly how high the peaks are when you come near them; such, my dear Lucilius, is our true philosopher, true by his acts and not by his tricks. He stands in a high place, worthy of admiration, lofty, and really great. He does not stretch himself or walk on tiptoe like those who seek to improve their height by deceit, wishing to seem taller than they really are; he is content with his own greatness. And why should he not be content with having grown to such a height that Fortune cannot reach her hands to it? He is therefore above earthly things, equal to himself under all conditions, – whether the current of life runs free, or whether he is tossed and travels on troubled and desperate seas; but this steadfastness cannot be gained through such hair-splittings as I have just mentioned. The mind plays with them, but profits not a whit; the mind in such cases is simply dragging philosophy down from her heights to the level ground.

I would not forbid you to practise such exercises occasionally; but let it be at a time when you wish to do nothing. The worst feature, however, that these indulgences present is that they acquire a sort of self-made charm, occupying and holding the soul by a show of subtlety; although such weighty matters claim our attention, and a whole life seems scarcely sufficient to learn the single principle of despising life. "What? Did you not mean 'control' instead of 'despise'"? No; "controlling" is the second task; for no one has controlled his life aright unless he has first learned to despise it. Farewell.

Letter CXII - On Reforming Hardened Sinners

I am indeed anxious that your friend be moulded and trained, according to your desire. But he has been taken in a very hardened state, or rather (and this is a more difficult problem), in a very soft state, broken down by bad and inveterate habits.

I should like to give you an illustration from my own handicraft. It is not every vine that admits the grafting process; if it be old and decayed, or if it be weak and slender, the vine either will not receive the cutting, or will not nourish it and make it a part of itself, nor will it accommodate itself to the qualities and nature of the grafted part. Hence we usually cut off the vine above ground, so that if we do not get results at first, we may try a second venture, and on a second trial graft it below the ground.

Now this person, concerning whom you have sent me your message in writing, has no strength; for he has pampered his vices. He has at one and the same time become flabby and hardened. He cannot receive reason, nor can he nourish it. "But," you say, "he desires reason of his own free will." Don't believe him. Of course I do not mean that he is lying to you; for he really thinks that he desires it. Luxury has merely upset his stomach; he will soon become reconciled to it again. "But he says that he is put out with his former way of living." Very likely. Who is not? Men love and hate their vices at the same time. It will be the proper season to pass judgment on him when he has given us a guarantee that he really hates luxury; as it is now, luxury and he are merely not on speaking terms. Farewell.

Letter CXIII - On the Vitality of the Soul and Its Attributes

You wish me to write to you my opinion concerning this question, which has been mooted by our school – whether justice, courage, foresight, and the other virtues, are living things. By such niceties as this, my beloved Lucilius, we have made people think that we sharpen our wits on useless objects, and waste our leisure time in discussions that will be unprofitable. I shall, however, do as you ask, and shall set forth the subject as viewed by our school. For myself, I confess to another belief: I hold that there are certain things which befit a wearer of white shoes and a Greek mantle. But what the beliefs are that have stirred the ancients, or those which the ancients have stirred up for discussion, I shall explain to you.

The soul, men are agreed, is a living thing, because of itself it can make us living things, and because "living things" have derived their name therefrom. But virtue is nothing else than a soul in a certain condition; therefore it is a living thing. Again, virtue is active, and no action can take place without impulse. And if a thing has impulse, it must be a living thing; for none except a living thing possesses impulse. A reply to this is: "If virtue is a living thing, then virtue itself possesses virtue." Of course it possesses its own self! Just as the wise man does everything by reason of virtue, so virtue accomplishes everything by reason of itself. "In that case," say they, "all the arts also are living things, and all our thoughts and all that the mind comprehends. It therefore follows that many thousands of living things dwell in man's tiny heart, and that each individual among us consists of, or at least contains, many living beings."

Are you gravelled for an answer to this remark? Each of these will be a living thing; but they will not be many separate living things. And why? I shall explain, if you will apply your subtlety and your concentration to my words. Each living thing must have a separate substance; but since all the things mentioned above have a single soul, consequently they can be separate living things but without plurality. I myself am a living thing, and a man; but you cannot say that there are two of me for that reason. And why? Because, if that were so, they would have to be two separate existences. This is what I mean: one would have to be sundered from the other so as to produce two. But whenever you have that which is manifold in one whole, it falls into the category of a single nature, and is therefore single.

My soul is a living thing, and so am I; but we are not two separate persons. And why? Because the soul is part of myself. It will only be reckoned as a definite thing in itself when it shall exist by itself. But as long as it shall be part of another, it cannot be regarded as different. And why? I will tell you: it is because that which is different, must be personal and peculiar to itself, a whole, and complete within itself. I myself have gone on record as being of a different opinion; for if one adopts this belief, not only the virtues will be living things, but so will their contrary vices, and the emotions, like wrath, fear, grief, and suspicion. Nay, the argument will carry us still further – all opinions and all thoughts will be living things. This is by no means admissible; since anything that man does is not necessarily the man himself. "What is Justice?" people say. Justice is a soul that maintains itself in a certain attitude. "Then if the soul is a living being, so is Justice." By no means. For Justice is really a state, a kind of power, of the soul; and this same soul is transformed into various likenesses and does not become a different kind of living thing as often as it acts differently. Nor is the result of soul-action a living thing. If Justice, Bravery, and the other virtues have actual life, do they cease to be living things and then begin life over again, or are they always living things?

But the virtues cannot cease to be. Therefore, there are many, nay countless, living things, sojourning in this one soul. "No," is the answer, "not many, because they are all attached to the one, being parts and members of a single whole." We are then portraying for ourselves an image of the soul like that of a many-headed hydra – each separate head fighting and destroying independently. And yet there is no separate living thing to each head; it is the head of a living thing, and the hydra itself is one single living thing. No one ever believed that the Chimaera contained a living lion or a living serpent; these were merely parts of the whole Chimaera; and parts are not living things. Then how can you infer that Justice is a living thing? "Justice," people reply, "is active and helpful; that which acts and is helpful, possesses impulse; and that which possesses impulse is a living thing." True, if the impulse is its own; (but in the case of justice it is not its own;) the impulse comes from the soul. Every living thing exists as it began, until death; a man, until he dies, is a man, a horse is a horse, a dog a dog. They cannot change into anything else. Now let us grant that Justice – which is defined as "a soul in a certain attitude," is a living thing. Let us suppose this to be so. Then Bravery also is alive, being "a soul in a certain attitude." But which soul? That which was but now defined as Justice? The soul is kept within the first-named being, and cannot cross over into another; it must last out its existence in the medium where it had its origin. Besides, there cannot be one soul to two living things, much less to many living things. And if Justice, Bravery, Restraint, and all the other virtues, are living things, how will they have one soul? They must possess separate souls, or else they are not living things. Several living things cannot have one body; this is admitted by our very opponents. Now what is the "body" of justice? "The soul," they admit. And of bravery? "The soul also." And yet there cannot be one body of two living things. "The same soul, however," they answer, "assumes the guise of Justice, or Bravery, or Restraint." This would be possible if Bravery were absent when Justice was present, and if Restraint were absent when Bravery was present; as the case stands now, all the virtues exist at the same time. Hence, how can the separate virtues be living things, if you grant that there is one single soul, which cannot create more than one single living thing?

Again, no living thing is part of another living thing. But Justice is a part of the soul; therefore Justice is not a living thing. It looks as if I were wasting time over something that is an acknowledged fact; for one ought to decry such a topic rather than debate it. And no two living things are equal. Consider the bodies of all beings: every one has its particular colour, shape, and size. And among the other reasons for marvelling at the genius of the Divine Creator is, I believe, this, – that amid all this abundance there is no repetition; even seemingly similar things are, on comparison, unlike. God has created all the great number of leaves that we behold: each, however, is stamped with its special pattern. All the many animals: none resembles another in size – always some difference! The Creator has set himself the task of making unlike and unequal things that are different; but all the virtues, as your argument states, are equal. Therefore, they are not living things.

Every living thing acts of itself; but virtue does nothing of itself; it must act in conjunction with man. All living things either are gifted with reason, like men and gods, or else are irrational, like beasts and cattle. Virtues, in any case, are rational; and yet they are neither men nor gods; therefore they are not living things. Every living thing possessed of reason is inactive if it is not first stirred by some external impression; then the impulse comes, and finally assent confirms the impulse. Now what assent is, I shall explain. Suppose that I ought to take a walk: I do walk, but only after uttering the command to myself and approving this opinion of mine. Or suppose that I ought to seat myself; I do seat myself, but only after the same process. This assent is not a part of virtue. For let us suppose that it is Prudence; how will Prudence assent to the opinion: "I must take a walk"? Nature does not allow this. For Prudence looks after the interests of its possessor, and not of its own self. Prudence cannot walk or be seated. Accordingly, it does not possess the power of assent, and it is not a living thing possessed of reason. But if virtue is a living thing, it is rational. But it is not rational; therefore it is not a living thing. If virtue is a living thing, and virtue is a Good – is not, then, every Good a living thing? It is. Our school professes it.

Now to save a father's life is a Good; it is also a Good to pronounce one's opinion judiciously in the senate, and it is a Good to hand down just opinions; therefore the act of saving a father's life is a living thing, also the act of pronouncing judicious opinions. We have carried this absurd argument so far that you cannot keep from laughing outright: wise silence is a Good, and so is a frugal dinner; therefore silence and dining are living things. Indeed I shall never cease to tickle my mind and to make sport for myself by means of this nice nonsense. Justice and Bravery, if they are living things, are certainly of the earth. Now every earthly living thing gets cold or hungry or thirsty; therefore, Justice goes a-cold, Bravery is hungry, and Kindness craves a drink!

And what next? Should I not ask our honourable opponents what shape these living beings have? Is it that of man, or horse, or wild beast? If they are given a round shape, like that of a god, I shall ask whether greed and luxury and madness are equally round. For these, too, are "living things." If I find that they give a rounded shape to these also, I shall go so far as to ask whether a modest gait is a living thing; they must admit it, according to their argument, and proceed to say that a gait is a living thing, and a rounded living thing, at that!

Now do not imagine that I am the first one of our school who does not speak from rules but has his own opinion: Cleanthes and his pupil Chrysippus could not agree in defining the act of walking. Cleanthes held that it was spirit transmitted to the feet from the primal essence, while Chrysippus maintained that it was the primal essence in itself. Why, then, following the example of Chrysippus himself, should not every man claim his own freedom, and laugh down all these "living things," so numerous that the universe itself cannot contain them? One might say: "The virtues are not many living things, and yet they are living things. For just as an individual may be both poet and orator in one, even so these virtues are living things, but they are not many. The soul is the same; it can be at the same time just and prudent and brave, maintaining itself in a certain attitude towards each virtue." The dispute is settled, and we are therefore agreed. For I shall admit, meanwhile, that the soul is a living thing with the proviso that later on I may cast my final vote; but I deny that the acts of the soul are living beings. Otherwise, all words and all verses would be alive; for if prudent speech is a Good, and every Good a living thing, then speech is a living thing. A prudent line of poetry is a Good; everything alive is a Good; therefore, the line of poetry is a living thing. And so "Arms and the man I sing," is a living thing; but they cannot call it rounded, because it has six feet! "This whole proposition," you say, "which we are at this moment discussing, is a puzzling fabric." I split with laughter whenever I reflect that solecisms and barbarisms and syllogisms are living things, and, like an artist, I give to each a fitting likeness. Is this what we discuss with contracted brow and wrinkled forehead? I cannot say now, after Caelius, "What melancholy trifling!" It is more than this; it is absurd. Why do we not rather discuss something which is useful and wholesome to ourselves, seeking how we may attain the virtues, and finding the path which will take us in that direction?

Teach me, not whether Bravery be a living thing, but prove that no living thing is happy without bravery, that is, unless it has grown strong to oppose hazards and has overcome all the strokes of chance by rehearsing and anticipating their attack. And what is Bravery? It is the impregnable fortress for our mortal weakness; when a man has surrounded himself therewith, he can hold out free from anxiety during life's siege; for he is using his own strength and his own weapons. At this point I would quote you a saying of our philosopher Posidonius: "There are never any occasions when you need think yourself safe because you wield the weapons of Fortune; fight with your own! Fortune does not furnish arms against herself; hence men equipped against their foes are unarmed against Fortune herself."

Alexander, to be sure, harried and put to flight the Persians, the Hyrcanians, the Indians, and all the other races that the Orient spreads even to the Ocean; but he himself, as he slew one friend or lost another, would lie in the darkness lamenting sometimes his crime, and sometimes his loss; he, the conqueror of so many kings and nations, was laid low by anger and grief! For he had made it his aim to win control over everything except his emotions. Oh with what great mistakes are men obsessed, who desire to push their limits of empire beyond the seas, who judge themselves most prosperous when they occupy many provinces with their soldiery and join new territory to the old! Little do they know of that kingdom which is on an equality with the heavens in greatness! Self-Command is the greatest command of all. Let her teach me what a hallowed thing is the Justice which ever regards another's good and seeks nothing for itself except its own employment. It should have nothing to do with ambition and reputation; it should satisfy itself.

Let each man convince himself of this before all else – "I must be just without reward." And that is not enough; let him convince himself also of this: "May I take pleasure in devoting myself of my own free will to uphold this noblest of virtues." Let all his thoughts be turned as far as possible from personal interests. You need not look about for the reward of a just deed; a just deed in itself offers a still greater return. Fasten deep in your mind that which I remarked a short space above: that it makes no difference how many persons are acquainted with your uprightness. Those who wish their virtue to be advertised are not striving for virtue but for renown. Are you not willing to be just without being renowned? Nay, indeed you must often be just and be at the same time disgraced. And then, if you are wise, let ill repute, well won, be a delight. Farewell.

Letter CXIV - On Style as a Mirror of Character

You have been asking me why, during certain periods, a degenerate style of speech comes to the fore, and how it is that men's wits have gone downhill into certain vices – in such a way that exposition at one time has taken on a kind of puffed-up strength, and at another has become mincing and modulated like the music of a concert piece. You wonder why sometimes bold ideas – bolder than one could believe – have been held in favour, and why at other times one meets with phrases that are disconnected and full of innuendo, into which one must read more meaning than was intended to meet the ear. Or why there have been epochs which maintained the right to a shameless use of metaphor. For answer, here is a phrase which you are wont to notice in the popular speech – one which the Greeks have made into a proverb: "Man's speech is just like his life." Exactly as each individual man's actions seem to speak, so people's style of speaking often reproduces the general character of the time, if the morale of the public has relaxed and has given itself over to effeminacy. Wantonness in speech is proof of public luxury, if it is popular and fashionable, and not confined to one or two individual instances. A man's ability cannot possibly be of one sort and his soul of another. If his soul be wholesome, well-ordered, serious, and restrained, his ability also is sound and sober. Conversely, when the one degenerates, the other is also contaminated. Do you not see that if a man's soul has become sluggish, his limbs drag and his feet move indolently? If it is womanish, that one can detect the effeminacy by his very gait? That a keen and confident soul quickens the step? That madness in the soul, or anger (which resembles madness), hastens our bodily movements from walking to rushing?

And how much more do you think that this affects one's ability, which is entirely interwoven with the soul, – being moulded thereby, obeying its commands, and deriving therefrom its laws! How Maecenas lived is too well-known for present comment. We know how he walked, how effeminate he was, and how he desired to display himself; also, how unwilling he was that his vices should escape notice. What, then? Does not the looseness of his speech match his ungirt attire? Are his habits, his attendants, his house, his wife, any less clearly marked than his words? He would have been a man of great powers, had he set himself to his task by a straight path, had he not shrunk from making himself understood, had he not been so loose in his style of speech also. You will therefore see that his eloquence was that of an intoxicated man – twisting, turning, unlimited in its slackness.

What is more unbecoming than the words: "A stream and a bank covered with long-tressed woods"? And see how "men plough the channel with boats and, turning up the shallows, leave gardens behind them." Or, "He curls his lady-locks, and bills and coos, and starts a-sighing, like a forest lord who offers prayers with down-bent neck." Or, "An unregenerate crew, they search out people at feasts, and assail households with the wine-cup, and, by hope, exact death." Or, "A Genius could hardly bear witness to his own festival"; or "threads of tiny tapers and crackling meal"; "mothers or wives clothing the hearth."

Can you not at once imagine, on reading through these words, that this was the man who always paraded through the city with a flowing tunic? For even if he was discharging the absent emperor's duties, he was always in undress when they asked him for the countersign. Or that this was the man who, as judge on the bench, or as an orator, or at any public function, appeared with his cloak wrapped about his head, leaving only the ears exposed, like the millionaire's runaway slaves in the farce? Or that this was the man who, at the very time when the state was embroiled in civil strife, when the city was in difficulties and under martial law, was attended in public by two eunuchs – both of them more men than himself? Or that this was the man who had but one wife, and yet was married countless times? These words of his, put together so faultily, thrown off so carelessly, and arranged in such marked contrast to the usual practice, declare that the character of their writer was equally unusual, unsound, and eccentric. To be sure, we bestow upon him the highest praise for his humanity; he was sparing with the sword and refrained from bloodshed; and he made a show of his power only in the course of his loose living; but he spoiled, by such preposterous finickiness of style, this genuine praise, which was his due. For it is evident that he was not really gentle, but effeminate, as is proved by his misleading word-order, his inverted expressions, and the surprising thoughts which frequently contain something great, but in finding expression have become nerveless. One would say that his head was turned by too great success.

This fault is due sometimes to the man, and sometimes to his epoch. When prosperity has spread luxury far and wide, men begin by paying closer attention to their personal appearance. Then they go crazy over furniture. Next, they devote attention to their houses – how to take up more space with them, as if they were country-houses, how to make the walls glitter with marble that has been imported over seas, how to adorn a roof with gold, so that it may match the brightness of the inlaid floors. After that, they transfer their exquisite taste to the dinner-table, attempting to court approval by novelty and by departures from the customary order of dishes, so that the courses which we are accustomed to serve at the end of the meal may be served first, and so that the departing guests may partake of the kind of food which in former days was set before them on their arrival.

When the mind has acquired the habit of scorning the usual things of life, and regarding as mean that which was once customary, it begins to hunt for novelties in speech also; now it summons and displays obsolete and old-fashioned words; now it coins even unknown words or misshapes them; and now a bold and frequent metaphorical usage is made a special feature of style, according to the fashion which has just become prevalent. Some cut the thoughts short, hoping to make a good impression by leaving the meaning in doubt and causing the hearer to suspect his own lack of wit. Some dwell upon them and lengthen them out. Others, too, approach just short of a fault – for a man must really do this if he hopes to attain an imposing effect – but actually love the fault for its own sake. In short, whenever you notice that a degenerate style pleases the critics, you may be sure that character also has deviated from the right standard.

Just as luxurious banquets and elaborate dress are indications of disease in the state, similarly a lax style, if it be popular, shows that the mind (which is the source of the word) has lost its balance. Indeed you ought not to wonder that corrupt speech is welcomed not merely by the more squalid mob but also by our more cultured throng; for it is only in their dress and not in their judgments that they differ. You may rather wonder that not only the effects of vices, but even vices themselves, meet with approval. For it has ever been thus: no man's ability has ever been approved without something being pardoned. Show me any man, however famous; I can tell you what it was that his age forgave in him, and what it was that his age purposely overlooked. I can show you many men whose vices have caused them no harm, and not a few who have been even helped by these vices. Yes, I will show you persons of the highest reputation, set up as models for our admiration; and yet if you seek to correct their errors, you destroy them; for vices are so intertwined with virtues that they drag the virtues along with them. Moreover, style has no fixed laws; it is changed by the usage of the people, never the same for any length of time. Many orators hark back to earlier epochs for their vocabulary, speaking in the language of the Twelve Tables. Gracchus, Crassus, and Curio, in their eyes, are too refined and too modern; so back to Appius and Coruncanius! Conversely, certain men, in their endeavour to maintain nothing but well-worn and common usages, fall into a humdrum style. These two classes, each in its own way, are degenerate; and it is no less degenerate to use no words except those which are conspicuous, high-sounding, and poetical, avoiding what is familiar and in ordinary usage. One is, I believe, as faulty as the other: the one class are unreasonably elaborate, the other are unreasonably negligent; the former depilate the leg, the latter not even the armpit.

Let us now turn to the arrangement of words. In this department, what countless varieties of fault I can show you! Some are all for abruptness and unevenness of style, purposely disarranging anything which seems to have a smooth flow of language. They would have jolts in all their transitions; they regard as strong and manly whatever makes an uneven impression on the ear. With some others it is not so much an "arrangement" of words as it is a setting to music; so wheedling and soft is their gliding style. And what shall I say of that arrangement in which words are put off and, after being long waited for, just manage to come in at the end of a period? Or again of that softly-concluding style, Cicero-fashion, with a gradual and gently poised descent always the same and always with the customary arrangement of the rhythm! Nor is the fault only in the style of the sentences, if they are either petty and childish, or debasing, with more daring than modesty should allow, or if they are flowery and cloying, or if they end in emptiness, accomplishing mere sound and nothing more.

Some individual makes these vices fashionable – some person who controls the eloquence of the day; the rest follow his lead and communicate the habit to each other. Thus when Sallust was in his glory, phrases were lopped off, words came to a close unexpectedly, and obscure conciseness was equivalent to elegance. L. Arruntius, a man of rare simplicity, author of a historical work on the Punic War, was a member and a strong supporter of the Sallust school. There is a phrase in Sallust: exercitum argento fecit, meaning thereby that he recruited an army by means of money. Arruntius began to like this idea; he therefore inserted the verb facio all through his book. Hence, in one passage, fugam nostris fecere; in another, Hiero, rex Syracusanorum, bellum fecit; and in another, quae audita Panhormitanos dedere Romanis fecere. I merely desired to give you a taste; his whole book is interwoven with such stuff as this. What Sallust reserved for occasional use, Arruntius makes into a frequent and almost continual habit – and there was a reason: for Sallust used the words as they occurred to his mind, while the other writer went afield in search of them. So you see the results of copying another man's vices. Again, Sallust said: aquis hiemantibus. Arruntius, in his first book on the Punic War, uses the words: repente hiemavit tempestas. And elsewhere, wishing to describe an exceptionally cold year, he says: totus hiemavit annus. And in another passage: inde sexaginta onerarias leves praeter militem et necessarios nautarum hiemante aquilone misit; and he continues to bolster many passages with this metaphor. In a certain place, Sallust gives the words: inter arma civilia aequi bonique famas petit; and Arruntius cannot restrain himself from mentioning at once, in the first book, that there were extensive "reminders" concerning Regulus.

These and similar faults, which imitation stamps upon one's style, are not necessarily indications of loose standards or of debased mind; for they are bound to be personal and peculiar to the writer, enabling one to judge thereby of a particular author's temperament; just as an angry man will talk in an angry way, an excitable man in a flurried way, and an effeminate man in a style that is soft and unresisting. You note this tendency in those who pluck out, or thin out, their beards, or who closely shear and shave the upper lip while preserving the rest of the hair and allowing it to grow, or in those who wear cloaks of outlandish colours, who wear transparent togas, and who never deign to do anything which will escape general notice; they endeavour to excite and attract men's attention, and they put up even with censure, provided that they can advertise themselves. That is the style of Maecenas and all the others who stray from the path, not by hazard, but consciously and voluntarily. This is the result of great evil in the soul. As in the case of drink, the tongue does not trip until the mind is overcome beneath its load and gives way or betrays itself; so that intoxication of style – for what else than this can I call it? – never gives trouble to anyone unless the soul begins to totter. Therefore, I say, take care of the soul; for from the soul issue our thoughts, from the soul our words, from the soul our dispositions, our expressions, and our very gait. When the soul is sound and strong, the style too is vigorous, energetic, manly; but if the soul lose its balance, down comes all the rest in ruins.

> *If but the king be safe, your swarm will live*
> *Harmonious; if he die, the bees revolt.*

The soul is our king. If it be safe, the other functions remain on duty and serve with obedience; but the slightest lack of equilibrium in the soul causes them to waver along with it. And when the soul has yielded to pleasure, its functions and actions grow weak, and any undertaking comes from a nerveless and unsteady source. To persist in my use of this simile – our soul is at one time a king, at another a tyrant. The king, in that he respects things honourable, watches over the welfare of the body which is entrusted to his charge, and gives that body no base, no ignoble commands. But an uncontrolled, passionate, and effeminate soul changes kingship into that most dread and detestable quality – tyranny; then it becomes a prey to the uncontrolled emotions, which dog its steps, elated at first, to be sure, like a populace idly sated with a largess which will ultimately be its undoing, and spoiling what it cannot consume. But when the disease has gradually eaten away the strength, and luxurious habits have penetrated the marrow and the sinews, such a soul exults at the sight of limbs which, through its overindulgence, it has made useless; instead of its own pleasures, it views those of others; it becomes the go-between and witness of the passions which, as the result of self-gratification, it can no longer feel. Abundance of delights is not so pleasing a thing to that soul as it is bitter, because it cannot send all the dainties of yore down through the over-worked throat and stomach, because it can no longer whirl in the maze of eunuchs and mistresses, and it is melancholy because a great part of its happiness is shut off, through the limitations of the body.

Now is it not madness, Lucilius, for none of us to reflect that he is mortal? Or frail? Or again that he is but one individual? Look at our kitchens, and the cooks, who bustle about over so many fires; is it, think you, for a single belly that all this bustle and preparation of food takes place? Look at the old brands of wine and store-houses filled with the vintages of many ages; is it, think you, a single belly that is to receive the stored wine, sealed with the names of so many consuls, and gathered from so many vineyards? Look, and mark in how many regions men plough the earth, and how many thousands of farmers are tilling and digging; is it, think you, for a single belly that crops are planted in Sicily and Africa? We should be sensible, and our wants more reasonable, if each of us were to take stock of himself, and to measure his bodily needs also, and understand how little he can consume, and for how short a time! But nothing will give you so much help toward moderation as the frequent thought that life is short and uncertain here below; whatever you are doing, have regard to death. Farewell.

Letter CXV - On the Superficial Blessings

I wish, my dear Lucilius, that you would not be too particular with regard to words and their arrangement; I have greater matters than these to commend to your care. You should seek what to write, rather than how to write it – and even that not for the purpose of writing but of feeling it, that you may thus make what you have felt more your own and, as it were, set a seal on it. Whenever you notice a style that is too careful and too polished, you may be sure that the mind also is no less absorbed in petty things. The really great man speaks informally and easily; whatever he says, he speaks with assurance rather than with pains.

You are familiar with the young dandies, natty as to their beards and locks, fresh from the bandbox; you can never expect from them any strength or any soundness. Style is the garb of thought: if it be trimmed, or dyed, or treated, it shows that there are defects and a certain amount of flaws in the mind. Elaborate elegance is not a manly garb. If we had the privilege of looking into a good man's soul, oh what a fair, holy, magnificent, gracious, and shining face should we behold – radiant on the one side with justice and temperance, on another with bravery and wisdom! And, besides these, thriftiness, moderation, endurance, refinement, affability, and – though hard to believe – love of one's fellow-men, that Good which is so rare in man, all these would be shedding their own glory over that soul. There, too, forethought combined with elegance and, resulting from these, a most excellent greatness of soul (the noblest of all these virtues) – indeed what charm, O ye heavens, what authority and dignity would they contribute! What a wonderful combination of sweetness and power! No one could call such a face lovable without also calling it worshipful. If one might behold such a face, more exalted and more radiant than the mortal eye is wont to behold, would not one pause as if struck dumb by a visitation from above, and utter a silent prayer, saying: "May it be lawful to have looked upon it!"? And then, led on by the encouraging kindliness of his expression, should we not bow down and worship? Should we not, after much contemplation of a far superior countenance, surpassing those which we are wont to look upon, mild-eyed and yet flashing with life-giving fire – should we not then, I say, in reverence and awe, give utterance to those famous lines of our poet Vergil:

> *O maiden, words are weak! Thy face is more*
> *Than mortal, and thy voice rings sweeter far*
> *Than mortal man's; . . . .*
> *Blest be thou; and, whoe'er thou art, relieve*
> *Our heavy burdens.*

And such a vision will indeed be a present help and relief to us, if we are willing to worship it. But this worship does not consist in slaughtering fattened bulls, or in hanging up offerings of gold or silver, or in pouring coins into a temple treasury; rather does it consist in a will that is reverent and upright.

There is none of us, I declare to you, who would not burn with love for this vision of virtue, if only he had the privilege of beholding it; for now there are many things that cut off our vision, piercing it with too strong a light, or clogging it with too much darkness. If, however, as certain drugs are wont to be used for sharpening and clearing the eyesight, we are likewise willing to free our mind's eye from hindrances, we shall then be able to perceive virtue, though it be buried in the body – even though poverty stand in the way, and even though lowliness and disgrace block the path. We shall then, I say, behold that true beauty, no matter if it be smothered by unloveliness. Conversely, we shall get a view of evil and the deadening influences of a sorrow-laden soul – in spite of the hindrance that results from the widespread gleam of riches that flash round about, and in spite of the false light – of official position on the one side or great power on the other – which beats pitilessly upon the beholder.

Then it will be in our power to understand how contemptible are the things we admire – like children who regard every toy as a thing of value, who cherish necklaces bought at the price of a mere penny as more dear than their parents or than their brothers. And what, then, as Aristo says, is the difference between ourselves and these children, except that we elders go crazy over paintings and sculpture, and that our folly costs us dearer? Children are pleased by the smooth and variegated pebbles which they pick up on the beach, while we take delight in tall columns of veined marble brought either from Egyptian sands or from African deserts to hold up a colonnade or a dining-hall large enough to contain a city crowd; we admire walls veneered with a thin layer of marble, although we know the while what defects the marble conceals. We cheat our own eyesight, and when we have overlaid our ceilings with gold, what else is it but a lie in which we take such delight? For we know that beneath all this gilding there lurks some ugly wood.

Nor is such superficial decoration spread merely over walls and ceilings; nay, all the famous men whom you see strutting about with head in air, have nothing but a gold-leaf prosperity. Look beneath, and you will know how much evil lies under that thin coating of titles. Note that very commodity which holds the attention of so many magistrates and so many judges, and which creates both magistrates and judges – that money, I say, which ever since it began to be regarded with respect, has caused the ruin of the true honour of things; we become alternately merchants and merchandise, and we ask, not what a thing truly is, but what it costs; we fulfil duties if it pays, or neglect them if it pays, and we follow an honourable course as long as it encourages our expectations, ready to veer across to the opposite course if crooked conduct shall promise more. Our parents have instilled into us a respect for gold and silver; in our early years the craving has been implanted, settling deep within us and growing with our growth. Then too the whole nation, though at odds on every other subject, agrees upon this; this is what they regard, this is what they ask for their children, this is what they dedicate to the gods when they wish to show their gratitude – as if it were the greatest of all man's possessions! And finally, public opinion has come to such a pass that poverty is a hissing and a reproach, despised by the rich and loathed by the poor.

Verses of poets also are added to the account – verses which lend fuel to our passions, verses in which wealth is praised as if it were the only credit and glory of mortal man. People seem to think that the immortal gods cannot give any better gift than wealth – or even possess anything better:

> *The Sun-god's palace, set with pillars tall,*
> *And flashing bright with gold.*
> *Or they describe the chariot of the Sun:*
> *Gold was the axle, golden eke the pole,*
> *And gold the tires that bound the circling wheels,*
> *And silver all the spokes within the wheels.*

And finally, when they would praise an epoch as the best, they call it the "Golden Age." Even among the Greek tragic poets there are some who regard pelf as better than purity, soundness, or good report:

> *Call me a scoundrel, only call me rich!*
> *All ask how great my riches are, but none*
> *Whether my soul is good.*
> *None asks the means or source of your estate,*
> *But merely how it totals.*
> *All men are worth as much as what they own.*
> *What is most shameful for us to possess?*
> *Nothing!*
> *If riches bless me, I should love to live;*
> *Yet I would rather die, if poor.*
> *A man dies nobly in pursuit of wealth.*
> *Money, that blessing to the race of man,*
> *Cannot be matched by mother's love, or lisp*
> *Of children, or the honour due one's sire.*
> *And if the sweetness of the lover's glance*
> *Be half so charming, Love will rightly stir*
> *The hearts of gods and men to adoration.*

When these last-quoted lines were spoken at a performance of one of the tragedies of Euripides, the whole audience rose with one accord to hiss the actor and the play off the stage. But Euripides jumped to his feet, claimed a hearing, and asked them to wait for the conclusion and see the destiny that was in store for this man who gaped after gold. Bellerophon, in that particular drama, was to pay the penalty which is exacted of all men in the drama of life. For one must pay the penalty for all greedy acts; although the greed is enough of a penalty in itself. What tears and toil does money wring from us! Greed is wretched in that which it craves and wretched in that which it wins! Think besides of the daily worry which afflicts every possessor in proportion to the measure of his gain! The possession of riches means even greater agony of spirit than the acquisition of riches. And how we sorrow over our losses –

losses which fall heavily upon us, and yet seem still more heavy! And finally, though Fortune may leave our property intact, whatever we cannot gain in addition, is sheer loss!

"But," you will say to me, "people call yonder man happy and rich; they pray that some day they may equal him in possessions." Very true. What, then? Do you think that there is any more pitiable lot in life than to possess misery and hatred also? Would that those who are bound to crave wealth could compare notes with the rich man! Would that those who are bound to seek political office could confer with ambitious men who have reached the most sought-after honours! They would then surely alter their prayers, seeing that these grandees are always gaping after new gain, condemning what is already behind them. For there is no one in the world who is contented with his prosperity, even if it comes to him on the run. Men complain about their plans and the outcome of their plans; they always prefer what they have failed to win.

So philosophy can settle this problem for you, and afford you, to my mind, the greatest boon that exists – absence of regret for your own conduct. This is a sure happiness; no storm can ruffle it; but you cannot be steered safely through by any subtly woven words, or any gently flowing language. Let words proceed as they please, provided only your soul keeps its own sure order, provided your soul is great and holds unruffled to its ideals, pleased with itself on account of the very things which displease others, a soul that makes life the test of its progress, and believes that its knowledge is in exact proportion to its freedom from desire and its freedom from fear. Farewell.

Letter CXVI - On Self-Control

The question has often been raised whether it is better to have moderate emotions, or none at all. Philosophers of our school reject the emotions; the Peripatetics keep them in check. I, however, do not understand how any half-way disease can be either wholesome or helpful. Do not fear; I am not robbing you of any privileges which you are unwilling to lose! I shall be kindly and indulgent towards the objects for which you strive – those which you hold to be necessary to our existence, or useful, or pleasant; I shall simply strip away the vice. For after I have issued my prohibitions against the desires, I shall still allow you to wish that you may do the same things fearlessly and with greater accuracy of judgment, and to feel even the pleasures more than before; and how can these pleasures help coming more readily to your call, if you are their lord rather than their slave!

"But," you object, "it is natural for me to suffer when I am bereaved of a friend; grant some privileges to tears which have the right to flow! It is also natural to be affected by men's opinions and to be cast down when they are unfavourable; so why should you not allow me such an honourable aversion to bad opinion?"

There is no vice which lacks some plea; there is no vice that at the start is not modest and easily entreated; but afterwards the trouble spreads more widely. If you allow it to begin, you cannot make sure of its ceasing. Every emotion at the start is weak. Afterwards, it rouses itself and gains strength by progress; it is more easy to forestall it than to forgo it. Who does not admit that all the emotions flow as it were from a certain natural source? We are endowed by Nature with an interest in our own well-being; but this very interest, when overindulged, becomes a vice. Nature has intermingled pleasure with necessary things – not in order that we should seek pleasure, but in order that the addition of pleasure may make the indispensable means of existence attractive to our eyes. Should it claim rights of its own, it is luxury.

Let us therefore resist these faults when they are demanding entrance, because, as I have said, it is easier to deny them admittance than to make them depart. And if you cry: "One should be allowed a certain amount of grieving, and a certain amount of fear." I reply that the "certain amount" can be too long-drawn-out, and that it will refuse to stop short when you so desire. The wise man can safely control himself without becoming over-anxious; he can halt his tears and his pleasures at will; but in our case, because it is not easy to retrace our steps, it is best not to push ahead at all. I think that Panaetius gave a very neat answer to a certain youth who asked him whether the wise man should become a lover: "As to the wise man, we shall see later; but you and I, who are as yet far removed from wisdom, should not trust ourselves to fall into a state that is disordered, uncontrolled, enslaved to another, contemptible to itself. If our love be not spurned, we are excited by its kindness; if it be scorned, we are kindled by our pride. An easily won love hurts us as much as one which is difficult to win; we are captured by that which is compliant, and we struggle with that which is hard. Therefore, knowing our weakness, let us remain quiet. Let us not expose this unstable spirit to the temptations of drink, or beauty, or flattery, or anything that coaxes and allures."

Now that which Panaetius replied to the question about love may be applied, I believe, to all the emotions. In so far as we are able, let us step back from slippery places; even on dry ground it is hard enough to take a sturdy stand. At this point, I know, you will confront me with that common complaint against the Stoics: "Your promises are too great, and your counsels too hard. We are mere manikins, unable to deny ourselves everything. We shall sorrow, but not to any great extent; we shall feel desires, but in moderation; we shall give way to anger, but we shall be appeased." And do you know why we have not the power to attain this Stoic ideal? It is because we refuse to believe in our power. Nay, of a surety, there is something else which plays a part: it is because we are in love with our vices; we uphold them and prefer to make excuses for them rather than shake them off. We mortals have been endowed with sufficient strength by nature, if only we use this strength, if only we concentrate our powers and rouse them all to help us or at least not to hinder us. The reason is unwillingness, the excuse, inability. Farewell.

Letter CXVII - On Real Ethics as Superior to Syllogistic Subtleties

You will be fabricating much trouble for me, and you will be unconsciously embroiling me in a great discussion, and in considerable bother, if you put such petty questions as these; for in settling them I cannot disagree with my fellow-Stoics without impairing my standing among them, nor can I subscribe to such ideas without impairing my conscience. Your query is, whether the Stoic belief is true: that wisdom is a Good, but that being wise is not a Good. I shall first set forth the Stoic view, and then I shall be bold enough to deliver my own opinion.

We of the Stoic school believe that the Good is corporeal, because the Good is active, and whatever is active is corporeal. That which is good, is helpful. But, in order to be helpful, it must be active; so, if it is active, it is corporeal. They (the Stoics) declare that wisdom is a Good; it therefore follows that one must also call wisdom corporeal. But they do not think that being wise can be rated on the same basis. For it is incorporeal and accessory to something else, in other words, wisdom; hence it is in no respect active or helpful.

"What, then?" is the reply; "Why do we not say that being wise is a Good?" We do say so; but only by referring it to that on which it depends – in other words, wisdom itself. Let me tell you what answers other philosophers make to these objectors, before I myself begin to form my own creed and to take my place entirely on another side. "Judged in that light," they say, "not even living happily is a Good. Willy nilly, such persons ought to reply that the happy life is a Good, but that living happily is not a Good." And this objection is also raised against our school: "You wish to be wise. Therefore, being wise is a thing to be desired. And if it be a thing to be desired it is a Good." So our philosophers are forced to twist their words and insert another syllable into the word "desired," – a syllable which our language does not normally allow to be inserted. But, with your permission, I shall add it. "That which is good," they say, "is a thing to be desired; the desirable thing is that which falls to our lot after we have attained the Good. For the desirable is not sought as a Good; it is an accessory to the Good after the Good has been attained."

I myself do not hold the same view, and I judge that our philosophers have come down to this argument because they are already bound by the first link in the chain and for that reason may not alter their definition. People are wont to concede much to the things which all men take for granted; in our eyes the fact that all men agree upon something is a proof of its truth. For instance, we infer that the gods exist, for this reason, among others – that there is implanted in everyone an idea concerning deity, and there is no people so far beyond the reach of laws and customs that it does not believe at least in gods of some sort. And when we discuss the immortality of the soul, we are influenced in no small degree by the general opinion of mankind, who either fear or worship the spirits of the lower world. I make the most of this general belief: you can find no one who does not hold that wisdom is a Good, and being wise also. I shall not appeal to the populace, like a conquered gladiator; let us come to close quarters, using our own weapons.

When something affects a given object, is it outside the object which it affects, or is it inside the object it affects? If it is inside the object it affects, it is as corporeal as the object which it affects. For nothing can affect another object without touching it, and that which touches is corporeal. If it is outside, it withdraws after having affected the object. And withdrawal means motion.

And that which possesses motion, is corporeal. You expect me, I suppose, to deny that "race" differs from "running," that "heat" differs from "being hot," that "light" differs from "giving light." I grant that these pairs vary, but hold that they are not in separate classes. If good health is an indifferent quality, then so is being in good health; if beauty is an indifferent quality, then so is being beautiful. If justice is a Good, then so is being just. And if baseness is an evil, then it is an evil to be base – just as much as, if sore eyes are an evil, the state of having sore eyes is also an evil. Neither quality, you may be sure, can exist without the other. He who is wise is a man of wisdom; he who is a man of wisdom is wise. So true it is that we cannot doubt the quality of the one to equal the quality of the other, that they are both regarded by certain persons as one and the same.

Here is a question, however, which I should be glad to put: granted that all things are either good or bad or indifferent – in what class does being wise belong? People deny that it is a Good; and, as it obviously is not an evil, it must consequently be one of the "media." But we mean by the "medium," or the "indifferent" quality that which can fall to the lot of the bad no less than to the good – such things as money, beauty, or high social position. But the quality of being wise can fall to the lot of the good man alone; therefore being wise is not an indifferent quality. Nor is it an evil, either; because it cannot fall to the lot of the bad man; therefore, it is a Good. That which the good man alone can possess, is a Good; now being wise is the possession of the good man only; therefore it is a Good. The objector replies: "It is only an accessory of wisdom." Very well, then, I say, this quality which you call being wise – does it actively produce wisdom, or is it a passive concomitant of wisdom? It is corporeal in either case. For that which is acted upon and that which acts, are alike corporeal; and, if corporeal, each is a Good. The only quality which could prevent it from being a Good, would be incorporeality.

The Peripatetics believe that there is no distinction between wisdom and being wise, since either of these implies the other also. Now do you suppose that any man can be wise except one who possesses wisdom? Or that anyone who is wise does not possess wisdom? The old masters of dialectic, however, distinguish between these two conceptions; and from them the classification has come right down to the Stoics. What sort of a classification this is, I shall explain: A field is one thing, and the possession of the field another thing; of course, because "possessing the field" refers to the possessor rather than to the field itself. Similarly, wisdom is one thing and being wise another. You will grant, I suppose, that these two are separate ideas – the possessed and the possessor: wisdom being that which one possesses, and he who is wise its possessor. Now wisdom is Mind perfected and developed to the highest and best degree. For it is the art of life. And what is being wise? I cannot call it "Mind Perfected," but rather that which falls to the lot of him who possesses a "mind perfected"; thus a good mind is one thing, and the so-called possession of a good mind another.

"There are," it is said, "certain natural classes of bodies; we say: 'This is a man,' 'this is a horse.' Then there attend on the bodily natures certain movements of the mind which declare something about the body. And these have a certain essential quality which is sundered from body; for example: 'I see Cato walking.' The senses indicate this, and the mind believes it. What I see, is body, and upon this I concentrate my eyes and my mind. Again, I say: 'Cato walks.' What I say," they continue, "is not body; it is a certain declarative fact concerning body – called variously an 'utterance,' a 'declaration,' a 'statement.' Thus, when we say 'wisdom,' we mean something pertaining to body; when we say 'he is wise,' we are speaking concerning body. And it makes considerable difference whether you mention the person directly, or speak concerning the person."

Supposing for the present that these are two separate conceptions (for I am not yet prepared to give my own opinion); what prevents the existence of still a third – which is none the less a Good? I remarked a little while ago that a "field" was one thing, and the "possession of a field" another; of course, for possessor and possessed are of different natures; the latter is the land, and the former is the man who owns the land. But with regard to the point now under discussion, both are of the same nature – the possessor of wisdom, and wisdom itself. Besides, in the one case that which is possessed is one thing, and he who possesses it is another; but in this case the possessed and the possessor come under the same category. The field is owned by virtue of law, wisdom by virtue of nature. The field can change hands and go into the ownership of another; but wisdom never departs from its owner. Accordingly, there is no reason why you should try to compare things that are so unlike one another. I had started to say that these can be two separate conceptions, and yet that both can be Goods – for instance, wisdom and the wise man being two separate things and yet granted by you to be equally good. And just as there is no objection to regarding both wisdom and the possessor of wisdom as Goods, so there is no objection to regarding as a good both wisdom and the possession of wisdom, – in other words, being wise. For I only wish to be a wise man in order to be wise. And what then? Is not that thing a Good without the possession of which a certain other thing cannot be a Good? You surely admit that wisdom, if given without the right to be used, is not to be welcomed! And wherein consists the use of wisdom? In being wise; that is its most valuable attribute; if you withdraw this, wisdom becomes superfluous. If processes of torture are evil, then being tortured is an evil – with this reservation, indeed, that if you take away the consequences, the former are not evil. Wisdom is a condition of "mind perfected," and being wise is the employment of this "mind perfected." How can the employment of that thing not be a Good, which without employment is not a Good? If I ask you whether wisdom is to be desired, you admit that it is. If I ask you whether the employment of wisdom is to be desired, you also admit the fact; for you say that you will not receive wisdom if you are not allowed to employ it. Now that which is to be desired is a Good. Being wise is the employment of wisdom, just as it is of eloquence to make a speech, or of the eyes to see things. Therefore, being wise is the employment of wisdom, and the employment of wisdom is to be desired. Therefore being wise is a thing to be desired; and if it is a thing to be desired, it is a Good.

Lo, these many years I have been condemning myself for imitating these men at the very time when I am arraigning them, and of wasting words on a subject that is perfectly clear. For who can doubt that, if heat is an evil, it is also an evil to be hot? Or that, if cold is an evil, it is an evil to be cold? Or that, if life is a Good, so is being alive? All such matters are on the outskirts of wisdom, not in wisdom itself. But our abiding-place should be in wisdom itself. Even though one takes a fancy to roam, wisdom has large and spacious retreats: we may investigate the nature of the gods, the fuel which feeds the constellations, or all the varied courses of the stars; we may speculate whether our affairs move in harmony with those of the stars, whether the impulse to motion comes from thence into the minds and bodies of all, and whether even these events which we call fortuitous are fettered by strict laws and nothing in this universe is unforeseen or unregulated in its revolutions. Such topics have nowadays been withdrawn from instruction in morals, but they uplift the mind and raise it to the dimensions of the subject which it discusses; the matters, however, of which I was speaking a while ago, wear away and wear down the mind, not (as you and yours maintain) whetting, but weakening it. And I ask you, are we to fritter away that necessary study which we owe to greater and better themes, in discussing a matter which may perhaps be wrong and is certainly of no avail? How will it profit me to know whether wisdom is one thing, and being wise another? How will it profit me to know that the one is, and the other is not, a Good? Suppose I take a chance, and gamble on this prayer: "Wisdom for you, and being wise for me!" We shall come out even.

Try rather to show me the way by which I may attain those ends. Tell me what to avoid, what to seek, by what studies to strengthen my tottering mind, how I may rebuff the waves that strike me abeam and drive me from my course, by what means I may be able to cope with all my evils, and by what means I can be rid of the calamities that have plunged in upon me and those into which I myself have plunged. Teach me how to bear the burden of sorrow without a groan on my part, and how to bear prosperity without making others groan; also, how to avoid waiting for the ultimate and inevitable end, and to beat a retreat of my own free will, when it seems proper to me to do so. I think nothing is baser than to pray for death. For if you wish to live, why do you pray for death? And if you do not wish to live, why do you ask the gods for that which they gave you at birth? For even as, against your will, it has been settled that you must die some day, so the time when you shall wish to die is in your own hands. The one fact is to you a necessity, the other a privilege.

I read lately a most disgraceful doctrine, uttered (more shame to him!) by a learned gentleman: "So may I die as soon as possible!" Fool, thou art praying for something that is already thine own! "So may I die as soon as possible!" Perhaps thou didst grow old while uttering these very words! At any rate, what is there to hinder? No one detains thee; escape by whatsoever way thou wilt! Select any portion of Nature, and bid it provide thee with a means of departure! These, namely, are the elements, by which the world's work is carried on – water, earth, air. All these are no more the causes of life than they are the ways of death. "So may I die as soon as possible!" And what is thy wish with regard to this "as soon as possible"? What day dost thou set for the event? It may be sooner than thy prayer requests. Words like this come from a weak mind, from one that courts pity by such cursing; he who prays for death does not wish to die. Ask the gods for life and health; if thou art resolved to die, death's reward is to have done with prayers.

It is with such problems as these, my dear Lucilius, that we should deal, by such problems that we should mould our minds. This is wisdom, this is what being wise means — not to bandy empty subtleties in idle and petty discussions. Fortune has set before you so many problems — which you have not yet solved — and are you still splitting hairs? How foolish it is to practise strokes after you have heard the signal for the fight! Away with all these dummy-weapons; you need armour for a fight to the finish. Tell me by what means sadness and fear may be kept from disturbing my soul, by what means I may shift off this burden of hidden cravings. Do something! "Wisdom is a Good, but being wise is not a Good;" such talk results for us in the judgment that we are not wise, and in making a laughing-stock of this whole field of study — on the ground that it wastes its effort on useless things. Suppose you knew that this question was also debated: whether future wisdom is a Good? For, I beseech you, how could one doubt whether barns do not feel the weight of the harvest that is to come, and that boyhood does not have premonitions of approaching young manhood by any brawn and power? The sick person, in the intervening period, is not helped by the health that is to come, any more than a runner or a wrestler is refreshed by the period of repose that will follow many months later. Who does not know that what is yet to be is not a Good, for the very reason that it is yet to be? For that which is good is necessarily helpful. And unless things are in the present, they cannot be helpful; and if a thing is not helpful, it is not a Good; if helpful, it is already. I shall be a wise man some day; and this Good will be mine when I shall be a wise man, but in the meantime it is non-existent. A thing must exist first, then may be of a certain kind. How, I ask you, can that which is still nothing be already a Good? And in what better way do you wish it to be proved to you that a certain thing is not, than to say: "It is yet to be"? For it is clear that something which is on the way has not yet arrived. "Spring will follow": I know that winter is here now. "Summer will follow:" I know that it is not summer. The best proof to my mind that a thing is not yet present is that it is yet to be. I hope some day to be wise, but meanwhile I am not wise. For if I possessed that Good, I should now be free from this Evil. Some day I shall be wise; from this very fact you may understand that I am not yet wise. I cannot at the same time live in that state of Good and in this state of Evil; the two ideas do not harmonize, nor do Evil and Good exist together in the same person.

Let us rush past all this clever nonsense, and hurry on to that which will bring us real assistance. No man who is anxiously running after a midwife for his daughter in her birth-pangs will stop to read the praetor's edict or the order of events at the games. No one who is speeding to save his burning house will scan a checker-board to speculate how the imprisoned piece can be freed. But good heavens! — In your case all sorts of news are announced on all sides — your house afire, your children in danger, your country in a state of siege, your property plundered. Add to this shipwreck, earthquakes, and all other objects of dread; harassed amid these troubles, are you taking time for matters which serve merely for mental entertainment? Do you ask what difference there is between wisdom and being wise? Do you tie and untie knots while such a ruin is hanging over your head? Nature has not given us such a generous and free-handed space of time that we can have the leisure to waste any of it. Mark also how much is lost even when men are very careful: people are robbed of one thing by ill-health and of another thing by illness in the family; at one time private, at another public, business absorbs the attention; and all the while sleep shares our lives with us.

Out of this time, so short and swift, that carries us away in its flight, of what avail is it to spend the greater part on useless things? . Besides, our minds are accustomed to entertain rather than to cure themselves, to make an aesthetic pleasure out of philosophy, when philosophy should really be a remedy. What the distinction is between wisdom and being wise I do not know; but I do know that it makes no difference to me whether I know such matters or am ignorant of them. Tell me: when I have found out the difference between wisdom and being wise, shall I be wise?

Why then do you occupy me with the words rather than with the works of wisdom? Make me braver, make me calmer, make me the equal of Fortune, make me her superior. And I can be her superior, if I apply to this end everything that I learn. Farewell.

Letter CXVIII - On the Vanity of Place-Seeking

You have been demanding more frequent letters from me. But if we compare the accounts, you will not be on the credit side. We had indeed made the agreement that your part came first, that you should write the first letters, and that I should answer. However, I shall not be disagreeable; I know that it is safe to trust you, so I shall pay in advance, and yet not do as the eloquent Cicero bids Atticus do: "Even if you have nothing to say, write whatever enters your head." For there will always be something for me to write about, even omitting all the kinds of news with which Cicero fills his correspondence: what candidate is in difficulties, who is striving on borrowed resources and who on his own; who is a candidate for the consulship relying on Caesar, or on Pompey, or on his own strong-box; what a merciless usurer is Caecilius, out of whom his friends cannot screw a penny for less than one per cent each month.

But it is preferable to deal with one's own ills, rather than with another's – to sift oneself and see for how many vain things one is a candidate, and cast a vote for none of them. This, my dear Lucilius, is a noble thing, this brings peace and freedom – to canvass for nothing, and to pass by all the elections of Fortune. How can you call it enjoyable, when the tribes are called together and the candidates are making offerings in their favourite temples – some of them promising money gifts and others doing business by means of an agent, or wearing down their hands with the kisses of those to whom they will refuse the least finger-touch after being elected – when all are excitedly awaiting the announcement of the herald, do you call it enjoyable, I say, to stand idle and look on at this Vanity Fair without either buying or selling? How much greater joy does one feel who looks without concern, not merely upon the election of a praetor or of a consul, but upon that great struggle in which some are seeking yearly honours, and others permanent power, and others the triumph and the prosperous outcome of war, and others riches, or marriage and offspring, or the welfare of themselves and their relatives! What a great-souled action it is to be the only person who is canvassing for nothing, offering prayers to no man, and saying: "Fortune, I have nothing to do with you. I am not at your service. I know that men like Cato are spurned by you, and men like Vatinius made by you. I ask no favours." This is the way to reduce Fortune to the ranks.

These, then, are the things about which we may write in turn, and this is the ever fresh material which we may dig out as we scan the restless multitudes of men, who, in order to attain something ruinous, struggle on through evil to evil, and seek that which they must presently shun or even find surfeiting. For who was ever satisfied, after attainment, with that which loomed up large as he prayed for it? Happiness is not, as men think, a greedy thing; it is a lowly thing; for that reason it never gluts a man's desire. You deem lofty the objects you seek, because you are on a low level and hence far away from them; but they are mean in the sight of him who has reached them. And I am very much mistaken if he does not desire to climb still higher; that which you regard as the top is merely a rung on the ladder. Now all men suffer from ignorance of the truth; deceived by common report, they make for these ends as if they were good, and then, after having won their wish, and suffered much, they find them evil, or empty, or less important than they had expected. Most men admire that which deceives them at a distance, and by the crowd good things are supposed to be big things.

Now, lest this happen also in our own case, let us ask what is the Good. It has been explained in various ways; different men have described it in different ways. Some define it in this way. "That which attracts and calls the spirit to itself is a Good." But the objection at once comes up – what if it does attract, but straight to ruin? You know how seductive many evils are. That which is true differs from that which looks like the truth; hence the Good is connected with the true, for it is not good unless it is also true. But that which attracts and allures, is only like the truth; it steals your attention, demands your interest, and draws you to itself. Therefore, some have given this definition: "That is good which inspires desire for itself, or rouses towards itself the impulse of a struggling soul." There is the same objection to this idea; for many things rouse the soul's impulses, and yet the search for them is harmful to the seeker. The following definition is better: "That is good which rouses the soul's impulse towards itself in accordance with nature, and is worth seeking only when it begins to be thoroughly worth seeking." It is by this time an honourable thing; for that is a thing completely worth seeking.

The present topic suggests that I state the difference between the Good and the honourable. Now they have a certain quality which blends with both and is inseparable from either: nothing can be good unless it contains an element of the honourable, and the honourable is necessarily good. What, then, is the difference between these two qualities? The honourable is the perfect Good, and the happy life is fulfilled thereby; through its influence other things also are rendered good. I mean something like this: there are certain things which are neither good nor bad – as military or diplomatic service, or the pronouncing of legal decisions. When such pursuits have been honourably conducted, they begin to be good, and they change over from the "indifferent" class into the Good. The Good results from partnership with the honourable, but the honourable is good in itself. The Good springs from the honourable, but the latter from itself. What is good might have been bad; what is honourable could never have been anything but good.

Some have defined as follows: "That is good which is according to nature." Now attend to my own statement: that which is good is according to nature, but that which is according to nature does not also become immediately good; for many things harmonize with nature, but are so petty that it is not suitable to call them good. For they are unimportant and deserve to be despised. But there is no such thing as a very small and despicable good, for, as long as it is scanty, it is not good, and when it begins to be good, it ceases to be scanty. How, then, can the Good be recognized? Only if it is completely according to nature.

People say: "You admit that that which is good is according to nature; for this is its peculiar quality. You admit, too, that there are other things according to nature, which, however, are not good. How then can the former be good, and the latter not? How can there be an alteration in the peculiar quality of a thing, when each has, in common with the other, the special attribute of being in accord with nature?" Surely because of its magnitude. It is no new idea that certain objects change as they grow. A person, once a child, becomes a youth; his peculiar quality is transformed; for the child could not reason, but the youth possesses reason. Certain things not only grow in size as they develop, but grow into something else. Some reply: "But that which becomes greater does not necessarily become different. It matters not at all whether you pour wine into a flask or into a vat; the wine keeps its peculiar quality in both vessels. Small and large quantities of honey are not distinct in taste." But these are different cases which you mention; for wine and honey have a uniform quality; no matter how much the quantity is enlarged, the quality is the same. For some things endure according to their kind and their peculiar qualities, even when they are enlarged.

There are others, however, which, after many increments, are altered by the last addition; there is stamped upon them a new character, different from that of yore. One stone makes an archway – the stone which wedges the leaning sides and holds the arch together by its position in the middle. And why does the last addition, although very slight, make a great deal of difference? Because it does not increase; it fills up. Some things, through development, put off their former shape and are altered into a new figure. When the mind has for a long time developed some idea, and in the attempt to grasp its magnitude has become weary, that thing begins to be called "infinite." And then this has become something far different from what it was when it seemed great but finite. In the same way we have thought of something as difficult to divide; at the very end, as the task grows more and more hard, the thing is found to be "indivisible." Similarly, from that which could scarcely or with difficulty be moved we have advanced on and on – until we reach the "immovable." By the same reasoning a certain thing was according to nature; its greatness has altered it into some other peculiar quality and has rendered it a Good. Farewell.

Letter CXIX - On Nature as our Best Provider

Whenever I have made a discovery, I do not wait for you to cry "Shares!" I say it to myself in your behalf. If you wish to know what it is that I have found, open your pocket; it is clear profit. What I shall teach you is the ability to become rich as speedily as possible. How keen you are to hear the news! And rightly; I shall lead you by a short cut to the greatest riches. It will be necessary, however, for you to find a loan; in order to be able to do business, you must contract a debt, although I do not wish you to arrange the loan through a middle-man, nor do I wish the brokers to be discussing your rating. I shall furnish you with a ready creditor, Cato's famous one, who says: "Borrow from yourself!" No matter how small it is, it will be enough if we can only make up the deficit from our own resources. For, my dear Lucilius, it does not matter whether you crave nothing, or whether you possess something. The important principle in either case is the same – freedom from worry.

But I do not counsel you to deny anything to nature – for nature is insistent and cannot be overcome; she demands her due – but you should know that anything in excess of nature's wants is a mere "extra" and is not necessary. If I am hungry, I must eat. Nature does not care whether the bread is the coarse kind or the finest wheat; she does not desire the stomach to be entertained, but to be filled. And if I am thirsty, Nature does not care whether I drink water from the nearest reservoir, or whether I freeze it artificially by sinking it in large quantities of snow. Nature orders only that the thirst be quenched; and it does not matter whether it be a golden, or crystal, or murrine goblet, or a cup from Tibur, or the hollow hand. Look to the end, in all matters, and then you will cast away superfluous things. Hunger calls me; let me stretch forth my hand to that which is nearest; my very hunger has made attractive in my eyes whatever I can grasp. A starving man despises nothing.

Do you ask, then, what it is that has pleased me? It is this noble saying which I have discovered: "The wise man is the keenest seeker for the riches of nature." "What", you ask, "will you present me with an empty plate? What do you mean? I had already arranged my coffers; I was already looking about to see some stretch of water on which I might embark for purposes of trade, some state revenues that I might handle, and some merchandise that I might acquire. That is deceit – showing me poverty after promising me riches." But, friend, do you regard a man as poor to whom nothing is wanting? "It is, however," you reply, "thanks to himself and his endurance, and not thanks to his fortune." Do you, then, hold that such a man is not rich, just because his wealth can never fail? Would you rather have much, or enough? He who has much desires more – a proof that he has not yet acquired enough; but he who has enough has attained that which never fell to the rich man's lot – a stopping-point. Do you think that this condition to which I refer is not riches, just because no man has ever been proscribed as a result of possessing them? Or because sons and wives have never thrust poison down one's throat for that reason? Or because in war-time these riches are unmolested? Or because they bring leisure in time of peace? Or because it is not dangerous to possess them, or troublesome to invest them?

"But one possesses too little, if one is merely free from cold and hunger and thirst." Jupiter himself however, is no better off. Enough is never too little, and not-enough is never too much. Alexander was poor even after his conquest of Darius and the Indies. Am I wrong? He seeks something which he can really make his own, exploring unknown seas, sending new fleets over the Ocean, and, so to speak, breaking down the very bars of the universe. But that which is enough for nature, is not enough for man. There have been found persons who crave something more after obtaining everything; so blind are their wits and so readily does each man forget his start after he has got under way. He who was but lately the disputed lord of an unknown corner of the world, is dejected when, after reaching the limits of the globe, he must march back through a world which he has made his own. Money never made a man rich; on the contrary, it always smites men with a greater craving for itself. Do you ask the reason for this? He who possesses more begins to be able to possess still more.

To sum up, you may hale forth for our inspection any of the millionaires whose names are told off when one speaks of Crassus and Licinus. Let him bring along his rating and his present property and his future expectations, and let him add them all together: such a man, according to my belief, is poor; according to yours, he may be poor some day. He, however, who has arranged his affairs according to nature's demands, is free from the fear, as well as from the sensation, of poverty. And in order that you may know how hard it is to narrow one's interests down to the limits of nature – even this very person of whom we speak, and whom you call poor, possesses something actually superfluous. Wealth, however, blinds and attracts the mob, when they see a large bulk of ready money brought out of a man's house, or even his walls crusted with abundance of gold, or a retinue that is chosen for beauty of physique, or for attractiveness of attire. The prosperity of all these men looks to public opinion; but the ideal man, whom we have snatched from the control of the people and of Fortune, is happy inwardly. For as far as those persons are concerned, in whose minds bustling poverty has wrongly stolen the title of riches – these individuals have riches just as we say that we "have a fever," when really the fever has us. Conversely, we are accustomed to say: "A fever grips him." And in the same way we should say: "Riches grip him." There is therefore no advice – and of such advice no one can have too much – which I would rather give you than this: that you should measure all things by the demands of Nature; for these demands can be satisfied either without cost or else very cheaply. Only, do not mix any vices with these demands. Why need you ask how your food should be served, on what sort of table, with what sort of silver, with what well-matched and smooth-faced young servants? Nature demands nothing except mere food.

Dost seek, when thirst inflames thy throat, a cup of gold?
Dost scorn all else but peacock's flesh or turbot
When the hunger comes upon thee?

Hunger is not ambitious; it is quite satisfied to come to an end; nor does it care very much what food brings it to an end. Those things are but the instruments of a luxury which is not "happiness"; a luxury which seeks how it may prolong hunger even after repletion, how to stuff the stomach, not to fill it, and how to rouse a thirst that has been satisfied with the first drink. Horace's words are therefore most excellent when he says that it makes no difference to one's thirst in what costly goblet, or with what elaborate state, the water is served. For if you believe it to be of importance how curly-haired your slave is, or how transparent is the cup which he offers you, you are not thirsty.

Among other things, Nature has bestowed upon us this special boon: she relieves sheer necessity of squeamishness. The superfluous things admit of choice; we say: "That is not suitable"; "this is not well recommended"; "that hurts my eyesight." The Builder of the universe, who laid down for us the laws of life, provided that we should exist in well-being, but not in luxury. Everything conducive to our well-being is prepared and ready to our hands; but what luxury requires can never be got together except with wretchedness and anxiety.

Let us therefore use this boon of Nature by reckoning it among the things of high importance; let us reflect that Nature's best title to our gratitude is that whatever we want because of sheer necessity we accept without squeamishness. Farewell.

Letter CXX - More about Virtue

Your letter roamed, over several little problems, but finally dwelt upon this alone, asking for explanation: "How do we acquire a knowledge of that which is good and that which is honourable?" In the opinion of other schools, these two qualities are distinct; among our followers, however, they are merely divided. This is what I mean: Some believe the Good to be that which is useful; they accordingly bestow this title upon riches, horses, wine, and shoes; so cheaply do they view the Good, and to such base uses do they let it descend. They regard as honourable that which agrees with the principle of right conduct – such as taking dutiful care of an old father, relieving a friend's poverty, showing bravery on a campaign, and uttering prudent and well-balanced opinions. We, however, do make the Good and the honourable two things, but we make them out of one: only the honourable can be good; also, the honourable is necessarily good. I hold it superfluous to add the distinction between these two qualities, inasmuch as I have mentioned it so many times. But I shall say this one thing – that we regard nothing as good which can be put to wrong use by any person. And you see for yourself to what wrong uses many men put their riches, their high position, or their physical powers.

To return to the matter on which you desire information: "How we first acquire the knowledge of that which is good and that which is honourable." Nature could not teach us this directly; she has given us the seeds of knowledge, but not knowledge itself. Some say that we merely happened upon this knowledge; but it is unbelievable that a vision of virtue could have presented itself to anyone by mere chance. We believe that it is inference due to observation, a comparison of events that have occurred frequently; our school of philosophy hold that the honourable and the good have been comprehended by analogy. Since the word "analogy" has been admitted to citizen rank by Latin scholars, I do not think that it ought to be condemned, but I do think it should be brought into the citizenship which it can justly claim. I shall, therefore, make use of the word, not merely as admitted, but as established.

Now what this "analogy" is, I shall explain. We understood what bodily health was: and from this basis we deduced the existence of a certain mental health also. We knew, too, bodily strength, and from this basis we inferred the existence of mental sturdiness. Kindly deeds, humane deeds, brave deeds, had at times amazed us; so we began to admire them as if they were perfect. Underneath, however, there were many faults, hidden by the appearance and the brilliancy of certain conspicuous acts; to these we shut our eyes. Nature bids us amplify praiseworthy things – everyone exalts renown beyond the truth. And thus from such deeds we deduced the conception of some great good. Fabricius rejected King Pyrrhus's gold, deeming it greater than a king's crown to be able to scorn a king's money. Fabricius also, when the royal physician promised to give his master poison, warned Pyrrhus to beware of a plot. The selfsame man had the resolution to refuse either to be won over by gold or to win by poison. So we admired the hero, who could not be moved by the promises of the king or against the king, who held fast to a noble ideal, and who – is anything more difficult? – was in war sinless; for he believed that wrongs could be committed even against an enemy, and in that extreme poverty which he had made his glory, shrank from receiving riches as he shrank from using poison. "Live," he cried, "O Pyrrhus, thanks to me, and rejoice, instead of grieving as you have done till now, that Fabricius cannot be bribed!"

Horatius Cocles blocked the narrow bridge alone, and ordered his retreat to be cut off, that the enemy's path might be destroyed; then he long withstood his assailants until the crash of the beams, as they collapsed with a huge fall, rang in his ears. When he looked back and saw that his country, through his own danger, was free from danger, "Whoever," he cried, "wishes to pursue me this way, let him come!" He plunged headlong, taking as great care to come out arm'd from the midst of the dashing river-channel as he did to come out unhurt; he returned, preserving the glory of his conquering weapons, as safely as if he had come back over the bridge.

These deeds and others of the same sort have revealed to us a picture of virtue. I will add something which may perhaps astonish you: evil things have sometimes offered the appearance of what is honourable, and that which is best has been manifested through, its opposite. For there are, as you know, vices which are next-door to virtues; and even that which is lost and debased can resemble that which is upright. So the spendthrift falsely imitates the liberal man – although it matters a great deal whether a man knows how to give, or does not know how to save, his money. I assure you, my dear Lucilius, there are many who do not give, but simply throw away and I do not call a man liberal who is out of temper with his money. Carelessness looks like ease, and rashness like bravery. This resemblance has forced us to watch carefully and to distinguish between things which are by outward appearance closely connected, but which actually are very much at odds with one another; and in watching those who have become distinguished as a result of some noble effort, we have been forced to observe what persons have done some deed with noble spirit and lofty impulse, but have done it only once. We have marked one man who is brave in war and cowardly in civil affairs, enduring poverty courageously and disgrace shamefacedly; we have praised the deed but we have despised the man. Again, we have marked another man who is kind to his friends and restrained towards his enemies, who carries on his political and his personal business with scrupulous devotion, not lacking in long-suffering where there is anything that must be endured, and not lacking in prudence when action is to be taken. We have marked him giving with lavish hand when it was his duty to make a payment, and, when he had to toil, striving resolutely and lightening his bodily weariness by his resolution. Besides, he has always been the same, consistent in all his actions, not only sound in his judgment but trained by habit to such an extent that he not only can act rightly, but cannot help acting rightly. We have formed the conception that in such a man perfect virtue exists.

We have separated this perfect virtue into its several parts. The desires had to be reined in, fear to be suppressed, proper actions to be arranged, debts to be paid; we therefore included self-restraint, bravery, prudence, and justice – assigning to each quality its special function. How then have we formed the conception of virtue? Virtue has been manifested to us by this man's order, propriety, steadfastness, absolute harmony of action, and a greatness of soul that rises superior to everything. Thence has been derived our conception of the happy life, which flows along with steady course, completely under its own control. How then did we discover this fact? I will tell you: that perfect man, who has attained virtue, never cursed his luck, and never received the results of chance with dejection; he believed that he was citizen and soldier of the universe, accepting his tasks as if they were his orders. Whatever happened, he did not spurn it, as if it were evil and borne in upon him by hazard; he accepted it as if it were assigned to be his duty. "Whatever this may be," he says, "it is my lot; it is rough and it is hard, but I must work diligently at the task."

Necessarily, therefore, the man has shown himself great who has never grieved in evil days and never bewailed his destiny; he has given a clear conception of himself to many men; he has shone forth like a light in the darkness and has turned towards himself the thoughts of all men, because he was gentle and calm and equally compliant with the orders of man and of God. He possessed perfection of soul, developed to its highest capabilities, inferior only to the mind of God – from whom a part flows down even into this heart of a mortal. But this heart is never more divine than when it reflects upon its mortality, and understands that man was born for the purpose of fulfilling his life, and that the body is not a permanent dwelling, but a sort of inn (with a brief sojourn at that) which is to be left behind when one perceives that one is a burden to the host. The greatest proof, as I maintain, my dear Lucilius, that the soul proceeds from loftier heights, is if it judges its present situation lowly and narrow, and is not afraid to depart. For he who remembers whence he has come knows whither he is to depart. Do we not see how many discomforts drive us wild, and how ill-assorted is our fellowship with the flesh? We complain at one time of our headaches, at another of our bad digestions, at another of our hearts and our throats. Sometimes the nerves trouble us, sometimes the feet; now it is diarrhea, and again it is catarrh; we are at one time full-blooded, at another anemic; now this thing troubles us, now that, and bids us move away: it is just what happens to those who dwell in the house of another.

But we, to whom such corruptible bodies have been allotted, nevertheless set eternity before our eyes, and in our hopes grasp at the utmost space of time to which the life of man can be extended, satisfied with no income and with no influence. What can be more shameless or foolish than this? Nothing is enough for us, though we must die some day, or rather, are already dying; for we stand daily nearer the brink, and every hour of time thrusts us on towards the precipice over which we must fall. See how blind our minds are! What I speak of as in the future is happening at this minute, and a large portion of it has already happened; for it consists of our past lives. But we are mistaken in fearing the last day, seeing that each day, as it passes, counts just as much to the credit of death. The failing step does not produce, it merely announces, weariness. The last hour reaches, but every hour approaches, death. Death wears us away, but does not whirl us away.

For this reason the noble soul, knowing its better nature, while taking care to conduct itself honourably and seriously at the post of duty where it is placed, counts none of these extraneous objects as its own, but uses them as if they were a loan, like a foreign visitor hastening on his way. When we see a person of such steadfastness, how can we help being conscious of the image of a nature so unusual? Particularly if, as I remarked, it was shown to be true greatness by its consistency. It is indeed consistency that abides; false things do not last. Some men are like Vatinius or like Cato by turns; at times they do not think even Curius stern enough, or Fabricius poor enough, or Tubero sufficiently frugal and contented with simple things; while at other times they vie with Licinus in wealth, with Apicius in banqueting, or with Maecenas in daintiness. The greatest proof of an evil mind is unsteadiness, and continued wavering between pretence of virtue and love of vice.

> He'd have sometimes two hundred slaves at hand
> And sometimes ten. He'd speak of kings and grand
> Moguls and naught but greatness. Then he'd say:
> "Give me a three-legged table and a tray
> Of good clean salt, and just a coarse-wove gown
> To keep the cold out." If you paid him down
> (So sparing and content!) a million cool,
> In five short days he'd be a pence-less fool.

The men I speak of are of this stamp; they are like the man whom Horatius Flaccus describes – a man never the same, never even like himself; to such an extent does he wander off into opposites. Did I say many are so? It is the case with almost all. Everyone changes his plans and prayers day by day. Now he would have a wife, and now a mistress; now he would be king, and again he strives to conduct himself so that no slave is more cringing; now he puffs himself up until he becomes unpopular; again, he shrinks and contracts into greater humility than those who are really unassuming; at one time he scatters money, at another he steals it. That is how a foolish mind is most clearly demonstrated: it shows first in this shape and then in that, and is never like itself – which is, in my opinion, the most shameful of qualities. Believe me, it is a great role – to play the role of one man. But nobody can be one person except the wise man; the rest of us often shift our masks. At times you will think us thrifty and serious, at other times wasteful and idle. We continually change our characters and play a part contrary to that which we have discarded. You should therefore force yourself to maintain to the very end of life's drama the character which you assumed at the beginning. See to it that men be able to praise you; if not, let them at least identify you. Indeed, with regard to the man whom you saw but yesterday, the question may properly be asked: "Who is he?" So great a change has there been! Farewell.

Letter CXXI - On Instinct in Animals

You will bring suit against me, I feel sure, when I set forth for you to-day's little problem, with which we have already fumbled long enough. You will cry out again: "What has this to do with character?" Cry out if you like, but let me first of all match you with other opponents, against whom you may bring suit – such as Posidonius and Archidemus; these men will stand trial. I shall then go on to say that whatever deals with character does not necessarily produce good character. Man needs one thing for his food, another for his exercise, another for his clothing, another for his instruction, and another for his pleasure. Everything, however, has reference to man's needs, although everything does not make him better. Character is affected by different things in different ways: some things serve to correct and regulate character, and others investigate its nature and origin. And when I seek the reason why Nature brought forth man, and why she set him above other animals, do you suppose that I have left character-study in the rear? No; that is wrong. For how are you to know what character is desirable, unless you have discovered what is best suited to man? Or unless you have studied his nature? You can find out what you should do and what you should avoid, only when you have learned what you owe to your own nature.

"I desire," you say, "to learn how I may crave less, and fear less. Rid me of my unreasoning beliefs. Prove to me that so-called felicity is fickle and empty, and that the word easily admits of a syllable's increase." I shall fulfil your want, encouraging your virtues and lashing your vices. People may decide that I am too zealous and reckless in this particular; but I shall never cease to hound wickedness, to check the most unbridled emotions, to soften the force of pleasures which will result in pain, and to cry down men's prayers. Of course I shall do this; for it is the greatest evils that we have prayed for, and from that which has made us give thanks comes all that demands consolation.

Meanwhile, allow me to discuss thoroughly some points which may seem now to be rather remote from the present inquiry. We were once debating whether all animals had any feelings about their "constitution." That this is the case is proved particularly by their making motions of such fitness and nimbleness that they seem to be trained for the purpose. Every being is clever in its own line. The skilled workman handles his tools with an ease born of experience; the pilot knows how to steer his ship skilfully; the artist can quickly lay on the colours which he has prepared in great variety for the purpose of rendering the likeness, and passes with ready eye and hand from palette to canvas. In the same way an animal is agile in all that pertains to the use of its body. We are apt to wonder at skilled dancers because their gestures are perfectly adapted to the meaning of the piece and its accompanying emotions, and their movements match the speed of the dialogue. But that which art gives to the craftsman, is given to the animal by nature. No animal handles its limbs with difficulty, no animal is at a loss how to use its body. This function they exercise immediately at birth. They come into the world with this knowledge; they are born full-trained.

But people reply: "The reason why animals are so dexterous in the use of their limbs is that if they move them unnaturally, they will feel pain. They are compelled to do thus, according to your school, and it is fear rather than will-power which moves them in the right direction." This idea is wrong. Bodies driven by a compelling force move slowly; but those which move of their own accord possess alertness. The proof that it is not fear of pain which prompts them thus, is, that even when pain checks them they struggle to carry out their natural motions. Thus the child who is trying to stand and is becoming used to carry his own weight, on beginning to test his strength, falls and rises again and again with tears until through painful effort he has trained himself to the demands of nature. And certain animals with hard shells, when turned on their backs, twist and grope with their feet and make motions side-ways until they are restored to their proper position. The tortoise on his back feels no suffering; but he is restless because he misses his natural condition, and does not cease to shake himself about until he stands once more upon his feet.

So all these animals have a consciousness of their physical constitution, and for that reason can manage their limbs as readily as they do; nor have we any better proof that they come into being equipped with this knowledge than the fact that no animal is unskilled in the use of its body. But some object as follows: "According to your account, one's constitution consists of a ruling power in the soul which has a certain relation towards the body. But how can a child comprehend this intricate and subtle principle, which I can scarcely explain even to you? All living creatures should be born logicians, so as to understand a definition which is obscure to the majority of Roman citizens!" Your objection would be true if I spoke of living creatures as understanding "a definition of constitution," and not "their actual constitution." Nature is easier to understand than to explain; hence, the child of whom we were speaking does not understand what "constitution" is, but understands its own constitution. He does not know what "a living creature" is, but he feels that he is an animal. Moreover, that very constitution of his own he only understands confusedly, cursorily, and darkly. We also know that we possess souls, but we do not know the essence, the place, the quality, or the source, of the soul. Such as is the consciousness of our souls which we possess, ignorant as we are of their nature and position, even so all animals possess a consciousness of their own constitutions. For they must necessarily feel this, because it is the same agency by which they feel other things also; they must necessarily have a feeling of the principle which they obey and by which they are controlled. Every one of us understands that there is something which stirs his impulses, but he does not know what it is. He knows that he has a sense of striving, although he does not know what it is or its source. Thus even children and animals have a consciousness of their primary element, but it is not very clearly outlined or portrayed.

"You maintain, do you," says the objector, "that every living thing is at the start adapted to its constitution, but that man's constitution is a reasoning one, and hence man is adapted to himself not merely as a living, but as a reasoning, being? For man is dear to himself in respect of that wherein he is a man. How, then, can a child, being not yet gifted with reason, adapt himself to a reasoning constitution?" . But each age has its own constitution, different in the case of the child, the boy, and the old man; they are all adapted to the constitution wherein they find themselves. The child is toothless, and he is fitted to this condition. Then his teeth grow, and he is fitted to that condition also. Vegetation also, which will develop into grain and fruits, has a special constitution when young and scarcely peeping over the tops of the furrows, another when it is strengthened and stands upon a stalk which is soft but strong enough to bear its weight, and still another when the colour changes to yellow, prophesies threshing-time, and hardens in the ear – no matter what may be the constitution into which the plant comes, it keeps it, and conforms thereto. The periods of infancy, boyhood, youth, and old age, are different; but I, who have been infant, boy, and youth, am still the same. Thus, although each has at different times a different constitution, the adaptation of each to its constitution is the same. For nature does not consign boyhood or youth, or old age, to me; it consigns me to them. Therefore, the child is adapted to that constitution which is his at the present moment of childhood, not to that which will be his in youth. For even if there is in store for him any higher phase into which he must be changed, the state in which he is born is also according to nature. First of all, the living being is adapted to itself, for there must be a pattern to which all other things may be referred. I seek pleasure; for whom? For myself. I am therefore looking out for myself. I shrink from pain; on behalf of whom? Myself. Therefore, I am looking out for myself. Since I gauge all my actions with reference to my own welfare, I am looking out for myself before all else. This quality exists in all living beings – not engrafted but inborn.

Nature brings up her own offspring and does not cast them away; and because the most assured security is that which is nearest, every man has been entrusted to his own self. Therefore, as I have remarked in the course of my previous correspondence, even young animals, on issuing from the mother's womb or from the egg, know at once of their own accord what is harmful for them, and avoid death-dealing things. They even shrink when they notice the shadow of birds of prey which flit overhead.

No animal, when it enters upon life, is free from the fear of death. People may ask: "How can an animal at birth have an understanding of things wholesome or destructive?" The first question, however, is whether it can have such understanding, and not how it can understand. And it is clear that they have such understanding from the fact that, even if you add understanding, they will act no more adequately than they did in the first place. Why should the hen show no fear of the peacock or the goose, and yet run from the hawk, which is a so much smaller animal not even familiar to the hen? Why should young chickens fear a cat and not a dog.? These fowls clearly have a presentiment of harm – one not based on actual experiments; for they avoid a thing before they can possibly have experience of it. Furthermore, in order that you may not suppose this to be the result of chance, they do not shrink from certain other things which you would expect them to fear, nor do they ever forget vigilance and care in this regard; they all possess equally the faculty of avoiding what is destructive. Besides, their fear does not grow as their lives lengthen.

Hence indeed it is evident that these animals have not reached such a condition through experience; it is because of an inborn desire for self-preservation. The teachings of experience are slow and irregular; but whatever Nature communicates belongs equally to everyone, and comes immediately. If, however, you require an explanation, shall I tell you how it is that every living thing tries to understand that which is harmful? It feels that it is constructed of flesh; and so it perceives to what an extent flesh may be cut or burned or crushed, and what animals are equipped with the power of doing this damage; it is of animals of this sort that it derives an unfavourable and hostile idea. These tendencies are closely connected; for each animal at the same time consults its own safety, seeking that which helps it, and shrinks from that which will harm it. Impulses towards useful objects, and revulsion from the opposite, are according to nature; without any reflection to prompt the idea, and without any advice, whatever Nature has prescribed, is done.

Do you not see how skillful bees are in building their cells? How completely harmonious in sharing and enduring toil? Do you not see how the spider weaves a web so subtle that man's hand cannot imitate it; and what a task it is to arrange the threads, some directed straight towards the centre, for the sake of making the web solid, and others running in circles and lessening in thickness – for the purpose of tangling and catching in a sort of net the smaller insects for whose ruin the spider spreads the web? This art is born, not taught; and for this reason no animal is more skilled than any other. You will notice that all spider-webs are equally fine, and that the openings in all honeycomb cells are identical in shape. Whatever art communicates is uncertain and uneven; but Nature's assignments are always uniform. Nature has communicated nothing except the duty of taking care of themselves and the skill to do so; that is why living and learning begin at the same time. No wonder that living things are born with a gift whose absence would make birth useless. This is the first equipment that Nature granted them for the maintenance of their existence – the quality of adaptability and self-love. They could not survive except by desiring to do so. Nor would this desire alone have made them prosper, but without it nothing could have prospered. In no animal can you observe any low esteem, or even any carelessness, of self. Dumb beasts, sluggish in other respects, are clever at living. So you will see that creatures which are useless to others are alert for their own preservation. Farewell.

Letter CXXII - On Darkness as a Veil for Wickedness

The day has already begun to lessen. It has shrunk considerably, but yet will still allow a goodly space of time if one rises, so to speak, with the day itself. We are more industrious, and we are better men if we anticipate the day and welcome the dawn; but we are base churls if we lie dozing when the sun is high in the heavens, or if we wake up only when noon arrives; and even then to many it seems not yet dawn. Some have reversed the functions of light and darkness; they open eyes sodden with yesterday's debauch only at the approach of night. It is just like the condition of those peoples whom, according to Vergil, Nature has hidden away and placed in an abode directly opposite to our own:

When in our face the Dawn with panting steeds
Breathes down, for them the ruddy evening kindles
Her late-lit fires.

It is not the country of these men, so much as it is their life, that is "directly opposite" to our own. There may be Antipodes dwelling in this same city of ours who, in Cato's words, "have never seen the sun rise or set." Do you think that these men know how to live, if they do not know when to live? Do these men fear death, if they have buried themselves alive? They are as weird as the birds of night. Although they pass their hours of darkness amid wine and perfumes, although they spend the whole extent of their unnatural waking hours in eating dinners – and those too cooked separately to make up many courses – they are not really banqueting; they are conducting their own funeral services. And the dead at least have their banquets by daylight.

But indeed to one who is active no day is long. So let us lengthen our lives; for the duty and the proof of life consist in action. Cut short the night: use some of it for the day's business. Birds that are being prepared for the banquet, that they may be easily fattened through lack of exercise, are kept in darkness; and similarly, if men vegetate without physical activity, their idle bodies are overwhelmed with flesh, and in their self-satisfied retirement the fat of indolence grows upon them. Moreover, the bodies of those who have sworn allegiance to the hours of darkness have a loathsome appearance. Their complexions are more alarming than those of anemic invalids; they are lackadaisical and flabby with dropsy; though still alive, they are already carrion. But this, to my thinking, would be among the least of their evils. How much more darkness there is in their souls! Such a man is internally dazed; his vision is darkened; he envies the blind. And what man ever had eyes for the purpose of seeing in the dark?

You ask me how this depravity comes upon the soul – this habit of reversing the daylight and giving over one's whole existence to the night? All vices rebel against Nature; they all abandon the appointed order. It is the motto of luxury to enjoy what is unusual, and not only to depart from that which is right, but to leave it as far behind as possible, and finally even take a stand in opposition thereto. Do you not believe that men live contrary to Nature who drink fasting, who take wine into empty veins, and pass to their food in a state of intoxication? And yet this is one of youth's popular vices – to perfect their strength in order to drink on the very threshold of the bath, amid the unclad bathers; nay even to soak in wine and then immediately to rub off the sweat which they have promoted by many a hot glass of liquor! To them, a glass after lunch or one after dinner is bourgeois; it is what the country squires do, who are not connoisseurs in pleasure. This unmixed wine delights them just because there is no food to float in it, because it readily makes its way into their muscles; this boozing pleases them just because the stomach is empty.

Do you not believe that men live contrary to Nature who exchange the fashion of their attire with women? Do not men live contrary to Nature who endeavour to look fresh and boyish at an age unsuitable for such an attempt? What could be more cruel or more wretched? Cannot time and man's estate ever carry such a person beyond an artificial boyhood? Do not men live contrary to Nature who crave roses in winter, or seek to raise a spring flower like the lily by means of hot-water heaters and artificial changes of temperature? Do not men live contrary to Nature who grow fruit-trees on the top of a wall? Or raise waving forests upon the roofs and battlements of their houses – the roots starting at a point to which it would be outlandish for the tree-tops to reach? Do not men live contrary to Nature who lay the foundations of bathrooms in the sea and do not imagine that they can enjoy their swim unless the heated pool is lashed as with the waves of a storm?

When men have begun to desire all things in opposition to the ways of Nature, they end by entirely abandoning the ways of Nature. They cry: "It is daytime – let us go to sleep! It is the time when men rest: now for exercise, now for our drive, now for our lunch! Lo, the dawn approaches: it is dinner-time! We should not do as mankind do. It is low and mean to live in the usual and conventional way. Let us abandon the ordinary sort of day. Let us have a morning that is a special feature of ours, peculiar to ourselves!" Such men are, in my opinion, as good as dead. Are they not all but present at a funeral – and before their time too – when they live amid torches and tapers? I remember that this sort of life was very fashionable at one time: among such men as Acilius Buta, a person of praetorian rank, who ran through a tremendous estate and on confessing his bankruptcy to Tiberius, received the answer: "You have waked up too late!" Julius Montanus was once reading a poem aloud he was a middling good poet, noted for his friendship with Tiberius, as well as his fall from favour. He always used to fill his poems with a generous sprinkling of sunrises and sunsets. Hence, when a certain person was complaining that Montanus had read all day long, and declared that no man should attend any of his readings, Natta Pinarius remarked: "I couldn't make a fairer bargain than this: I am ready to listen to him from sunrise to sunset!" Montanus was reading, and had reached the words:

'Gins the bright morning to spread forth his flames clear-burning; the red dawn
Scatters its light; and the sad-eyed swallow returns to her nestlings,
Bringing the chatterers' food, and with sweet bill sharing and serving.

Then Varus, a Roman knight, the hanger-on of Marcus Vinicius, and a sponger at elegant dinners which he earned by his degenerate wit, shouted: "Bed-time for Buta!" And later, when Montanus declaimed

Lo, now the shepherds have folded their flocks, and the slow-moving darkness
'Gins to spread silence o'er lands that are drowsily lulled into slumber,

this same Varus remarked: "What? Night already? I'll go and pay my morning call on Buta!" You see, nothing was more notorious than Buta's upside-down manner of life. But this life, as I said, was fashionable at one time. And the reason why some men live thus is not because they think that night in itself offers any greater attractions, but because that which is normal gives them no particular pleasure; light being a bitter enemy of the evil conscience, and, when one craves or scorns all things in proportion as they have cost one much or little, illumination for which one does not pay is an object of contempt. Moreover, the luxurious person wishes to be an object of gossip his whole life; if people are silent about him, he thinks that he is wasting his time. Hence he is uncomfortable whenever any of his actions escape notoriety.

Many men eat up their property, and many men keep mistresses. If you would win a reputation among such persons, you must make your programme not only one of luxury but one of notoriety; for in such a busy community wickedness does not discover the ordinary sort of scandal. I heard Pedo Albinovanus, that most attractive story-teller, speaking of his residence above the town-house of Sextus Papinius. Papinius belonged to the tribe of those who shun the light. "About nine o'clock at night I hear the sound of whips. I ask what is going on, and they tell me that Papinius is going over his accounts. About twelve there is a strenuous shouting; I ask what the matter is, and they say he is exercising his voice. About two A.M. I ask the significance of the sound of wheels; they tell me that he is off for a drive. And at dawn there is a tremendous flurry-calling of slaves and butlers, and pandemonium among the cooks. I ask the meaning of this also, and they tell me that he has called for his cordial and his appetizer, after leaving the bath. His dinner," said Pedo, "never went beyond the day, for he lived very sparingly; he was lavish with nothing but the night. Accordingly, if you believe those who call him tight-fisted and mean, you will call him also a 'slave of the lamp.'"

You should not be surprised at finding so many special manifestations of the vices; for vices vary, and there are countless phases of them, nor can all their various kinds be classified. The method of maintaining righteousness is simple; the method of maintaining wickedness is complicated, and has infinite opportunity to swerve. And the same holds true of character; if you follow nature, character is easy to manage, free, and with very slight shades of difference; but the sort of person I have mentioned possesses badly warped character, out of harmony with all things, including himself. The chief cause, however, of this disease seems to me to be a squeamish revolt from the normal existence. Just as such persons mark themselves off from others in their dress, or in the elaborate arrangement of their dinners, or in the elegance of their carriages; even so they desire to make themselves peculiar by their way of dividing up the hours of their day. They are unwilling to be wicked in the conventional way, because notoriety is the reward of their sort of wickedness. Notoriety is what all such men seek – men who are, so to speak, living backwards.

For this reason, Lucilius, let us keep to the way which Nature has mapped out for us, and let us not swerve therefrom. If we follow Nature, all is easy and unobstructed; but if we combat Nature, our life differs not a whit from that of men who row against the current. Farewell.

Letter CXXIII - On the Conflict between Pleasure and Virtue

Wearied with the discomfort rather than with the length of my journey, I have reached my Alban villa late at night, and I find nothing in readiness except myself. So I am getting rid of fatigue at my writing-table: I derive some good from this tardiness on the part of my cook and my baker. For I am communing with myself on this very topic – that nothing is heavy if one accepts it with a light heart, and that nothing need provoke one's anger if one does not add to one's pile of troubles by getting angry. My baker is out of bread; but the overseer, or the house-steward, or one of my tenants can supply me therewith. "Bad bread!" you say. But just wait for it; it will become good. Hunger will make even such bread delicate and of the finest flavour. For that reason I must not eat until hunger bids me; so I shall wait and shall not eat until I can either get good bread or else cease to be squeamish about it. It is necessary that one grow accustomed to slender fare: because there are many problems of time and place which will cross the path even of the rich man and one equipped for pleasure, and bring him up with a round turn. To have whatsoever he wishes is in no man's power; it is in his power not to wish for what he has not, but cheerfully to employ what comes to him. A great step towards independence is a good-humoured stomach, one that is willing to endure rough treatment.

You cannot imagine how much pleasure I derive from the fact that my weariness is becoming reconciled to itself; I am asking for no slaves to rub me down, no bath, and no other restorative except time. For that which toil has accumulated, rest can lighten. This repast, whatever it may be, will give me more pleasure than an inaugural banquet. For I have made trial of my spirit on a sudden – a simpler and a truer test. Indeed, when a man has made preparations and given himself a formal summons to be patient, it is not equally clear just how much real strength of mind he possesses; the surest proofs are those which one exhibits off-hand, viewing one's own troubles not only fairly but calmly, not flying into fits of temper or wordy wranglings, supplying one's own needs by not craving something which was really due, and reflecting that our habits may be unsatisfied, but never our own real selves. How many things are superfluous we fail to realize until they begin to be wanting; we merely used them not because we needed them but because we had them. And how much do we acquire simply because our neighbours have acquired such things, or because most men possess them! Many of our troubles may be explained from the fact that we live according to a pattern, and, instead of arranging our lives according to reason, are led astray by convention.

There are things which, if done by the few, we should refuse to imitate; yet when the majority have begun to do them, we follow along – just as if anything were more honourable because it is more frequent! Furthermore, wrong views, when they have become prevalent, reach, in our eyes, the standard of righteousness. Everyone now travels with Numidian outriders preceding him, with a troop of slave-runners to clear the way; we deem it disgraceful to have no attendants who will elbow crowds from the road, or will prove, by a great cloud of dust, that a high dignitary is approaching! Everyone now possesses mules that are laden with crystal and myrrhine cups carved by skilled artists of great renown; it is disgraceful for all your baggage to be made up of that which can be rattled along without danger. Everyone has pages who ride along with ointment-covered faces so that the heat or the cold will not harm their tender complexions; it is disgraceful that none of your attendant slave-boys should show a healthy cheek, not covered with cosmetics.

You should avoid conversation with all such persons: they are the sort that communicate and engraft their bad habits from one to another. We used to think that the very worst variety of these men were those who vaunted their words; but there are certain men who vaunt their wickedness. Their talk is very harmful; for even though it is not at once convincing, yet they leave the seeds of trouble in the soul, and the evil which is sure to spring into new strength follows us about even when we have parted from them. Just as those who have attended a concert carry about in their heads the melodies and the charm of the songs they have heard – a proceeding which interferes with their thinking and does not allow them to concentrate upon serious subjects, – even so the speech of flatterers and enthusiasts over that which is depraved sticks in our minds long after we have heard them talk. It is not easy to rid the memory of a catching tune; it stays with us, lasts on, and comes back from time to time. Accordingly, you should close your ears against evil talk, and right at the outset, too; for when such talk has gained an entrance and the words are admitted and are in our minds, they become more shameless. And then we begin to speak as follows: "Virtue, Philosophy, Justice – this is a jargon of empty words. The only way to be happy is to do yourself well. To eat, drink, and spend your money is the only real life, the only way to remind yourself that you are mortal. Our days flow on, and life – which we cannot restore – hastens away from us. Why hesitate to come to our senses? This life of ours will not always admit pleasures; meantime, while it can do so, while it clamours for them, what profit lies in imposing thereupon frugality? Therefore get ahead of death, and let anything that death will filch from you be squandered now upon yourself. You have no mistress, no favourite slave to make your mistress envious; you are sober when you make your daily appearance in public; you dine as if you had to show your account-book to 'Papa'; but that is not living, it is merely going shares in someone else's existence. And what madness it is to be looking out for the interests of your heir, and to deny yourself everything, with the result that you turn friends into enemies by the vast amount of the fortune you intend to leave! For the more the heir is to get from you, the more he will rejoice in your taking-off! All those sour fellows who criticize other men's lives in a spirit of priggishness and are real enemies to their own lives, playing schoolmaster to the world – you should not consider them as worth a farthing, nor should you hesitate to prefer good living to a good reputation."

These are voices which you ought to shun just as Ulysses did; he would not sail past them until he was lashed to the mast. They are no less potent; they lure men from country, parents, friends, and virtuous ways; and by a hope that, if not base, is ill-starred, they wreck them upon a life of baseness. How much better to follow a straight course and attain a goal where the words "pleasant" and "honourable" have the same meaning! This end will be possible for us if we understand that there are two classes of objects which either attract us or repel us. We are attracted by such things as riches, pleasures, beauty, ambition, and other such coaxing and pleasing objects; we are repelled by toil, death, pain, disgrace, or lives of greater frugality. We ought therefore to train ourselves so that we may avoid a fear of the one or a desire for the other. Let us fight in the opposite fashion: let us retreat from the objects that allure, and rouse ourselves to meet the objects that attack.

Do you not see how different is the method of descending a mountain from that employed in climbing upwards? Men coming down a slope bend backwards; men ascending a steep place lean forward. For, my dear Lucilius, to allow yourself to put your body's weight ahead when coming down, or, when climbing up, to throw it backward is to comply with vice. The pleasures take one down hill but one must work upwards toward that which is rough and hard to climb; in the one case let us throw our bodies forward, in the others let us put the check-rein on them.

Do you believe me to be stating now that only those men bring ruin to our ears, who praise pleasure, who inspire us with fear of pain – that element which is in itself provocative of fear? I believe that we are also in injured by those who masquerade under the disguise of the Stoic school and at the same time urge us on into vice. They boast that only the wise man and the learned is a lover. "He alone has wisdom in this art; the wise man too is best skilled in drinking and feasting. Our study ought to be this alone: up to what age the bloom of love can endure!" All this may be regarded as a concession to the ways of Greece; we ourselves should preferably turn our attention to words like these: "No man is good by chance. Virtue is something which must be learned. Pleasure is low, petty, to be deemed worthless, shared even by dumb animals – the tiniest and meanest of whom fly towards pleasure. Glory is an empty and fleeting thing, lighter than air. Poverty is an evil to no man unless he kick against the goads. Death is not an evil; why need you ask? Death alone is the equal privilege of mankind. Superstition is the misguided idea of a lunatic; it fears those whom it ought to love; it is an outrage upon those whom it worships. For what difference is there between denying the gods and dishonouring them?"

You should learn such principles as these, nay rather you should learn them by heart; philosophy ought not to try to explain away vice. For a sick man, when his physician bids him live recklessly, is doomed beyond recall. Farewell.

Letter CXXIV - On the True Good as Attained by Reason

Full many an ancient precept could I give,
Didst thou not shrink, and feel it shame to learn
Such lowly duties.

But you do not shrink, nor are you deterred by any subtleties of study. For your cultivated mind is not wont to investigate such important subjects in a free-and-easy manner. I approve your method in that you make everything count towards a certain degree of progress, and in that you are disgruntled only when nothing can be accomplished by the greatest degree of subtlety. And I shall take pains to show that this is the case now also. Our question is, whether the Good is grasped by the senses or by the understanding; and the corollary thereto is that it does not exist in dumb animals or little children.

Those who rate pleasure as the supreme ideal hold that the Good is a matter of the senses; but we Stoics maintain that it is a matter of the understanding, and we assign it to the mind. If the senses were to pass judgment on what is good, we should never reject any pleasure; for there is no pleasure that does not attract, no pleasure that does not please. Conversely, we should undergo no pain voluntarily; for there is no pain that does not clash with the senses. Besides, those who are too fond of pleasure and those who fear pain to the greatest degree would in that case not deserve reproof. But we condemn men who are slaves to their appetites and their lusts, and we scorn men who, through fear of pain, will dare no manly deed. But what wrong could such men be committing if they looked merely to the senses as arbiters of good and evil? For it is to the senses that you and yours have entrusted the test of things to be sought and things to be avoided!

Reason, however, is surely the governing element in such a matter as this; as reason has made the decision concerning the happy life, and concerning virtue and honour also, so she has made the decision with regard to good and evil. For with them the vilest part is allowed to give sentence about the better, so that the senses – dense as they are, and dull, and even more sluggish in man than in the other animals, – pass judgment on the Good. Just suppose that one should desire to distinguish tiny objects by the touch rather than by the eyesight! There is no special faculty more subtle and acute than the eye, that would enable us to distinguish between good and evil. You see, therefore, in what ignorance of truth a man spends his days and how abjectly he has overthrown lofty and divine ideals, if he thinks that the sense of touch can pass judgment upon the nature of the Supreme Good and the Supreme Evil! He says: "Just as every science and every art should possess an element that is palpable and capable of being grasped by the senses (their source of origin and growth), even so the happy life derives its foundation and its beginnings from things that are palpable, and from that which falls within the scope of the senses. Surely you admit that the happy life takes its beginnings from things palpable to the senses." But we define as "happy" those things that are in accord with Nature. And that which is in accord with Nature is obvious and can be seen at once – just as easily as that which is complete. That which is according to Nature, that which is given us as a gift immediately at our birth, is, I maintain, not a Good, but the beginning of a Good. You, however, assign the Supreme Good, pleasure, to mere babies, so that the child at its birth begins at the point whither the perfected man arrives. You are placing the tree-top where the root ought to be. If anyone should say that the child, hidden in its mother's womb, of unknown sex too, delicate, unformed, and shapeless – if one should say that this child is already in a state of goodness, he would clearly seem to be astray in his ideas. And yet how little difference is there between one who has just lately received the gift of life, and one who is still a hidden burden in the bowels of the mother! They are equally developed, as far as their understanding of good or evil is concerned; and a child is as yet no more capable of comprehending the Good than is a tree or any dumb beast.

But why is the Good non-existent in a tree or in a dumb beast? Because there is no reason there, either. For the same cause, then, the Good is non-existent in a child, for the child also has no reason; the child will reach the Good only when he reaches reason. There are animals without reason, there are animals not yet endowed with reason, and there are animals who possess reason, but only incompletely; in none of these does the Good exist, for it is reason that brings the Good in its company. What, then, is the distinction between the classes which I have mentioned? In that which does not possess reason, the Good will never exist. In that which is not yet endowed with reason, the Good cannot be existent at the time. And in that which possesses reason but only incompletely, the Good is capable of existing, but does not yet exist. This is what I mean, Lucilius: the Good cannot be discovered in any random person, or at any random age; and it is as far removed from infancy as last is from first, or as that which is complete from that which has just sprung into being. Therefore, it cannot exist in the delicate body, when the little frame has only just begun to knit together. Of course not – no more than in the seed. Granting the truth of this, we understand that there is a certain kind of Good of a tree or in a plant; but this is not true of its first growth, when the plant has just begun to spring forth out of the ground. There is a certain Good of wheat: it is not yet existent, however, in the swelling stalk, nor when the soft ear is pushing itself out of the husk, but only when summer days and its appointed maturity have ripened the wheat. Just as Nature in general does not produce her Good until she is brought to perfection, even so man's Good does not exist in man until both reason and man are perfected. And what is this Good? I shall tell you: it is a free mind, an upright mind, subjecting other things to itself and itself to nothing. So far is infancy from admitting this Good that boyhood has no hope of it, and even young manhood cherishes the hope without justification; even our old age is very fortunate if it has reached this Good after long and concentrated study. If this, then, is the Good, the good is a matter of the understanding.

"But," comes the retort, "you admitted that there is a certain Good of trees and of grass; then surely there can be a certain Good of a child also." But the true Good is not found in trees or in dumb animals the Good which exists in them is called good only by courtesy. "Then what is it?" you say. Simply that which is in accord with the nature of each. The real Good cannot find a place in dumb animals – not by any means; its nature is more blest and is of a higher class. And where there is no place for reason, the Good does not exist. There are four natures which we should mention here: of the tree, animal, man, and God. The last two, having reasoning power, are of the same nature, distinct only by virtue of the immortality of the one and the mortality of the other. Of one of these, then – to wit God – it is Nature that perfects the Good; of the other – to wit man – pains and study do so. All other things are perfect only in their particular nature, and not truly perfect, since they lack reason.

Indeed, to sum up, that alone is perfect which is perfect according to nature as a whole, and nature as a whole is possessed of reason. Other things can be perfect according to their kind. That which cannot contain the happy life cannot contain that which produces the happy life; and the happy life is produced by Goods alone. In dumb animals there is not a trace of the happy life, nor of the means whereby the happy life is produced; in dumb animals the Good does not exist. The dumb animal comprehends the present world about him through his senses alone. He remembers the past only by meeting with something which reminds his senses; a horse, for example, remembers the right road only when he is placed at the starting-point. In his stall, however, he has no memory of the road, no matter how often he may have stepped along it. The third state – the future – does not come within the ken of dumb beasts.

How, then, can we regard as perfect the nature of those who have no experience of time in its perfection? For time is three-fold, – past, present, and future. Animals perceive only the time which is of greatest moment to them within the limits of their coming and going – the present. Rarely do they recollect the past – and that only when they are confronted with present reminders. Therefore the Good of a perfect nature cannot exist in an imperfect nature; for if the latter sort of nature should possess the Good, so also would mere vegetation. I do not indeed deny that dumb animals have strong and swift impulses toward actions which seem according to nature, but such impulses are confused and disordered. The Good however, is never confused or disordered.

"What!" you say, "do dumb animals move in disturbed and ill-ordered fashion?" I should say that they moved in disturbed and ill-ordered fashion, if their nature admitted of order; as it is, they move in accordance with their nature. For that is said to be "disturbed" which can also at some other time be "not disturbed"; so, too, that is said to be in a state of trouble which can be in a state of peace. No man is vicious except one who has the capacity of virtue; in the case of dumb animals their motion is such as results from their nature. But, not to weary you, a certain sort of good will be found in a dumb animal, and a certain sort of virtue, and a certain sort of perfection – but neither the Good, nor virtue, nor perfection in the absolute sense. For this is the privilege of reasoning beings alone, who are permitted to know the cause, the degree, and the means. Therefore, good can exist only in that which possesses reason.

Do you ask now whither our argument is tending, and of what benefit it will be to your mind? I will tell you: it exercises and sharpens the mind, and ensures, by occupying it honourably, that it will accomplish some sort of good. And even that is beneficial which holds men back when they are hurrying into wickedness. However, I will say this also: I can be of no greater benefit to you than by revealing the Good that is rightly yours, by taking you out of the class of dumb animals, and by placing you on a level with God. Why, pray, do you foster and practise your bodily strength? Nature has granted strength in greater degree to cattle and wild beasts. Why cultivate your beauty? After all your efforts, dumb animals surpass you in comeliness. Why dress your hair with such unending attention? Though you let it down in Parthian fashion, or tie it up in the German style, or, as the Scythians do, let it flow wild – yet you will see a mane of greater thickness tossing upon any horse you choose, and a mane of greater beauty bristling upon the neck of any lion. And even after training yourself for speed, you will be no match for the hare. Are you not willing to abandon all these details – wherein you must acknowledge defeat, striving as you are for something that is not your own and come back to the Good that is really yours?

And what is this Good? It is a clear and flawless mind, which rivals that of God, raised far above mortal concerns, and counting nothing of its own to be outside itself. You are a reasoning animal. What Good, then, lies within you? Perfect reason. Are you willing to develop this to its farthest limits – to its greatest degree of increase? Only consider yourself happy when all your joys are born of reason, and when – having marked all the objects which men clutch at, or pray for, or watch over – you find nothing which you will desire; mind, I do not say prefer. Here is a short rule by which to measure yourself, and by the test of which you may feel that you have reached perfection: "You will come to your own when you shall understand that those whom the world calls fortunate are really the most unfortunate of all." Farewell.

THE ENCHIRIDION

By Epictetus

1

Of all existing things some are in our power, and others are not in our power. In our power are thought, impulse, will to get and will to avoid, and, in a word, everything which is our own doing. Things not in our power include the body, property, reputation, office, and, in a word, everything which is not our own doing. Things in our power are by nature free, unhindered, untrammelled; things not in our power are weak, servile, subject to hindrance, dependent on others. Remember then that if you imagine that what is naturally slavish is free, and what is naturally another's is your own, you will be hampered, you will mourn, you will be put to confusion, you will blame gods and men; but if you think that only your own belongs to you, and that what is another's is indeed another's, no one will ever put compulsion or hindrance on you, you will blame none, you will accuse none, you will do nothing against your will, no one will harm you, you will have no enemy, for no harm can touch you.

Aiming then at these high matters, you must remember that to attain them requires more than ordinary effort; you will have to give up some things entirely, and put off others for the moment. And if you would have these also—office and wealth—it may be that you will fail to get them, just because your desire is set on the former, and you will certainly fail to attain those things which alone bring freedom and happiness.

Make it your study then to confront every harsh impression with the words, 'You are but an impression, and not at all what you seem to be'. Then test it by those rules that you possess; and first by this—the chief test of all—'Is it concerned with what is in our power or with what is not in our power?' And if it is concerned with what is not in our power, be ready with the answer that it is nothing to you.

2

Remember that the will to get promises attainment of what you will, and the will to avoid promises escape from what you avoid; and he who fails to get what he wills is unfortunate, and he who does not escape what he wills to avoid is miserable. If then you try to avoid only what is unnatural in the region within your control, you will escape from all that you avoid; but if you try to avoid disease or death or poverty you will be miserable.

Therefore let your will to avoid have no concern with what is not in man's power; direct it only to things in man's power that are contrary to nature. But for the moment you must utterly remove the will to get; for if you will to get something not in man's power you are bound to be unfortunate; while none of the things in man's power that you could honourably will to get is yet within your reach. Impulse to act and not to act, these are your concern; yet exercise them gently and without strain, and provisionally.

3

When anything, from the meanest thing upwards, is attractive or serviceable or an object of affection, remember always to say to yourself, 'What is its nature?' If you are fond of a jug, say you are fond of a jug; then you will not be disturbed if it be broken. If you kiss your child or your wife, say to yourself that you are kissing a human being, for then if death strikes it you will not be disturbed.

4

When you are about to take something in hand, remind yourself what manner of thing it is. If you are going to bathe put before your mind what happens in the bath—water pouring over some, others being jostled,. some reviling, others stealing; and you will set to work more securely if you say to yourself at once: 'I want to bathe, and I want to keep my will in harmony with nature,' and so in each thing you do; for in this way, if anything turns up to hinder you in your bathing, you will be ready to say, 'I did not want only to bathe, but to keep my will in harmony with nature, and I shall not so keep it, if I lose my temper at what happens'.

5

What disturbs men's minds is not events but their judgements on events: For instance, death is nothing dreadful, or else Socrates would have thought it so. No, the only dreadful thing about it is men's judgement that it is dreadful. And so when we are hindered, or disturbed, or distressed, let us never lay the blame on others, but on ourselves, that is, on our own judgements. To accuse others for one's own misfortunes is a sign of want of education; to accuse oneself shows that one's education has begun; to accuse neither oneself nor others shows that one's education is complete.

6

Be not elated at an excellence which is not your own. If the horse in his pride were to say, 'I am handsome', we could bear with it. But when you say with pride, 'I have a handsome horse', know that the good horse is the ground of your pride. You ask then what you can call your own. The answer is—the way you deal with your impressions. Therefore when you deal with your impressions in accord with nature, then you may be proud indeed, for your pride will be in a good which is your own.

7

When you are on a voyage, and your ship is at anchorage, and you disembark to get fresh water, you may pick up a small shellfish or a truffle by the way, but you must keep your attention fixed on the ship, and keep looking towards it constantly, to see if the Helmsman calls you; and if he does, you have to leave everything, or be bundled on board with your legs tied like a sheep. So it is in life. If you have a dear wife or child given you, they are like the shellfish or the truffle, they are very well in their way. Only, if the Helmsman call, run back to your ship, leave all else, and do not look behind you. And if you are old, never go far from the ship, so that when you are called you may not fail to appear.

8

Ask not that events should happen as you will, but let your will be that events should happen as they do, and you shall have peace.

9

Sickness is a hindrance to the body, but not to the will, unless the will consent. Lameness is a hindrance to the leg, but not to the will. Say this to yourself at each event that happens, for you shall find that though it hinders something else it will not hinder you.

10

When anything happens to you, always remember to turn to yourself and ask what faculty you have to deal with it. If you see a beautiful boy or a beautiful woman, you will find continence the faculty to exercise there; if trouble is laid on you, you will find endurance; if ribaldry, you will find patience. And if you train yourself in this habit your impressions will not carry you away.

11

Never say of anything, 'I lost it', but say, 'I gave it back'. Has your child died? It was given back. Has your wife died? She was given back. Has your estate been taken from you? Was not this also given back? But you say, 'He who took it from me is wicked'. What does it matter to you through whom the Giver asked it back? As long as He gives it you, take care of it, but not as your own; treat it as passers-by treat an inn.

12

If you wish to make progress, abandon reasonings of this sort: 'If I neglect my affairs I shall have nothing to live on'; 'If I do not punish my son, he will be wicked.' For it is better to die of hunger, so that you be free from pain and free from fear, than to live in plenty and be troubled in mind. It is better for your son to be wicked than for you to be miserable. Wherefore begin with little things. Is your drop of oil spilt? Is your sup of wine stolen? Say to yourself, 'This is the price paid for freedom from passion, this is the price of a quiet mind.' Nothing can be had without a price. When you call your slave-boy, reflect that he may not be able to hear you, and if he hears you, he may not be able to do anything you want. But he is not so well off that it rests with him to give you peace of mind.

13

If you wish to make progress, you must be content in external matters to seem a fool and a simpleton; do not wish men to think you know anything, and if any should think you to be somebody, distrust yourself. For know that it is not easy to keep your will in accord with nature and at the same time keep outward things; if you attend to one you must needs neglect the other.

14

It is silly to want your children and your wife and your friends to live for ever, for that means that you want what is not in your control to be in your control, and what is not your own to be yours. In the same way if you want your servant to make no mistakes, you are a fool, for you want vice not to be vice but something different. But if you want not to be disappointed in your will to get, you can attain to that.

Exercise yourself then in what lies in your power. Each man's master is the man who has authority over what he wishes or does not wish, to secure the one or to take away the other. Let him then who wishes to be free not wish for anything or avoid anything that depends on others; or else he is bound to be a slave.

15

Remember that you must behave in life as you would at a banquet. A dish is handed round and comes to you; put out your hand and take it politely. It passes you; do not stop it. It has not reached you; do not be impatient to get it, but wait till your turn comes. Bear yourself thus towards children, wife, office, wealth, and one day you will be worthy to banquet with the gods. But if when they are set before you, you do not take them but despise them, then you shall not only share the gods' banquet, but shall share their rule. For by so doing Diogenes and Heraclitus and men like them were called divine and deserved the name.

16

When you see a man shedding tears in sorrow for a child abroad or dead, or for loss of property, beware that you are not carried away by the impression that it is outward ills that make him miserable. Keep this thought by you: 'What distresses him is not the event, for that does not distress another, but his judgement on the event.' Therefore do not hesitate to sympathize with him so far as words go, and if it so chance, even to groan with him; but take heed that you do not also groan in your inner being.

17

Remember that you are an actor in a play, and the Playwright chooses the manner of it: if he wants it short, it is short; if long, it is long. If he wants you to act a poor man you must act the part with all your powers; and so if your part be a cripple or a magistrate or a plain man. For your business is to act the character that is given you and act it well; the choice of the cast is Another's.

18

When a raven croaks with evil omen, let not the impression carry you away, but straightway distinguish in your own mind and say, 'These portents mean nothing to me; but only to my bit of a body or my bit of property or name, or my children or my wife. But for me all omens are favourable if I will, for, whatever the issue may be, it is in my power to pt benefit therefrom.'

19

You can be invincible, if you never enter on a contest where victory is not in your power. Beware then that when you see a man raised to honour or great power or high repute you do not let your impression carry you away. For if the reality of good lies in what is in our power, there is no room for envy or jealousy. And you will not wish to be praetor, or prefect or consul, but to be free; and there is but one way to freedom—to despise what is not in our power.

20

Remember that foul words or blows in themselves are no outrage, but your judgement that they are so. So when any one makes you angry, know that it is your own thought that has angered you. Wherefore make it your first endeavour not to let your impressions carry you away. For if once you gain time and delay, you will find it easier to control yourself.

21

Keep before your eyes from day to day death and exile and all things that seem terrible, but death most of all, and then you will never set your thoughts on what is low and will never desire anything beyond measure.

22

If you set your desire on philosophy you must at once prepare to meet with ridicule and the jeers of many who will say, 'Here he is again, turned philosopher. Where has he got these proud looks?' Nay, put on no proud looks, but hold fast to what seems best to you, in confidence that God has set you at this post. And remember that if you abide where you are, those who first laugh at you will one day admire you, and that if you give way to them, you will get doubly laughed at.

23

If it ever happen to you to be diverted to things outside, so that you desire to please another, know that you have lost your life's plan. Be content then always to be a philosopher; if you wish to be regarded as one too, show yourself that you are one and you will be able to achieve it.

24

Let not reflections such as these afflict you: 'I shall live without honour, and never be of any account'; for if lack of honour is an evil, no one but yourself can involve you in evil any more than in shame. Is it your business to get office or to be invited to an entertainment?

Certainly not.

Where then is the dishonour you talk of? How can you be 'of no account anywhere', when you ought to count for something in those matters only which are in your power, where you may achieve the highest worth? 'But my friends,' you say, 'will lack assistance.'

What do you mean by 'lack assistance'? They will not have cash from you and you will not make them Roman citizens. Who told you that to do these things is in our power, and not dependent upon others? Who can give to another what is not his to give?

'Get them then,' says he, 'that we may have them.'

If I can get them and keep my self-respect, honour, magnanimity, show the way and I will get them. But if you call on me to lose the good things that are mine, in order that you may win things that are not good, look how unfair and thoughtless you are. And which do you really prefer? Money, or a faithful, modest friend? Therefore help me rather to keep these qualities, and do not expect from me actions which will make me lose them.

'But my country,' says he, 'will lack assistance, so far as lies in me.'

Once more I ask, What assistance do you mean? It will not owe colonnades or baths to you. What of that? It does not owe shoes to the blacksmith or arms to the shoemaker; it is sufficient if each man fulfils his own function. Would you do it no good if you secured to it another faithful and modest citizen?

'Yes.'

Well, then, you would not be useless to it.

'What place then shall I have in the city?'

Whatever place you can hold while you keep your character for honour and self-respect. But if you are going to lose these qualities in trying to benefit your city, what benefit, I ask, would you have done her when you attain to the perfection of being lost to shame and honour?

25

Has some one had precedence of you at an entertainment or a levée or been called in before you to give advice? If these things are good you ought to be glad that he got them; if they are evil, do not be angry that you did not get them yourself. Remember that if you want to get what is not in your power, you cannot earn the same reward as others unless you act as they do. How is it possible for one who does not haunt the great man's door to have equal shares with one who does, or one who does not go in his train equality with one who does; or one who does not praise him with one who does? You will be unjust then and insatiable if you wish to get these privileges for nothing, without paying their price. What is the price of a lettuce? An obol perhaps. If then a man pays his obol and gets his lettuces, and you do not pay and do not get them, do not think you are defrauded. For as he has the lettuces so you have the obol you did not give. The same principle holds good too in conduct. You were not invited to some one's entertainment? Because you did not give the host the price for which he sells his dinner. He sells it for compliments, he sells it for attentions. Pay him the price then, if it is to your profit. But if you wish to get the one and yet not give up the other, nothing can satisfy you in your folly.

What! you say, you have nothing instead of the dinner?

Nay, you have this, you have not praised the man you did not want to praise, you have not had to bear with the insults of his doorstep.

26

It is in our power to discover the will of Nature from those matters on which we have no difference of opinion. For instance, when another man's slave has broken the wine-cup we are very ready to say at once, 'Such things must happen'. Know then that when your own cup is broken, you ought to behave in the same way as when your neighbour's was broken. Apply the same principle to higher matters. Is another's child or wife dead? Not one of us but would say, 'Such is the lot of man'; but when one's own dies, straightway one cries, 'Alas! miserable am I'. But we ought to remember what our feelings are when we hear it of another.

27

As a mark is not set up for men to miss it, so there is nothing intrinsically evil in the world.

28

If any one trusted your body to the first man he met, you would be indignant, but yet you trust your mind to the chance comer, and allow it to be disturbed and confounded if he revile you; are you not ashamed to do so?

In everything you do consider what comes first and what follows, and so approach it. Otherwise you will come to it with a good heart at first because you have not reflected on any of the consequences, and afterwards, when difficulties have appeared, you will desist to your shame. Do you wish to win at Olympia? So do I, by the gods, for it is a fine thing. But consider the first steps to it, and the consequences, and so lay your hand to the work. You must submit to discipline, eat to order, touch no sweets, train under compulsion, at a fixed hour, in heat and cold, drink no cold water, nor wine, except by order; you must hand yourself over completely to your trainer as you would to a physician, and then when the contest comes you must risk getting hacked, and sometimes dislocate your hand, twist your ankle, swallow plenty of sand, sometimes get a flogging, and with all this suffer defeat. When you have considered all this well, then enter on the athlete's course, if you still wish it. If you act without thought you will be behaving like children, who one day play at wrestlers, another day at gladiators, now sound the trumpet, and next strut the stage. Like them you will be now an athlete, now a gladiator, then orator, then philosopher, but nothing with all your soul. Like an ape, you imitate every sight you see, and one thing after another takes your fancy. When you undertake a thing you do it casually and halfheartedly, instead of considering it and looking at it all round. In the same way some people, when they see a philosopher and hear a man speaking like Euphrates (and indeed who can speak as he can?), wish to be philosophers themselves.

29

Man, consider first what it is you are undertaking; then look at your own powers and see if you can bear it. Do you want to compete in the pentathlon or in wrestling? Look to your arms, your thighs, see what your loins are like. For different men are born for different tasks. Do you suppose that if you do this you can live as you do now—eat and drink as you do now, indulge desire and discontent just as before? Nay, you must sit up late, work hard, abandon your own people, be looked down on by a mere slave, be ridiculed by those who meet you, get the worst of it in everything—in honour, in office, in justice, in every possible thing. This is what you have to consider: whether you are willing to pay this price for peace of mind, freedom, tranquillity. If not, do not come near; do not be, like the children, first a philosopher, then a tax-collector, then an orator, then one of Caesar's procurators. These callings do not agree. You must be one man, good or bad; you must develop either your Governing Principle, or your outward endowments; you must study either your inner man, or outward things—in a word, you must choose between the position of a philosopher and that of a mere outsider.

30

Appropriate acts are in general measured by the relations they are concerned with. 'He is your father.' This means you are called on to take care of him, give way to him in all things, bear with him if he reviles or strikes you.

'But he is a bad father.'

Well, have you any natural claim to a good father? No, only to a father.

'My brother wrongs me.'

Be careful then to maintain the relation you hold to him, and do not consider what he does, but what you must do if your purpose is to keep in accord with nature. For no one shall harm you, without your consent; you will only be harmed, when you think you are harmed. You will only discover what is proper to expect from neighbour, citizen, or praetor, if you get into the habit of looking at the relations implied by each.

31

For piety towards the gods know that the most important thing is this: to have right opinions about them—that they exist, and that they govern the universe well and justly—and to have set yourself to obey them, and to give way to all that happens, following events with a free will, in the belief that they are fulfilled by the highest mind. For thus you will never blame the gods, nor accuse them of neglecting you. But this you cannot achieve, unless you apply your conception of good and evil to those things only which are in our power, and not to those which are out of our power. For if you apply your notion of good or evil to the latter, then, as soon as you fail to get what you will to get or fail to avoid what you will to avoid, you will be bound to blame and hate those you hold responsible. For every living creature has a natural tendency to avoid and shun what seems harmful and all that causes it, and to pursue and admire what is helpful and all that causes it. It is not possible then for one who thinks he is harmed to take pleasure in what he thinks is the author of the harm, any more than to take pleasure in the harm itself. That is why a father is reviled by his son, when he does not give his son a share of what the son regards as good things; thus Polynices and Eteocles were set at enmity with one another by thinking that a king's throne was a good thing. That is why the farmer, and the sailor, and the merchant, and those who lose wife or children revile the gods. For men's religion is bound up with their interest. Therefore he who makes it his concern rightly to direct his will to get and his will to avoid, is thereby making piety his concern. But it is proper on each occasion to make libation and sacrifice and to offer first-fruits according to the custom of our fathers, with purity and not in slovenly or careless fashion, without meanness and without extravagance.

32

When you make use of prophecy remember that while you know not what the issue will be, but are come to learn it from the prophet, you do know before you come what manner of thing it is, if you are really a philosopher. For if the event is not in our control, it cannot be either good or evil. Therefore do not bring with you to the prophet the will to get or the will to avoid, and do not approach him with trembling, but with your mind made up, that the whole issue is indifferent and does not affect you and that, whatever it be, it will be in your power to make good use of it, and no one shall hinder this. With confidence then approach the gods as counsellors, and further, when the counsel is given you, remember whose counsel it is, and whom you will be disregarding if you disobey. And consult the oracle, as Socrates thought men should, only when the whole question turns upon the issue of events, and neither reason nor any art of man provides opportunities for discovering what lies before you. Therefore, when it is your duty to risk your life with friend or country, do not ask the oracle whether you should risk your life. For if the prophet warns you that the sacrifice is unfavourable, though it is plain that this means death or exile or injury to some part of your body, yet reason requires that even at this cost you must stand by your friend and share your country's danger. Wherefore pay heed to the greater prophet, Pythian Apollo, who cast out of his temple the man who did not help his friend when he was being killed.

33

Lay down for yourself from the first a definite stamp and style of conduct, which you will maintain when you are alone and also in the society of men. Be silent for the most part, or, if you speak, say only what is necessary and in a few words. Talk, but rarely, if occasion calls you, but do not talk of ordinary things—of gladiators, or horse-races, or athletes, or of meats or drinks—these are topics that arise everywhere—but above all do not talk about men in blame or compliment or comparison. If you can, turn the conversation of your company by your talk to some fitting subject; but if you should chance to be isolated among strangers, be silent. Do not laugh much, nor at many things, nor without restraint.

Refuse to take oaths, altogether if that be possible, but if not, as far as circumstances allow.

Refuse the entertainments of strangers and the vulgar. m-5 But if occasion arise to accept them, then strain every nerve to avoid lapsing into the state of the vulgar. For know that, if your comrade have a stain on him, he that associates with him must needs share the stain, even though he be clean in himself.

For your body take just so much as your bare need requires, such as food, drink, clothing, house, servants, but cut down all that tends to luxury and outward show.

Avoid impurity to the utmost of your power before marriage, and if you indulge your passion, let it be done lawfully. But do not be offensive or censorious to those who indulge it, and do not be always bringing up your own chastity. If some one tells you that so and so speaks ill of you, do not defend yourself against what he says, but answer, 'He did not know my other faults, or he would not have mentioned these alone.'

It is not necessary for the most part to go to the games; but if you should have occasion to go, show that your first concern is for yourself; that is, wish that only to happen which does happen, and him only to win who does win, for so you will suffer no hindrance. But refrain entirely from applause, or ridicule, or prolonged excitement. And when you go away do not talk much of what happened there, except so far as it tends to your improvement. For to talk about it implies that the spectacle excited your wonder.

Do not go lightly or casually to hear lectures; but if you do go, maintain your gravity and dignity and do not make yourself offensive. When you are going to meet any one, and particularly some man of reputed eminence, set before your mind the thought, 'What would Socrates or Zeno have done?' and you will not fail to make proper use of the occasion.

When you go to visit some great man, prepare your mind by thinking that you will not find him in, that you will be shut out, that the doors will be slammed in your face, that he will pay no heed to you. And if in spite of all this you find it fitting for you to go, go and bear what happens and never say to yourself, 'It was not worth all this'; for that shows a vulgar mind and one at odds with outward things.

In your conversation avoid frequent and disproportionate mention of your own doings or adventures; for other people do not take the same pleasure in hearing what has happened to you as you take in recounting your adventures.

Avoid raising men's laughter; for it is a habit that easily slips into vulgarity, and it may well suffice to lessen your neighbour's respect.

It is dangerous too to lapse into foul language; when anything of the kind occurs, rebuke the offender, if the occasion allow, and if not, make it plain to him by your silence, or a blush or a frown, that you are angry at his words.

34

When you imagine some pleasure, beware that it does not carry you away, like other imaginations. Wait a while, and give yourself pause. Next remember two things: how long you will enjoy the pleasure, and also how long you will afterwards repent and revile yourself. And set on the other side the joy and self-satisfaction you will feel if you refrain. And if the moment seems come to realize it, take heed that you be not overcome by the winning sweetness and attraction of it; set in the other scale the thought how much better is the consciousness of having vanquished it.

35

When you do a thing because you have determined that it ought to be done, never avoid being seen doing it, even if the opinion of the multitude is going to condemn you. For if your action is wrong, then avoid doing it altogether, but if it is right, why do you fear those who will rebuke you wrongly?

36

The phrases, 'It is day' and 'It is night', mean a great deal if taken separately, but have no meaning if combined. In the same way, to choose the larger portion at a banquet may be worth while for your body, but if you want to maintain social decencies it is worthless. Therefore, when you are at meat with another, remember not only to consider the value of what is set before you for the body, but also to maintain your self-respect before your host.

37

If you try to act a part beyond your powers, you not only disgrace yourself in it, but you neglect the part which you could have filled with success.

38

As in walking you take care not to tread on a nail or to twist your foot, so take care that you do not harm your Governing Principle. And if we guard this in everything we do, we shall set to work more securely.

39

Every man's body is a measure for his property, as the foot is the measure for his shoe. If you stick to this limit, you will keep the right measure; if you go beyond it, you are bound to be carried away down a precipice in the end; just as with the shoe, if you once go beyond the foot, your shoe puts on gilding, and soon purple and embroidery. For when once you go beyond the measure there is no limit.

40

Women from fourteen years upwards are called 'madam' by men. Wherefore, when they see that the only advantage they have got is to be marriageable, they begin to make themselves smart and to set all their hopes on this. We must take pains then to make them understand that they are really honoured for nothing but a modest and decorous life.

41

It is a sign of a dull mind to dwell upon the cares of the body, to prolong exercise, eating, drinking, and other bodily functions. These things are to be done by the way; all your attention must be given to the mind.

42

When a man speaks evil or does evil to you, remember that he does or says it because he thinks it is fitting for him. It is not possible for him to follow what seems good to you, but only what seems good to him, so that, if his opinion is wrong, he suffers, in that he is the victim of deception. In the same way, if a composite judgement which is true is thought to be false, it is not the judgement that suffers, but the man who is deluded about it. If you act on this principle you will be gentle to him who reviles you, saying to yourself on each occasion, 'He thought it right.'

43

Everything has two handles, one by which you can carry it, the other by which you cannot. If your brother wrongs you, do not take it by that handle, the handle of his wrong, for you cannot carry it by that, but rather by the other handle—that he is a brother, brought up with you, and then you will take it by the handle that you can carry by.

44

It is illogical to reason thus, 'I am richer than you, therefore I am superior to you', 'I am more eloquent than you, therefore I am superior to you.' It is more logical to reason, 'I am richer than you, therefore my property is superior to yours', 'I am more eloquent than you, therefore my speech is superior to yours.' You are something more than property or speech.

45

If a man wash quickly, do not say that he washes badly, but that he washes quickly. If a man drink much wine, do not say that he drinks badly, but that he drinks much. For till you have decided what judgement prompts him, how do you know that he acts badly? If you do as I say, you will assent to your apprehensive impressions and to none other.

46

On no occasion call yourself a philosopher, nor talk at large of your principles among the multitude, but act on your principles. For instance, at a banquet do not say how one ought to eat, but eat as you ought. Remember that Socrates had so completely got rid of the thought of display that when men came and wanted an introduction to philosophers he took them to be introduced; so patient of neglect was he. And if a discussion arise among the multitude on some principle, keep silent for the most part; for you are in great danger of blurting out some undigested thought. And when some one says to you, 'You know nothing', and you do not let it provoke you, then know that you are really on the right road. For sheep do not bring grass to their shepherds and show them how much they have eaten, but they digest their fodder and then produce it in the form of wool and milk. Do the same yourself; instead of displaying your principles to the multitude, show them the results of the principles you have digested.

47

When you have adopted the simple life, do not pride yourself upon it, and if you are a water-drinker do not say on every occasion, 'I am a water-drinker.' And if you ever want to train laboriously, keep it to yourself and do not make a show of it. Do not embrace statues. If you are very thirsty take a good draught of cold water, and rinse you mouth and tell no one.

48

The ignorant man's position and character is this: he never looks to himself for benefit or harm, but to the world outside him. The philosopher's position and character is that he always look to himself for benefit and harm.

The signs of one who is making progress are: he blames none, praises none, complains of none, accuses none, never speaks of himself as if he were somebody, or as if he knew anything. And if any one compliments him he laughs in himself at his compliment; and if one blames him, he makes no defence. He goes about like a convalescent, careful not to disturb his constitution on its road to recovery, until it has got firm hold. He has got rid of the will to get, and his will to avoid is directed no longer to what is beyond our power but only to what is in our power and contrary to nature. In all things he exercises his will without strain. If men regard him as foolish or ignorant he pays no heed. In one word, he keeps watch and guard on himself as his own enemy, lying in wait for him.

49

When a man prides himself on being able to understand and interpret the books of Chrysippus, say to yourself, 'If Chrysippus had not written obscurely this man would have had nothing on which to pride himself.'

What is my object? To understand Nature and follow her. I look then for some one who interprets her, and having heard that Chrysippus does

I come to him. But I do not understand his writings, so I seek an interpreter. So far there is nothing to be proud of. But when I have found the interpreter it remains for me to act on his precepts; that and that alone is a thing to be proud of. But if I admire the mere power of exposition, it comes to this—that I am turned into a grammarian instead of a philosopher, except that I interpret Chrysippus in place of Homer. Therefore, when some one says to me, 'Read me Chrysippus', when I cannot point to actions which are in harmony and correspondence with his teaching, I am rather inclined to blush.

50

Whatever principles you put before you, hold fast to them as laws which it will be impious to transgress. But pay no heed to what any one says of you; for this is something beyond your own control.

51

How long will you wait to think yourself worthy of the highest and transgress in nothing the clear pronouncement of reason? You have received

the precepts which you ought to accept, and you have accepted them. Why then do you still wait for a master, that you may delay the amendment of yourself till he comes? You are a youth no longer, you are now a full-grown man. If now you are careless and indolent and are always putting off, fixing one day after another as the limit when you mean to begin attending to yourself, then, living or dying, you will make no progress but will continue unawares in ignorance. Therefore make up your mind before it is too late to live as one who is mature and proficient, and let all that seems best to you be a law that you cannot transgress. And if you encounter anything troublesome or pleasant or glorious or inglorious, remember that the hour of struggle is come, the Olympic contest is here and you may put off no longer, and that one day and one action determines whether the progress you have achieved is lost or maintained.

This was how Socrates attained perfection, paying heed to nothing but reason, in all that he encountered. And if you are not yet Socrates, yet ought you to live as one who would wish to be a Socrates.

52

The first and most necessary department of philosophy deals with the application of principles; for instance, 'not to lie'. The second deals with demonstrations; for instance, 'How comes it that one ought not to lie?' The third is concerned with establishing and analysing these processes; for instance, 'How comes it that this is a demonstration? What is demonstration, what is consequence, what is contradiction, what is true, what is false?' It follows then that the third department is necessary because of the second, and the second because of the first. The first is the most necessary part, and that in which we must rest. But we reverse the order: we occupy ourselves with the third, and make that our whole concern, and the first we completely neglect. Wherefore we lie, but are ready enough with the demonstration that lying is wrong.

53

On every occasion we must have these thoughts at hand,
'Lead me, O Zeus, and lead me, Destiny,
Whither ordainèd is by your decree.
I'll follow, doubting not, or if with will
Recreant I falter, I shall follow still.'
'Who rightly with necessity complies
In things divine we count him skilled and wise.'

MARCUS AURELIUS BIOGRAPHY

By

John Lord

MARCUS AURELIUS A.D. 121-180

Marcus Aurelius is immortal, not so much for what he did as for what he was. His services to the State were considerable, but not transcendent. He was a great man, but not pre-eminently a great emperor. He was a meditative sage rather than a man of action; although he successfully fought the Germanic barbarians, and repelled their fearful incursions. He did not materially extend the limits of the Empire, but he preserved and protected its provinces. He reigned wisely and ably, but made mistakes. His greatness was in his character; his influence for good was in his noble example. When we consider his circumstances and temptations, as the supreme master of a vast Empire, and in a wicked and sensual age, he is a greater moral phenomenon than Socrates or Epictetus. He was one of the best men of Pagan antiquity. History furnishes no example of an absolute monarch so pure and spotless and lofty as he was, unless it be Alfred the Great or St. Louis. But the sphere of the Roman emperor was far greater than that of the Mediaeval kings. Marcus Aurelius ruled over one hundred and twenty millions of people, without check or hindrance or Constitutional restraint. He could do what he pleased with their persons and their property. Most sovereigns, exalted to such lofty dignity and power, have been either cruel, or vindictive, or self-indulgent, or selfish, or proud, or hard, or ambitious, -men who have been stained by crimes, whatever may have been their services to civilization. Most of them have yielded to their great temptations. But Marcus Aurelius, on the throne of the civilized world, was modest, virtuous, affable, accessible, considerate, gentle, studious, contemplative, stained by novices, -a model of human virtue. Hence he is one of the favorite characters of history. No Roman emperor was so revered and loved as he, and of no one have so many monuments been preserved. Everybody had his picture or statue in his house. He was more than venerated in his day, and his fame as a wise and good man has increased with the flight of ages.

This illustrious emperor did not belong to the family of the great Caesar. That family became extinct with Nero, the sixth emperor. Like Trajan and Hadrian, Marcus Aurelius derived his remote origin from Spain, although he was born in Rome. His great-grandfather was a Spaniard, and yet attained the praetorian rank. His grandfather reached the consulate. His father died while praetor, and when he himself was a child. He was adopted by his grandfather Annius Verus. But his marvellous moral beauty, even as a child, attracted the attention of the Emperor Hadrian, who bestowed upon him the honor of the aequestrian rank, at the age of six. At fifteen he was adopted by Antoninus Pius, then, as we might say, "Crown Prince." Had he been older, he would have been adopted by Hadrian himself. He thus, a mere youth, became the heir of the Roman world. His education was most excellent. From Fronto, the greatest rhetorician of the day, he learned rhetoric; from Herodes Atticus he acquired a knowledge of the world; from Diognotus he learned to despise superstition; from Apollonius, undeviating steadiness of purpose; from Sextus of Chaeronea, toleration of human infirmities; from Maximus, sweetness and dignity; from Alexander, allegiance to duty; from Rusticus, contempt of sophistry and display. This stoical philosopher created in him a new intellectual life, and opened to him a new world of thought. But the person to whom he was most indebted was his adopted father and father-in-law, the Emperor Antoninus Pius. For him he seems to have had the greatest reverence. "In him," said he, "I noticed mildness of manner with firmness of resolution, contempt of vain-glory, industry in business, and accessibility of person. From him I learned to acquiesce in every fortune, to exercise foresight in public affairs, to rise superior to vulgar praises, to serve mankind without ambition, to be sober and steadfast, to be content with little, to be practical and active, to be no dreamy bookworm, to be temperate, modest in dress, and not to be led away by novelties." What a picture of an emperor! What a contrast to such a man as Louis XIV!

We might draw a parallel between Marcus Aurelius and David, when he was young and innocent. But the person in history whom he most resembled was St. Anselm. He was a St. Anselm on the throne. Philosophical meditations seem to have been his delight and recreation; and yet he could issue from his retirement and engage in active pursuits. He was an able general as well as a meditative sage, -heroic like David, capable of enduring great fatigue, and willing to expose himself to great dangers.

While his fame rests on his "Meditations," as that of David rests upon his Psalms, he yet rendered great military services to the Empire. He put down a dangerous revolt under Avidius Cassius in Asia, and did not punish the rebellious provinces. Not one person suffered death in consequence of this rebellion. Even the papers of Cassius, who aimed to be emperor, were burned, that a revelation of enemies might not be made, -a signal instance of magnanimity. Cassius, it seems, was assassinated by his own officers, which assassination Marcus Aurelius regretted, because it deprived him of granting a free pardon to a very able but dangerous man.

But the most signal service he rendered the Empire was a successful resistance to the barbarians of Germany, who had formed a general union for the invasion of the Roman world. They threatened the security of the Empire, as the Teutons did in the time of Marius, and the Gauls and Germans in the time of Julius Caesar. It took him twenty years to subdue these fierce warriors. He made successive campaigns against them, as Charlemagne did against the Saxons. It cost him the best years of his life to conquer them, which he did under difficulties as great as Julius surmounted in Gaul. He was the savior and deliverer of his country, as much as Marius or Scipio or Julius. The public dangers were from the West and not the East. Yet he succeeded in erecting a barrier against barbaric inundations, so that for nearly two hundred years the Romans were not seriously molested. There still stands in "the Eternal City" the column which commemorates his victories, -not so beautiful as that of Trajan, which furnished the model for Napoleon's column in the Place Vendome, but still greatly admired. Were he not better known for his writings, he would be famous as one of the great military emperors, like Vespasian, Diocletian, and Constantine. Perhaps he did not add to the art of war; that was perfected by Julius Caesar. It was with the mechanism of former generals that he withstood most dangerous enemies, for in his day the legions were still well disciplined and irresistible.

The only stains on the reign of this good and great emperor -for there were none on his character -were in allowing the elevation of his son Commodus as his successor, and his persecution of the Christians.

In regard to the first, it was a blunder rather than a fault. Peter the Great caused his heir to be tried and sentenced to death, because he was a sot, a liar, and a fool. He dared not intrust the interests of his Empire to so unworthy a son; the welfare of Russia was more to him than the interest of his family. In that respect this stern and iron man was a greater prince than Marcus Aurelius; for the law of succession was not established at Rome any more than in Russia. There was no danger of civil war should the natural succession be set aside, as might happen in the feudal monarchies of Europe. The Emperor of Rome could adopt or elect his successor. It would have been wise for Aurelius to have selected one of the ablest of his generals, or one of the wisest of his senators, as Hadrian did, for so great and responsible a position, rather than a wicked, cruel, dissolute son. But Commodus was the son of Faustina also, -an intriguing and wicked woman, whose influence over her husband was unfortunately great; and, what is common in this world, the son was more like the mother than the father. (I think the wife of Eli the high-priest must have been a bad woman.) All his teachings and virtues were lost on such a reprobate. She, as an unscrupulous and ambitious woman, had no idea of seeing her son supplanted in the imperial dignity; and, like Catherine de'Medici and Agrippina, probably she connived at and even encouraged the vices of her children, in order more easily to bear rule. At any rate, the succession of Commodus to the throne was the greatest calamity that could have happened. For five reigns the Empire had enjoyed peace and prosperity; for five reigns the tide of corruption had been stayed: but the flood of corruption swept all barriers away with the accession of Commodus, and from that day the decline of the Empire was rapid and fatal. Still, probably nothing could have long arrested ruin. The Empire was doomed.

The other fact which obscured the glory of Marcus Aurelius as a sovereign was his persecution of the Christians, -for which it is hard to account, when the beneficent character of the emperor is considered. His reign was signalized for an imperial persecution, in which Justin at Rome, Polycarp at Smyrna, and Ponthinus at Lyons, suffered martyrdom. It was not the first persecution. Under Nero the Christians had been cruelly tortured, nor did the virtuous Trajan change the policy of the government. Hadrian and Antoninus Pius permitted the laws to be enforced against the Christians, and Marcus Aurelius saw no reason to alter them. But to the mind of the Stoic on the throne, says Arnold, the Christians were "philosophically contemptible, politically subversive, and morally abominable." They were regarded as statesmen looked upon the Jesuits in the reign of Louis XV, as we look upon the Mormons, -as dangerous to free institutions. Moreover, the Christians were everywhere misunderstood and misrepresented. It was impossible for Marcus Aurelius to see the Christians except through a mist of prejudices. "Christianity grew up in the Catacombs, not on the Palatine." In allowing the laws to take their course against a body of men who were regarded with distrust and aversion as enemies of the State, the Emperor was simply unfortunate. So wise and good a man, perhaps, ought to have known the Christians better; but, not knowing them, he cannot be stigmatized as a cruel man. How different the fortunes of the Church had Aurelius been the first Christian emperor instead of Constantine! Or, had his wife Faustina known the Christians as well as Marcia the mistress of Commodus, perhaps the persecution might not have happened, and perhaps it might. Earnest and sincere men have often proved intolerant when their peculiar doctrines have been assailed, like Athanasius and St. Bernard. A Stoical philosopher was trained, like a doctor of the Jewish Sandhedrim, in a certain intellectual pride.

The fame of Marcus Aurelius rests, as it has been said, on his philosophical reflections, as his "Meditations" attest. This remarkable book has come down to us, while most of the annals of the age have perished; so that even Niebuhr confesses that he knows less of the reign of Marcus Aurelius than of the early kings of Rome. Perhaps that is one reason why Gibbon begins his history with later emperors. But the "Meditations" of the good emperor survive, like the writings of Epictetus, St. Augustine, and Thomas a Kempis: one of the few immortal books, immortal, in this case, not for artistic excellence, like the writings of Thucydides and Tacitus, but for the loftiness of thoughts alone; so precious that the saints of the Middle Ages secretly preserved them as in accord with their own experiences. It is from these "Meditations" that we derive our best knowledge of Marcus Aurelius. They reveal the man, -and a man of sorrows, as the truly great are apt to be, when brought in contact with a world of wickedness, as were Alfred and Dante.

In these "Meditations" there is a striking resemblance to the discourses of Epictetus, which alike reveal the lofty and yet sorrowful soul, and are among the most valuable fragments which have come down from Pagan antiquity; and this is remarkable, since Epictetus was a Phrygian slave, of the lowest parentage. He belonged to the secretary and companion of Nero, whose name was Epaphroditus, and who treated this poor Phrygian with great cruelty. And yet, what is very singular, the master caused the slave to be indoctrinated in the Stoical philosophy, on account of a rare intelligence which commanded respect. He was finally manumitted, but lived all his life in the deepest poverty, to which he attached no more importance than Socrates did at Athens. In his miserable cottage he had no other furniture than a straw pallet and an iron lamp, which last somebody stole. His sole remark on the loss of the only property he possessed was, that when the thief came again he would be disappointed to find only an earthen lamp instead of an iron one. This earthen lamp was subsequently purchased by a hero-worshipper for three thousand drachmas. Epictetus, much as he despised riches and display and luxury and hypocrisy and pedantry and all phariseeism, living in the depths of poverty, was yet admired by eminent men, among whom was the Emperor Hadrian himself; and he found a disciple in Arrian, who was to him what Xenophon was to Socrates, committing his precious thoughts to writing; and these thoughts were to antiquity what the "Imitation of Christ" was to the Middle Ages, -accepted by Christians as well as by pagans, and even to-day regarded as one of the most beautiful treatises on morals ever composed by man. The great peculiarity of the "Manual" and the "Discourses" is the elevation of the soul over external evils, the duty of resignation to whatever God sends, and the obligation to do right because it is right. Epictetus did not go into the dreary dialectics of the schools, but, like Socrates, confined himself to practical life, -to the practice of virtue as the greatest good, -and valued the joys of true intellectual independence. To him his mind was his fortune, and he desired no better. We do not find in the stoicism of the Phrygian slave the devout and lofty spiritualism of Plato, -thirsting for God and immortality; it may be doubted whether he believed in immortality at all: but he did recognize what is most noble in human life, -the subservience of the passions to reason, the power of endurance, patience, charity, and disinterested action. He did recognize the necessity of divine aid in the struggles of life, the glory of friendship, the tenderness of compassion, the power of sympathy. His philosophy was human, and it was cheerful; since he did not believe in misfortune, and exalted gentleness and philanthropy. Above everything, he sought inward approval, not the praises of the world, that happiness which lies within one's self, in the absence of all ignoble fears, in contentment, in that peace of the mind which can face poverty, disease, exile, and death.

Such were the lofty views which, embodied in the discourses of Epictetus, fell into the hands of Marcus Aurelius in the progress of his education, and exercised such a great influence on his whole subsequent life. The slave became the teacher of the emperor, which it is impossible to conceive of unless their souls were in harmony. As a Stoic, the emperor would not be less on his throne than the slave in his cottage. The trappings and pomps of imperial state became indifferent to him, since they were external, and were of small moment compared with that high spiritual life which he desired to lead. If poverty and pain were nothing to Epictetus, so grandeur and power and luxury should be nothing to him, -both alike being merely outward things, like the clothes which cover a man. And the fewer the impediments in the march after happiness and truth the better. Does a really great and preoccupied man care what he wears? "A shocking bad hat" was perhaps as indifferent to Gladstone as a dirty old cloak was to Socrates. I suppose if a man is known to be brainless, it is necessary for him to wear a disguise, -even as instinct prompts a frivolous and empty woman to put on jewels. But who expects a person recognized as a philosopher to use a mental crutch or wear a moral mask? Who expects an old man, compelling attention by his wisdom, to dress like a dandy? It is out of place; it is not even artistic, -it is ridiculous. That only is an evil which shackles the soul. Aurelius aspired to its complete emancipation. Not for the joys of a future heaven did he long, but for the realities and certitudes of earth, -the placidity and harmony and peace of his soul, so long as it was doomed to the trials and temptations of the world, and a world, too, which he did not despise, but which he sought to benefit.

So, what was contentment in the slave became philanthropy in the emperor. He would be a benefactor, not by building baths and theatres, but by promoting peace, prosperity, and virtue. He would endure cheerfully the fatigue of winter campaigns upon the frozen Danube, if the Empire could be saved from violence. To extend its boundaries, like Julius, he cared nothing; but to preserve what he had was a supreme duty. His watchword was duty, to himself, his country, and God. He lived only for the happiness of his subjects. Benevolence became the law of his life. Self-abnegation destroyed self-indulgence. For what was he placed by Providence in the highest position in the world, except to benefit the world? The happiness of one hundred and twenty millions was greater than the joys of any individual existence. And what were any pleasures which ended in vanity to the sublime placidity of an emancipated soul? Stoicism, if it did not soar to God and immortality, yet aspired to the freedom and triumph of what is most precious in man. And it equally despised, with haughty scorn, those things which corrupted and degraded this higher nature, the glorious dignity of unfettered intellect. The accidents of earth were nothing in his eyes, -neither the purple of kings nor the rags of poverty. It was the soul, in its transcendent dignity, which alone was to be preserved and purified.

This was the exalted realism which appears in the "Meditations" of Marcus Aurelius, and which he had learned from the inspirations of a slave. Yet such was the inborn, almost supernatural, loftiness of Aurelius, that, had he been the slave and Epictetus the emperor, the same moral wisdom would have shone in the teachings and life of each; for they both were God's witnesses of truth in an age of wickedness and shame. It was He who chose them both, and sent them out as teachers of righteousness, -the one from the humblest cottage, the other from the most magnificent palace of the capital of the world. In station they were immeasurably apart; in aim and similarity of ideas they were kindred spirits, -one of the phenomena of the moral history of our race; for the slave, in his physical degradation, had all the freedom and grandeur of an aspiring soul, and the emperor, on his lofty throne, had all the humility and simplicity of a peasant in the lowliest state of poverty and suffering. Surely circumstances had nothing to do with this marvellous exhibition. It was either the mind and soul triumphant over and superior to all outward circumstances, or it was God imparting an extraordinary moral power.

I believe it was the inscrutable design of the Supreme Governor of the universe to show, perhaps, what lessons of moral wisdom could be taught by men under the most diverse influences and under the greatest contrasts of rank and power, and also to what heights the souls of both slave and king could rise, with His aid, in the most corrupt period of human history. Noah, Abraham, and Moses did not stand more isolated amidst universal wickedness than did the Phrygian slave and the imperial master of the world. And as the piety of Noah could not save the antediluvian empires, as the faith of Abraham could not convert idolatrous nations, as the wisdom of Moses could not prevent the sensualism of emancipated slaves, so the lofty philosophy of Aurelius could not save the Empire which he ruled. And yet the piety of Noah, the faith of Abraham, the wisdom of Moses, and the stoicism of Aurelius have proved alike a spiritual power, -the precious salt which was to preserve humanity from the putrefaction of almost universal selfishness and vice, until the new revelation should arouse the human soul to a more serious contemplation of its immortal destiny.

The imperial "Meditations" are without art or arrangement, -a sort of diary, valuable solely for their precious thoughts; not lofty soarings in philosophical and religious contemplation, which tax the brain to comprehend, like the thoughts of Pascal, but plain maxims for the daily intercourse of life, showing great purity of character and extraordinary natural piety, blended with pithy moral wisdom and a strong sense of duty. "Men exist for each other: teach them or bear with them," said he. "Benevolence is invincible, if it be not an affected smile." "When thou risest in the morning unwillingly, say, 'I am rising to the work of a human being; why, then, should I be dissatisfied if I am going to do the things for which I was brought into the world?'" "Since it is possible that thou mayest depart from this life this very moment, regulate every act and thought accordingly (... for death hangs over thee whilst thou livest), while it is in thy power to be good." "What has become of all great and famous men, and all they desired and loved? They are smoke and ashes, and a tale." "If thou findest in human life anything better than justice, temperance, fortitude, turn to it with all thy soul; but if thou findest anything else smaller (and of no value) than this, give place to nothing else." "Men seek retreats for themselves, -houses in the country, seashores, and mountains; but it is always in thy power to retire within thyself, for nowhere does a man retire with more quiet or freedom than into his own soul." Think of such sayings, written down in his diary on the evenings of the very days of battle with the barbarians on the Danube or in Hungarian marshes! Think of a man, O ye Napoleons, ye conquerors, who can thus muse and meditate in his silent tent, and by the light of his solitary lamp, after a day of carnage and of victory! Think of such a man, -not master of a little barbaric island or a half-established throne in a country no bigger than a small province, but the supreme sovereign of a vast empire, at the time of its greatest splendor and prosperity, with no mortal power to keep his will in check, nothing but the voice within him; nothing but the sense of duty; nothing but the desire of promoting the happiness of others: and this man a Pagan!

But the state of that Empire, with all its prosperity, needed such a man to arise. If anything or anybody could save it, it was that succession of good emperors of whom Marcus Aurelius was the last, in the latter part of the second century. Let us glance, in closing, at the real condition of the Empire at that time. I take leave of the man, this "laurelled hero and crowned philosopher," stretching out his hands to the God he but dimly saw, and yet enunciating moral truths which for wisdom have been surpassed only by the sacred writers of the Bible, to whom the Almighty gave his special inspiration. I turn reluctantly from him to the Empire he governed.

Gibbon says, in his immortal History, "If a man were called to fix the period in the history of the world during which the condition of the human race was most happy and prosperous, he would, without hesitation, name that which elapsed from the death of Domitian to the accession of Commodus."

This is the view that Gibbon takes of the prosperity of the old Roman world under such princes as the Antonines. Niebuhr, however, a greater critic, though not so great an artist, takes a different view; and both are great authorities. If Gibbon meant simply that this period was the happiest and most prosperous during the imperial reigns, he may not have been far from the truth, according to his standpoint of what human happiness consists in, -that external prosperity which was the blessing of the Old Testament, and which Macaulay exalts as proudly as Gibbon before him. There was this external prosperity, so far as we know, and we know but little aside from monuments and medals. Even Tacitus shrank from writing contemporaneous history, and the period he could have painted is to us dark, mysterious, and unknown. Still, it is generally supposed and conceded that the Empire at this time was outwardly splendid and prosperous. Certainly there was a period of peace, when no wars troubled the State but those which were distant, on the very confines of the Empire, and that with rude barbarians, no more formidable in the eyes of the luxurious citizens of the capital than a revolt of the Sepoys to the eyes of the citizens of London, or Indian raids among the Rocky Mountains to the eyes of the people of New York. And there was the reign of law and order, a most grateful thing to those who had read of the conspiracy of Catiline and the tumults of Clodius, two hundred and fifty years before. And there was doubtless a magnificent material civilization which promised to be eternal, and of which every Roman was proud. There was a centralization of power in the Eternal City such as had never been seen before and has never been seen since, a solid Empire so large that the Mediterranean, which it enclosed, was a mere central lake, around the vast circuit of whose shores were temples and palaces and villas of unspeakable beauty, and where a busy population pursued unmolested its various trades. There was commerce on every river which empties itself into this vast basin; there were manufactures in every town, and there were agricultural skill and abundance in every province. The plains of Egypt and Mesopotamia rejoiced in the richest harvests of wheat; the hills of Syria and Gaul, and Spain and Italy, were covered with grape-vines and olives. Italy boasted of fifty kinds of wine, and Gaul produced the same vegetables that are known at the present day. All kinds of fruit were plenty and luscious in every province. There were game-preserves and fish-ponds and groves. There were magnificent roads between all the great cities, -an uninterrupted highway, mostly paved, from York to Jerusalem. The productions of the East were consumed in the West, for ships whitened the sea, bearing their precious gems, and ivory, and spices, and perfumes, and silken fabrics, and carpets, and costly vessels of gold and silver, and variegated marbles; and all the provinces of an empire which extended fifteen hundred miles from north to south and three thousand from east to west were dotted with cities, some of which almost rivalled the imperial capital in size and magnificence. The little island of Rhodes contained twenty-three thousand statues, and Antioch had a street four miles in length, with double colonnades throughout its whole extent. The temple of Ephesus covered as much ground as does the cathedral of Cologne, and the library of Alexandria numbered seven hundred thousand volumes. Rome, the proud metropolis, had a diameter of eleven miles, and was forty-five miles in circuit, with a population, according to Lipsius, larger than modern London. It had seventeen thousand palaces, thirty theatres, nine thousand baths, and eleven amphitheatres, -one of which could seat eighty-seven thousand spectators. The gilding of the roof of the capitol cost fifteen millions of our money. The palace of Nero was more extensive than Versailles. The mausoleum of Hadrian became the most formidable fortress of Mediaeval times. And then, what gold and silver vessels ornamented every palace, what pictures and statues enriched every room, what costly and gilded and carved furniture was the admiration of every guest, what rich dresses decorated the women who supped at gorgeous tables of solid silver, whose very sandals were ornamented with precious stones, and whose necks were hung with priceless pearls and rubies and diamonds! Paulina wore a pearl which, it is said, cost two hundred and fifty thousand dollars of our money. All the masterpieces of antiquity were collected in this centre of luxury and pride, -all those arts which made Greece immortal, and which we can only copy. What vast structures, ornamented with pillars and marble statues, were crowded together near the Forum and Capitoline Hill! The museums of Italy contain to-day twenty thousand specimens of ancient sculpture, which no modern artist could improve. More than a million of dollars were paid for a single picture for the imperial bed-chamber, -for painting was carried to as great perfection as sculpture.

Such were the arts of the Pagan city, such the material civilization in all the cities; and these cities were guarded by soldiers who were trained to the utmost perfection of military discipline, and presided over by governors as elegant, as polished, and as intelligent as the courtiers of Louis XIV. The genius for war was only equalled by genius for government. How well administered were all the provinces! The Romans spread their laws, their language, and their institutions everywhere without serious opposition. They were great civilizers, as the English have been. "Law" became as great an idea as "glory;" and so perfect was the mechanism of government that the happiness of the people was scarcely affected by the character of the emperors. Jurisprudence, the indigenous science of the Romans, is still studied and adopted for its political wisdom.

Such was the civilization of the Roman world in the time of Marcus Aurelius, -that external grandeur, that outward prosperity, to which Gibbon points with such admiration and pride, and to which he ascribed the highest happiness which the world has ever enjoyed. Far different, probably, would have been the verdict of the good and contemplative emperor who then ruled the civilized world, when he saw the luxury, the pride, the sensuality, the selfishness, the irreligion, the worldliness, which marked all classes; producing vices too horrible to be even named, and undermining the moral health, and secretly and surely preparing the way for approaching violence and ruin.

What, then, is the reverse of the picture which Gibbon admired? What established facts have we as an offset to these gilded material glories? What should be the true judgment of mankind as to this lauded period?

The historian speaks of peace, and the prosperity which naturally flowed from it in the uninterrupted pursuit of the ordinary occupations of life. This is indisputable. There was the increase of wealth, the enjoyment of security, the absence of fears, and the reign of law. Life and property were guarded. A man could travel from one part of the Empire to the other without fear of robbers or assassins. All these things are great blessings. Materially we have no higher civilization. But with peace and prosperity were idleness, luxury, gambling, dissipation, extravagance, and looseness of morals of which we have no conception, and which no subsequent age of the world has seen. It was the age of most scandalous monopolies, and disproportionate fortunes, and abandonment to the pleasures of sense. Any Roman governor could make a fortune in a year; and his fortune was spent in banquets and fêtes and races and costly wines, and enormous retinues of slaves. The theatres, the chariot races, the gladiatorial shows, the circus, and the sports of the amphitheatre were then at their height. The central spring of society was money, since it purchased everything which Epicureanism valued. No dignitary was respected for his office, -only for the salary or gains which his office brought. All professions which were not lucrative gradually fell into disrepute; and provided they were lucrative, it was of no consequence whether or not they were infamous. Dancers, cooks, and play-actors received the highest consideration, since their earnings were large. Scholars, poets, and philosophers -what few there were -pined in attics. Epictetus lived in a miserable cottage with only a straw pallet and a single lamp. Women had no education, and were disgracefully profligate; even the wife of Marcus Aurelius (the daughter of Antoninus Pius) was one of the most abandoned women of the age, notwithstanding all the influence of their teachings and example. Slavery was so great an institution that half of the population were slaves. There were sixty millions of them in the Empire, and they were generally treated with brutal cruelty. The master of Epictetus, himself a scholar and philosopher, broke wantonly the leg of his illustrious slave to see how well he could bear pain. There were no public charities. The poor and miserable and sick were left to perish unheeded and unrelieved. Even the free citizens were fed at the public expense, not as a charity, but to prevent revolts. About two thousand people owned the whole civilized world, and their fortunes were spent in demoralizing it. What if their palaces were grand, and their villas beautiful, and their dresses magnificent, and their furniture costly, if their lives were spent in ignoble and enervating pleasures, as is generally admitted. There was a low religious life, almost no religion at all, and what there was was degrading by its superstition. Everywhere were seen the rites of magical incantations, the pretended virtue of amulets and charms, soothsayers laughing at their own predictions, nowhere the worship of the one God who created the heaven and the earth, nor even a genuine worship of the Pagan deities, but a general spirit of cynicism and atheism. What does St. Paul say of the Romans when he was a prisoner in the precincts of the imperial palace, and at a time of no greater demoralization? We talk of the glories of jurisprudence; but what was the practical operation of laws when such a harmless man as Paul could be brought to trial, and perhaps execution! What shall we say of the boasted justice, when judgments were rendered on technical points, and generally in favor of those who had the longest purses; so that it was not only expensive to go to law, but so expensive that it was ruinous? What could be hoped of laws, however good, when they were made the channels of extortion, when the occupation of the Bench itself was the great instrument by which powerful men protected their monopolies? We speak of the glories of art; but art was prostituted to please the lower tastes and inflame the passions. The most costly pictures were hung up in the baths, and were disgracefully indecent. Even literature was directed to the flattery of tyrants and rich men. There was no manly protest from literary men against the increasing vices of society, -not even from the philosophers. Philosophy continually declined, like literature and art. Nothing strikes us more forcibly than the absence of genius in the second century. There was no reward for genius except when it flattered and pandered to what was demoralizing. Who dared to utter manly protests in the Senate? Who discussed the principles of government? Who would venture to utter anything displeasing to the imperial masters of the world? In this age of boundless prosperity, where were the great poets, where the historians, where the writers on political economy, where the moralists? For one hundred years there were scarcely ten eminent men in any department of literature whose writings have come down to us. There was the most marked decay in all branches of knowledge, except in that knowledge which could be utilized for making money. The imperial regime cast a dismal shadow over all the efforts of independent genius, on all lofty aspirations, on all individual freedom. Architects, painters, and sculptors there were in abundance, and they were employed and well paid; but where were poets, scholars, sages? -where were politicians even? The great and honored men were the tools of emperors, -the prefects of their guards, the generals of their armies, the architects of their palaces, the purveyors of their banquets. If the emperor happened to be a good administrator of this complicated despotism, he was sustained, like Tiberius, whatever his character. If he was weak or frivolous, he was removed by assassination. It was a government of absolute physical forces, and it is most marvellous that such a man as Marcus Aurelius could have been its representative. And what could he have done with his philosophical inquiries had he not also been a great general and a practical administrator, -a man of business as well as a man of thought?

But I cannot enumerate the evils which coexisted with all the boasted prosperity of the Empire, and which were preparing the way for ruin, -evils so disgraceful and universal that Christianity made no impression at all on society at large, and did not modify a law or remove a single object of scandal. Do you call that state of society prosperous and happy when half of the population was in base bondage to cruel masters; when women generally were degraded and slighted; when money was the object of universal idolatry; when the only pleasures were in banquets and races and other demoralizing sports; when no value was placed upon the soul, and infinite value on the body; when there was no charity, no compassion, no tenderness; when no poor man could go to law; when no genius was encouraged unless for utilitarian ends; when genius was not even appreciated or understood, still less rewarded; when no man dared to lift up his voice against any crying evil, especially of a political character; when the whole civilized world was fettered, deceived, and mocked, and made to contribute to the power, pleasure, and pride of a single man and the minions upon whom he smiled? Is 'all this to be overlooked in our estimate of human happiness? Is there nothing to be considered but external glories which appeal to the senses alone? Shall our eyes be diverted from the operation of moral law and the inevitable consequences of its violation? Shall we blind ourselves to the future condition of our families and our country in our estimate of happiness? Shall we ignore, in the dazzling life of a few favored extortioners, monopolists, and successful gamblers all that Christianity points out as the hope and solace and glory of mankind? Not thus would we estimate human felicity. Not thus would Marcus Aurelius, as he cast his sad and prophetic eye down the vistas of succeeding reigns, and saw the future miseries and wars and violence which were the natural result of egotism and vice, have given his austere judgment on the happiness of his Empire. In all his sweetness and serenity, he penetrated the veil which the eye of the worldly Gibbon could not pierce. He declares that "those things which are most valued are empty, rotten, and trifling," these are his very words; and that the real life of the people, even in the days of Trajan, had ceased to exist, that everything truly precious was lost in the senseless grasp after what can give no true happiness or permanent prosperity.

18001751R00326

Made in the USA
San Bernardino, CA
23 December 2014